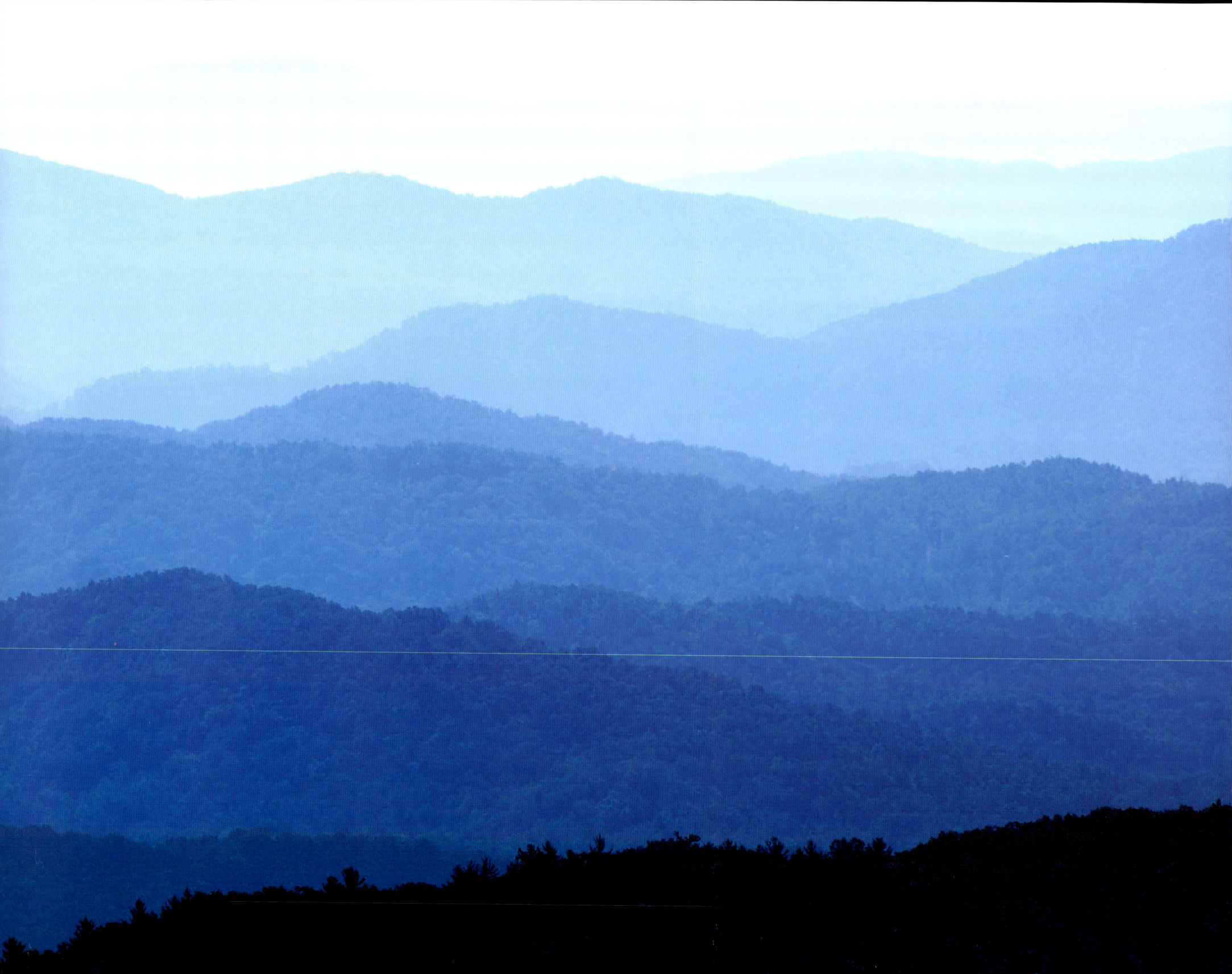

# THE MOUNTAIN LAKE SYMPOSIUM AND WORKSHOP

## ART IN LOCALE

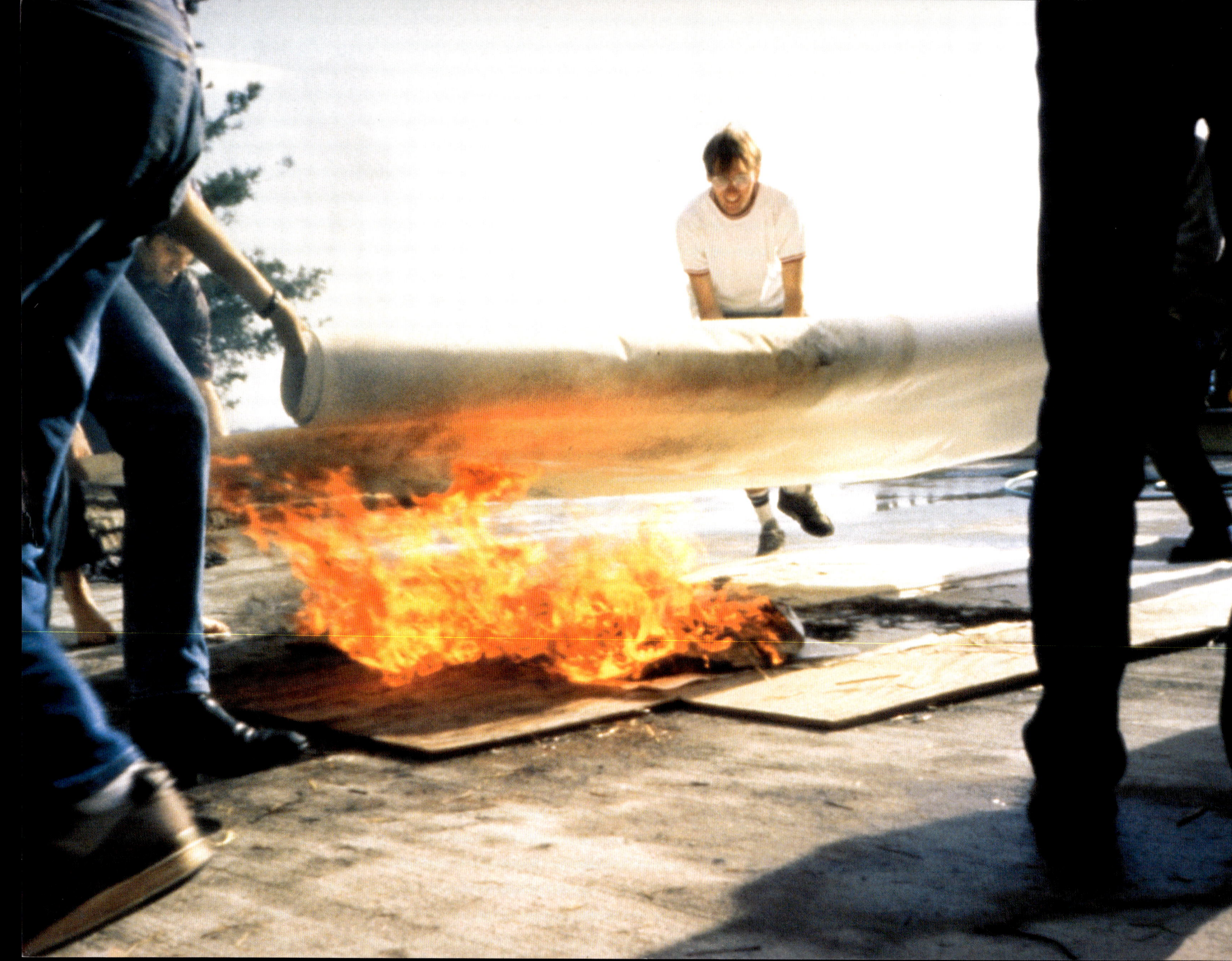

# THE MOUNTAIN LAKE SYMPOSIUM AND WORKSHOP

## ART IN LOCALE

RAY KASS & HOWARD RISATTI

# TABLE OF CONTENTS

# TABLE OF CONTENTS

# APPRECIATON &
# ACKNOWLEDGEMENTS

*We would like to thank everyone who, over the years, participated in Mountain Lake Programs and contributed essays to this book–and extend special thanks to Donald B. Kuspit for his long-standing commitment to the Mountain Lake Symposium and his always reliable advice. These contributions reveal the spirit of Mountain Lake Symposium and Workshops and tell the story of what happened there over the past 35 or so years. We wish to express our appreciation for John Link, Victor Huggins, Robert Porter, Trudie Grace, Elaine King, Linda McGreevy and Patricia Matthews for the important roles that they played in the the Mountain Lake Symposium conferences, and to Peter Lau, Joe Kelley, Bruce McClure, Sarah Johnson, Brian Sieveking, Robin Boucher, Holli Drewry, Ginger Wagoner, J.J. Watson, Dan Yates, Greg Byson, Paris Carter, Jeff Cornwell, and Robert Camicia Jr., who comprised the core volunteers in the early Mountain Lake Workshops with John Cage, Howard Finster and Jiro Okura. We are grateful for Mason Peterson and David Whaley's contribution in undertaking the design of this complex and long-evolving book. Thank you to the School of Visual Arts at Virginia Tech, the Virginia Tech Foundation, the Mountain Lake Lodge (Hotel), Miles Horton Jr. and Ruth Horton, and especially the Mary Moody Northen Endowment and Edward L. Protz, and Eugene Lucas of Galveston, Texas, for their encouragement and support.*

*Finally, we would like to thank Rachel Ivers and the Longwood Center for the Visual Arts of Longwood University for organizing the ambitious exhibition that made this publication necessary and possible.*

*Ray Kass & Howard Risatti*

From their earliest days, the symposia and workshops at Mountain Lake were collaborative. Collaborations tend to grow organically, and the development of the Mountain Lake programs over the next few decades was no exception. Like the Mountain Lake Symposium and Workshops, this book — published in conjunction with the first exhibition to examine the corpus of Mountain Lake — took shape organically. As a collaborative museum, the LCVA provides a supportive environment for creative process in all activities. This book, with its multiple voices and perspectives, is no exception.

Chief among the chorus that is Mountain Lake are Ray Kass and Howard Risatti, Mountain Lake Symposium co-directors and co-editors of this publication. Their importance to all things Mountain Lake cannot be overstated. They have been supported in this endeavor by the essay contributors, each one responsible either for creating and/or supporting programming firsthand within the Mountain Lake community or for building on projects initiated at Mountain Lake and carrying them to a wider, even international audience. We are deeply grateful to Robin Sedgwick for her sage editorial guidance and commitment to excellence, and to Mason Peterson for his tireless work with the editors to ensure a publication of both beauty and clarity. He was complemented in his efforts by Longwood University's Director of Design, David Whaley. Mark Saunders at the University of Virginia Press provided words of support for the project that buoyed us through its daunting early days. Roger Manley and the Gregg Museum of Art & Design at North Carolina State University similarly helped with their early and enthusiastic expression of interest in participating in the exhibition's eventual tour. Alex Grabiec coordinated countless details for both publication and exhibition in his role as project manager for the Longwood Center for the Visual Arts.

The LCVA could not do what it does without the unwavering support of the members of our advisory board under the leadership of Dr. Helen Warriner-Burke. We thrive because of their genuine love of and dedication to our organization and our community. We are also grateful for the support of Longwood University's administration, particularly the encouragement of President W. Taylor Reveley IV, Dr. Joan Neff, Dr. Larissa Fergeson, and Justin Pope. Together with our board, they guide and inspire the confidence needed to take creative risks.

Rachel Talent Ivers

Executive Director
Longwood Center for the Visual Arts

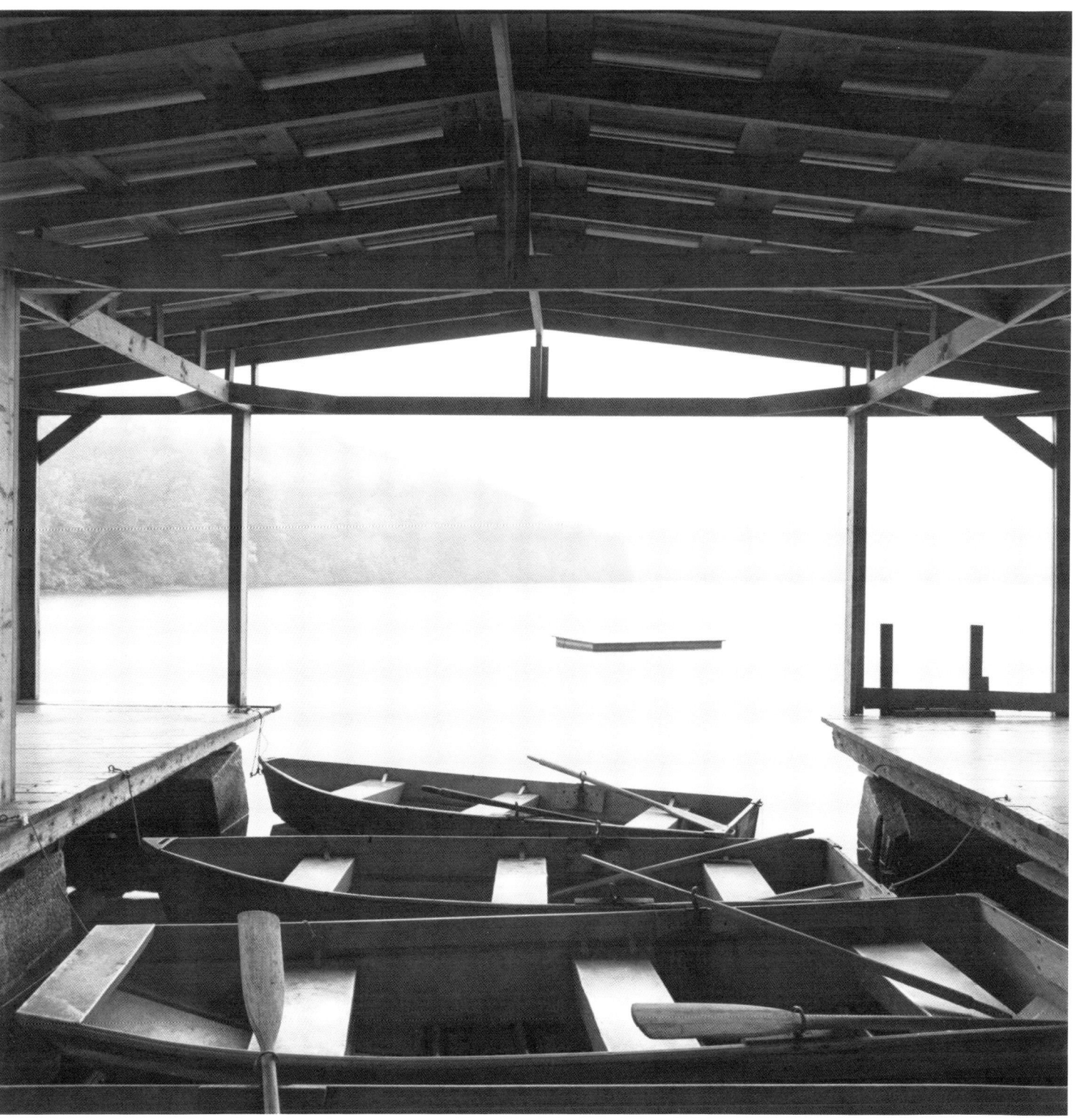

# PREFACE: REVISITING MOUNTAIN LAKE

ASHLEY KISTLER

Mountain Lake, a rural retreat in southwestern Virginia far removed from any large urban center, may seem like an unlikely venue for the multifarious activities focused on contemporary art and criticism that took place there, beginning in 1980. But the unconventional character — and natural beauty — of this location were of course part of its appeal. Foremost among the other key ingredients instrumental in the success and longevity of the Mountain Lake programs were the creative vision, passionate commitment, and unflagging curiosity of artist and Virginia Tech Emeritus Professor Ray Kass and Virginia Commonwealth University (VCU) Emeritus Professor Howard Risatti, whose enterprising DIY approach enlisted a host of enthusiastic collaborators to accomplish amazing things on mostly a shoestring budget.

Organized each year around a timely, always provocative theme, the Mountain Lake Symposium expanded the context for art in a multitude of meaningful ways by involving not only artists and art critics, but also writers and scholars from such fields as philosophy, music, sociology, anthropology, psychology, and religious studies. This early recognition of the merits of cross-disciplinary engagement also informed the conception and development of other programs, including workshops that bridged art and science, designed to merge the academic, vernacular, and natural resources of the area. The favorable outcome of each project depended, too, on both collaboration at every level and the welcoming ambience this mode of implementation fostered, which offered students as well as community participants direct exposure to creative processes, while attracting different audiences, both art-savvy and not. Long before these attributes of

successful contemporary-art programming had become standard practice, a flexible model for the imaginative engagement of artists (and others), capable of inspiring new paths of discovery anchored in the specifics of locale, had taken hold at Mountain Lake.

In our present era, opportunities to experience the immersive atmosphere, intellectual rigor, fertile interaction, and serious intent that defined the Mountain Lake Symposium are more limited now than they once were, at least beyond the academic campus and in most communities outside of a few major cities. Media and institutional support for in-depth critical commentary and analysis in the visual arts, particularly on a local and regional level, has steadily declined under pressure for more populist offerings. Certainly, access to online periodicals, publications, websites, and blogs has far outstripped anything we could have possibly imagined a few decades ago; and yet, as indispensable as these virtual sources have become, they nonetheless pale in comparison to firsthand, real-time encounters with makers and thinkers, and the lively debates thus engendered, as a way of promoting both a deeper critical awareness of art and the exhilarating sense of discovery that comes with it.

In this regard, attending the Mountain Lake Symposium was for me, first as a graduate student and then as a young museum professional, a formative, highly motivating experience. Recalling these events inevitably conjures a desire for the absorption in salient issues stimulated by the original research and substantive papers presented at each symposium, and by the ensuing discussions among speakers and audience members, which was bolstered by the

benefits of informal social interaction enabled by the setting, duration, and relative intimacy of this annual convening.

Many notable artists participated during the eleven years of the symposium's existence and indeed formed an essential component of every program. Especially memorable for this attendee was meeting Mierle Laderman Ukeles, whose pioneering work as artist-in-residence with the New York City Department of Sanitation has only recently received the long-overdue recognition it deserves. On a second visit, Ukeles returned to Mountain Lake for a collaborative workshop with Virginia Tech's Anaerobic Lab and its microbiologists, creating a body of work later exhibited in Richmond. Now, when art students at VCU, engaged as many of them are in social practice and performance, express their stunned admiration for this artist, I remember having the same response when introduced to her audacious initiatives over 25 years ago at Mountain Lake.

Reading through the many entries collected here, representing a wonderfully rich chorus of voices, I am also once again amazed by the plethora of other venturous Mountain Lake programs and activities that occurred over more than three decades. Especially through annual workshops, as mentioned above, vital relationships were forged with an impressive roster of artists. Among them was composer John Cage who, at Kass' invitation, made workshop visits to Mountain Lake in 1983 and 1988, producing on the latter occasion his *New River Watercolors*, so named for the nearby source of the river stones that he collected to make the work. The exhibition of selections from this stunning group of paintings, organized by curator Julia Boyd at the suggestion of Risatti, had its première later that year at the Virginia Museum of Fine Arts (VMFA), before embarking on a three-venue tour that concluded at The Phillips Collection in Washington, D.C.

Stepping into the completed installation of these paintings for the first time was a mind-blowing experience that defied my expectations: at once serenely spare and full of gestural incident, they appeared to embody such a distinctive sensibility, despite Cage's characteristic application of chance procedures intended to discourage any semblance of personal style. This and subsequent exhibitions of the New River Watercolors, as well as other events and performances that grew out of the extremely fruitful partnership between Cage and the Mountain Lake cohort, offered fresh insights into this seminal figure's concept of the interconnection between chance and choice, while also bringing much greater visibility to his work as a visual artist, which at the time was virtually unknown to a wider audience. As Boyd observes in her VMFA catalogue introduction, referring to Kass, "The opportunity he orchestrated was an extraordinary event for everyone concerned, and we are the beneficiaries."[1]

However, Cage was only one of numerous contributors to the creative culture of Mountain Lake. The array of artists invited to participate in these programs reflected a nonhierarchical attitude toward artmaking on the part of Kass and his associates, absent of any particular formula, format, or outlook but instead indicative of a generous, open-minded spirit of experimental investigation necessarily guided by diverse perspectives and ideas. The rewards of this approach were clearly evident in

*The Mountain Lake Workshop: Artists in Locale*, the first major exhibition of works assembled from the workshops, which opened at the Anderson Gallery of the VCU School of the Arts in August 1996, accompanied by a catalogue of the same title by Risatti.[2] Reinforcing what strikes me as the most abiding conviction of the Mountain Lake endeavor, the show also made clear that the connection between artists as radically different as Cage and Howard Finster rested, as one critic noted, "on a shared belief that art must be actively engaged with the world."[3]

The present book is an invaluable, multifaceted resource that comprehensively revisits an important and instructive history, thanks to the tenacious efforts of Ray, Howard, and their collaborators, and the support of the Longwood Center for the Visual Arts. In this brief preface, I've mentioned only a few highlights that personally shaped my experience of Mountain Lake. Much more of this singular legacy remains to be discovered and savored in these pages.

[1] "Acknowledgements" in *John Cage, New River Watercolors* (Richmond: Virginia Museum of Fine Arts, 1988), v.

[2] Howard Risatti, *The Mountain Lake Workshop: Artists in Locale*, exhibition catalogue published by the Anderson Gallery, Virginia Commonwealth University, Richmond, in association with the Mountain Lake Workshop of the Virginia Tech Foundation, Blacksburg, 1996.

[3] CeCe Bullard, "Rural Workshop Links Artworks at Anderson," *Richmond Times-Dispatch*, Sept. 27, 1996: C3.

# COMMENTARY: THE MOUNTAIN LAKE SYMPOSIUM

DONALD B. KUSPIT

The Mountain Lake Symposia were part of the larger ensemble of Mountain Lake programs that also include artists' conferences, lectures, exhibitions, and collaborative workshops conducted by guest artists. The symposia, in their focus on issues in contemporary art and art criticism, were a utopian idea. They're over now — they lasted over a decade — and it's still a utopian idea, one that succeeded. Every year critics of every stripe gathered together in an idyllic — non-academic — setting to debate a more or less urgent issue (one never ran out of urgent issues) in the company of various artists, art educators, and other critics. The audience vigorously participated, the debate was lively, sometimes heated, and we were all stuck together for two days, so that we had to be congenial however much our ideas differed. Friendships did in fact form, and continue to the present day. I was present at each one of the symposia, thanks to Ray Kass, without whose remarkable efforts and personality the symposia never would have occurred — each year was a scramble for funding, Ray somehow managing to pull it off — and I, of course, regularly change my stripes, so that I fitted into every debate, adding my touch of controversy.

Why were the symposia utopian? Because they were premised on the assumption that there is a community of devoted yet critical individuals who understand that one can't really appreciate art without intellectually and passionately engaging and questioning it. Indeed, it doesn't really give itself except through critical consciousness, and the whole point of the symposia was to develop critical consciousness of art beyond the usual academic rules for doing so. This seems extraordinarily utopian — naïve? — in a society where the celebrity culture of spectacle has assimilated much of the art world, bringing with it a certain cynicism about the purpose of art and art criticism. The symposia were a beacon in this depressing situation, so inimical to the creativity of both. They reaffirmed Baudelaire's idea that the best criticism must be "passionate, partisan, and political," but within the "widest horizon of understanding." That is, it must always be in touch with "metaphysics" or theory so that it understands its own premises and can justify its belief in this or that art. The symposia were metaphysical in that they brought a variety of horizons of understanding — some very wide indeed — to bear on art, testing art as well as theory itself. Whether there was a clash of or a fit between the diverse ways of engaging art — whether each stretched the other out of shape or made it seem narrow — the result was always vitalizing and thought-provoking.

I remember the shock and pleasure of arriving at Roanoke airport after the grubbiness of New York, and the even greater shock and pleasure of the drive to Mountain Lake — up the mountain on a narrow road that seemed to have been freshly cut through the forest — and the sense of relief and freedom at finally arriving at the lodge with its rustic amenities, fresh air, steep grounds, lush greenery, and above all the glassy lake. We were on a magic mountain where we could discuss art to our hearts' and minds' content, but fortunately, it has a much happier atmosphere than the one that prevailed on Thomas Mann's magic mountain.

I am nostalgic for the Mountain Lake Symposia on art and art criticism. Like all good things, they had to end; but, I never quite understood why. I suppose it was because the bad world couldn't understand why art and critical consciousness should be taken so seriously. The spirit of the symposia continues in the on going workshops conducted by guest artists at Mountain Lake, but it can't be the same without critical consciousness to complete their art.

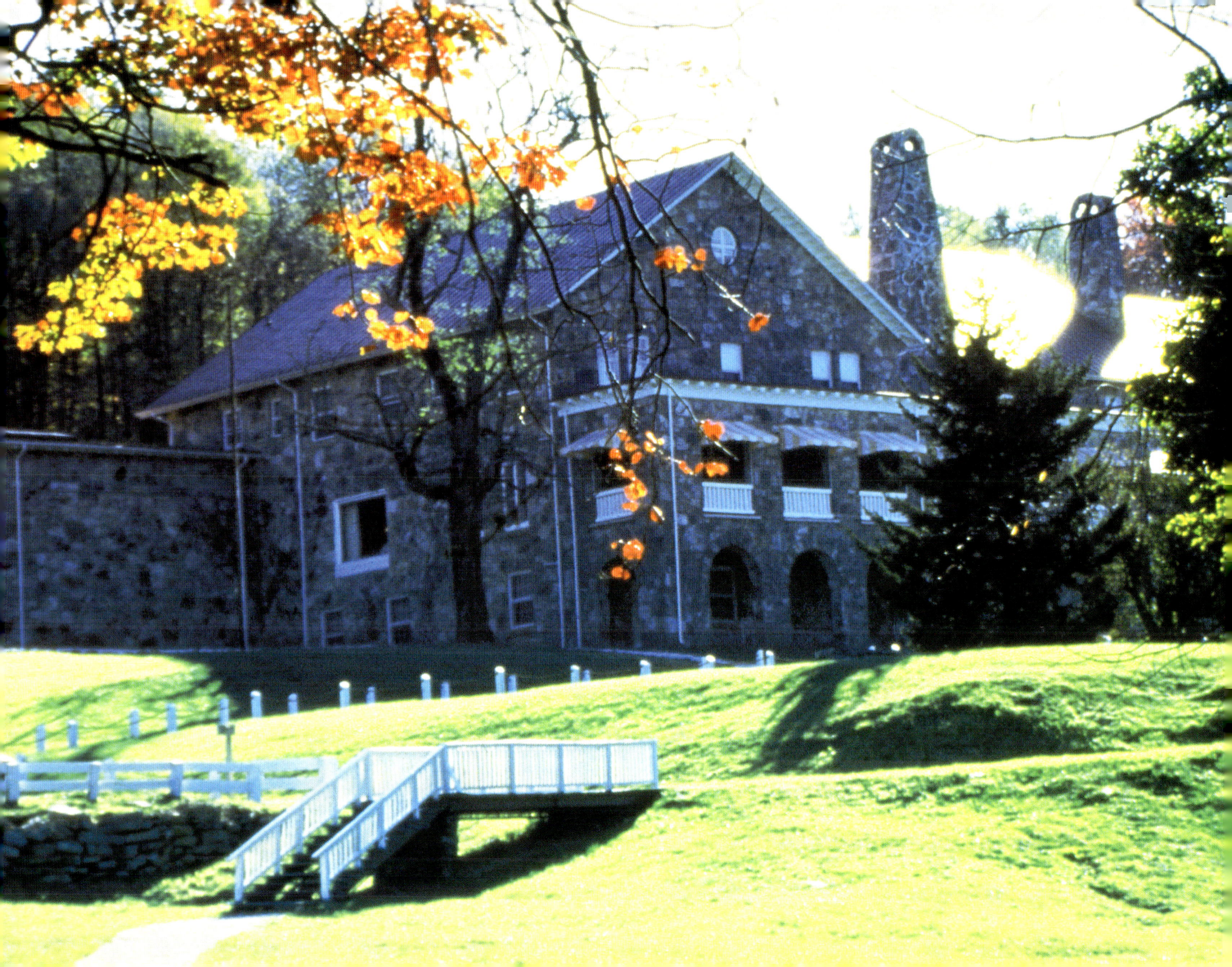

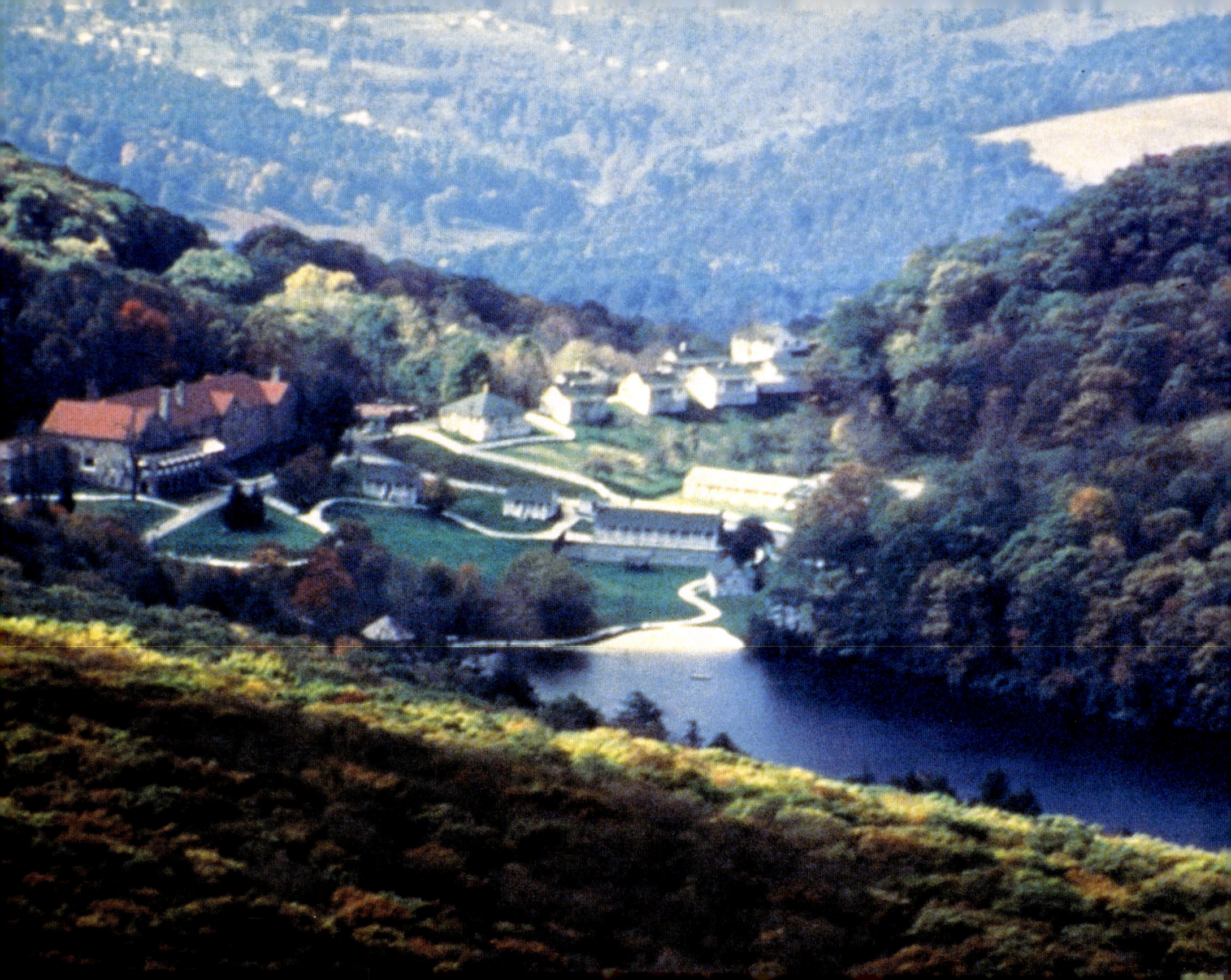

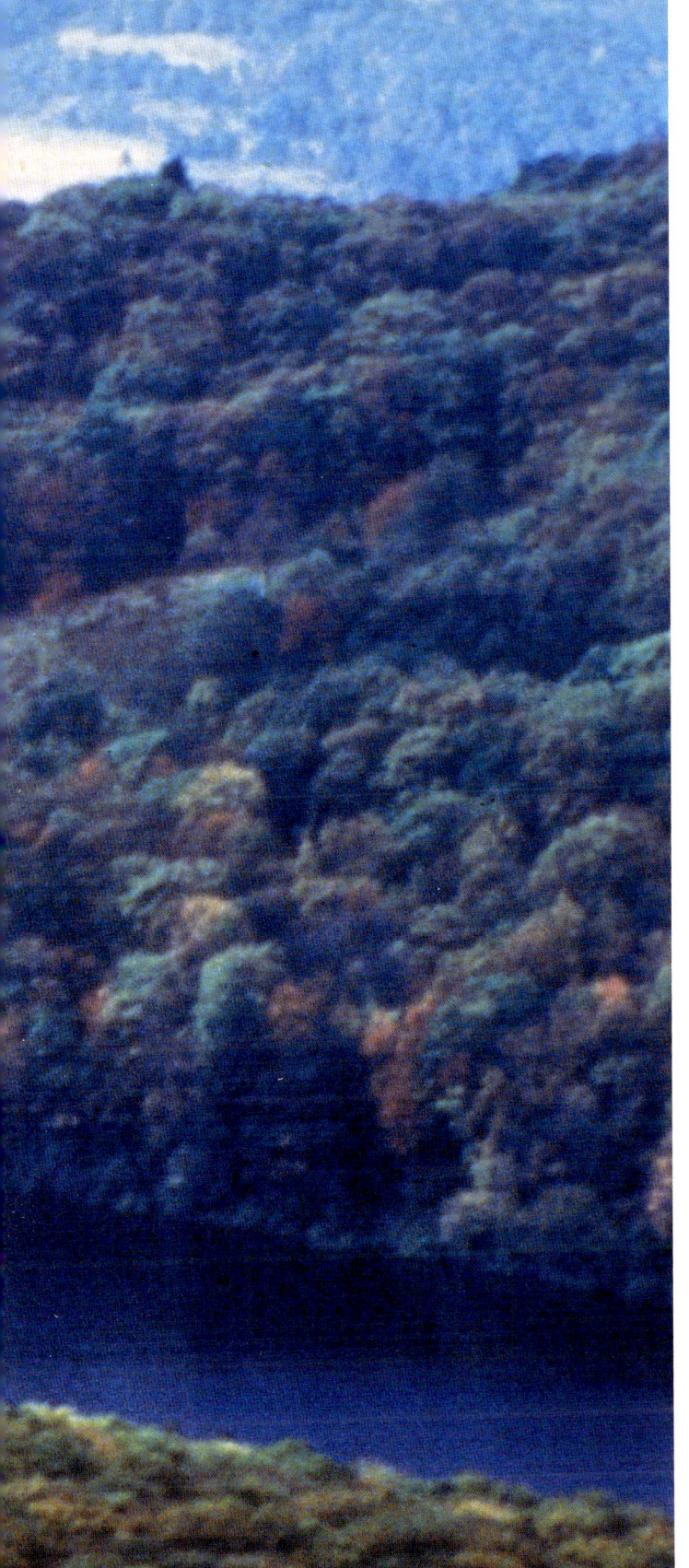

The Mountain Lake Hotel
as seen from above.

# *The Mountain Lake Symposium 1980–1990*

# THE MOUNTAIN LAKE SYMPOSIUM AND WORKSHOPS — THE EFFECT

## GARY (CHICO) HARKRADER

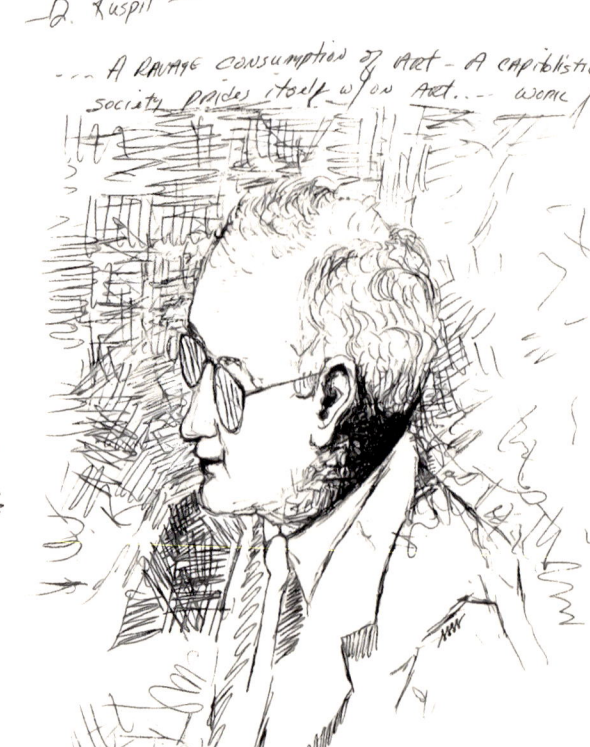

*Regionalism – MAINSTREAM*

A Virginian may be MAINSTREAM
A New Yorker may be a Regionalist.
To be a Non-MAINSTREAM is not
to be less diminished status.
An Artist work at present may
be mainstream at a later date.

— *Kuspit.*

*D. Kuspit — cont.*

... A RAVAGE consumption of ART – A capitalistic
society prides itself w/ on Art ... *work.*

*Ellen Handler Spitz.*
Columbia Psychoanalytic Institute
Author: Art & People

*Dr. Elaine A. King:*
*Director: ART Gallery, CARNEGIE–MELLON Univ.*
"CREATIVE ART in the CRUNCH of Technology"
A SOCIAL ANALYSIS
CURATOR & AUTHOR
: WHY has individualism died?
: CORPORATE collection RADICALLY RISES
: CORPORATE giving – MEDIA HYPE
: Proliferation of PREdetermined
  success

: STATEMENT: NOT STYLE
: NEXT YEAR – THIS YEAR
  will be history
: "The Speilberg effect"

Rawlings
McCallum  Artist
Sa        examples

"Neo Geo"

Absence of SENSUALITY
Lack of PASSION : wit

— *Howard Risatti —*
WRITER: New Art Examiner
: ART FORUM

*Charles Miller – NEW YORK*
*ARTCRITIC Art Forum*
Scholium – German Lit.
"The International MAINSTREAM"

Fitch: sculpture
grand elephant
Banquet table
w/ 32 figures

Seated Hollow –
A public edifice
empir ... The town
& Flooding the
Market.

ART SERVICES NETWORK

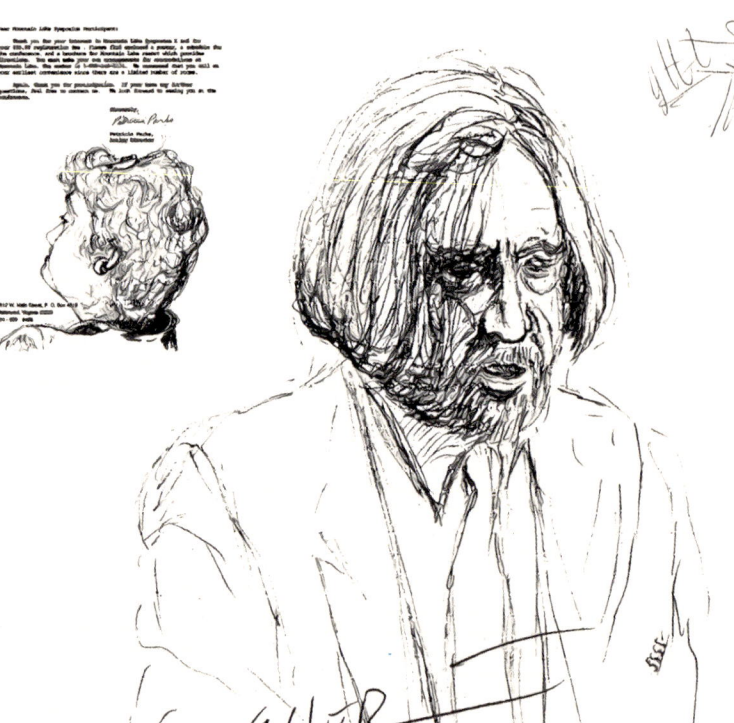

*Vidler*

*Judith Russi Kirshner*
Chicago

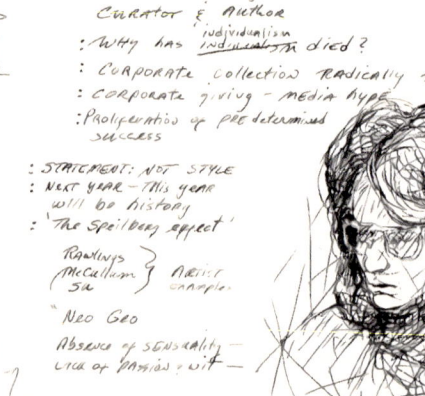

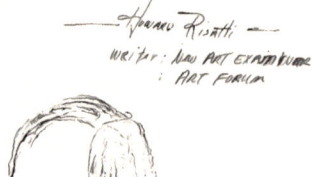

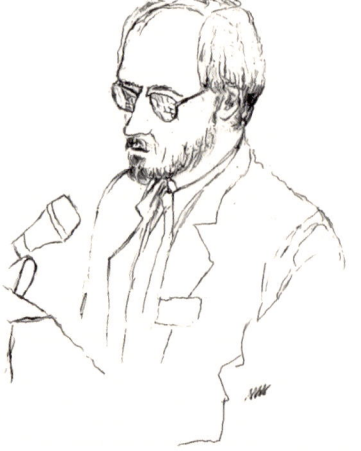

MOUNTAIN LAKE SYMPOSIUM X AT MT. LAKE
"Artists' Intentions: Enduring Values/Discounted Goods"
November 3–5, 1989

**Agenda**

**Friday, November 3**
Afternoon check-in. Participants should arrive by 6:00 p.m.
5:30 p.m.    Cocktails
5:30–10:00 p.m.    Dinner served

**Saturday, November 4**
7:30–9:00 a.m.    Breakfast
9:00 a.m.    Welcome and introductions – Howard Risatti
9:15    Presentation of Papers
             Maureen Sherlock
10:00    Sydney Tillim
11:00    Break
11:15    Suzi Gablik
12 noon–2 p.m.    Lunch
             Others ...
2:00 p.m.    Nancy ...
3:00    Ron ...
3:45    Break
4:00    Din ...
5:30    Reception ... anniversary of the Mt. Lake
             Sympo ...

**Sunday, November 5**
7:30–9:00 a.m.    Breakfast
9:00 a.m.    Marcus Raskin
9:45–12 noon    Panel Discussion and Audience Questions with the seven
             speakers, as well as Abram Hidani and Charles V. Miller.
12:00 noon    Conference ends.

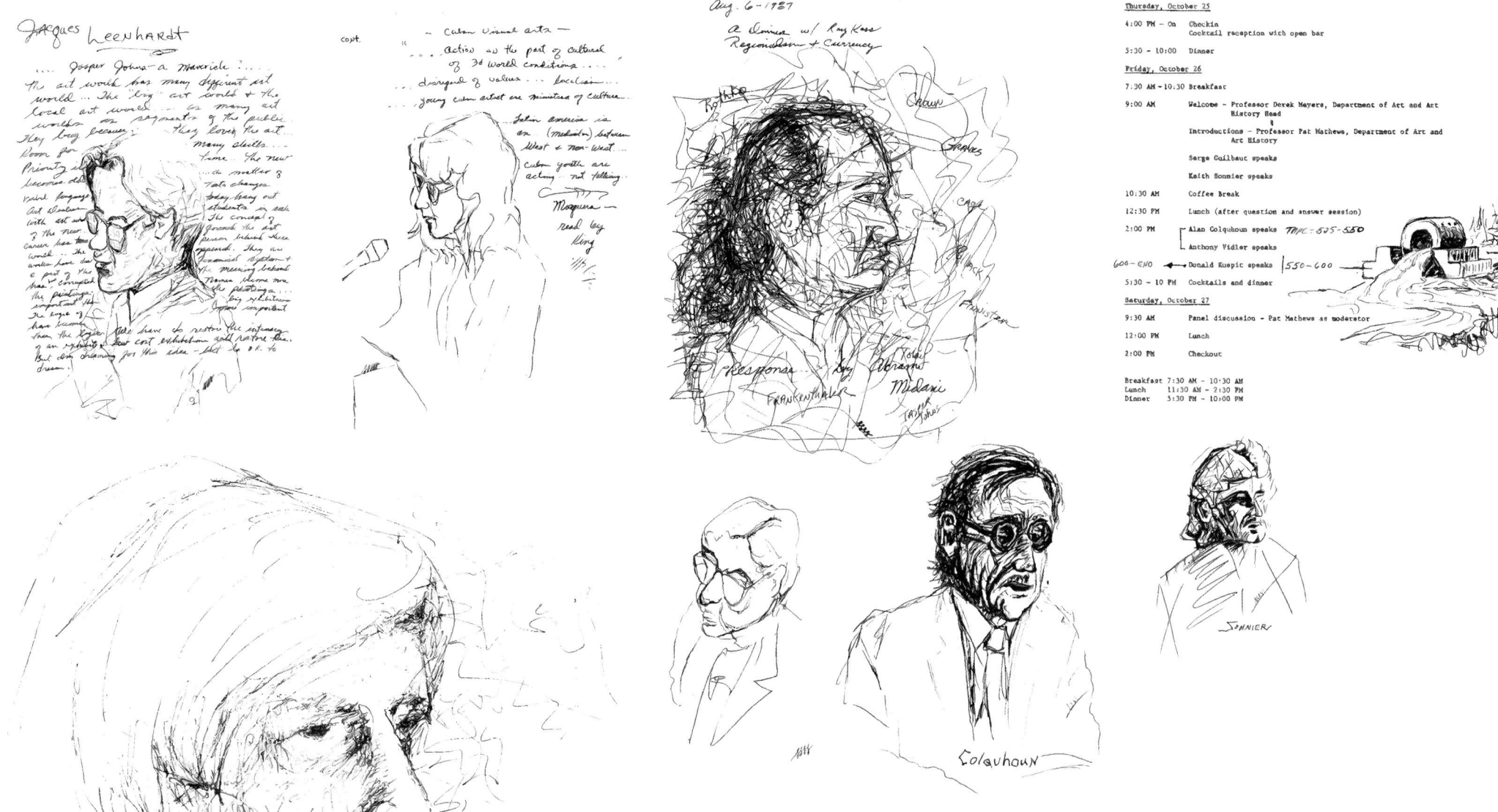

**Thursday, October 25**

4:00 PM - On    Checkin
     Cocktail reception with open bar
5:30 - 10:00    Dinner

**Friday, October 26**

7:30 AM -10:30 Breakfast
9:00 AM      Welcome - Professor Derek Meyers, Department of Art and Art
           History Head
           Introductions - Professor Pat Mathews, Department of Art and
           Art History
           Serge Guilbaut speaks
           Keith Sonnier speaks
10:30 AM      Coffee Break
12:30 PM      Lunch (after question and answer session)
2:00 PM      Alan Colquhoun speaks
           Anthony Vidler speaks
           Donald Kuspic speaks
5:30 - 10 PM    Cocktails and dinner

**Saturday, October 27**

9:30 AM      Panel discussion - Pat Mathews as moderator
12:00 PM      Lunch
2:00 PM      Checkout

Breakfast 7:30 AM - 10:30 AM
Lunch     11:30 AM - 2:30 PM
Dinner     5:30 PM - 10:00 PM

I attended almost all of the Mountain Lake Symposium conferences and Workshop programs during the 1980s, and I sketched, from life, many of the important invited lecturers. These events had a profound impact on my art, education, and philosophy. Now, in retrospect, I think of those historic gatherings of creative artists and intellectuals as a giant "salon" convened in a remote lodge in the Appalachian Mountains of Virginia. There was a creative and explorative environment where attendees could contemplate humanity and absorb spirituality against the backdrop of nature, art, music, and words. John Cage, composer and avant-garde artist, had nothing to say, and he said it!

I recall special workshops that included unique gatherings of renowned personalities. Imagine visual artists painting plein air, dispersed around the fields and valleys at the Mountain Lake

Hotel. California artist Wayne Thiebaud led night critiques of area artists' works and painted landscapes from the balcony of the lodge. Artist and writer Robert Berlind meandered in the vicinity, visiting local artists at their easels as he made critiques and conversation. Photographer Marie Cosindas led a Polaroid camera workshop inside the hotel, posing a very young Sally Mann as her model. And chamber musicians played their instruments and music flowed through the trees and across the hills, creating a magical environment. At the same time, John Cage, also a mycologist, was exploring the remotest part of nearby Salt Pond Mountain with mycology groups; later, at the evening panel discussions, he reported having found a new species of mushroom.

It was enchanting.

19

# THE MOUNTAIN LAKE SYMPOSIUM: CRITICAL ENGAGEMENT

HOWARD RISATTI

The Mountain Lake Symposium, which began in 1980, was inspired by a panel on realism in art at the 1977 Southeastern College Art Conference (SECAC) that was hosted by Virginia Polytechnic and State University in Blacksburg. Organized by Virginia Tech Department of Art Studio Professor Ray Kass, "The Realist Panel" included art critics Donald B. Kuspit and Clement Greenberg and artists Duane Hanson, Janet Fish, and Richard Estes, and was moderated by Virginia Tech Art History Professor Robert Porter. In featuring both artists and art critics, the panel became an important model for the Mountain Lake Symposium as a way of addressing critical issues that had a bearing on contemporary art. From its inception, professionals from the art world and related fields such as religious studies, philosophy, music, sociology, anthropology, and psychology were invited to participate in the symposium, which was named after the Mountain Lake Hotel, a nearby seasonal resort where most of the symposia were held. The Mountain Lake Hotel with its lake and surrounding woods presented an idyllic retreat for the serious contemplation of important issues in art and culture.[1]

From the outset the symposium intended to view art within a larger context that went well beyond the sometimes parochial confines of contemporary "art world" discourse. This is clear from the very first symposium, which was held October 1–3, 1980, and focused on the issue of "Moral Philosophy, Aesthetics, and Contemporary Art." It included Greenberg and Kuspit from "The Realist Panel" as well as New York art critic Robert Pincus-Witten, curator Jan van der Marck, and art historians and religious studies professors John Dixon and Giles Gunn.[2] The following year, 1981, the symposium went from October 9

to 11; this second Mountain Lake Symposium addressed the related topic "Art Criticism/Social Criticism." Kuspit was again included along with poet and anthropologist Stanley Diamond, art critic/writer Rosalind E. Krauss, and art historian Irving Sandler.

The titles of their papers give some sense of the serious tone of Symposium II as well as the expansive approach taken by the participants in their analysis of contemporary art: Kuspit, "An End to Autonomy: Art Criticism as Social Science"; Krauss, "The Discourses of Originality"; Sandler, "The Social Uses of Modern Art: The Constructive Tradition"; and Diamond, "The Reification of Art — The Individual in Art." Diamond's paper was an analysis of what he saw as the disenfranchisement of modern man from what he termed the primitive "entitledness" to the art experience.[3]

The focus of Symposium III, held October 7–9, 1982, was "Art and Its Publics." Kuspit, who by this time was a regular contributor, titled his paper "Maligned and Mystified Audiences: The Artist's Sense of the Public" and addressed what he believed was the cause of the public's disdain for the avant-garde. Composer George Rochberg, who titled his paper "The Marvelous Art," had concerns similar to Kuspit's about what he termed "alienated audiences." He had recently abandoned avant-garde 12-tone serial composition for what he felt were more melodic forms that did not alienate audiences. With music as his example, he called for "art to mediate the audience's 'desire and hunger' for ontological fullness in life. Profound meaning," he stated, "intersects the marvelous, and life wrests itself away from the literal." Literary critic and writer Gerald Graff titled his presentation "The Decay of Carping"; it was

an attack on literary critics and teachers overly infected with what he considered academic "promotionalism," a kind of closed system in which academics basically write for each other, ignoring the general public. This was something that the symposium tried to avoid by insisting on the use of vernacular, non-specialized language whenever possible by presenters.[4] New York Conceptual artist Joseph Kosuth's paper was titled "Comments on the Institutionalization of Art"; this "institutionalization," he believed, led to the commodification of art. And in her paper, "Keypunching Creativity," Ingrid Sischy bemoaned the media's obsession with the aura of art, with its celebrity nature and superficial features surrounding it and the maker.[5] (This, unfortunately, is something that has only become more pronounced with the staggering increase in prices in the art market.)

It is important to note that from the outset of the symposium a significant percentage of its audience was made up of artists. This is not only because all of the symposia, now regularly held in the fall, intentionally had artists on their panels. It is also because other Mountain Lake events that occurred in the spring, events like "artists' conferences" and various studio demonstrations/workshops, and even lectures, were conducted by artists. A symbiotic relationship thereby developed between these serious but less theoretical events and the symposium, because the critical and theoretical discussion of contemporary art issues the symposium engaged provided a philosophical background for the artistic concerns developing in the workshops.

It also should be pointed out that the way the symposium

[1] Movie goers might be interested to know that the hotel provided the setting for the 1987 movie *Dirty Dancing*. In the early years Kass continued to organize the symposium with the help of the Virginia Tech art department faculty including Department Head Victor Huggins and art historians Robert Porter, Trudie Grace, and Patricia Mathews. By the second symposium other college and university art departments were invited to join the Mountain Lake Symposium as a consortium by paying a simple, modest fee that would help support the symposium and then allow their faculty and students to attend the symposium programs. Old Dominion University was soon followed by Carnegie Mellon University, University of Richmond, Virginia Commonwealth University (where I was on the art history faculty), Cornell University, and the Virginia Museum of Fine Arts (VMFA). In 1985 Julia Boyd from the VMFA and I involved our respective institutions in a more substantial financial commitment to the symposium and became co-organizers with Kass.

[2] From here on, all titles of participants are as of the time of the symposium. Kuspit was a philosopher and professor of art, SUNY at Stony Brook; Dixon, professor of art, UNC, Chapel Hill; van der Marck, art historian and director, Center for Fine Arts, Miami; Gunn, professor of American and religious studies, UNC, Chapel Hill.

[3] Krauss, professor of art at Hunter College and also co-editor of the art journal *October*; Sandler, professor of art history, SUNY–Purchase; Diamond, professor of anthropology at the New School of Social Research, NY.

[4] For more on this issue of specialized writing in academia see Russell Jacoby, *The Last Intellectuals: American Culture in the Age of Academe* (New York: Noonday Press, 1987).

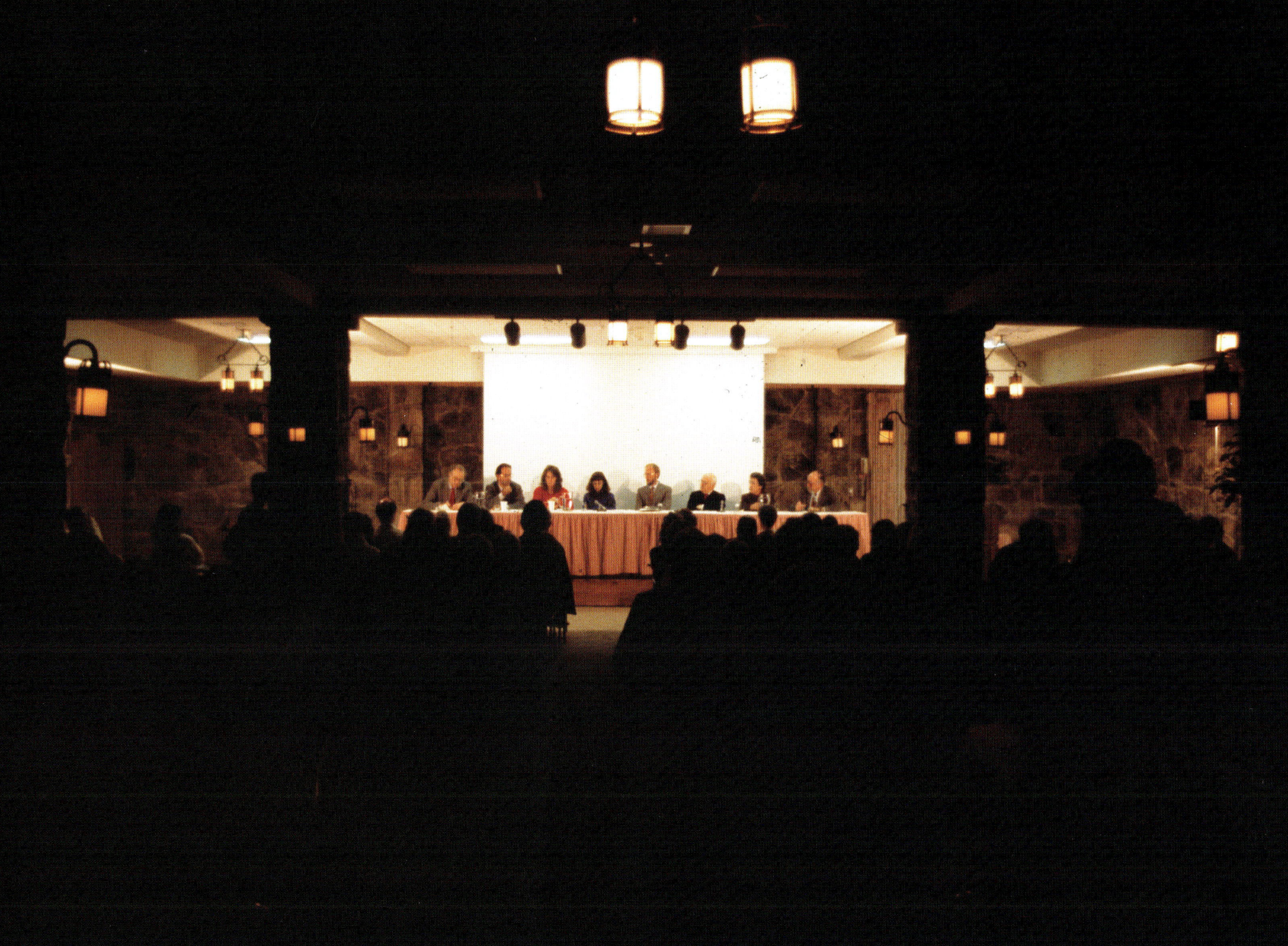

was organized encouraged an interaction between speakers, panelists, and audience. On Friday evening, the day before the symposium's formal papers were presented, a makeshift bar/reception area was open to everyone in attendance, giving all an opportunity to informally meet and greet the presenters. The same situation was arranged for Saturday evening following the presentation of the formal papers. Again audience members had an opportunity to speak casually and informally with presenters about specific issues raised in papers during the day. This kind of intimate, one-on-one situation encouraged audience members who were not necessarily experts in the field to discuss ideas that they may have felt awkward or even intimidated to bring up before a large audience. The final part of the symposium, which occurred on Sunday morning, included a panel discussion among the presenters and then a public forum open to the audience.

"Media: Artists, Imagery, and Influences" was the title of Symposium IV that convened 13–15 October 1983.[6] The stated goal was "to stimulate an investigation into the use and influence of mass media in the visual arts." Kuspit, now an advisor and regular presenter at the symposium, spoke on "Evading the Media: A Source of Artistic 'Progress'?" He noted how Dadaism, in becoming a media event, "had lost its negativity, and with that its progressive character — its autonomy as critical resistance to convention."[7] This is a theme that would surface again and again in the coming symposia. Painter and critic Thomas Lawson, co-founder of REALLIFE, a magazine by and about artists, spoke about Modernism's denial of history and its desire "to negate the past in an ever-present longing for a better future. Tomorrow

and tomorrow and tomorrow — the relentless optimism of irresponsible advance to a superior homogeneity." With this subtle allusion to Shakespeare's *Macbeth*, he went on to warn that "an organism without history is without life." Russell Keziere, critic and editor of *Vanguard*, an influential Vancouver, British Columbia, publication, titled his paper "Media: Artists, Imagery and Influences"; he noted that "the hallmark of mass culture is mass media, and its influence is a coercive rather than a persuasive force." Sociologist Howard Becker from Northwestern University, continuing in this vein, spoke about "Distributing Modern Art" and about how the way "works are publicized and distributed affects how those works are made ... and understood" by their audience. Artist Edward Paschke, a noted member of the Chicago Imagists group that eschewed popular New York art trends in favor of the grotesque and surreal, was invited because his paintings not only engage media images but also echo TV and video stylistic features such as acid colors and blurred images. He titled his presentation "Notes on a Work Process" and discussed his relationship to media as part of his working method.

The variety and range of speakers at the symposium attest to a desire to engage as wide a theoretical and philosophical perspective as possible. It was a genuine attempt to move away from a mainstream, but narrow, art-world perspective centered in New York to one that engaged other parts of the country and in this case even Canada.

Topics for both the 1984 and the 1985 symposia concerned Postmodern architecture, something that, on the surface, would seem far afield from the visual art and mass media focus of the

previous symposia. However, these topics provided an approach to the critiquing of International Modernism's non-localized, non-regional identity by examining the role indigenous and regional architecture played in establishing a sense of place and locale because of localized customs as well as physical environment. The first of these, Symposium V, went from 25 to 27 October 1984 and was titled "Revisionism/Criticism: Directions in Postmodern Art and Architecture." The symposium poster invited "speakers and audience participants to propose and examine alternatives to traditional formalist approaches in Art, Architecture, Art History and Criticism."[8] Featured speakers were architect and Professor of Architecture at Princeton University Alan Colquhoun and architect and architectural historian Kenneth Frampton from Columbia University. However, the symposium also included Serge Guilbaut, professor of art history, University of British Columbia; multi-media and video artist Keith Sonnier; and Kuspit.

The second symposium dedicated to Postmodernism, Symposium VI, held from 10 to 12 October 1985, was titled "Dislocated Sources: Historicism in Post-Modern Art & Architecture." The intent was to address issues arising from Postmodern attitudes towards the market and the historical past that have led to widespread use of appropriated (borrowed) imagery in contemporary art:

*In an art world in which all identity is circumscribed by the market-related standards of the media, many contemporary artists are appropriating historical modes of imagery and narrative in an attempt to renew an independent aesthetic identity.*

[5] Graff, professor of English, Northwestern University; Rochberg, professor of humanities, University of Pennsylvania; Sischy, critic and editor-in-chief, *Artforum*, NY; respondent Derek Guthrie, critic and publisher, *New Art Examiner*. For a critical response to the conference see Linda F. McGreevy, "*Art and Its Publics — Inspired but inconclusive symposium*," *New Art Examiner* (Dec. 1982), vol. 10, no. 2, pp. 8–9.

[6] Symposium IV was organized by Kass and professor and curator Elaine King, Carnegie Mellon University.

[7] For Kuspit's remarks as well as those of the other panelists see "The 1983 Mountain Lake Symposium," *New Art Examiner* (Jan. 1984), Section III, pp. 1–7.

[8] See statement on symposium poster. Organizers were Kass, Mathews, Gregory Hunt (Virginia Tech), McGreevy (Old Dominion University), and Humberto Rodriguez-Camilloni, Virginia Tech professor of architecture.

*The historicism in works by [various Postmodern] artists ... differs significantly in meaning from the modernist's use of collage-like historical references as a protest against the authority of tradition. ...*

*This conference will address the historicist mentality as it may be expressed by individual artists and architects: critical formulations will pivot on specific productions of art and architecture.* [9]

The presenters who were invited to address these issues represented a wide range of art-related fields from various parts of the country. They included California artist John Baldessari, who unfortunately could not attend; New York critic, curator, and rock-and-roll singer Dan Cameron; New Haven, Connecticut, architect Allan Greenberg; University of Virginia Professor of Architectural History Carroll William Westfall; curator and Director of the Carnegie Mellon Art Gallery Elaine King; and, as usual, Kuspit.

In the fall of 1986 the symposium shifted venues, moving from the Mountain Lake Hotel to the Virginia Museum of Fine Arts in Richmond. This seventh symposium in the series was held on the 17th and 18th of October, 1986. Besides shifting locations, it also shifted in topic, from Postmodern architecture to "The Evaluative Process in Contemporary Art." As the title suggests, the intention of the symposium was to probe the criteria for making judgments of works of art by asking where those criteria come from, who establishes them, and what values they imply on the part of artist and audience. The role of the media again came into focus in a very prescient

way and raised questions that are still deeply relevant today:

*Is the Modernist notion of art's privileged position being subsumed by a media culture? Is art becoming just another mode of communication, another type of mass entertainment — or even theatre? The status of aesthetic value appears to be undergoing radical transformation. What evaluative principles must be applied to new forms arising from such a transformation in order to make judgments and derive meaning when the old formulae for making such judgments no longer seem to apply?* [10]

The topic was to be addressed "through the discussion of individual artists' works, societal attitudes about art and artists, and the role of critical discourse in giving form to the evaluative process."

The speakers invited to specifically address this topic were Yve-Alain Bois, curator, critic, and professor of art history, Johns Hopkins University; Suzi Gablik, author, critic, and corresponding editor from London to *Art in America*; Annette Michelson, co-editor and co-founder of *October* magazine and visiting professor, Yale University; Allan Kaprow, performance artist and writer who is credited with inventing the New York "Happenings" of the 1950s and '60s; and Kuspit. [11]

Closely related and complementary to Symposium VII was the conference of the following year, Symposium VIII. Returning to the Mountain Lake Hotel, it convened from 29 to 31 October 1987. Its title, "Making Psychoanalytical Sense of Art," clearly shows the influence of Kuspit, whose critical methods

increasingly looked to psychoanalysis as a way of understanding art and artistic motives. He, more than anyone else in the field, consistently developed this approach in his critical writings on contemporary art. And, as he increasingly brought this approach to the symposia, the role the psyche plays in the formation of a sense of self and a sense of place — the sense of what it means to belong somewhere — became clearer, and its influence on the development of workshop strategies became more pronounced. The title of Kuspit's paper, "A Psychological Approach to the Unintelligible in Modern Art," echoes the symposium description, which was premised on the belief that "psychoanalysis has a profound basis in philosophical discourse, and its procedures may be formally associated with the quest for a transcendental sense-of-self that is also a goal of artistic expression and experience."

The description goes on to state that:

*a number of contemporary critical writers, artists, and architects have taken a psychoanalytic approach in their work that may be identified with post-modern imagery: viewed as a movement, the current "psychoanalytic" dimension in art is the most significant revival of the "unconscious" as an expression of our belief in the authority of art since the efforts of the surrealists in the 30s and abstract expressionists in the 50s.* [12]

In the sense stated above, the psychoanalytic approach to art attempts to uncover the psychological make-up of the artist, thought to be responsible for the true "authorial" voice in the work. This approach placed emphasis on the personal history and biography of the artist, as seen in the presentation by

[9] See statement on Mountain Lake Symposium VI poster.

[10] This and the quotation that follows are from the Mountain Lake in Richmond poster. The poster lists Professor Wieland Schmied of the German Academic Exchange Service (DAAD) and professor of art history, Academy of Fine Arts, Munich, as one of the speakers; unfortunately, Professor Schmied was unable to attend. Boyd of the VMFA and I (VCU) were the conference directors.

[11] Paper titles: Gablik, "The Evaluative Process in Contemporary Art: What Is Art For?"; Kaprow, "The Conference as Performance"; Kuspit, "The Subjective Aspect of Critical Evaluation"; Michelson, "Utopia & Possible Worlds"; Bois's tentative title was "The Political Morality of Art"; Schmied's proposed paper was titled "Expressionism after Expressionism" or "Expressionism as Post-Expressionism — The Situation in Germany."

[12] See Symposium VIII poster.

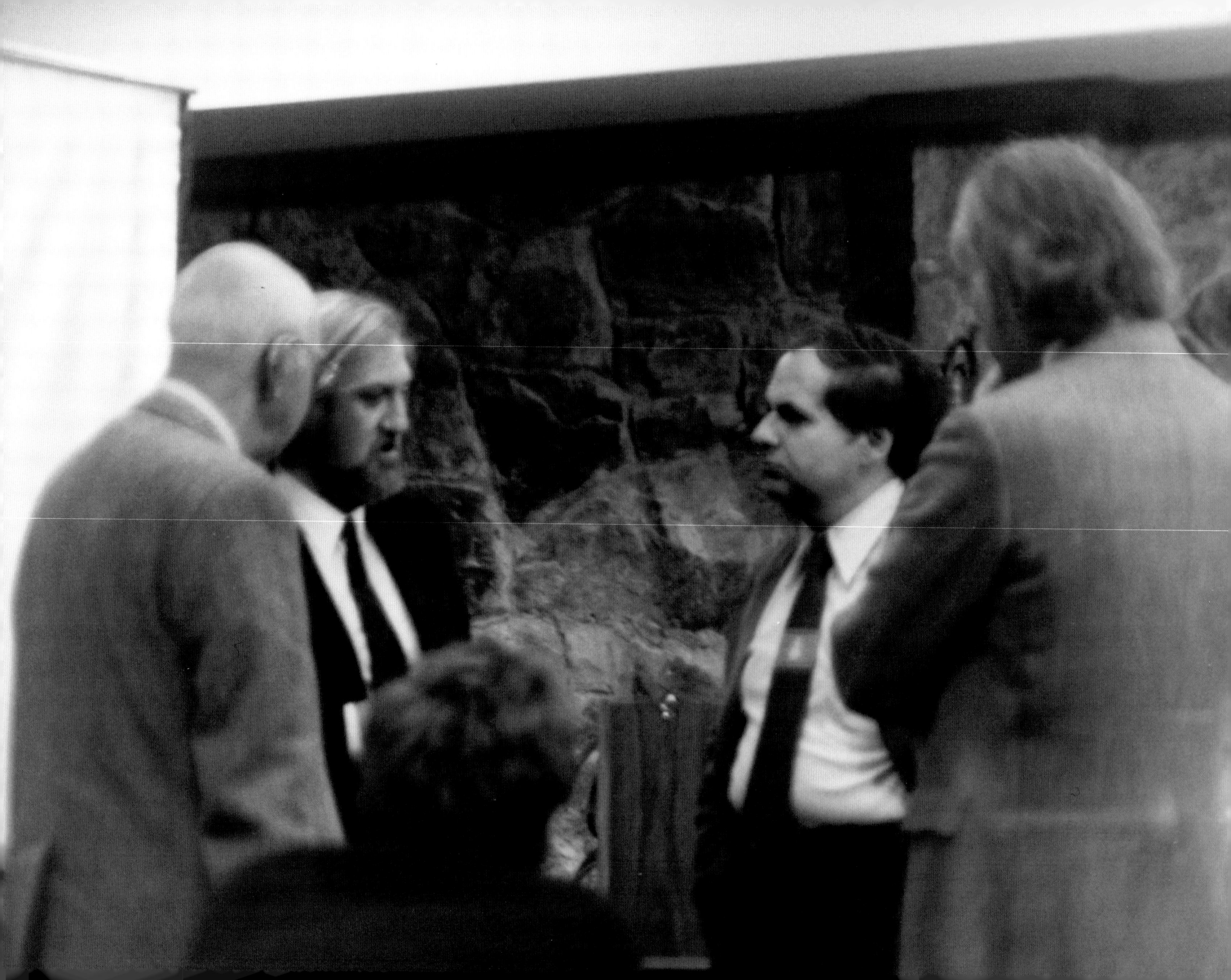

Mary Mathews Gedo. A clinical psychologist and art historian, Gedo titled her paper "An Autobiography in the Shape of Alabama: The Art of Roger Brown" and related Chicago artist Roger Brown's childhood life in Alabama and inter-family relationships to the content of his paintings.[13] In a similar approach Ellen Handler Spitz, a research candidate at the Columbia Psychoanalytic Institute with degrees in art history and aesthetics, presented a psychoanalytical account of the phenomenon of urban graffiti art and the motivation of its adolescent practitioners in a paper titled after Shakespeare "An Insubstantial Pageant Faded."

Also presenting papers were Jacques Leenhardt, professor at the Ecole des Hautes Etudes en Sciences Sociales (EHESS), Paris; Juan Pablo Bonta, formerly of the University of Buenos Aires and currently professor of architecture, University of Maryland, who spoke about the "Hidden Assumptions in Architectural Criticism"; and John E. Gedo, M.D., an analyst at the Institute for Psychoanalysis in Chicago, whose paper was titled "Looking with the Third Eye."

Befitting the regional make-up of the Mountain Lake Consortium as well as its ideological/theoretical position, the 1988 symposium, number IX in the series, again took place in another region, this time in Pittsburgh at Carnegie Mellon University. It convened from 18 to 20 November, a month later than usual so as to overlap with the 50th Carnegie International Exhibition at the Carnegie Museum of Art. This was just a few months after John Cage's first workshop at Mountain Lake. Symposium IX was significant in that it

seemed to articulate the intentions of all of the Mountain Lake activities to date, giving them a clearer focus by discussing various ideas of identity and various concepts of "community." Titled "Artists in Locale: Beyond a Regional Critique," the symposium questioned the hegemony of modernism in the face of more regionalist approaches to art that were occurring at the time. The symposium statement as it appeared on the poster along with names of the speakers made this quite explicit:

*The art of the 1980s was much more pluralistic in style, content, and purpose which contrasts with the stylistic hegemony of earlier modernism. Such greater diversity suggests that the art of this decade reflects a de-centered international aesthetic culture in which the very definitions of "mainstream" and individual artistic purpose should be re-examined. An examination of current "regional" art may clarify that works may be strongly associated with diverse regional and personal backgrounds.*

To allay any fears that this was a call for an insular or provincial art, the symposium statement went on to say:

*In this definition, regionalism does not imply the reactionary or parochial nature of historical American regionalism; rather, it focuses on the importance of ... artists in the international aesthetic culture whose works are the products of their information-rich environments. The activities of such artists face ongoing challenge without the need to concede to the "mainstream."*

Among the participants were Judith Russi Kirshner, curator,

critic, and professor of art history, School of the Art Institute of Chicago; Charles Miller, managing editor of *Artforum* and formerly editor-in-chief of *Dialogue*, a cooperative art journal in Columbus, Ohio; critic and curator Gerardo Mosquera from the Centro Wifredo Lam in Havana, Cuba, where he had organized the Havana Biennial Exhibition and was a regular contributor to the Cuban publications *Granma* and *Revolucion y Cultura*; artist Tim Rollins, director of K.O.S (Kids of Survival); Jacques Leenhardt, who again came from Paris; and Kuspit.[14]

The range and scope of the issues engaged by the symposium, which was moderated by Elaine A. King, Carnegie Mellon professor and university art gallery director, can be judged from Mosquera's presentation. Titled "New Cuban Art: Identity and Popular Culture," it focused on the unique character of contemporary Cuban art. Even though this art has been localized within Cuba and the Caribbean Basin for various geographic and political reasons, Mosquera showed that it has remained deeply rooted in the Cuban experience for genuine cultural reasons; it was an art expressing a people, not an international art world. Coming from the completely opposite direction was Rollins. An artist and former public school art teacher, he talked about the ongoing collaborative community-action workshop that he began doing with "kids" after school in the South Bronx. Called K.O.S. (Kids of Survival, The Art and Knowledge Workshop), his workshop used art as an educational tool in the inner-city neighborhood of the South Bronx to help young people develop a sense of self and community identity while also learning about history, literature, politics, and culture.[15]

[13] For the complete text of Mary Mathews Gedo's essay, see Howard Risatti, *Postmodern Perspectives: Issues in Contemporary Art*, 2nd edition (New Jersey: Prentice Hall, 1998), pp. 241–54.

[14] I also presented at the symposium as professor of art history and criticism at VCU and as Richmond editor of the regional-based *New Art Examiner*. I spoke about the development of community around shared interests, whether economic, cultural, or political, using feminism as an example of a way of finding a meaningful set of values that create a "shared realm" of cultural/social meaning.

[15] Some of the activities Rollins did with K.O.S. were to have young students/participants each paint something on a collaborative canvas that best expressed/characterized their response to a given piece of literature they had all read. In one project, each participant painted a letter A in the style/script that best represented their response to Nathaniel Hawthorne's *The Scarlet Letter*. For more on Tim Rollins and K.O.S., see Suzi Gablik, "Making Art as if the World Mattered: Some Models of Creative Partnership," *UTNE Reader* (July/Aug 1989), pp.75–76. Leenhardt's paper was titled "The Artistic Subjectivity Facing the Objectivity of the Art Scene and of Art History," Kuspit's "The Will to Unintelligibility in Modern Art, Understood Psychoanalytically."

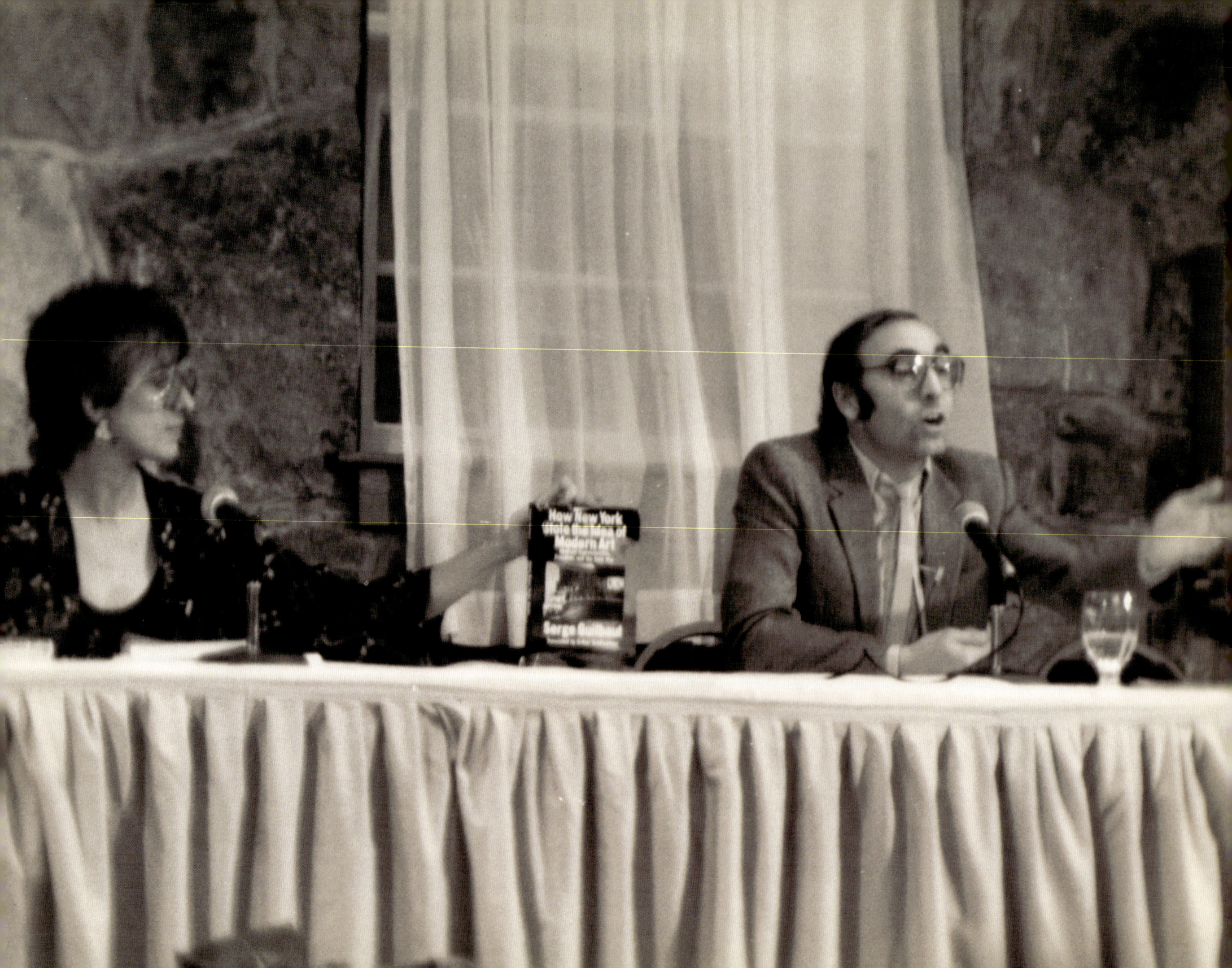

In their various ways the activities reported on by the symposium presenters paralleled the collaborative activities that had been going on at Mountain Lake. They helped make clear certain motivational features of the Mountain Lake activities. While all of the activities used art as a way to create a critical dialogue about contemporary issues in a place distant from the centers of mainstream culture, it became apparent that they all shared in addition an underlying philosophical position. This position had to do with more than just creating critical art discourses in a local region. In one way or another, all the activities — symposia, workshops, exhibitions, talks — were actually concerned with how to create a meaningful context or "culture" for art that would emerge out of the idea of community. What the symposium "Artists and Locale" made clear was that such a context could not simply be "borrowed" from an art world hundreds of miles away (i.e., New York or Chicago) by imitating the stylistic features of the art of these centers. Rather, the discourse that evolved from this particular symposium, in emphasizing how place and community must be understood as a dynamic interplay of the psychological, physical, and historical setting in which everyday life is lived and shared, underscored the conviction that art cannot be created out of dead bones or a barren psyche. To be viable and meaningful, art must also be grounded in a community and place of shared and vital (or re-vitalized) experiences. The creation of a "context for art," a way of locating art meaningfully within the larger cultural and social complex, had commonly been a driving force behind the Mountain Lake programs, not only the symposium, but also the workshops. For these reasons, the symposia, but especially the workshops, began to convene at sites in the wider community,

not just the Mountain Lake Hotel and the Miles C. Horton Center, sometimes as far away as France, Japan, and China. Symposium X, which returned to Mountain Lake, was titled "Artists' Intentions: Enduring Values/Discounted Goods." Held November 3–5, 1989, it also approached the idea of "art in locale," but from a critical/theoretical perspective. Again it featured a variety of presenters from different backgrounds and different fields of study including Akram Midani, multidisciplinary fine arts professor and dean of the College of Fine Arts, Carnegie Mellon University; Marcus Raskin, co-founder of the Institute for Policy Studies, Washington, D.C.; Maureen Sherlock, teacher of philosophy and critical theory in the film department, Art Institute of Chicago; New York feminist artist Nancy Spero; "realist" painter Sidney Tillim, former professor of painting and art history, Bennington College in Vermont; artist and critic Ronald Jones from Yale University; and returning presenters Charles Miller, Donald Kuspit, and Suzi Gablik.

The focus of Symposium X had to do with the aftermath of early Modernism, which was at one time, indeed, revolutionary in nature. The issue posed to the presenters, however, questioned the results of this Modernist revolution for the individual in today's world:

*Looking at the current "art world," it is not clear whether the modernist "revolution" has served to expand individual and social consciousness, or whether it actually has had a narrowing effect by limiting artistic content to style, and implicitly accommodating the homogenizing spirit and mass commodification of post-industrialism.*

It went on to wonder whether artists "outside of mainstream art activity" are, in fact, "addressing issues more broadly significant to society" than mainstream artists.[16] At one point a lively exchange occurred between Sidney Tillim and Maureen Sherlock when, in her remarks, Sherlock seemed to be lauding Eastern European Communism. Tillim, who was an old-line liberal, reminded her that "people in the Eastern Block are voting with their feet, risking their lives to cross the Berlin Wall to get to the West."

In her presentation Gablik raised provocative criticisms about the hermetic nature of so much contemporary art which produced, through what she called its "art for art's sake" values, "discrete aesthetic objects" without context. She was referring to art that is international in nature, unbounded by place or cultural context. Gablik implored artists to rethink their positions, to "make art as if the world mattered."[17]

Symposium X turned out to be the last gathering of its kind at Mountain Lake. And Symposium XI proved to be the last of Mountain Lake's challenging, thought-provoking, and diverse symposia, anywhere. It, like the 1986 gathering, was held at the Virginia Museum in Richmond. Titled "Decadence and Conscience: What Is Art Doing?," it convened November 2–4, 1990, and re-engaged issues raised by the previous symposium. The panelists were: Lowry Burgess, Conceptual/environmental artist and dean, College of Fine and Performing Arts at Carnegie Mellon, with a paper titled "Art and Global Issues: Summary Statements"; African-American painter Robert Colescott with a paper titled "The Form of Social Discourse"; Conceptual/

[16] From Conference Statement on Symposium X poster. The symposium was organized by Kass, Boyd, and the author, who also was the symposium moderator.

[17] Suzi Gablik, "Deconstructing Aesthetics," *New Art Examiner* (Jan 1989), p. 32. For more on Gablik's position, see her book *The Reenchantment of Art* (New York: Thames and Hudson, 1991). Paper titles: Kuspit, "The Good Enough Artist: Beyond the Mainstream Avant-Garde Artist"; Sherlock, "Agoraphobia: The Contradiction of Culture"; Jones, "If I Knew, Do You Really Expect that I Would Tell You?"; Spero, "The Continuous Presence."

Sidney Tillim and artist Gail
Nathan, currently Executive
Director, Bronx River Art
Center, Bronx, NY

environmental/performance artist Mierle Laderman Ukeles, who was artist-in-residence at the New York Sanitation Department; German-born Uruguayan Conceptual artist and critic Luis Camnitzer, whose work explores political issues such as social justice, repression, and institutional critique, with a paper titled "Screaming in a Room Filled with Jello"; Kay Rosen, a painter/word artist and art writer with a paper titled "RSTUVW, or Volkswagons Rust"; critic Kay Larson with "Truth and Consequences: The Crisis of Interpretation"; and Kuspit with "Super Ego Issues in Contemporary Art." Larson and Kuspit also conducted a very ambitious one-day criticism workshop as part of the symposium. This was a way to directly engage an audience with art issues in a "hands on" manner by having them do critical writing about works of art in the museum. Their stated focus was on critical issues and mechanics and style in writing, as well as critiques which they gave of two papers written by each participant.[18]

As in previous symposia, Symposium XI had a very specific focus which presenters were invited to address:

*Many artists today are seeking a more accessible relationship with the viewer. They are attempting to more fully engage the moral values and social responsibilities of the individual, both as a developing self and as a person responsive to the needs and realities of a particular locale.*[19]

In her presentation, Kay Rosen, in the way she uses forms and fragments of language in her paintings to address issues such as AIDS, rejected any sense of a hermetically sealed International Modernism. Instead she focused on pressing

social and moral issues of which AIDS was one because of its association with gay culture. In one example of her work, she re-configured the words *torsos rot* into TOR/SOS/ROT. Legible both forward and backwards, it has a call for action (SOS) in the center to draw attention to a health crisis that was sweeping across America but also had become politicized. She clearly showed how artists could engage pressing issues that went beyond mere style and polite formal design.

Much the same was apparent in the work of Camnitzer and Colescott. Using traditional European art media, Colescott's large canvases parody racial stereotypes through his manipulation of historical settings and skin color, thereby raising questions about cultural values and standards of beauty in a multicultural and multiethnic society. Mierle Laderman Ukeles also engages political and social issues through her concerns with finite systems, especially garbage disposal and its effects on the environment. In her presentation she worried that the "minimalist and process art of the 60s were unconnected to the human labor, processes, and industrial systems out of which their ordering and procedures sprang."[20]

While Symposium XI was the last in the series, it was clear that symposium participants over the previous decade were attempting to foster an art that was responsible and engaged, one that took physical, social, political, and environmental issues seriously as part of a meaningful cultural production. Over the last decades, these ideas have become even more pressing as an international art has developed along with a market to serve it that tends to be unconnected to place and lacks any sense of urgency. Such discrete aesthetic objects

devoid of context give added meaning and urgency to Suzi Gablik's exhortation to "make art as if the world mattered."

Why did the Mountain Lake Symposium come to an end? It is difficult to say exactly. Ray Kass and I were both teaching full-time at our respective universities and also doing our own research — Ray painting and exhibiting his work nationally while I was actively researching in my area of art history. Moreover, we also needed to write grants, usually to the National Endowment for the Arts, to fund the Symposium using Consortium fees as matching funds. What this meant, because of grant deadlines, is that we had to formalize the topic and a list of possible speakers for the coming year's symposium so we could submit a grant, all of which had to be done before the current symposium had even convened. As one can image, this made for a very hectic fall semester. After the current symposium was over, much of the remainder of the academic year was spent contacting possible speakers before they left for summer vacation so we could formalize the upcoming symposium. It became a very difficult schedule to maintain, especially without a great deal of support from our respective institutions.

To make matters worse, in 1990 there was a downturn in the economy and many universities implemented budget recensions, a practice that continued for many years to "instigate new efficiencies." As Mountain Lake Consortium support declined, and with it our ability to raise matching funds for grant applications, we finally decided to end the Symposium. It was intense but wonderful while it lasted.

---

[18] For further details see "Mountain Lake Criticism Workshop, 1990," which follows on p. §.

[19] From Statement on Symposium XI poster. The author moderated this symposium.

[20] Ukeles, in personal correspondence with the author, 16 July 1996. See Ukeles as quoted in Suzi Gablik, "Art and Audience in a Model Partnership," *New Art Examiner* (Jan. 1989), p. 33.

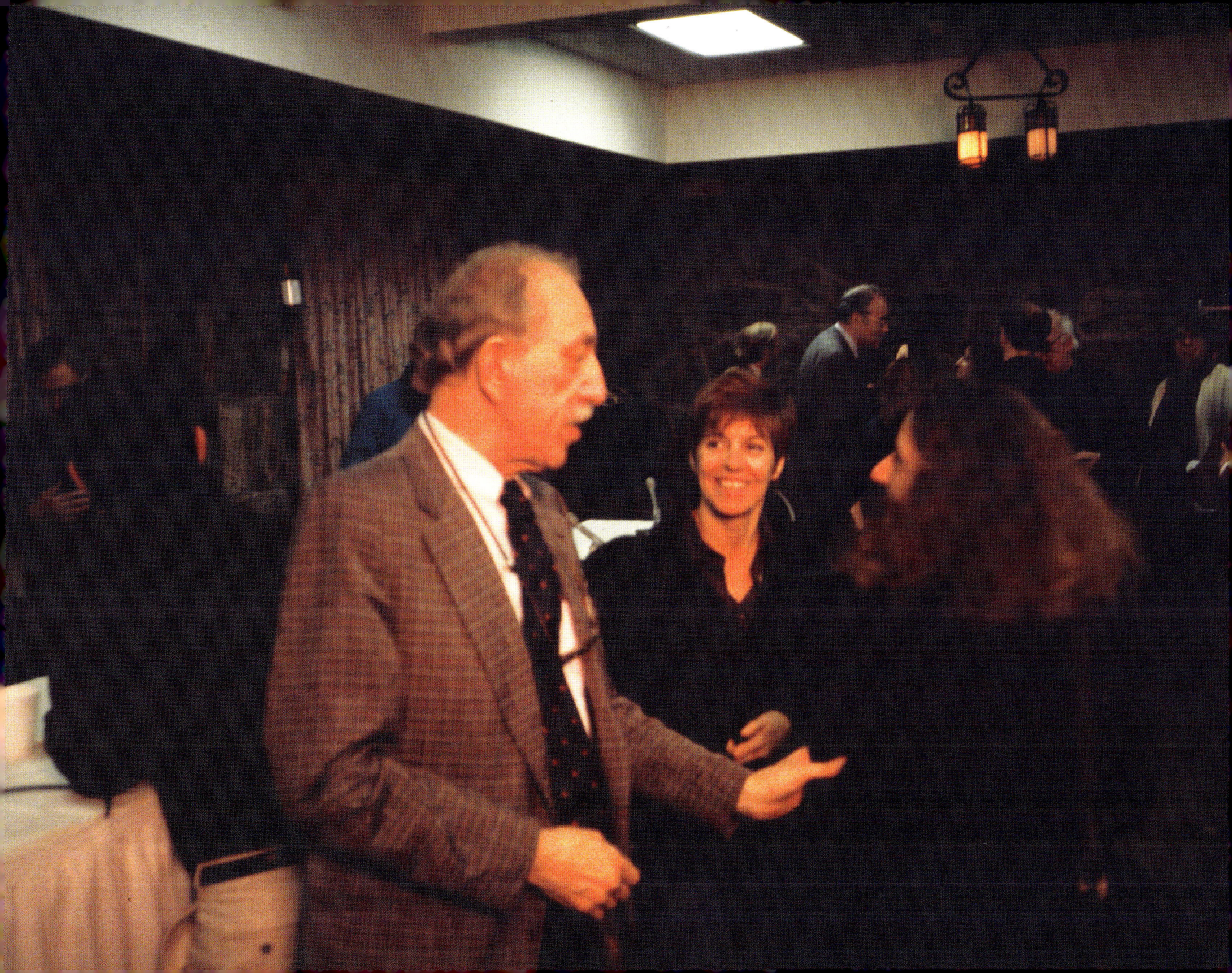

# MOUNTAIN LAKE
# CRITICISM WORKSHOP

**HOWARD RISATTI**

In the fall of 1990, the day before Mountain Lake Symposium XI was to meet at the Virginia Museum of Fine Arts in Richmond, Donald Kuspit and critic and art writer Kay Larson from *New York Magazine* conducted an intense criticism-writing workshop at the museum. About twenty members from the Richmond community and elsewhere participated in the day-long workshop, which was essentially a master class in criticism. In the spirit of the symposium, the title of which was "Decadence and Conscience: What Is Art Doing?," the morning session involved a broad discussion of theoretical and critical ideas about art. Led by Kuspit and Larson, who at times engaged in a friendly but serious debate over differing approaches to critical art writing, participants were invited to join in the discussion with comments and questions.

As the morning session was ending, participants were given an assignment to do during their two-hour lunch break. They were to go into the museum and select a work of art that was on display and write a critical review about it. When participants returned at the beginning of the afternoon session, they were asked to hand in their reviews — there were about twenty in all. Kuspit and Larson then took turns carefully reading aloud each review, after which they did an exhaustive critique of that review addressing writing style, clarity, and, of course, content. It was an extremely impressive display not only of critical acumen on the part of Kuspit and Larson, but also of generosity of spirit as they engaged each writer individually with suggestions about how to improve their writing and offering insights about critical ideas concerning the work of art in question.

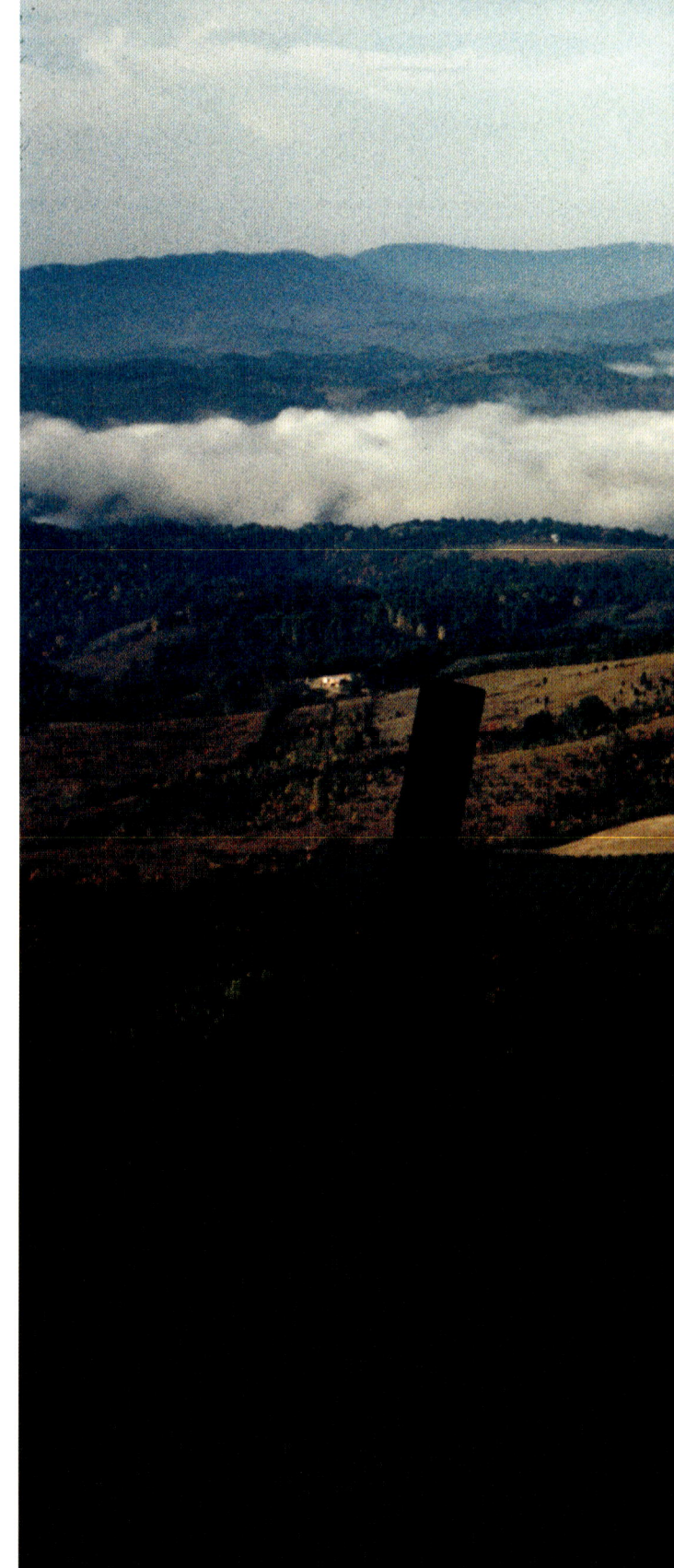

New River Valley from Salt
Pond Mountain with "Sleeping
Lady" Mountain in view

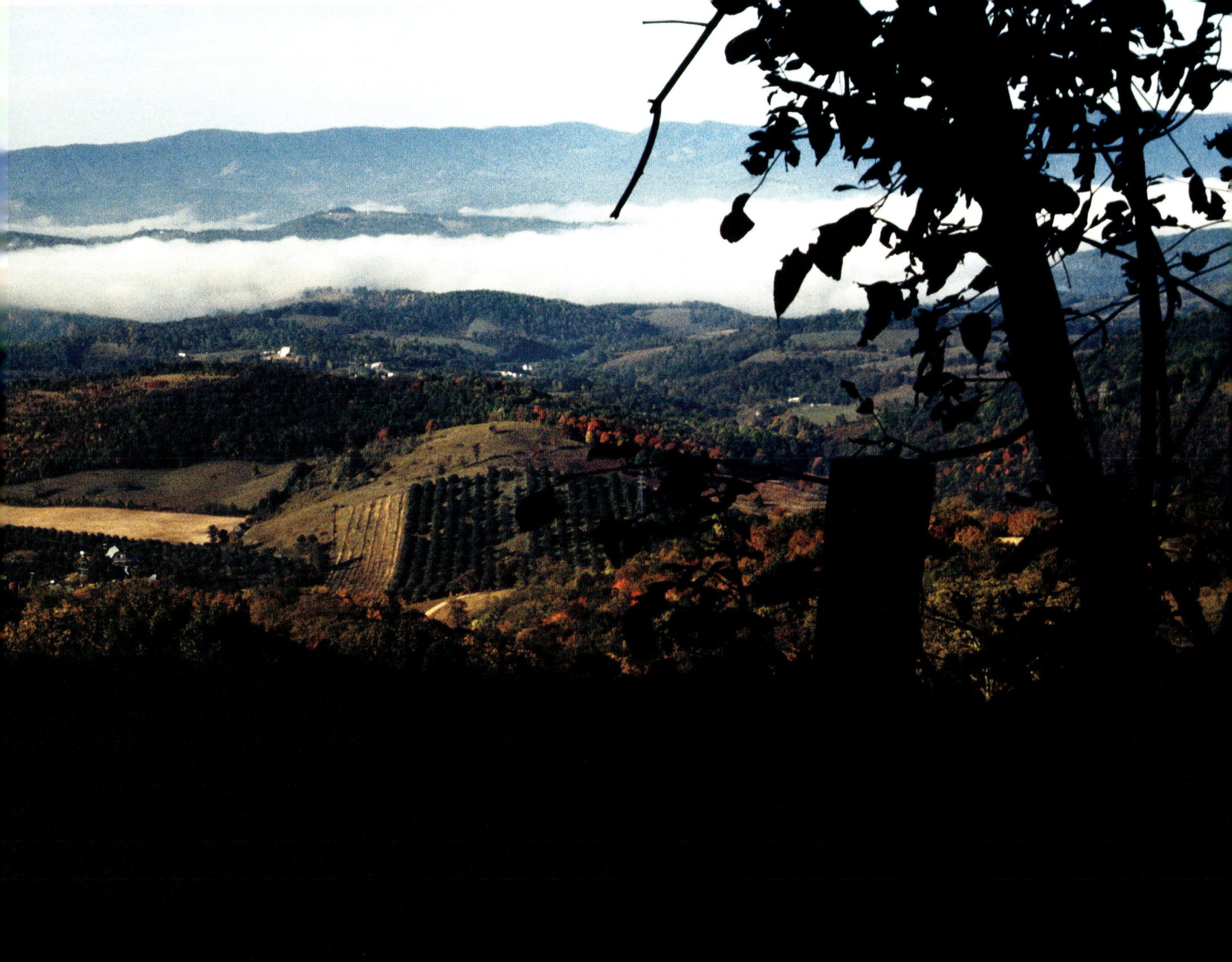

# DONALD KUSPIT AT THE MOUNTAIN LAKE SYMPOSIUM

HOWARD RISATTI with RAY KASS

During the decade of the 1980s New York critic Donald Kuspit was a familiar presence at Mountain Lake, a small hotel complex located in the Appalachian region of southwest Virginia. Built sometime in the 1930s beside a natural lake perched high atop a mountain in Giles County, one of only two such lakes in the United States, the Mountain Lake complex was the site of a decade-long series of art criticism conferences called the Mountain Lake Symposium. Begun in the fall of 1980, the symposium recalled in many ways the type of intellectual interchange that occurred decades earlier at Black Mountain College in North Carolina. The pastoral beauty and rural isolation of the Mountain Lake site appealed to artists and critics alike, especially those coming from large metropolitan areas such as New York City, Chicago, Los Angeles, Paris, and Havana. Despite a cosmopolitan draw, the principal audience for these art symposia was mid-life artists, scholars, and some students, all living within a day's driving distance of the hotel, which would include Blacksburg, Roanoke, Norfolk, Richmond, and Washington, D.C.

Kuspit's connection to the Mountain Lake Symposium has its origin in an annual meeting of the Southeastern College Art Conference (SECAC) that was held in the fall of 1977 at nearby Virginia Tech University in Blacksburg. One of the conference programs was "The Realist Panel," which focused on the new realism in art. Kuspit and fellow critic Clement Greenberg participated on the panel along with artists Janet Fish, Richard Estes, and Duane Hanson. The exchange between the artists, critics, and audience was extraordinary and gathered a momentum that resulted in many invitations for Greenberg and Kuspit to return to the New River Valley community

around Virginia Tech. These invitations continued even as the Mountain Lake Symposium began to take shape three years later in the form of meetings convening each spring and fall. The spring meetings created opportunities for invited artists and critics to meet with community artists and discuss issues that they felt pertinent to their work. The fall meetings, on the other hand, developed into carefully organized symposia with an interdisciplinary focus on theories of criticism and the relationship between artistic practice and abstract theoretical constructs such as Formalism, Structuralism, and Post Structuralism. Typically, participants, who came from a wide range of disciplines including art, architecture, philosophy, theater, sociology, religion, history, and psychology, presented formal papers on specific subjects related to the symposium topic for that year.

Kuspit's role at Mountain Lake was crucial because he participated in every one of the criticism symposia throughout the decade of the 1980s. In a sense, the trajectory of all of the symposia topics reflects the development of his own critical ideas as the symposia increasingly grappled with the issues of contemporary art's relationship to the wider culture. The symposia were undertaken with a hope that critical discourse could and indeed should play a vital role in shaping culture, that critical discourse could help make the cultural realm a vehicle for social transformation. This was evident from the very outset as the title of the first conference, convened in October of 1980, was "Moral Philosophy, Aesthetics, and Contemporary Art."

It was at this symposium that Kuspit staked out the basic premises of his critical stance in the presence of older or more established

critics such as Robert Pincus-Witten and Greenberg. Kuspit's role in the conference also became strategic at this time, and a pattern developed — one that was to continue throughout all of the symposia — in which he was always the last of the invited speakers to present a paper. As it happened, for this first symposium he had prepared a paper titled "Art Incommunicado" as his contribution to the question of moral philosophy's relationship to aesthetics and to contemporary art. However, after having heard the papers presented by the day's previous speakers, he made revisions in his text and renamed it, with a bow to Hegel's influential idea of the divided or contradictory self, "The Unhappy Consciousness of Modernism." Kuspit described the moral dimension in wholly existential terms premised on Nietzsche's contention in *Beyond Good and Evil* that imposing moral judgments on experience interferes with the perception of the psychological and is thus a barrier to an understanding of psycho/social reality. Kuspit contended that a sense of the moral can properly exist in art — rather than in the artist, even an artist unencumbered by judgmental moral concepts — because it resides in how artists feel about making art. In other words, an artist's assumptions about how art should be seen and understood in the social world constitute its moral dimension.

Kuspit's and Greenberg's lively interaction provided fertile ground for many of the artists in the audience and helped establish the direction and critical development of the Mountain Lake Symposium and, perhaps, even Kuspit's own work, for the ensuing decade. During their exchanges Kuspit could appear to be countering Greenberg, and there was occasionally the feeling of palpable antagonism between the two, but they had much

*"Criticism begins with a responsibility to experience, moves to an awareness of practice, and ends with theory that seems to clarify the depth with which a particular practice is experienced. ...*

*"I think the wish for one true [theoretical] model reflects anxiety about the abundance and complexity of art today. It is a kind of arrogance masking fear of engulfment."**

–Donald Kuspit

*Redeeming Art: Critical Reveries (New York: Allworth Press, 2000), pp. 274-75

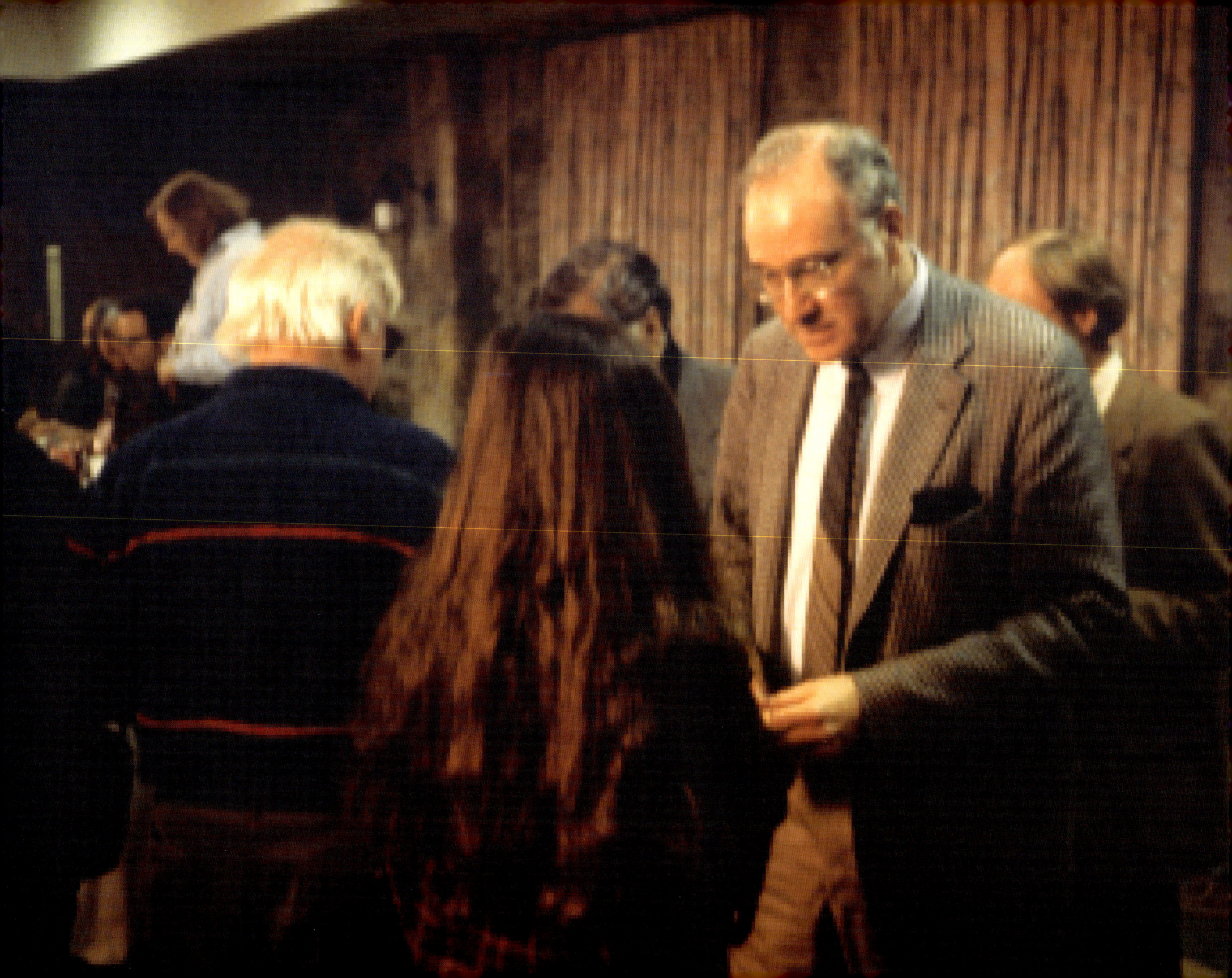

in common. Kuspit certainly took Greenberg's art criticism and theory seriously; the very first two lines of *Clement Greenberg, Art Critic*, the book Kuspit published in 1979 (two years after he and Greenberg appeared together on the SECAC realism panel), state this unequivocally. "The significance of Clement Greenberg," wrote Kuspit, "cannot be overestimated. He is the designer and subtle manipulator of modernism, which is the single most important and influential theory of modern art."[1]

Both Greenberg and Kuspit demonstrated a conviction that artists did not have to live and work in New York City. Greenberg's sense of "stylistic competence" supported Kuspit's idea of the "good enough artist." Moreover, Greenberg and Kuspit were decidedly artist-centered critics and visited many artists' studios over a period of years. These visits and the dynamic exchange of ideas at the Mountain Lake Symposium laid the foundation for a new critical culture for many of the artists in the area that more closely resembled the "localized" culture of the "Neo Expressionist" artists who were emerging in Europe at the time, especially those in Germany in whom Kuspit took a special interest, than the parochial, inward-looking character of traditional southern regionalism. From what was happening in artists' studios in the New River Valley community around Mountain Lake, it became clear that intense critical interaction could result in the creation of culture and, as artist and Mountain Lake participant Mierle Laderman Ukeles later observed during her 1994 Mountain Lake workshop, the Mountain Lake Symposium, along with related workshops, did indeed create a culture.[2]

The second Mountain Lake Symposium convened the following October (1981). Like the first, it too focused on issues of greater consequence than that of insular art-world politics in order to explore the relationship between critical discourse in art and social issues. Titled "Art Criticism/Social Criticism," it was an attempt to move away from a criticism based primarily on what could be characterized as a second-generation Greenbergian Formalism, a formalism that, unfortunately, lacked the critical urgency that gave weight and meaning to Greenberg's best writings, those done between 1939 and the later 1950s when the Depression and World War II still haunted the American psyche.[3] With the economic prosperity of the 1960s, this critical urgency quickly dissipated, and the question of whether culture itself would survive, something that had deeply troubled Greenberg in the '40s and '50s, no longer seemed relevant, and a kind of "art in a vacuum" approach to formalist criticism developed.

Besides Kuspit, critic/art historian Rosalind Krauss from Hunter College was also a participant in the symposium. She was co-editor with Annette Michelson of *October*, a magazine that prided itself on being the forum for "advanced" critical ideas, apparently in the spirit of Russia's October Revolution. Greenberg, who was joined by English sculptor Anthony Caro, Canadian painter and critic Terry Fenton, American painter Walter Darby Bannard, and *Artforum* editor Charles Millard at the spring 1981 artists' conference, was not at the fall symposium that year, nor at any of the subsequent symposia. However, he remained in the background as a larger-than-life critical force because of his ideas and reputation. Krauss and Greenberg had an uneasy relationship at times, especially after she wrote a widely read article contesting his order to strip paint from five of the late David Smith's sculptures.[4] However, when all was said and done, Krauss's critical approach to art was closer to Greenberg's (especially his late, post 1950s "hermetic formalism") than to Kuspit's. Like Greenberg, she was intent on establishing an all-encompassing theoretical system that could account for all aspects of artistic production. This is something she apparently found in French Structuralism/Post Structuralism with its penchant for valuing abstract formal schemas more than individual artists and artistic practice. For his part, Kuspit was also influenced by Greenbergian theory in some sense. Greenberg's international reputation as the most important theorist and critic of modernism is one reason why Kuspit felt obliged to take him on with a critique of him and his theory. But Kuspit's interest in individual artists' work was acute enough and his critical background wide enough that his approach to art was also able to encompass the ideas of a critic as different from Greenberg as Harold Rosenberg, Greenberg's critical nemesis since the 1940s and the rise of Abstract Expressionism. Rosenberg, who coined the term "action painting," rejected the idea of a "pure" art and spoke about the moral element inherent in the struggle of the artist.[5] In a similar way Kuspit was inclined to critically locate each work of art or group of works within the context of culture at large. Furthermore, like Rosenberg, Kuspit was not inclined toward system-making; he once remarked that he regularly changed his stripes so he could fit into every debate, adding his own touch of controversy. In contrast to various Structural/Post Structural and Deconstruction theories that were sweeping through the field of critical writing in the 1980s and '90s, and that were increasingly shaped by abstract academic theory rather than actual works of art, Kuspit, again reflecting

---

[1] Donald Kuspit, "Issues and Attitudes," *Clement Greenberg, Art Critic* (Madison: University of Wisconsin Press, 1979), p. 3.

[2] According to Ray Kass in conversation with the author, Ukeles repeated this remark to him a few years later when they happened to meet at the Ronald Feldman Gallery in New York City.

[3] See, for example, Greenberg's "Avant-Garde and Kitsch," published in 1939 on the eve of WWII, and his "Plight of Culture" from 1953, both reprinted in Greenberg, *Art and Culture: Critical Essays* (Boston: Beacon Press, 1961), pp. 3–33.

[4] At the time Greenberg was an executor of Smith's estate and believed that paint on sculpture violated the dictum of medium purity. Controversy broke out when Krauss, in an *Art in America* article (September 1974), charged Greenberg with changing Smith's sculptures.

[5] See Harold Rosenberg, "The American Action Painters," *Art News* (December 1952), reprinted in his *The Tradition of the New*, 2nd Edition (New York, Toronto: McGraw-Hill Book Company, 1959), pp. 23–39.

Rosenberg, championed individual human agency in all its forms as the source of art's meaning and the locus of its importance.

The titles of subsequent conferences show that they continued to echo the flow of Kuspit's ideas and attempted to tie critical discourse to larger social and moral imperatives in a kind of give-and-take between artist, critic, and viewer. For example, the third symposium, "Art and Its Publics," in fall 1982, occurred at the same time that the new German painting's reprise of the stylistic expressionism of pre–World War II German art began receiving international attention through exhibitions in Europe and America. Regional in its expression, but international in its outlook, this art was laden with historical and psychological tension conveyed through a linking of subject matter and style; thus it offered another lens through which to view the role of place and region in the development of an art outside of the established mainstream. The social and political connotations of this new work were unmistakable to Kuspit, and he quickly became involved in framing a discourse that made his concerns clear. He outlined the relevance of this new painting in "Acts of Aggression: German Painting Today," an essay published in *Art in America* in two parts that acted as book ends to the third symposium, the first part appearing in September of 1982, one month before the symposium, and the second in January of 1983, two months afterwards.[6]

The critical discourse at "Art and Its Publics" questioned the long-held modernist attitude that artists make their work strictly on their own terms without regard for the public. Following this way of thinking, the public was left with little choice:

either get on board or be deemed philistines unable to embrace the future exemplified by new art. The noted Conceptual artist Joseph Kosuth, who was one of the last presenters at this symposium, had a strong view of these developments. Not only did he see a vacuum of meaning in the newest contemporary styles, but he singled out Neo Expressionism as indicative of a loss of belief in modernist tenets. To some people, however, these so-called modernist tenets seemed increasingly less modern and more questionable in view of what was happening at this stage of contemporary art production. Moreover, by this time the modernist movement was already nearly 100 years old and seemed less "modern" and more conventional as part of a commercial art/gallery establishment.

Kuspit's paper, titled "Maligned and Mystified Audiences: The Artist's Sense of the Public," was, in a sense, a response to Leo Steinberg's 1962 article "Contemporary Art and the Plight of Its Public," in which Steinberg posited a teleological view of art forever marching forward into an uncharted future while discarding the past along the way.[7] As usual, Kuspit's was the last paper presented. Following directly after Kosuth's paper, it was awaited by the audience with much anticipation. By now the editor of the Contemporary American Art Critics series for UMI Research Press and soon to be the recipient of the 1983 Frank Jewett Mather Award for Distinction in Art Criticism from the College Art Association (CAA), Kuspit was well known for philosophical discourse. Linda McGreevy, who was in the audience that day, recalled that as Kuspit took the podium for his presentation, the audience "settled in for the 'truly theoretical' paper they expected."[8]

MOUNTAIN LAKE SYMPOSIUM X AT MT. LAKE
"Artists' Intentions: Enduring Values/Discounted Goods"
November 3-5, 1989

Agenda

Friday, November 3
Afternoon check-in. Participants should arrive by 6:00 p.m.
5:30 p.m.          Cocktails
5:30-10:00 p.m.    Dinner served

Saturday, November 4
7:30-9:00 a.m.     Breakfast
9:00 a.m.          Welcome and Introductions - Howard Risatti
9:15               Presentation of Papers
                   Maureen Sherlock
10:00              Sydney Tillim
11:00              Break
11:15              Suzi Gablik
12 noon-2 p.m.     Lunch (provided for registrants who have paid $35 fee.
                   Others may pay directly).
2:00 p.m.          Nancy Spero
3:00               Ron Jones
3:45               Break
4:00               Donald Kuspit
5:30               Reception celebrating the 10th Anniversary of the Mt. Lake
                   Symposium, followed by dinner.

Sunday, November 5
7:30-9:00 a.m.     Breakfast
9:00 a.m.          Marcus Raskin
9:45-12 noon       Panel Discussion and Audience Questions with the seven
                   speakers, as well as Akram Midani and Charles V. Miller.
12:00 noon         Conference ends.

Gary "Chico" Harkrader, sketch of Mary Matthews Gedo at Symposium VIII, "Making Psychoanalytic Sense of Art," 1987

[6] Kuspit, Part I, *Art in America* (September 1982), pp. 140–51, and Part II (January 1983), pp. 90–101, 131–35. For a hint of the controversy surrounding the new art see Kuspit, "Flak from 'Radicals': The American Case Against German Expressionism," *Expressions: New Art from Germany*, exhibition catalogue (Munich: Prestel, in association with the St. Louis Museum of Art, 1983).

[7] See Leo Steinberg, "Contemporary Art and the Plight of Its Public," *Harper's Magazine* (March 1962), reprinted in his *Other Criteria: Confrontations with Twentieth-Century Art* (London, Oxford, New York: Oxford University Press, 1972), pp. 3–16.

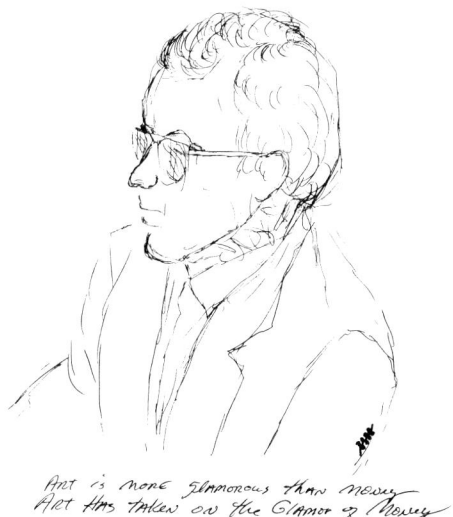

*Donald Kuspit — New York*
*Editor, Critic, Author*

*iNoPK — YNAPRBSPONSEdLtobPKirshNevxP — PxyI*
*the "Everything wrong w/ Everything"*

*A problem w/ Art in the Age of Glamor*
*Every Art has its Historical Price*
*... Art as A gesture of Glamor — Salle*

*Art is more glamorous than money*
*Art has taken on the Glamor of Money*

Gary "Chico" Harkrader, sketch of Donald B. Kuspit at
Symposium VIII, "Making Psychoanalytic Sense of Art," 1987

As usual, Kuspit did not disappoint. He discussed the making of art as the making of new codes or systems, but within an established language of art. He also went on to argue that the audiences for art are complex and break down into at least three groups, not all of whom are hostile to the artist.

A subtext of the third symposium was the growing belief that the concept of a "mainstream art world" as the foundation of modernism's internationalism was no longer as valid as it once had been. This view was being challenged as the notion of the postmodern and a "new historicism" began to gain influence among critics and many younger artists. As a cultural matrix, the "mainstream art world" seemed to be devolving into a commercial world with art as its center. And, as Kuspit implied, while it may still be possible to universalize in modernist fashion various of the themes found in the new art (say, those found in German Neo Expressionist painting — war, aggression, power), nonetheless to universalize the psychological dimension (especially the psychological impact) of these themes and hence the painting's reception with its different audiences would be far more difficult. This was true because of the varied dynamics of history and personal experience, that is to say, how the effects of war, aggression, and power were different for different people — as they certainly were for younger Germans who had to live in the shadow of Hitler's oppression as opposed to those who were actual survivors of that oppression. It was becoming increasingly clear, as Kuspit's writing about the new German art indicated: culture and history are not so easily separated — nor so easily abstracted into universal concepts — as modernist theory had indicated.[9]

The next three symposia carried forward related themes by focusing on the role of the media in art and society and by raising questions about revisionism, historicism, and criticism in Postmodern art and architecture as the symposium titles indicate: "Artists, Imagery and Influences" (1983), "Revisionism/Criticism: Directions in Postmodern Art and Architecture" (1984), and "Dislocated Sources: Historicism in Postmodern Art and Architecture" (1985). In the general spirit of postmodernist thinking, which deployed a critique of the placeless internationalism of late modernity's non-localized, non-regional identity, Kuspit explored the role that the indigenous and regional could play in the development of culture. His own continuing interest in German Neo Expressionism and the phenomenon of Outsider Art are two examples of his approach to this issue.

At Symposium VII in 1986, "The Evaluative Process in Contemporary Art," critical methodology was itself being questioned. The old relationships between art, critical thought, and the public at large were no longer being taken for granted. The long-held view that contemporary art's relationship to the dominant culture was still one of confrontation, rather than complicity, was also being challenged as part of this critical evaluative process. Kuspit's thinking was central to examining the criteria for making judgments about works of art, and for asking where those criteria come from, who establishes them, and what values they imply on the part of artist and audience.

The topic of Symposium VIII in 1987, "Making Psychoanalytical Sense of Art," came directly from Kuspit. By this time his ideas about the local and regional had become more concentrated,

[9] See Linda F. McGreevy, "*Art and Its Publics*: Inspired but inconclusive symposium," *New Art Examiner*, vol. 10, no. 2 (Dec. 1982), pp. 8–9.

[9] Kuspit, fluent in German, earned a PhD in Philosophy under Theodor W. Adorno at Universität Frankfurt in 1963, giving him a unique insight into the German "situation" being explored by Neo Expressionist artists in Germany.

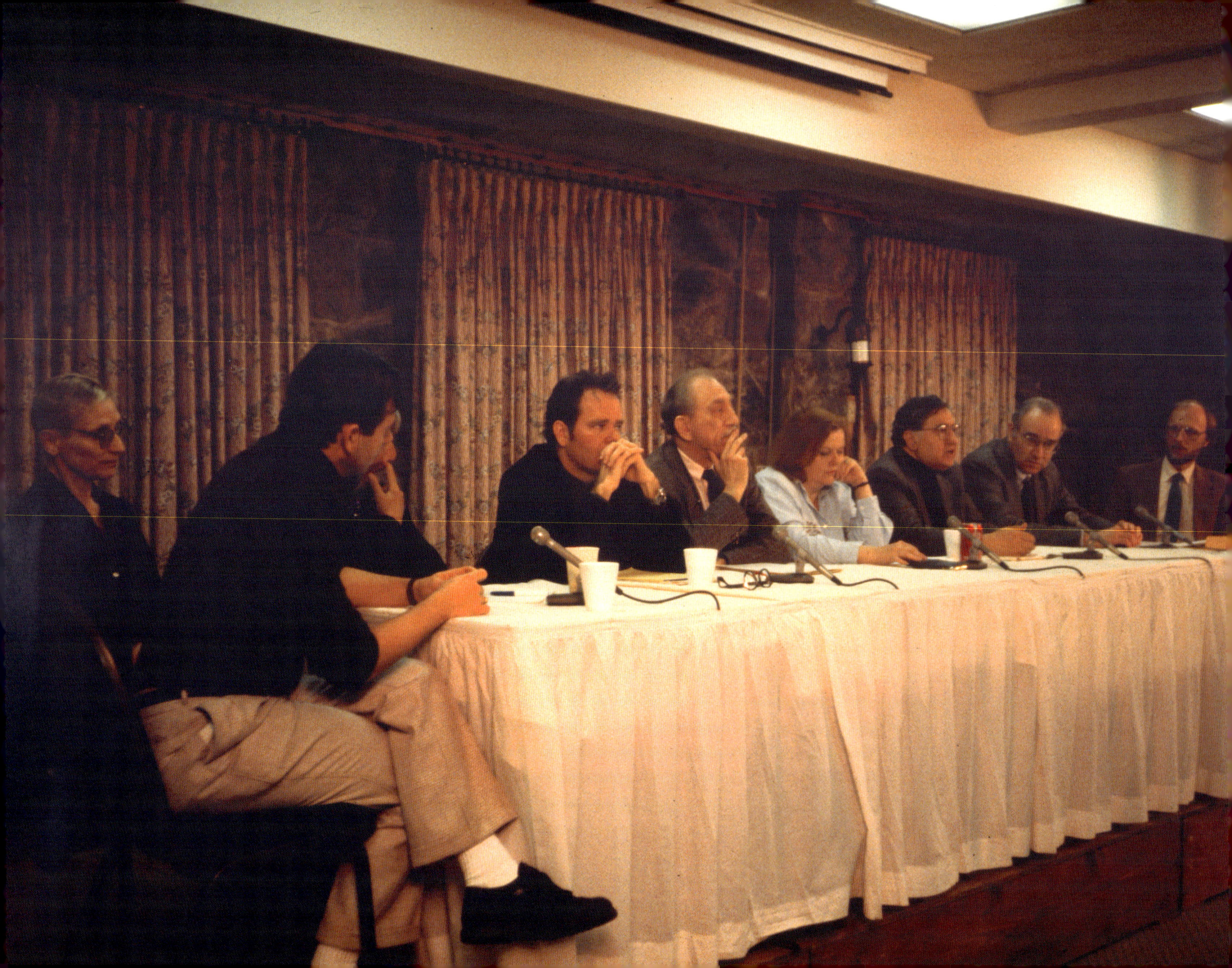

in the sense that his focus had shifted to the individual person as a psychic entity. More than anyone else at the time, Kuspit explored these ideas in his symposium papers and his writings. Few art critics could match the insight and experience that he brought to the subject through his knowledge of psychoanalysis.[10] Because of this, the panelists for Symposium VIII were less a gathering of distinguished art professionals than professionals from the field of psychoanalysis. Among them were John E. Gedo from the Institute for Psychoanalysis in Chicago; art historian and clinical psychologist Mary Mathews Gedo; and Ellen Handler Spitz, research candidate at the Columbia Psychoanalytic Institute in New York. Through the papers presented, the role the psyche plays in formation of the self and development of a sense of place, that is, a sense of what it means to "be" someone and to "be" somewhere, became clearer and took on greater meaning for the local Appalachian region and its artists. This symposium also influenced other Mountain Lake strategies — for example, those of the collaborative painting workshops that were held in the spring and featured invited artists and interested members of the local community.

Unlike other more academically oriented critics, Kuspit continued to place great stock in art because his thinking continued to be artist-centered. This is evident from his essay "Artist Envy," which appeared in *Artforum* in November 1987, the month following Symposium VIII. In this essay about the parallel relationship between the psychoanalyst and the artist, he came down on the side of the artist by placing great emphasis on the creative agency of the artist; he concluded that it is because of this creativity that the artist is envied by the analyst.

Such ideas continued to be the focus of Kuspit's work and of the symposium in general. Symposium IX in 1988, "Artists in Locale: Beyond a Regional Critique," expanded the critical exploration of the local by opposing it to the mainstream. The question that was being asked was whether art could continue to exist as a meaningful activity if completely dislocated from its sources. Kuspit was engaging these issues in his own writings at the time. In May of 1988 he published "Crowding the Picture: Notes on American Activist Art Today," an essay that questioned the motives behind the new political art in the United States that was currently the rage in New York galleries.[11] He began by looking at the loneliness of the individual in mass society, at how the individual is actually alienated from and within what Jacques Ellul termed the "lonely crowd."[12] From here Kuspit went on to raise questions about the new political art itself. Was this art as genuinely and constructively confrontational of the system as the old avant-garde had been? Or was it just another fashionable stance assumed by artists as part of mainstream commercial gallery practice? What was being asked, in other words, was whether the new political art might be less a meaningful attempt at social transformation as some advocates had argued and more of what amounted to a self-congratulatory claim to the moral high ground that art had held since the mid-nineteenth century. Clearly Kuspit was a critic concerned more deeply with critical analysis of art in society than with "cheerleading" the newest art-world wrinkle.

Mountain Lake Symposia X and XI, in 1989 and 1990, the last two symposia held, were titled respectively "Artists' Intentions: Enduring Values/Discounted Goods" and "Decadence and Conscience: What Is Art Doing?" Perhaps even more blatantly than the first few, these last two symposia questioned art and its capacity to inspire, if not actually implement social change. By this time a decade of symposia had convened and Kuspit had become one of the premier art critics in America.

Over this decade his critical ideas both shaped and were shaped by the Mountain Lake Symposium with all of its various participants and audiences and points of view. And a small hotel on a mountain top in rural southwest Virginia had become a locus for intense critical discussions about art and culture.

---

[10] Besides PhDs in philosophy and art history, Kuspit eventually completed the equivalent in psychoanalysis from New York University's School of Medicine in the 1990s.

[11] See Donald Kuspit, "Crowding the Picture," *Artforum* (May 1988), p. 112. Reprinted in Howard Risatti, *Postmodern Perspectives: Issues in Contemporary Art*, 2nd Edition (Upper Saddle River, NJ: Prentice Hall, 1997), pp. 108–120.

[12] Kuspit quoting Ellul, *Propaganda: The Formation of Men's Attitudes (first published in France as Propaganda*, 1962) (New York: Alfred A. Knopf, 1972), pp. 8–9. See also David Riesman, *The Lonely Crowd* (New Haven, CT: Yale University Press, 1950 and 1961).

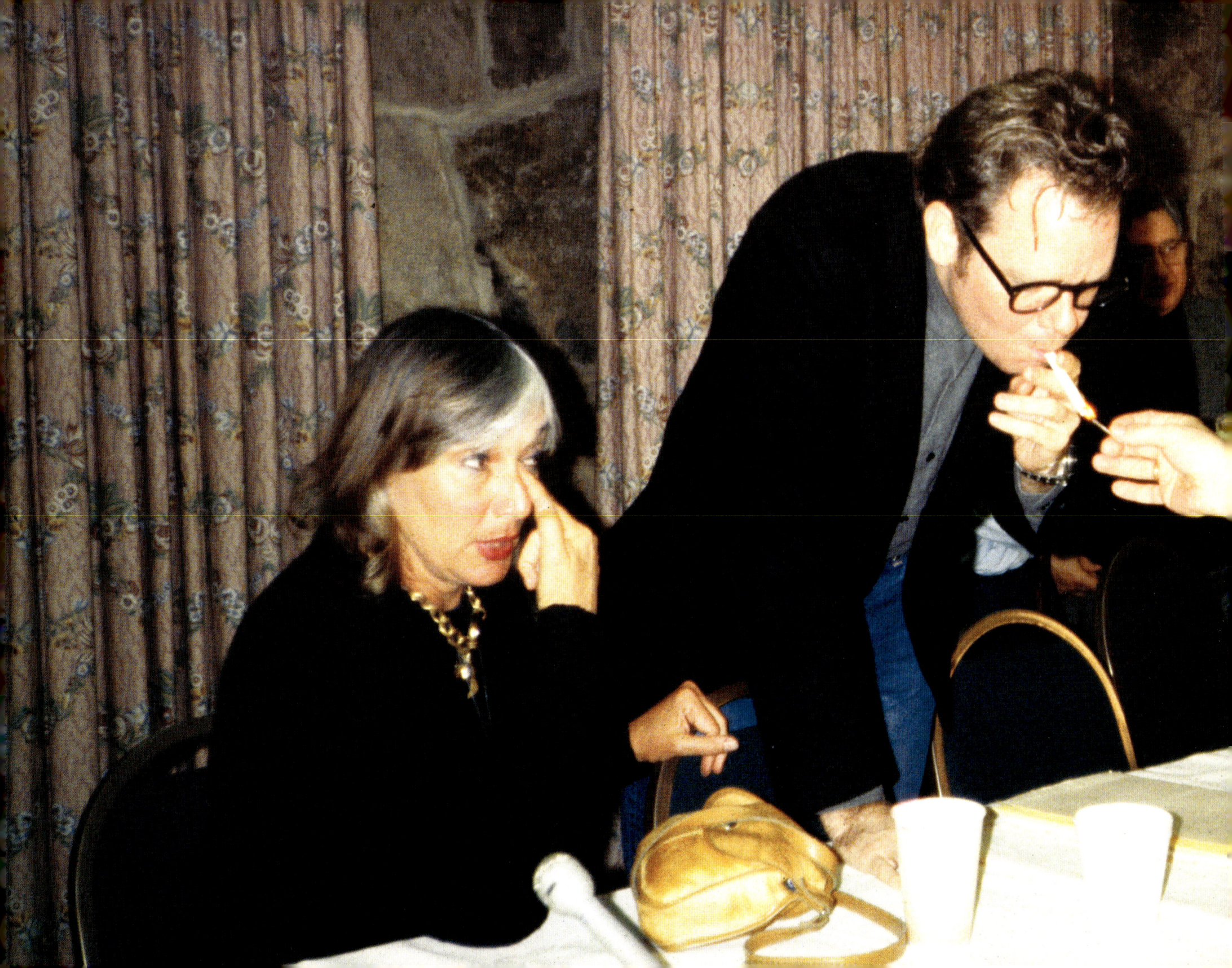

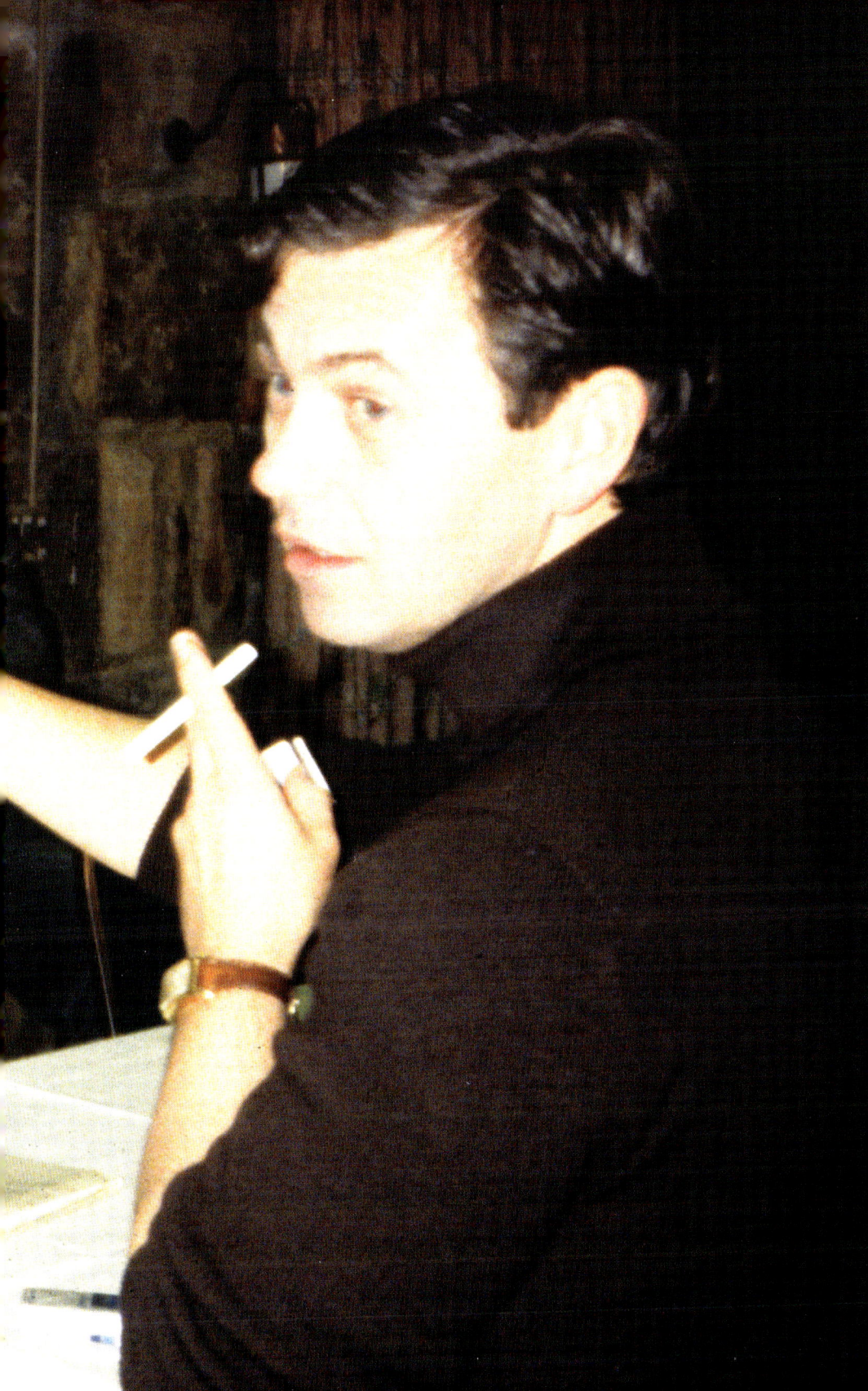

(L-R) Suzi Gablik, Ron Jones,
Akram Midani, Charles V. Miller

# II

## *Origins of the Mountain Lake Symposium and Workshops*

# SOME MEMOIR / SOME CONTEXT

RAY KASS

*We were on a magic mountain where we could discuss art to our hearts' and minds' content. ...*

Donald B. Kuspit[1]

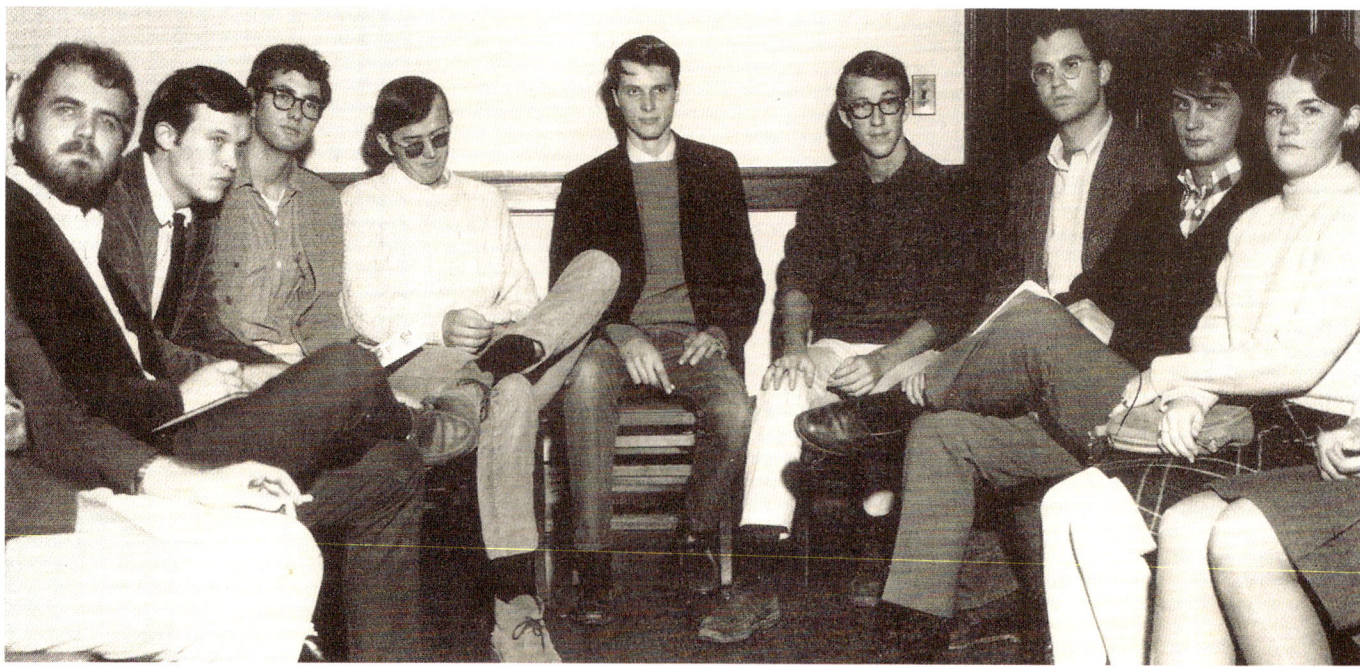

Staff of the *The Carolina Quarterly*, 1965-66, (L-R) Unidentified, Russell Banks, Bill Hicks, Dan Tartaglia, Lucius Shepard, Ray Kass, David Forster, Mike Goldstein, Bob Simmons, Kitty Hawthorne, unidentified

In retrospect, I realize that the Mountain Lake Symposium and Workshops had essential roots in the southern literary fermentation in Chapel Hill, North Carolina, in the 1960s. In 1965, as an undergraduate at the University of North Carolina (UNC), I was serving as subscriptions and circulation editor of *The Carolina Quarterly*, the university's literary magazine. At the time, I was an aspiring poet and painter whose only previous experience with publishing was as a co-editor and a cartoonist for *The Golden Wave*, my high school newspaper, and *The Daily Tar Heel*, UNC's campus newspaper. Unexpectedly, I became the Quarterly's editor-in-chief. In this role I had the good fortune to be joined by an extraordinary group of gifted editor/friends, including Russell Banks and Lucius Shepard. Unfortunately, we published only two issues of *The Carolina Quarterly* before the Publications Board of North Carolina pulled the remainder of our annual funding.[2]

My brief stint as editor proved of lasting value to me, however. Through it I met artists and writers who visited the UNC campus. Perhaps most importantly, I met Jonathan Williams, who had founded the Jargon Society press in 1951 while a student at Black Mountain College. Through Jonathan, I would meet many artists and writers who had been part of the extraordinary Black Mountain College community.

The following year, 1966, *Lillabulero* magazine and press was founded by Russell Banks, William Matthews, Newton Smith, and David Maleson as a platform for their literary endeavors and for those of emerging and established artists and writers they admired. As my first experience of a community of like-minded young artists collaborating to create an actual forum for their own ideas, the example of *Lillabulero* magazine was probably the most important influence on my personal development; it made me realize that I, too, could be an event organizer, or "convener."

During this time I also was inspired by a class in small press publishing co-taught by poet Carolyn Kizer and Professor Dougald McMillan, a James Joyce and Samuel Beckett scholar. The central focus was twofold: publishing a literature and art magazine we called *Sample Copy* and examining at our weekly seminars earlier twentieth-century literary journals. Particular emphasis was placed on the ground-breaking, avant-garde Parisian magazine *Transition* (1927–1938).[3] This journal was intended as a platform for experimental writing and featured modernist contributions by visual artists, critics, and political activists. From my limited perspective at the time, I thought of *Transition* as an apt model for what my literary friends in Chapel Hill were attempting to do with *Sample Copy*, *The Carolina Quarterly*, and then *Lillabulero*. We were trying to be modern and interdisciplinary and provide an outlet for experimental literary texts and critical essays along with photographs and illustrations by visual artists.

[1] This sentence is taken from Kuspit's "Commentary" in this volume.

[2] During the spring of 1966, the writer and scion of the "Beat Generation," Jack Kerouac, was dropped off at my house, and a week-long visit commenced that has been variously documented. It was rumored that Kerouac wanted me to publish a text of his, loosely based on the Diamond Sutra, that Grove Press founder and editor Barney Rosset thought was too pornographic for his *Evergreen Review*. I personally find this hard to believe since Rosset was not timid about pushing the envelope when it came to freedom of speech and the arts. Kerouac and I had some follow-up correspondence, but I never received the text. However, just the rumor of it provoked a scandal that was my undoing. I was to be the last undergraduate to serve as editor of the magazine, which is now ensconced in the graduate program of the UNC English department.

[3] *Transition* was founded in Paris by the poet Eugène Jolas in 1927, and twenty-seven issues were published before the magazine ceased publication in 1938. According to Jolas, writing in *Transition*'s April 1927 "Manifesto," "We should like to think of the readers as a homogeneous group of friends, united by a common appreciation of the beautiful — idealists of a sort — and to share with them what has seemed significant to us."

[4] Day began teaching at Humboldt in 1959, and over the course of his career he combined the vocations of teaching and writing. In the 1960s and '70s he was instrumental in bringing major poets and writers to teach and read at Humboldt. Throughout his tenure he supported *Toyon*, a literary journal founded by poet and fiction writer Jim Dodge. Day is the author of *When in Florence* (New York: Doubleday Press, 1986) and *Something for the Journey*

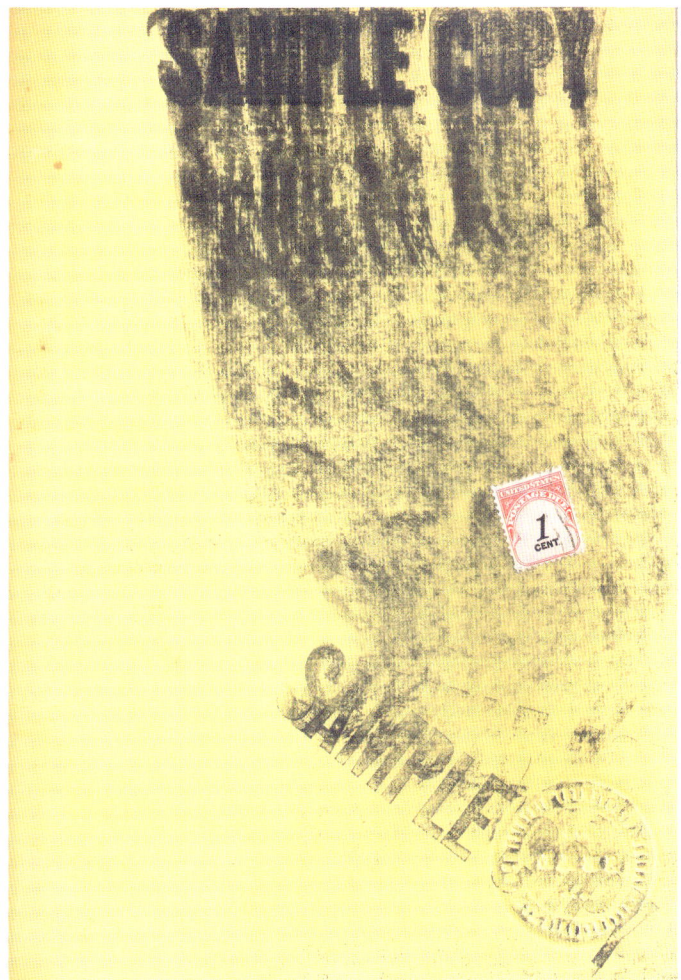

*Sample Copy* magazine, 1968, UNC-Chapel Hill. Advisors: Faculty Carolyn Kizer and Dougald McMillan; Editor: Marc Haynes; Art Editor: Ray Kass; Poetry Editor: Carol Moore; Staff: Tyna Austin, Jim Cloud, Richard Gatling, Laurence Naumoff, Sandy Treadwell, Diane Warman, Shari Willis

Morris Graves, *Chalice*, 1941, gouache, chalk, and sumi ink on paper, 27 x 30 in. (68.58 X 76.2 cm). Collection of The Phillips Collection, acquired 1942; ©Morris Graves Foundation

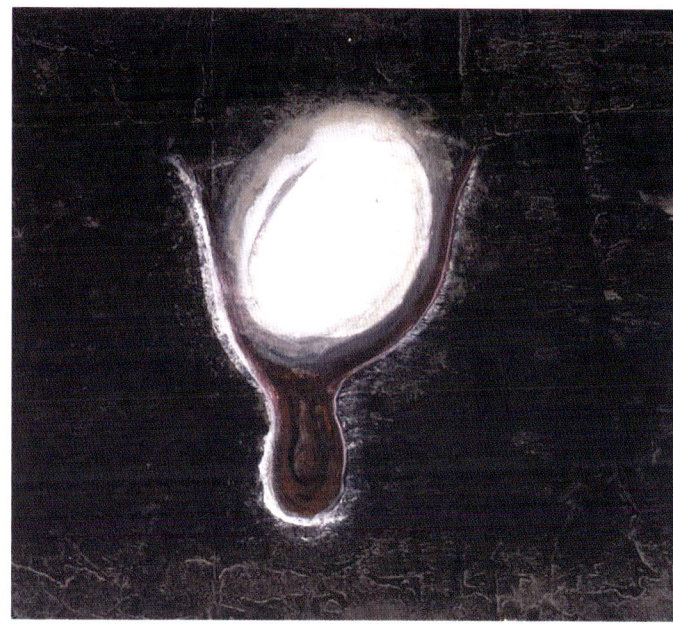

survive there. Richard Cortez Day, a renowned teacher of fiction in the English department, quickly recruited me, among others, to help with the active program of poetry readings that he had organized with members of the community.[4] He created an expanding local culture for these readings, which everyone looked forward to with excited anticipation. Day's example was not lost on me. At Humboldt I also met the poets Robert Bly, Robert Creeley, and Gary Snyder and the reclusive mystic artist Morris Graves, who lived nearby on a deeply wooded compound. We became friends, and Graves would later be a very consequential figure in my life.[5]

I left Humboldt State to be closer to New York City as I was preparing for my first solo exhibition in 1972 at the Allan Stone Gallery. I lived in a somewhat communal environment in Northwood Narrows, New Hampshire, with Russell Banks and his wife, Mary Gunst.[6] At Northwood I had a unique opportunity to observe the development of *Lillabulero* magazine and press and meet many of the writers and artists associated with the salon-like atmosphere that grew up around it. For me it was a profoundly important example of what it meant to create a local culture that could prosper and blossom.[7]

By the mid '70s I had moved from New Hampshire to a big studio in Boston at 655 Atlantic Avenue, a building occupied by artists across the street from South Station. I had started a small business in fine art delivery and display, working principally for my dealer Allan Stone, who had me delivering and hanging paintings for his clients between Boston, New York, and Washington, D.C. The fine art handling industry didn't

exist at that time. I had the benefit of meeting Allan's clients and seeing their extraordinary private collections. With Allan's introduction, I soon had more business than I could handle.

Then in fall of 1975 Virginia Tech invited me to be a visiting artist for the eight-week-long Winter Quarter starting in January. I arrived in Blacksburg on New Year's Day, 1976. Victor Huggins, a Chapel Hill friend and colleague and senior painter in the art department at Tech, had arranged the eight-week residency for me. My first night in town was especially memorable. I slept on a cot in the Huggins' basement, and when the temperature plunged to zero the adjacent water pipes froze solid and burst! By February we were experiencing spring-like weather, and I was able to get out into the Appalachian Mountains to explore the region. Missing my studio in Boston, I began painting landscapes outdoors in watercolor: wide panoramic views of the extraordinary pastel-colored winter mountains, and denser, more up-close images of the abundant streams and waterfalls that formed the grottoes and valleys. It was during this time of personal exploration that I came upon the Mountain Lake Hotel tucked beside its lake in a recess on top of Salt Pond Mountain.

After receiving an MFA in painting and art criticism in 1969, I accepted a teaching position in the art department at Humboldt State College in Arcata, a remote coastal hamlet in northern California. The area was renowned for its majestic redwoods, rocky coastline, abundant rainfall, impenetrable fog, and an impressive presence of indigenous Native American culture. Something about the remoteness of the place and its acute isolation seemed to require creative initiative if one was to

(Cheney, WA: Eastern Washington University, 2005). Because of his commitment as a teacher, mentor, and guide to students with an interest in the art of fiction writing, perhaps most notably Raymond Carver, in 2012 *Toyon* renamed its Advisors Award the Dick Day Award. http://www.toyonliterarymagazine.org/richard-cortez-day-award

[5] Graves was born August 28, 1910, in Fox Valley, Oregon. His childhood was marked by frequent bouts of pneumonia, which prevented him from attending school on a regular basis and likely contributed to his solitary nature. Early described as a "reclusive mystic" in the publicity that he received as a young artist, Graves quickly became something of a legend reinforcing the enthusiastic popular reception for his work and that of the Northwest School of Visionary Artists with which he was closely

associated and that his notoriety helped to define and bring to national prominence in the 1940s. Graves was a vigorous and catalytic figure who shared an unusual critical synergy with a small, emerging community of other important artists of the region in the 1930s, in particular the older artist and mentor figure Mark Tobey and the youthful composer John Cage.

[7] I rented a large studio in Concord, New Hampshire, and lived in a guesthouse with Mary's younger sister Laurie. Russell Banks and I were brothers-in-law for a few years in the 1970s.

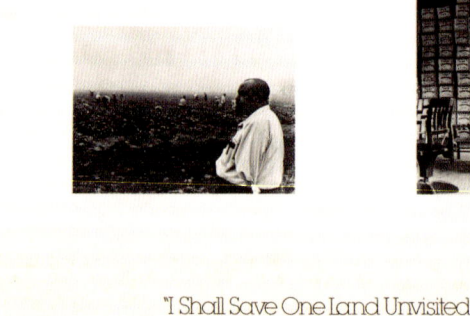

Mountain Lake is 3000 feet above sea level and is one of only two natural lakes in Virginia; it became my favorite place to paint. The hotel was closed for the winter, and the "no trespassing" signs were abundant. But I befriended the caretakers, Robert and Josephine Dollinger, and they advised me to write to Robert Eugene ("Gene") Lucas, then president of Gal-Tex Hotel Corporation in Galveston, Texas, and request permission to paint on the hotel property — which he granted. Exploring, looking, painting, I fell in love with the old hotel and the beautiful environmental features of the 3000-plus acres surrounding the lake. Eventually I met Mac McMillan, the hotel manager, and Edward L. Protz, legal representative for the hotel's owner, Mary Moody Northen. At the time she was almost 90 years old and visited the hotel during the summer. Often there were no other guests; despite the beautiful lake and forests, the place had seen better days.

While I was in residence in Blacksburg, Virginia Tech offered me a position for another quarter. I was delighted to stay on and paint through the spring, spending some of my time traveling around the Southeast reconnecting with old friends and making new ones who would soon become important contributors to my future projects. In Lexington, Virginia, I visited photographer Sally Mann, whom I had met in 1963 when I visited her parents' home with her brother Chris Munger, a friend from my Chapel Hill days and the civil rights movement. Maryann Harman, my colleague in the studio program at Tech, introduced me to Clement Greenberg. On a visit to Chapel Hill I met the art critic Donald Kuspit at a dinner party at the house of Dennis Zaborowski, a painter in the UNC art department, where Kuspit was teaching in the art

history program. I also re-connected with Jonathan Williams, and through him and my subsequent participation on the board of directors of the Jargon Society, I met folklorist and curator Roger Manley, writer and art critic Tom Patterson, and the visionary "outsider artist" Reverend Howard Finster, whom I visited at Paradise Garden, his extraordinary handmade environment in Summerville, Georgia. I returned to Chapel Hill later that spring to attend the Spring Arts Festival that had been co-organized by my friend Michelle Patterson, one of Kuspit's art history graduate students, and there I met John Cage and Meredith Monk. During the festival I was surprised when I received a midnight phone call at the home of a friend asking if I would come over to Dennis Zaborowski's house and play chess with Cage.[8]

Shortly after returning to Boston and New Hampshire for the summer, I was offered a one-year teaching position at Virginia Tech that had been assigned to the art department by the Division of Humanities, a new interdisciplinary program at the university. This opportunity was a great alternative to my fine art delivery business; I was delighted to accept it and take on the challenge of making myself useful in this new and innovative academic program. An opportunity soon presented itself when Dean Carter, a sculptor and chairman of the art department, agreed to host the annual meeting of the Southeastern College Art Conference (SECAC) in Blacksburg in 1977. My participation in SECAC became my inspiration to organize ambitious interdisciplinary visual arts projects.

Responsibility for organizing the on-campus programs for the SECAC meeting fell largely on art historian Robert

Porter and Victor Huggins and myself. I wrote a grant application to the National Endowment for the Arts to support the program; it was to be the first of a number of grants I would write over the years. One of the sessions organized for SECAC was "The Realist Panel," which included critics Donald Kuspit and Clement Greenberg and artists Richard Estes, Duane Hanson, and Janet Fish.[9]

Encouraged by the success of "The Realist Panel," I organized a traveling exhibition of southern photography titled *I Shall Save One Land Unvisited*. It was my first experience in coordinating virtually every aspect of a large exhibition and

Northwood was an interesting extended-family experience that included frequent visits by artists and poets including local neighbors poet Charles Simic, sculptor Silvana Cenci, and artists Sigmund Abeles and Caroline May, as well as a multitude of other artists and poets who were visiting houseguests including Graves, James Tate, Cynthia Lasky, Bill and Marie Matthews, Mark Strand, Charles Wright, and Bill and Beverly Corbett.

[8] I arrived about midnight and played several games of chess with Cage's friend, the pianist Grete Sultan, while Cage intently watched. I learned later that Cage often played with Teeny Duchamp while Marcel Duchamp looked on.

[9] "The Realist Panel" was Studio Session II: Photo Realism, 9:30 a.m. – 12 noon. The SECAC conference was made possible in part by a grant from the National Endowment for the Arts.

[10] The NEA grant we received to support the catalogue, which was published by Gnomon Press, Frankfort, Kentucky, was for $10,000.

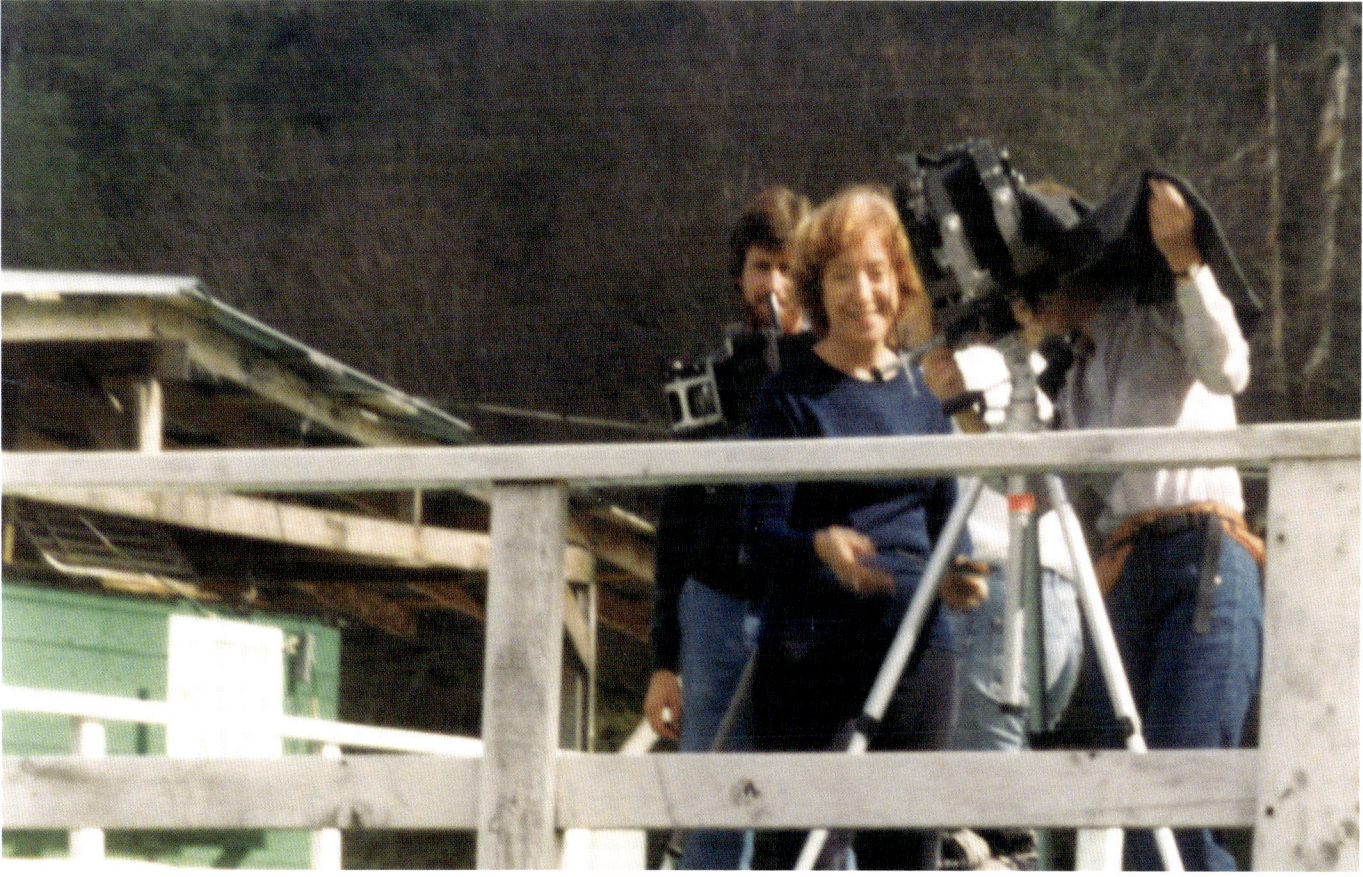

Marie Cosindas (1925-2017) (center) and her large-format Polaroid camera on the dock at Mountain Lake, 1981. Photo: Gary "Chico" Harkrader

related publication. I invited Jonathan Williams to guest-curate the exhibition although I ensured that two artists in whose work I was especially interested — John Menapace and Sally Mann — were included. Philanthropist and art patron R. Phillip Hanes and Ted Potter, then director of the Southeastern Center for Contemporary Art, located on the Hanes family compound in Winston-Salem, North Carolina, supported and encouraged me in developing this project. I wrote another grant to the National Endowment for the Arts to support the exhibition catalogue, and, with Hanes' help and underwriting, the exhibition opened at the Corcoran Gallery of American Art in Washington, D.C., and closed at the International Center of Photography in New York City, traveling to a dozen additional venues in between.[10]

The experience of organizing the exhibition engaged my interest in the creative role of curator that would later become an important component of the Mountain Lake Workshop activities. Another curatorial opportunity presented itself quite soon afterwards, when I began exhibiting my paintings at Washington, D.C., galleries. In 1979 I met James McLaughlin, chief curator at The Phillips Collection, at the reception for my first solo exhibition in D.C. at Ramon Osuna's Pyramid Gallery.[11] We talked about the reclusive Pacific Northwest artist Morris Graves, a favorite of Duncan Phillips and someone I remembered well from the time I lived in northern California. McLaughlin invited me to visit him at The Phillips Collection the next day, and we looked at some of the Graves paintings that Duncan Phillips, the museum's founder, had acquired for the permanent collection in the 1940s and '50s. Graves's originality and the creative dialogue between Eastern and Western culture that was apparent

in his art were of great interest to Phillips, who associated Graves with the broader movement of modernist innovation to which he was committed.[12] McLaughlin was impressed that I knew Graves, who was notorious for not answering letters of inquiry even from museums that owned his works and initially had even refused to show his paintings at the Museum of Modern Art in a 1942 exhibition that brought him overnight fame.[13] He asked me if I would be willing to act as an intermediary for the museum and contact Graves about a potential retrospective exhibition at The Phillips. I called Graves and he was interested; a few weeks later I was invited to guest-curate the exhibition *Morris Graves: Vision of the Inner Eye* and author the accompanying publication.[14]

Graves provided the circumstances for my re-introduction to Cage; they had become close friends in Seattle in the 1930s.[15] Although Graves had once invited me to have dinner with Cage at his house, I was unable to attend and did not meet Cage until that midnight when I played chess in Chapel Hill. However, The Phillips Collection retrospective necessitated that I interview Cage, which I did several times in New York in 1980 and '81 when I was writing the text for the catalogue. These meetings led to Cage's participation in the Mountain Lake Workshop in 1983 (and also that of Merce Cunningham, but that was much later).

But I have gotten ahead of myself; we are still working our way

[11] McLaughlin, an accomplished still life painter, began his association with Duncan Phillips when he was a student at the Phillips Gallery School in 1932. He worked at The Phillips for 50 years until his death in 1982. He played an active role in the museum's activities and hired art students as museum guards. McLaughlin died shortly after the exhibition was planned, and I worked closely with his successor, the painter Willem de Looper, and registrar Martha Carey, who both became good friends.

[12] Graves' paintings characteristically embraced influences from Asian art and culture and were cross-cultural and interdisciplinary from the outset. He may be associated with the late Romantic outlook in art reflected in his interest in occult sciences and mysticism as well as his evocation of the sublime in cosmic space and imagery characteristically expressed throughout his art.

[13] Dorothy Miller, curator of the exhibition *Americans 1942: 18 Artists from 9 States* at the Museum of Modern Art, told me in an interview in 1980 that Graves initially refused her invitation to participate in the exhibition, noting that in her long experience at MoMA this was the only time she could recall an artist refusing such an invitation. Her friends in Seattle and New York, Nancy Wilson Ross and Marian Willard, who knew Graves, acted as intermediaries and prevailed upon him to reconsider, which he did. Thirty of his paintings were included.

[14] Ray Kass, *Morris Graves: Vision of the Inner Eye* (New York: George Braziller, Inc., in association with The Phillips Collection, Washington, D.C., 1983). The exhibition traveled to Greenville County Museum of Art, Greenville, SC; the Whitney Museum of American Art, NY; the Oakland Museum, Oakland, CA; the Seattle Art Museum, Seattle, WA; and the San Diego Museum of Art, San Diego, CA.

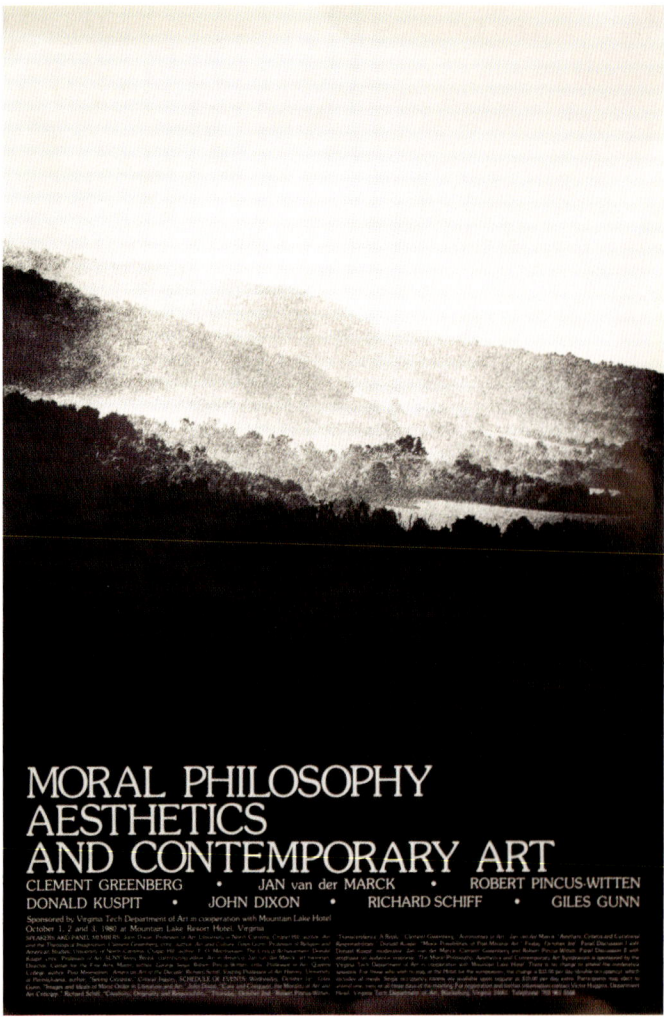

to the adventure at Mountain Lake. In 1977 I had attempted to organize two extended workshops at the Mountain Lake Hotel; they were to run from May 2 through June 10, 1977. One was to be a plein air landscape watercolor workshop that I would direct and the other a ceramics workshop that would be taught by Stephen LeQuire, the ceramist at Tech. We called it the "Salt Pond Mountain Art Center at Mountain Lake." The assumption was that many of the workshop participants would stay at the Mountain Lake Hotel, which provided rooms and three meals a day at very reasonable rates.[16] No one signed up. This was my introduction to the importance of marketing.

In 1980 Edward Protz, president of the Mary Moody Northen Endowment and a person with whom I was now in regular correspondence, began providing funds to the Virginia Tech Foundation for the purpose of supporting programs in the arts at the Mountain Lake Hotel.[17] With Mrs. Northen's financial

support as an incentive, despite the poor response to the 1977 workshops I organized a new workshop of shorter duration at the hotel for the spring of 1980. I wrote another grant to the National Endowment for the Arts and invited Boston photographer Marie Cosindas to lead a workshop in color Polaroid photography and, in particular, the larger-format prints that had recently become possible.[18] This time I organized the

publicity myself, using the SECAC mailing list and sending posters to every art program in the Southeast and the Mid-Atlantic states. Unlike the earlier workshops, Cosindas's workshop was well attended, and she returned to lead workshops for the next three years; her workshops were the beginning of a series of regular springtime visiting artist workshops and conferences alternating with fall symposium programs in art criticism that for many years were a staple at Mountain Lake. The Mountain Lake Symposium and Workshops were starting to take shape.

Recalling the success of "The Realist Panel" at SECAC, I thought that organizing an interdisciplinary art criticism conference specifically directed at the local art community and regional academic programs might be timely. I consulted with Donald Kuspit about a topic for discussion; this was the beginning of Kuspit's crucial decade-long involvement in what was to become the Mountain Lake Symposium.[19]

Kuspit was an art critic of special interest to artists working from nature, especially given the late modernist sensibility of the New York City–dominated art world of the 1970s and '80s, where a kind of hermetic abstraction and Conceptual art flourished. His writing in the late 1970s expressed an interest in transcendentalism and the experience of nature in art; it was not a criticism narrowly addressing the semiotic, Post Structuralist, and Deconstructivist theories about the conditions of language and visual art or about imagery deriving from the forms of urban culture such as in Pop art, for example.[20]

The new conference was called the Mountain Lake Symposium

[15] Cage had come to Seattle in 1937 to work as a piano accompanist for the dance classes at the Cornish School of Art. Their first encounter occurred when Graves attended a concert of Cage's percussion compositions. Graves, who by this time was gaining a reputation for Dada antics, arrived with friends at the concert carrying a bag of peanuts and a lorgnette with dolls' eyes suspended in it. At one point in the concert he cried out, "Jesus in Everywhere," which thoroughly disrupted the proceedings. Theater attendants, who had been warned about Graves, immediately ejected him. That same evening Cage and Graves were introduced and their long friendship began.

[16] The Donaldson Brown Continuing Education Center at Tech sponsored the workshops and Robert Fields, Tech's graphic design professor, created an elegant brochure to advertise it.

[17] In all, Protz directed three separate gifts of $100,000 each to the Virginia Tech Foundation to support Mountain Lake programs in the arts and humanities.

[18] The NEA "Grant for Artist's Forum" for the Cosindas workshop was for $2000.

[19] Kuspit's involvement is detailed in Howard Risatti's "Donald Kuspit at the Mountain Lake Symposium" in Chapter 1.

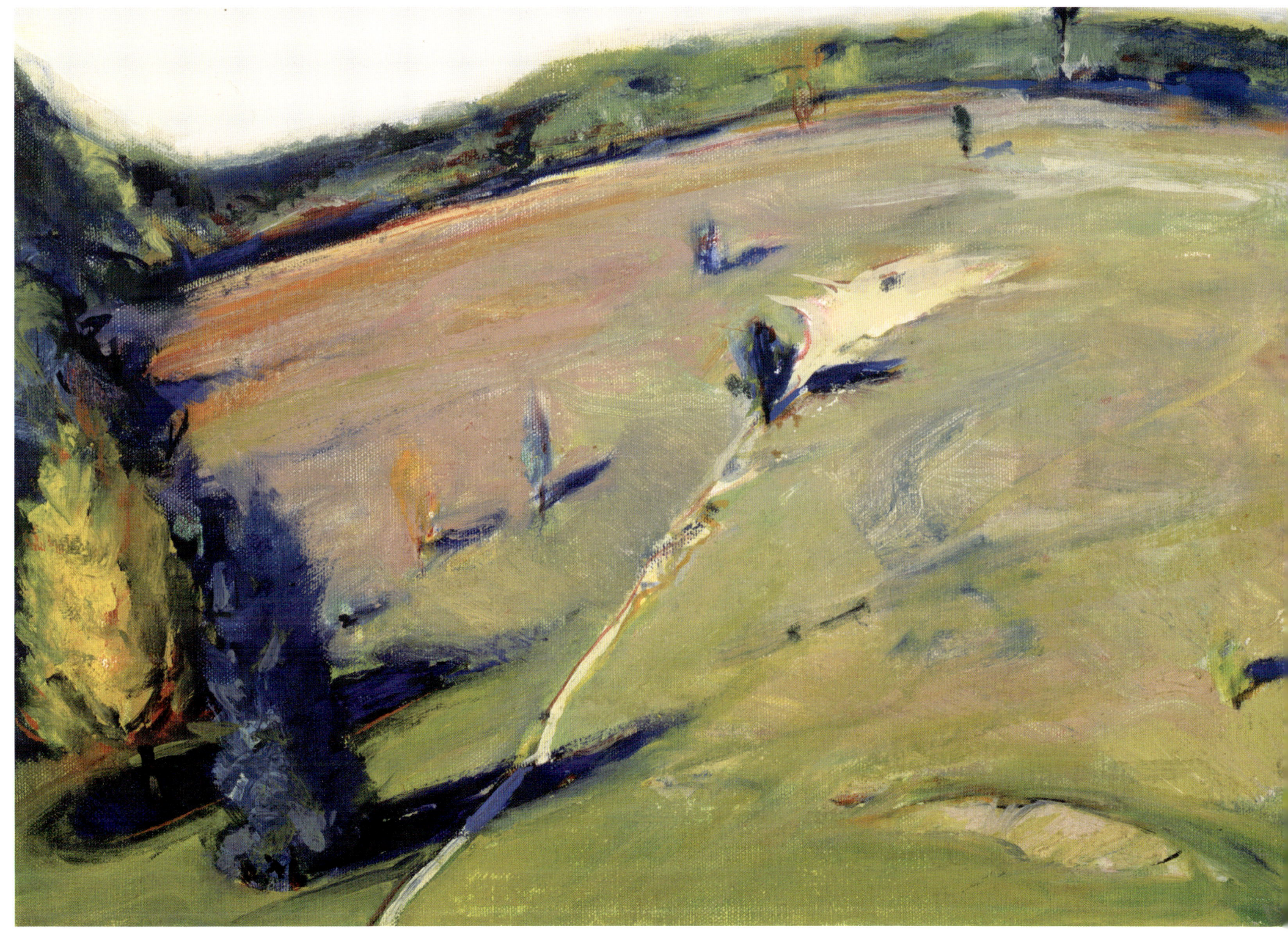

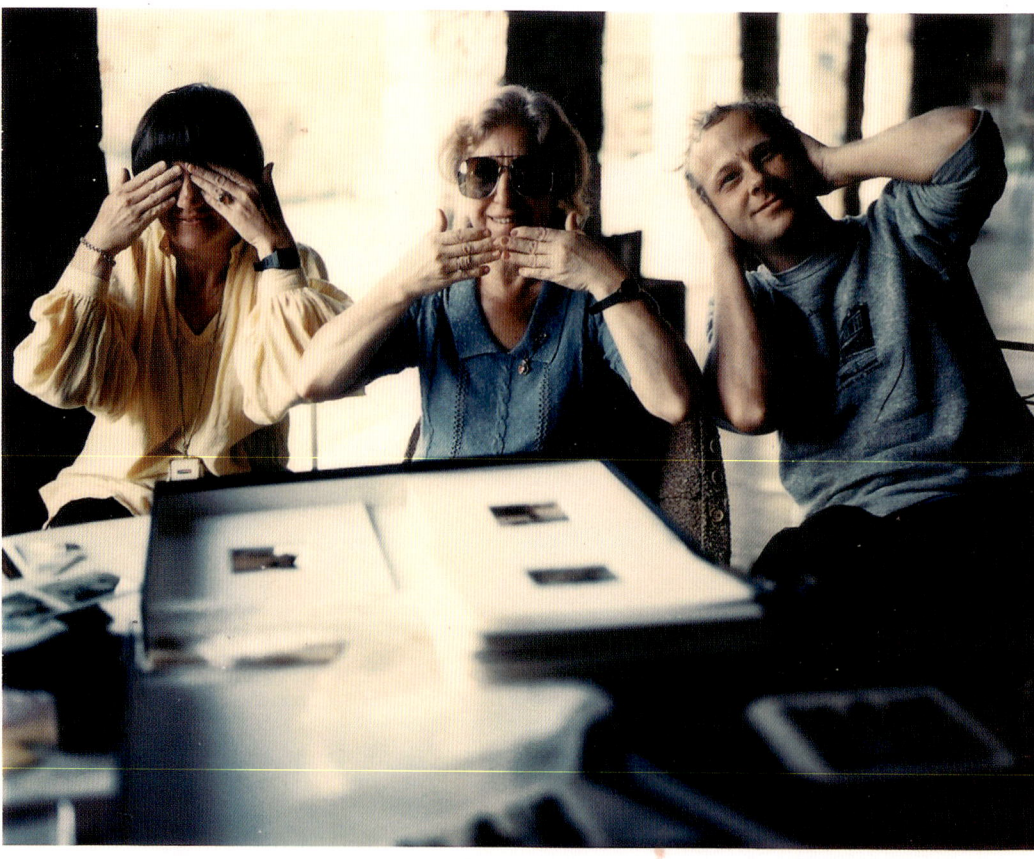

at the Mountain Lake Hotel. It convened in October 1980 with the unlikely title "Moral Philosophy, Aesthetics, and Contemporary Art." Unlike my first attempt, it was a great success with more than 100 registrants, and it filled all of the available rooms in the hotel and cabins. While attendees were mostly area artists and academics, there were notable individuals who traveled some distance to attend including New York City gallery impresario Richard Bellamy (he came with Seattle art collector and patron Virginia Wright), Glenn Lowery, director of the Muscarelle Museum at the College of William and Mary (he later became MoMA director), art critic Hal Foster, and artist and critic Peter Plagens.

The enthusiastic response to the symposium encouraged me to organize another spring workshop/visiting artist program and a second symposium for the following fall, both to be held at the Mountain Lake Hotel. The visiting artists who came in the spring of 1981 were Wayne Thiebaud (painting) and Marie Cosindas (Polaroid photography). The ensuing fall symposium, titled "Art Criticism/Social Criticism" and co-directed with Trudie Grace, ran from 9 to 11 October 1981. Participants included Stanley Diamond (poet and professor of anthropology, New School of Social Research, New York), Rosalind E. Krauss (professor of art at Hunter College in New York and co-editor of *October* magazine), Kuspit (critic and professor of art history, SUNY–Stony Brook), Irving Sandler (writer and professor of art history, SUNY–Purchase), and Richard Schiff (visiting professor of art history, University of Pennsylvania).

The Mountain Lake Symposium continued with the help of regular grants and a growing consortium of contributing institutions called the Mountain Lake Consortium. Consortium representatives met at the end of each fall symposium to review and discuss preliminary topics for the next year's program. By 1983 consortium members included my principal symposium co-director, the art historian Howard Risatti (Virginia Commonwealth University); curators Julia Boyd, Margo Crutchfield, and Ashley Kistler (the Virginia Museum of Fine Arts); gallery director and art historian Elaine A. King (Carnegie Mellon University); painter Victor Kord (art department head, Cornell University); art historian and critic Linda McGreevy (Old Dominion University); and, of course, Kuspit.

[20] For more on these issues see Risatti, "The Loneliness of the Regional Artist," *Ralph Harvey: A History of Studio Glass Education in the Rural South* exhibition catalogue (Department of Visual Art: Georgia Southwestern State University, 2015) and Risatti "Part Three: Cognitive and Communicative Structure of Art," *Postmodern Perspectives: Issues in Contemporary Art* (Englewood Cliffs, NJ: Prentice Hall, 1990), pp. 199ff. The conference was funded by a $5,000 grant from the National Endowment for the Humanities. Professor John Link, department head, and I were the principal investigators on the project.

[21] Though addressing a range of different topics, all embraced the ideal of the city as a model for social interaction and political life and advocated for the necessity of architectural theory grounded in practical collectivism as the basis of invention. Architectural theory and criticism in this sense constitute a special kind of literature and, similar to art criticism, can be understood as a unique literary genre. The presenters were Alan Colquhoun, Anthony Vidler, Allan Greenberg, Carroll William Westfall, and Juan Pablo Bonta.

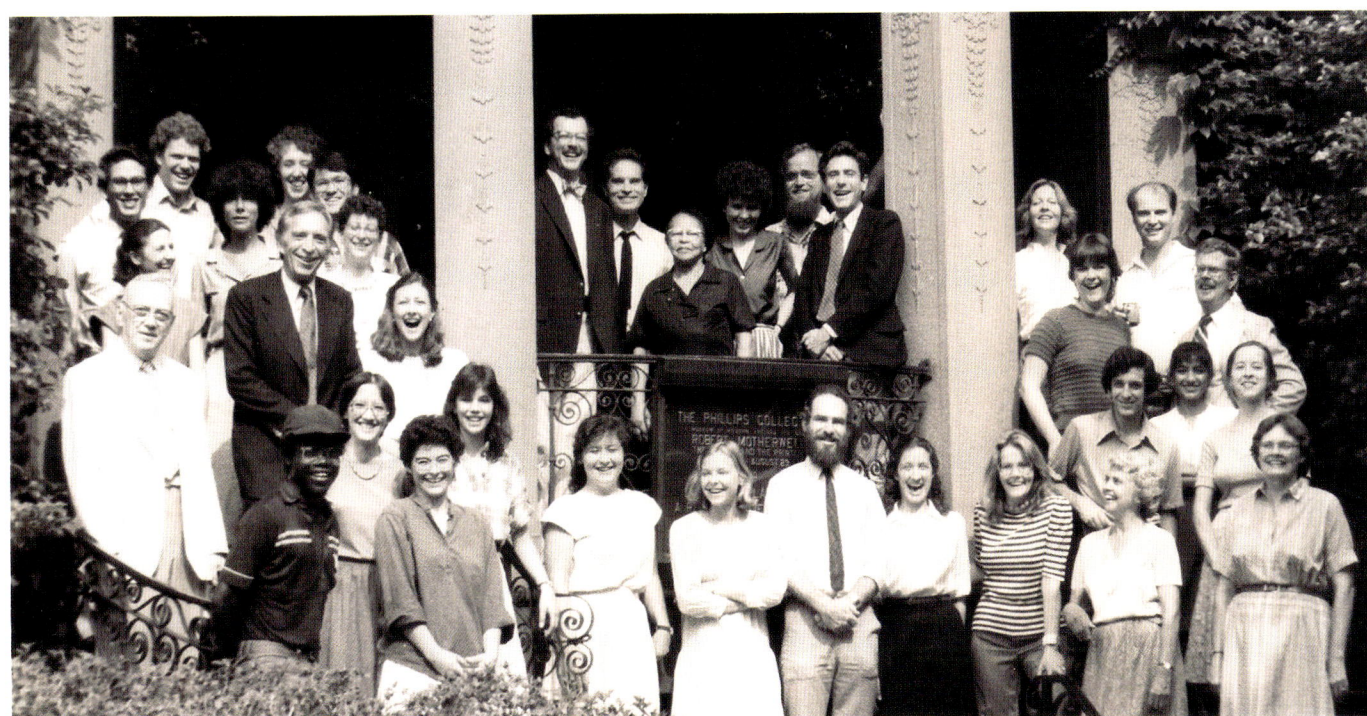

The Phillips Collection staff, circa 1980 (photographer unknown). Photo courtesy The Phillips Collection

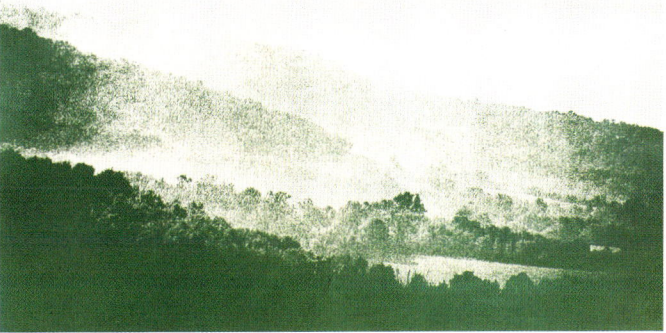

ANTHONY CARO · CLEMENT GREENBERG · CHARLES MILLARD
WALTER DARBY BANNARD · TERRY FENTON

**THREE WORKSHOPS**
&
**CONTEMPORARY SCULPTURE CONFERENCE**
MAY 12-14 — MAY 14-16, 1982

WORKSHOP LEADERS & PANEL MEMBERS: Anthony Caro is a major sculptor from Britain working with steel and other metals. He will conduct the sculpture workshop and participate in the Contemporary Sculpture Conference. Clement Greenberg, significant American art critic whose formalist theory is integrally involved with the work of David Smith and Anthony Caro, will conduct the Criticism Workshop and also participate in the sculpture conference; Walter Darby Bannard is a well-known artist and critic whose work has been identified with the mainstream concerns of formalist-oriented contemporary painting. He will conduct the Painting Workshop and participate in the conference. Charles Millard is curator of Contemporary Art at the Hirshhorn Museum in Washington, DC. Mr. Millard and Terry Fenton, Director of the Edmonton Art Gallery in Alberta, Canada, will join the workshop leaders on Friday to participate in the Contemporary Sculpture Conference.

REGISTRATION INFORMATION: The three workshops are limited to 20 participants each, and will directly precede the Contemporary Sculpture Conference. There is a $30 registration fee for each workshop, which includes participation in the Contemporary Sculpture Conference. Individuals wishing to attend only the Contemporary Sculpture Conference may do so for a registration fee of $20. Hotel charges are $38/day double occupancy and $48/day single occupancy, plus $1.00/day room charge and 4% tax (includes all meals). Accommodations charges must be paid to Mountain Lake Hotel upon departure from the workshops and/or conference. Reservations for hotel accommodations are guaranteed upon confirmation of workshop/conference registration and receipt of appropriate registration fees. For further information call or write Victor Huggins, Head, Department of Art, Virginia Tech, Blacksburg, Virginia 24061. Phone (703) 961-5598. To register send appropriate fee payable to Virginia Polytechnic Institute and State University to Victor Huggins.

PUBLIC LECTURE
On Thursday, May 13 at 8:30 PM, Anthony Caro and Walter Darby Bannard will give lectures and their formal remarks. These lectures are open to the public.

**LANDSCAPE PAINTING**
MAY 23-26

MARJORIE PORTNOW, a noted landscape painter painting in oil medium directly from nature in the out-of-doors, whose work has been included in numerous national exhibitions and is represented by the Odessa Gallery in New York City, will conduct a workshop in Landscape Painting for twenty participants.

**MOUNTAIN LAKE RESORT HOTEL, VIRGINIA**

Artists, architects, and practitioners of architectural theory and criticism were often invited to make presentations at the fall symposium; they tended to represent very contrasting views on the social utility of their respective practices. The architecture presenters generally aspired to a unifying theory of form, a philosophy of architecture that embraced the necessity of its functional social role.[21] In contrast, the symposium presentations by artists were essentially deconstructive; their individual work tended to be conceptual and based in language and images that were in reaction to social, urban, and technological culture, challenging familiar premises in art-world society.[22]

Insight into an artist's inner moorings, however, was more likely to be revealed in the visiting artist critiques offered at spring workshops. Cosindas was an important contributor in this regard. She shared her creative energy with the group by arranging tableaux to photograph with them; she also talked about her personal experiences in bringing the lives of her subjects into play in her portrait photography as she took photographs alongside workshop participants. During his 1981 visit Thiebaud painted and made drawings with local artists. His slide lectures and critiques were very rich in personal commentary, and he brought a broad art-historical perspective to his public presentations and individual discussions with artists. He talked about the implicit sensuality of paint and painting, describing oil paint as "meat." Thiebaud often critiqued artists' works after dinner at the hotel, sometimes until after 2:00 a.m. Walter Darby Bannard also painted in public when he was the visiting artist in 1982; he interjected exclamatory, spontaneous comments as he composed his juicy abstract compositions. I felt he was only one step away from inviting observers' participation in the process. He was "watching" what took place on the canvas, and I was impressed by his confident bravado. His openness as an artist and a teacher, like that of both Cosindas and Thiebaud, made him an artist of stature in my mind, a willing bearer of a culture.[23]

An important goal of the Mountain Lake Workshop was to live out a belief that every community should and can make its own "high" art — high in the sense that the community participants at Mountain Lake, to varying degrees, were simultaneously the makers and the primary audience for the artworks that were created in the workshop collaborations and subsequently exhibited on site or in nearby venues. To put it in more Marxist terms, the idea that developed out of the collaboration process

[22] Joseph Kosuth, Allan Kaprow, Douglas Davis, Ronald Jones, and Kay Rosen were essentially conceptual language-based artists. Thomas Lawson engaged with appropriated images from popular media, as did Davis, but was nevertheless a genuine painter, as were Sidney Tillim, Ed Pashke, and Robert Colescott, who addressed media and social imagery in their paintings and in their conference presentations. Similar to Pashke and Colescott, Keith Sonnier's presentation indicated the personal multicultural influences at play in his installed neon constructions that expressed a level of "localism" that was becoming increasingly interesting to me. I had organized for the symposium a retrospective of his black and white experimental videos at Virginia Tech's Armory Art Gallery that was decidedly conceptual. This special exhibition was underwritten and provided by Leo Castelli.

[23] There also were visiting artists who led critiques but did not make art alongside community participants. Sculptors James Wolfe and Anthony Caro, painters Susan Shatter, Jane Freilicher, Robert Berlind, Andrew Tavarelli, Katherine Porter, Carol Goldberg, James Poppitz (Fashion Moda), and Willem de Looper led critiques with community artists but did not make art with them.

[24] See M. C. Richards, *Centering: In Pottery, Poetry, and the Person* (Hanover, NH: Wesleyan University Press, 1964).

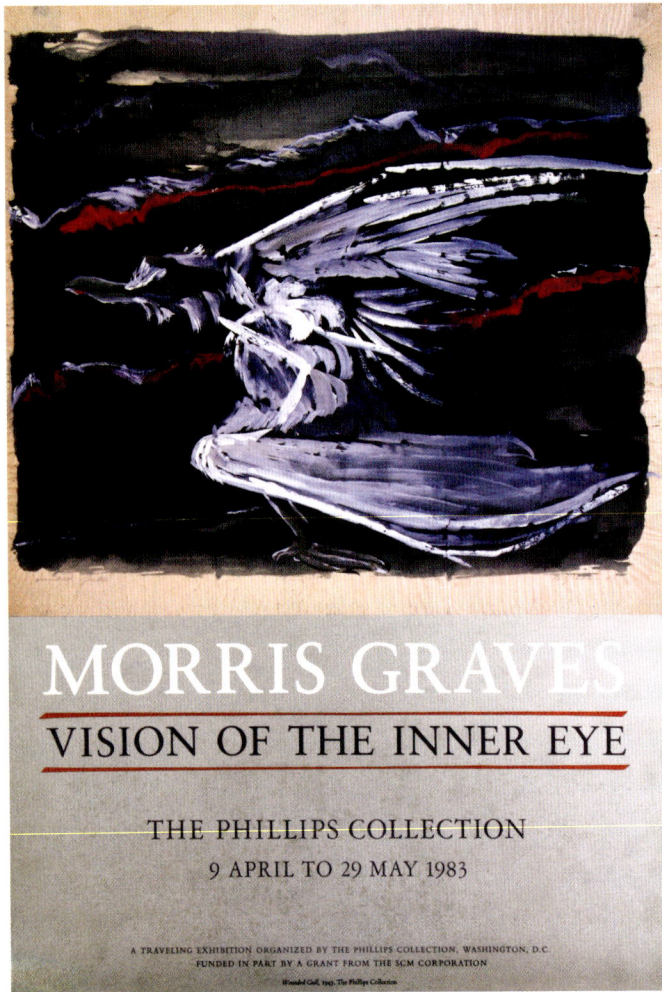

1983 poster for *Morris Graves: Vision of the Inner Eye*.

**MORRIS GRAVES**

**VISION OF THE INNER EYE**

**THE PHILLIPS COLLECTION**

9 APRIL TO 29 MAY 1983

A TRAVELING EXHIBITION ORGANIZED BY THE PHILLIPS COLLECTION, WASHINGTON, D.C.
FUNDED IN PART BY A GRANT FROM THE SCM CORPORATION

*Wounded Gull, 1943, The Phillips Collection*

was that the people who make the art should also be its consumers, something very different from the modern gallery system as it exists in major metropolitan centers. I think that the ideas M. C. Richards expressed in *Centering*, a book I had read in the 1960s, encouraged my development toward this goal.[24] Also, very important to my thinking about art made in collaboration with community was Howard Becker's 1983 symposium

presentation in which he proposed that the art object be defined in terms of all of the social contributors to its existence — a rejection of the traditional idea of artist as *sole auteur*. The architecture presentations at the symposia also inspired my efforts to begin the spring workshop collaborations. Juan Pablo Bonta's concept of the relationship of architectural form and architectural criticism as a means to identify socially shared values and their role in influencing design impressed me very much, and I thought that they could be applied to art making in the community. The interdisciplinary concept for the symposium often resulted in insightful, serendipitous comparative points of view.

The interdisciplinary collaborative art projects of the Mountain Lake Workshop that commenced after 1983 developed out of a fusion of the criticism symposium and artists' conferences and the visiting artists' critiques. John Cage's first visit to co-direct the "Mycological Foray and Conference" with Dr. Orson Miller of Virginia Tech established an important new direction, inviting an established artist to work collaboratively with community members in a new medium or discipline. The mycological foray program also invited other discipline-centered and value-oriented communities in the sciences and humanities at Virginia Tech to join with artists. The presentations made at the mycological foray placed Cage on a panel alongside Miller, a renowned mycologist.[25] This visit also was the occasion of Cage's introduction to watercolor painting in my studio.

The Reverend Howard Finster's visit in 1985 was hosted at the Miles C. Horton Sr. Center near the Mountain Lake Hotel. Miles C. Horton Jr. and his wife, Ruth, had become supporters

of my projects, and I received annual contributions from them which I used as matching funds for grants. Finster's visit was co-sponsored by the Appalachian Studies program in Tech's Center for Programs in the Humanities. During his week-long visit, Finster preached, made a public presentation on campus, and sang and played his banjo at public gatherings at the Horton Center; he seemed to paint night and day, sleeping only in short intervals. Additionally, his workshop was the subject of two video documentaries.[26] Finster's "workout" (his term for his workshop) was the first in which workshop participants literally made all of the artworks, with Finster working with them and beside them. The experience of workshop participants actually making the artwork became a strategic goal in future workshops, though not a necessary part of all of them.

Finster and Cage were defining figures in the evolution of the Mountain Lake Workshop. They came from very different cultural backgrounds and perspectives but both were on crusades of sorts, trying to offer society alternatives to convention. Finster's notion of "sacred art" became his ministry when he realized that he could reach far more people through image-making than by preaching in a church. Cage's use of "chance operations" and "indeterminacy" in his music, visual art, and writing offered a strategic philosophical counterpoint that challenged the empirical, logically rational, deterministic Western mind. Both artists had followings much wider than the respective audiences for folk art/Outsider art and musicology.

Cage was always interested in what we were doing in the workshop, and he attended the opening of Finster's retrospective

[25] Cage — a co-founder of the New York Mycological Society — and Orson Miller were aware of each other by reputation, but had never met. The foray was an opportunity for them to meet and to bring people — not just artists — from all walks of life together around their mutual interest in fungi, the happy assumption being that all parties would benefit from their interaction. This first major interdisciplinary and collaborative project of the Mountain Lake Workshop was a richly eventful program: Dr. Miller gave a detailed slide presentation about spore formation in fungi; Cosindas and Berlind conducted plein air workshops in Polaroid photography and painting; British artist Ray Cowell had a small exhibition and made a public presentation of her detailed fungi illustrations for the British Museum. Last but not least, Cage, commissioned to give a lecture relating his interest in mushrooms to his writing and music, composed and read

the first four sections of *Mushrooms et Variationes*. For more on this, see Ray Kass, *The Sight of Silence: John Cage's Complete Watercolors* (New York: National Academy Museum and the Taubman Museum of Art, 2011), p. 42.

[26] Videographer and producer Robert Walker made a particularly good documentary titled *Well Known Stranger: Howard Finster's Workout*. It is available online at: http://www.folkstreams.net/film,207

[27] The exhibition was titled *The Road to Heaven Is Paved by Good Works: The Art of Reverend Howard Finster* and ran from September 21, 1989, to January 5, 1990; it was curated by John Turner for the PaineWebber Gallery in New York City.

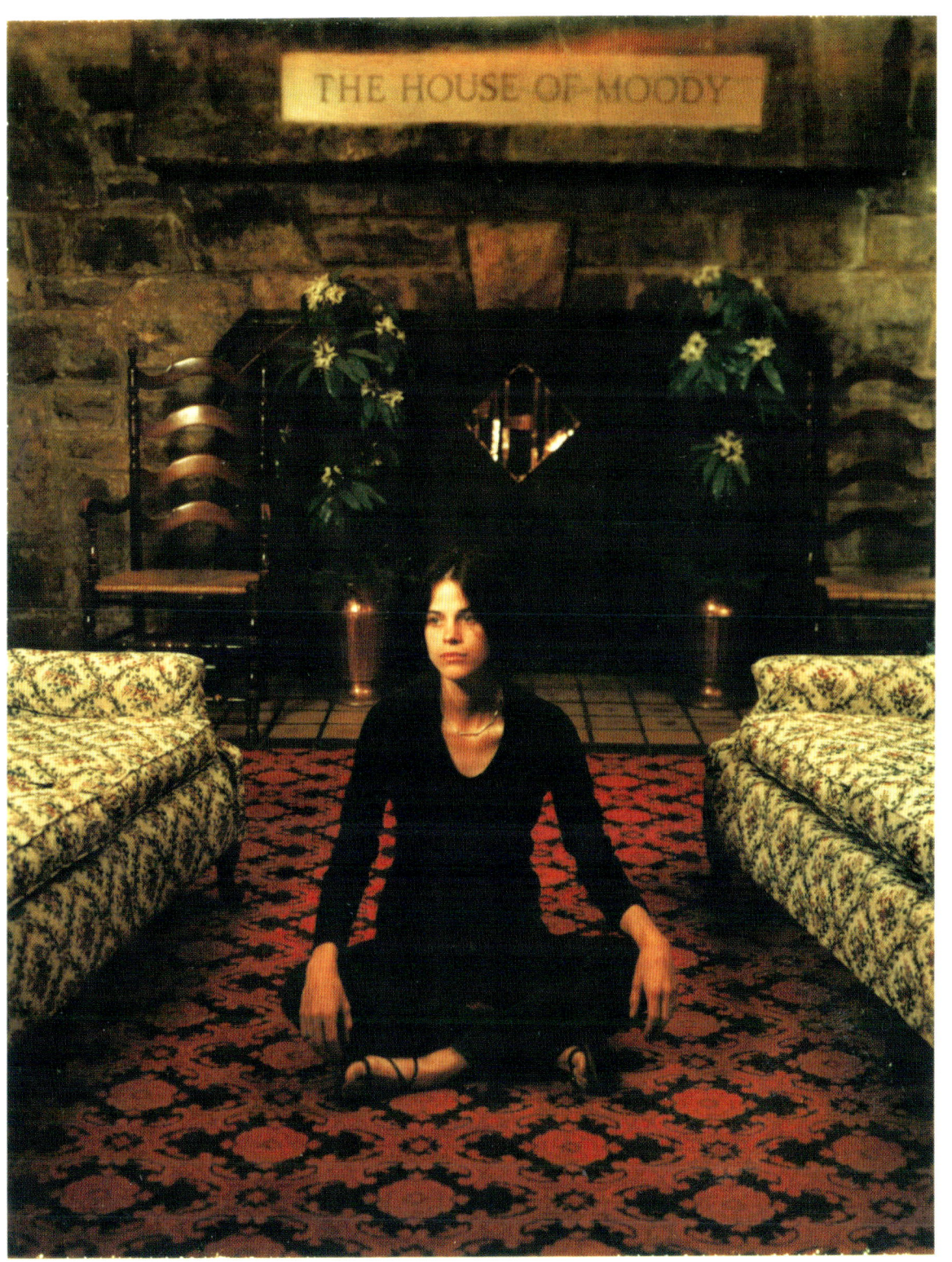

exhibition that was organized by the American Folk Art Museum at the Paine Webber Gallery in New York City in 1989.[27] He called me later that night to tell me that he had had an opportunity to talk with Finster at the reception and thought that he was wonderful — "absolutely the real thing." This reminded me of Cage's often-quoted remark that the goal of art is not "self expression — but self alteration," an openness to new experience. He saw Finster's disciplined authenticity and admired it; it corresponded to his personal credo in encouraging experimentation: "permission given, but not to do anything. ..." During the mycological foray in 1983 we invited a local bluegrass band to play at a dance party at the hotel. Cage said to me, "This is beautiful music"; shortly he was out on the dance floor moving to our mountain music.[28]

Neither Cage nor Finster thought that it mattered "who held the brush." When Cage came to do his first painting workshop in 1988, we asked him to hold the brush when he painted around the stones that he used to make the *New River Watercolors*. I noticed that working in a new medium allowed Cage to explore his own performance in refreshing ways that welcomed new characteristics into his work. Gestural expression is implicit in painting, and Cage had to accept his role as performer in his paintings.[29] The early Cage and Finster workshops expanded my efforts to organize experiences that included greater and more authorial participation by the community.

The alignment of the local art community with its aspects of traditional Appalachian cultural practices and the advanced technological communities at Virginia Tech seems inevitable to me now — but it was not something that I foresaw at the outset. A workshop by definition does not "teach" a specified curriculum but is a process that, like an unscripted performance, must remain open to unpredictable developments. However, as Mierle Laderman Ukeles observed during her visit in 1994, "the Mountain Lake Symposium and Workshops had created a culture. It was a culture of community anticipation that attracted participants into the program from a wide range of backgrounds."

[28] Les Melichamp, a retired Virginia Tech professor and friend, arranged for Big Al and the Crocodiles, the bluegrass band he played in, to perform at the hotel.

[29] When composer George Rochberg said at the symposium that his abandoning avant-garde serial compositions to return to harmonics was not an announcement that "I would never write a twelve tone piece again," he was newly exploring conventional expressionism while leaving a door open to Post Modern possibility. I later related Rochberg's conditional return to more conventional lyrical composing to Cage's opening of himself as an "indeterminate" performer in his own visual artworks, particularly in his acceptance of his own gesture in his late watercolors, about which he said, "I have to accept what I do"— which I related to the indeterminate nature of the "number" pieces that he was composing in the same period.

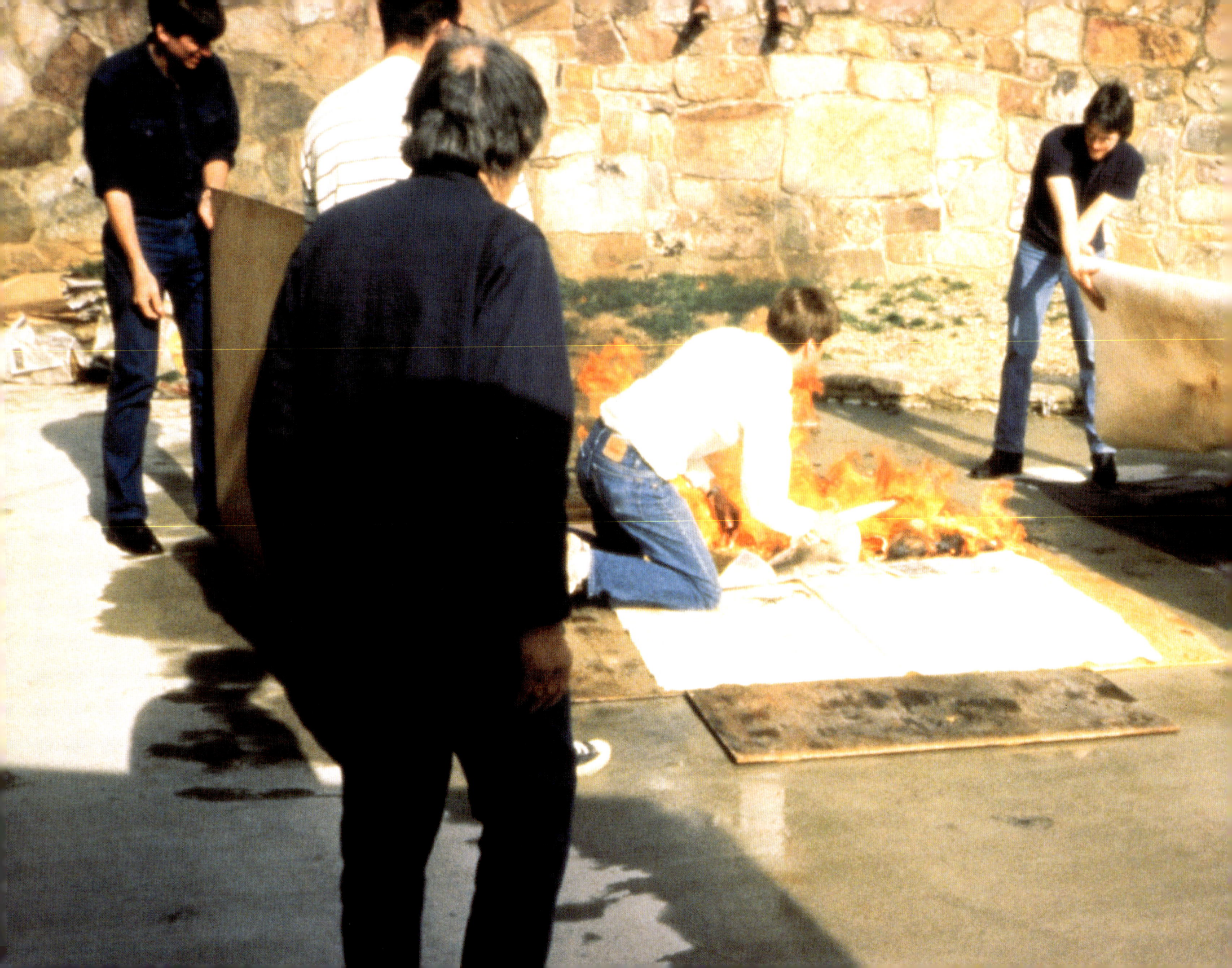

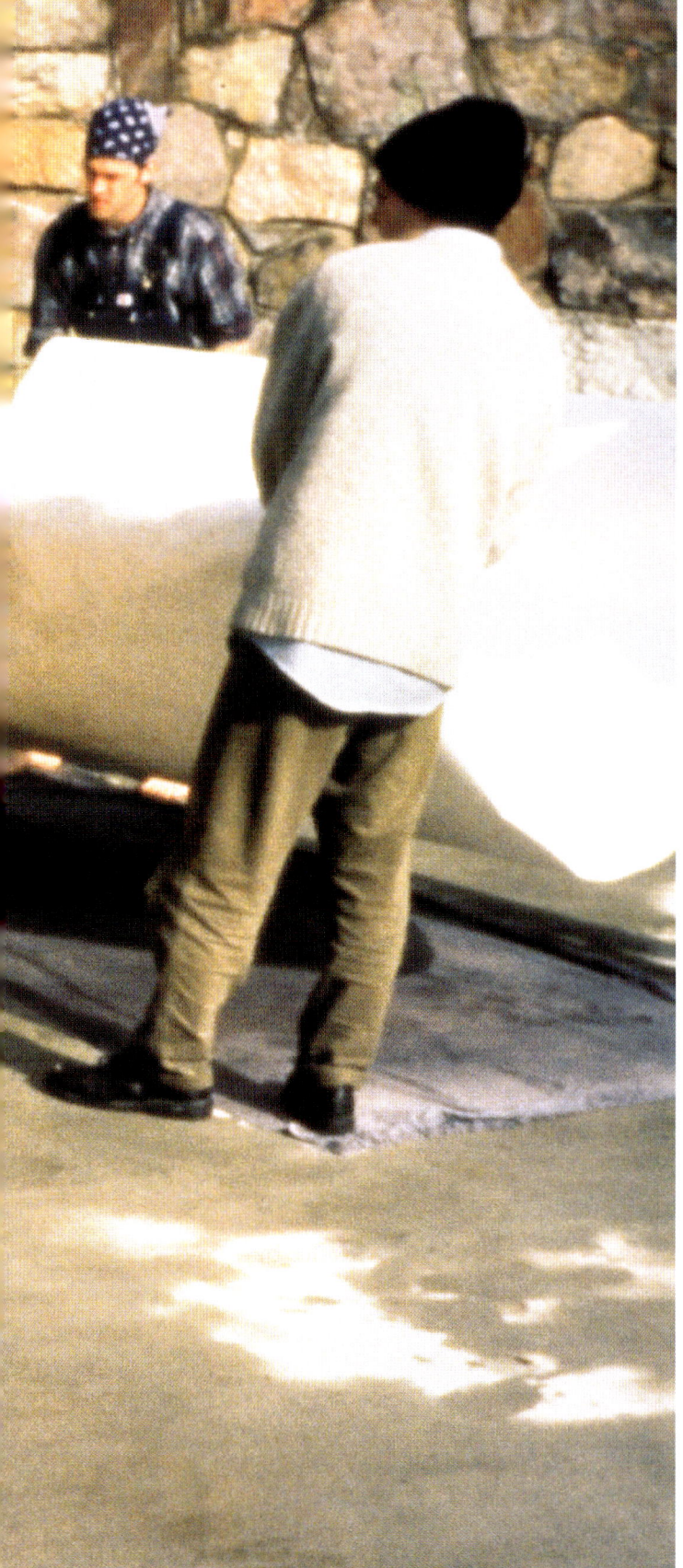

# III

# John Cage at the Mountain Lake Workshop

# THE 1983 MYCOLOGICAL FORAY AND *WHERE R = RYOANJI*

RAY KASS & HOWARD RISATTI

(right) The mycological foray group, 1983, including John Cage (far left), Orson Miller (center), Howard Risatti (2nd from right)

(below) John Cage, *Where R = Ryoanji (7R/15)*, 8/1983, pencil on Japanese paper, 9.875 x 19 in. (25.08 x 48.26 cm)

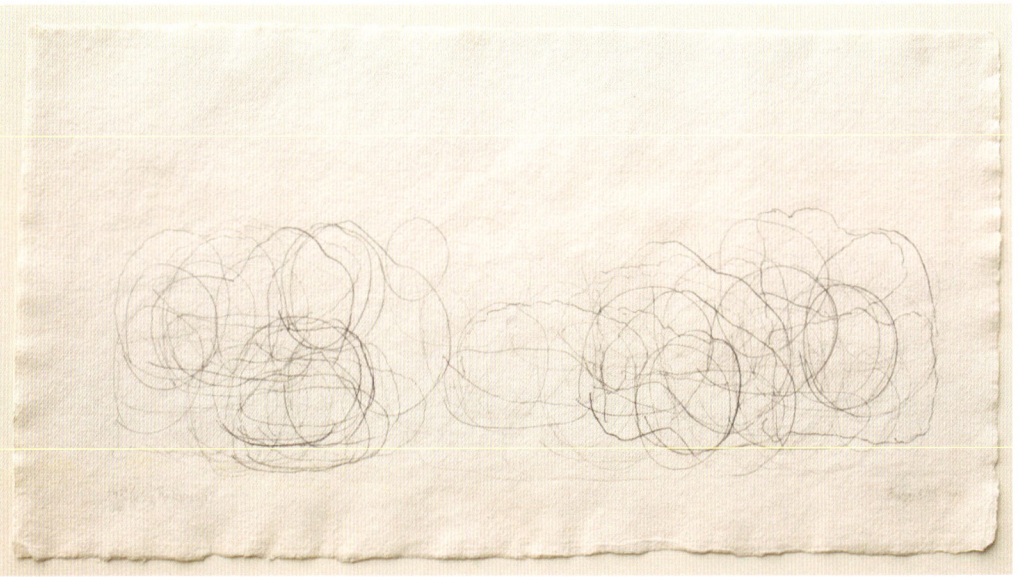

One of the key events in the evolution of both the conceptual ideas and practical working methods that would become central to future workshops occurred during John Cage's visit to Mountain Lake in the fall of 1983 at the invitation of Ray Kass.[1] Cage, who had developed a great interest in mushrooms in the '50s, was one of the founders in 1962 of the New York Mycological Society. Widely recognized as an expert in the field of mycology, Cage was invited to Mountain Lake to participate in what was hoped would be the beginning of a cross-disciplinary program in art and science. Such programs actually came to fruition in 1994 with the Methanogenesis workshop, but the 1983 "mycological foray," as the program involving Cage came to be called, already suggested how to use not only the resources of the locale, its physical materials such as plants and rocks as well as its customs, but also the resources of the scientific community at nearby Virginia Tech.

In October Cage came to Mountain Lake to co-direct the mycological foray with noted Virginia Tech mycologist Orson Miller and to participate in art workshops with Polaroid photographer Marie Cosindas and painter Robert Berlind. As part of the program, Miller gave a slide presentation about spore formation in fungi and British artist Ray Cowell gave a talk to accompany the small exhibition of her detailed fungi illustrations that she had made for the British Museum. Then it was Cage's turn to speak. Previously asked by Kass to speak about his interest in mushrooms as they relate to his writing and music, Cage read parts of *Mushrooms et Variationes*, a text that he had prepared for the foray.[2]

The foray itself, which was actually a mushroom hunt, might seem to be of little significance for the art workshops, but in fact Cage concerned himself with many "discipline-centered" activities that required paying close attention to things. He used chance operations in his compositions to encourage the audience to do the same thing, to be more attentive to the world around them. The mycological foray required just such disciplined attention; without it, it was simply impossible to see mushrooms in the midst of foliage and other objects on the forest floor.[3]

Cage also lectured at Virginia Tech for the opening of an exhibition of graphic works he had made over several years at Crown Point Press in Oakland, California. To this exhibition, which Kass organized as part of the program, Cage suggested adding some of the prints and drawings from a new series he had just finished that year at Crown Point Press.[4] These new works are titled *Where R = Ryoanji* and relate to *Ryoanji*,

a series for solo instruments that Cage began composing in 1983 inspired by the Zen-style Ryoanji Garden in Kyoto, Japan.[5] Surrounded by walls, this dry-landscape rock garden is an isolated precinct for the solitary contemplation of nature. The overlapping circular configurations found in the Ryoanji drawings were made by drawing around stones of various sizes using seventeen pencils of differing weights. The number of

[1] Kass came to know Cage while interviewing him as part of research for a Morris Graves exhibition catalogue. See related discussion in Kass' "Origin of the Mountain Lake Symposium and Workshops: Some Memoir/Some Context," p. §.

[2] For more on this, see Ray Kass, *The Sight of Silence: John Cage's Complete Watercolors*, exhibition catalogue (National Academy Museum, New York, and Taubman Museum of Art, Roanoke, Virginia, 2011), p. 42.

[3] Participating in Cage's spring 1988 workshop and mycological foray, the authors found it virtually impossible to see the morel mushrooms they were seeking. Only by intense concentration was it possible to separate the mushrooms from leaves, shadows, and foliage. Once they learned to concentrate in this way, mushrooms seemed to appear as if by magic.

[4] Cage experimented with painting as a youth; during this period he went door-to-door offering art lessons to neighbors and friends of his parents in their Los Angeles neighborhood as a means of making pocket money. Although Cage's musical scores are very interesting visually, his first real visual art creation since his student days was probably the *Automobile Tire Print* that he made with Robert Rauschenberg in 1953. In 1969 his graphic work began with *Not Wanting to Say Anything About Marcel*, a work done with Calvin Sumsion and printed on eight sheets of Plexiglas to commemorate the death of Marcel Duchamp, who had been Cage's friend for many years. Beginning in 1978 Cage did numerous graphic works at Crown Point Press at the invitation of Kathan Brown. These works were based on chance procedures and include *Changes and Disappearances* (1979–82) and *17 Drawings by Thoreau* (1978). For more on these works, see *John Cage Etchings, 1978–1982* (Oakland CA: Crown Point Press, 1982).

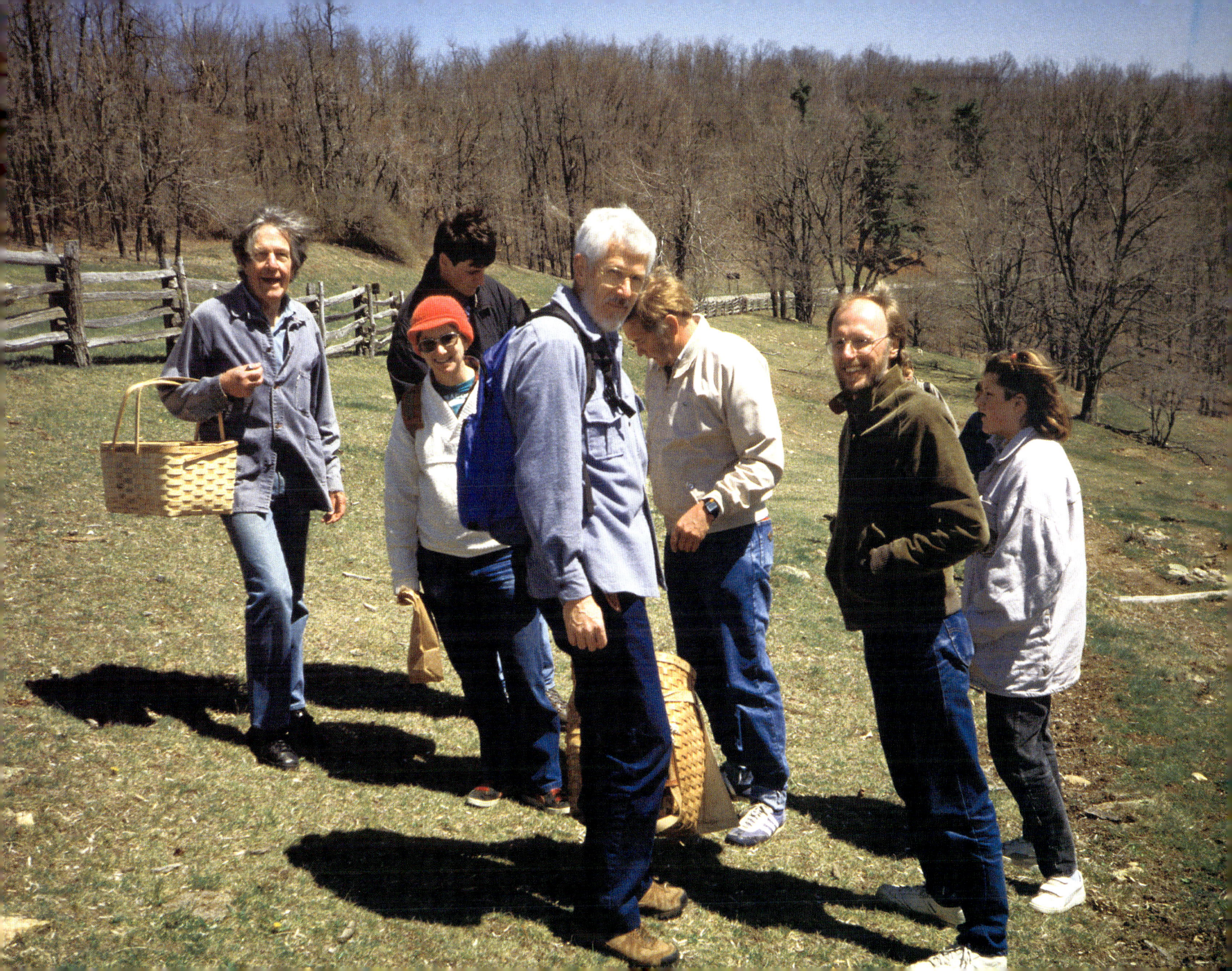

stones to be drawn around, fifteen, reflects the fifteen rocks of the Ryoanji Garden, rocks carefully arranged within the 360 square yards of raked gravel that forms the rectangular garden area.

Like Cage's earlier graphic works, various aspects of these drawings were created using chance methods derived from the *I Ching*, an ancient Chinese book variously known as the *Chinese Book of Changes* or the *Chinese Book of Wisdom*.[6] Cage came to be interested in chance ideas and indeterminacy in the 1930s, partly as a result of a lecture he attended at the Cornish School in Seattle on "Zen and Dada" by the noted writer Nancy Wilson Ross, a close friend of the Seattle painters Morris Graves and Mark Tobey.[7] In the early 1950s in New York, wanting to get away from certain predetermined dramatic musical structures connected to the sonata form, he turned to a serious study of chance as a way of writing music. In 1951 he wrote *Music of Changes* (for piano) and *Imaginary Landscape No. 4* (for twelve radios) using the *I Ching* as a method to determine what "musical events" should happen, when they would happen, and how long they would last. Following the *I Ching*, three coins (replacements for the prescribed yarrow sticks) were tossed six times to determine a number which was then matched to a chart of prearranged, pre-composed numbered musical events.[8]

When Cage was invited by Kathan Brown to Crown Point Press to do graphic works, he developed ways in which "visual events" could likewise be determined by using chance operations. For example, the position on the paper of an impression, the size or shape of that impression, the color ink to be used, and even the "bite" (the length of time the plate is in the acid) could all be determined through chance procedures. This is how

the tiny drawings Henry David Thoreau made to illustrate his journal were selected and manipulated for Cage's 1978 suite of prints titled *17 Drawings by Thoreau*.

Although the 1983 Ryoanji drawings follow the same chance procedures used in the graphic works, they differ in an important aspect from all of Cage's earlier works. Once the stone, pencil, and position on the paper had been determined through the "objective," impersonal procedures of chance, Cage then had to take pencil in hand and draw around the stone. Thus, despite the fact that most elements of the works were "mechanistically" determined in an effort to avoid compositional decisions and a "personally expressive" stylistic manner, an implicit quality of hand gesture is inherent in the drawing procedure itself.

Cage tried to minimize the self-expressive gestural potential of drawing by using chance to randomly select the weights of the pencils, by maintaining a sharp point, and by applying a constant drawing pressure. He also restricted the shapes the drawing marks could take by drawing around stones. Although the stones are not treated so procedurally as to become mere silhouettes, drawing around them removes certain expressive drawing features (such as shape and size) from the choices available to the artist. By doing this, Cage hoped to minimize the personal expressive qualities usually associated with the formal conventions of

drawing. The result is that what would normally have been self-expressive gestures now seem more like randomly made marks conditioned by the stones around which they are drawn. The marks now become the subject matter of the drawings, a subject matter generated from the shapes of the stones as a kind of afterimage or trace memory that links the stones — as a part of nature — to a human presence. They share something of the sensibility of Zen ink paintings in which solitary, spontaneous calligraphic marks reflect both inner and outer nature.

[5] Interestingly, the shape of the lines created by the stones Cage drew around in his graphic work *Where R = Ryoanji* determines the pitches the solo instrument plays. For more on this see John Pritchett, *The Music of John Cage* (Cambridge: Cambridge University Press, 1993), pp. 189–91.

[6] Used for divination, the *I Ching* is a book of sayings that are accessed through chance operations that involve throwing three yarrow sticks six times to arrive at a number which is then matched to the number corresponding to a saying in the book. Cage began employing a slightly modified version of this technique for composing music in 1951, when Christian Wolff, a young composer who was studying with him, gave him a copy of the *I Ching* which his father, Kurt Wolff, founder of Pantheon Press, had just published in an English edition. See Calvin Tomkins, *The Bride and the Bachelors: Five Masters of the Avant-Garde* (London and New York: Penguin Books, 1976), p. 108.

[7] In his *Morris Graves: Visions of the Inner Eye* (New York: Braziller in association with The Phillips Collection, Washington, D.C.,1983), p. 28, Ray Kass quotes Cage's reference to Nancy Wilson Ross's lecture and the impact it had on his method of composition: "It was very important to me, it drew a parallel for me with its insistence on experience and the irrational, rather than on logic and understanding."

[8] For *Music of Changes*, Cage used twenty-six large charts listing sounds, tempi, durations, rhythms, even silences, all of which were numbered. For the *Imaginary Landscape No. 4*, chance was used to determine many things including which stations each radio would be tuned to and for how long. At its premier, the performance was so late in the program that few radio stations were still on the air; the result, as most everyone agreed, was not very successful. See Tomkins, *The Bride*, p. 111 and pp. 113–14.

# RIPPLEMEAD WATERCOLOR EXPERIMENT IN KASS' STUDIO

**HOWARD RISATTI**

As the mycological foray unfolded over several days' time, there were opportunities for exploration of the area, including a stretch along the New River (reportedly the oldest river in the Western Hemisphere) called Ripplemead. Ripplemead is a site where the river rocks are particularly impressive. Knowing this and Cage's interest in the large stones from the Ryoanji Garden, Kass and several students took Cage to Ripplemead to see the rocks. They so impressed Cage that he selected a group that were brought back to Kass' studio and later transported to Cage's apartment in New York.[1]

Before returning to New York at the conclusion of the mycological foray, Cage visited Kass' studio, where he was surprised by a "painting experiment/situation" that Kass had carefully arranged the night before. He had mixed colors, prepared paper, arranged brushes, and provided the studio expertise in terms of washes and the knowledge of how certain desired effects could be achieved. In other words, Kass provided a studio practice for Cage that would enable him to paint. What Cage had to do was to come up with the artistic motivation for his own involvement.

Based on the procedures Cage had used for the Ryoanji drawings,[2] a selection of papers, brushes, colors, and the Ripplemead rocks had been arranged and numbered, and Cage was invited to apply his chance procedures in a "painting experiment" by treating these materials as the elements to be manipulated. Using *I Ching*–derived numbers, the paper, rocks, positions, colors, and brushes were selected as Cage did three paintings following the same methods he had employed in the Ryoanji drawings. At their completion, Cage felt something was missing from the paintings; and Kass suggested that, to bring together

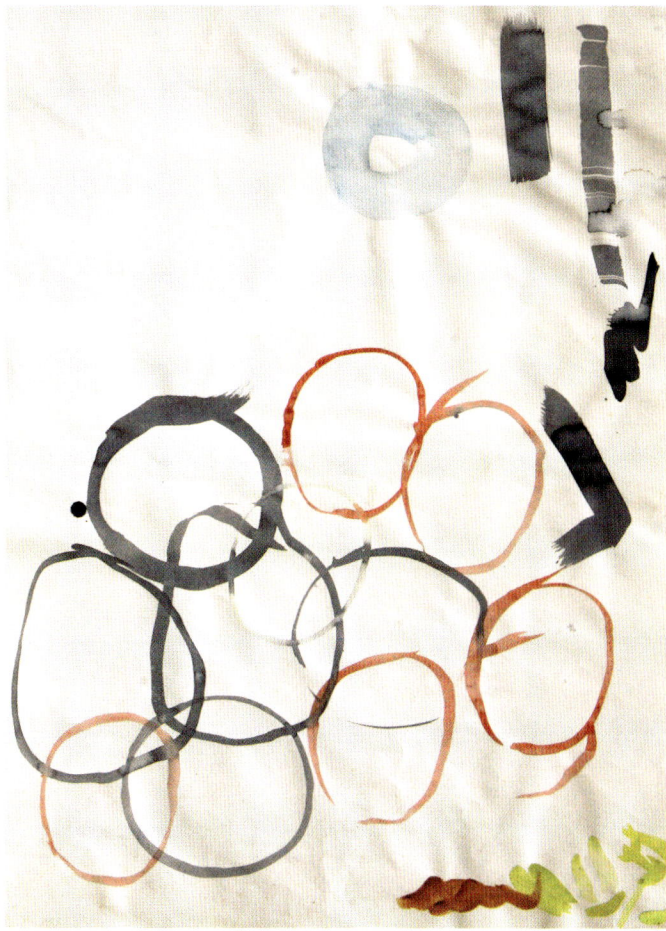

John Cage's first test painting, 1983, watercolor on paper, 24 x 18 in. (60.9 x 45.7 cm)

the marks made by painting around the rocks, a transparent wash should be applied to the works to "finish" them.

Although Cage felt positive about the results of the painting experiment, he still had some general reservations about painting

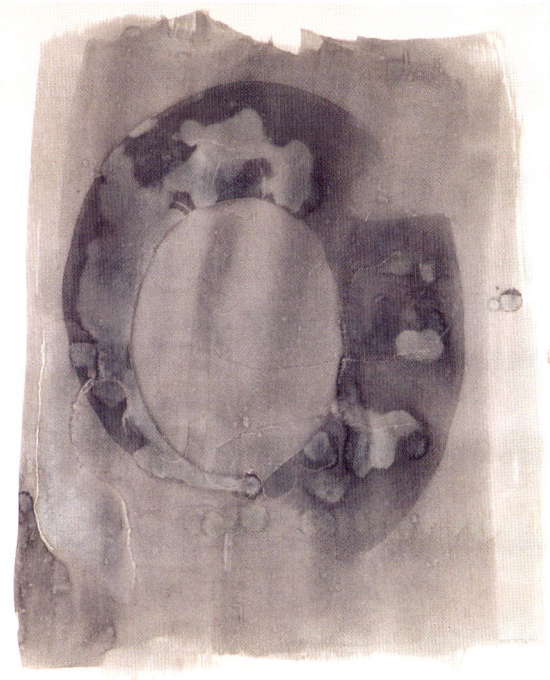

John Cage's second test painting, 1983, watercolor on paper, 36.5 x 31 in. (92.7 x 78.7 cm)

which stemmed, in part, from doubt that he could pursue such a complicated new studio activity. And, more importantly, he had concerns over the question of self-expression associated with painting. Self-expression conflicted with his deeply held aesthetic ideas. Cage had been closely connected with the New York Abstract Expressionist Gesture painters during the 1940s and early '50s. He had worked with Robert Motherwell and Harold Rosenberg editing the only issue of the art and literary magazine *Possibilities* and he even titled a musical composition of 1943 *Totem Ancestor*, recalling the titles of Jackson Pollock's *Totem Lesson I* and *Totem Lesson II* from the same time. In the early '50s he also spoke about chance ideas at The Club, the East 8th Street loft that was the Abstract Expressionist

[1] Many of these rocks were later presented as the Cunningham Dance Foundation Award for Distinguished Support of the Arts. See Ray Kass, "The Mountain Lake Workshop" in *John Cage/New River Watercolors* exhibition catalogue (Richmond: Virginia Museum of Fine Arts, 1988), p. 2. The essay is reprinted from *Drawing*, vol. 10, no. 3 (Sept/Oct 1988).

[2] See p. X in "The 1983 Mycological Foray and *Where R = Ryoanji*."

[3] See Calvin Tomkins, *The Bride and the Bachelors: Five Masters of the Avant-Garde* (London and New York: Penguin Books, 1976), p. 110. For more on The Club, see Irving Sandler, *The Triumph of American Painting: A History of Abstract Expressionism* (New York: Praeger Publishers, 1970), pp. 213ff.

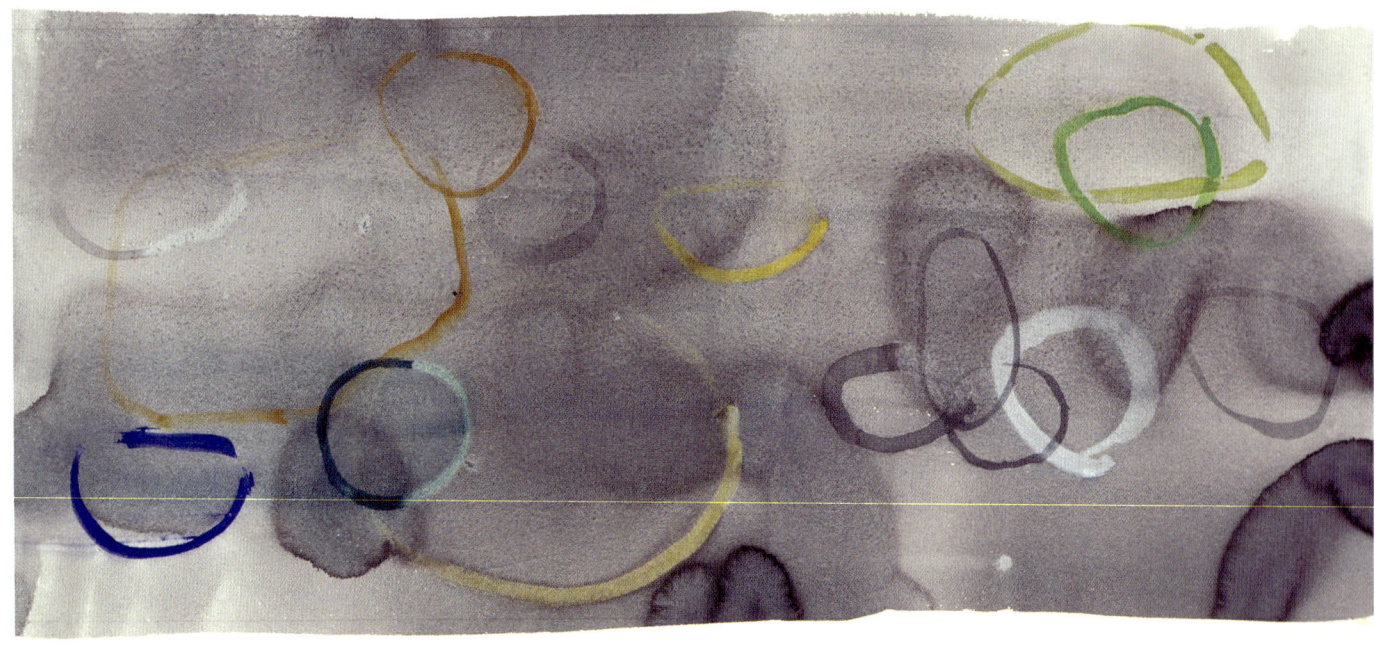

John Cag's first complete and signed watercolor painting, *New River Stones*, 1983, watercolor, 24 in. x 51 (60.9 x 129.5 cm)

As he delved into these ideas of Indian aesthetic, which he further studied with Gita Sarabhai, a young music student from India, Cage seriously began as well to study Japanese Zen concepts.[7] In 1945–47, he studied Zen Buddhism while attending the classes of Dr. Daisetz T. Suzuki at Columbia University, learning to open his mind to the world around him, to blur the line between art and life. What he came to realize, according to Calvin Tomkins, was "that Zen, like psychoanalysis, was an attempt to open the mind from within to a more intense awareness (enlightenment, or *satori*) of everyday life."[8]

By the late 1940s, in part because of his work composing music for the Cunningham Dance Foundation (music which must fit the amount of time dancers are performing rather than tell a story), Cage began to conceive his non-dance music as a space (a certain length of time) into which the composer "put" sounds. Later, with the composition titled *4'33"* (often referred to simply as *Silence*), music became a space in which to "let" sounds occur. The sounds that occurred in *4'33"* as pianist David Tudor sat on stage silently at the piano were the ambient sounds of nature and the audience. What this piece represented was the Zen spirit of acceptance rather than a method of control; it was a way of practically and symbolically opening the self to the world around it.

The problem that the painting experiment in Kass' studio raised for Cage had to do with how to let events occur in the space of the painting as opposed to controlling them with a self-expressive, personal gesture. This was a practical problem with deep aesthetic and philosophical implications with which Cage had to come to grips. Nonetheless, despite these concerns, he agreed to consider doing a full-fledged painting workshop in the near future. Unfortunately, because of the great number of other demands placed upon him, including his commitment to the Cunningham Dance Foundation, he would not be able to find time to do a workshop at Mountain Lake incorporating his new interest in visual art until the late spring of 1988.

meeting place. One of these lectures, composed using chance, was titled "Lecture on Nothing"; it was followed by "Lecture on Something" devoted to the music of Morton Feldman.[3]

However, while Abstract Expressionists like Willem de Kooning, Franz Kline, and Philip Guston considered the painted gesture a personal signature, an expression of the inner self, Cage had been at pains to avoid this in his own work since the mid-1940s. As composer and *New York Herald Tribune* music critic Virgil Thomson noted, the friends Cage made in Seattle while at the Cornish School in the '30s, friends such as composer Lou Harrison, dancer Merce Cunningham, and painters Morris Graves and Mark Tobey, "stimulated his take-off as a composer toward Eastern art principles."[4] These "Eastern art principles," which in time would lead Cage away from reliance upon the self and self-expression in music, became apparent in Cage's thinking around 1945. His *Sonatas and Interludes* (for piano), begun in 1946 and completed in 1948, was an attempt, as Thomson understood it,

to avoid progress and change, to avoid developing a piece that had a beginning, middle, and end.[5] It was also an attempt to express the nine permanent emotions of the Indian aesthetic tradition. These emotions — the heroic, the erotic, the wondrous, the mirthful, sorrow, fear, anger, the odious, and their common tendency toward tranquility — were part of a concept of art and nature that Cage e ncountered in the writings of Ananda K. Coomaraswamy.[6] A curator of Indian art, Coomaraswamy discussed Indian aesthetic ideas in documents that were widely read, especially his 1934 book *The Transformation of Nature in Art*. It is likely that Cage encountered these writings while in Seattle, because both Tobey and Graves were very interested in Coomaraswamy's ideas, especially his notion that in art one should imitate nature, not in "her appearance, but in her manner of operation." This idea, which would become very important for the workshops at Mountain Lake, reinforced Cage's concern to avoid self-expression because self-expression seemed too personal, too ego-centered, to express a larger concept of nature.

[4] Virgil Thomson, *American Music Since 1910* (New York: Holt, Rinehart, and Winston, 1970), p. 70. Cage recounted that Tobey gave him a lesson in looking without prejudice, without comparing one thing with something seen before. This was an important principle for Cage's work at Mountain Lake. See Cage conversation with Daniel Charles in *For the Birds: John Cage in Conversation with Daniel Charles* (Boston and London: Marion Boyars, 1981), p. 158.

[5] Thomson, American Music, p. 71.

[6] Tomkins, *The Bride*, pp. 98–99. Coomaraswamy was a curator at the Museum of Fine Arts, Boston. For the emotions and Cage's music, see Paul Griffiths, *Modern Music: A Concise History from Debussy to Boulez* (New York: Thames and Hudson, 1985), p. 127.

[7] See Tomkins, *The Bride*, p. 99.

[8] See Tomkins, *The Bride*, p. 100.

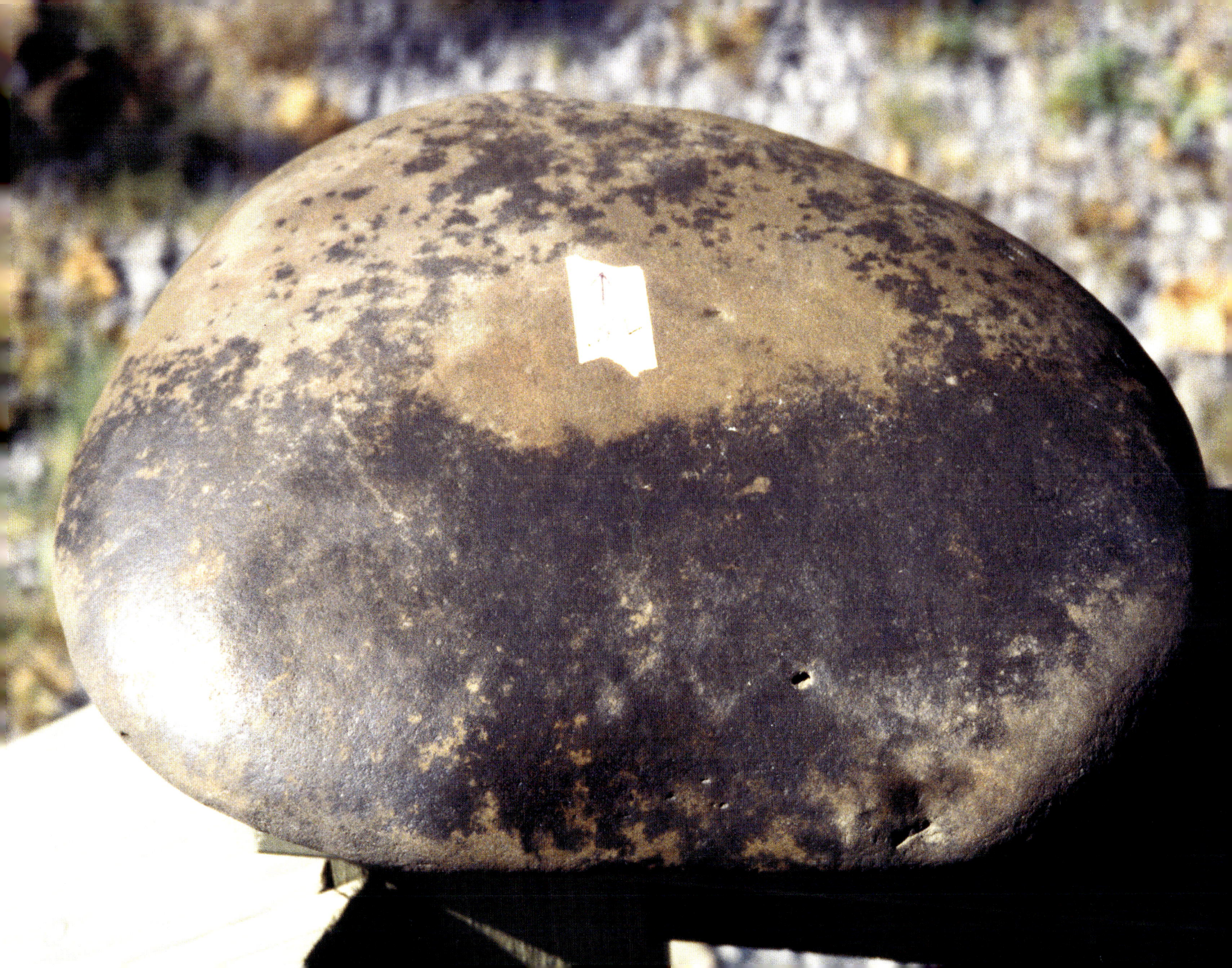

# JOHN CAGE: NEW RIVER WATERCOLORS, 1988

**HOWARD RISATTI**

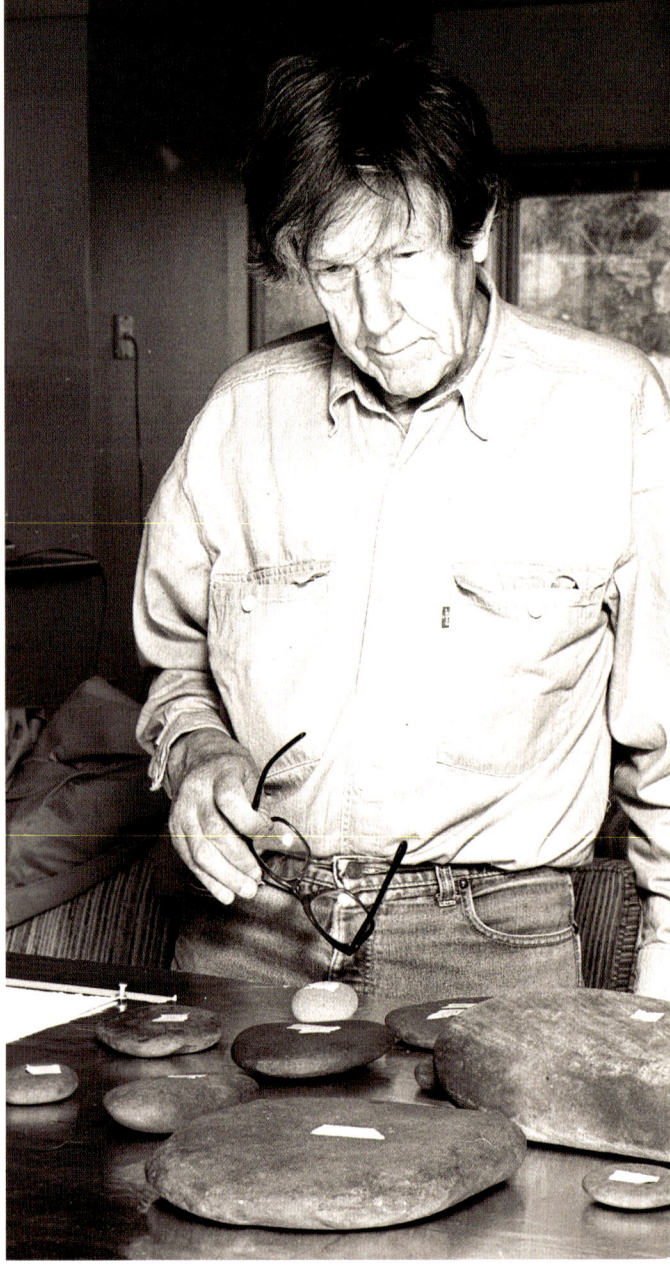

Cage at the Horton Studio, 1988
Photo: Stephanie Klein-Davis

In 1985 when Howard Finster conducted a collaborative workshop at Mountain Lake he brought with him cut-outs of enlarged images taken from comic books, newspapers, and other contemporary sources. These "dementions," as he called them, were used by participants as stencils to create their own personal visual art. Finster's conception of his dementions fostered a new attitude about the creative aspects of the collaborative process. The visionary aspect of the image, its sacred wonder and immutable resonance, showed that the process of artistic production through collaboration, if carried out with a sincere artistic effort, could be linked to the creative motive for the work. Finster did not have to make every single work himself for his vision to be conveyed by his dementions.

Because of their mutual connection with Mountain Lake, John Cage made an effort to acquaint himself with Finster and his work, perhaps because he saw parallels between Finster's thinking about art and his own. When Finster's retrospective exhibition opened at the American Folk Art Museum, Cage made a point of going there to meet him. After the opening he called Ray Kass, saying how much he enjoyed the conversation and how completely sincere and genuine Finster seemed to him.[1]

Though there are differences in where their ideas come from, Finster's from an evangelical religious background and Cage's from a background of modern music influenced by Asian philosophy, there are implicit parallels in their thinking. Finster saw his work in religious terms in which the image takes on a spiritual quality conveyed by the maker; hence the idea that it doesn't matter who executes the work as long as

their attitude is sincere and in the spirit of the work. For Cage's part, as a composer he necessarily had to involve performers in the collaborative process of actually playing his music. This has always been an accepted practice in music. After all, the composer writes the musical score with the understanding that others will play it. Once this realization came to the fore in Cage's thinking, it allowed him to expand the possibilities of the collaborative process in relation to his own work and aesthetic ideas. When it came to doing visual art, Cage gradually came to reassess the implications of the painted mark, especially regarding its expressive content. He too came to embrace the idea that it doesn't matter who "holds the brush" as long as they work with sincere commitment to the spirit of the work.

It was not until 1988 that Cage's schedule finally permitted him to return to Mountain Lake. At the beginning of April he arrived at the Horton Center and remained for a week-long workshop during which four series of works were produced. Following upon the 1983 "painting experiment," stones collected from the New River were sorted into three groups according to size, which were separately numbered; numerous and varied brushes were divided into two separately numbered groups; likewise, feathers to paint with, colors and washes, and papers were also divided and numbered.[2] In this way, chance procedures using pages of random numbers that were now generated by a computer program — a technology that Cage only recently had put to work to serve his novel purposes — could be used to determine the specific materials and processes to be utilized for each painting — which painting instruments, what type of paper and which colors, how many washes, which stones

---

[1] Related to the author by Ray Kass in conversation, February 21, 2017. The retrospective was *The Road to Heaven Is Paved by Good Works: The Art of Reverend Howard Finster*, American Folk Art Museum, 2 Sept. 1989–Jan. 1990, curated by John Turner/Paine Webber Gallery, NY.

[2] There were 14 types of paper numbered 1–14; 40 brushes arranged into two separately numbered groups; 33 colors numbered 1–33; and 131 rocks in three separately numbered groups of small (4" or less), medium (4"–9"), and large (9"–23"). Glide feathers were also used to paint with and were added to the brushes; they were provided by Dr. Walter Gross from birds at the Virginia Tech Poultry Laboratories.

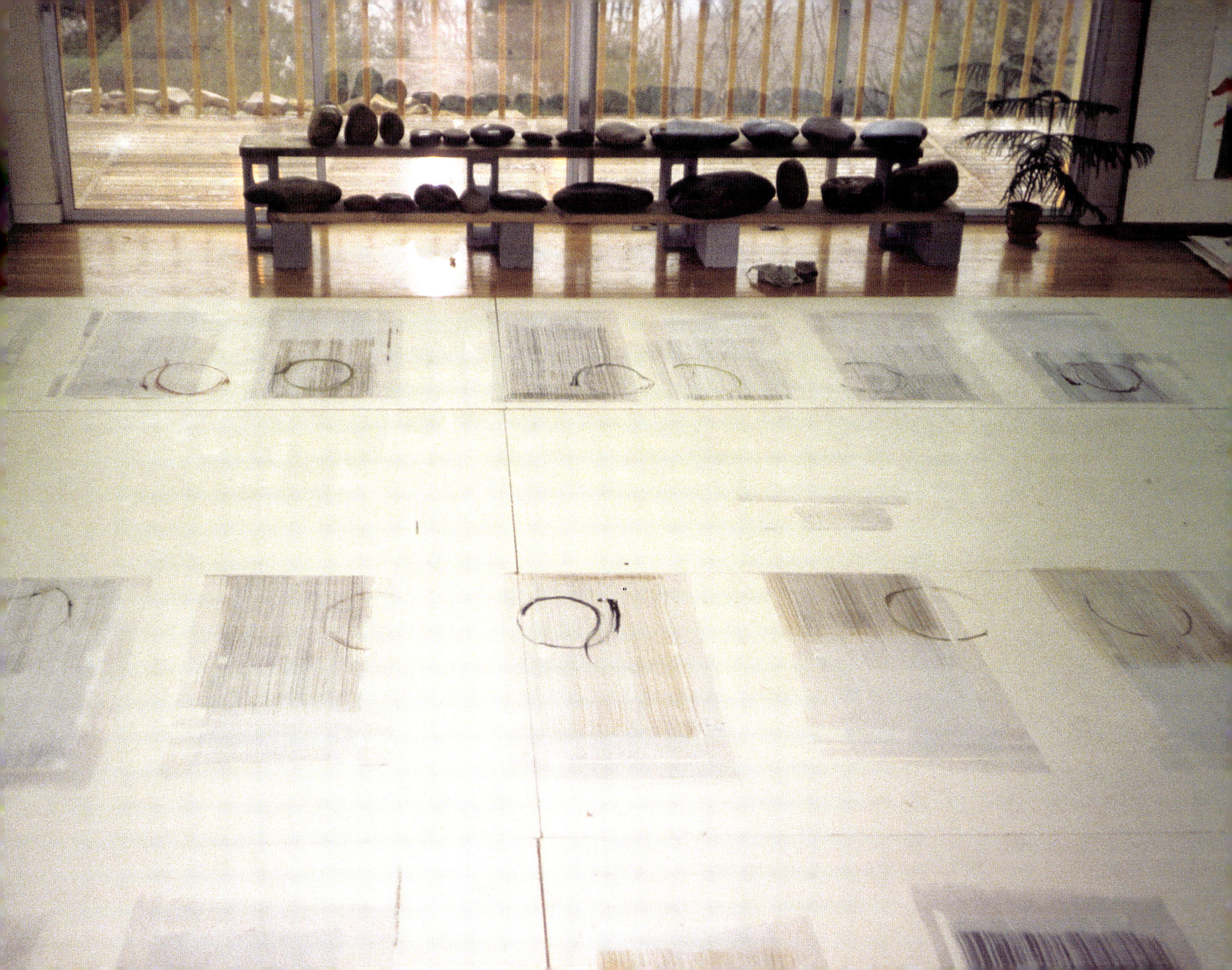

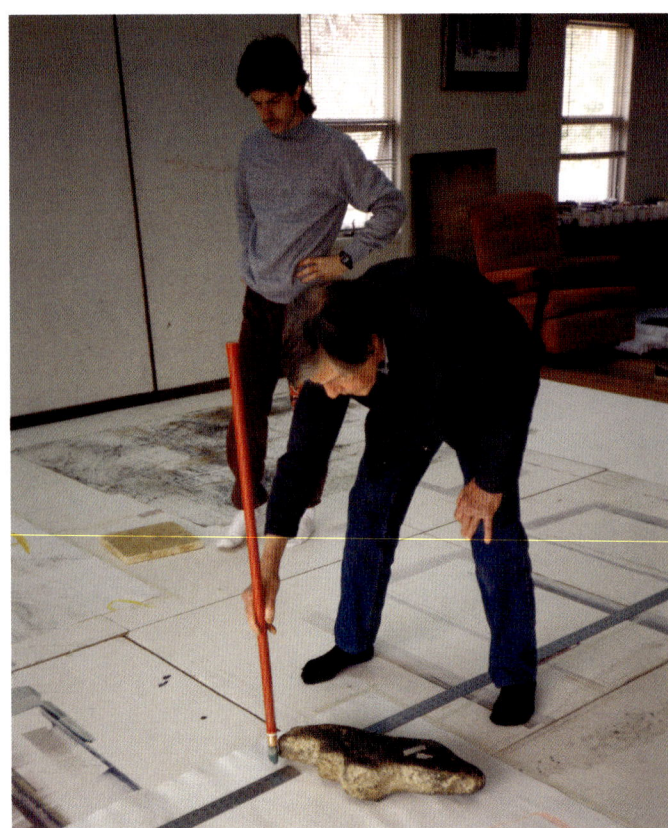

John Cage painting at the Horton Center Studio at Mountain Lake with Greg Bryson assisting.

to paint around, where to locate the stones on the paper.[3]

Because chance is generally considered the opposite of the predictable and the rational, the use of chance procedures has been one of the most controversial aspects of Cage's work since he began using the *I Ching* in 1951 to compose *Music of Changes* and Imaginary *Landscape No. 4*. Even French composer Pierre Boulez, who had been a close friend of Cage for years, finally broke with him in 1962 over the use of chance.[4] The reason Cage turned to chance was that although he was interested in expression, he was not interested in self-expression. From Zen Buddhism he came to believe that to truly experience the world around oneself, one had to free the mind and the self from control by the ego. Ego, according to Zen, is the one barrier to

experience because ego, which is connected to emotion, taste, memory, and desire, fixates on preconceived expectations and aesthetic possibilities, on the already known. In this way it prevents exploration and experience of the new. Cage realized that chance, on the other hand, offered the artist a way to rise above control by the ego into new and unexplored territory. This could happen, because, once an overall format for a work was consciously created, chance allowed unexpected things to happen; chance allowed musical or visual "events" to occur without the ego's intervention. The artist then would be in a new situation which required a conscious, disciplined response. Chance, when understood properly, still involved discipline, discipline to not do just anything, but to free oneself from, as Cage said, "likes and dislikes," in order to explore and experiment.[5] For Cage, chance was to be used as a discipline and not, as some people allege, as a way of giving up choices. "My choices," Cage said "consist in choosing what questions to ask."[6]

It is extremely important to understand that Cage used chance procedures only after a format for a work had been chosen. In organizing the format (i.e., numbering the painting materials and the formal painting procedures), Cage was choosing what questions to ask! In this way, chance was being asked to answer specific questions (to make "choices") about the specific kinds of details that would normally be dictated by individual habits of taste. Cage wanted to avoid those habits in order to discover new ways of looking so as to see and experience the world with fresh and revelatory insight.

When Cage understood his own philosophical and aesthetic ideas

in relation to Finster's convictions about the inherent visionary power of his dementions, he came to an important realization about the collaborative painting process and his own aesthetic ideas: once the format for a series of paintings was chosen, it didn't matter who held the brush![7] The result would be an expression of something larger than the individual ego/self.

Cage now brought his chance procedures to the workshop with a new sense of opportunity. He decided to do several series of works. In Series I (five works, each 18" x 36"), fifteen stones of widely varying sizes would be used in reference to the fifteen stones of the Zen-inspired Ryoanji Garden in Kyoto, Japan, and the feathers rather than brushes would be used to paint around them. Cage decided that colors and washes should be a mixture of two colors so they would be somewhat muted. The exact position and length of the washes would be determined by chance. In Series II (thirteen works, each 26" x 72"), seven or fewer stones would be used in each work with unmixed, bright colors used around the stones and mixed colors for the washes; again, the length and position of the washes were to be determined by chance, and feathers instead of brushes would again be used.

At the beginning of the third day of the workshop, Cage reported that he had had a dream during the night about what the works in Series III (twenty-four works, each 36" x 15") should be like. Following this, he chose to paint around a single mandala-like stone to create a circular shape near the bottom of each work that recalls the enso ("circle") paintings of Japanese Zenga (Zen calligraphic painting). Each of these works would have a wash covering all of the paper, with a final neutral wash added

[3] In 1984, composer Andrew Culver created a computer program for Cage to generate pages of random numbers, which saved a great deal of time. Before this, generating numbers was a very tedious and time-consuming process, and Cage spent hours tossing coins, even while riding on the subway. Author's conversation with Cage, May 1988.

[4] Not only Boulez, but in a 1964 concert the New York Philharmonic Orchestra with Leonard Bernstein at the helm, was openly hostile to Cage's *Atlas Eclipticalis with Winter Music (Electronic Version)* during their performance of the work. See Calvin Tomkins, *The Bride and the Bachelors: Five Masters of the Avant-Garde* (London and New York: Penguin Books, 1976), pp. 141 - 42.

[5] Cage quoted from interview by Richard Kostelanetz with an introduction by Laura Kuhn, "John Cage," *High Performance* (Sept. 1986), p. 30.

[6] Richard Kostelanetz, *Conversing with Cage* (New York: Limelight Editions, 1988), p. 58. Cage also noted that he was led to Eastern ideas through Dada (see Kostelanetz, p. 54). This is not surprising, for his remarks reflect the ideas of Dada artist Hans Arp, who saw Dada as closely connected to chance. Arp declared that "Dada stands for art without sense. ... [However,] this does not mean nonsense." (Arp went on to say that "Dada is without meaning, as nature is.") Arp quoted in Hans Richter, *Dada: Art and Anti-Art* (New York and Toronto: Oxford University Press, 1965), p. 37.

John Cage, *New River Watercolors, Series III, #23*, 1988, watercolor on rag paper, 36 x 15 in. (91.44 x 38.10 cm)

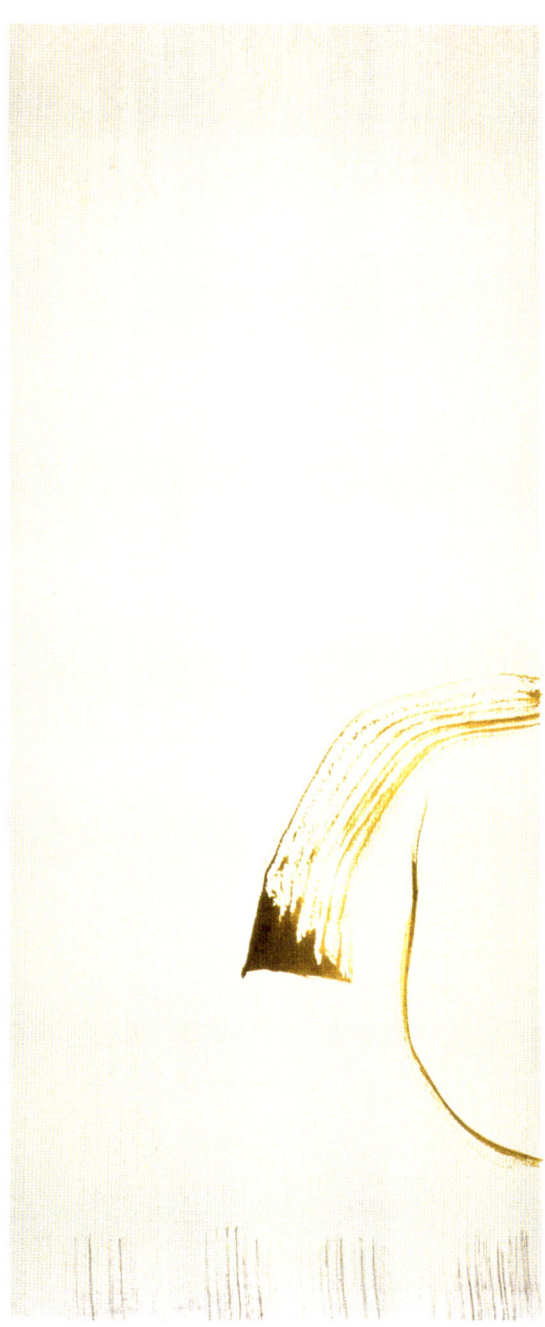

John Cage, *New River Watercolors, Series III, #24*, 1988, watercolor on rag paper, 36 x 15 in. (91.44 x 38.10 cm)

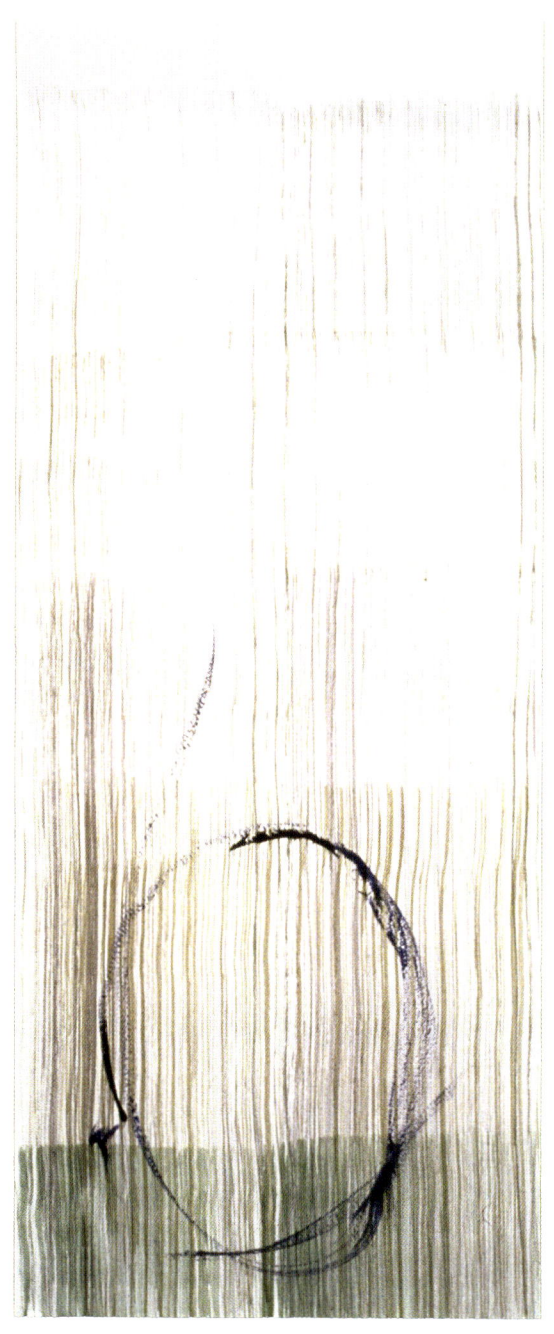

John Cage, *New River Watercolors, Series III, #8*, 1988, watercolor on rag paper, 36 x 15 in. (91.44 x 38.10 cm). Collection The Phillips Collection, Washington. D.C.

John Cage, *New River Watercolors, Series II, #1*, 1988, watercolor, 72 x 26 in. (182.88 x 66.04 cm)

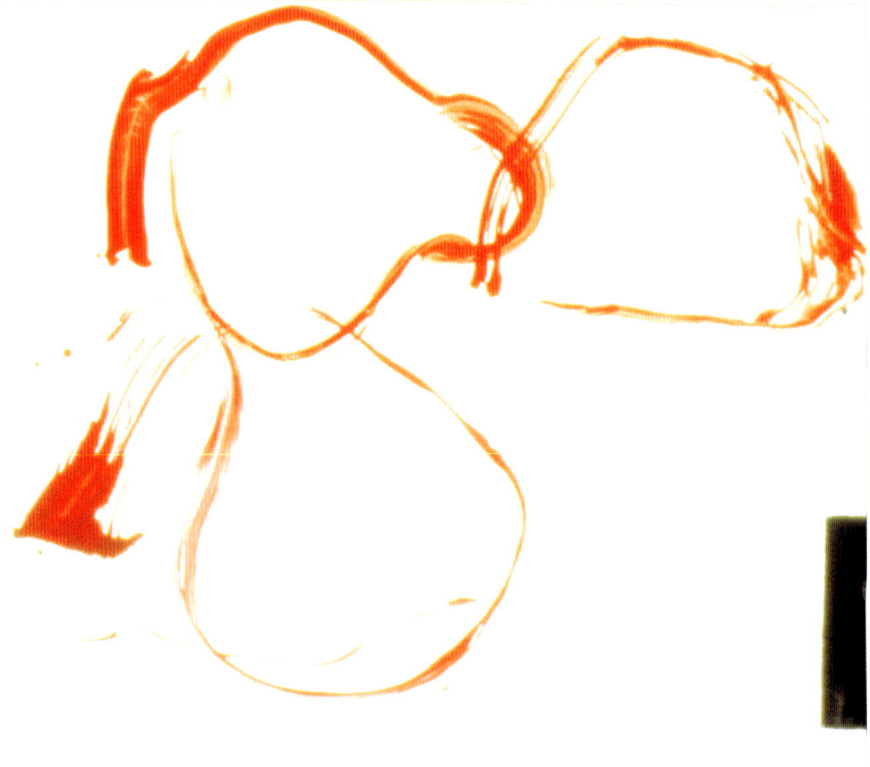

as well; colors were to be light and dry. Unlike the central placement of the enso in traditional Zenga paintings, the stone's position along the horizontal axis was determined by chance so that the circular shape would often be cropped by the edges of the paper on either right or left, but seldom centered.

In the initial stages of the workshop, Cage was still tentative enough to want to use feathers as a way of further avoiding the implications of the painted mark associated with the brush. By the final works, Series IV (eight works, each 26½ x 40 inches), Cage had gained enough confidence in the workshop procedures and his sense of the studio practice that he decided to abandon feathers and to use brushes for the first time.

He restricted the stones to the lower part of the paper representing the "golden rectangle," something he also had done in his Ryoanji pencil drawings of 1983. The first work in the series, done on a Thursday, had 195 "moves" (positions for stones to be painted around) and took a whole day to complete. The remaining seven works in the series had fewer moves and were all painted on Friday, the last day of the workshop.

Inspecting these watercolors, Cage became much more appreciative of how the expressive qualities of a painted mark could be tied to the intrinsic properties of the painting instrument and the rock (as opposed to being a gesture overtly expressive of a bodily motion). By being executed in a spirit of equanimity

(constancy of pressure and motion) and by being shaped by the rock around which it is formed, the painted mark symbolizes a balanced relationship between the individual self and the material world outside without being re-presented (i.e., painted and modeled realistically). In leaving a sign of their presence on the paper, the rocks are the ostensible subject matter of the paintings and serve to maintain the connection between the material world of nature and the artist. However, at a deeper level, the randomly overlapping circular marks and broad washes become the very principle of creation and are essential to the process of making art because they establish a conceptual link to nature in the way they are cropped by chance procedures. In this way, the painting process itself imitates nature's processes

7 Because of this, it was generally decided that Cage would do all of the painting during the workshop while participants would assist by mixing washes, carrying rocks, and helping position them on the paper following a numbered grid.

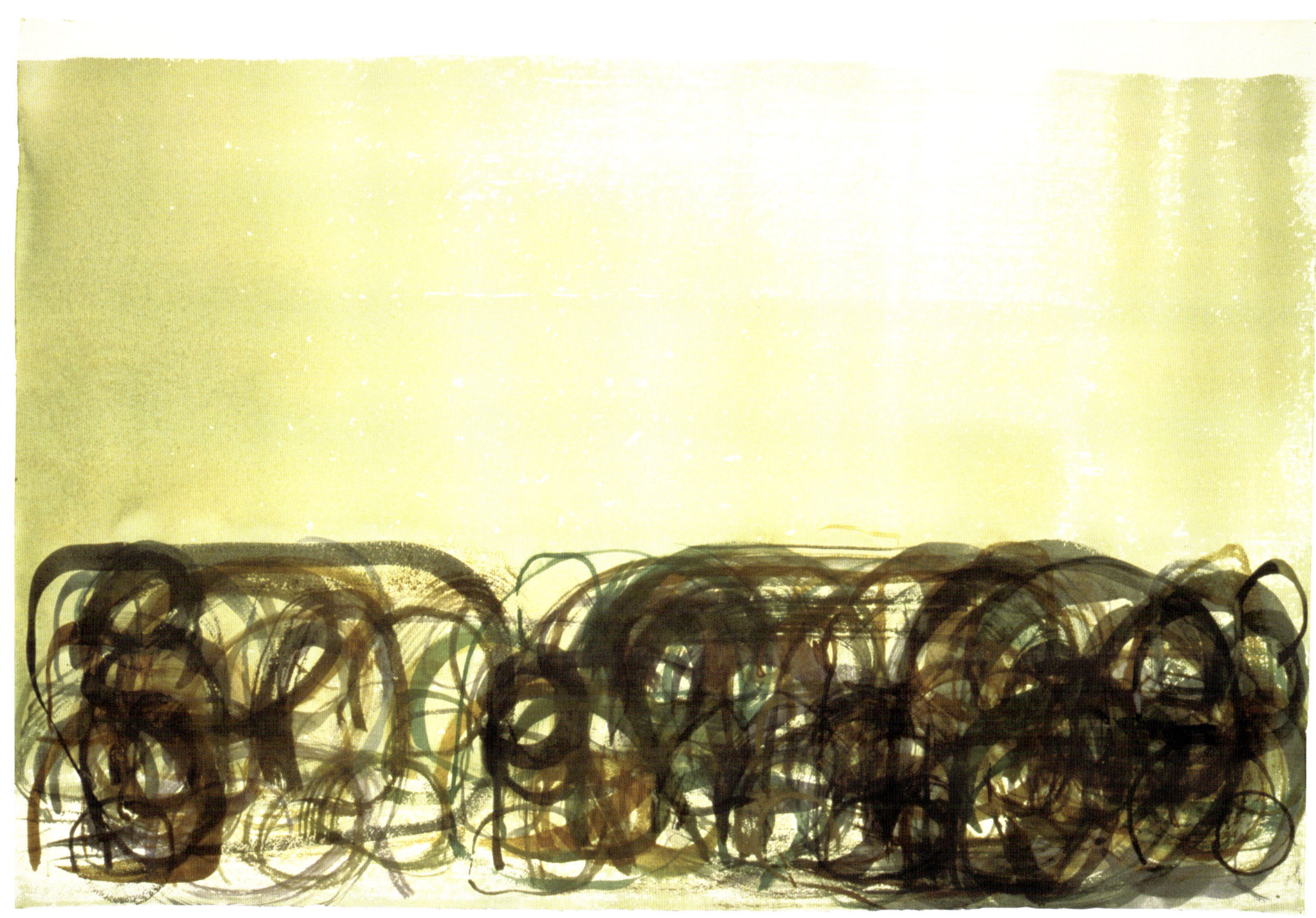

John Cage, *New River Watercolors, Series IV, #1*, 1988, watercolor on rag paper, 26 1/2 x 40 in. (67.31 x 101.6 cm).
Colllection Virginia Museum of Fine Arts, Richmond, Gift of Ray Kass and the Mountain
Lake Art Workshop, and the Horton Fund of the Virginia Tech Foundation

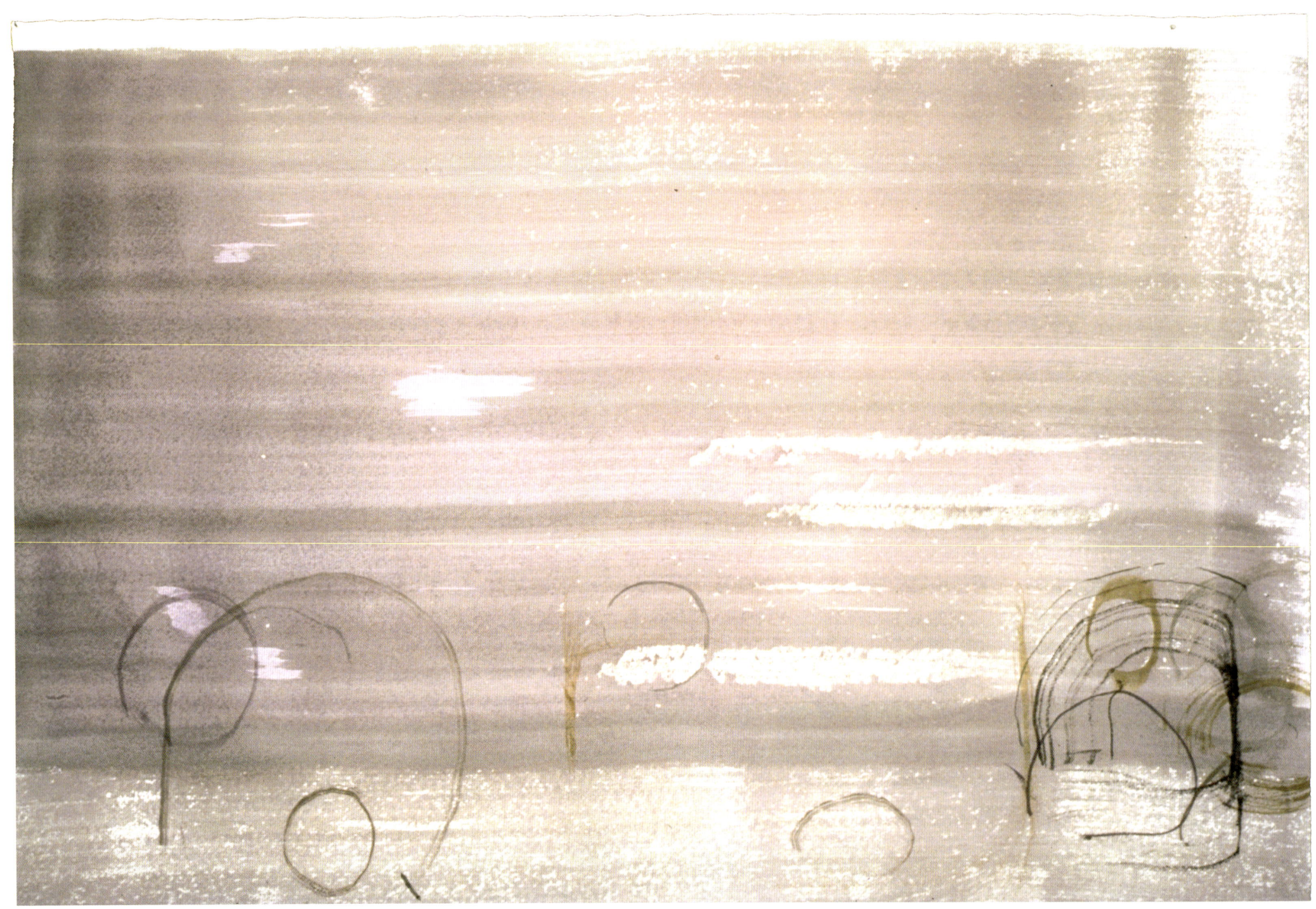

John Cage, *New River Watercolors,
Series IV, #2*, 1988, watercolor, 26
x 40 in. (101.60 x 66.04 cm)

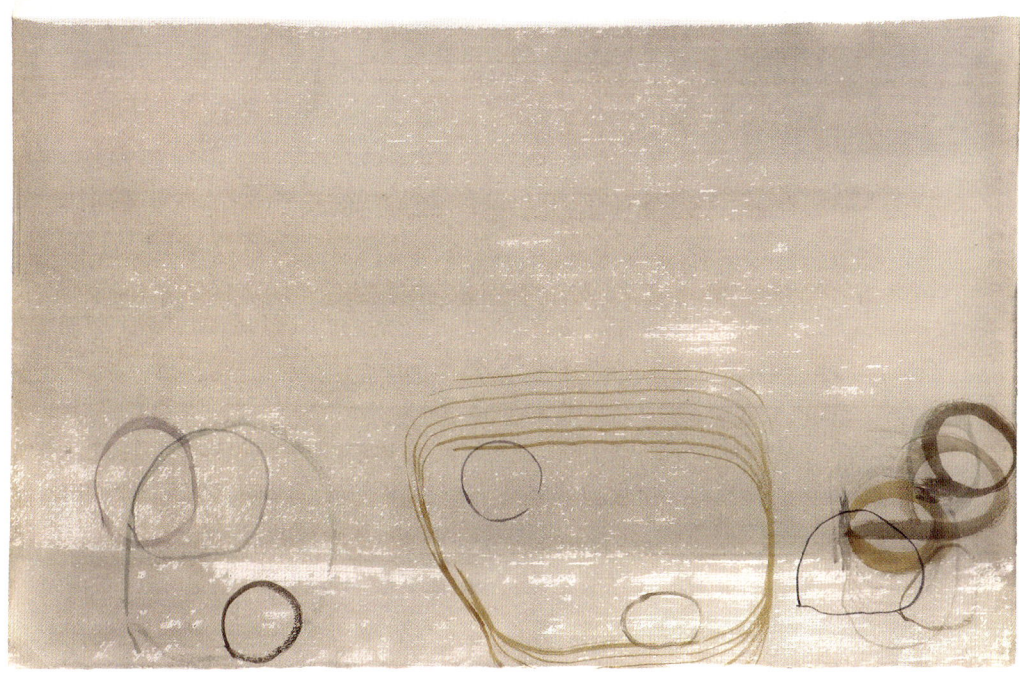

John Cage and Peter Lau, *New River Watercolors, Series IV, variant #2a*, 1988, watercolor, 26 x 40 in. (101.60 x 66.04 cm)

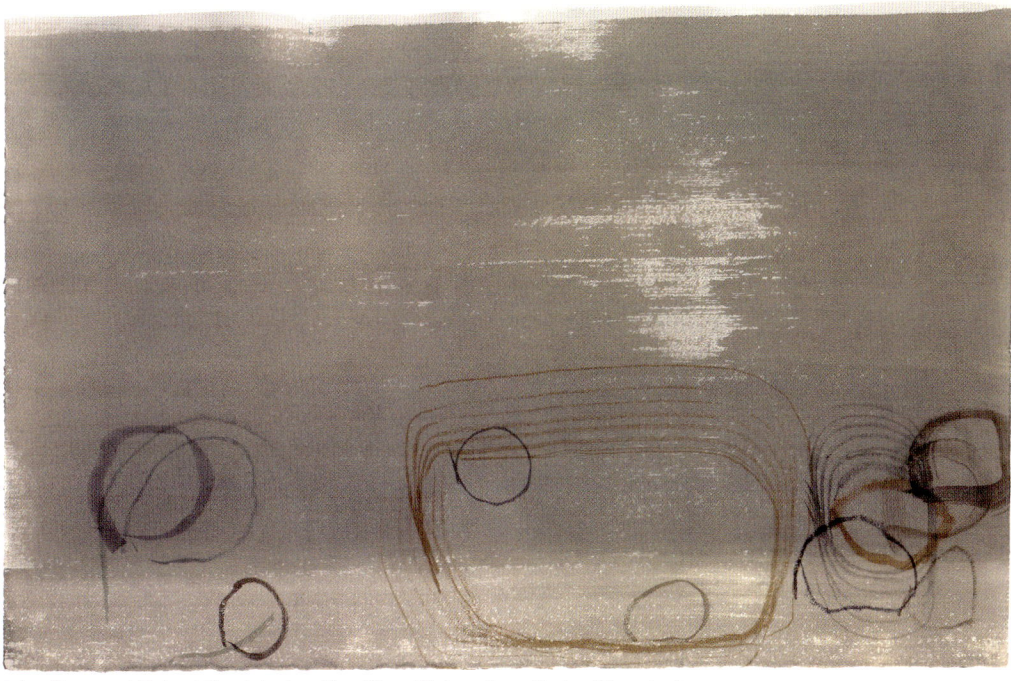

John Cage and Robert Camicia Jr., *New River Watercolors, Series IV, variant #2c*, 1988, watercolor, 26 x 40 in. (101.60 x 66.04 cm)

John Cage, *New River Watercolors, Series IV, variant #2b*, 1988, watercolor, 26 x 40 in. (101.60 x 66.04 cm)

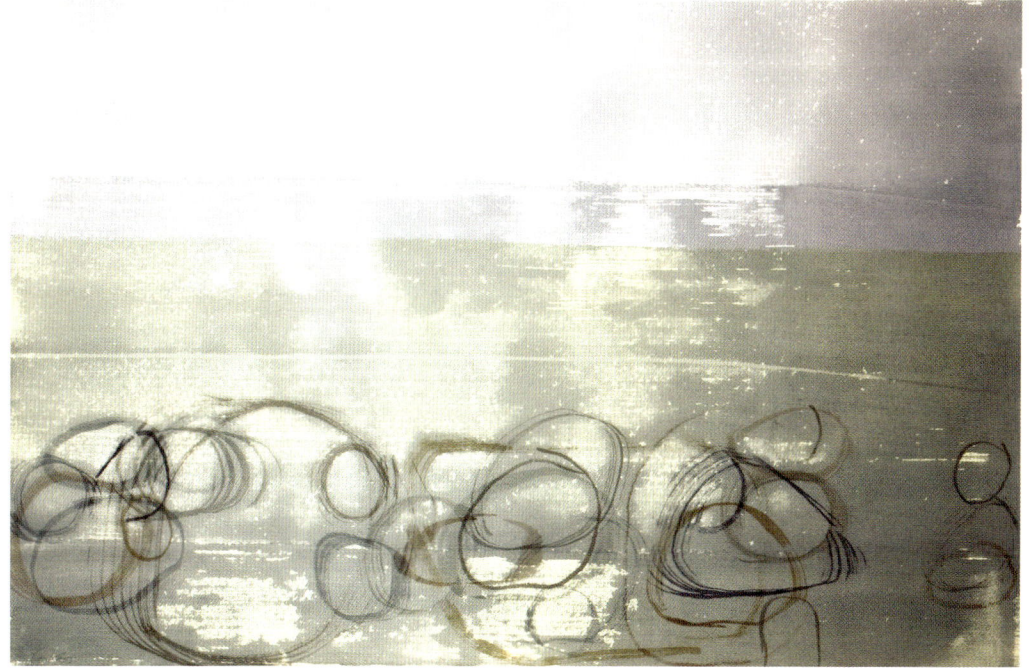

John Cage and Ray Kass, *New River Watercolors, Series IV, variant #2d*, 1988, watercolor, 26 x 40 in. (101.60 x 66.04 cm)
Collection: Jordi Soley, Barcelona, Spain

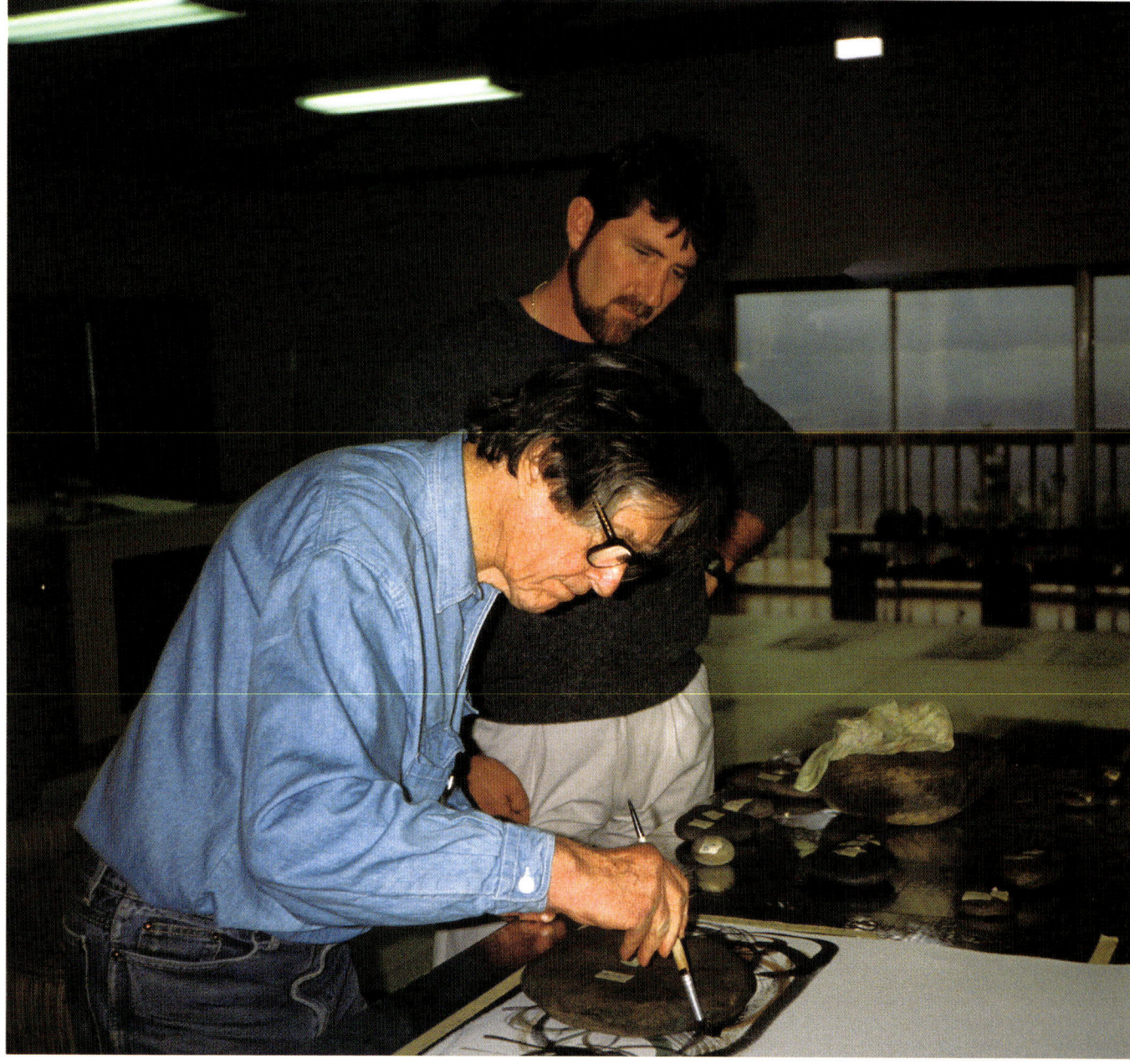

John Cage at work on
*New River Watercolors,
Series I*

John Cage, *New River
Watercolors, Series I*, #5, 1988,
watercolor on parchment, 18 x
36 in. (45.72 x 91.44 cm)

of operation following the Indian aesthetic described by Ananda K. Coomaraswamy.[8] The paintings, as visual images, develop almost the way elements develop in natural settings, the blooming of flowers in a field, the disposition of rocks in a stream bed, or the variety of trees in a forest. As Kass has pointed out, Fluxus artist George Brecht, who Cage knew in New York in the late 1950s, related chance images made by artists to such "chance images" in nature in an attempt to place them in the same conceptual category.[9] These ideas were at the heart of Cage's efforts in the workshop.[10] They have a basis in Dada thought, especially that of Arp, who believed that there are "laws of chance" and that these laws embrace all other laws and reveal a deeper sense of nature, a sense of nature beyond comprehension by purely rational means or in purely rational terms.

Like Arp and Brecht before him, Cage didn't adhere to accepted aesthetic rules and patterns for the construction of works of art; he deliberately eschewed the idea that art is created solely through personal taste manipulating elements of visual form. Instead, as is especially evident in the works from Series I of this workshop, Cage insured that marks unfold in sequence and remain clearly layered in "time" as a series of "chance occurrences" "scattered" within the "space" of the paper, a space that is both a real and a metaphorical place in which to "let" things happen.

Cage's desire to sublimate the individual, Freudian ego was an attempt to get the self to exist more harmoniously with the world and be more open to its possibilities. Chance procedures were a way to do this, to open the work of art — and the mind — to new experiences, especially the experiences of life as it exists

[8] For more on Cage's interest in Coomaraswamy's thought, see p. §.

[9] Kass, "The Mountain Lake Workshop," *John Cage/New River Watercolors* exhibition catalogue (Richmond: Virginia Museum of Fine Arts, 1988), p. 14. The essay is reprinted from *Drawing*, vol. 10, no. 3 (Sept/Oct 1988), p. 2. Brecht was in the course on writing experimental music that Cage began teaching in 1956 at the New School for Social Research in New York; other members of the class included Allan Kaprow, Jackson MacLow, Al Hansen, Allan Watts, and Dick Higgins. Roselee Goldberg, *Performance: Live Art, 1909 to the Present* (New York: Abrams, 1979), p. 82. See also Yve-Alain Bois, "George Brecht," *Artforum* (April 2006), p. 241.

[10] See Richter, *Dada: Art and Anti-Art*, p. 55. For more on this, also see David J. Clarke, *The Influence of Oriental Thought on Postwar American Painting and Sculpture* (New York and London: Garland Publishing, 1988), pp. 124–25. Clarke also claims that Arp was influenced by Eastern thought in his beliefs.

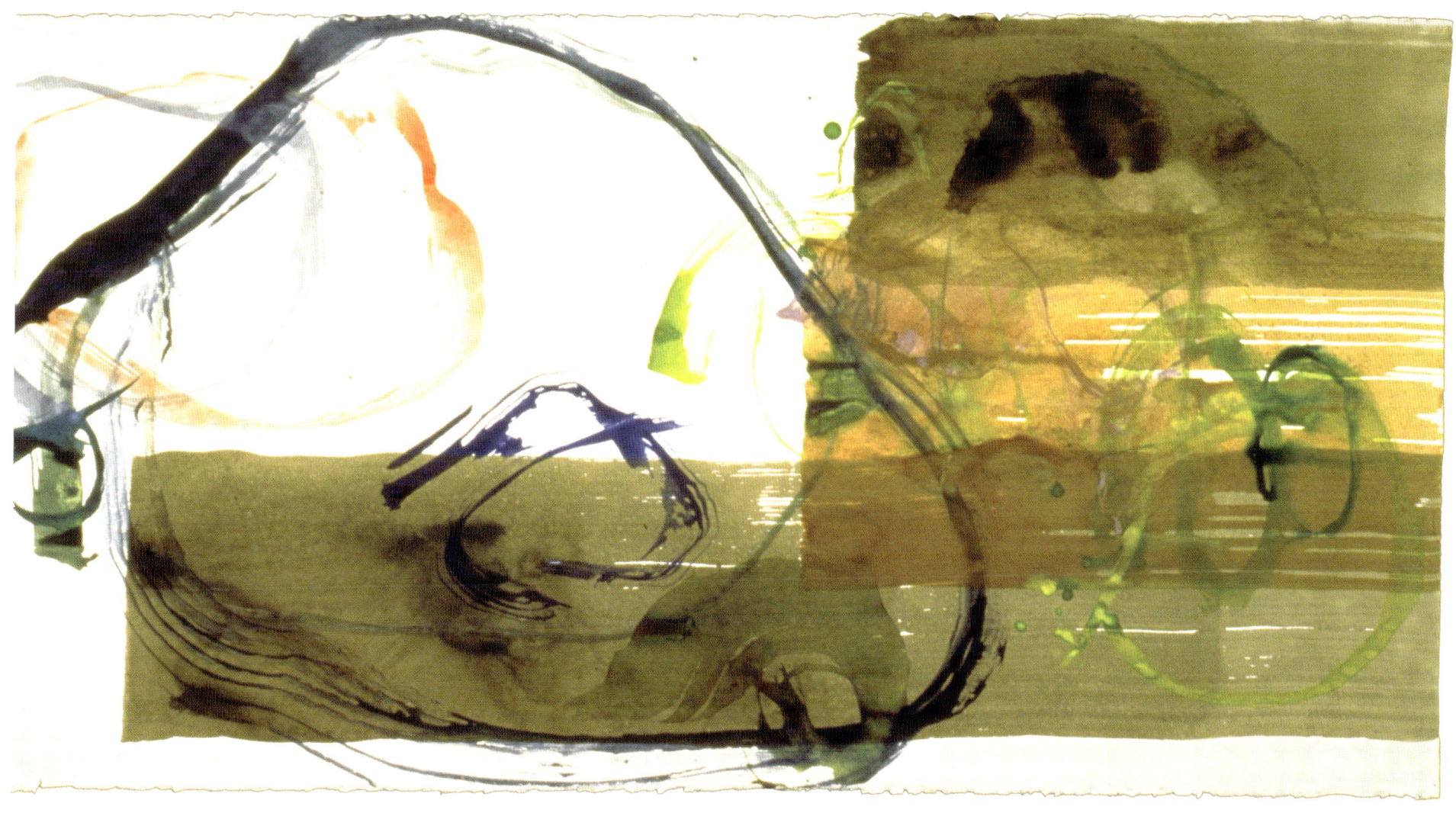

around us. To do this, Cage formulated a structure in which chance procedures can be activated; then, as a consequence of these procedures, he applied aesthetic choice to impart an overall character to works without actually having dictated the specific course of details. Thus, in these works the circular forms that are "afterimages" of the rocks, in their shape and randomness provide direct links to the landscape and symbolize and embody the chance aspects of nature. At the same time, their overall format fulfills Cage's desire to evoke the "look" of Japanese Zen painting.

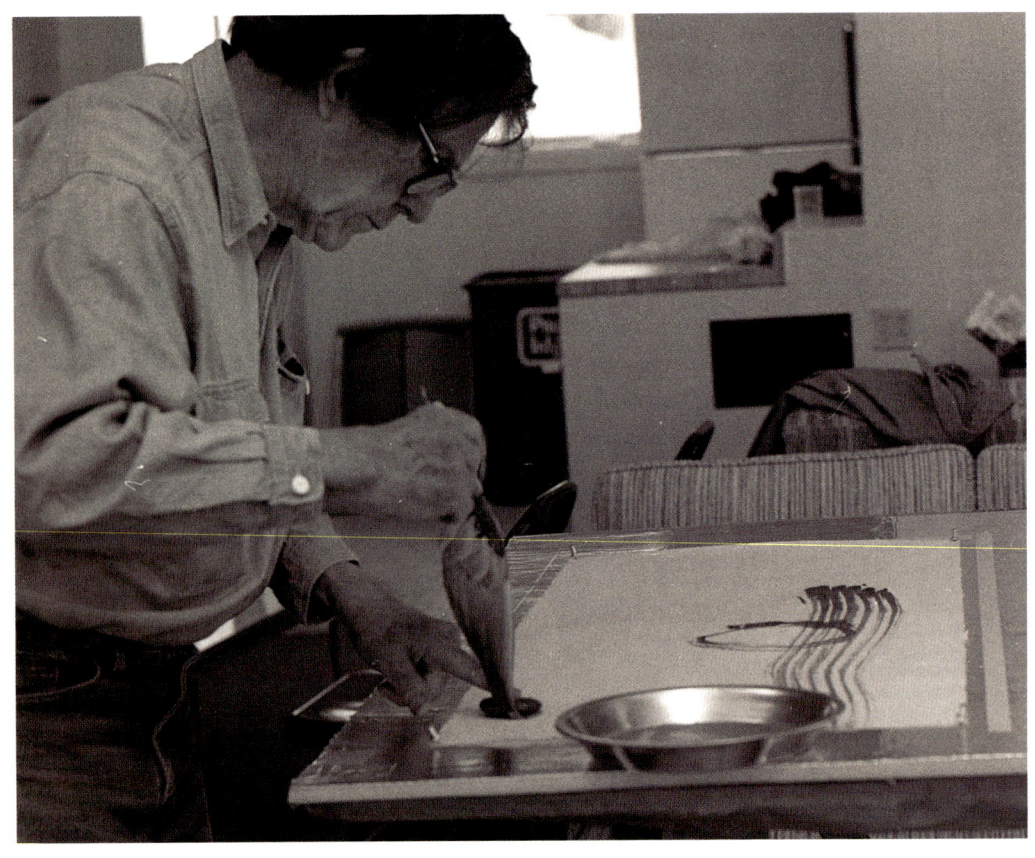

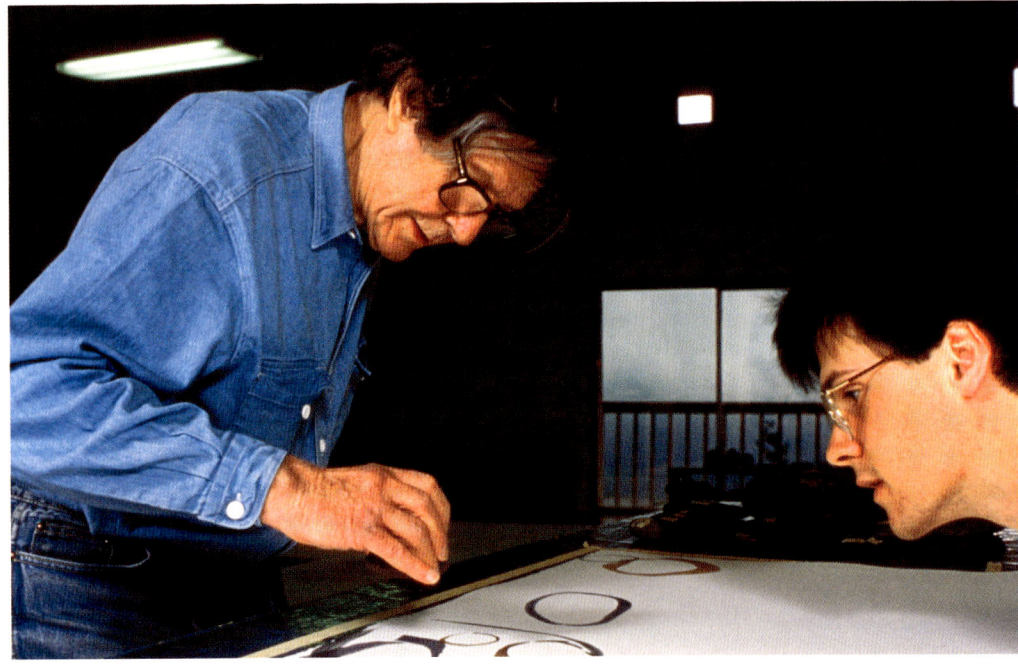

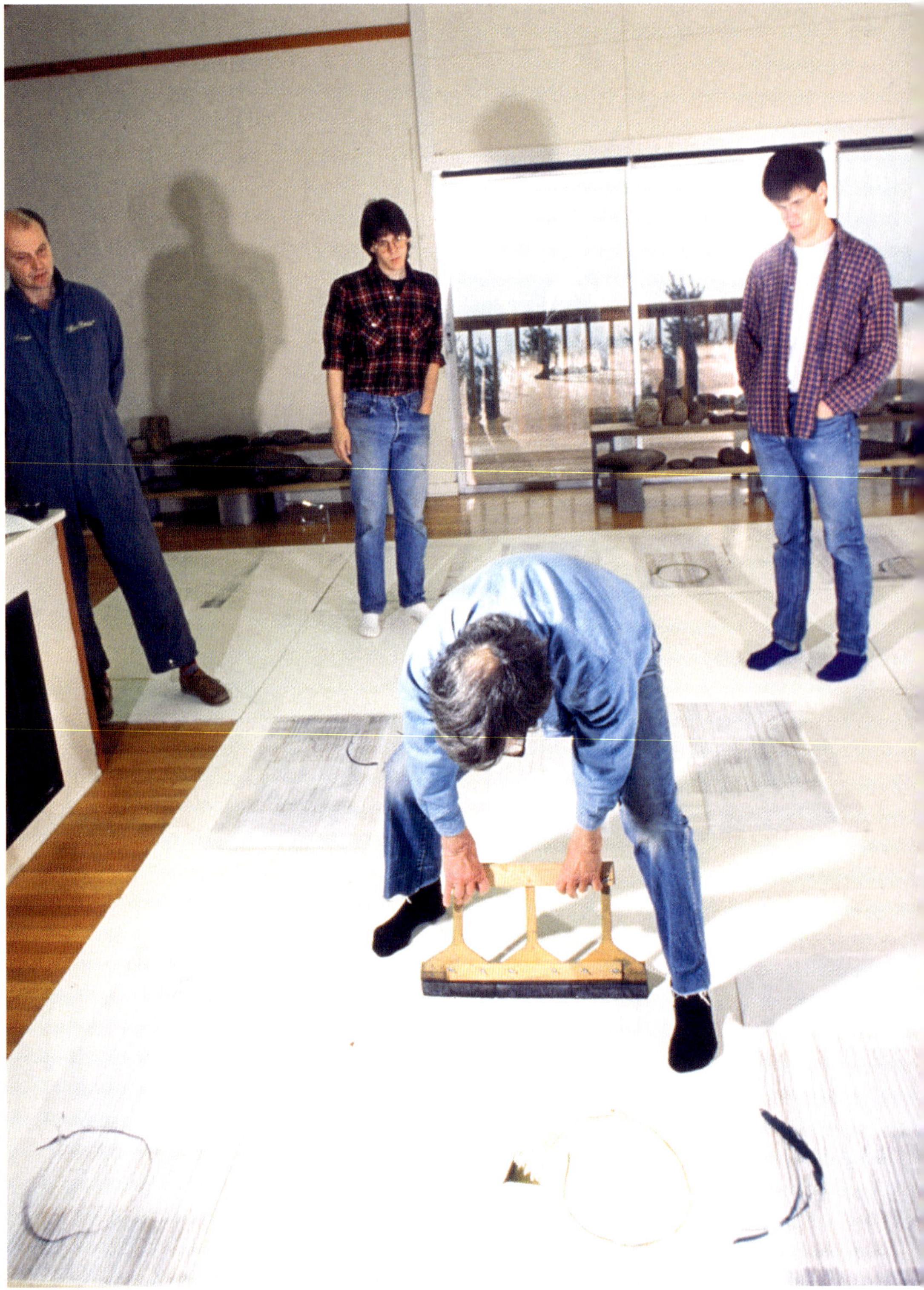

# JOHN CAGE'S 1989
# *STEPS* WORKSHOP

HOWARD RISATTI

In February of 1989 John Cage returned to Virginia as a guest of Radford University, which is located near Mountain Lake, to attend an exhibition of his *New River Watercolors* painted the previous year. In the weeks preceding his visit he and Ray Kass had several phone discussions about experimenting with new materials and techniques for another watercolor painting workshop at Mountain Lake. As a result of these discussions, Kass made a 56-inch-wide brush by connecting eight 7-inch-wide Asia-style "hake" brushes to a simple wooden armature; he also made a large mixing trough with which to load the brush with paint. Cage had agreed that before leaving Virginia he would visit Kass' studio in nearby Christiansburg. In advance, Kass prepared his studio with the big brush, the trough, and paper, and on the morning of Cage's departure for the airport, they stopped at the studio so Kass could show him the new materials and encourage him to experiment with them. The sheer size of the brush suggested some new painting possibilities that Cage and Kass had previously discussed via telephone. Offering new possibilities was important because Cage would get involved in a project only if it provided a new situation for exploration; he was not interested in doing the same thing over and over again. By its very nature, this brush certainly did offer new possibilities.

Another impetus for agreeing to do a new painting project was Kass' suggestion that Cage could perform something similar to Robert Rauschenberg's 1953 *Automobile Tire Print* — a work in which Cage had collaborated by driving a car with an inked rear tire down a length of connected pieces of paper — but this time without the car.[1] Kass said it could be a kind of homage to Rauschenberg. However, instead of the long, continuous

imprint of an automobile tire that suggests the world of modern mechanized movement and industrial production, it could be a kind of "Zen" painting featuring the isolated imprints of Cage's feet and, like 12th-century Chinese Sung paintings of lonely travelers among remote mountains and streams, it would raise the timeless image of a solitary figure walking in nature.

Cage liked the suggestion but was uncomfortable with the idea of stepping barefoot into trays of ink, so he decided to wear shoes which had a very strong molded sole imprint. A sample work was made of one shoe imprint in black paint on paper, which Cage inscribed "Soul of One Foot for Ray Kass." After this initial experiment Cage became more comfortable with Kass' idea, so Kass and two assistants mixed a wash using several tubes of neutral tint and black watercolor in the 60-inch-wide wooden trough and poured black ink and watercolor into two aluminum roasting pans placed at the end of a 208-inch-long sheet of 72-inch-wide rag paper that had been rolled out onto the studio floor. The 56-inch-wide brush was loaded with the dark grey-black watercolor in the trough and handed to Cage.

As he stepped backwards out of the two pans of black ink and onto the paper, trailing the large brush, a remarkable effect was achieved. By walking backwards along the length of the paper pulling the brush, he made imprints of his inked shoes which were immediately toned and blurred under a layer of wash. Because of the sheer size and weight of the brush the wash was not evenly applied but irregular and striated in a very humanly idiosyncratic way, thus adding another layer of complexity to the image. The effect was quite extraordinary.

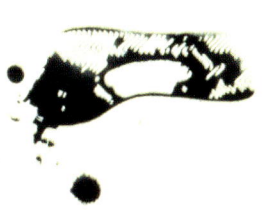

Cage remarked, "It does not matter who holds the brush."

Although *STEPS*, as the piece was named, resembles a giant Zen ink-wash painting of footprints in a river bed (water/river being a recurrent theme in Cage's Mountain Lake paintings), the footprints in this painting are real; they are not pictorial re-creations or artistic conceits, but the actual, physical impressions of Cage's movement in real time across the real space of the paper. They are an "afterimage" record of his active being in the world, something the sheer scale of this painting impresses upon the eye. As the "steps" in this haunting work slowly fade away toward one end of the painting, seemingly being washed away — perhaps purified — by water, a ghostly impression of someone's passing presence lingers.[2]

[1] *Automobile Tire Print*, which measures 16½" x 264½", was done on Fulton Street in lower Manhattan by inking the pavement and then driving a rear tire of a Model A Ford through the ink and over twenty pieces of paper that had been attached together to form a long, scroll-like sheet. Cage drove the car while Rauschenberg directed, urging him to "just stay on the paper." See *Robert Rauschenberg*, exhibition catalogue, National Collection of Fine Arts, Smithsonian Institution, Washington, D.C., 1976, p. 65.

[2] The brush and wooden trough Cage used in 1989 have been exhibited with the *STEPS* painting on several occasions. His original performance painting is now in the permanent collection of the Kunsthalle Bremen.

# NOTATION:
# JOHN CAGE'S *STEPS*

by RAY KASS

In 2006, at the request of Laura Kuhn, Director of the John Cage Trust, I wrote the notation, *John Cage's STEPS: A Composition for a Painting*, documenting the details of Cage's original performance of the painting in 1989. Also, Laura encouraged me to write a "second notation" at that time titled *John Cage's STEPS: A Composition for a Painting to be Performed by Individuals or Groups*. The Mountain Lake Workshop has organized or directed more than twenty performances of the piece since 2006. The eminent music publisher C.F. Peters Corporation plans to publish the notation in 2017 in time for performances of the piece that are being planned for a celebratory gathering (Oct. 2 – 7, 2017) in Halberstadt, Germany.[1]

The published notation of the piece will have a new, simplified title corresponding to the style of C. F. Peters' numerous other scores by Cage. The published title will be: *John Cage, STEPS, A Composition for a Painting*.

An explanatory text will accompany the illustrated notation which may be performed by individuals or groups and is open to the use of alternative materials. It will be available on September, 2017 from Henmar Press, INC, a member of the Edition Peters Group, (Leipzig, London, New York). For information please contact http://edition-peters.com/

[1] The medieval church of St. Burchardi in Halberstadt is the site of the world's longest concert, an on-going performance of John Cage's organ piece, *ORGAN²/ASLSP (As Slow As Possible)*. The performance began in 2001 on John Cage's birthday and is scheduled to continue for 639 years, ending in 2640. Halberstadt is also the site of the oldest documented organ in Europe, installed in Halberstadt Cathedral in 1361. The organizers of the performance determined that its duration would be 639 years, an homage to the time between the first organ installation and the year 2000, the original date proposed for the concert to begin.

The performances in Halberstadt in 2017 of *John Cage,- STEPS, A Composition for a Painting* and related exhibitions are sponsored by the *John Cage Organ Project* and organized by Harriett Watts and Georg Weckwerth.

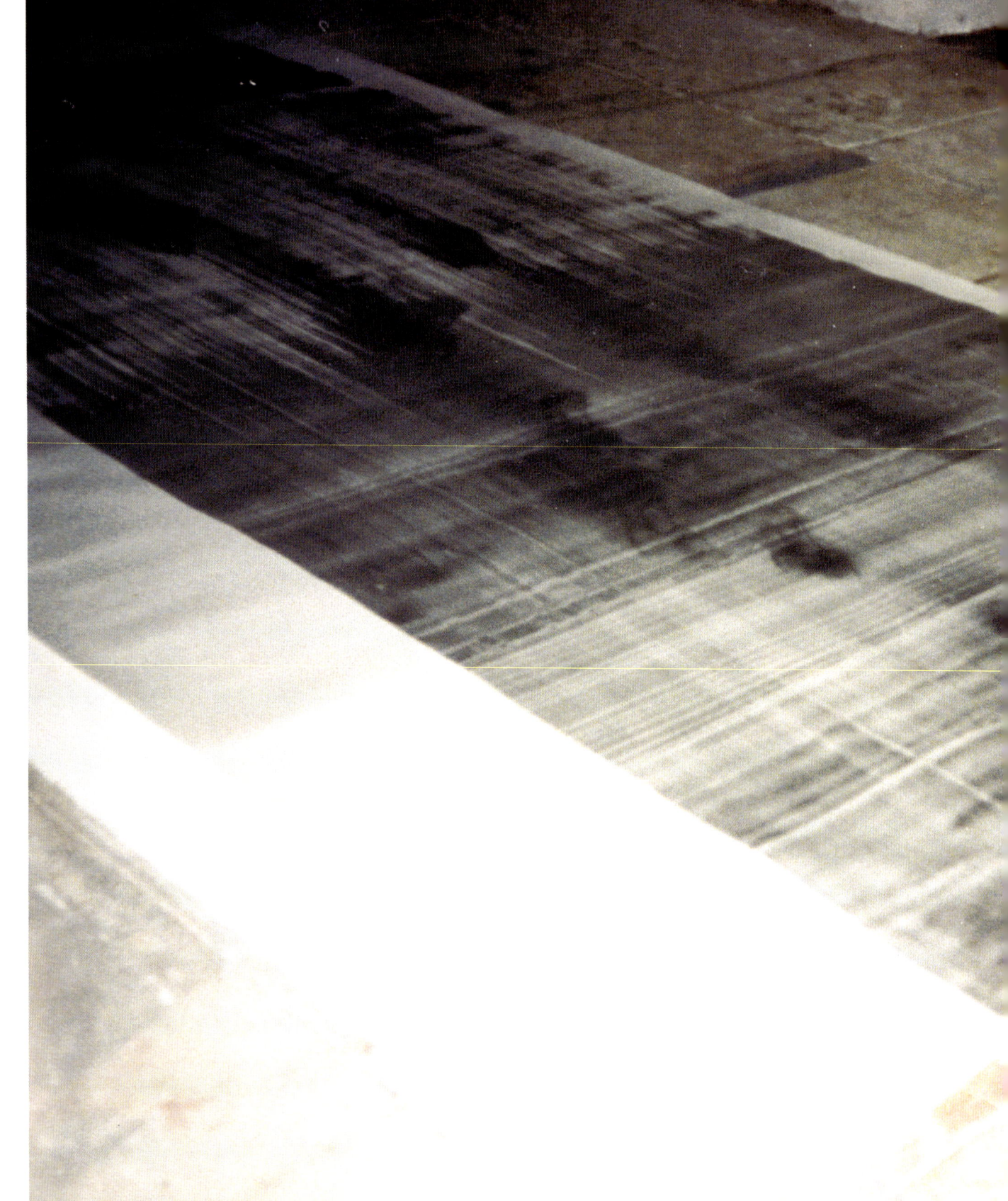

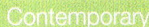

# CAGE

## STEPS,

A Composition for a Painting

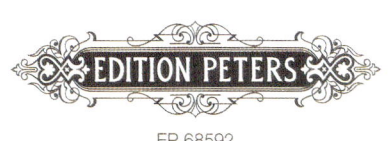

EP 68592

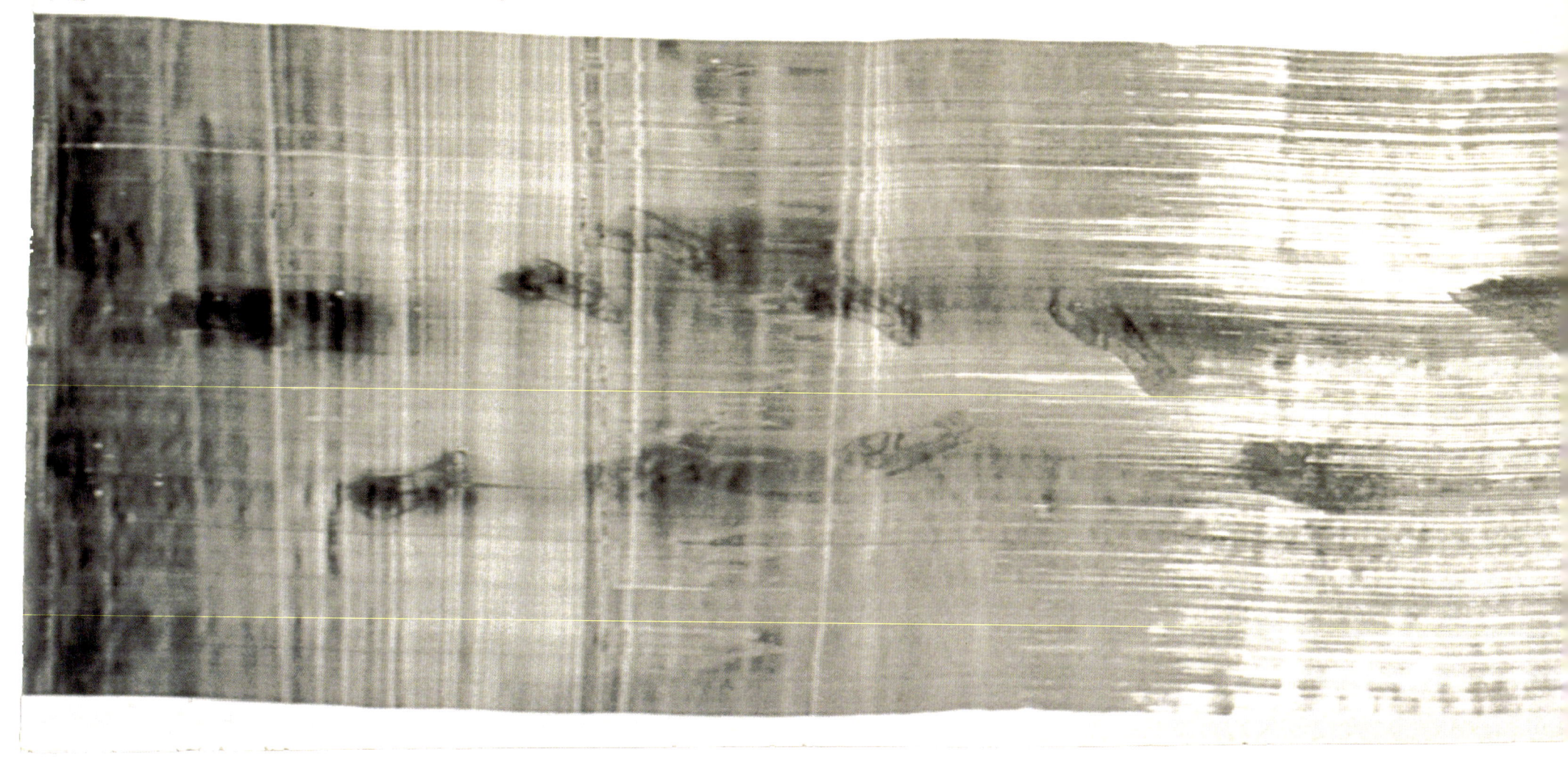

John Cage's *STEPS: A Composition for a Painting*, 1989, watercolor and ink on rag paper, 72 x 208 in. (182.88 x 528.32 cm) Collection: Bremen Kunsthalle, Bremen, Germany

# NEW RIVER ROCKS AND WASHES AND NEW RIVER ROCKS AND SMOKE, 1990

RAY KASS & HOWARD RISATTI

On Sunday the 8th of April 1990, Cage again came to the Horton Center to do another week-long workshop. His most recent print-making activities at Crown Point Press included various aspects of the "rock" imagery developed at Mountain Lake in 1983 and again in 1988. These activities included using etching acid to "paint" around stones placed on etching plates; then, with their "spit-bite" brushwork etched into the plates, the plates were inked and printed on paper that had been fired and smoked.

Using fired and smoked paper was new, though Cage had done something similar when he "branded" paper with a hot iron teakettle. The use of fired and smoked paper was done in an attempt, as Cage said,

*to understand a work that I love by Mark Tobey, and how he achieved the effect that's in it. Maybe it's a monoprint. There is almost nothing in it ... [just] reddish gray. I wanted to achieve the same sense of opposites — fire and water.*[1]

To fire and smoke the paper, assistants at Crown Point Press had placed crumpled newspaper on dampened printing paper. After igniting the newspaper, they immediately threw a wool printing blanket over the flames and passed the entire ensemble through the printing press. The result was that the paper retained bits of the newsprint and, of course, the gray smoke from the fire.

Before Cage arrived at the Horton Center, this firing/smoking process was replicated out-of-doors, first using newspaper sprinkled with mineral spirits. Because the newspaper produced unsightly sooty areas on the paper, other materials such as fine steel wool were tried until, finally, straw was substituted. Straw gave a greater range of color to the smoke, and the stalks left their marks on the paper as had the newspaper at Crown Point Press. However, unlike the newspaper, this method had the unintentional, but wonderful, effect of evoking the processes of natural forces through the impressions of straw left on the paper amidst the traces of fire and smoke. It was as if, in the finished works that were eventually made in Cage's workshop, the elemental forces of earth, air, fire, and water were combined through the painting procedure and the firing and smoking process. Once problems with handling the paper in the wind were solved and a system of "blanketing" the fire with 4 x 8 foot sheets of Masonite was developed, this "straw-writing on smoke," as it came to be called, became the method with which all the paper was treated in the weeks before Cage's visit.

Cage made four series of paintings during the workshop. The first day was very experimental, resulting in two versions of each of two paintings, one version with fired/smoked paper and another with a plain sheet. For the first group of paintings, on 72 x 48 inch paper, it was decided that sixty-five small to medium brushes would be employed and that 162 smooth, rounded stones from the Ripplemead site (the 129 stones used in the 1988 workshop plus an additional 33 stones) as well as 59 rather flat, angular stones from Sinking Creek at Eggleston Springs would be used. Each of the two groups of stones was divided into three categories according to size — small, medium, large — for a total of six. It was also decided that each piece of paper could have as many as six vertical divisions or "panels" (after the six groups of stones), their width to be determined by chance. Furthermore, it was decided that each vertical panel division would have a single stone that would "enter" from the left (always 4 inches from the bottom) to a position on the panel determined by chance. Because marks painted around the stones would not be allowed to cross into another panel, partial "images" of the stones were sometimes produced and some marks were so severely cropped by the adjacent panel as to be almost non-existent. As many as four washes could be applied (using chance procedures to determine number and color) to each individual panel.

For the second group in this series, the two versions would be done on 72 x 25 inch paper, again fired/smoked and unfired/unsmoked. Since these sheets of paper were narrower, Cage decided they could be divided into only three or fewer panels by chance procedures; otherwise, all the procedures were the same.

The result of these first experiments was to affect the procedures of the rest of the workshop. Cage felt that the four paintings of Series I lacked unity, although they had a rather dramatic appearance of vertical stripes caused by the different washes on the individual vertical panels. This lack of unity bothered Cage, who felt it was incompatible with the spirit of the "invisible" rocks which had guided his brush as he painted around them; he also disliked the fact that the washes obscured the smoke effect and the illusion of depth the smoke produced. Clearly Cage was willing to exercise his aesthetic judgment even though he was using chance procedures.

For Series II, Cage decided that no washes would be used so that even though the placement of the rocks would still

---

[1] Remarks made by Cage to Bruce McClure, workshop assistant, during the workshop and recorded by Dan Yates, April 1990.

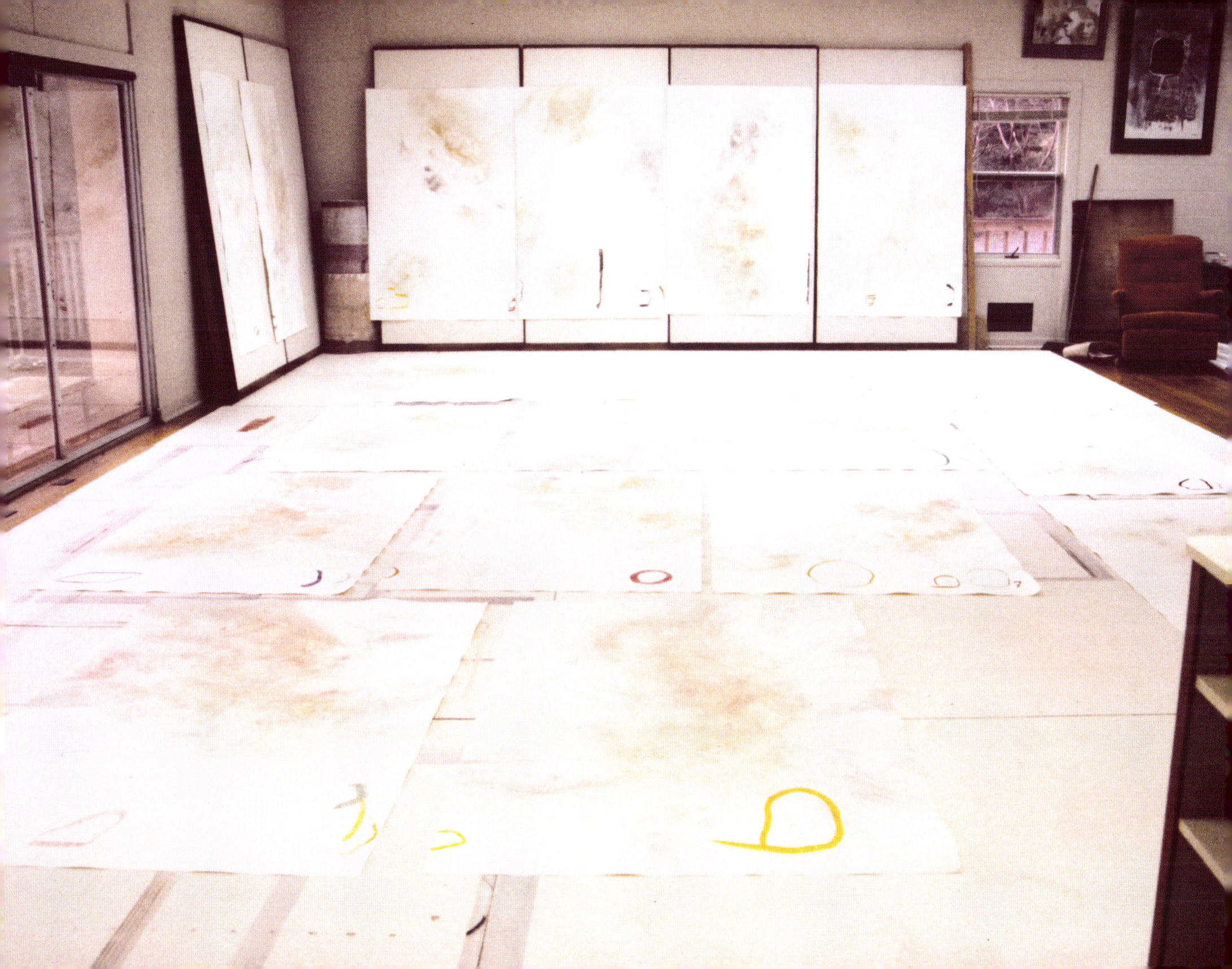

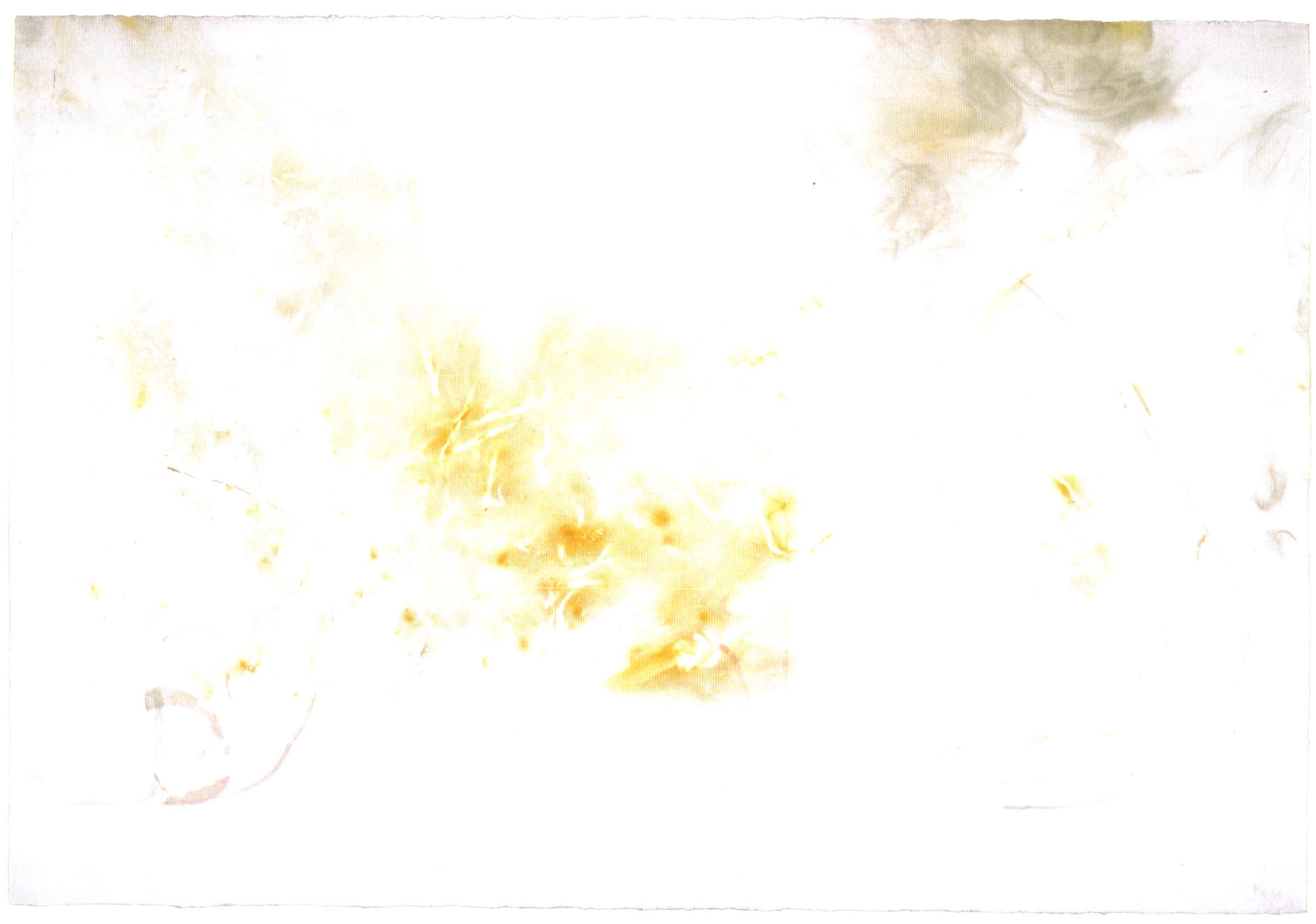

John Cage, *River Rocks and
Smoke, 4/10/90 #10*, watercolor
on "smoked" rag paper, 26.5 x
39.5 in. (67.31 x 100.33 cm)

John Cage, *4/10/90 #21*, 1990,
watercolor on "smoked" paper, 72
x 47.5 in. (182.88 x 120.65 cm)

John Cage, *4/13/90 #6*, 1990,
watercolor on "smoked" paper,
52.5 x 15 in. (133.35 x 5.91 cm)

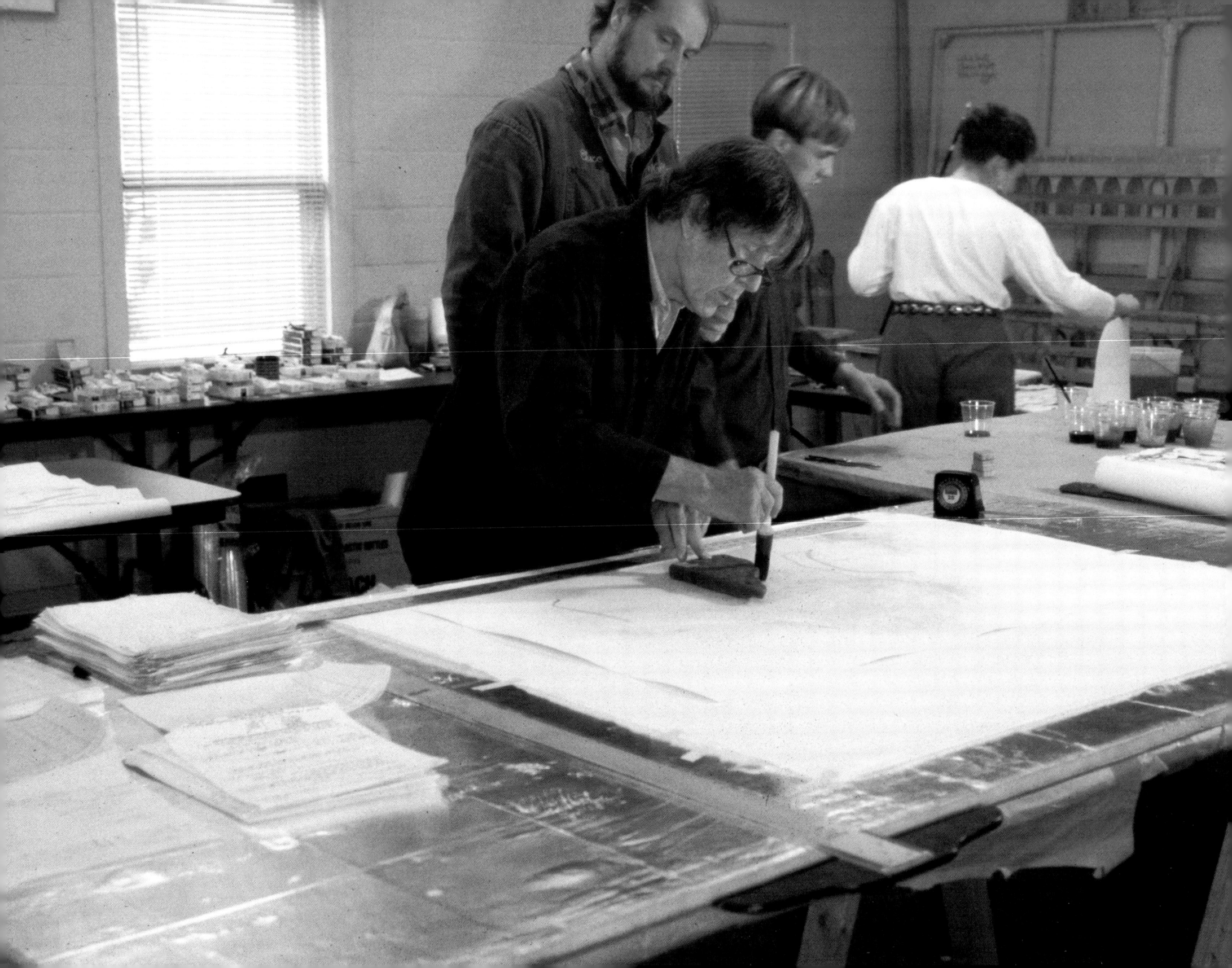

be determined by chance for each vertical panel, the panel divisions themselves would no longer be visible since they would not be treated with washes. The works in this series, sixteen in all (fourteen works 72 x 48 inches, one work 72 x 35 inches, and one work 72 x 25 inches), are vertically oriented and, without washes, the effect of the smoke is to create an ambiguous space within which the weightless "afterimages" of the rocks are held as if in suspension. This pleased Cage, as did the two narrowest works which, as a result of chance, each contain the afterimage of only a single stone.

After these initial works, the activity of the workshop proceeded much faster. In Series III, chance decided that for all nineteen works in the series, fifteen stones could be used. Cage decided that the stones would be placed 2 inches from the bottom and, even though the paper could have as many as fifteen possible vertical panel divisions, the positions of the stones would be determined in relation to the entire piece of paper, not according to individual panels. Although stones could still be cropped by the panel divisions, there was now the possibility of overlapping stones as occurred in the Ryoanji drawings and the *New River Watercolors* from 1988.

As these works progressed, Cage tried to achieve a drier, lighter brush mark so the marks would emerge from the smoke rather than appear to float on top of it. Small brushes were also added to the group of possible brushes for the final works in this series. The marks in these final works are so light as to be almost invisible. They reminded Cage, as he said, of the music of Morton Feldman, which was intended to be played very, very softly.[2]

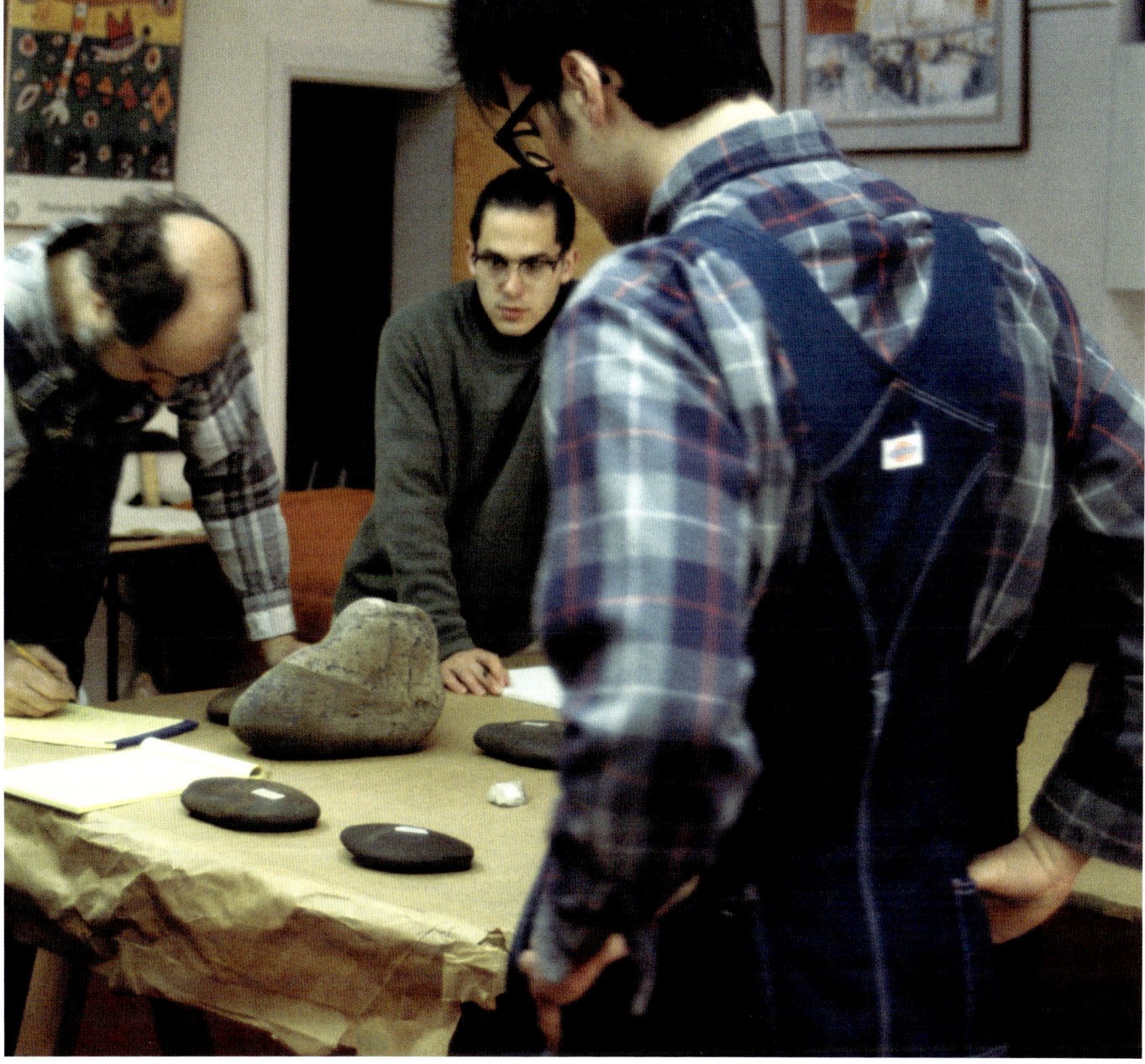

[2] Leaving a Philharmonic concert after having heard a performance of Anton Webern's Opus 21 and not wanting to hear the Rachmaninoff work that was to follow, Cage encountered Feldman, who was leaving for the same reason. They introduced themselves and began an "immediate friendship." See Calvin Tomkins, *The Bride and the Bachelors: Five Masters of the Avant-Garde* (New York: Penguin Books, Inc., 1976), p. 130.

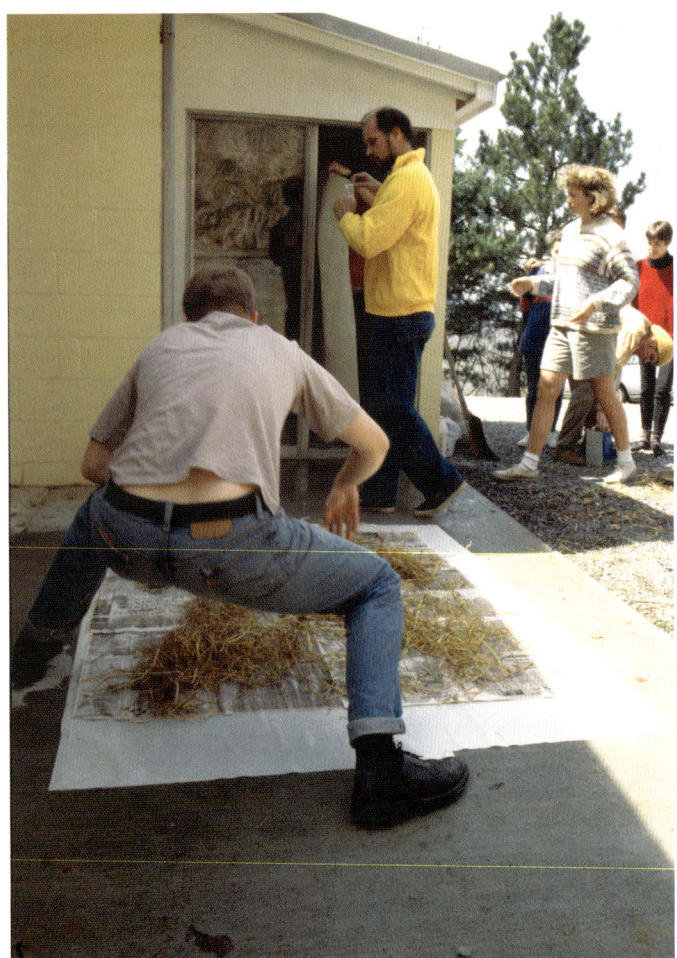 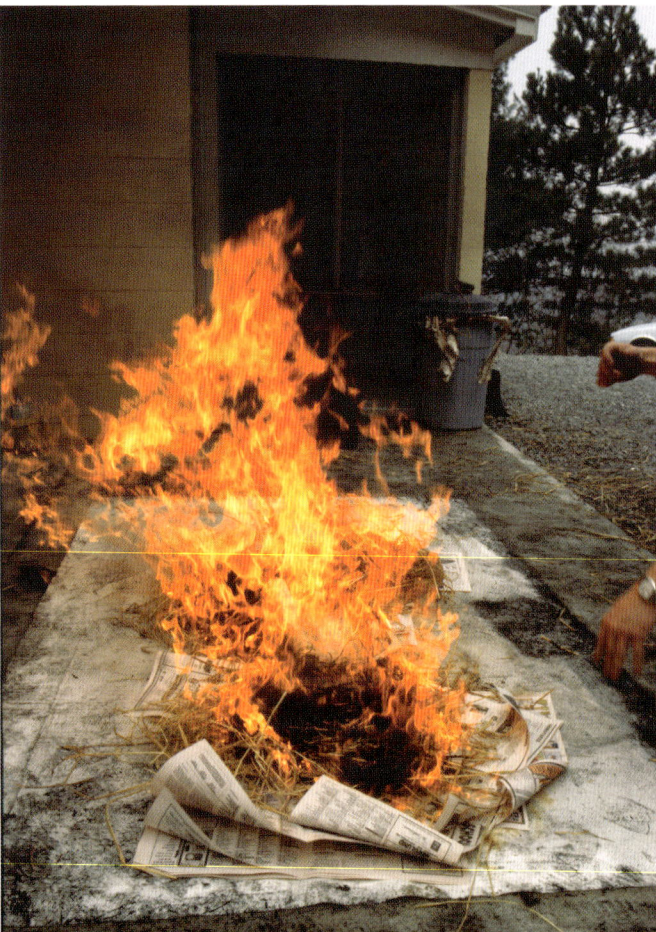 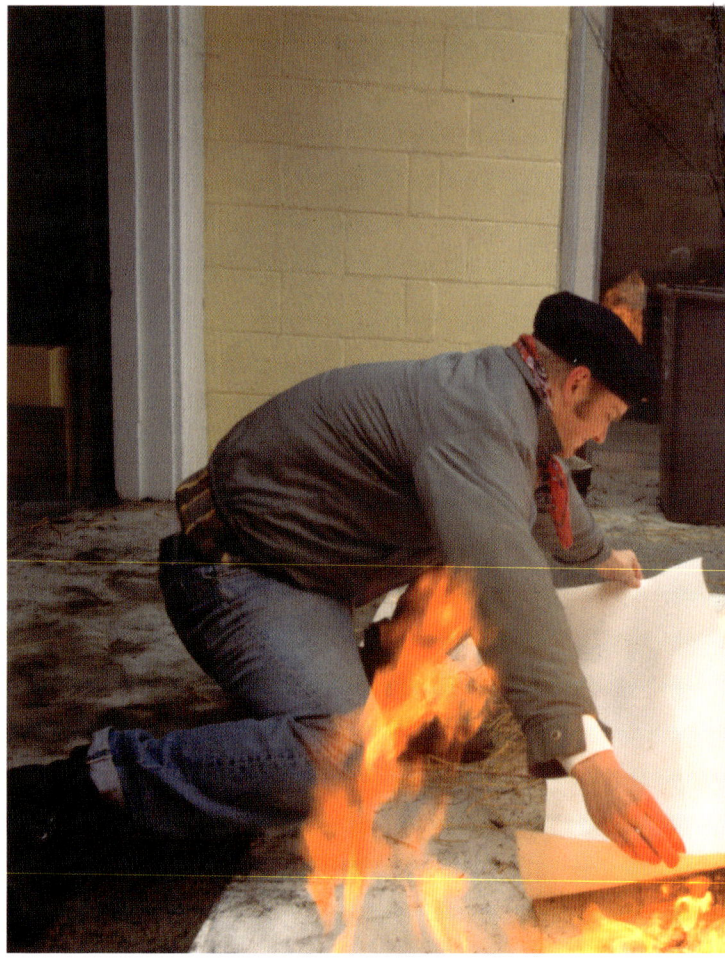

Paper smoking group: Charles Layman, Ray Kass, J.J. Watson (in background), Torolf Myklebust, and Joe Kelley

While Series III was being painted, assistants were firing and smoking more paper for the next series. Series IV includes twenty paintings (each 15 x 52½ inches) on fired/smoked paper. Chance decided that the color to be used for the marks around the stones was to be brighter and darker than in the previous series. Cage decided that one stone, 4 inches from the bottom, would be used; chance determined the position of the stone and to which side of the position point the stone

would be placed. In the Zen Buddhist sense, Cage thought of the afterimages of the rocks in these works as analogous to small persons in an enormous world; each was signified by a prominent dark mark, like an individual seeking harmony within nature as represented by the smoked ground of the paper.

Following Series IV, Cage created a large work (102 x 336 inches; that's over 8 feet high by 29 feet long) as a "parade of

stones" titled *New River Rocks and Washes*, using fifteen large stones centered on a line 12 inches from the bottom of a piece of paper which was divided into 168 panels (about six per foot).[3] Colors and large brushes were selected by chance; the overall wash, put on with the largest brush made at Mountain Lake (72 inches wide), consisted of all the leftover colors from the workshop. This brush was so large that Cage had to get inside of it to use it, as if he were a hang-glider pilot.

[3] This important painting was exhibited in Germany, near where Joseph Beuys was from. Beuys knew and admired Cage and shared some of his ideas about art as a means of transformation of the self, even though Beuys placed a great deal of importance on social transformation, which Cage did not.

[4] *New River Rocks and Smoke* was exhibited at the Peggy Guggenheim Museum in Venice, Italy, as part of the 45th Venice Biennale exhibition in 1993. For more details of the workshop, see Ray Kass, "Diario: John Cage, il Seminario di Mountain Lake," catalogue to the 45th Venice Biennale, 1993, pp. 79–82.

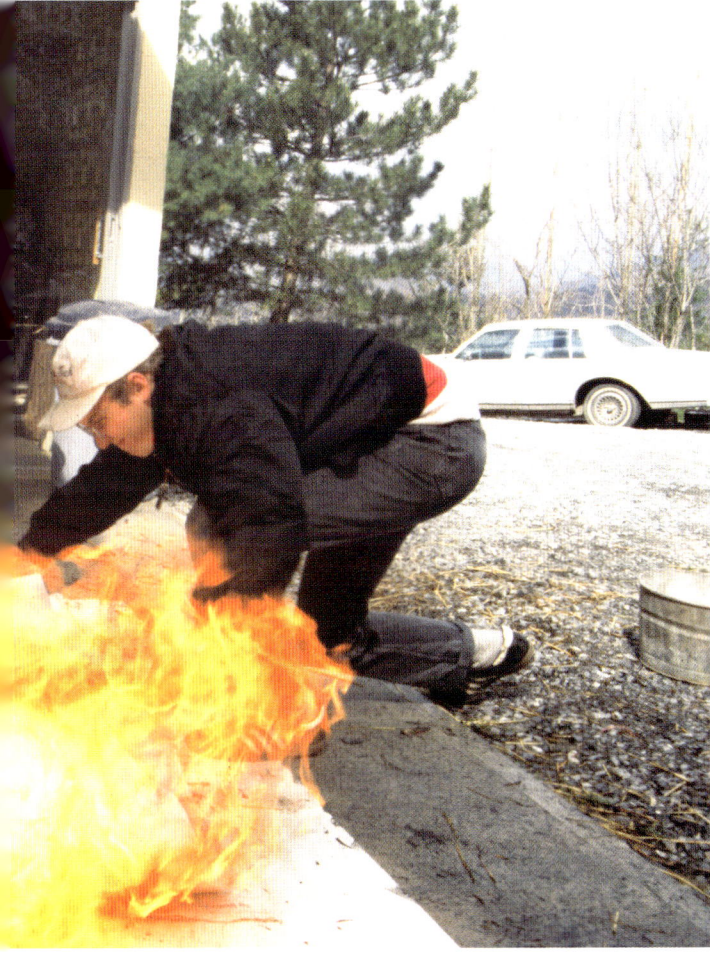
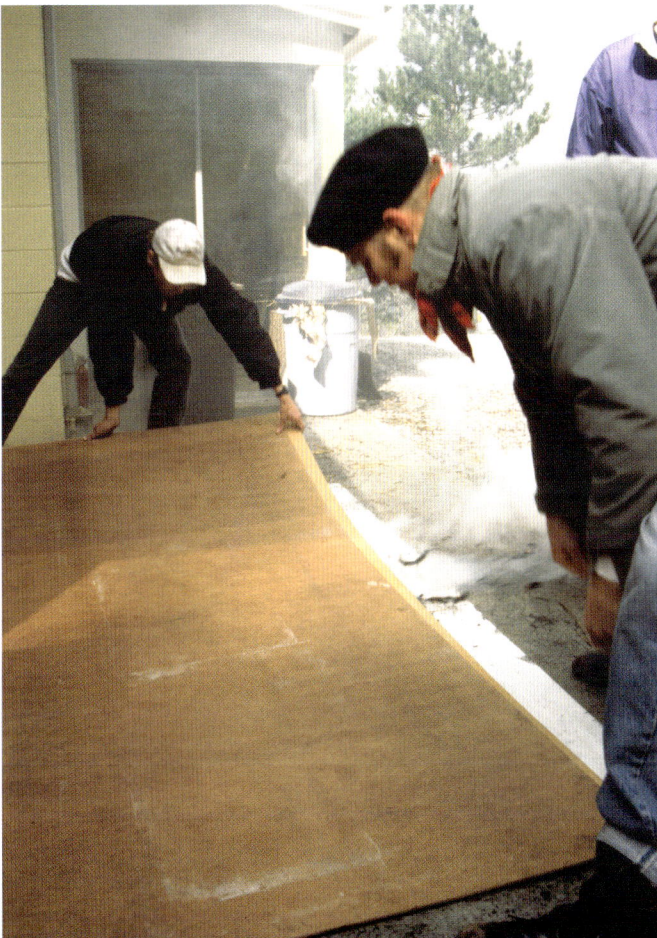
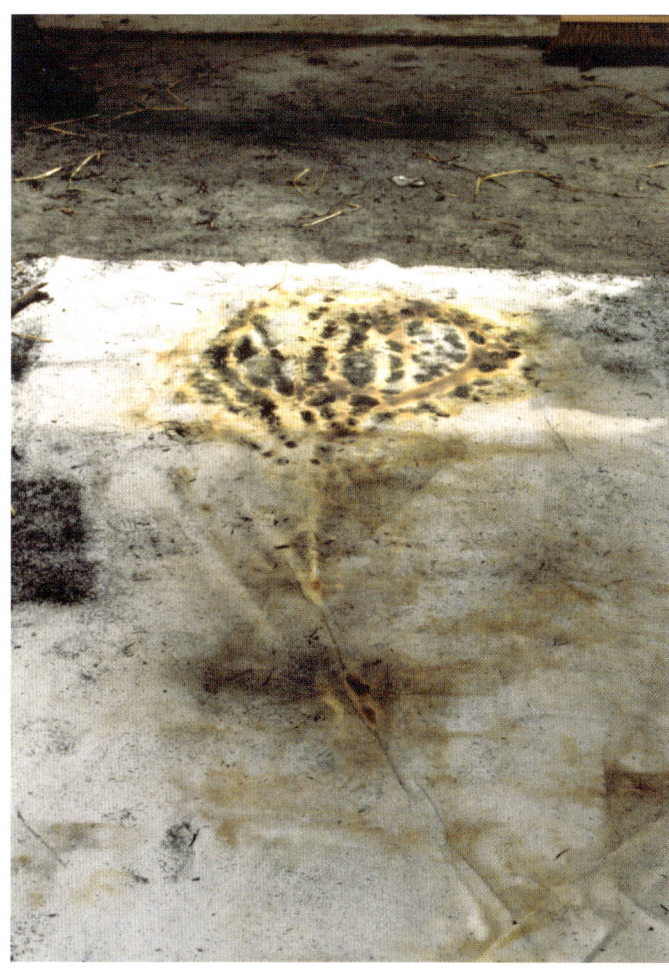

After a mycological foray with Orson and Hope Miller on Saturday, Cage returned to the center and made one last painting, executed on fired/smoked paper. It is the same size as *New River Rocks and Washes*, its companion piece, and it was painted using the same rocks, brushes, and positions, but with lighter colors. This painting is titled *New River Rocks and Smoke*. These two mural-sized works are the last paintings Cage made, and among the most beautiful.[4] They evoke Heracleitean opposites, of fire and water, as if seen through a complex, accordion-like spatial structure of reflected light. Their respective sober evocations led Cage to joke that he wanted "to change fire into water."

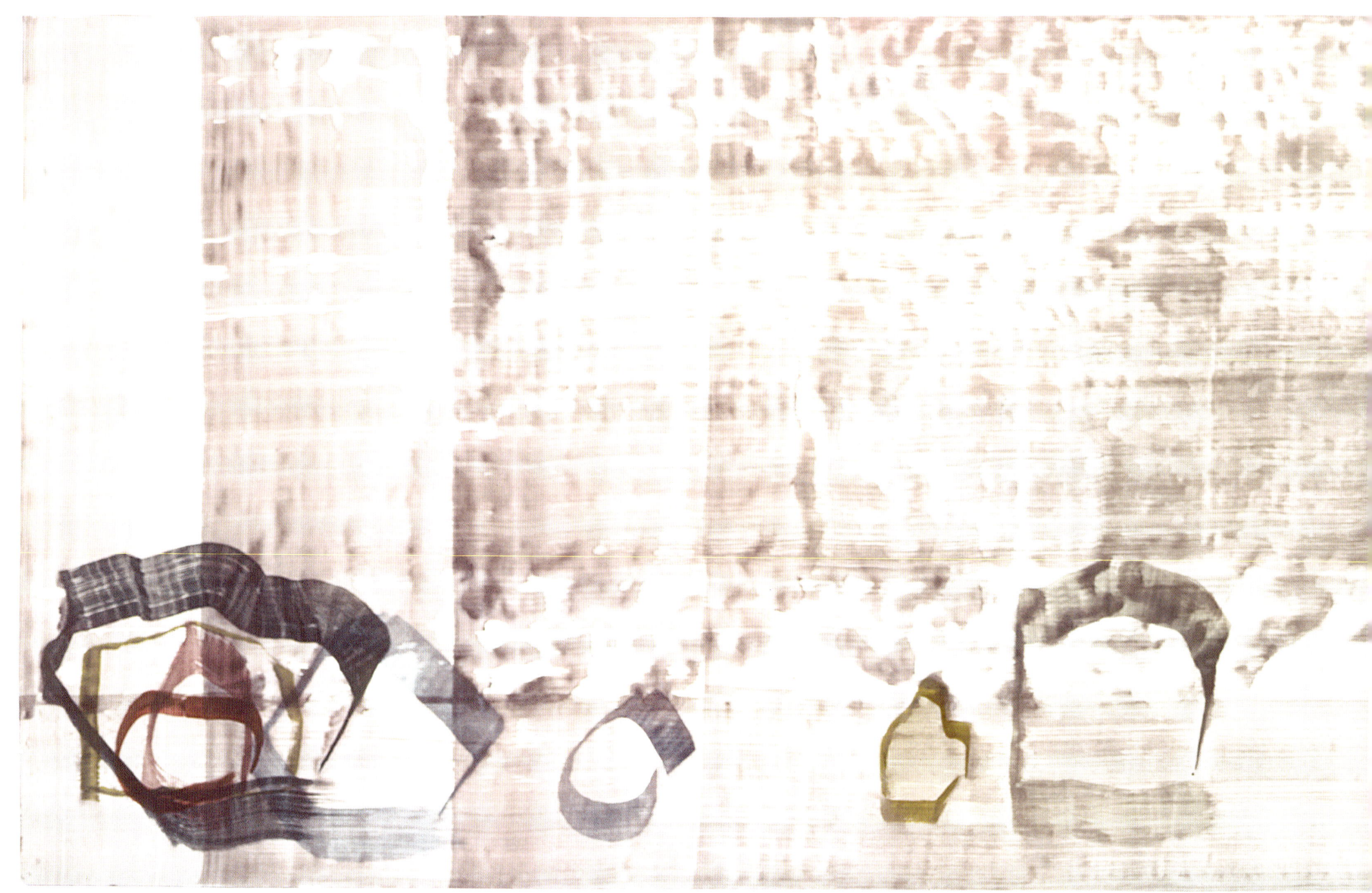

John Cage, *New River Rocks and Washes*, 1990, watercolor on rag paper,
102 x 336 in. (259.08 x 853.44 cm), Menil Collection, Houston.

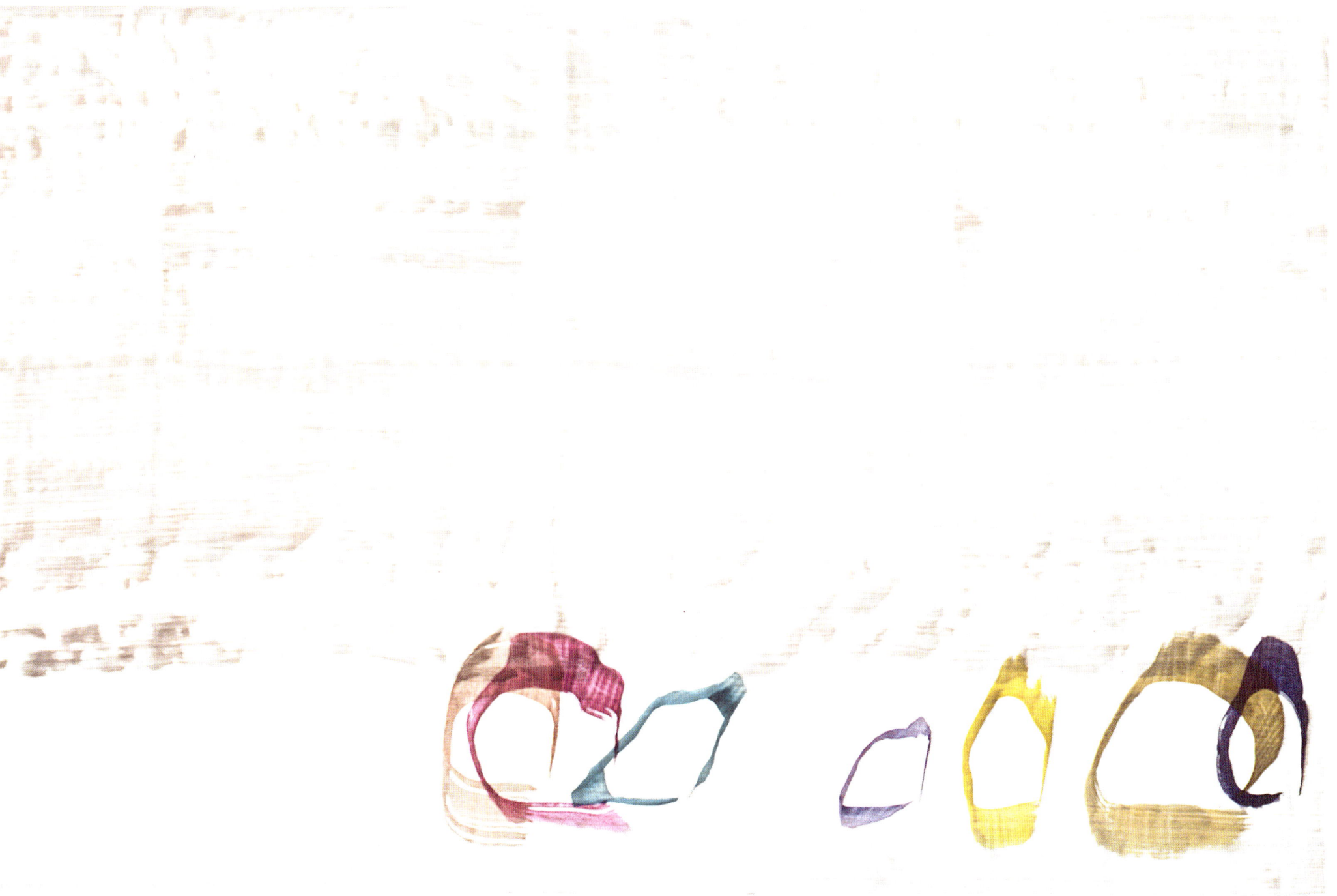

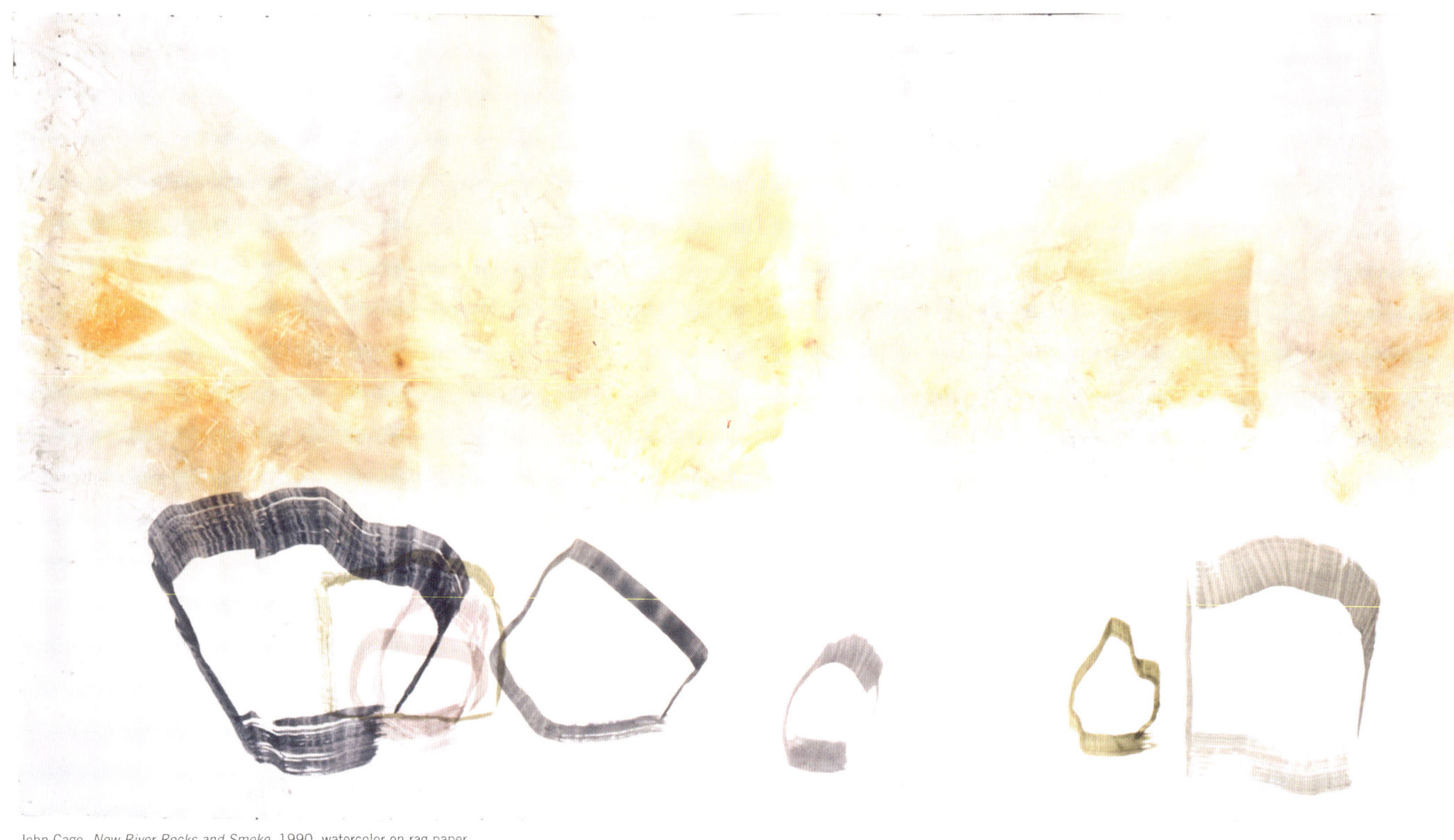

John Cage, *New River Rocks and Smoke*, 1990, watercolor on rag paper,
102 x 384 in. (259.08 x 975.36 cm), Menil Collection, Houston.

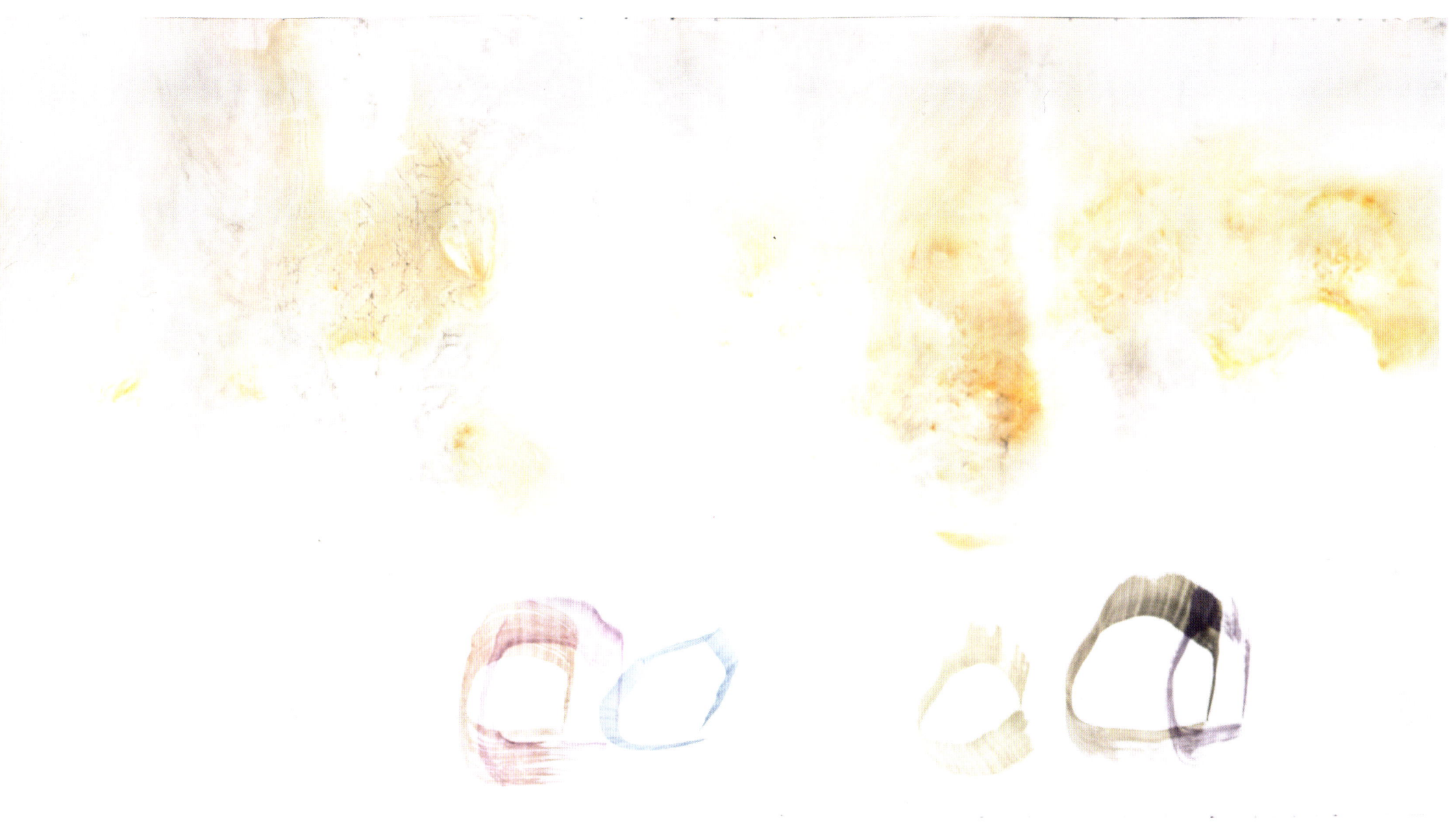

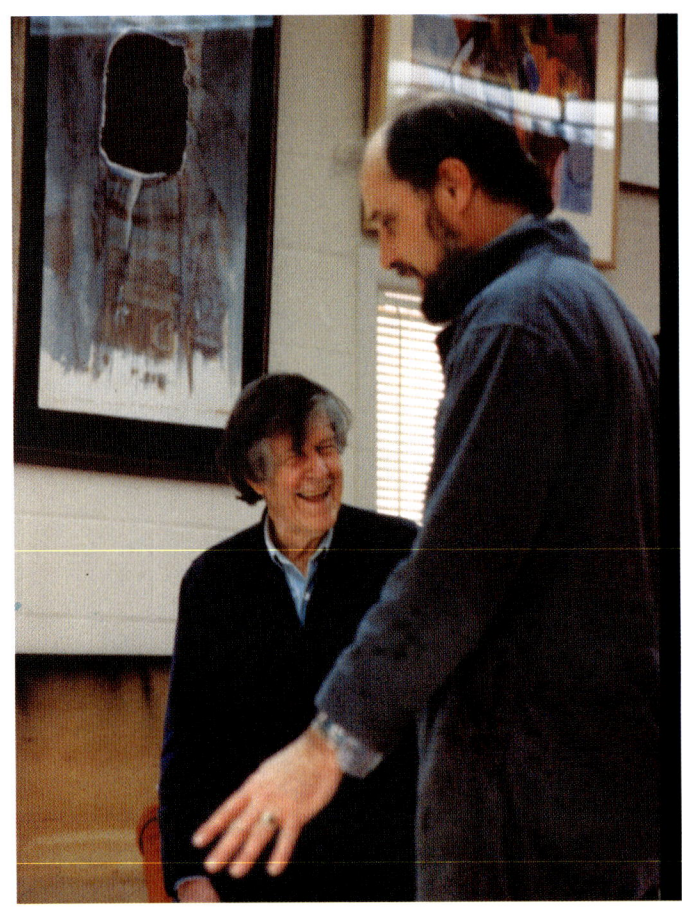
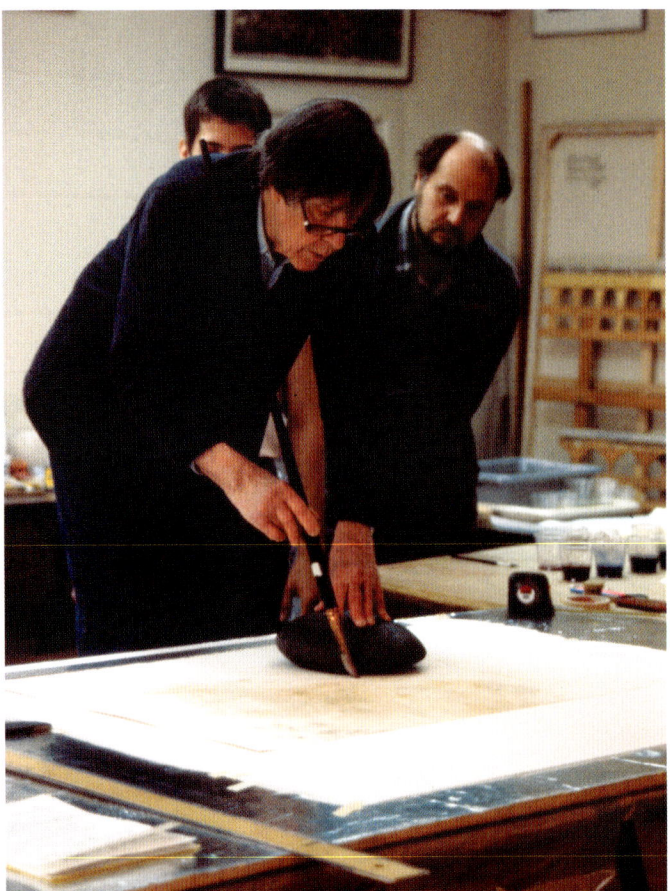
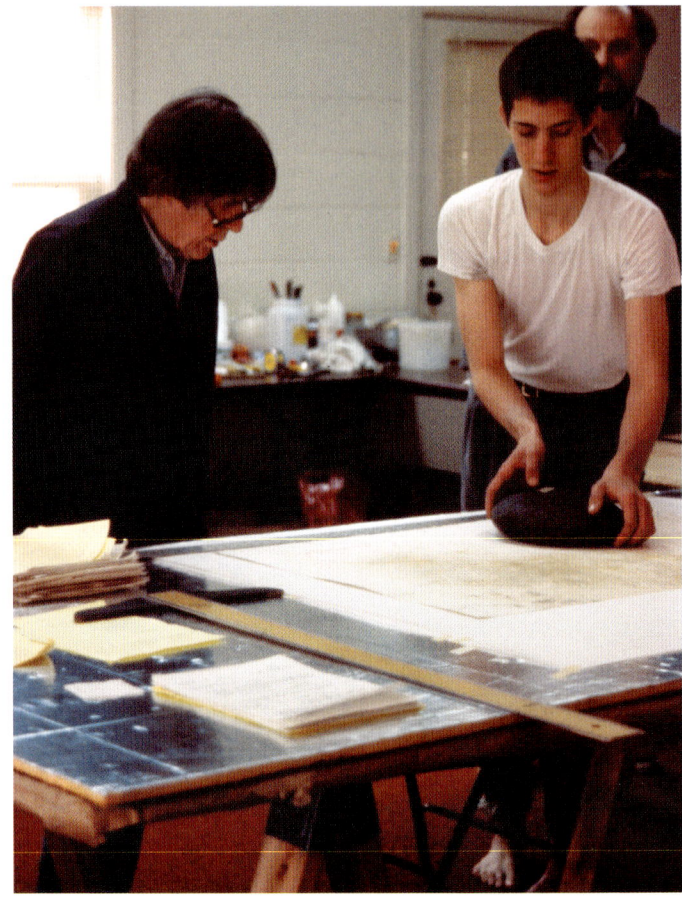
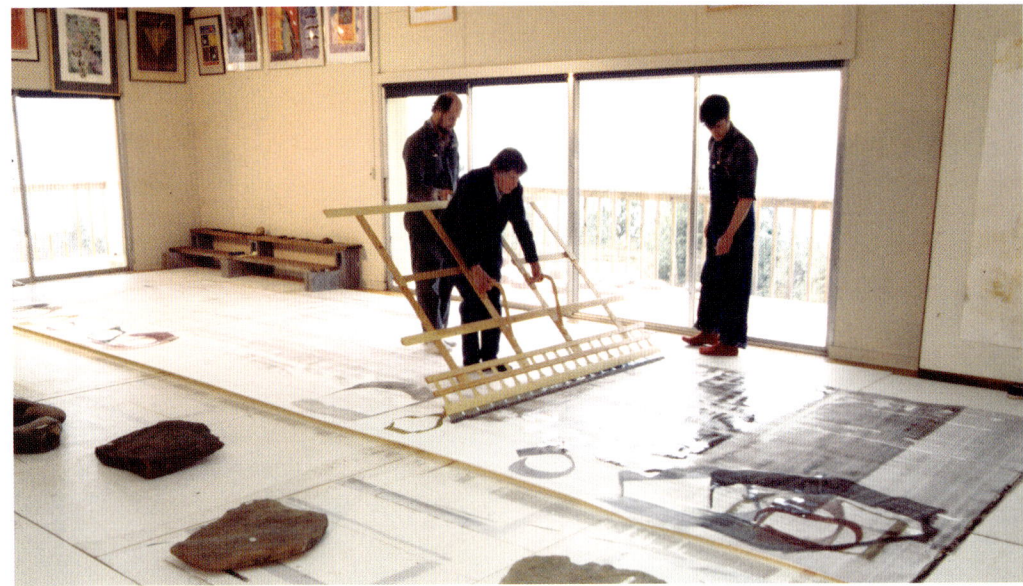
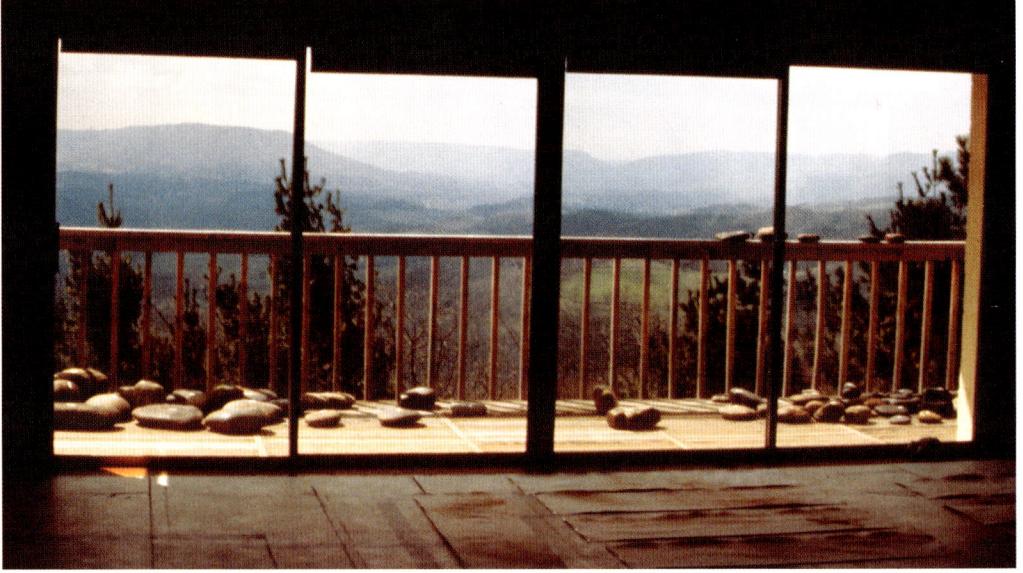

# "GIFT" (FOR JIRO OKURA), MAY 1990

**RAY KASS**

As John Cage was finishing his April 1990 workshop, he was encouraged by workshop participants to create a painting as a welcoming gift for Jiro Okura who was coming to Mountain Lake the following month. On a sheet of fired/smoked paper, Cage painted around the stone that had been used in early January as an altar for Okura's Shinto ceremony when trees in the Washington National Forest were blessed before harvesting. This was to be John Cage's last painting before he died and stands as a testament to the generosity of spirit that has pervaded the Mountain Lake programs.

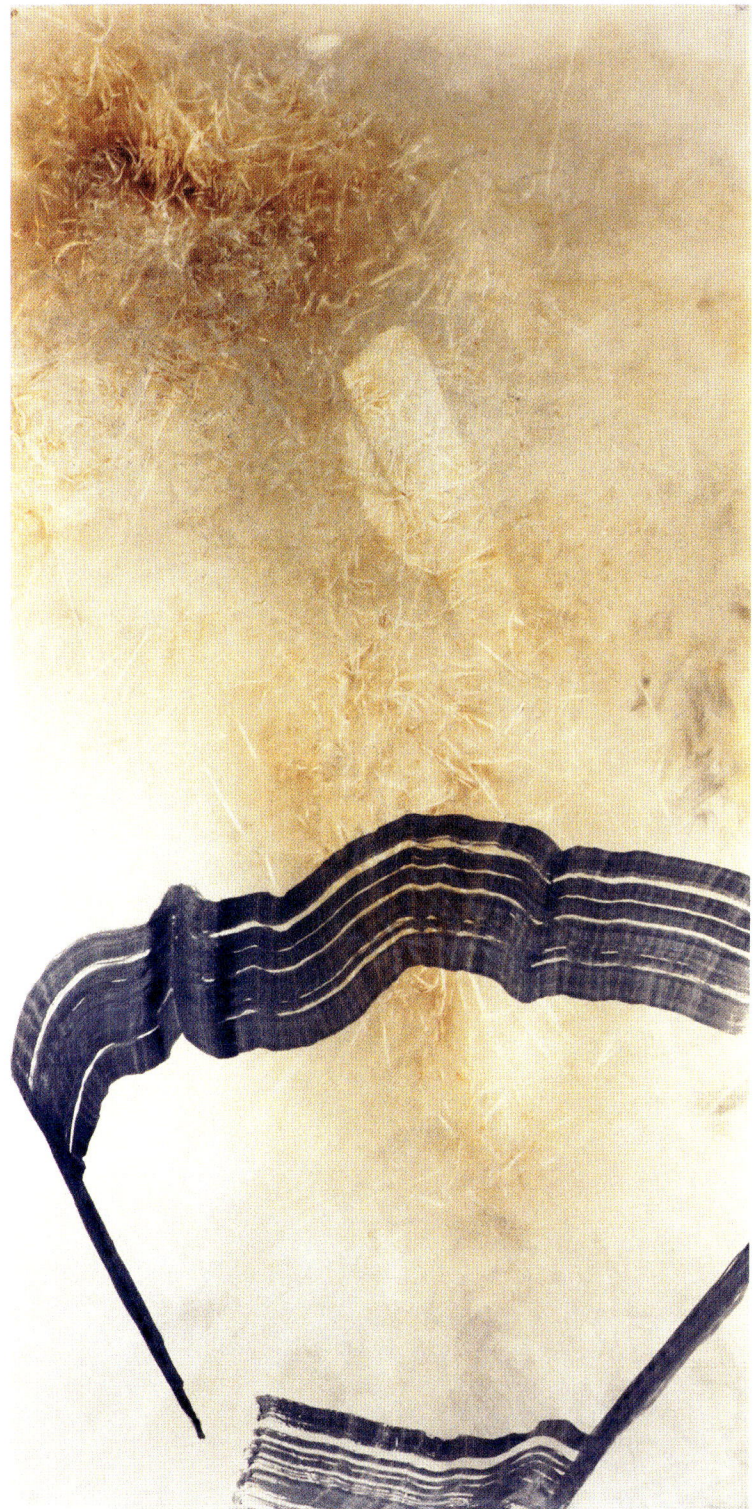

John Cage, *"Gift" (for Jiro Okura)* watercolor on "smoked" mulberry paper, 72 x 36 in. (182.88 x 91.44 cm). This painting was a gift to Okura welcoming him to his upcoming Mountain Lake Workshop which immediately followed Cage's workshop in 1990.

Photo: Jiro Okura family, Kyoto

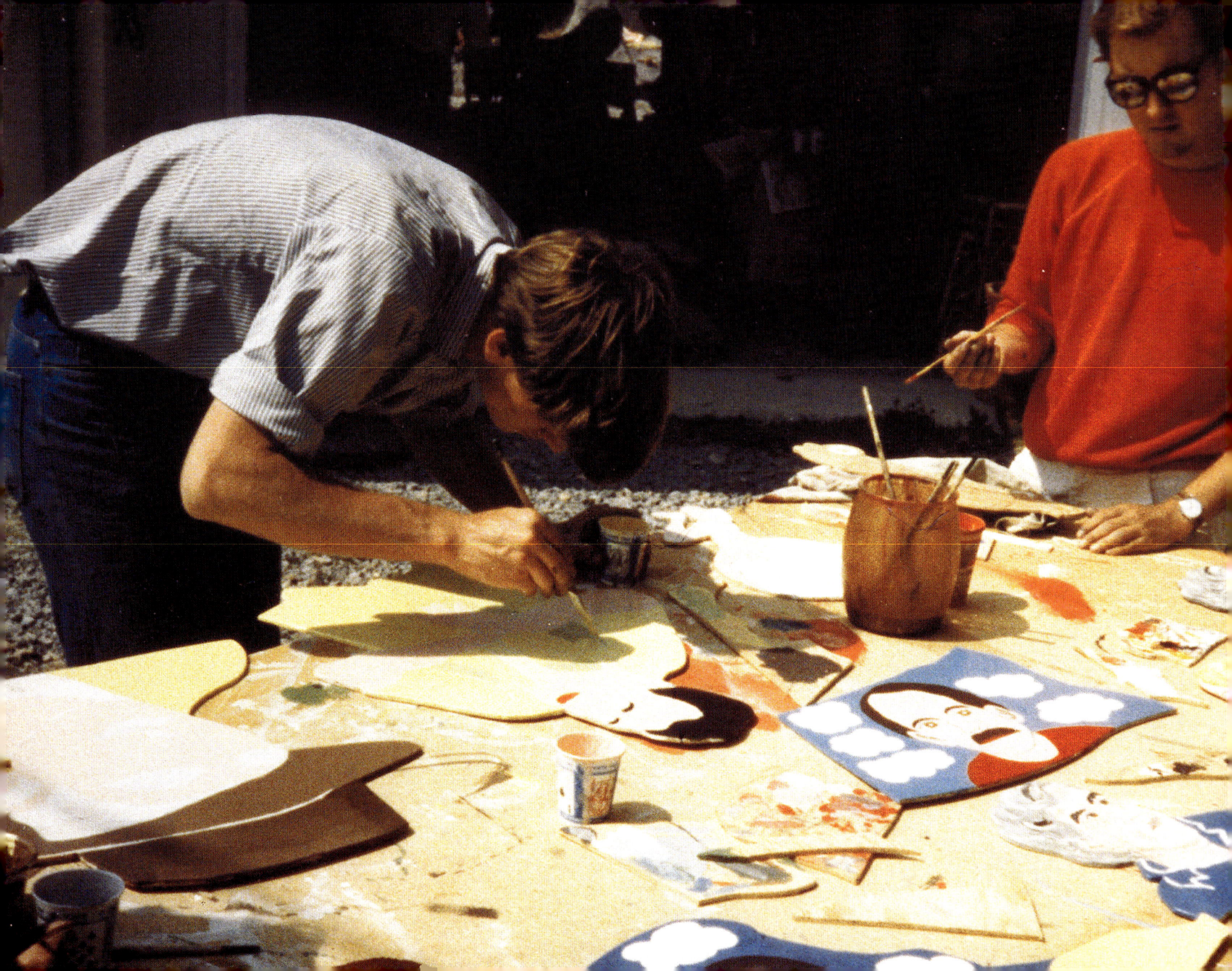

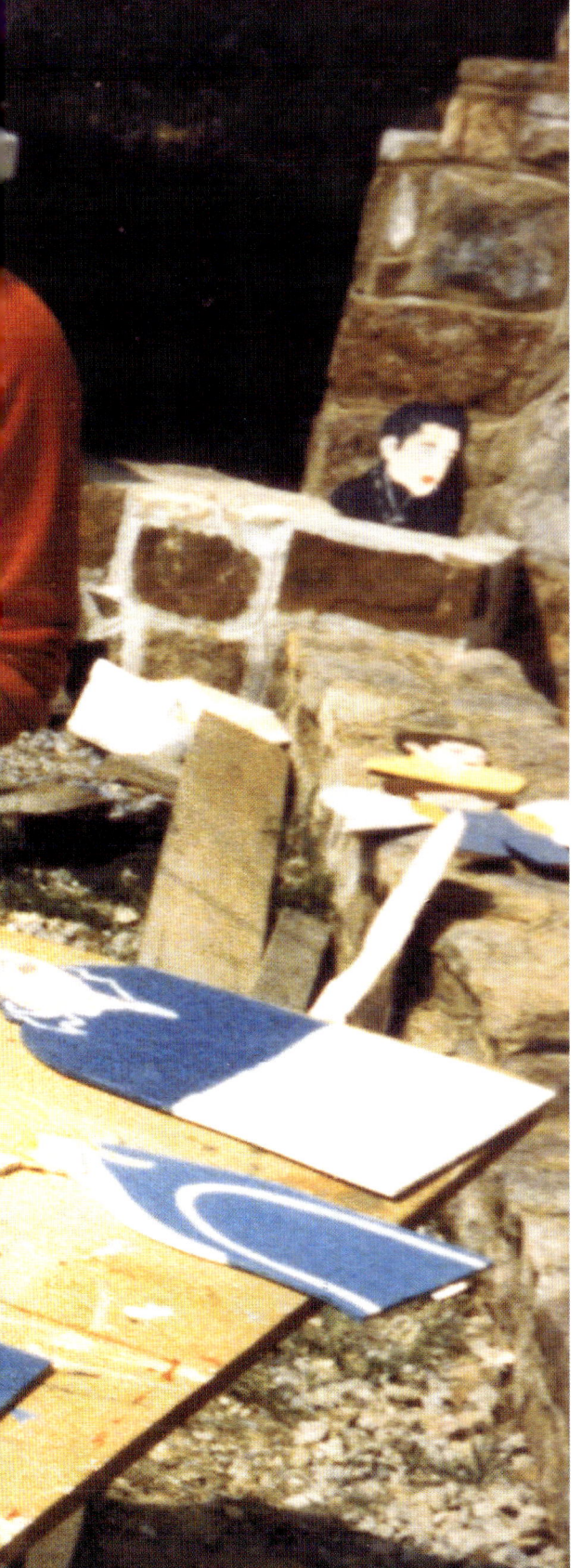

# IV

# *The Reverend Howard Finster*

# HOWARD FINSTER'S 1985 MOUNTAIN LAKE "WORKOUT" AND BEYOND

RAY KASS

I became acquainted with Howard Finster in 1984 through the efforts of the Appalachian poet and publisher Jonathan Williams, who had invited folklorist Roger Manley, Finster biographer Tom Patterson, and me (among others) to serve on the board of the Jargon Society. The Jargon Society was a small-press organization that Williams had developed out of his personal experience at Black Mountain College in North Carolina in the early 1950s. Williams always had an ear for the new, particularly regarding the special habitat of his beloved Appalachian "eco-art and literary world," and he had taken a decided interest in the "outsider art" phenomenon in the South, especially the work of Howard Finster.

As a result of this introduction, I met Finster and in 1985 organized the first Mountain Lake workshop involving him. Ann Oppenhimer (whom I had only spoken to on the telephone) and the writer Susan Hankla showed up for the week-long event prepared to take care of Finster and literally cooked all of his meals. I could not have coordinated the event without them.

More than 100 extraordinary pieces were produced during five long days of sawing wood, pouring concrete, and painting on plywood and discarded materials by Finster, Virginia Tech students, and many members of the Southwestern Virginia community. These pieces now reside in the permanent collection of the Taubman Museum of Art in Roanoke, Virginia. This collection of a Finster workshop is the only one that has been maintained in its entirety and is an excellent example of one of the artist's community "workouts"— as Finster liked to call them. Finster directed several such collaborative art events during the 1980s, mainly on university campuses. The "Howard Finster Mountain Lake Workshop Collection"

at the Taubman Museum demonstrates Finster's aesthetic awareness concerning the nature of art, its communicative power, and the essential and free vitality of art in society.

Sculpture and painting were indistinguishable categories of artistic discipline or practice to Finster. Only "sacred" art — a consequence and corollary of human experience — mattered to him. Once Finster recognized an image as revelatory by "setting his sight" on it and, with the help of an overhead projector, rendered it as a stencil (a "demention"; his term), it took on a life of its own that could not be repressed, but was free to exist as a potential experience and expressively creative image for anyone who embraced its form as audience participant or as artist.

In an important way, Finster's projects at Mountain Lake instigated the ideal that artist and audience could dynamically be brought together. This belief has become a primary motive of the community art collaborations of the Mountain Lake Workshop at Mountain Lake itself and in the wider community. In my opinion, only John Cage and Joseph Beuys have evinced concepts in their work that are as socially expansive and open in their embrace of the essential freedom of art.

The most important result of the many wonderful personal experiences that were shared during the 1985, 1989, and 1992 projects that the Mountain Lake Workshop undertook with Finster was the special relationship that he developed with Roanoke artist Brian Sieveking. Finster and Sieveking collaborated closely on the production of an extraordinary series of entirely original serigraphic prints that incorporated many of Finster's major visual themes. The many hours spent

working together at Finster's place in Summerville, Georgia, gave Sieveking an opportunity to develop a depth of personal friendship with Finster and his family that few have known.

Finster is arguably the most famous American artist since Andy Warhol. The work of both artists conveys a personal sense of the "weird," but the evangelical sign- and language-based art imagery that Finster inscribed on virtually every kind of natural or manmade surface has entered the world of both popular as well as high-art culture. Finster's inscriptions of spiritual admonishment actually aroused more controversy in the sophisticated art world than did Warhol's display of deviant, voyeuristic fetishism. Yet both artists confronted humanity, no matter how dark or troubled their visions, in the all-forgiving embrace of their unrepressed images. This is the gift of their art (and all great art): to open us to experience. Finster's genuinely sincere, persistently tough-minded and philosophically sublime art captured the largest audience for visual art in more than two decades, since the phenomena of Warhol's icons of advertising and dehumanized logos and Jasper Johns' language-based cryptic imagery of unremitting clues.

Finster's Georgia neighbor Leroy Almon Sr., the prominent folk artist, wood carver, and protégé of Elijah Pierce, once told Sieveking and me that Finster "was the father of us all. He opened the door to art for all of us. He was the man that put us [artists] on the map."[1]

Almon was right about that. The door is still wide open, and the energy is pouring through into the popular media, the New York art world, and the great beyond.

[1] Leroy R. Almon Sr., quoted in the *Folk Art Messenger* 54, vol. 14, no.3 (Fall/Winter 2001/02), p. 8.

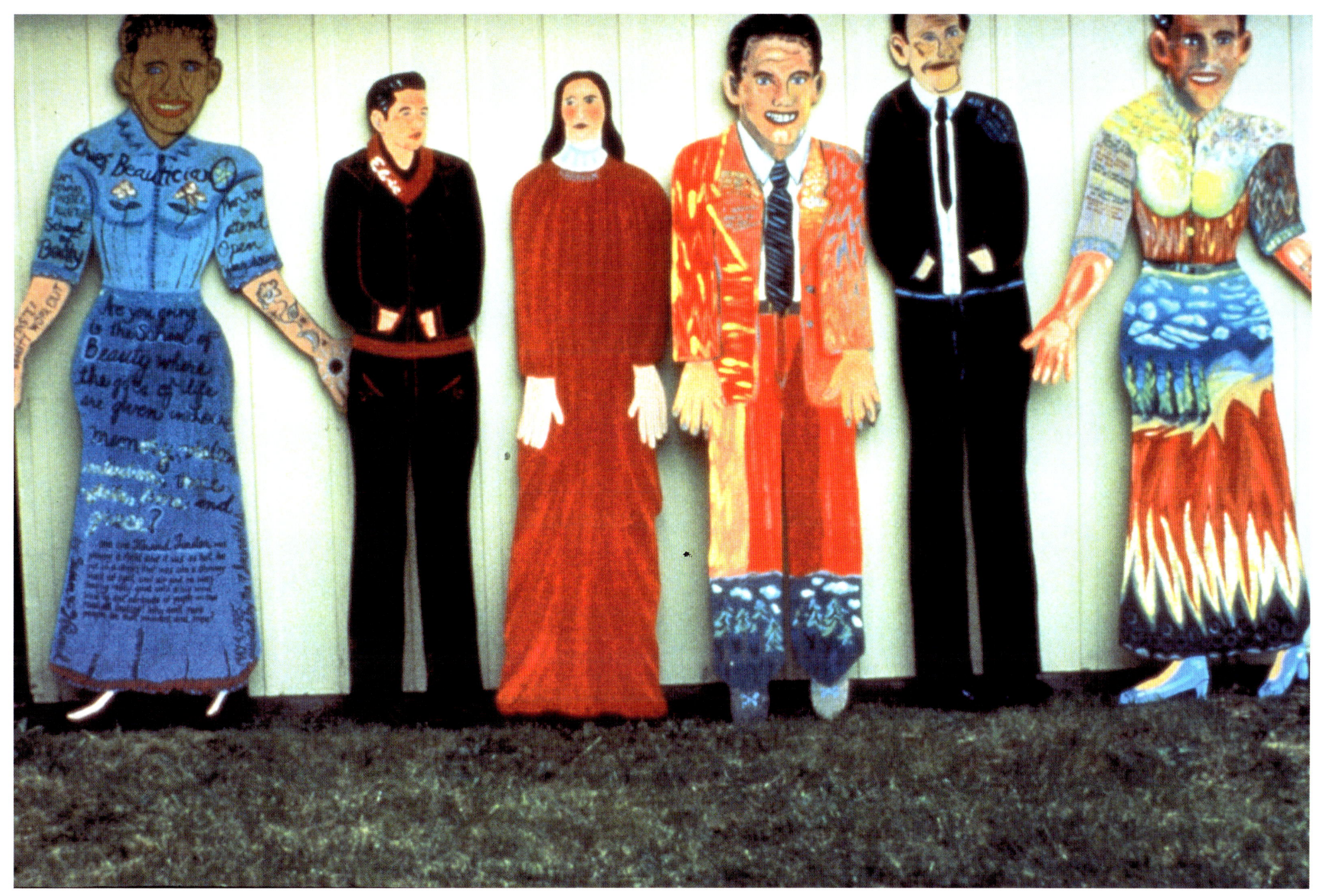

Life-sized cut-out plywood figures of Finster "dementions": (L-R) *Howard in his Little Dress*,
*Elvis Presley*, *Jesus Christ*, *Howard Finster*, *Abraham Lincoln*, *Howard in his Little Dress*.

# SPENDING TIME WITH HOWARD AT HIS "WORKOUT"

ANN OPPENHIMER

In 1985, Ray Kass, artist and assistant professor at Virginia Tech in Blacksburg, Virginia, said he was planning a five-day Mountain Lake Workshop with Howard Finster at the Miles C. Horton Center near the Mountain Lake Hotel. Ray said that Howard would be staying in a guest apartment at Miles and Ruth Hortons' home near the studio — or even in the studio — and that various students and local volunteers would come during the day to work with Howard. "What is Howard going to do for meals?" I asked.

"Oh, I'll get some food laid in, and he can fix his own food."

"Well, in that case, Susan Hankla and I will come and cook for him." Susan and I did, and that's how we came to spend almost a week with Howard and were able to participate in another of the artist's "workouts." The Mountain Lake Workshop was the third program sponsored in a university setting in which Howard Finster had taken part, after University of Colorado at Boulder and a program at the University of Richmond in 1984.

Finster arrived with a suitcase full of his "dementions," ready to share them with community participants and students from Virginia Tech and other area schools. He spread hundreds of these paper-stencil patterns on the floor of the cabin's large living room. Each person was free to select and use these patterns solo or in combinations. The choices were inspirational, and everyone set to work making multiple pieces. Most included written sayings in the manner of a Finster cutout. We were told we could make some to keep for ourselves as long as we made another for Virginia Tech.[1] Howard worked with each of us, showing us how to use a jigsaw correctly, how to sand the

[1] If participants made more than one piece during the workshop, they could take one home. The remaining piece(s) went to Virginia Tech and were eventually exhibited in Roanoke and ended up as part of the collection of the Taubman Museum.

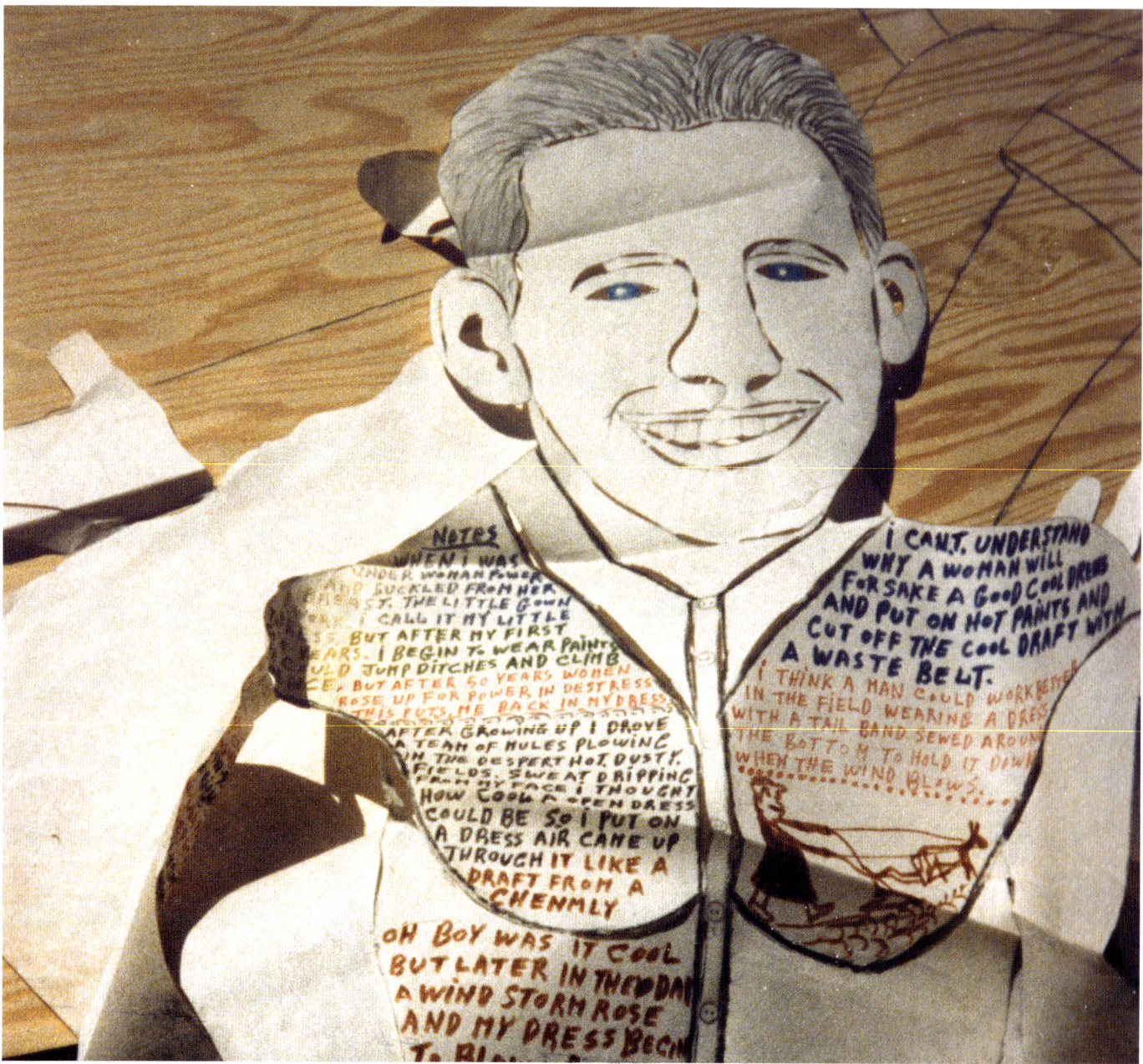

Cut-out paper stencil "demention" of Howard in his dress. He wore a dress sometimes when he had to plow the Georgia fields in the hot summer weather; he said it was much cooler than wearing overalls.

(right) Ray Kass painting *Howard Finster in his Li'l Dress*

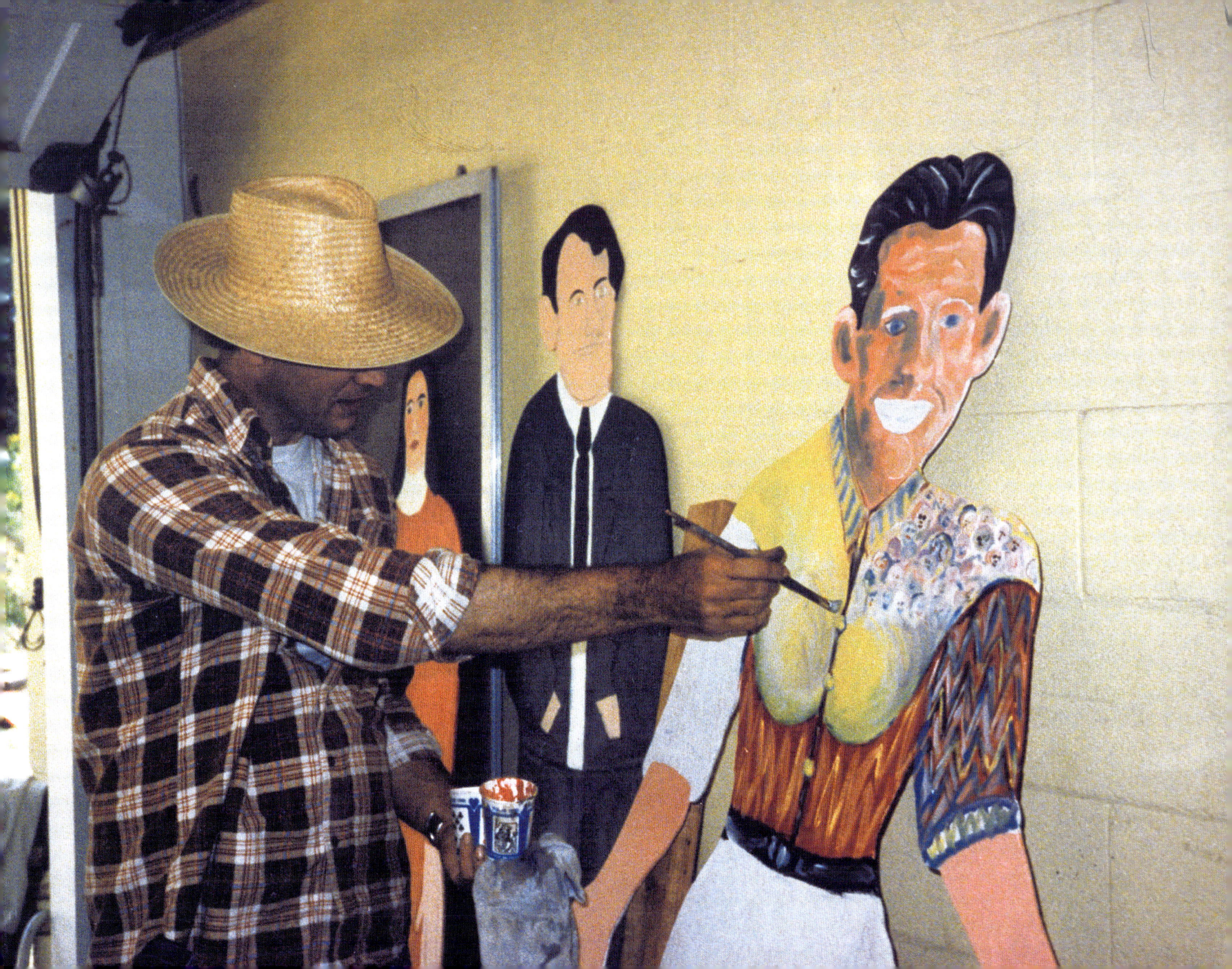

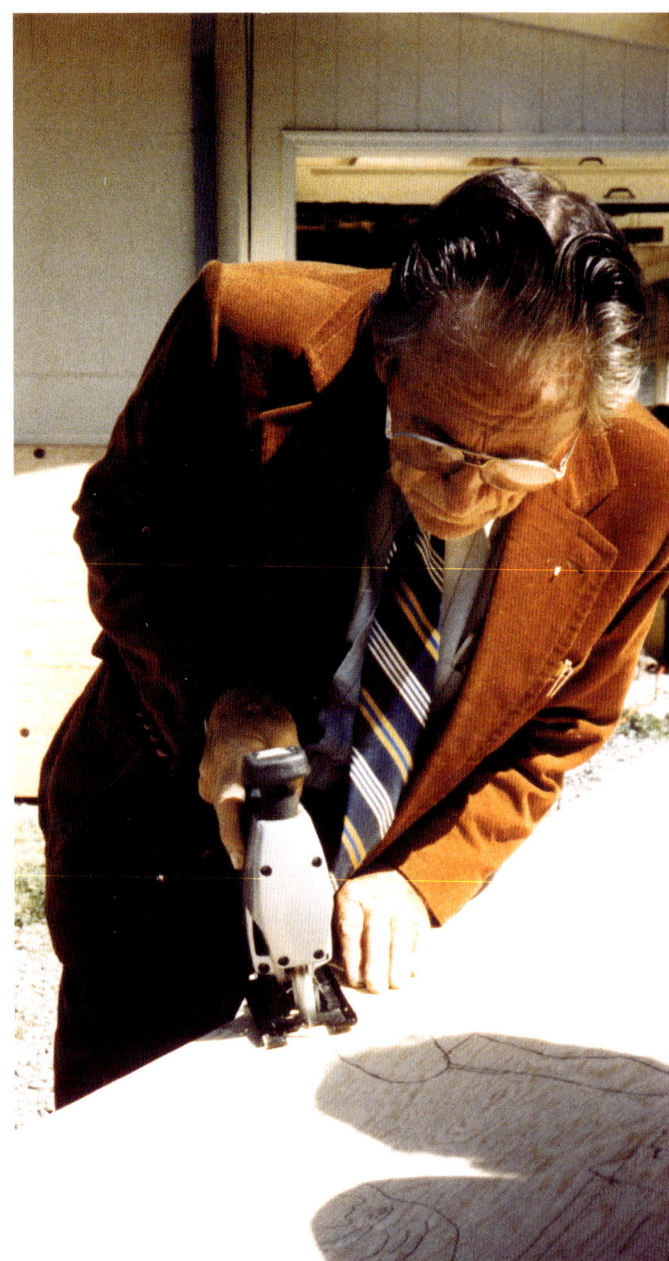

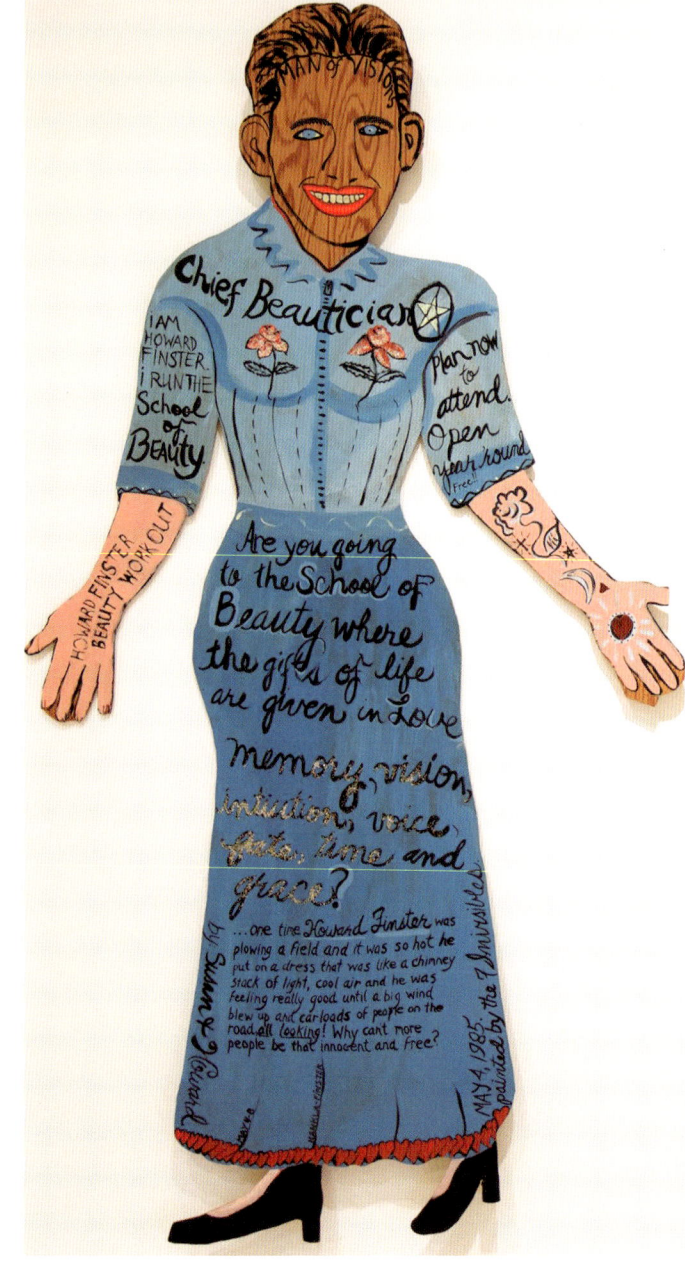

edges and prepare the paint. I even drew a few patterns of my own, making a portrait of my husband. Susan made a life-size version of "Howard in a Skirt," illustrating the artist's story of his late sister's appearance to him as an angel while he was working in the fields at about age six. When all the pieces were finished, they were assembled as giant collages on four-by-eight plywood sheets to be exhibited at the Roanoke Museum (now the Taubman Museum of Art) in Roanoke, Virginia.

Since Susan was a vegetarian, we had brought along a supply of peanut butter and plenty of vegetables. On our last day I recorded a video of Howard, who spent the first 30 minutes telling the history of the peanut in all its various forms and then extolling the values of peanut butter. All this before he began to play the banjo and sing a variety of old-time hymns, such as "Amazing Grace," and some of his original songs, such as "Just a Little Tack in the Shingle of Your Roof."

During the Mountain Lake Workshop, Finster personally interacted with each participant and visitor, and each person shared Finster's enthusiasm and the valuable lessons he taught all of us about carpentry as well as art-making. Susan and I were treated to the unique experience of sharing quiet time with Howard. On one unforgettable morning I sat on the front porch with Howard, looking across the valley to the green and blue mountains in the distance. Howard told me, "Last night, I journeyed beyond the light of the sun," and I am convinced that he did.

# REVEREND HOWARD FINSTER:
# THE MOUNTAIN LAKE
# "WORKOUT" 1985

HOWARD RISATTI

Most of the Mountain Lake workshops have come about through what seem like a series of fortuitous circumstances. While this may be so, they are nonetheless all closely linked together through their use of collaborative procedures and through profound conceptual and philosophical similarities. In fact, as seen in the Reverend Howard Finster's "workout" (his preferred name for a workshop) it is probably at this level that the most important influences they have had on each other have occurred.

Founded by Jonathan Williams in the 1950s, the Jargon Society published the poets associated with Black Mountain College located near Asheville, North Carolina. When Buckminster Fuller, who was on the board of directors of the society, died, Ray Kass and several others were invited to join the board. At this time, Williams and other members of the society were involved with folklorist and anthropologist Roger Manley, who, in turn, was interested in the emerging phenomenon of outsider art. Outsider art is usually understood as an art which represents a self-taught, home-grown tradition connected with what critic Kay Larson has called "local idiosyncrasies"; its locus seems to be the small towns and rural regions of the country rather than the large, mainstream urban art centers.[1] Through the Jargon Society, Manley, and Tom Patterson (a former director of the society who would eventually write a book on Finster), Kass also began to visit outsider artists and take an interest in their work; he felt their localism was somehow related to the community-based aspirations of the Mountain Lake programs.[2]

Around 1984 Kass became acquainted with Howard Finster, a retired Baptist minister who had served mostly rural

communities in the Deep South. Now living in Summerville, Georgia, Finster was just coming into prominence as an artist in the larger art world.[3] His self-taught visionary art relies on written text to communicate religious messages and reflects the religious preaching and sermonizing tradition of American Evangelicalism of which Finster is a part. With its special interest in apocalyptic themes, this tradition reflects Fundamentalist Christian attempts to understand contemporary worldly events within the context of the prophecies of Revelation.[4]

Finster's visual art, which he made to spread the word of God to an even larger audience, fuses Evangelicalism and apocalyptic themes to events in contemporary culture.[5] This is done through a process Finster referred to as "patterning," the "discovery" of images in contemporary popular cultural sources (comic books, magazines, newspapers, flyers, photographs, etc.) and their appropriation by directly tracing around them while they are enlarged with the aid of an overhead projector. These "discovered" images, when traced and enlarged this way, become "dementions," as Finster called them, which then may become stencils to form the visual imagery in his art.

Kass invited Finster to do an experimental workshop, and in the spring of 1985, Finster came for a week to the Miles C. Horton Sr. Center at Mountain Lake at St. John's Mountain.[6] In preparation for the actual workshop, which came to be called "Howard Finster's Mountain Lake 'Workout,'" public programs and talks about Finster were presented in the community. An artistic ambience was created around Finster and the workshop by inviting Jonathan Williams from North Carolina and art

critic John Yau from New York to Mountain Lake. A public gathering was held at the Horton Center with poetry readings; Finster played music, sang, and talked with the audience. This not only increased awareness of Finster and his art, but also injected and infused something of his spirit into the community.

Workshop organizers involved as many people as possible with Finster's work by informing and engaging the community so that the workshop would not be seen as something isolated from the community, something brought in merely to entertain the community in a show business sense, or educate it in the academic sense, but as an event that was an integral part of the community's cultural life. Out of these events, and through a process of self-selection, a group of people who were willing to give "body and soul" because of their special interest in Finster and his ideas participated in the week-long workshop. Materials were assembled including "tractor enamel" (commercial paint), plywood, brushes, saws, and other tools. Finster brought with him literally hundreds of his dementions, and workshop participants selected those they liked and used them as stencils, tracing around them and then cutting them out of plywood with jigsaws. These dementions were then given a white undercoat and painted by the participants. Finster painted the entire time, visiting everyone in the workshop, looking at what they were doing and sometimes painting on their pieces.

Finster felt no creative disruption to his own work in doing this kind of collaborative project because of the way he envisioned and understood his dementions. He would get upset if the dementions were talked about as tracings. For him, they were

[1] There is much debate about the differences between folk and outsider art. Finster's interest in mass-media images certainly makes him different from the traditional folk artist. Kay Larson noted in *The Village Voice* (9 June 1980), p. 72, that the "Primitives [outsider artists like Finster] are coming into fashion, ... because they certify local idiosyncrasies, giving America a cultural identity separate from centuries of European sophistication, and proclaiming that evangelism was and is our most important product." However, Peter Schjeldahl categorized Finster as a "modern naif" and defined naive art as "individualistic, even alienated — an eruptive singularity" before raising concerns about Finster's religious message. See Schjeldahl's "About Reverence," *The Village Voice* (31 Aug 1982), p. 73. Donald Kuspit raised a related issue, arguing that in the appropriation of the marginal by the mainstream, "the mainstream acquires the aura of authenticity and integrity supposedly innate to the marginal." See Kuspit's "The Appropriation of Marginal Art in the 80s," *American Art* (winter/spring 1991), pp. 133–141, esp. 134.

[2] Tom Patterson's book is *Howard Finster, Stranger from Another World: Man of Visions Now on this Earth* (New York: Abbeville Press, 1989).

[3] Finster's increasing prominence in the art world at this time is evident from the fact that he was included in *Paradise Lost/Paradise Regained: American Visions of the New Decade*, curated by Marcia Tucker of the New Museum of Contemporary Art in New York for the American Pavilion at the 1984 Venice Biennale.

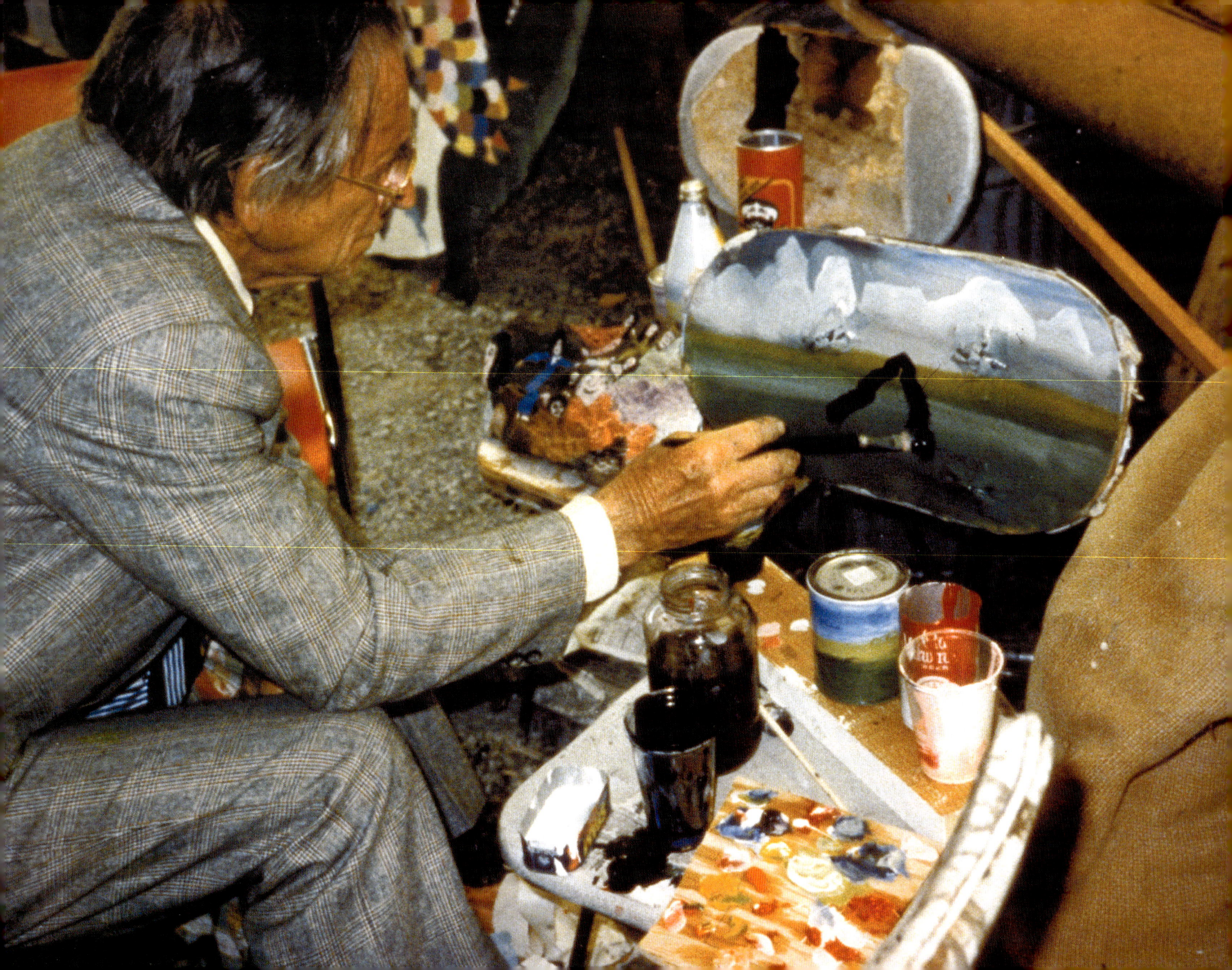

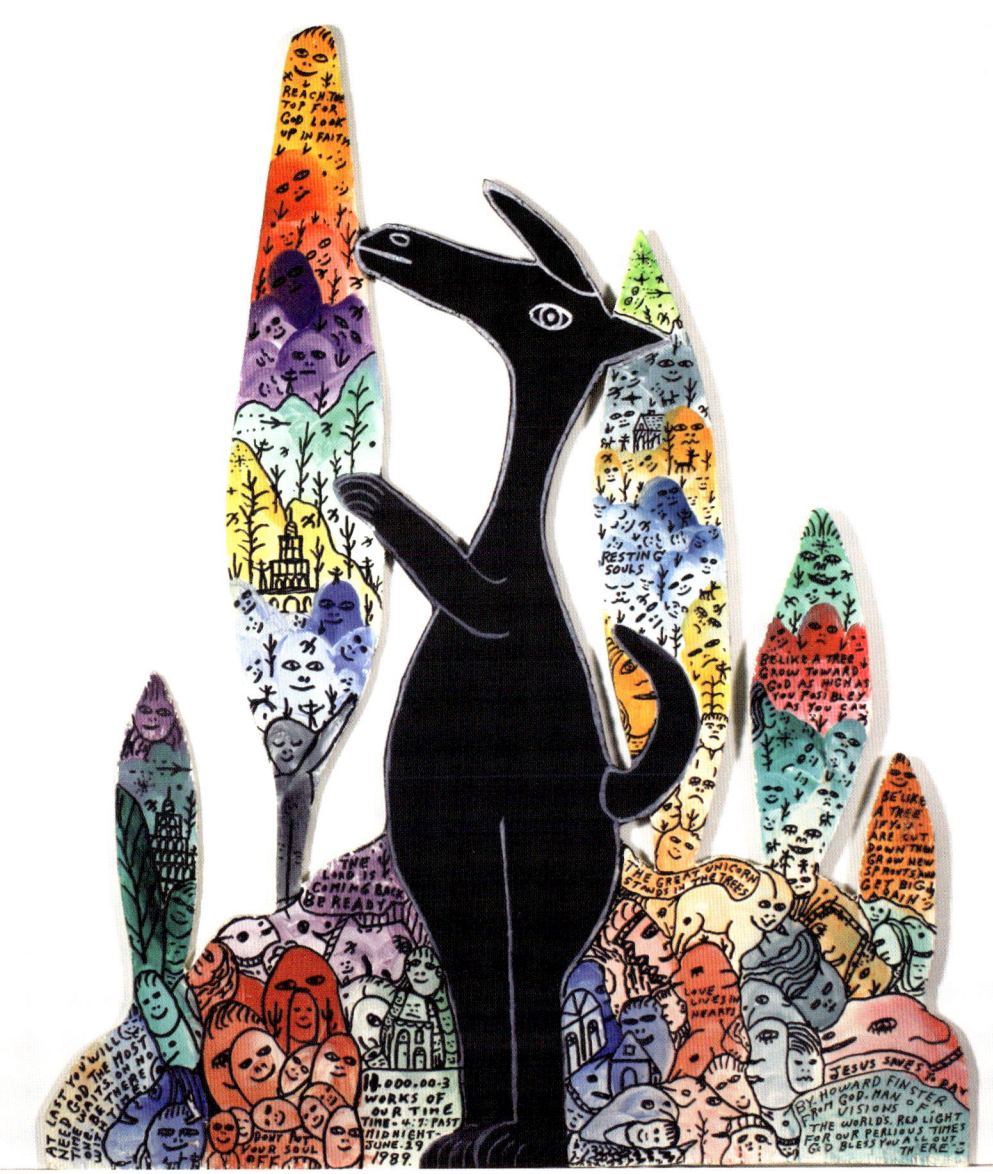

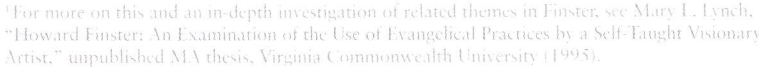

(left) Finster painting a chair at the Horton Studio, 1985

Howard Finster, *The Unicorn Stands in the Trees, #11,003 works of art*, June 29, 1989, oil paint on cut-out plywood, 26 1/4 X 21 1/2 in. (66.68 x 54.61 cm)

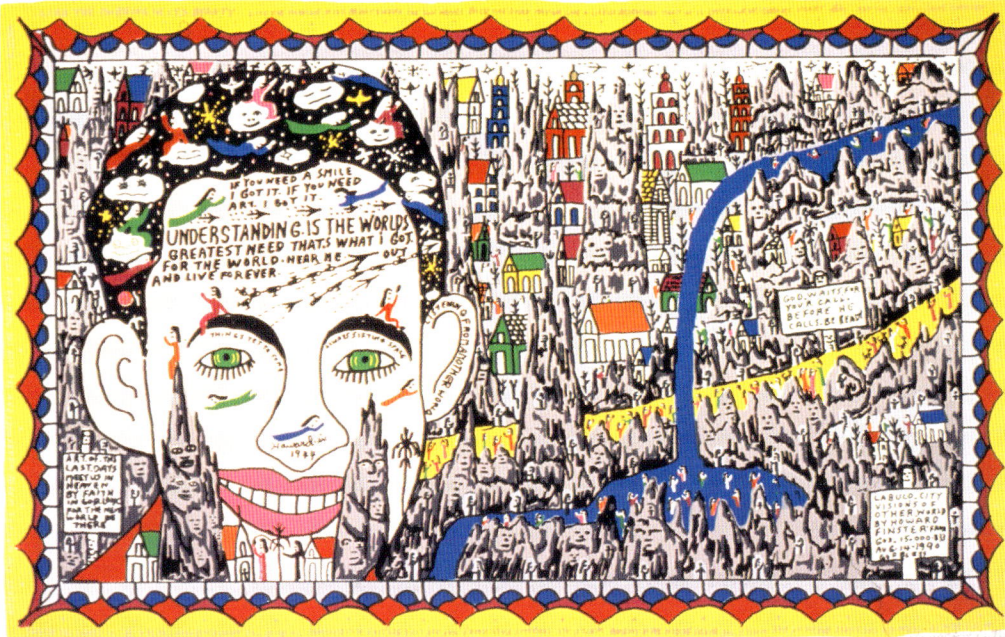

Howard Finster, *Labulo City*, 1990, serigraph, 24.5 x 34 in. (60.96 x 86.36 cm), edition 90, 10 artist's proof

not tracings but visionary symbols that he happened to "discover," symbols that, once they were "patterned," were taken out of society and the world of popular culture to speak with a divinely inspired energy. In Finster's view, even dementions that come from famous photographs like the one of Elvis at 3½ years of age become sacred art; even secular texts painted by other people on the dementions do not prevent them from possessing sacred resonance. In talking about secular texts written by participants, no matter how profane, Finster said they were all right because "God forgives everything — that which God wouldn't forgive, you couldn't imagine."

Finster's conception of his work — *that it doesn't matter who paints it*, that he is only the medium who discovered the demention — gave a profound philosophical and aesthetic basis to the workshop, making it clear that a collaborative project need not be any less conceptually rigorous or aesthetically demanding than the solo studio practice traditionally used by most artists. The finished paintings, which by agreement with Finster and the other participants were combined in specially designed panels or "vision boxes," demonstrate an essential aspect of Finster's aesthetic ideas, which center on the belief that *all images realized by the imagination are visionary and the communicative power of a visionary image is inherent within that image and can be conveyed by anyone's genuinely sincere artistic effort.*[7]

[4] For more on this and an in-depth investigation of related themes in Finster, see Mary L. Lynch, "Howard Finster: An Examination of the Use of Evangelical Practices by a Self-Taught Visionary Artist," unpublished MA thesis, Virginia Commonwealth University (1995).

[5] For people who mistakenly view Finster's art solely in terms of art-world market forces, his "workouts" seem just an attempt at commodification to increase production. See J. F. Turner, *Howard Finster, Man of Visions* (New York: Alfred A. Knopf, 1989), pp. 163–64.

[6] The Miles C. Horton Sr. Center is a Virginia Tech facility suitable for small conferences and meetings; it includes guest quarters and a 40' x 60' studio with a panoramic view of the New River Valley. Because Finster, who was in his late 60s at the time, didn't like to fly, workshop assistant Brian Sieveking drove to Summerville, Georgia, and brought Finster back with a large selection of his "dementions."

[7] Approximately 100 works were produced in the Finster "Workout" and, by agreement of the participants and Finster, they were given to the Art Museum of Western Virginia in Roanoke, today known as the Taubman Museum of Art.

# VISIONS OF ANOTHER WORLD: THE PENNVILLE WORKOUT, SUMMERVILLE, GEORGIA, 1989

RAY KASS

The author, accompanied by Mountain Lake assistants Peter Lau, Charles Layman, and Brian Sievenking drove to Summerville, Georgia, to assist Howard Finster in a two-week-long workshop that he called "The Pennville Workout" after the name of the neighborhood in Summerville where his Paradise Garden environment is located. We checked into the nearby Sequoyah Motel and arrived at the garden early in the morning with sawhorses, folding tables, power tools, paints, and sheets of pre-primed plywood. Our purpose was to provide studio assistance that would enable Howard to create large-scale "dementions" that he would not have been able to accomplish on his own. He created several new designs for this project including a life-size Marilyn Monroe, an elephant, and a new image of Jesus in a landscape. We cut out the new designs, sanded, and re-primed them, and did a great deal of the underpainting for him. Howard oversaw everything and did all of the detailed finishing work on each piece.

A tremendous amount of work was completed each day, with the exception of one day when an MTV crew arrived and interviewed Howard all day. Our visit coincided with the 125th anniversary of the nearby Battle of Chickamauga, and the local tourism office wanted to mark places of interest by placing Union and Confederate flags. Without Howard's consent, his grandson, Allen Wilson, gave them permission to fly a Confederate flag at Paradise Garden. It was the only time we saw Howard lose his temper. "Take it down!" he said. "I don't believe in glorifying war!" And it was quickly removed.

The man who had placed the flag said to Howard, "I don't think that you know what this flag stands for." Howard, who had now passed the point of being polite, responded, saying, "Son, I was born in Alabama in 1916 and I've lived here my whole life, and I know exactly what that flag means — and it's not flying over Paradise Garden."

Over forty independent major dementions were completed, as well as many smaller pieces that were combined in "vision boxes" similar to what we had done at Mountain Lake in 1985. Howard was a man of deeply felt principles, but he wasn't always dealing with like-minded people. The "Pennville Workout" project was underwritten by Peter Paul, then director of the dubious Spirit of America Foundation, a non-profit foundation that was best known for putting framed copies of the U.S. Constitution in public schools. Our understanding was that all of the artworks produced at this workshop were to be purchased by the foundation; Howard received a down payment. Afterwards Paul organized an extraordinary exhibition of the work at La Galeria on Rodeo Drive in Beverly Hills with a lavish reception hosted by celebrities Ann-Margret and Tom Bosley.[1] Peter Lau and Jorge Pardo packed all of the work into Howard's new Ford Club wagon and drove the show to California. Howard flew out for the opening — it was the first time that he had flown in a plane.

Howard said that, for reasons unexplained, he never received payment in full for this trove of important works, and they were eventually sold to the House of Blues in Chicago.

[1] The exhibition, *Paradise Garden: Visions of Another World*, opened in October 1989; it was designed by Peter Lau.

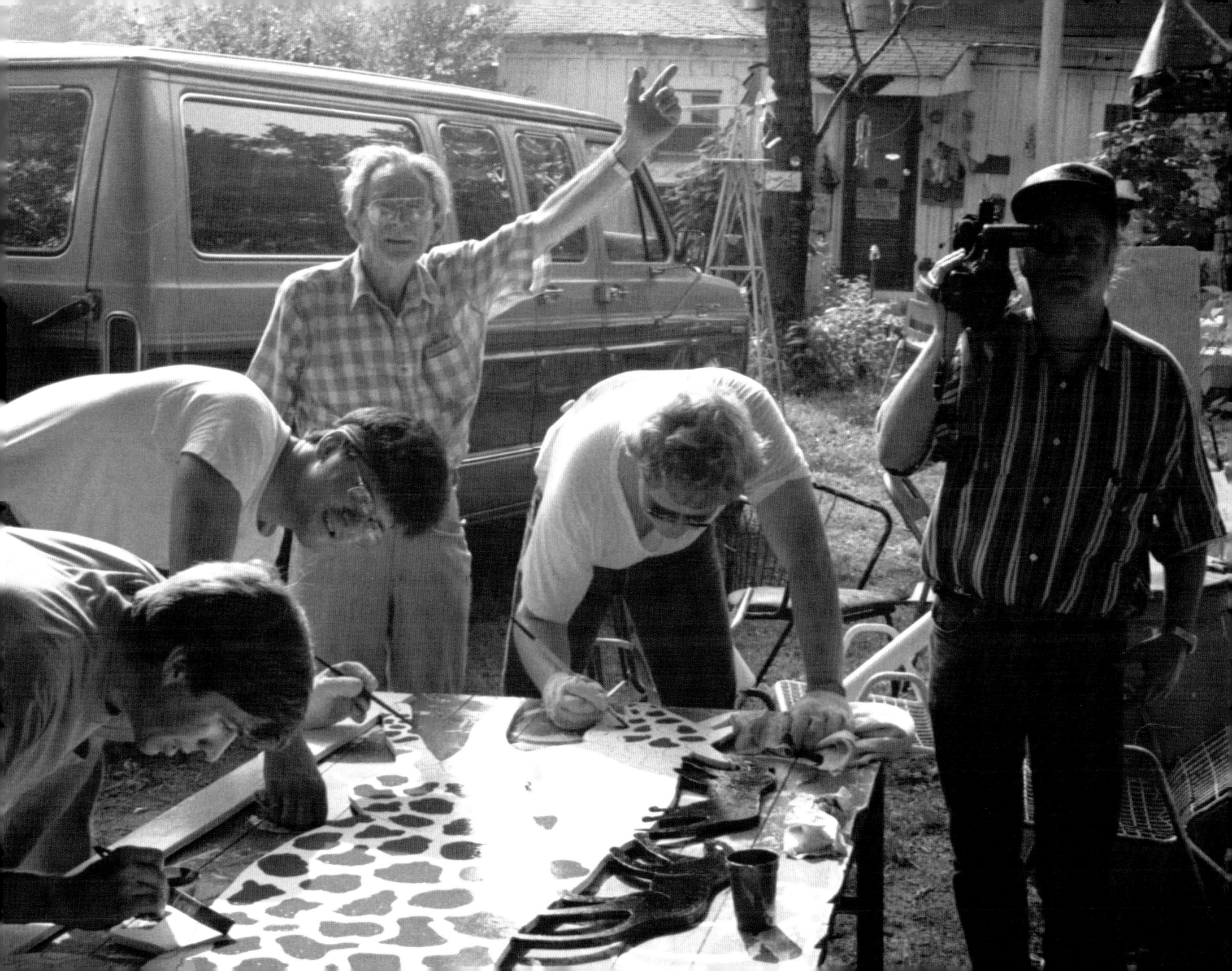

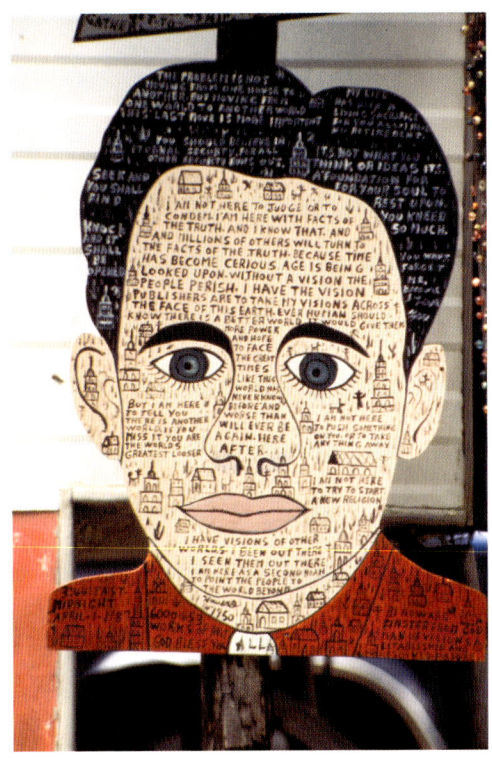
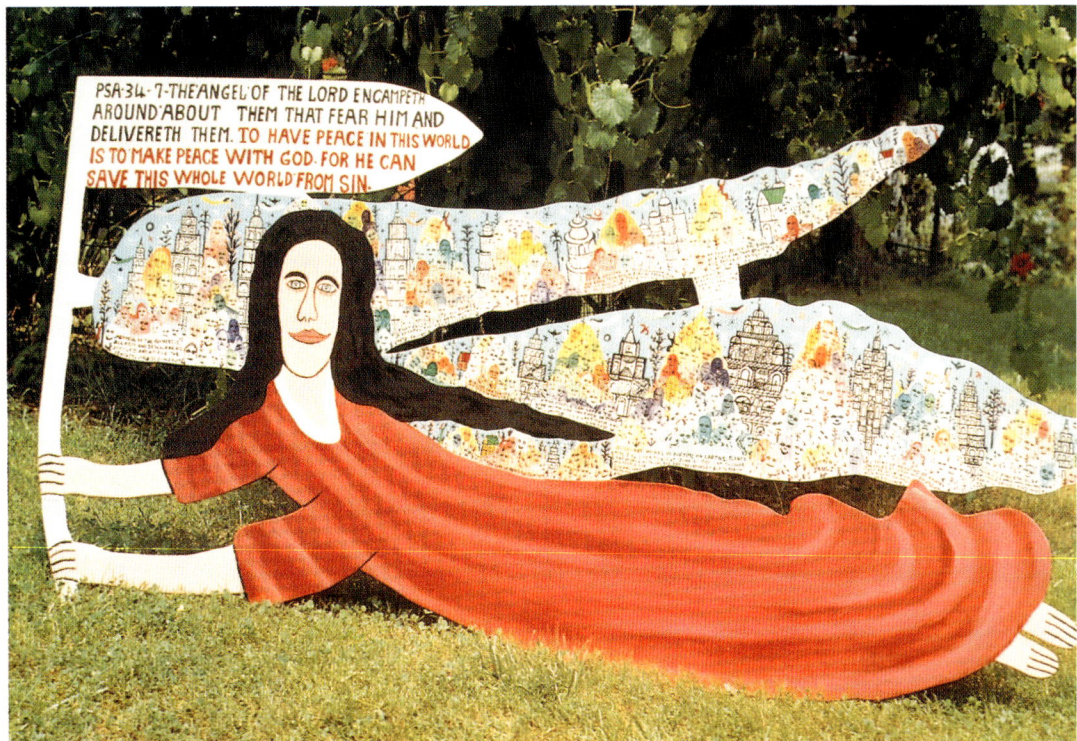
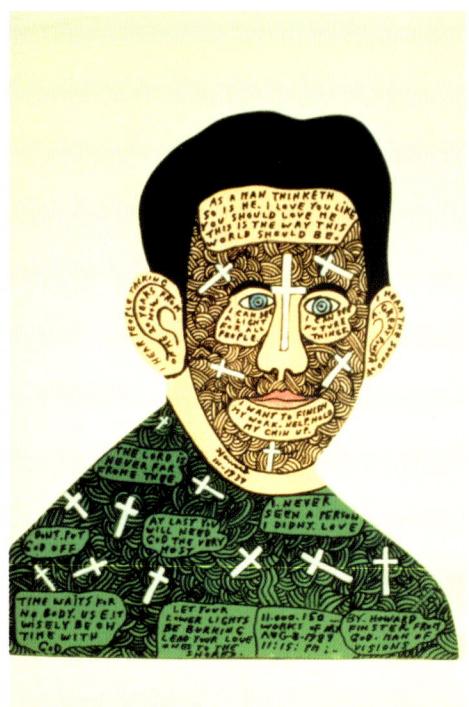
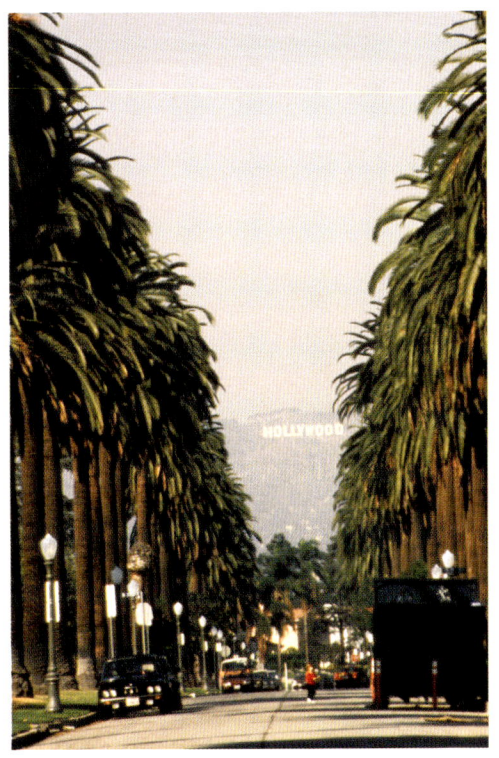
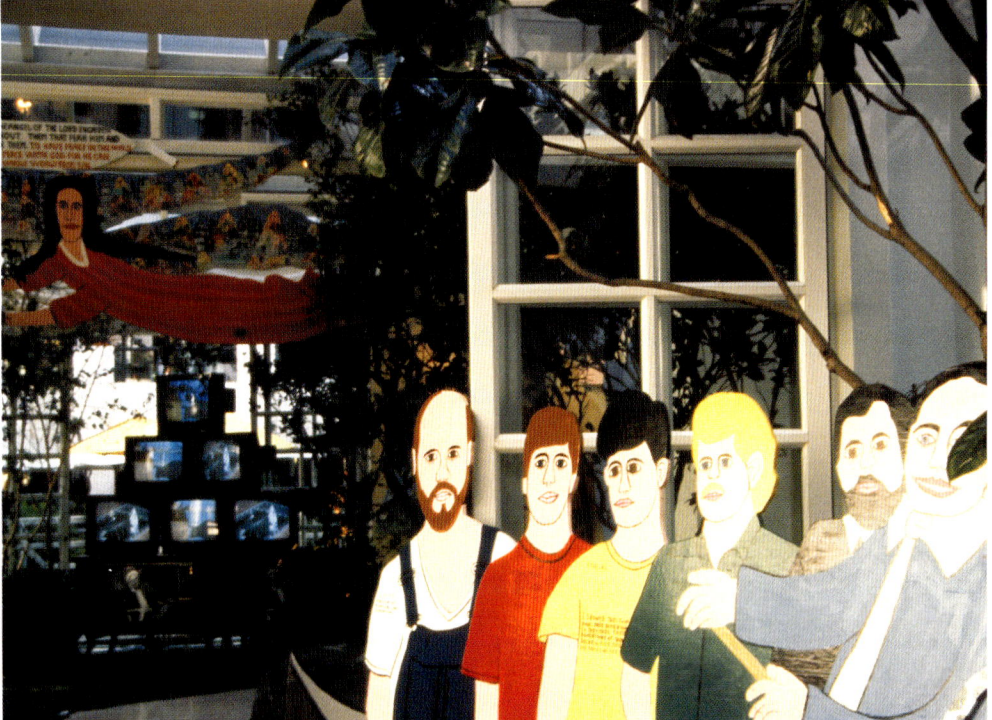
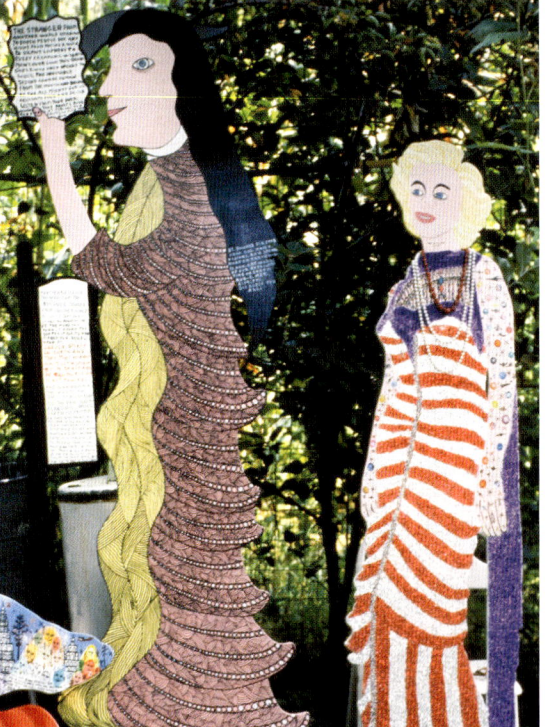

102

# HOWARD FINSTER: HIS WORKSHOPS AND HIS PRINTS

BRIAN SIEVEKING

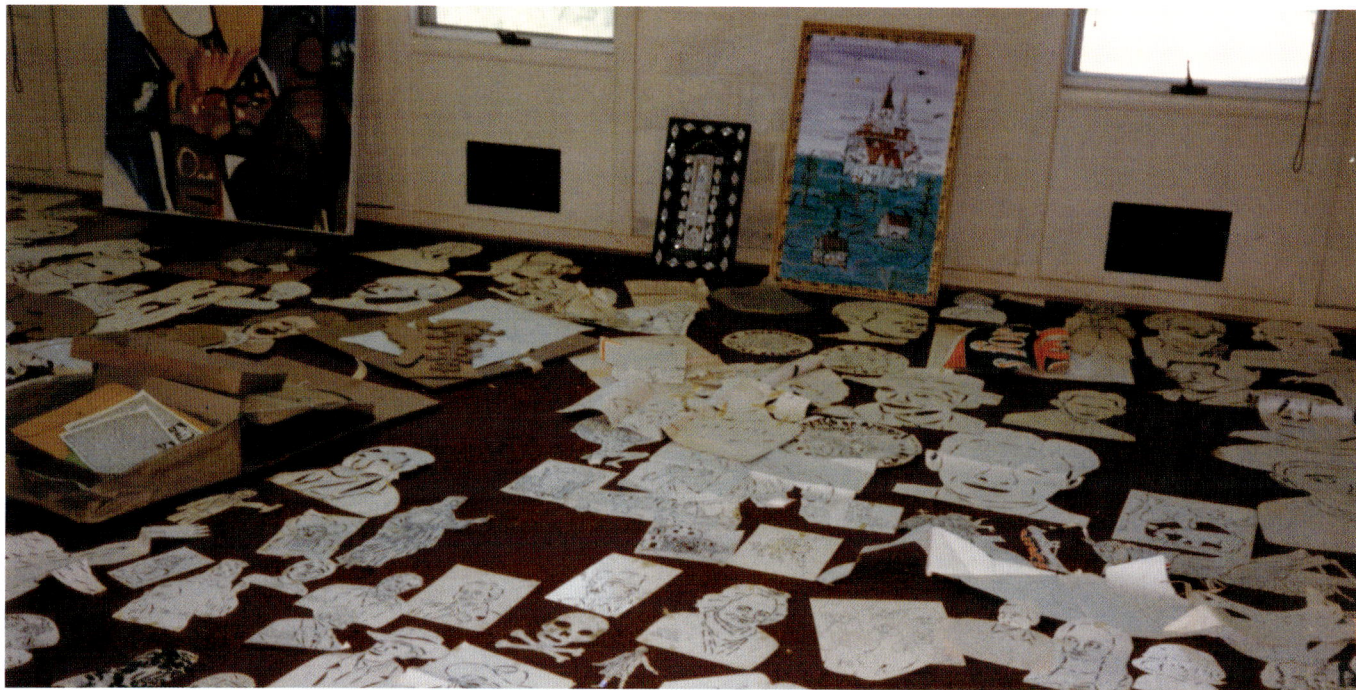

In the spring of 1985 Howard Finster — artist, poet, preacher, musician, and visionary — came to Mountain Lake. Initially this variously self-described "man of vision," "second Noah," and "garbage man of God" seemed an odd choice to invite to direct a Mountain Lake Workshop. Born into a hardscrabble life as one of thirteen children on a rural Appalachian family farm and largely self-taught in all things (family pressures forced him to leave school after the sixth grade), Finster received a call to preach at the age of 15.[1] While his background differed dramatically from that of most of our professors and Mountain Lake participants, we quickly came to understand the ways in which Finster's atypical experiences and influences had coalesced to form a truly personal aesthetic, a sort of postmodern backwoods Pop that bridged the gap between traditional regionalized pre-war folk art and the multifaceted art worlds of late-twentieth-century America.

Finster arrived at Mountain Lake ready to work and, dressed in hand-decorated work pants and shirt, quickly "got to it." As we laid out plywood, jigsaws, brushes, and tractor enamel, he unpacked and arranged hundreds of hand-cut stencils (which he referred to as "dementions") featuring historical figures, pop culture icons, and the "inventions of mankind." Taking a sip of coffee and placing a small plug of tobacco between his cheek and gum, he embarked on a speech and painting spree that seemed to last 100 uninterrupted hours.

In our pre-Google undergraduate world most of us were completely unaware that Finster had already been included in dozens of museum exhibits, profiled in major journals and magazines, and included in the United States Pavilion at the

41st Venice Biennale in 1984. Without referencing his art-world credentials, Finster quickly won us over with unique perspectives, humor, sincerity, and boundless energy and enthusiasm. Across the course of a week, Finster, eighteen workshop participants, several folk art authorities, many Virginia Tech students and faculty, and various local community members were immersed in a whirlwind series of exhibits, lectures, and collaborative art-making projects. The results of this "workout" would be collected, documented, mounted, exhibited, and added to the permanent collection of the Taubman Museum of Art in nearby Roanoke. More importantly Finster himself would begin a decade-long association with Mountain Lake that would lead to further workouts, exhibitions, documentary films, and the creation of a series of unique, limited-edition serigraphs as well as interactions both direct and indirect with cultural luminaries as diverse as David Byrne, Robert Duvall, Allen Ginsberg, Keith Haring, Michael Stipe, and William Styron.

This longer artistic collaboration really began with Ray Kass and me driving Finster back to his home and workplace in Pennville/Summerville, Georgia, where we first saw his Paradise Garden complex.[2] The garden was the center of Finster's art and life. The nearly 50,000 paintings that he created between 1976 and 2001 — experimental, lush, intricately detailed, at once both humorous and solemn, personal and universal, and combining inventive visuals with copious sprawling text — were inspired by and directly echoed the garden in form and content. Paradise Garden would also become the center of Mountain Lake's ongoing work with Finster. It would serve as the site of the 1988 Pennville workout and provide the documentary film's *mise en scène*. While his *bona fides* as an artist were unassailable,[3] it was the garden that most immediately tied Finster to the themes and goals of Mountain Lake and its multifaceted artists and participants. Locale, collaboration, environment, voice, and the intersection of art, identity, culture, and career

[1] Serving as a tent revivalist and circuit-rider evangelist as well as providing for his wife and five children as a mill worker, bicycle restorer, and TV repairman (Finster referred to himself as a "master of 22 trades"), he spent much of his life traveling throughout the rural South absorbing and recombining a steady stream of roadside attractions, revivalist educational banners, the illustrations that accompanied his biblical, technical, and news readings, and modern advertising.

[2] In 1961 Finster had purchased a large parcel of swamp land in northwest Georgia, cut brush, dug canals, removed "wheel barrows full" of snakes, and began to construct his greatest artistic achievement. Originally called the Plant Farm Museum, the astonishing collection of concrete sculpture, inlaid mosaics of broken glass and found objects, buildings and constructions

of repurposed bottles, mirrors, and bicycles would eventually be renamed Paradise Garden and become home to the World's Folk Art Church. The larger environmental pieces mingled with painted signs and pictures, compulsively arranged reflective spinners, chimes, and ornaments to create a multisensory experience that served as a "celebration of the inventions of mankind" and inspiration to musical and visual artists ranging from Michael Stipe and David Byrne to Jim Nutt and Keith Haring.

[3] For example, his cover painting for the Talking Heads' *Little Creatures* album (released soon after the initial workshop) set off a pop cultural explosion that granted him fame and celebrity rarely attained by any fine artist.

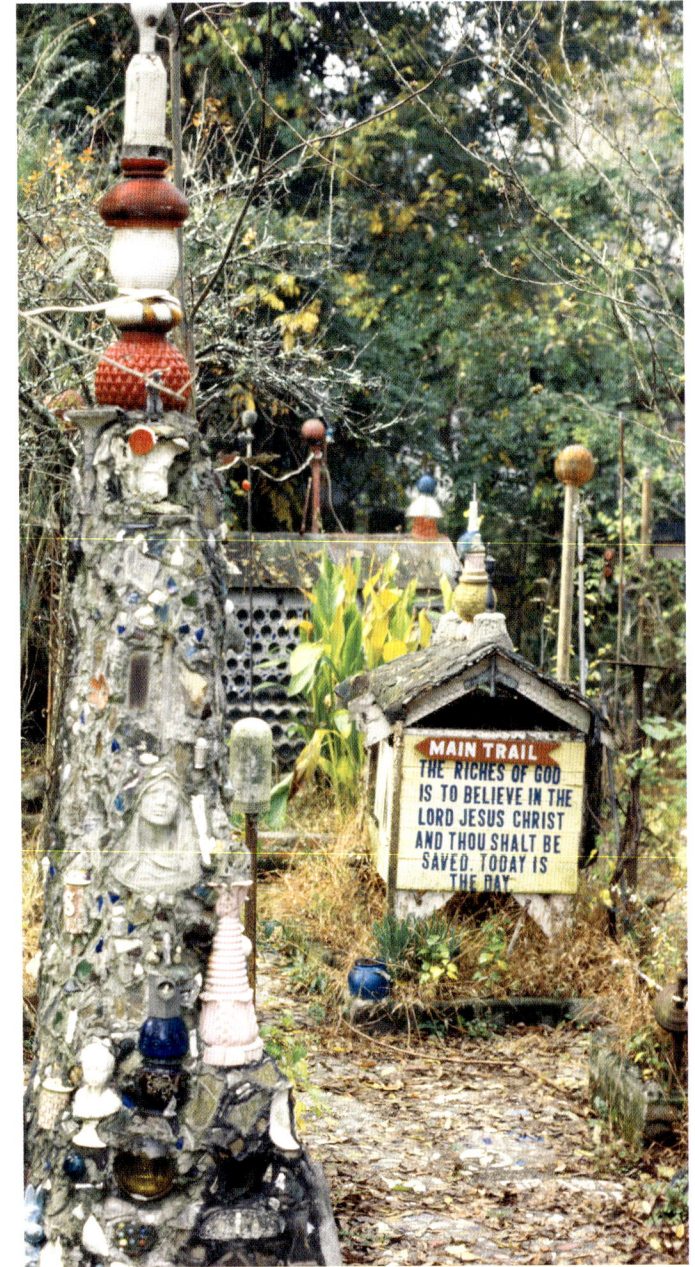

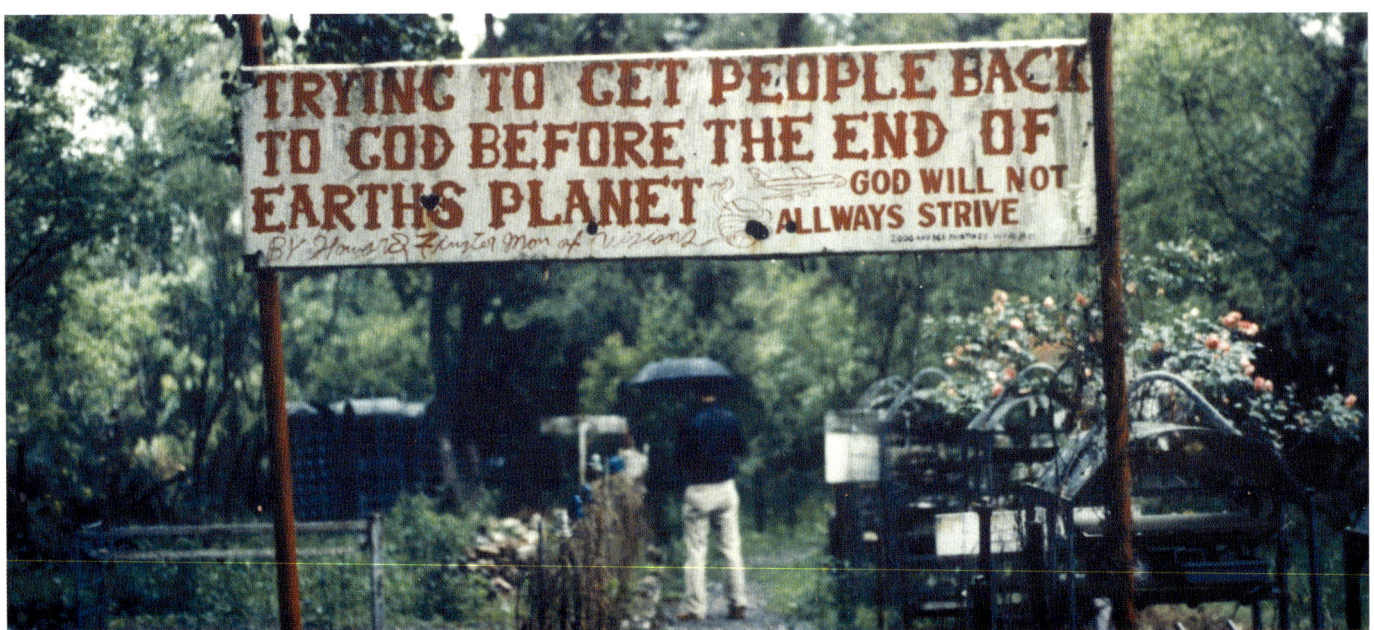

TRYING TO GET PEOPLE BACK TO GOD BEFORE THE END OF EARTHS PLANET   GOD WILL NOT ALLWAYS STRIVE

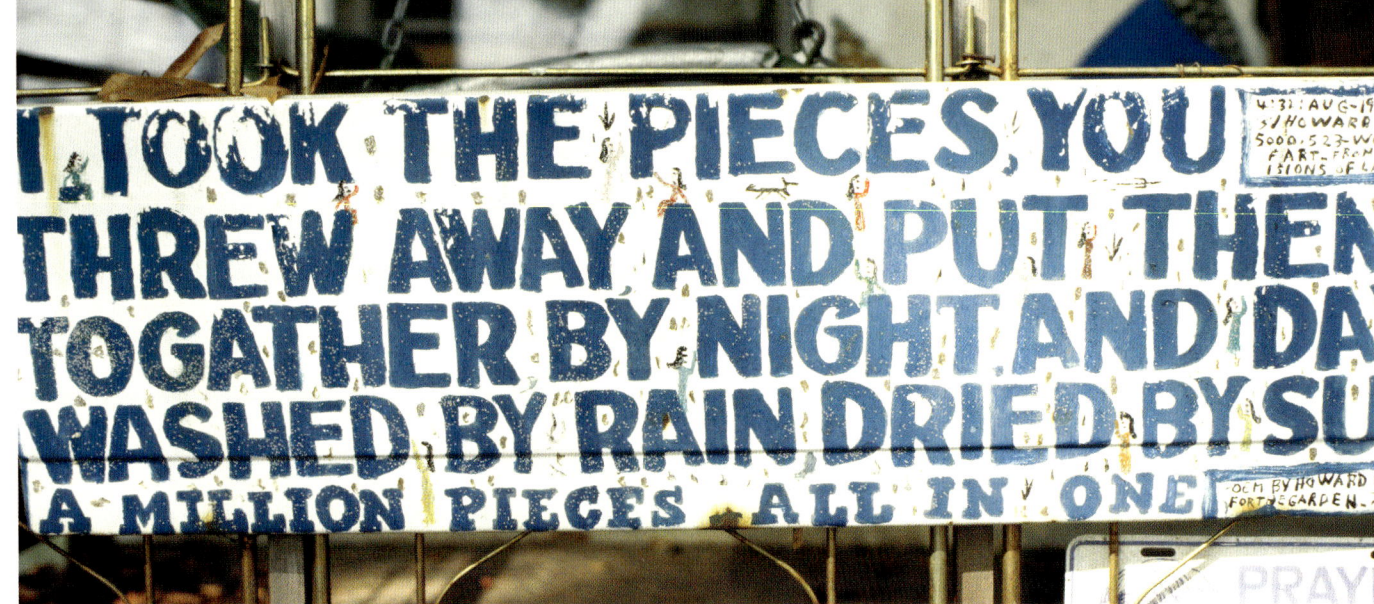

I TOOK THE PIECES YOU THREW AWAY AND PUT THEM TOGATHER BY NIGHT AND DAY WASHED BY RAIN DRIED BY SU A MILLION PIECES ALL IN ONE

MAIN TRAIL
THE RICHES OF GOD IS TO BELIEVE IN THE LORD JESUS CHRIST AND THOU SHALT BE SAVED. TODAY IS THE DAY

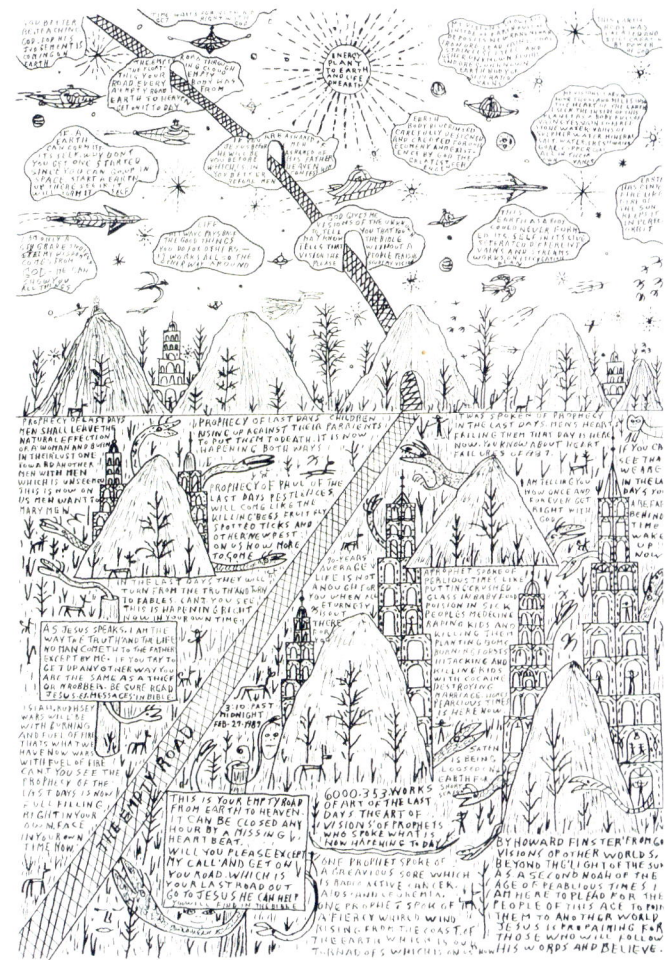

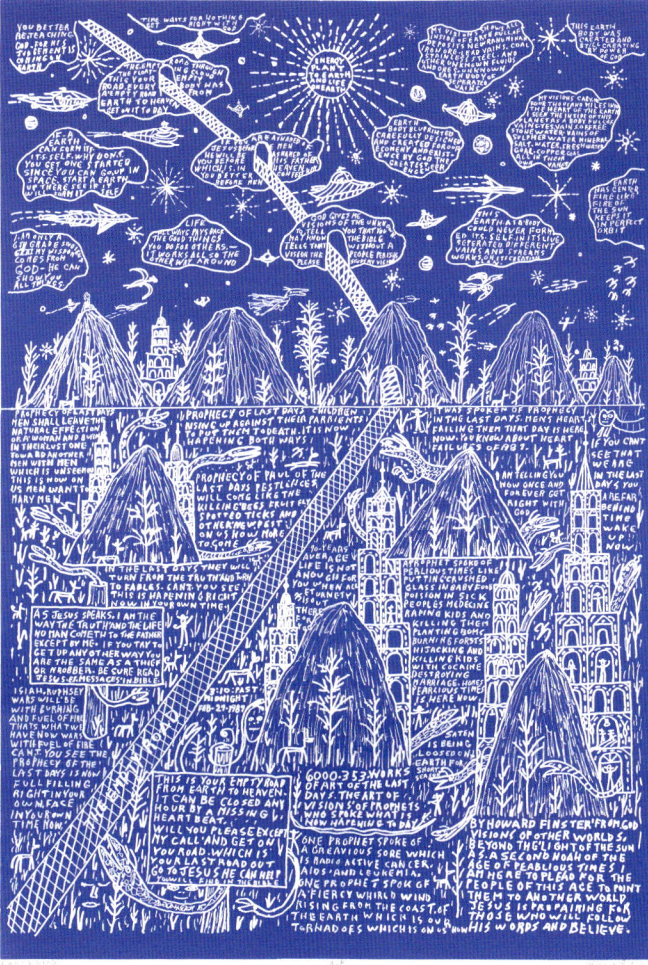

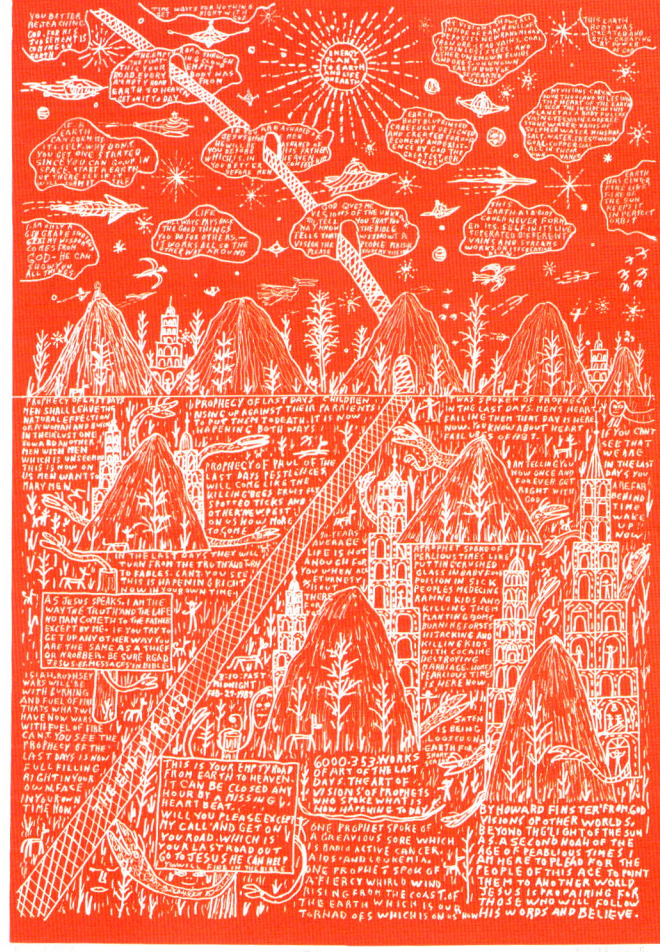

*Empty Road*, 1987, serigraph, 40.5 x 30 in. (102.87 x 76.2 cm), b&w edition of 150

*Empty Road*, 1987, serigraph, 40.5 x 30 in. (102.87 x 76.2 cm), blue edition 50, 10 artist's proofs

*Empty Road*, 1987, serigraph, 40.5 x 30 in. (102.87 x 76.2 cm), red edition 50, 10 artist's proofs

all found expression in Finster's lifelong project, philosophy, and work with and celebration of artists and creativity.

Finster believed the garden and his paintings to be directly inspired by God, and his work cannot be separated from his abiding dedication to spreading his religious messages and belief. In short, his call to preach was the center of his art and life. It provided meaning and motivation and supplied him with the communicative talents that made him the spokesperson and symbol of an art movement whose members were not noted for their gregariousness or social skills. It must be stressed and understood that Finster's religion was centered on caring communication; revelation, not damnation. He always emphasized Heaven and the possibility of perfection on Earth over Hell. Inquiry, interpretation, and investigation were integral to his preaching and process. Nowhere is this dedication more evident than in his approach to print making.[4]

[4] Finster had created prints before his workshop involvement — etchings at the University of Georgia, lithographs in Colorado, even early letterpress production of evangelical posters and tracts. He was fascinated by the various processes and captivated by their potential to spread his message more quickly and efficiently. His studio always had a vast array of offset black-and-white posters and cards offered as souvenirs and perfect for autographs. However, the limitations and complexities of adding color and large amounts of handwritten text to negative/positive printing surfaces ultimately led to frustration with intaglio and both fine-art and mass-production lithography.

[5] Ann Oppenhimer, "Art Works Presented to Museums," *Folk Art Messenger*, Winter 2002, p. 19.

[6] Camera crews from MTV, TBS, and other stations from around the world became regular garden visitors. When we chaperoned Finster to the 1992 Virginia Film Festival his crowds rivaled those of his fellow attendees Sidney Poitier and Robert Duvall.

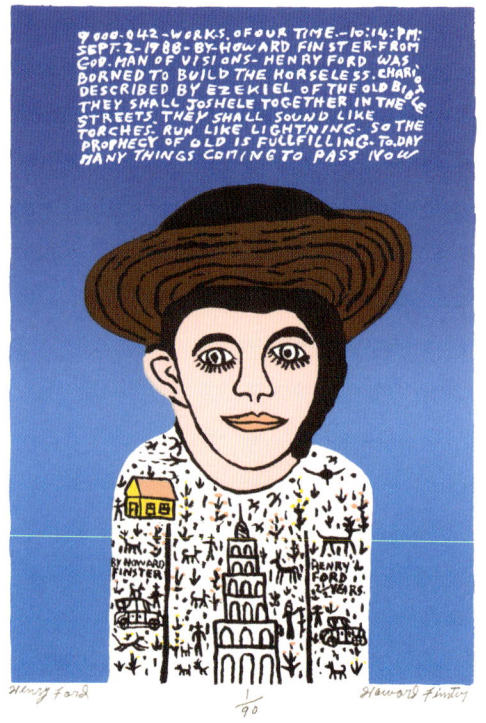

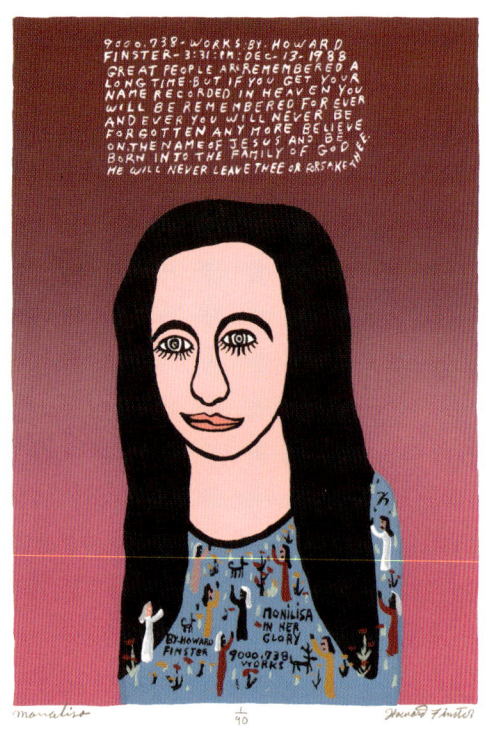

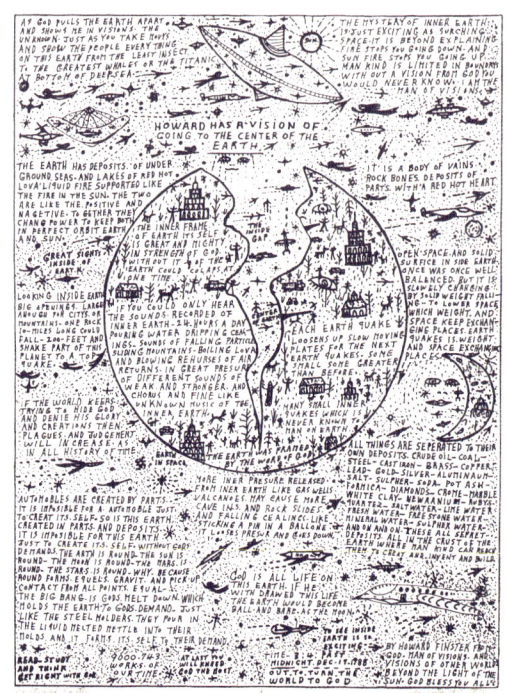

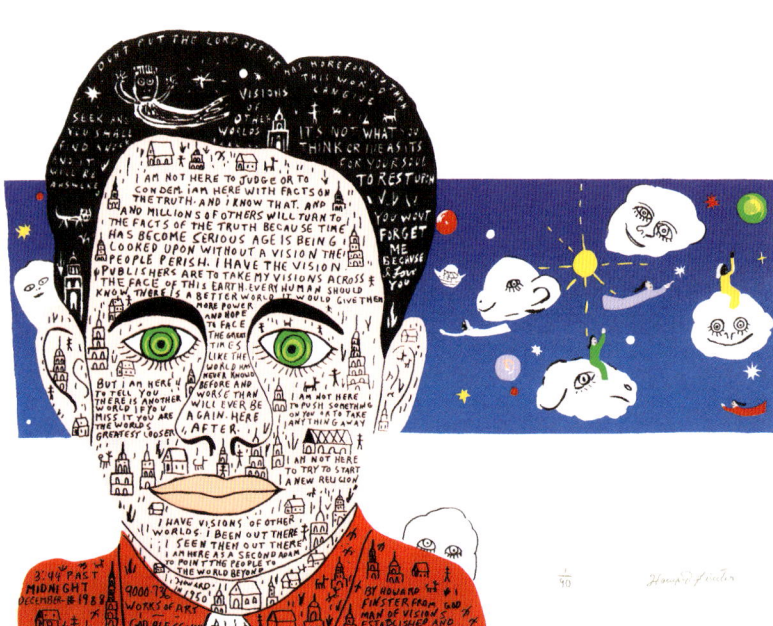

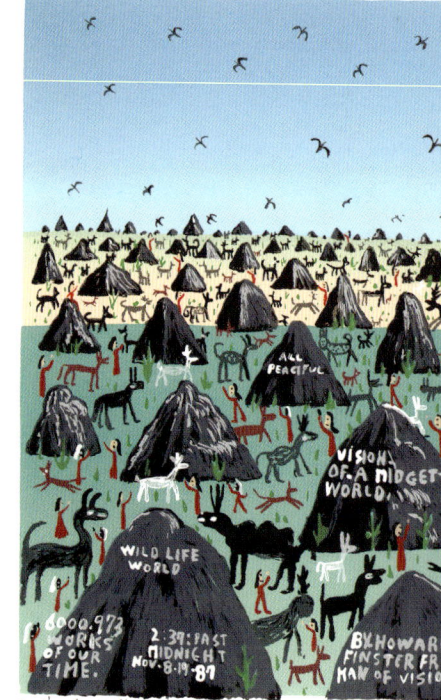

*Empty Road*, his first multiple produced with Mountain Lake, began as a lithograph but was quickly (if laboriously) converted to a serigraph available in three colors. Howard called this print "just about the most beautiful thing I ever made."[5] Finster quickly ascertained and was delighted by the increased size and color possibilities (blends and spot colors true to his tractor- enamel hues) offered by the silk screen. The ease of text application in a positive/positive surface transfer led him to fully embrace the medium. Always a quick study, Finster needed only three prints to fully comprehend the design and printing process. Across an eight-year period, conceptualizing and designing in Georgia, printing in Roanoke, Virginia, Finster and Mountain Lake produced thirteen fully original, hand-executed editions that explored the full range of Finster's vision and the serigraph process.

The print project as originally conceived served two purposes. The first, the creation of unique works of art via the introduction

Boxed Set of five serigraphs, 1988, each 22 x 17 in. (55.88 x 43.18 cm), edition 90, 10 artist's proofs

(clockwise from upper left) *Henry Ford, Mona Lisa, Center of Earth, Howard in 1950, Animal World*

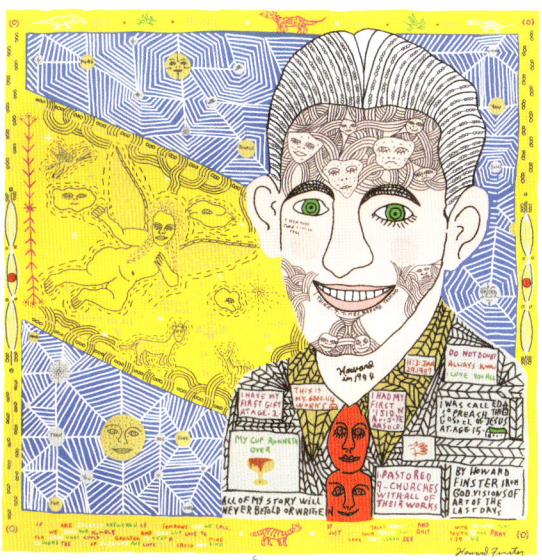

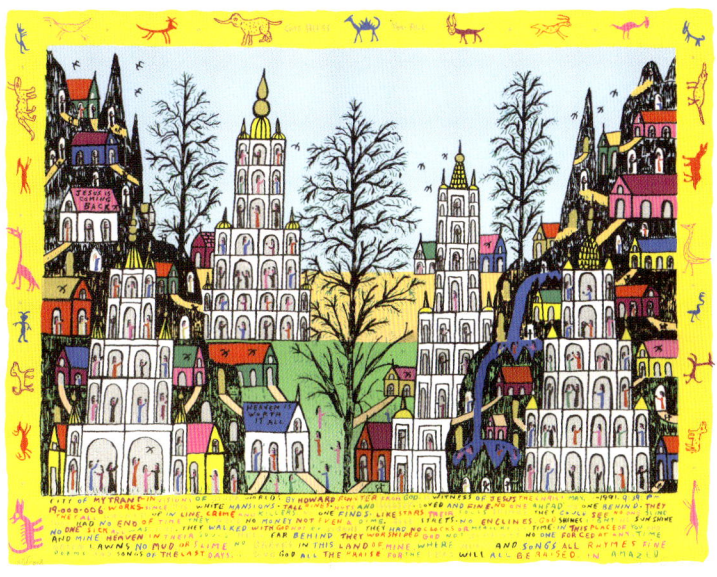

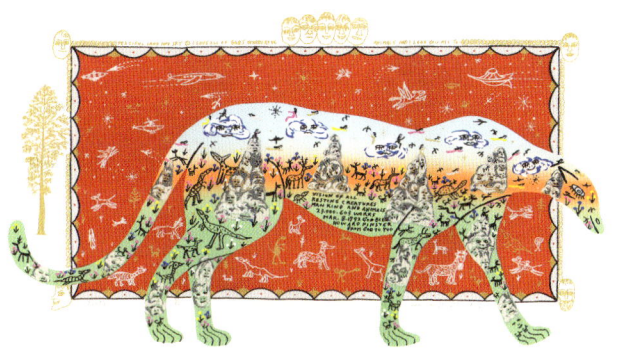

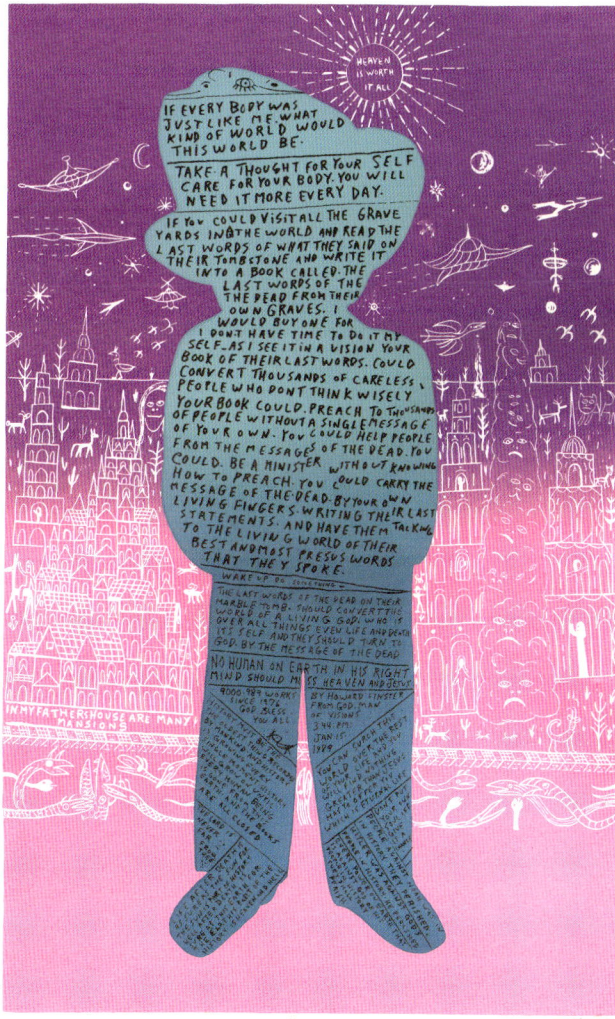

to and mastery of yet another "trade" for Finster, achieved splendid results. The second, freeing Finster from his perceived (by us) economic dependence on producing a steady stream of smaller production pieces to concentrate on what we considered his more important larger-scale paintings and the continuation of the garden, proved more difficult and complex than we imagined. As Finster's pop cultural star ascended,[6] his numeric art production increased commensurately. Many have quite reasonably and effectively argued that this increased output, simplification, and reliance on what Finster had once termed "souvenir" art in order to meet his ever-increasing demand negatively affected his work and reputation. He was still capable of producing great art. The final Mountain Lake print project (completed in 1995) involved him drawing improvisationally on each print. Some prints were altered so extensively that they were placed in a separate edition, an approach that was entirely

Finster's idea. While such moments of explosive creativity dwindled as Finster approached the new millennium and entered his eighties (a phenomenon not unseen in other artists), our frustration with the assembly line ignored the reality that Finster reveled in what he viewed as an enormous opportunity to more efficiently spread his vision across the country and around the world.

Ultimately it is all part of Howard Finster's extraordinary story — a celebration of life-affirming, superabundant artistry and vision that propelled a "simple man with a sixth grade education" into "the stranger from another world" whose warmth melted the often cynical icy veneer of the '80s art world and cemented his place as one of the late twentieth century's most celebrated and influential artists. It is a story in which the Mountain Lake Worshop played a small part

(clockwise from top)
*Howard in 1944*, serigraph, 1993-94, 30 x 30 in. (76.2 x 76.2 cm), edition 90 (75 completed with hand drawing, 15 heavily re-worked by hand and annotated with letters AO)
*City of Mytrant*, 1991, serigraph, 30 x 38 in. (76.2 x 96.52 cm), edition 90, 10 artist's proofs
*Cheetah*, 1992, serigraph, 24 x 40 in. (60.96 x 101.6 cm), edition 90, 10 artist's proofs
*Elvis at 3 & 1/2*, 1989, serigraph, 32 x 25 in. (81.28 x 63.5 cm), edition 90, 10 artist's proofs

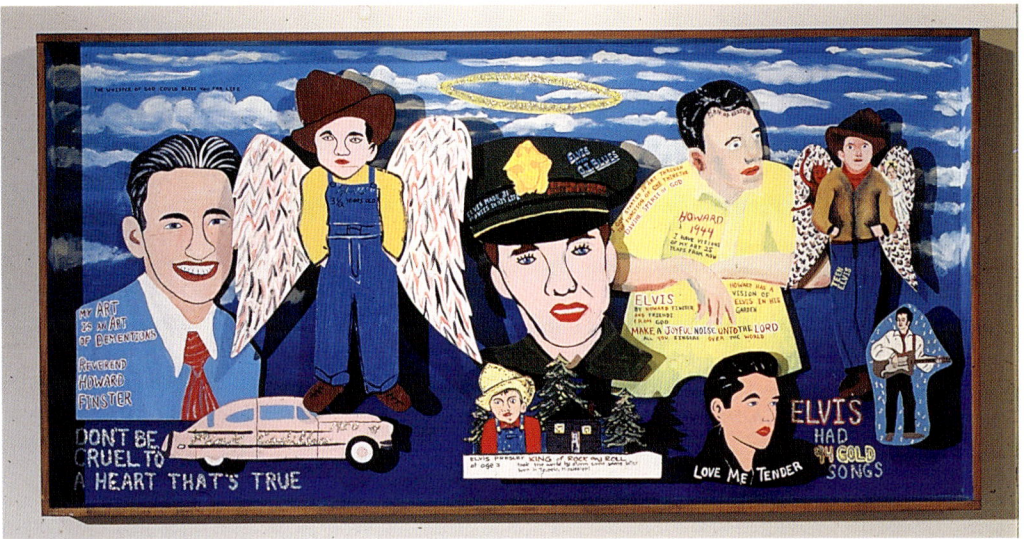

Howard Finster, *Elvis Had 94 Gold Songs*, 1985, oil paint on wood, assemblage of "dementions," 41 x 82 x 4.5 in. (104.14 x 208.28 x 12.06 cm). Collection Taubman Museum of Art, Roanoke

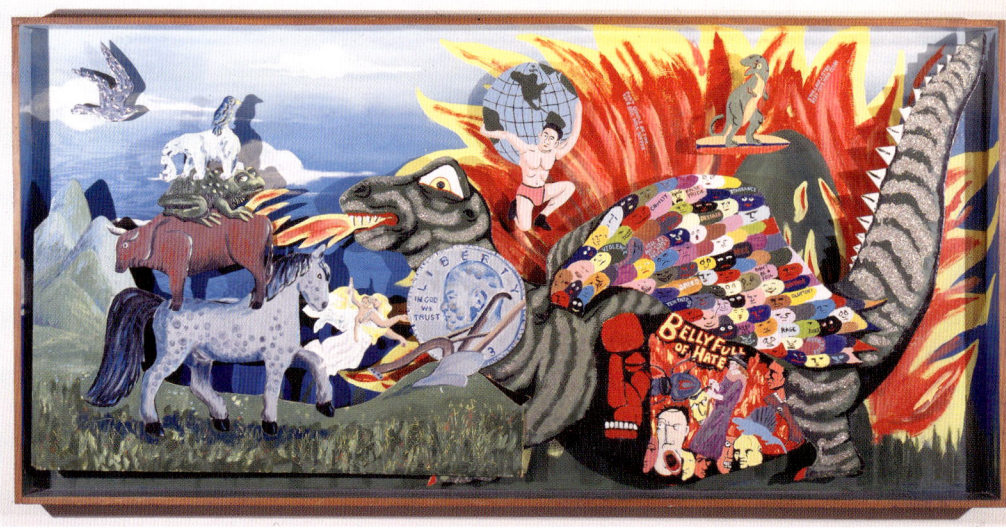

Howard Finster, *Belly Full of Hate*, 1985, oil paint on wood, assemblage of "dementions,", 47 x 98 x 4 3/4 in. (119.38 x 248.92 x 12.06 cm). Collection Taubman Museum of Art, Roanoke

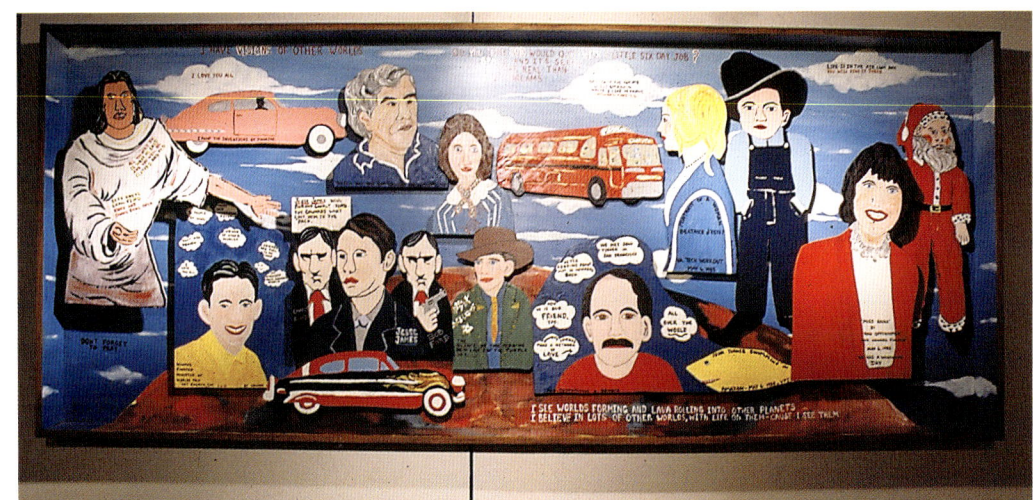

Howard Finster, *I Have Visions of Other Worlds*, 1985, oil paint on wood, assemblage of "dementions," 41 x 98 x 4.5 in. (104.14 x 248.92 x 12.06 cm). Collection Taubman Museum of Art, Roanoke

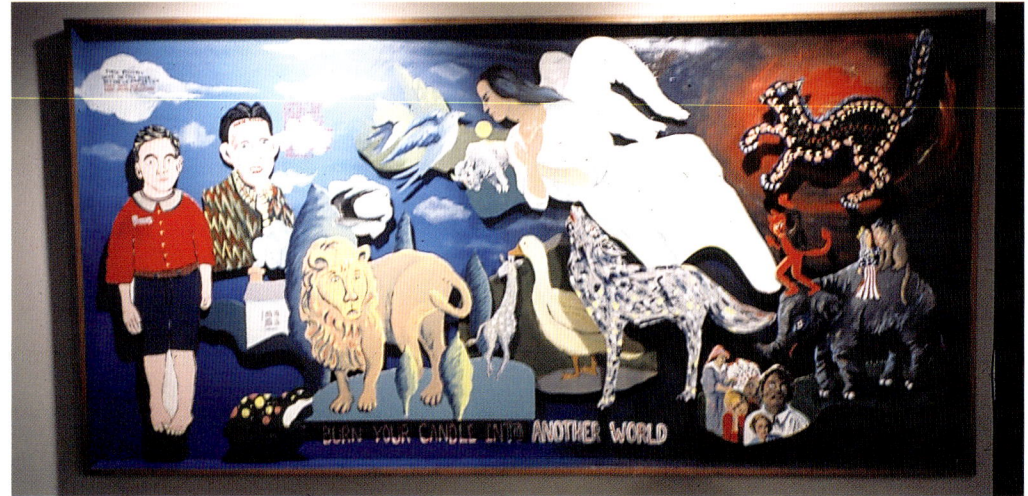

Howard Finster, *Burn Your Candle Into Another World*, 1985, oil paint on wood, assemblage of "dementions," 49 x 98 x 4 3/4 in. (124.46 x 248.92 x 12.06 cm). Collection Taubman Museum of Art, Roanoke

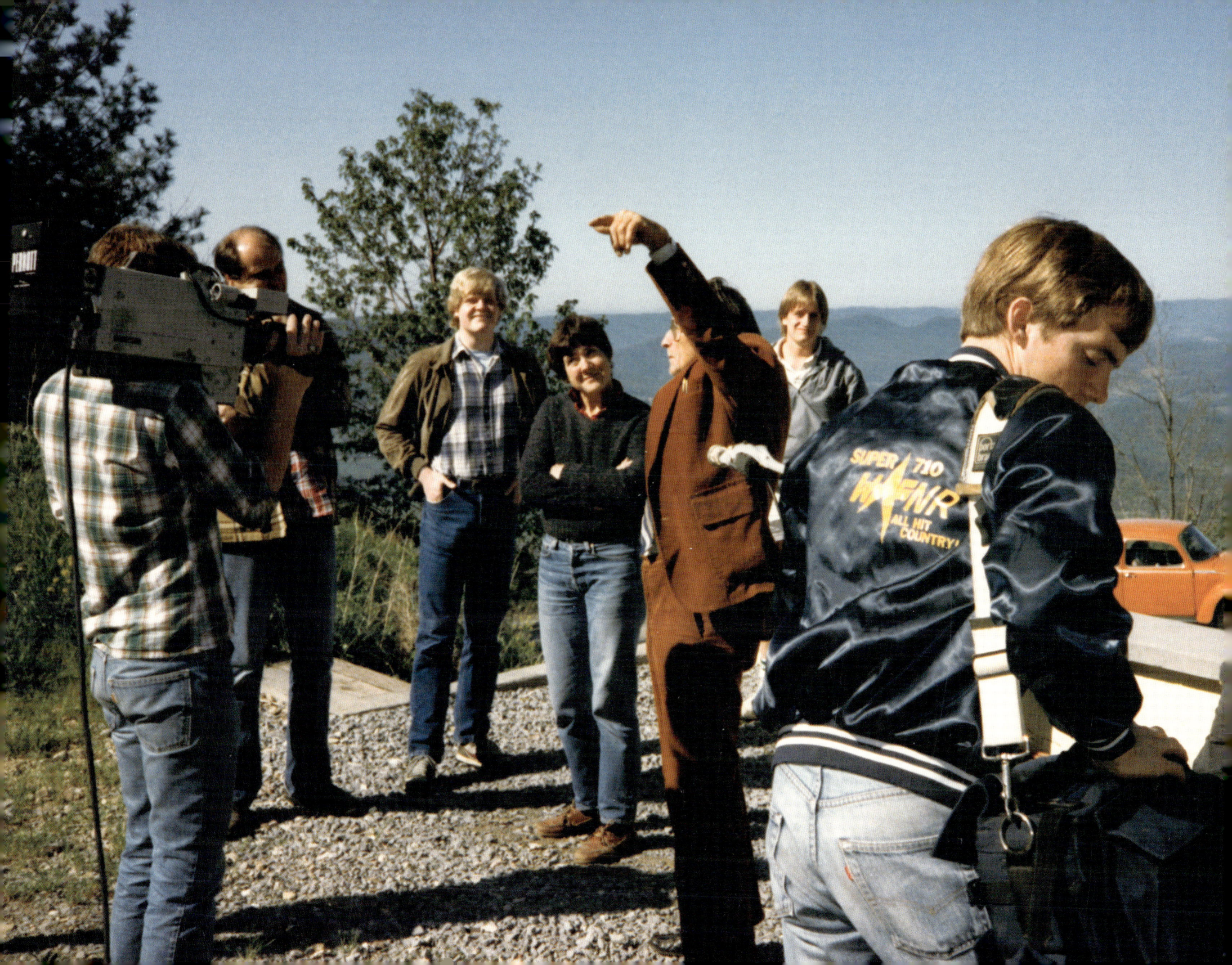

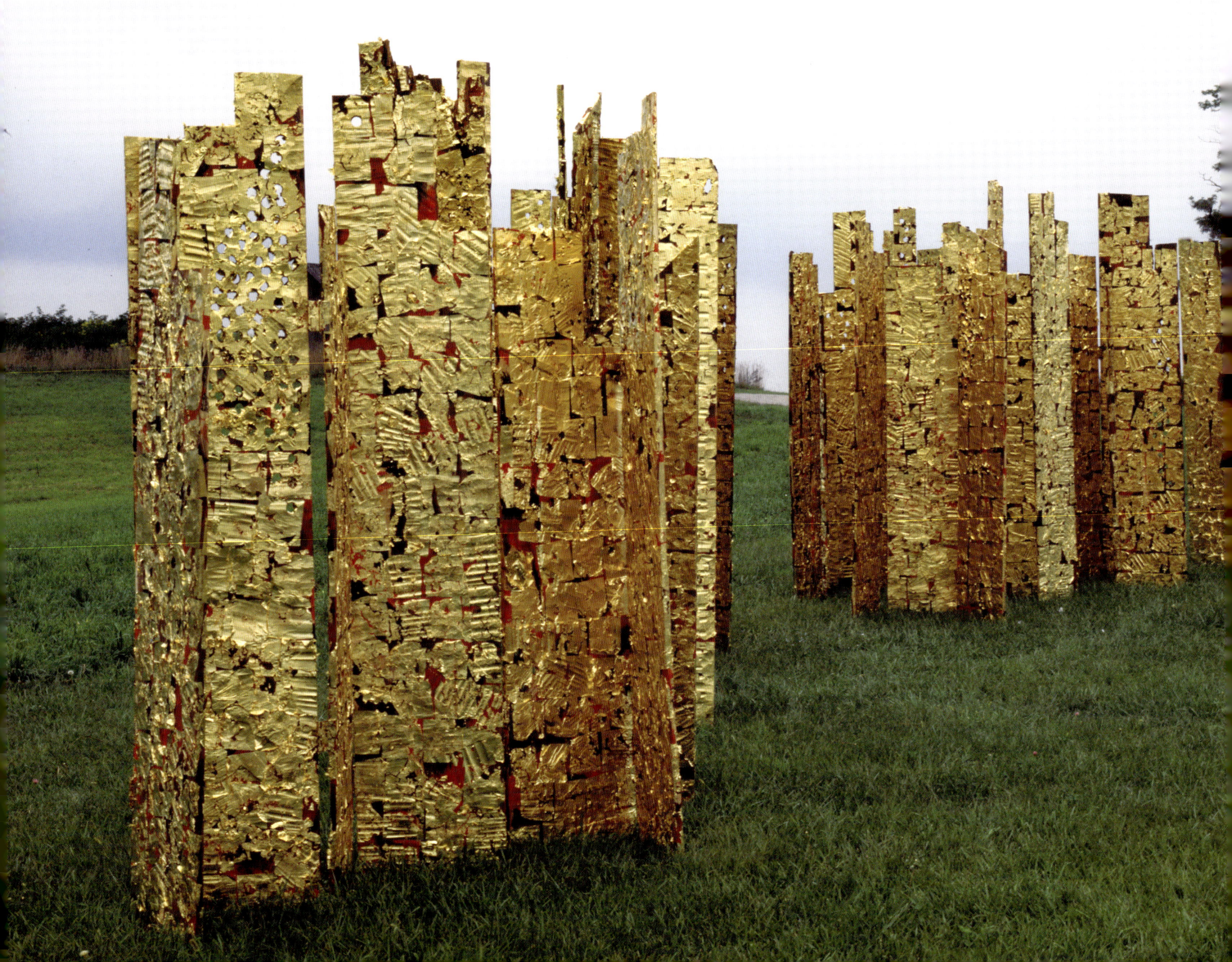

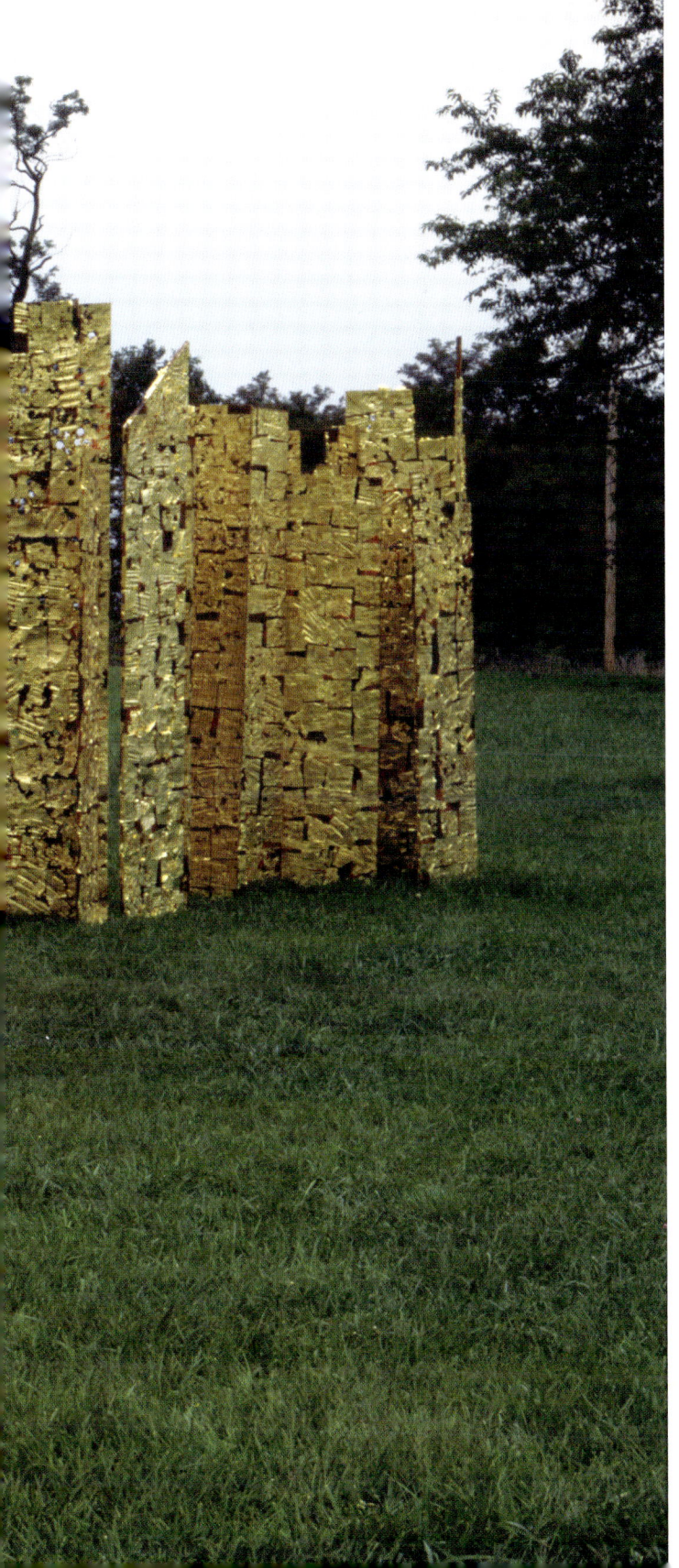

# V

## *Jiro Okura:*
## *Connecting Cultures*

# JIRO OKURA'S *MOUNTAIN LAKE SCREEN TACHI*, "THE MOVABLE WALL BETWEEN CULTURES," 1990

HOWARD RISATTI

Shinto ceremonial forest altar with offerings and traditional artifacts

Paintings from John Cage's 1988 workshop were shown in the fall of that year in an exhibition organized by Julia Boyd of the Virginia Museum of Fine Arts in Richmond. The exhibition opened in Richmond in October, traveled to various other venues in Virginia, and made its final stop at The Phillips Collection in Washington, D.C., in the spring of 1990.[1] When Kyoto-based "minimalist" sculptor Jiro Okura saw reproductions of the works in the exhibition catalogue, he was deeply moved. He already had been influenced by Cage's ideas about chance and indeterminacy, ideas that derived, in part, from Japanese Zen philosophy. Because the ideas in his own work shared an affinity with those of the Mountain Lake programs, after much discussion and planning, he was invited to be a guest artist in a collaborative workshop project.[2] Somehow it seems entirely fitting that Okura's "chance" viewing of the catalogue *John Cage/New River Watercolors* should lead him to Mountain Lake, where he eventually conducted workshops in 1990, 1992, and 1993.

The focus of Okura's workshops developed out of his deep respect for natural materials, especially wood. This respect is based on an understanding of the relationship between nature as an environment of material substance having physical location and nature as a concept of pure space. For Okura, substance and space acquire a sense of plenitude when the self grasps this relationship, which wood (or any other natural material) can symbolize if treated properly. Okura's ideas, which are expressed by his treatment of wood, are manifested in Eastern (Asian) belief systems through ritual practices that allow for chance and indeterminacy in the processing of materials. Obviously, such ideas paralleled the Mountain Lake conception

of the self and locale as related manifestations of both natural as well as psychic forces.

Okura began to use wood as a sculptural material after a momentous visit to the United States in 1969, several years after he completed a postgraduate course at Kyoto Kyoiku University. As he recalled, in his youth he had studied and trained in a Zen temple trying without success to attain what Zen Buddhism calls a "pure emptiness" of spirit. That pure emptiness of spirit came only years later while he was driving across the vast, empty expanses of desert in Arizona and New Mexico. Soon after his return to Japan, a carpenter in his neighborhood unexpectedly gave him a piece of wood, camphor laurel. He hadn't been thinking of making anything out of wood and, moreover, he didn't know the first thing about wood carving or carpentry. As he began working with this piece of wood, all this changed: "I was hooked on wood. By working with wood, I discovered a way to confirm not only my own existence, but also the vast presence of nature, of the entire cosmos, surrounding me."[3] In this piece of wood his experience of vast, empty space was fused with material substance into a powerful metaphor for a consciousness of existence.

Because Okura's Zen-like discovery of the symbolic importance of wood came after his fortuitous visit to America, it is hardly surprising that he would want to continue working with wood when he came to Mountain Lake. During the first week of January, 1990, eight black walnut trees from the Jefferson National Forest at Little Stone Mountain in Wise County, Virginia, were selected to be cut for the workshop.[4] This was done in cooperation with members of the local community, including the U.S. Forest Service, Louisiana-Pacific Corporation, and the Brooks Forest Products Center at Virginia Tech University. Black walnut was chosen because it is a wood very like zelkova, Japanese gray-bark elm, which is traditionally used for sacred objects in Japan.

Before the trees were cut, however, arrangements were made by special permission from the Ujigami Shrine near Okura's home

---

[1] The exhibition came about when Julia Boyd, a curator at the Virginia Museum, mentioned an opening in their fall exhibition schedule. I suggested the Cage paintings would make a very interesting exhibition. *The New River Watercolors* were shown at the Virginia Museum from 25 October to 27 November 1988. Subsequently, they were exhibited at the Flossie Martin Gallery at Radford University from 18 January to 17 February 1989, The Art Museum of Western Virginia, Roanoke, from 13 May to 16 July 1989, and finally, The Phillips Collection in Washington, D.C., from 14 April to 20 May 1990.

[2] It should be stressed that the arrangement of the workshop was the result of an impressive inter-cultural collaborative effort in itself, one that involved Okura's American sponsors — Joanne Wise of the Wise Collection in New York; Washington, D.C., curator Jane Farmer; and, of course, Ray Kass from Mountain Lake.

[3] Jiro Okura, "Artist's Statement" in the exhibition catalogue for *Jiro Okura: Wood, Paper, Water*, Sasakawa Peace Foundation USA Gallery, Washington, D.C., 29 March–31 May 1996, n.p.

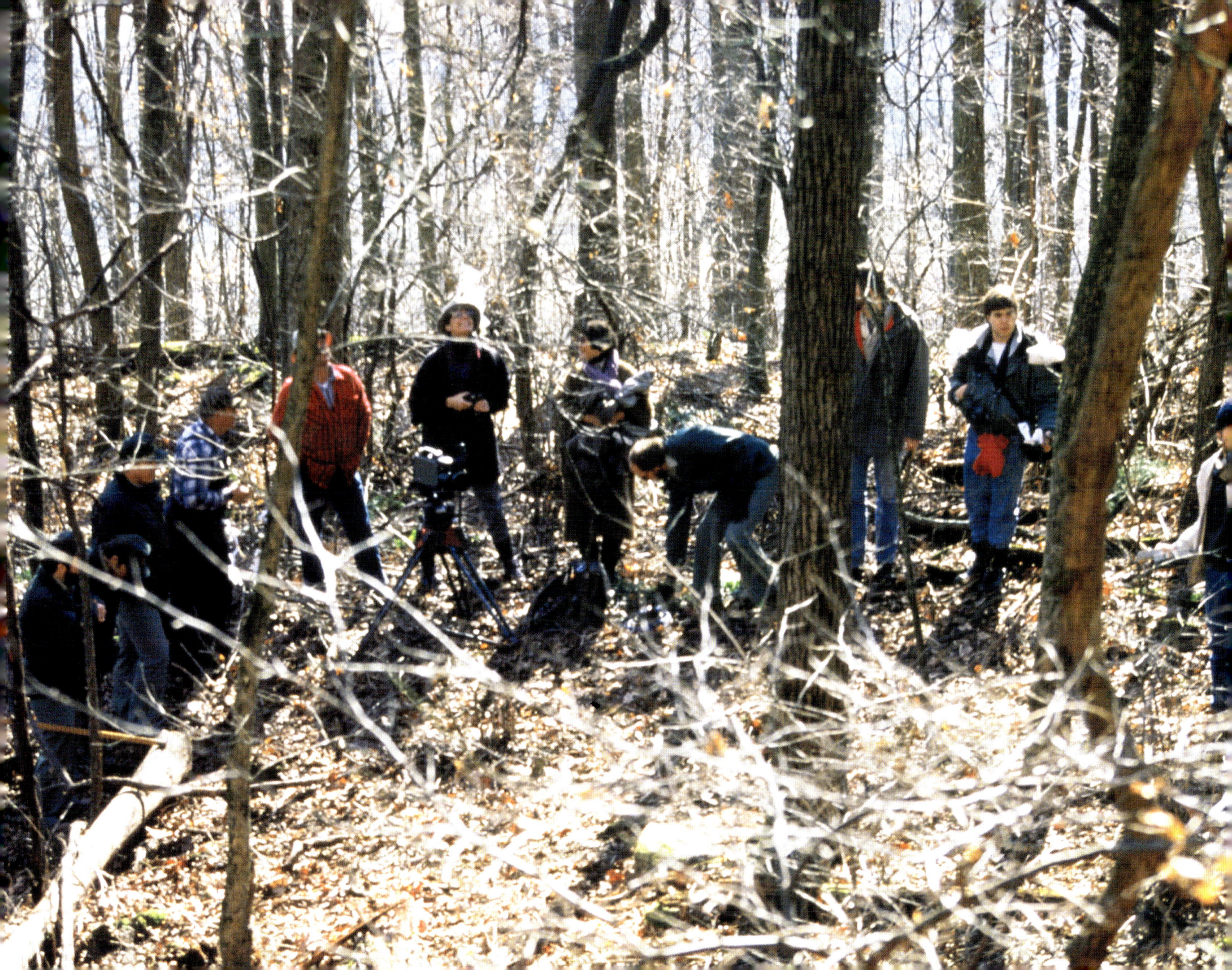

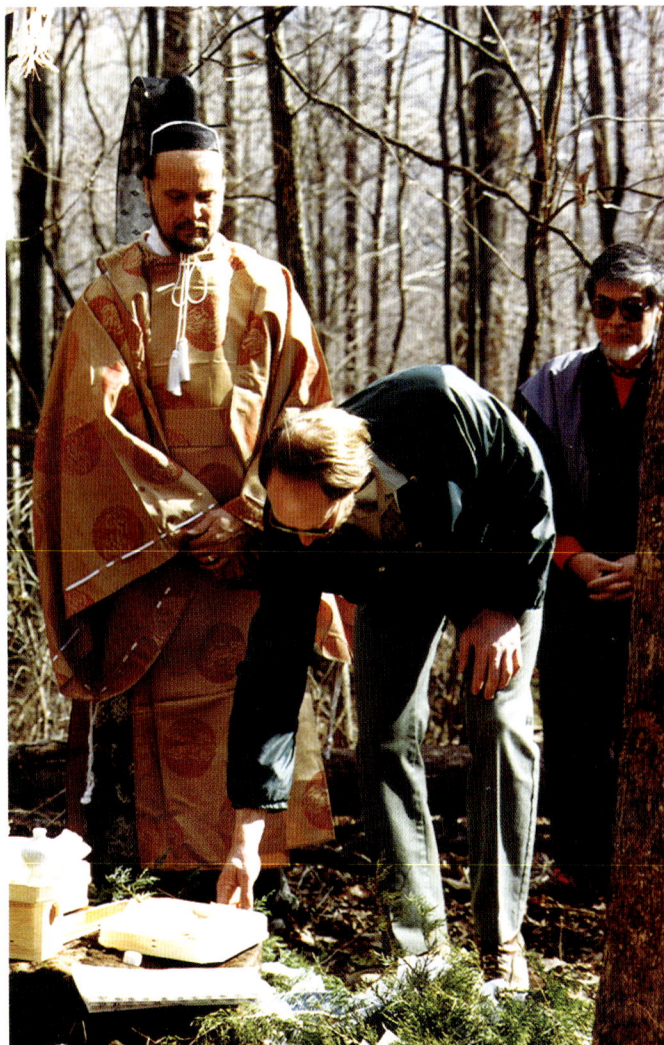

(left) Ray Kass wearing traditional Shinto priest vestments to conduct the "Forest Blessing Ceremony" on Little Stone Mountain in Wise County, Virginia

in Uji City, Kyoto Prefecture, to perform a traditional Shinto ceremony in the Virginia woods. According to Shinto beliefs, trees in nature are understood as a part of the "universe outside"; once they are cut for the artist to use, they become part of the artist's "universe within." A blessing honors the living spirit of the trees and releases this spirit to the artist to make something beautiful.

In accordance with these beliefs, Mountain Lake Director Ray Kass, in the role of a *kanushi* (a Shinto monk), donned full Shinto ceremonial robes and before a small audience including workshop participants, Forest Service officials, lumberjack Roger Bolling, and Okura himself, recited prayers in Japanese that had been especially prepared by the Shinto priests at Uji for the ceremony. Using a large, flat rock as an altar, he offered natural foods, sake, and water in a traditional Shinto ceremony of blessing.

The trees were cut following this ceremony emphasizing the sacredness of all nature and the interconnectedness of the living spirit inside of all things. They were then hauled to the Brooks Forest Products Center, where they were sawn into boards and left to cure until mid-summer when Okura would come back to Mountain Lake for the actual creation of the piece during the workshop.

From the Shinto ceremony used to bless and cut the trees, it became immediately clear that the workshop project would entail a cross-cultural orientation. A central consideration for the project would be the relationship between ecological responsibility and Eastern belief systems, traditional and contemporary sculpture

methods, and prescribed practices and the indeterminism of both materials and process favored at Mountain Lake.[5]

Upon returning from Japan in late July, Okura began working with about sixty members of the local community over what would turn out to be a seven-week period to complete the project. While intentionally exerting some control over them, he gave the participants a specific number of physical operations to perform on the boards after they had been glued together into four-board panels, sixteen in all. Each participant could perform these operations in a manner and location he or she judged appropriate, included planing, chiseling, gouging, drilling, and sanding. Carrying out these repetitive operations using both modern power tools and ancient Japanese hand tools, the participants slowly gained an appreciation for Okura's own working methods and his acceptance of indeterminacy and accidental effects. The length of time involved in laboriously working the wood with hand tools

[4] The trees to be cut were of pulp rather than milling quality because Kass and Okura were concerned with preserving the most valuable forest resources. Forest Ranger Chuck Sobaities arranged for permission to cut the trees and enlisted the help of Roger Bolling, who was Virginia's "lumberjack of the year" in 1989.

[5] Jerrie Pike, "Jiro Okura Exhibition — Roanoke Museum," *New Art Examiner* (June/Summer 1991).

and small power tools also gave the participants a feel for the wood's natural aspects, its randomness and its material substance.

Okura believes that the repetitiveness of the work offered a way of getting beyond preconceptions into a more random mode of working, a mode "without mind" (i.e., without total conscious control and planning). Doing something over and over is, for Okura, a kind of bodily (rather than verbal) "chanting" that induces a meditative state and clears the mind so one can find the universe that's inside oneself, the artistic spirit that will create the work.[6]

As the participants worked on the project, they came to understand how the creation of a work of art entails a dialogue among many forces. Their individual and combined actions could be seen as a kind of dialogue at the personal and communal levels, while the desire for control through the use of tools and the resistance of the physical properties of the material could be seen as a dialogue between the "self within" and the "world outside." To accept this dialogue between what can be called the "universe within" and the "universe outside" as part of the creative process is to acknowledge the existence of the individual self and a collaborative self that are fundamental concepts for any sense of community.

After the participants carried out these repetitive, physically taxing operations, these "bodily chants, as it were, they worked with Okura painting spontaneous calligraphic brush strokes in black and orange-red pigment on the boards. This completed, gold leaf was then loosely glued to the boards. Covered with

this gilding and colors traditionally associated with Japanese temples, the boards were then hinged and assembled as four-board sections into sixteen separate units; these units, which stand independently with space between them, form a large folding screen approximately 10 feet high and 120 feet long that Okura titled the *Mountain Lake Screen Tachi*.

The traditional Asian screen is understood by Okura as an elemental architectonic form that creates distinct physical spaces by defining and dividing space into discrete, controllable areas. *Screen Tachi*, however, with its drill holes, loose unit construction, and separations, articulates space, making the idea of vast, empty space comprehensible. And, because its units can be relocated and repositioned into new configurations at will, *Screen Tachi* conceptually transcends the limits of actual physical space plotted by the traditional, architectonic screen; it thereby symbolically opens up the vast and potent space of consciousness of the self in relation to all of nature.

⁶ Okura catalogue, Sasakawa Peace Foundation exhibition, n.p.

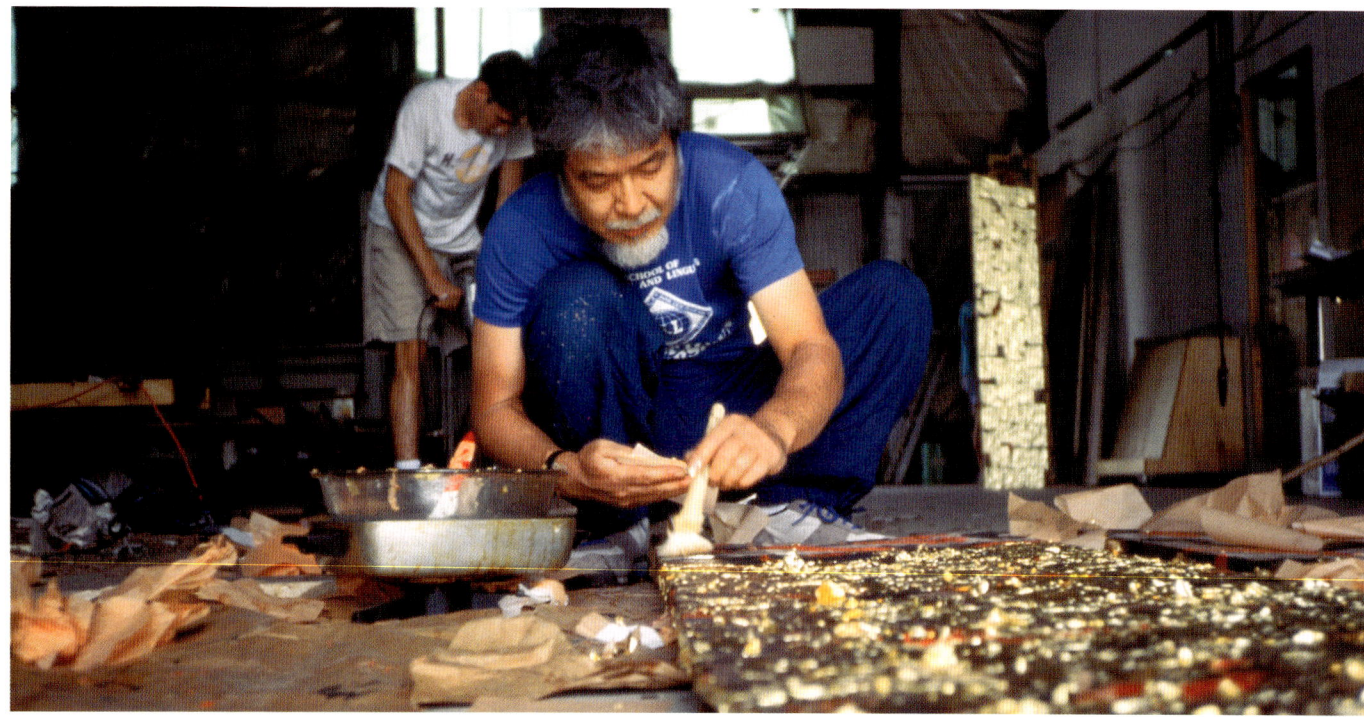

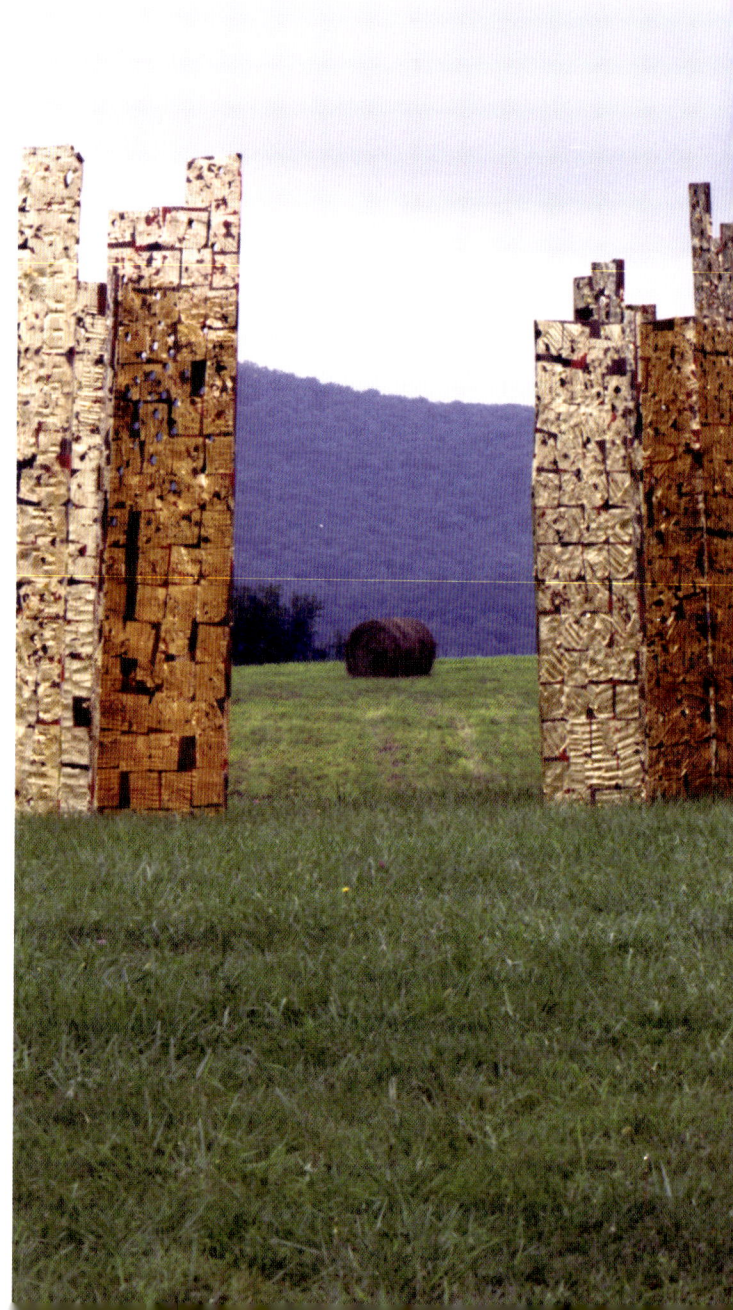

Glittering and shimmering in response to the least change in light or movement of air, *Screen Tachi* connects traditional Japanese art to modern Western sculpture in its acceptance of indeterminacy, randomness of appearance, and accidental effects. It also connects traditional Shinto beliefs to the modern ecology movement in the way the ritual and sacred aspects of its construction exhibit a reverence and respect for nature. In these ways, *Screen Tachi* spans the gap between tradition and modernity, becoming what Okura calls "the movable wall between Eastern and Western cultures." The collaborative efforts which brought it into existence underscore the need for a concept of communal and social action based on a philosophical understanding of our relationship to nature and to place.

In May of 1990, just a few weeks before Okura was to return to Mountain Lake from Japan to begin working on the boards that would eventually become *Screen Tachi*, John Cage was completing his second workshop. Cage took an avid interest

in the Mountain Lake projects of both Howard Finster and Okura. The Shinto ceremony held in preparation for cutting the walnut trees for Okura's workshop was particularly meaningful to Cage. The workshop participants encouraged Cage to make a special painting for Okura as a symbolic gift to welcome him to Mountain Lake. On paper that had been smoked in the manner of Cage's other workshops, Cage painted around the very same rock used as an altar for Okura's Shinto ceremony in early January. "*Gift*"(*for Jiro Okura*) is an extraordinarily haunting and poetic painting containing, in its lower half, a broadly painted outline of the altar rock floating within a smoky field. This painting, with its "afterimage" of the altar, represents a tangible connection between the aesthetic and philosophical beliefs of Cage and Okura and was officially presented to Okura at the completion of the "movable wall." As much as anything else, this painting expresses the spirit of collaboration and friendship that has surrounded the projects. It also demonstrates the intimate linkage — at the personal, artistic, and philosophical level — among the various workshops.

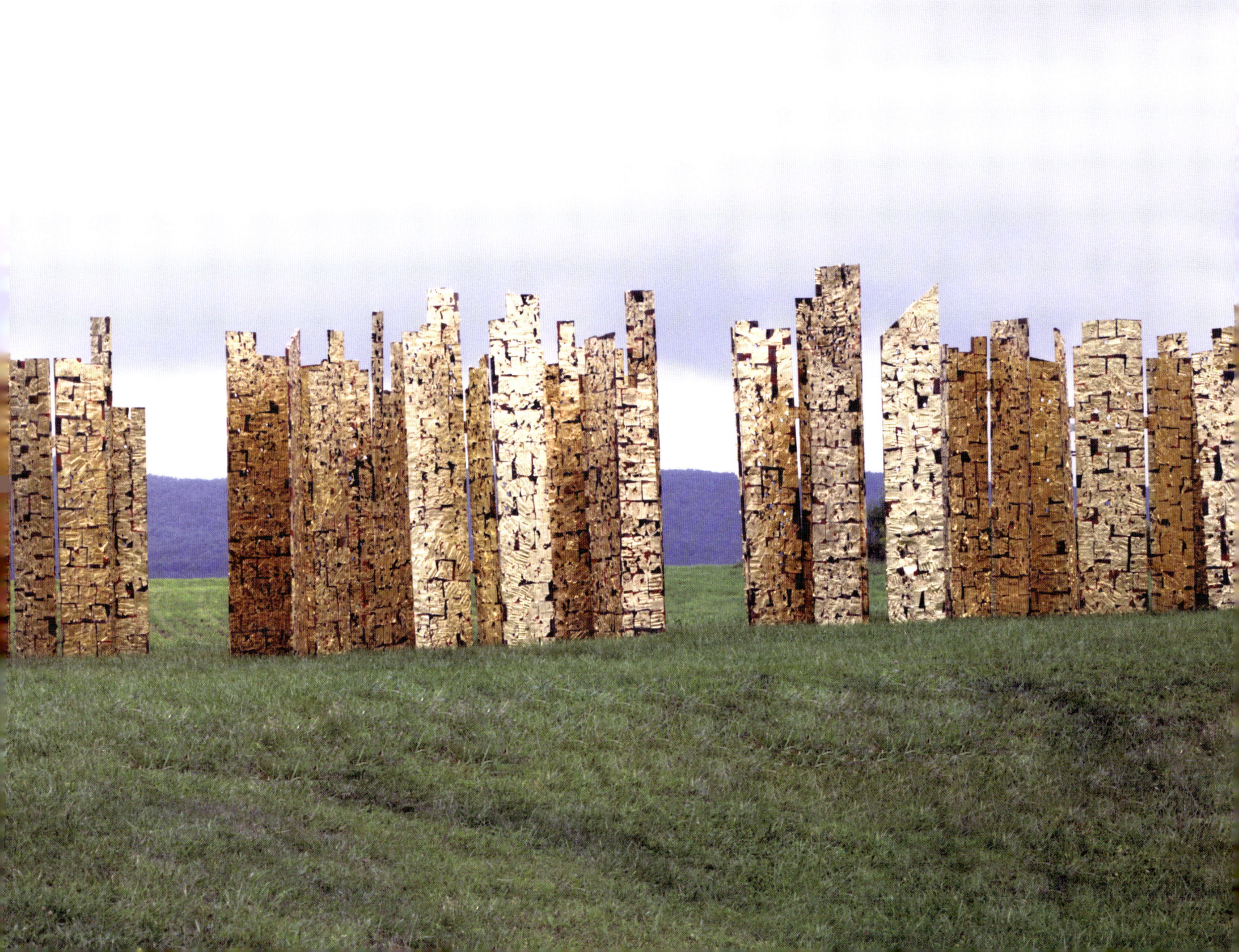

# OKURA'S 1992 SHISENDO GARDEN PAINTINGS: "BREATHING LINES"

HOWARD RISATTI

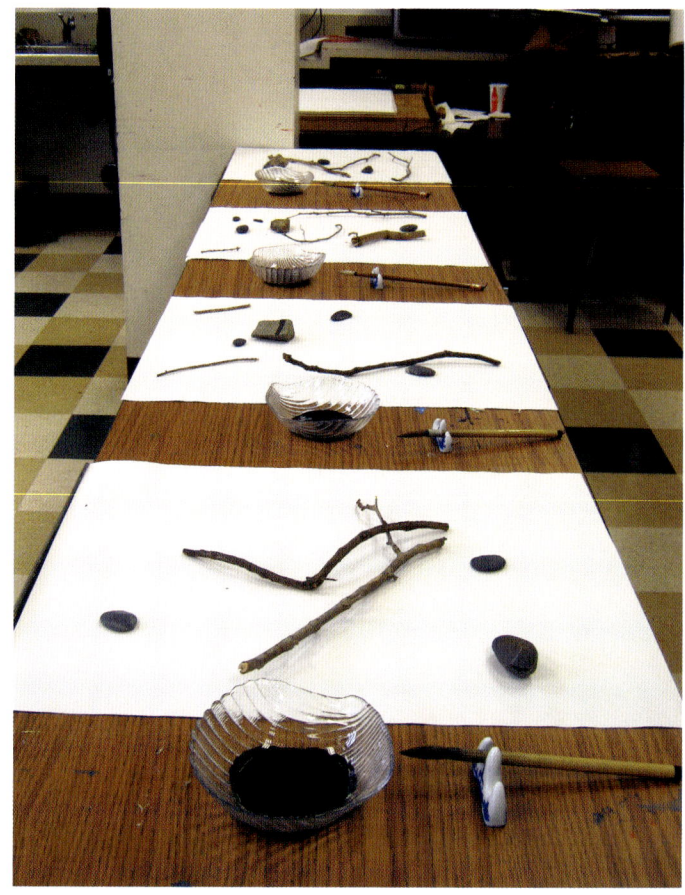

(right) Workshop participants at the College of William and Mary, 1993

In August of 1992, Okura returned to Mountain Lake to do a second workshop, this time on ink drawing.[1] The previous year, inspired by Cage's Mountain Lake paintings, Okura had done a series of drawings using a technique he had developed based on traditional Japanese Zen *sumi-e* (monochrome) ink painting. Echoing Cage's process of painting around stones, he painted long, undulating lines interrupted by leaves, twigs, or pebbles that had been placed on the paper. He called these works "Shisendo Garden Drawings" after the small garden in the Shisendo Temple in Kyoto. Like the more famous garden at Ryoanji, this garden is also a Zen-style rock garden; it was designed and built by Ishi Kawa Jozan in the seventeenth century as a personal retreat in which to meditate upon nature. Frequently visited by the poet and haiku master Matsuo Basho (1644–1694), it is a dry-landscape garden with its simple, open space visible from a small room especially designed so that visitors could gather in the autumn to watch the leaves from a lone tree fall onto the undulating pattern of carefully raked gravel.

To adapt Okura's *sumi-e*–derived technique to the collaborative workshop process, the notion that "it doesn't matter who holds the brush" was adopted for this workshop.[2] Members of the community, after rehearsal, painted with Okura using various inks and traditional Japanese brushes on paper. Imitating the artist's initial vertical brush stroke that changed width in a predictable rhythmic pattern of thick and thin, participants followed each other in painting a "matching" parallel stroke that fit into the pattern of the previous stroke. Concentrating upon this repetitive action was a kind of "bodily chanting" that cleared the mind, opening it up to a meditative state. As this painting process was unfolding, participants were placing objects such as branches and stones at random on the paper. These objects — chosen to symbolize nature — left their ghostly "traces," their "afterimages," as negative shapes among the linear brush strokes they interrupted. In the larger works, as the paper was being painted, it was slowly unrolled from one end and rolled up at the other so that the final patterning of landscape traces could not be dictated by personal taste, but would be a result of chance.

While the workshop was underway, word arrived that Cage had suddenly died. As a memorial to him, a piece of smoked paper remaining from Cage's previous workshop was painted in white tempera, gold and *sumi* ink, and gold pigment.[3] The painting, the *Untitled, Shisendo Garden Series (For John Cage)*, one of several produced on the spot in spontaneous homage to Cage remains as a special gesture to his spirit. Its autumnal quality of shimmering silver light is an acknowledgment that Cage's spirit infused the workshops with a sense of generosity and sharing. Cage's earlier painting around the Shinto ceremonial rock used on Little Stone Mountain, *"Gift" (for Jiro Okura)*, reflects the same remarkable spirit and the warm artistic friendships that developed at Mountain Lake.

---

[1] Okura would also do a third workshop using these techniques for an April 1993 exhibition of the Mountain Lake Workshops at the Muscarelle Museum of Art, College of William and Mary, Williamsburg, Virginia.

[2] In his 1985 Mountain Lake workshop, Howard Finster claimed that, since tracing images would take them out of society and make them a part of the self, it didn't matter who did the tracing or who made the painting using them. That "it didn't matter who held the brush" became one of the central ideas of the Mountain Lake workshops.

[3] At the time of Cage's rather sudden death at age 79 on the 12th of August, 1992, paper was being fired and smoked for his next workshop; this paper was subsequently used in Okura's ongoing workshop.

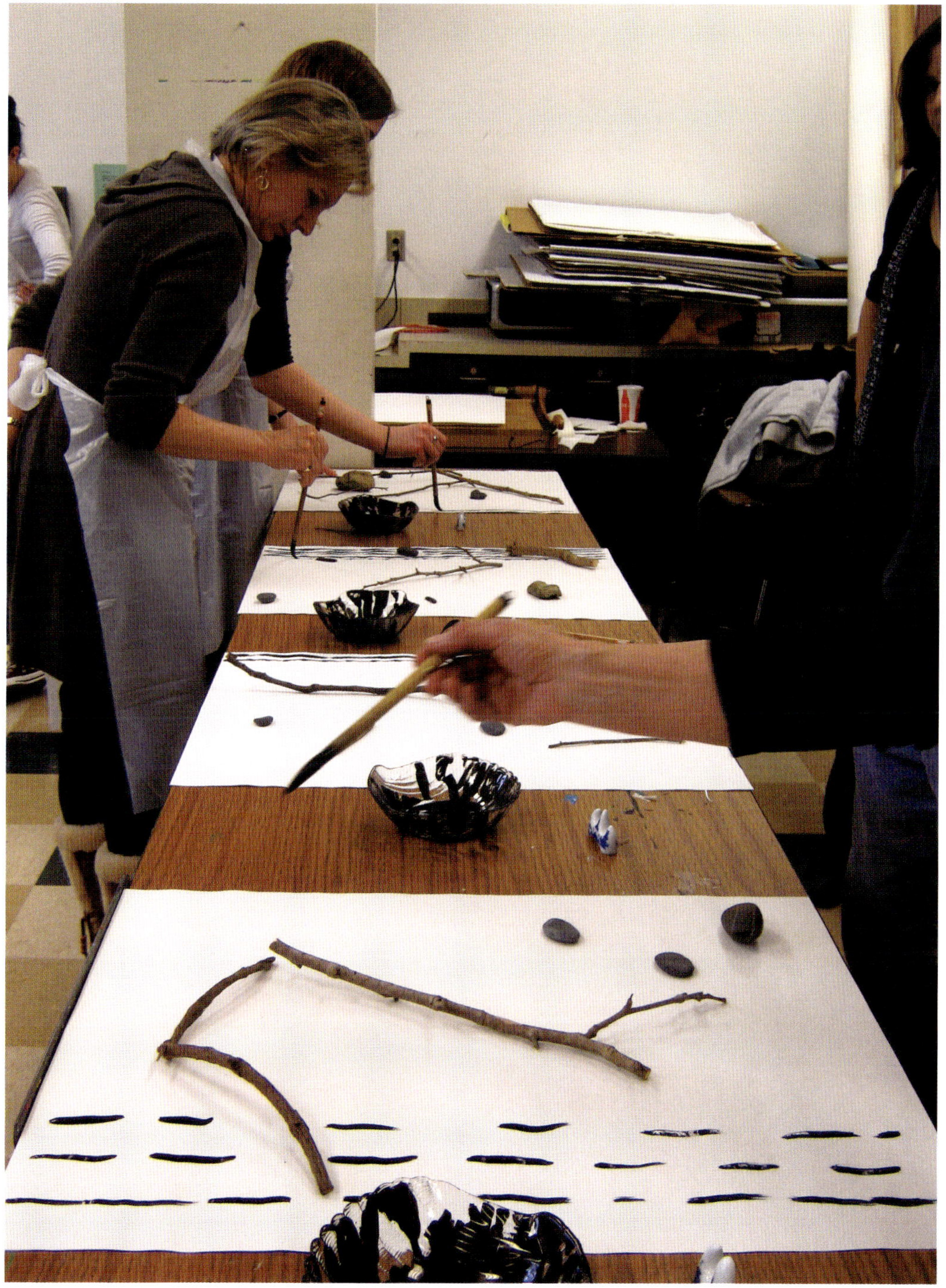

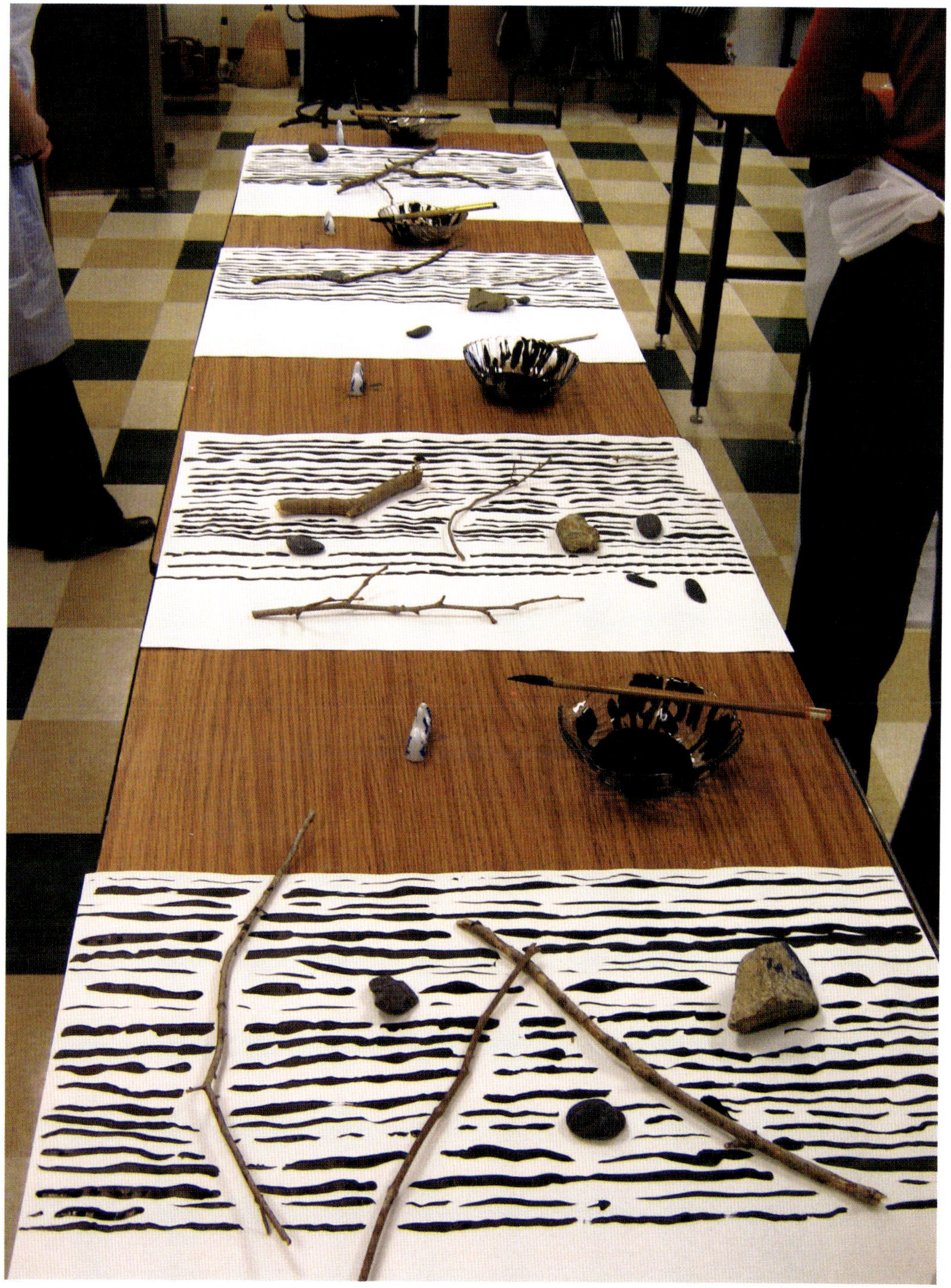

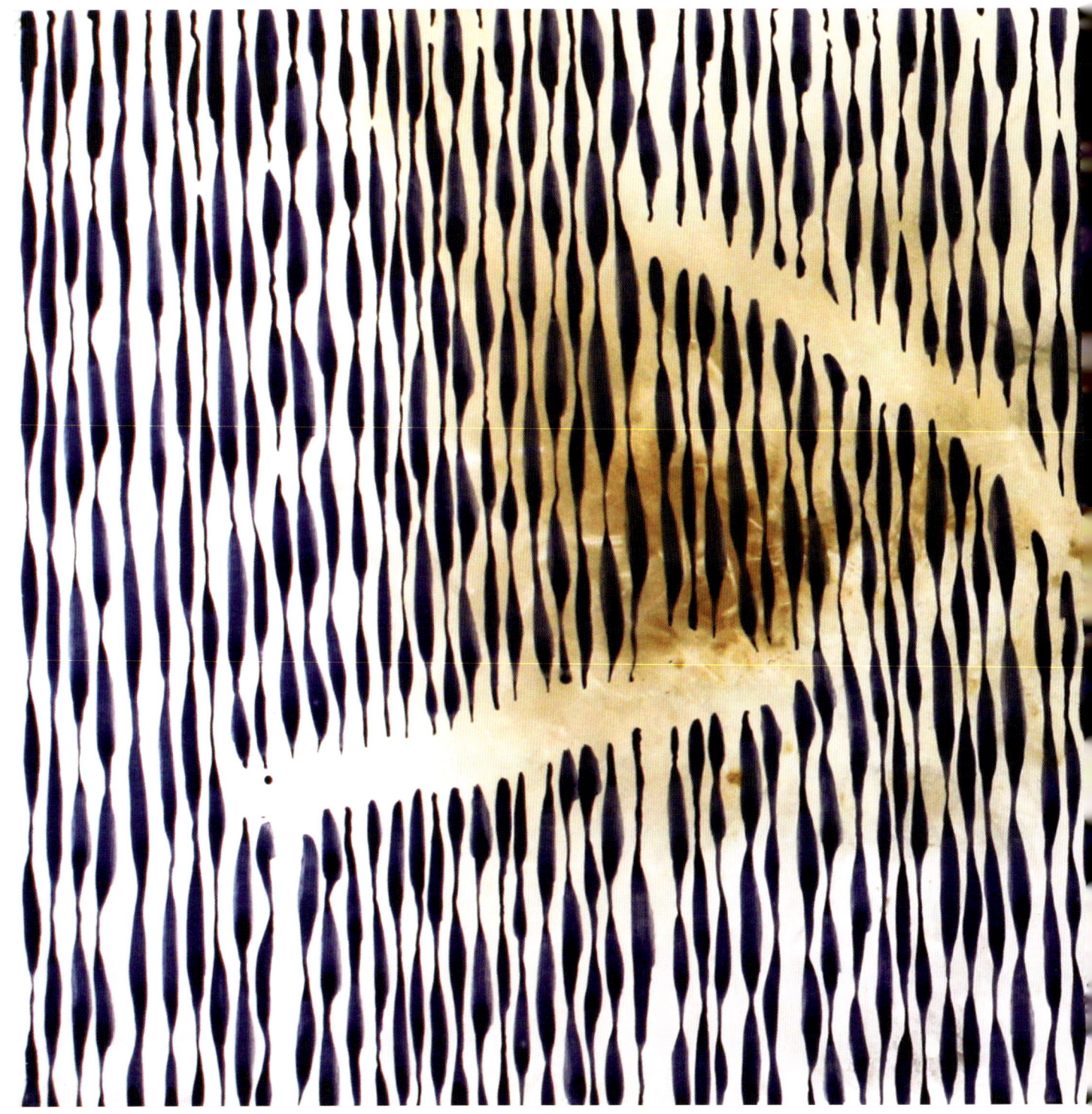

Jiro Okura's *Shisendo Garden, Breathing Lines #12, For John Cage*, August 12, 1992, blue ink on "smoked" paper, 28 x 72 in. (71.12 x 182.88 cm)

painted by Jiro Okura, Ray Kass, Gloria Heath, Rob Cole, Robin Boucher, and Joe Kelley

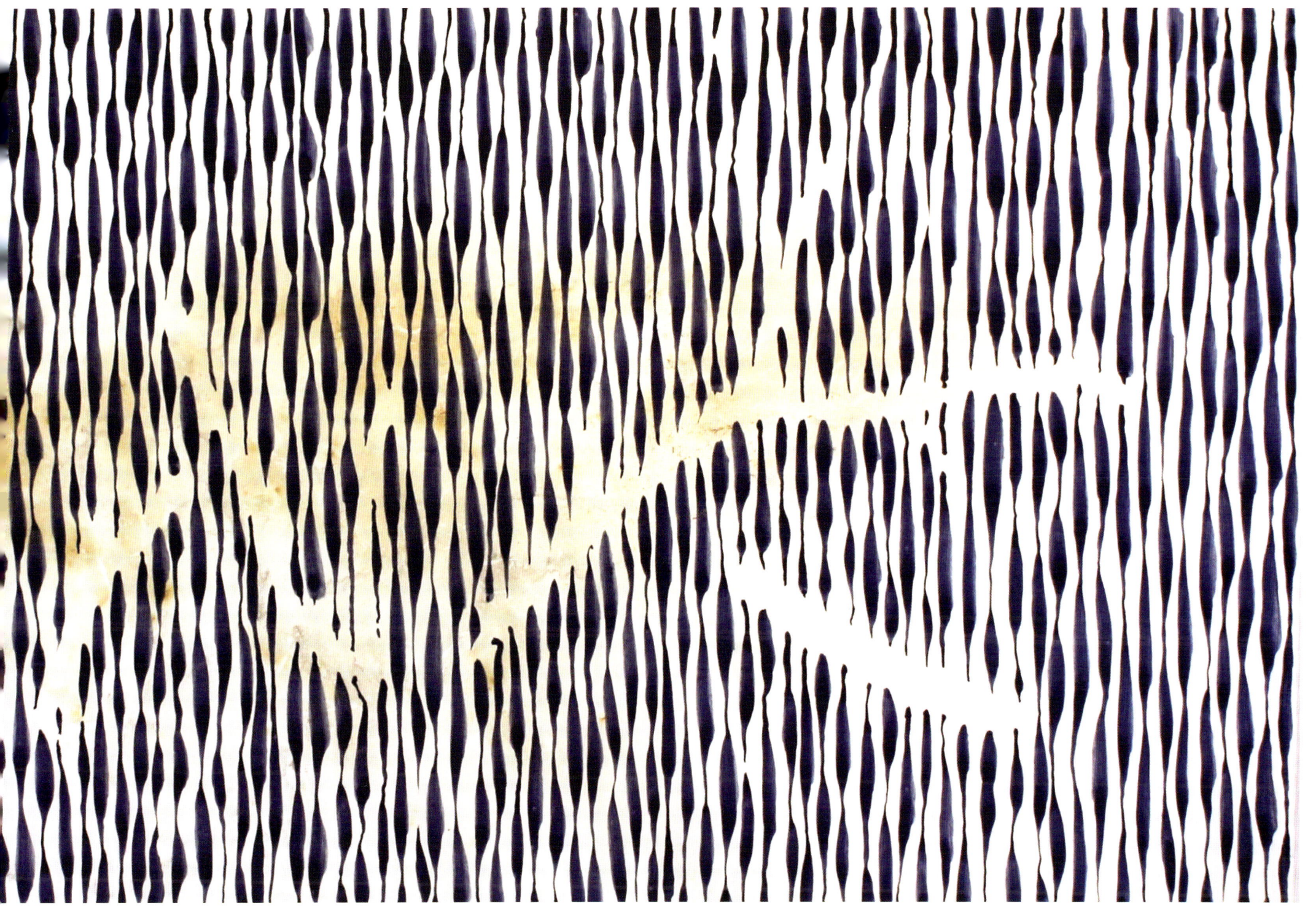

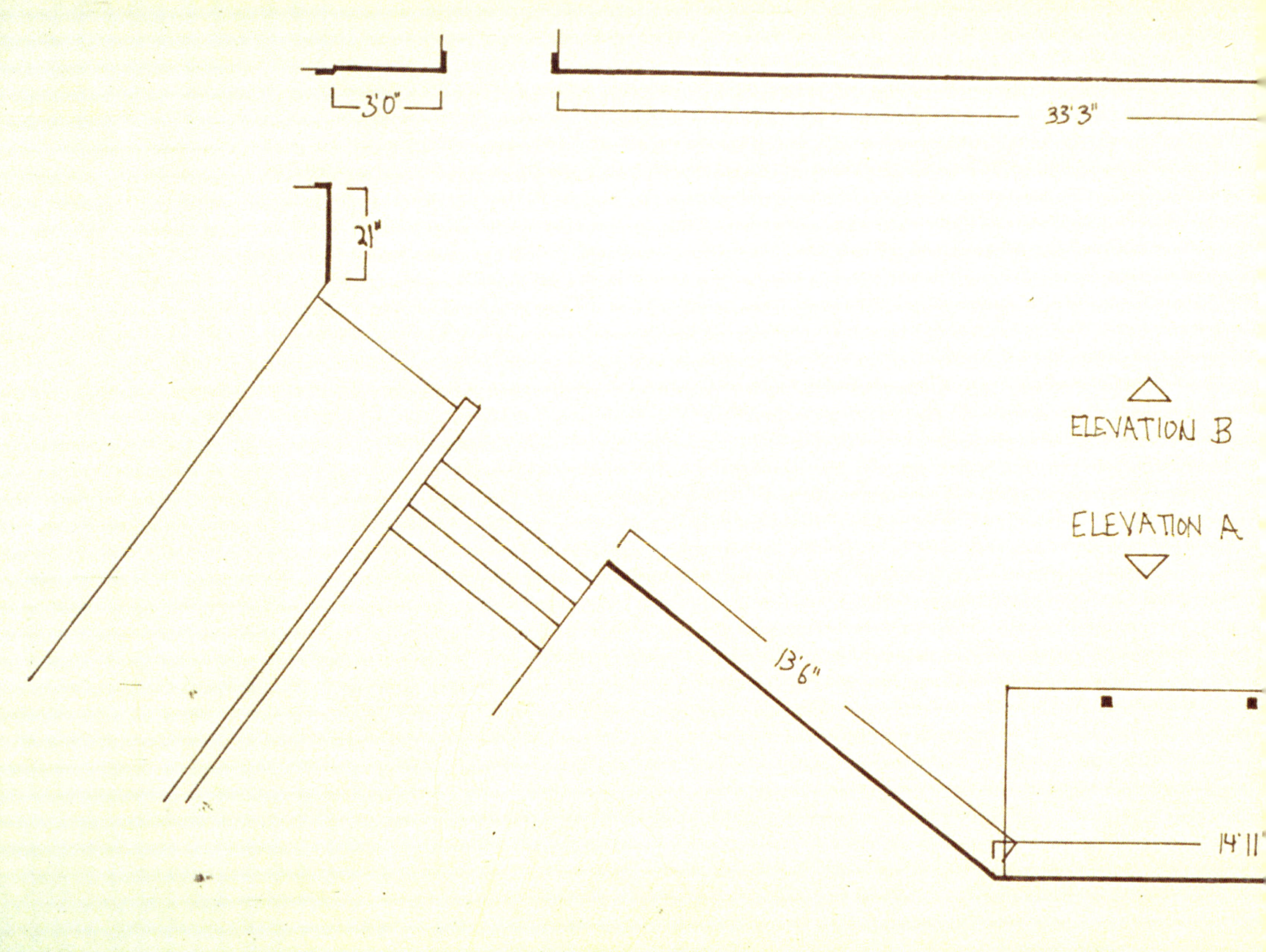

3'0"

33'3"

21"

ELEVATION B

ELEVATION A

13'6"

14'11"

Installation design drawn by architecture student Bryson VanNostrand for the *Broad Channel* and *Writing on the River* Polyptics at the Newman Library at Virginia Tech,, 1991. A photo on p. 127 shows the exhibition being installed

# VI

## *Ray Kass: Evolution of the Polyptychs*

# ARTISTIC DEVELOPMENT

HOWARD RISATTI

In 1991 it was impossible to bring a guest artist to Mountain Lake for financial reasons. In order to keep the workshop activities going and to keep people involved, Ray Kass decided to conduct a collaborative workshop project himself. Up to this point he had acted as organizer, studio coordinator, and assistant to the guest artists. The opportunity to do a workshop of his own allowed him to tailor the collaborative techniques that had evolved in the workshops to the working methods he had long been developing in his personal watercolors.

Following an initial foray into strictly nonrepresentational work in oil, Kass has essentially been committed to watercolor since the late 1960s, something which may explain the general watercolor focus of many of the workshops. In his work of the 1970s, Kass painted pastoral scenes and views of mountains, streams, waterfalls, and coastal areas. Recording the physical features of the landscape, these paintings are not bucolic or sentimental, but express a sense of the limitlessness of space, of nature seen as a vast panorama opening before the viewer.

This sense of expansive space originated with Kass' work in the late 1960s in northern California, where he began painting landscape views seen from the high bluffs overlooking the Pacific Ocean. Around this time he became reacquainted with watercolorist Keith Crown, with whom he had studied briefly while a student at the University of North Carolina at Chapel Hill. He also became friendly with Morris Graves, who was, by this time, a rather reclusive artist living near Arcata, California, where Kass was staying.

Both Crown and Graves influenced Kass by encouraging his

interest in landscape as well as advising him in his development of unconventional watercolor techniques, techniques that would form the basis of the studio practice that Kass would provide for John Cage's workshops at Mountain Lake in 1988 and 1990. Moving from abstractions in oil to landscapes in watercolor was liberating for Kass, something both Crown and Graves encouraged. Graves also suggested that Kass seal his watercolors with beeswax so that they wouldn't have to be framed under glass as is customarily done with works on paper; this would later prove valuable because it would allow for the creation of Kass' polyptychs (many-paneled paintings), the individual panels of which could not have been framed using glass.

Graves also influenced Kass in other more philosophical ways. As curator Margo Crutchfield has noted, he influenced Kass' use of "symbolic images as manifestations of other realities."[1] Without sharing Graves's deeply felt spiritualism, Kass learned how to mold the older artist's precepts for looking at the landscape and, by using abstracted forms, to convey a heightened sense of nature. In these watercolors, Kass' previous interest in abstraction reappears in the geometries formed by repeated patterns of rock formations or wave shapes. However, under the influence of Graves, these abstract patterns began to convey a heightened sense of the permanence of nature, even as subtle effects of light and atmosphere, which

transpose and transform those shapes, were also recorded. Kass came to understand Graves's philosophical approach to painting as a kind of meditative act that could lead to a unique vision of the world and came to understand what Graves meant when he said that the painting that tried to depict nature pictorially always failed because the subject always remained grander than the painting; it was the painting that captured the *idea* of nature that would be most successful.[2]

This period in northern California was very consequential for Kass because he came to understand how the art of the Pacific Northwest differed from that of New York where he grew up. The Pacific Northwest artists he had come to admire were inspired by nature but abstracted its forms. Mark Tobey, a friend of both Graves and John Cage, used abstract form to convey a cosmic sense of nature, Graves a more mystical and spiritual one. These ideas became more formalized in Kass' mind around 1980 when, because of his association with Graves in the

[1] See Margo Crutchfield's essay for *Ray Kass: Recent Paintings*, an exhibition she organized at the Virginia Museum of Fine Arts, 27 May–5 July 1987, p. 5

[2] Graves as quoted in Ray Kass, *Morris Graves: Vision of the Inner Eye*, exhibition catalogue (New York: Braziller in association with The Phillips Collection, Washington, D.C., 1983), p. 20

[3] As Kass related in his catalogue, Graves went to New York in 1946 to request support for his Guggenheim application to enter occupied Japan to study its culture and philosophy. During this trip east, he also went to Boston to enlist the support of Coomaraswamy, who was a curator at the Boston Museum of Fine Arts. See Kass, *Morris Graves*, pp. 50–51.

[4] Cage attended Suzuki's lectures at Columbia University sometime around the late 1940s or early 1950s. For more on this see David Revill, *The Roaring Silence: John Cage: A Life* (New York: Arcade Publishing, 1992), pp. 107–110

[5] See Crutchfield, *Ray Kass: Recent Paintings*, p. 5

[6] See Crutchfield, *Ray Kass: Recent Paintings*, p. 7

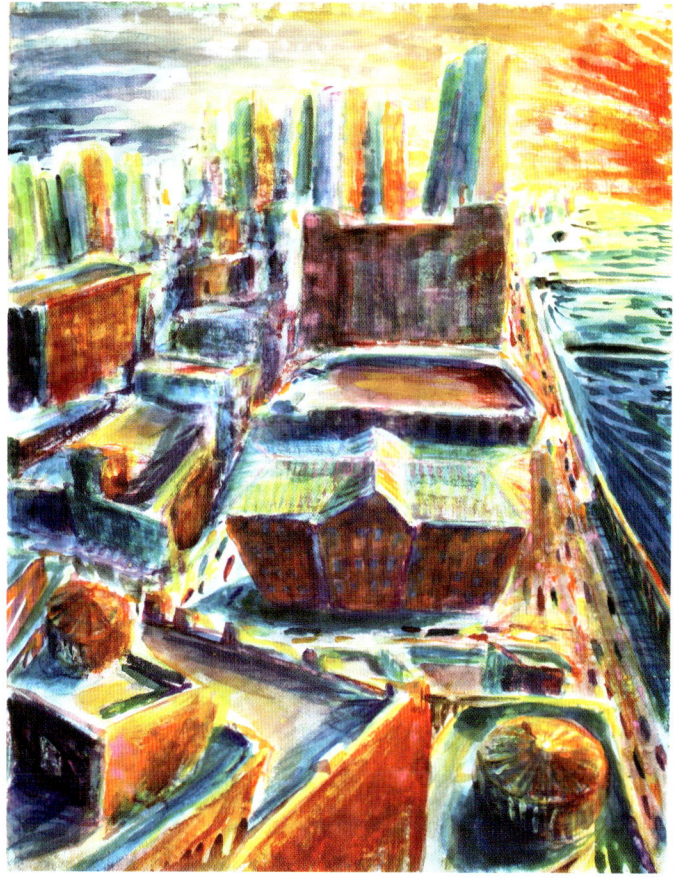

Ray Kass, NYC, *Looking South from Vestry St.*, 1985, watercolor on rag paper, 29 x 22 in. (73.66 x 58.88 cm)

previous decade, he was asked to guest-curate and write a book to accompany a Graves retrospective exhibition at The Phillips Collection in Washington, D.C. In doing the research for this project, Kass learned even more about the connections between Graves, Tobey, and Northwest Coast ideas about abstraction and nature and also about Ananda Coomaraswamy's notion of the transformation of nature in art. It was clear that Graves knew of Coomaraswamy's work, having visited him in Boston in 1946.[3]

Not only did this research for the Graves catalogue encourage Kass to develop and articulate his own ideas about art and nature, but it also led to his friendship with Cage. Because Cage had known both Tobey and Graves in Seattle during the '30s, Kass interviewed him for the catalogue. That Cage would be invited to Mountain Lake was not just a mere happenstance but one result of both his and Kass' long-time involvement with Pacific Northwest Coast culture, a culture that Cage did much to "transmit" to New York artists when his own interests in it were re-focused in the mid '40s through the Indian aesthetics of Coomaraswamy and Dr. Daisetz T. Suzuki's Zen.[4]

Kass' paintings of New York City of the 1980s must be understood against this rather complicated background. They transform the usual bustle-centered urban landscape by re-visioning it as part of the continuous space of nature. The views from high bluffs are now skylines seen from on high, from bird's-eye vantage points bleeding into distant, sweeping horizons in a play of undulating color, dizzyingly exaggerated perspective, and pulsating repeated forms reminiscent of organic forms of nature. In Kass' words, these are "environmental paintings," "dialogues with the natural world," created in an attempt to "paint the

city as if it were part of the natural world."[5] The similarities between the repeated patterns of forms found in nature and those found in the city reveal Kass attempting to "paint the land as if it were the ocean, or to paint the city as a waterfall."[6]

In a sense, this is a philosophical *rapprochement* with what critic Donald Kuspit identified as the nature/culture dichotomy so prominent in Western culture.[7] Cage and Jiro Okura expressed similar ideas in which the self and nature are seen as coterminous with the world. Kuspit has also pointed out that there is something of the 19th-century American Luminist tradition in Kass' work. This is especially apparent in the way the vastness of an almost sacred/religious space is articulated — is made visible — through the heightening of foreground detail; in these works, small detail, carefully rendered, makes the sense of limitless panoramic space comprehensible to the viewer.[8]

Around 1988 Kass moved away from the city scenes with their orientation toward a dramatic pictorial space and returned to a more abstract mode of painting in order to explore, in a more concentrated and systematic fashion, the idea of the interchangeability of formal elements and geometric patterns that occur throughout the visual world. This required adaptation of the personal techniques that he had developed over the previous decade painting the northern California coast, the city, and the Appalachian landscape of southwestern Virginia. Such techniques as the use of transparent color washes in layers, bright color in a wide range of hues, and the close observation of details often rendered as repeated abstract patterns of natural elements from the landscape were all incorporated into new paintings.

These paintings moved from diptychs and triptychs to many-paneled polyptychs with their grid-like construction. Because the grid shape, which is connected with utopian symbolism in Modernist painting, relates to the city via street plans and Modernist skyscraper architecture, the panelization of the polyptychal paintings was a way to "refresh" the grid and to bring the city back to nature in a more fundamental, abstract way. Thus the geometric shapes of the city survive as the geometry of the polyptych panels; even the technical problem involved in physically constructing the polyptychs suggests the city/skyscraper symbolism.

See Donald Kuspit essay for *Ray Kass: Images of the Winged Earth*, exhibition catalogue, the Art Museum of Western Virginia, 13 Nov. 1993–20 Feb. 1994, n.p.

See Kuspit, *Images of the Winged Earth*, n.p. Art historian John I. H. Baur sees "luminism as an attitude not only to light but to things in nature"; he goes on to say "that luminism is a mode of expression through a subjectivity so powerful that the artist's feeling is transferred directly to the object, with no sense of the artist as intermediary." For more on Luminism see Barbara Novak, *American Painting of the Nineteenth Century* (New York, Washington, London: Praeger Publishers, 1971), pp. 92–137.

# BROAD CHANNEL, WRITING ON THE RIVER, AND *MUSCARELLE POLYPTYCH*

HOWARD RISATTI

Kass' interests as a painter and his growing commitment to collaborative art making fostered by his work at Mountain Lake were leading him almost inevitably toward doing a Mountain Lake Workshop of his own. Earlier workshops, notably Cage's, had hinted at some of the themes that fascinated Kass: the interchangeability of abstracted natural forms and geometric patterns and the application of color in layered washes — an underlying Zen sensibility. The Mountain Lake setting itself with its sense of nature at work and maybe especially its light- and wind-struck water afforded inspiration that suited Kass' artistic temperament. When it became clear there wouldn't be a visiting artist at Mountain Lake in 1991, he decided to use the opportunity to organize workshops of his own.

Kass' first workshop resulted in two bodies of work, a series of paintings called *Writing on the River*, and a mural-sized painting titled *Broad Channel: The Vorticella Polyptych*. "Broad channel" refers to the main channel of a river; the vorticella is a single-celled micro-organism commonly found in rivers and streams, including the New River in Virginia. Kass learned of this micro-organism from Miles Horton, an amateur biologist for whom the vorticella was a favorite aquatic creature. While ill in the late 1980s and early '90s, Horton asked people to make drawings of the vorticella for him, which led Kass to the vorticella as the subject for paintings. Re-addressing the ambition he had imagined for the 1983 workshop with Cage, this eventually provided him with the opportunity to attempt to symbolize nature at a level deeper than simple visual representation.

Before reaching this stage in the workshop, however, Kass and workshop participants began working from electron microscope photographs of protozoa and vorticella, transforming these single-celled forms in fantasy renderings to facilitate their use as images in paintings. At a certain point, it became apparent that the workshop participants were merely rendering these images in studies based on their actual appearance or projecting cartoon-like exaggerations of them — in other words, they were simply illustrating the organism without understanding it at the deeper level of its activity. Without such an understanding, the vorticella could not be rendered as a symbol of nature's way of working, only of nature's outward appearance. The aspiration to capture nature in its manner of operation was the fundamental precept of Kass' workshops, something that he had learned from Graves and, through Graves, from Coomaraswamy. More and more, the choice of participating artists and the overall direction of the workshops at Mountain Lake were based on this goal.

Kass' workshop activities made it clear that nature must be understood not as a collection of objects or images but as a system of simultaneously occurring, interacting, and changing forces. To understand this, what was needed was a motivational exercise that was not limited to simple depiction. To get to this stage, techniques derived from Kass' earlier work were used. A system of painting on small panel boards was organized; the panels had dots on them, the positions of which had been determined by chance. Every participant repeatedly drew the wavy form of the vorticella and then worked on a panel, painting a simple, wavy form in the spirit of the vorticella, as a connection between the dots. Another participant could then work on the same panel, modifying the initial design by reconnecting the dots within a new perimeter, thus changing and expanding an existing drawing. After several similar applications were completed, the panels received layers of washes that eventually covered them, completely hiding the images; when they were subsequently washed with water, the images reappeared as if they were coming to the surface of a pool.

Through this elaborate process that employed not only collaborative effort but chance and indeterminacy — by now hallmarks of art making at Mountain Lake — the panel boards revealed a much more potent image of this aquatic life form than could any pictorial illustration. The final step in the process was to assemble the panels into polyptychal paintings that had an irregular "T" shape. Titled *Writing on the River*, this series of paintings, with their bright colors and undulating, floating shapes, capture something of the life activity at the micro level of nature. The process involved in their creation evokes a wide range of associations with organic things that seem to echo Coomaraswamy's dictum: "to imitate nature, not in her appearance, but in her manner of operation."

While painting the panel boards that were to constitute the *Writing on the River* series, participants also painted the panels for *Broad Channel: The Vorticella Polyptych*. The largest painting produced in this workshop, it has 68 panels and measures 97 inches x 350 inches. Procedures similar to those used for the panel boards were employed in painting it. However, the vorticella organism referred to in its title was used not as a specific subject but as a broad motif configured through washes that Kass selected to dramatically link several groupings of panels into a series of broad, interlocking patterns. These patterns, in their regular and inverted positions, resemble stepped pyramids or ziggurats as well as the vorticella shape. The appearance of the ziggurat shape, however, occurred completely by chance;

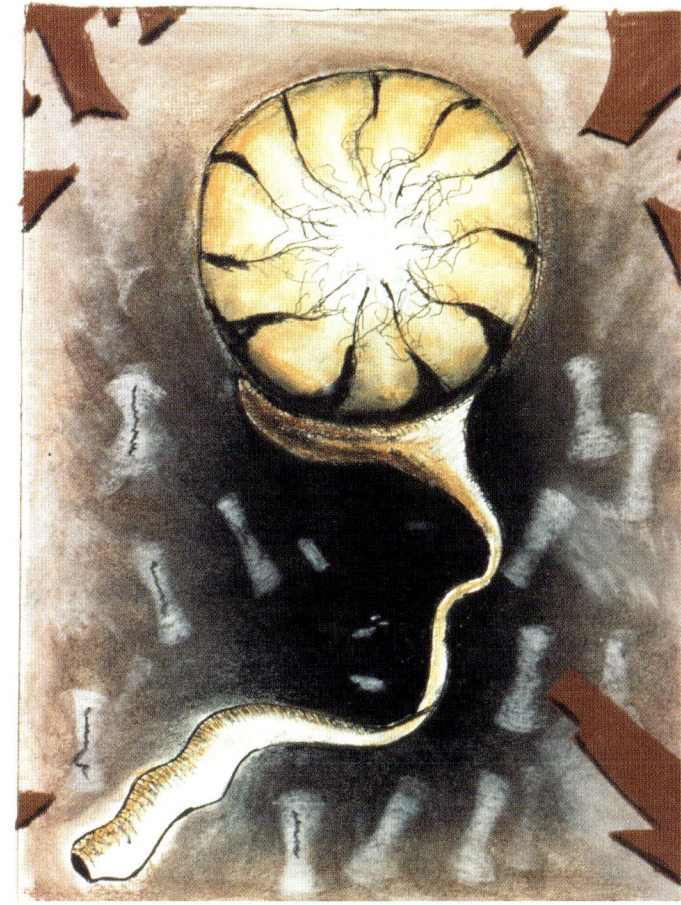

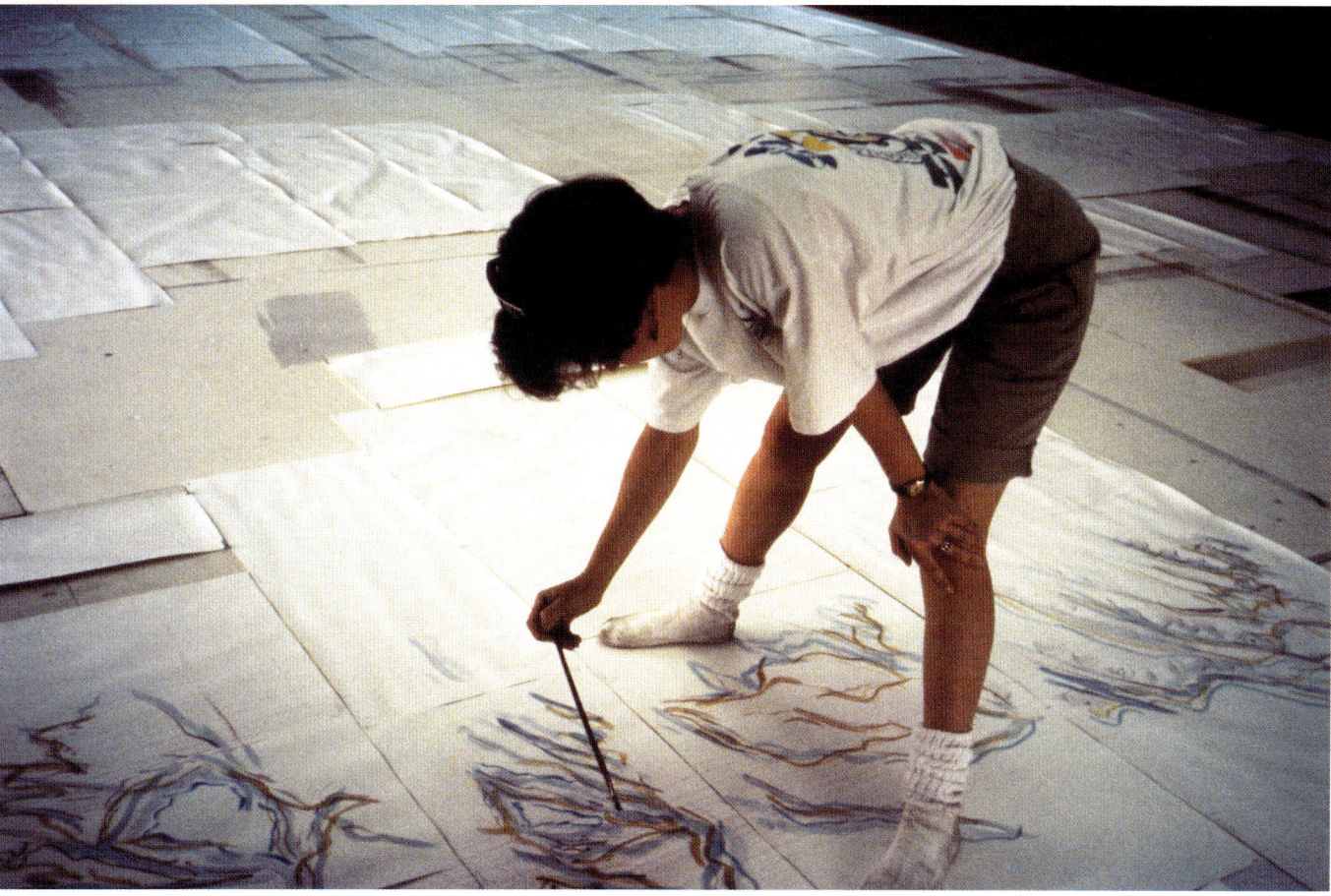

it was not intentional. Amazingly, it offered a geometric parallel to the organic form of the vorticella. In addition to these shapes, vine and other natural motifs that had been traced directly from nature onto numbered glass plates were also used. The motifs from these plates and the individual panels into which they would be incorporated were determined by chance — in other words, the collaborative/participatory process had been employed to infuse a sense of random naturalness into an image of nature.

After having carefully rehearsed on practice sheets of paper, participants executed the vine-like motifs selected for them

by the use of chance. Executed as subtle underpaintings on what would become the interlocking groupings of panel, individual motifs were layered so that they eventually formed complex configurations that became the structural underpainting for transparent washes that were applied over them. Kass first applied the washes using chance; then, using choice, he brought the individual panels together into a seamless whole, creating a work that seems to reflect a single artistic hand as a presence of humanity, not as an individual action. Even after the separate panels had been assembled into the mural-sized polyptych using chance, they retained

an organic unity that transcends its individual parts.

In *Broad Channel*, the result of varied hands and activities is a single field of shimmering light and "movemented" water that seems paced in a slow, deliberate rhythm by the repetitive motivic series of large ziggurat/vorticella shapes. The clean edges of these irregular shapes, which are locked together as a motif of alternating upright and inverted forms seen against a translucent blue light that could be reflected sky or water, create a monumental contrapuntal structure the complexity of which echoes the complex structure beneath.

127

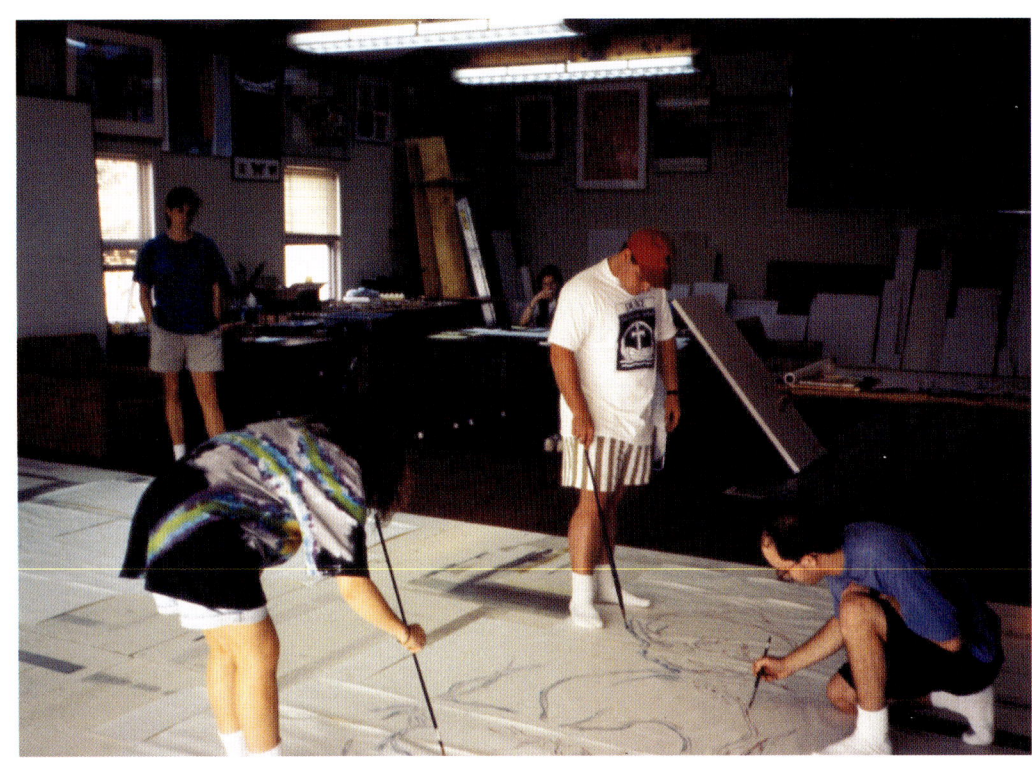

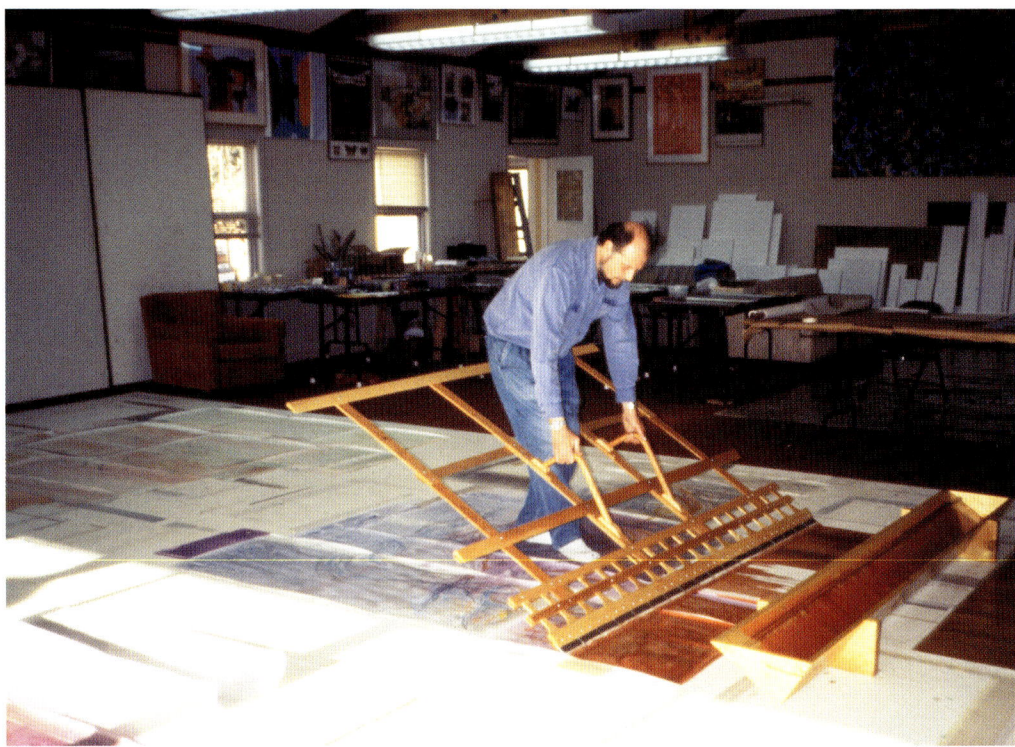

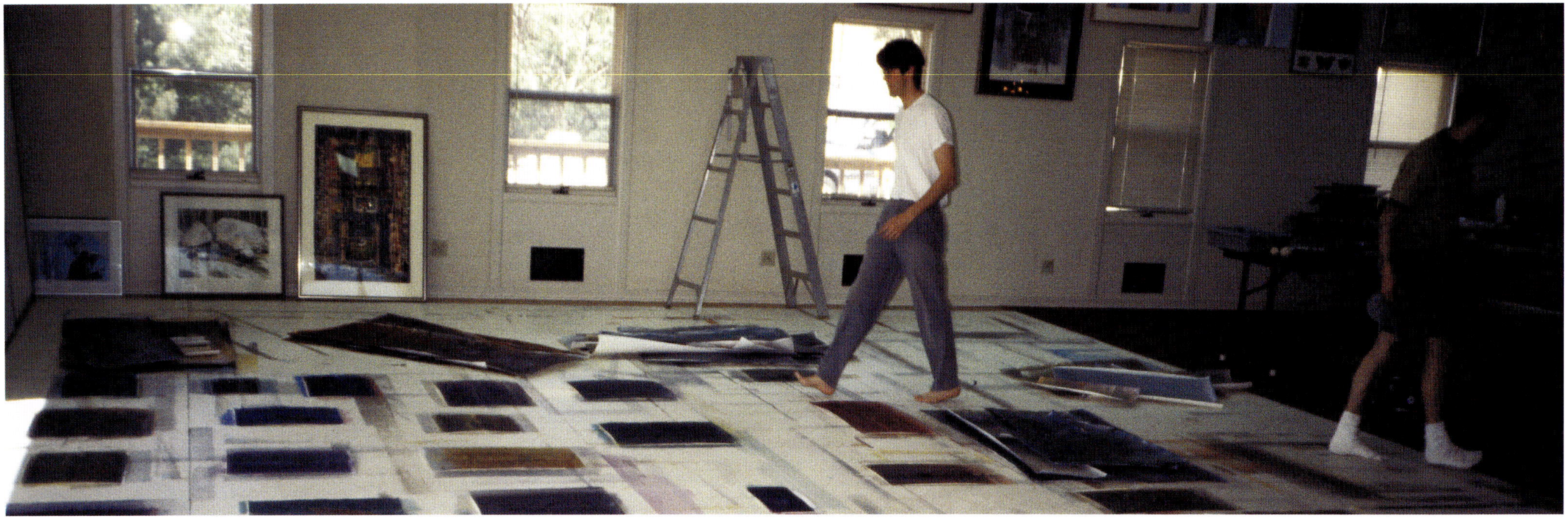

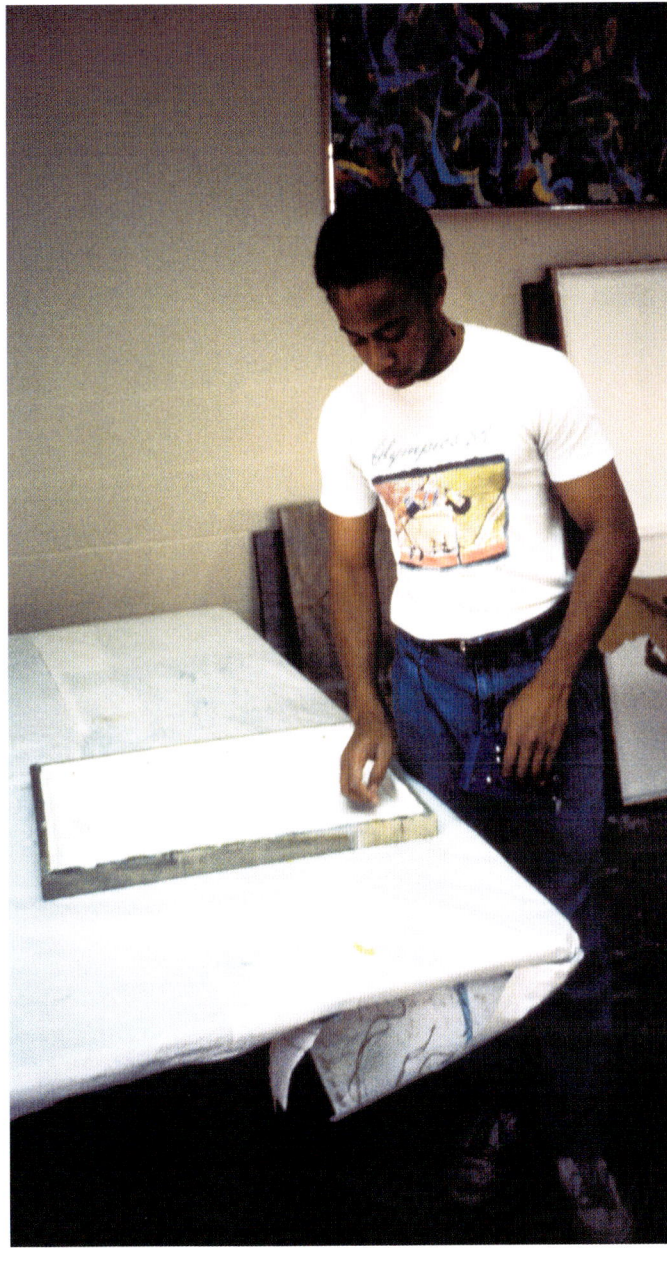

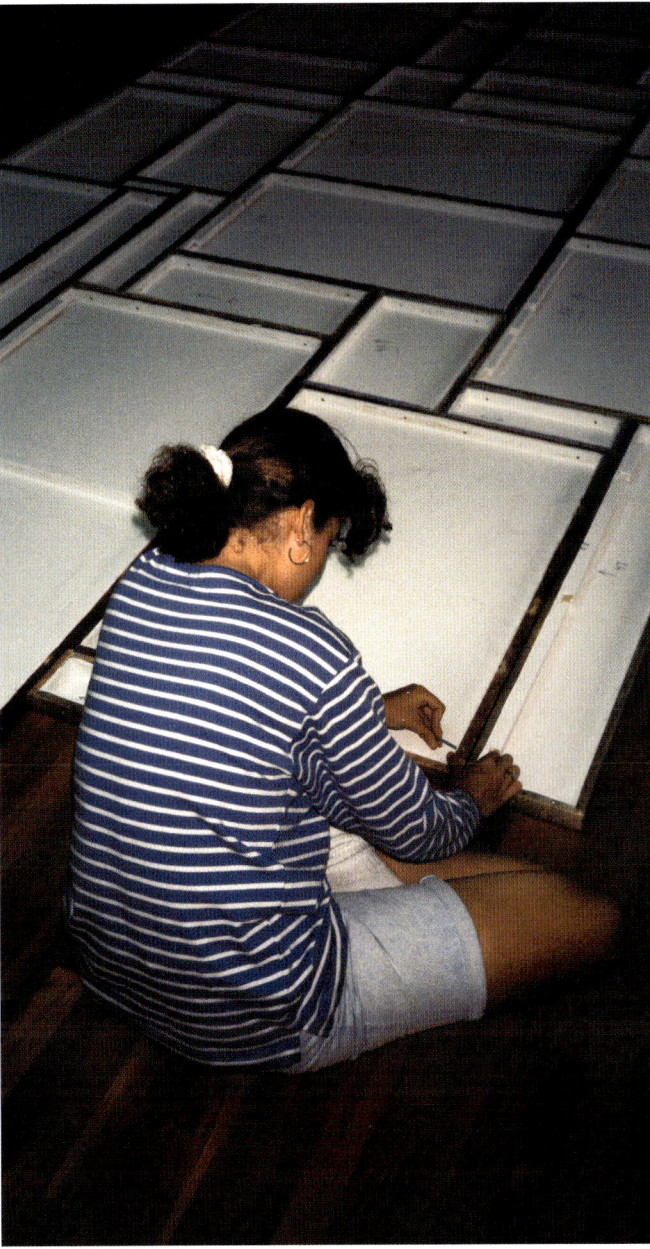

Foreground detail and the vast, broad space such detail makes comprehensible are held in a delicate balance within this luminous wall of light. *Broad Channel* evokes at once nature's intimacy and nature's grandeur, localized, minute detail and panoramic sweep on a scale that is almost sublime.

As in the works of Cage and Okura, the process of development of Kass' work also imitates the chance processes of nature, especially the serendipitous way vines and grasses grow into complex configurations. Through these methods, including the process of collaboration, Kass was able to maintain a direct, tangible connection to nature via natural motifs in his painting even as his translucent washes evoke the subtle, shifting play of light in the local landscape.

Just as his early work provided a technical resource for Cage, in this workshop Kass gave his work a new presence by incorporating into it strategies from all the previous workshops. He extended both the size and the complexity of his paintings by configuring individually painted panels into larger, multi-panel works whose overall compositional structures could not have been predetermined.[1] At the same time, the works retain their connection to the space of nature as subject matter, although now this subject matter has become more conceptual than pictorial or illusionistic.

Kass conducted a second workshop early in 1993 that resulted in the *Muscarelle Polyptych*. Painted in his studio, it was a collaborative project done in preparation for an exhibition and a special Mountain Lake Workshop program at the

[1] The process that Kass developed resembles somewhat the Surrealist "game" called the Exquisite Corpse (*Cadavre Exquis*), in which several people work independently, in sequence, on a single drawing without seeing each other's contribution until the last section of the drawing is completed. For more on this see William S. Rubin, *Dada, Surrealism, and Their Heritage* (New York: The Museum of Modern Art, 1968), p. 83.

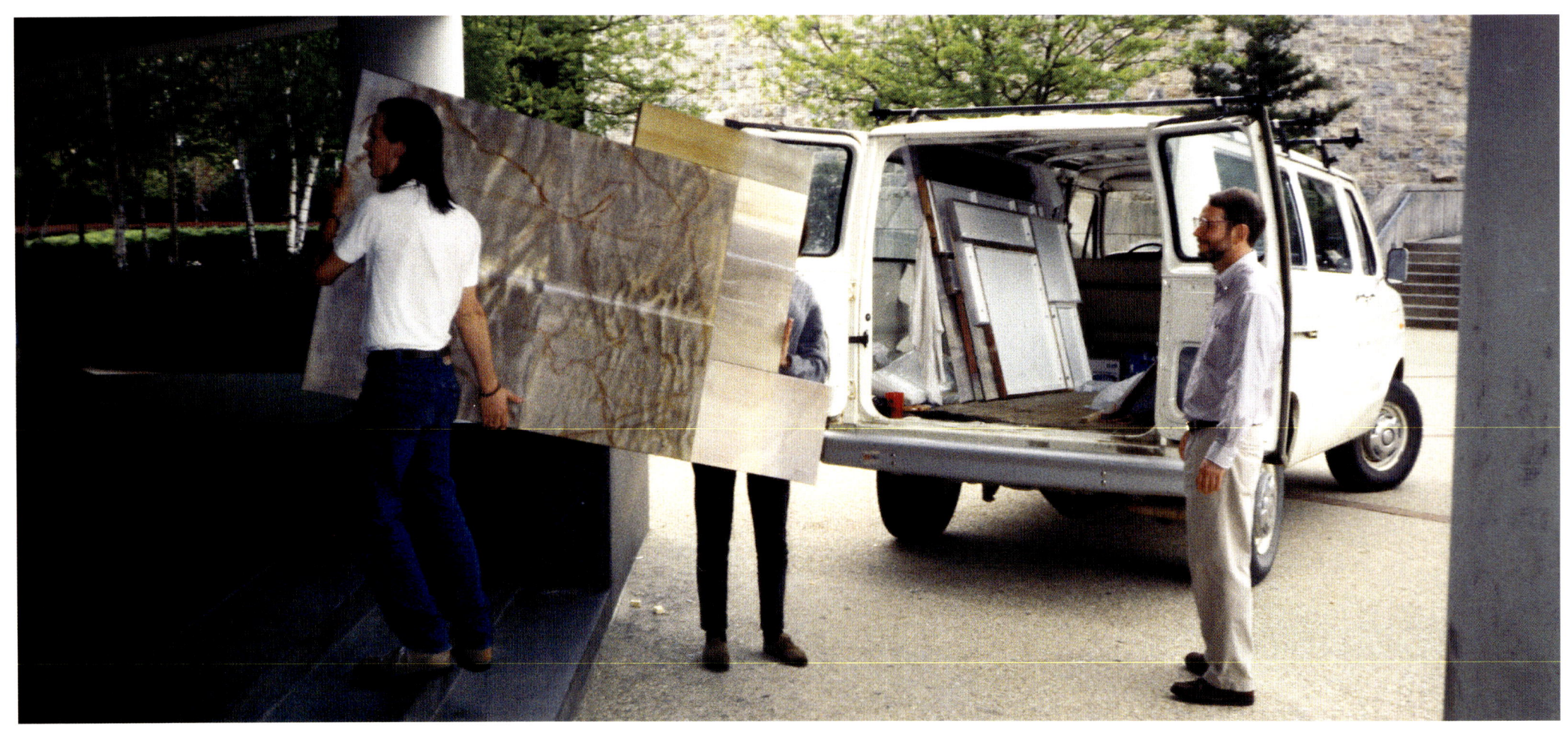

Muscarelle Museum of the College of William and Mary
in Williamsburg, Virginia. The painting is quite large —
over 10 feet high x 12 feet wide — and is composed of 17 panels
painted separately with the help of workshop assistants.
Like *Writing on the River* it too has an irregular "T" shape,
but in its flowing, rippling patterns — they seem currents of air
almost as much as swirls of river water — and in its shimmer
and overall movement, it more closely echoes *Broad Channel*. [2]

[2] The *Muscarelle Polyptych* was first exhibited in *Collaboration: Mountain Lake Workshop*; the exhibition ran from
3 April to 16 May, 1993. The painting was again exhibited in 1997 in *Uncommon Ground* at the Virginia Museum
of Fine Arts in Richmond and was subsequently purchased by Longwood University in Farmville, Virginia.

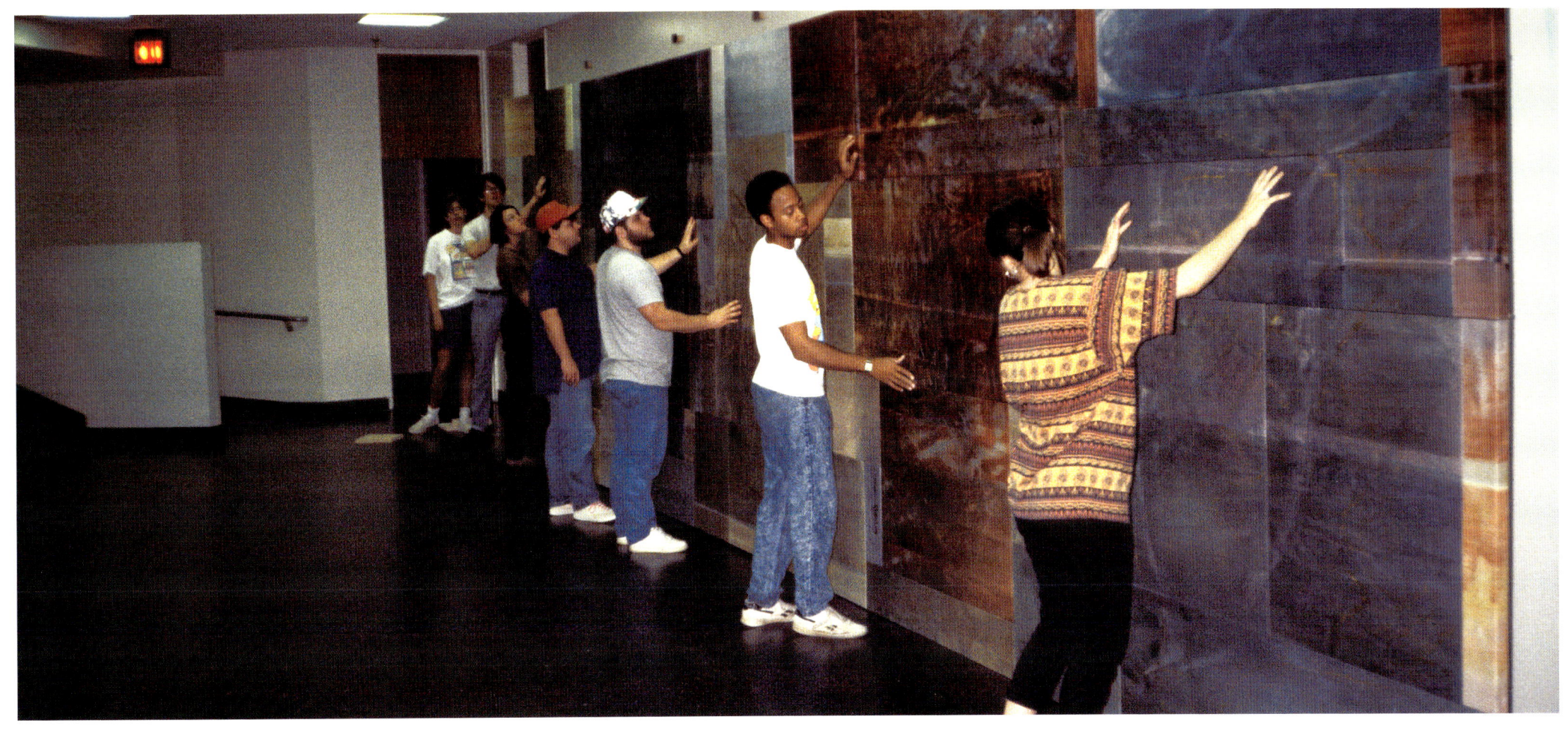

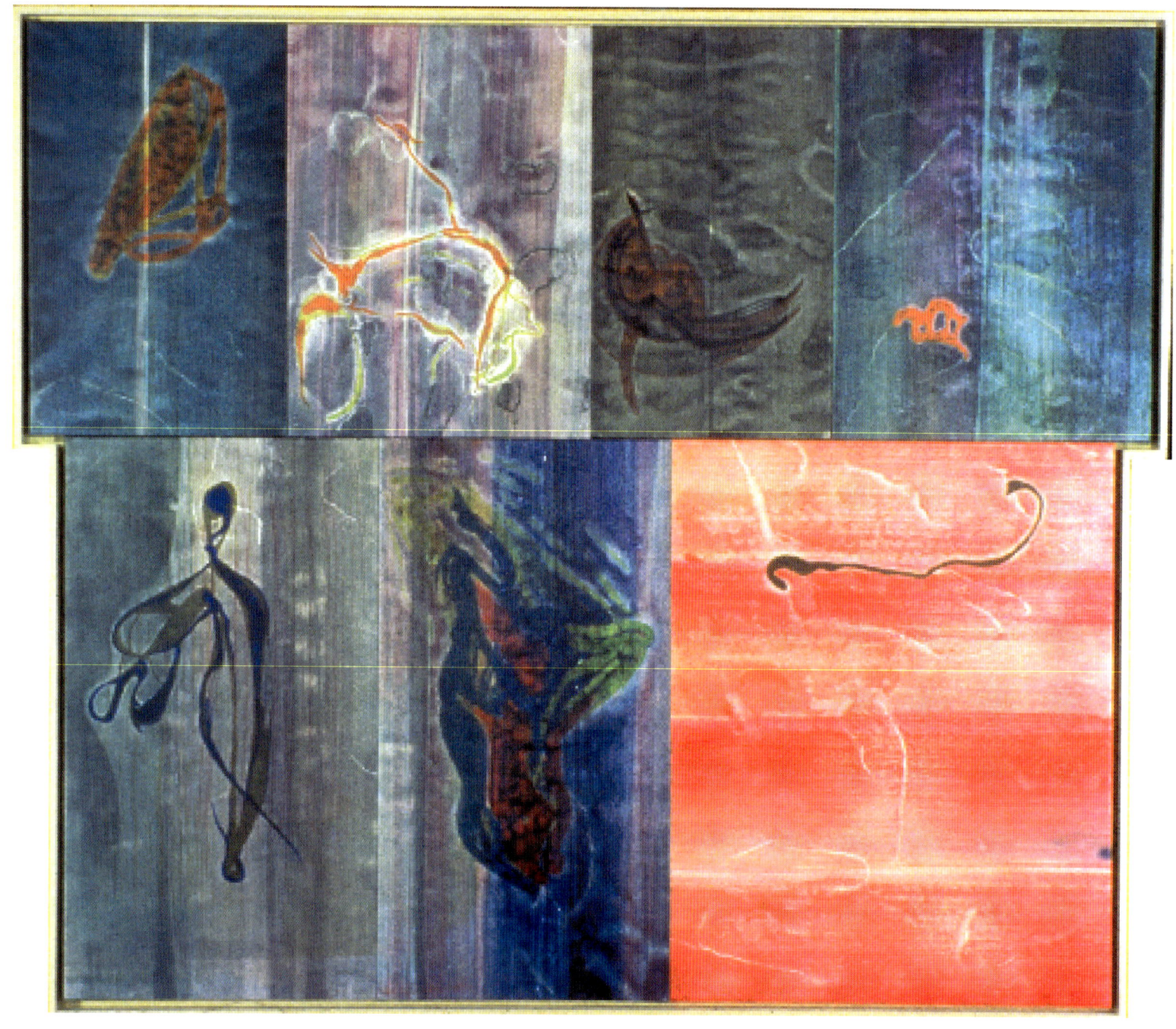

Ray Kass and the Mountain Lake Workshop, *Writing on the River I*, 1991, watercolor on rag paper, under beeswax, mounted on primed wood panels, 7 panels, 45 x 53.25 in. (114.3 x 135.26 cm)

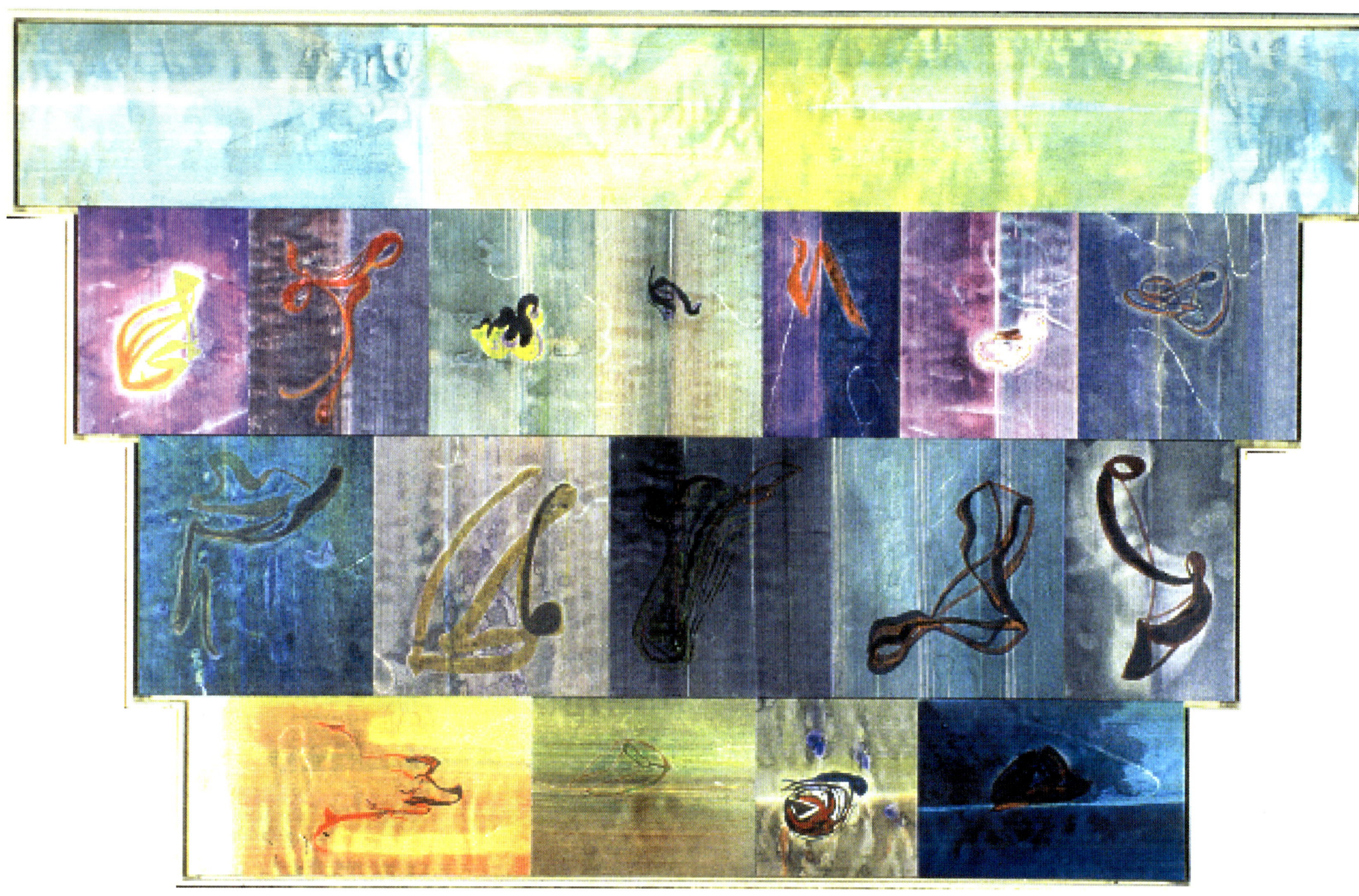

Ray Kass and the Mountain Lake Workshop, *Writing on the River II*, 1991, watercolor on rag paper, under beeswax, mounted on primed wood panels, 18 panels, 56 x 91.25 in. (142.24 x 231.78 cm)

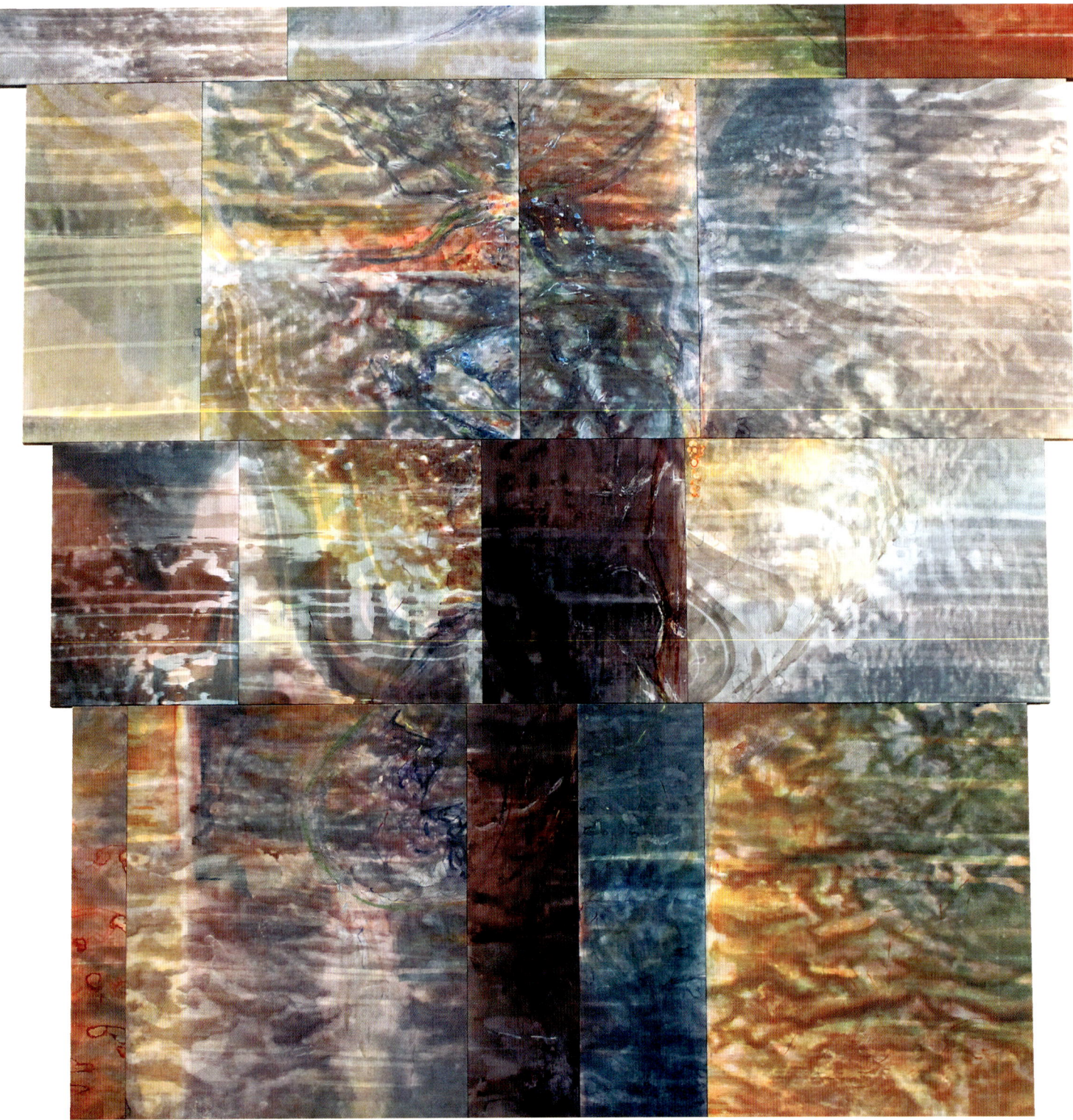

Ray Kass and the Mountain Lake Workshop, *Muscarelle Polyptych*, 1993, watercolor on rag paper, under beeswax and methylcellulose, mounted on canvas, 17 panels, 127 x 145 in. (322.58 x 368.3 cm), permanent collection of the Longwood Center for the Visual Arts

Longwood University president
W. Taylor Reveley IV meeting
with students in the Stallard
Boardroom at Longwood where
*Muscarelle Polyptych* is installed

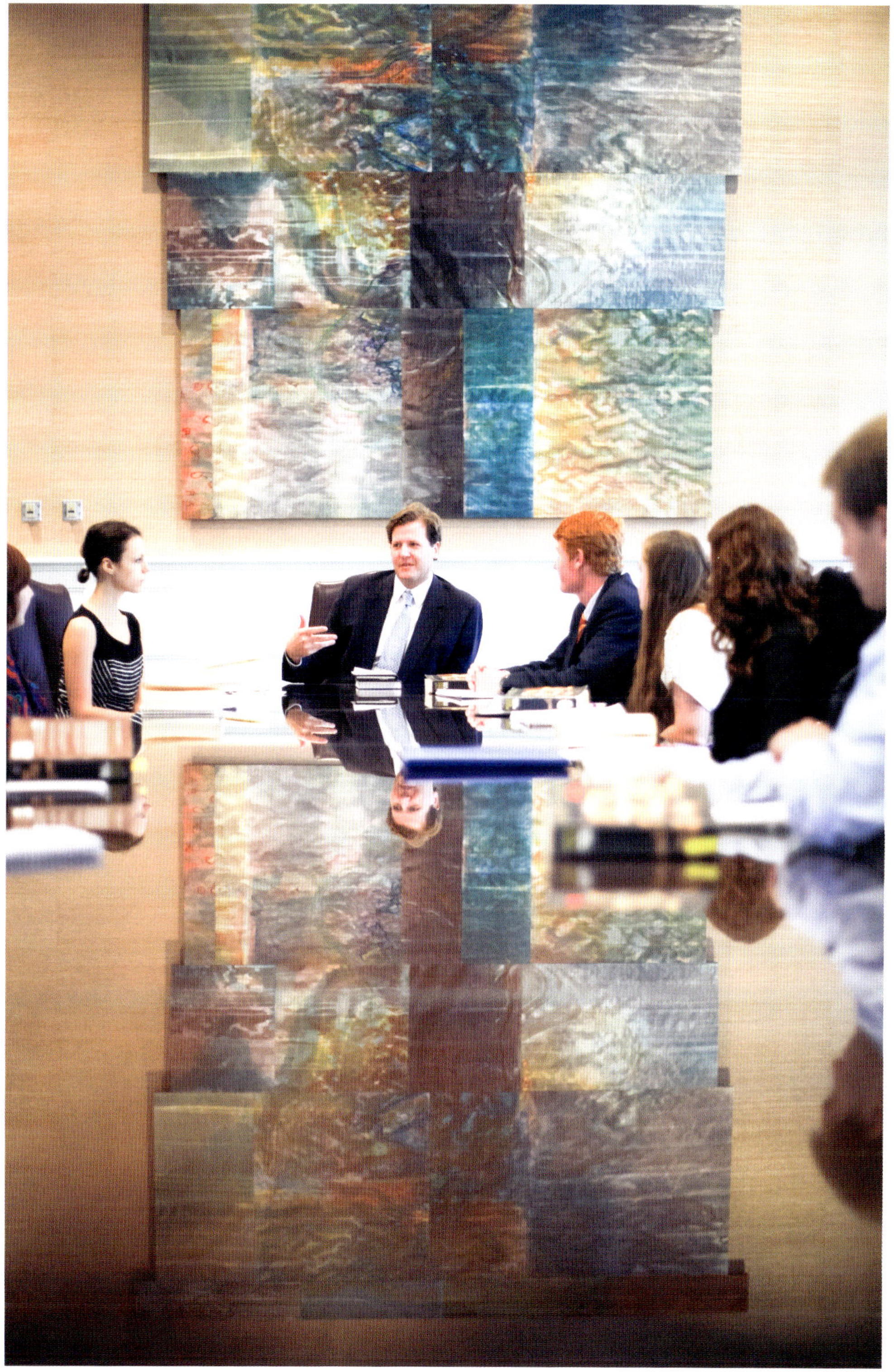

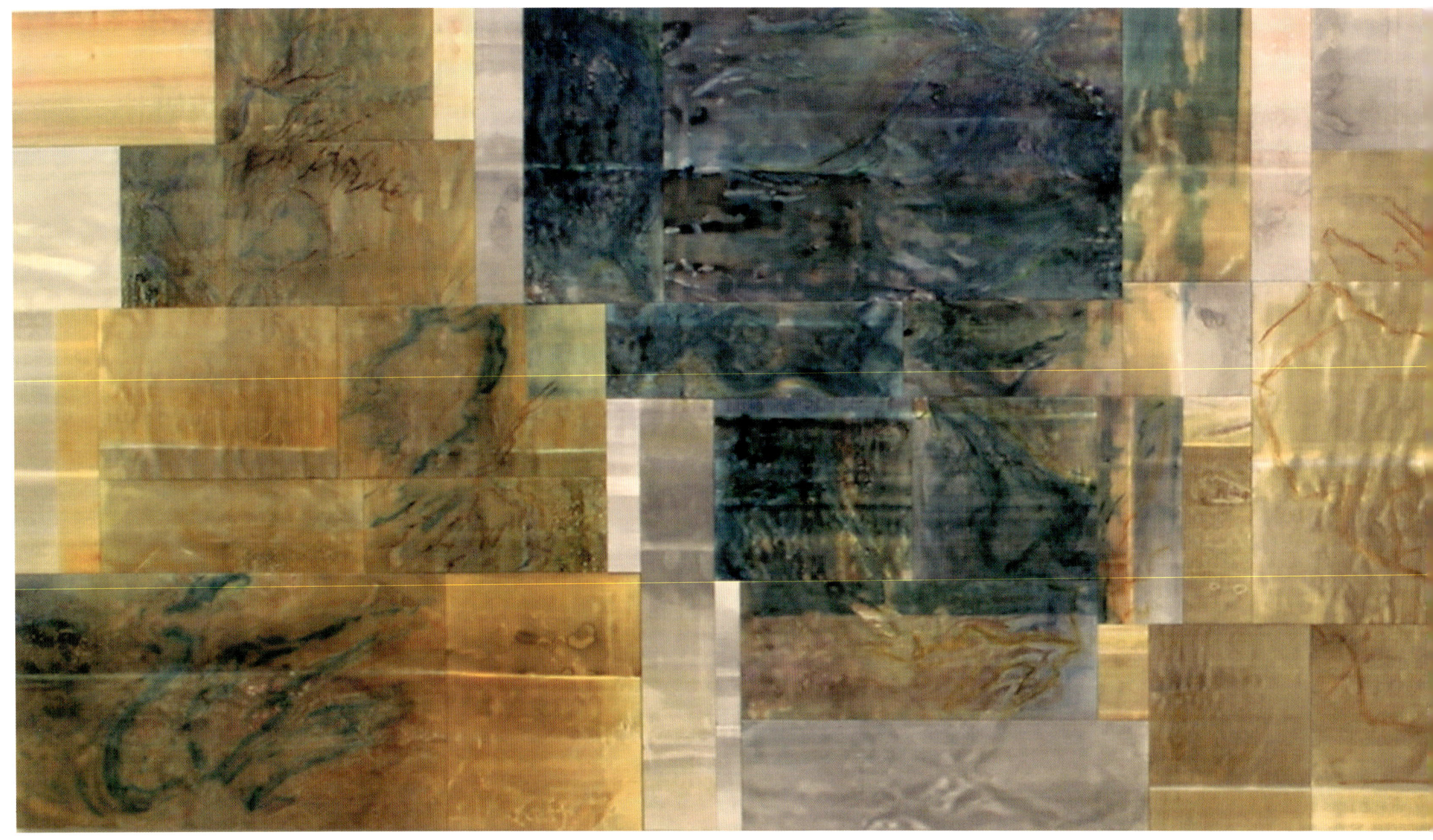

Ray Kass and the Mountain Lake Workshop, *Broad Channel: Vorticella Polyptych*, 1991
watercolor on rag paper, under shaved beeswax, mounted on 68 primed wood panels
97 x 350 in. (246.38 x 889 cm), Collection of the Nevada Museum of Art,
gift of Howard Risatti in memory of James Risatti

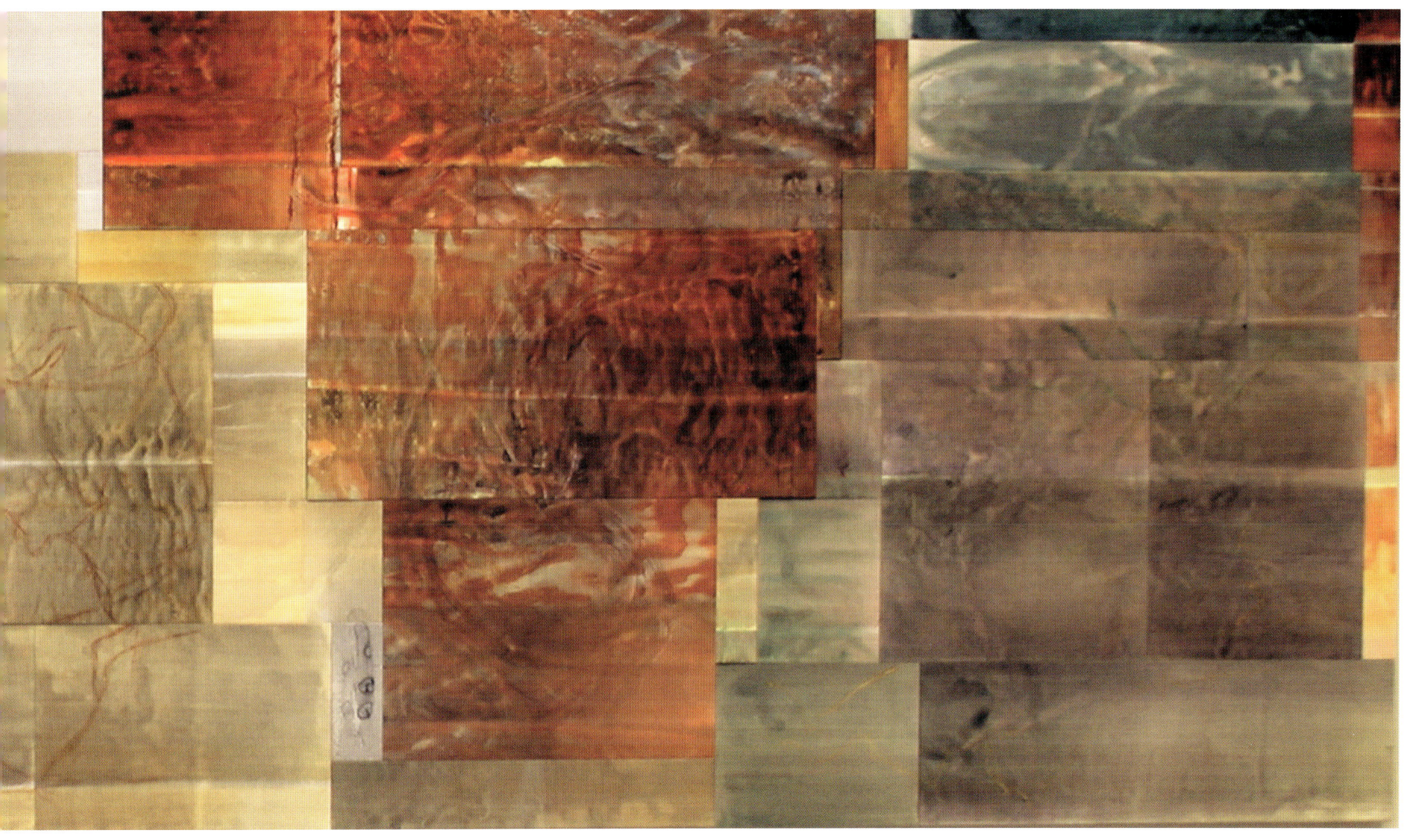

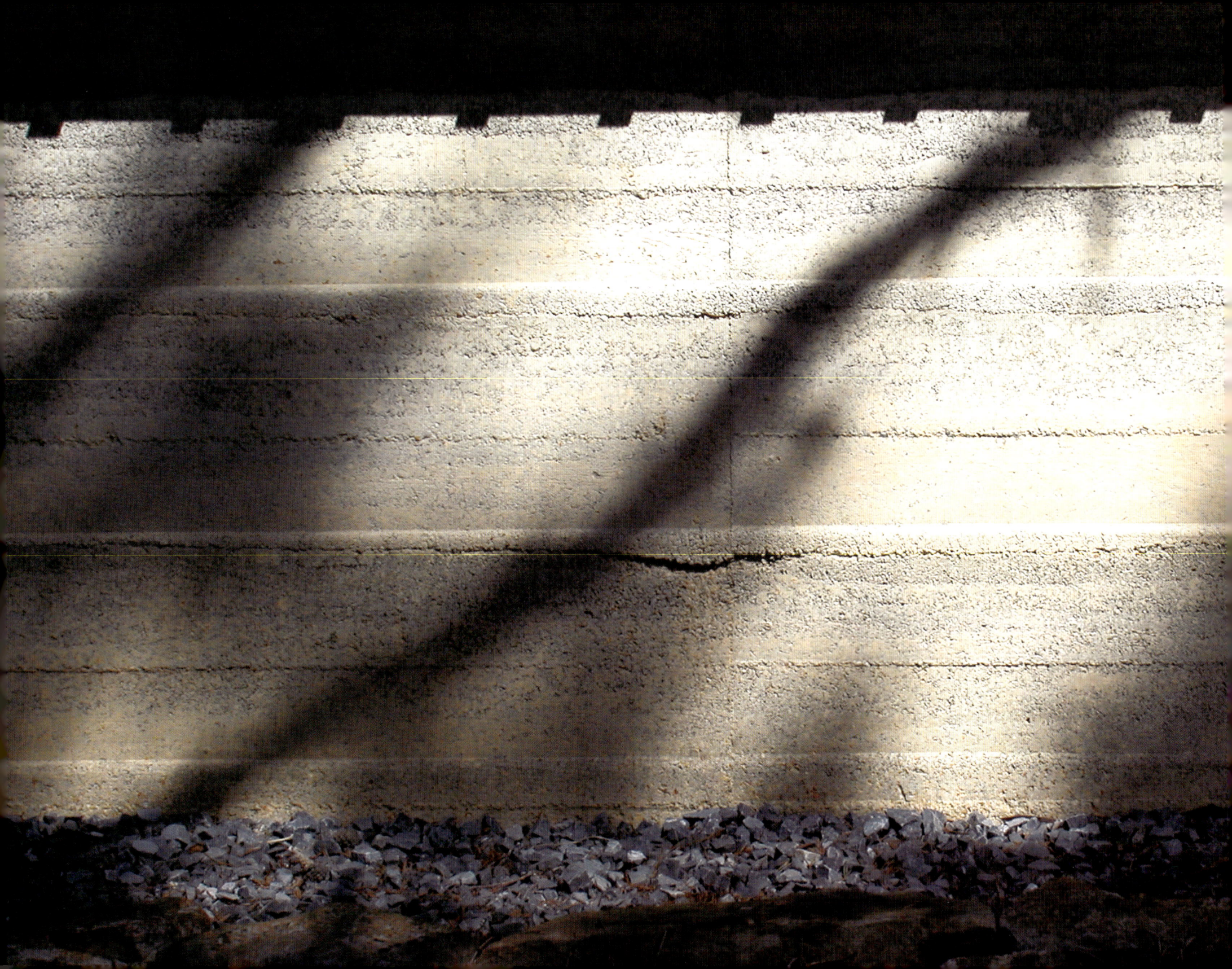

# VII

*Ki no Ichiku*
*(Relocating the Tree)*

# *KI NO ICHIKU*: AN INTRODUCTION

HOWARD RISATTI with RAY KASS

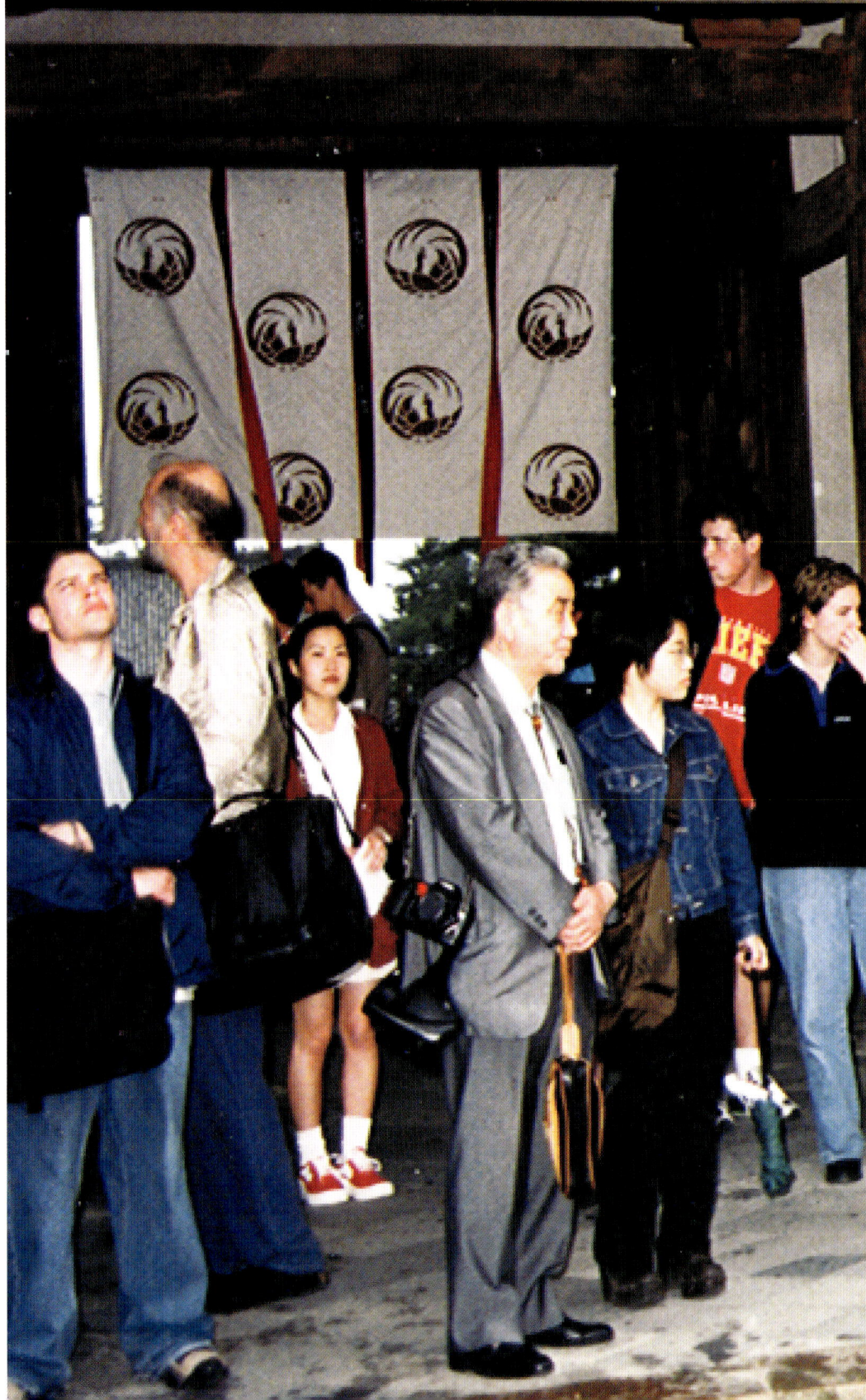

Participants gather at the temple gate of Horyu-ji to listen to Mitsuo Ogawa, master carpenter.
Photo Credit: Peter Laws

*Ki no Ichiku*, "Relocating the Tree," was a three-year-long interdisciplinary study-abroad project in art and design sponsored by Virginia Tech's Honors Program. The project encouraged the participation of students from a broad range of academic programs.

In the spring of 1997, project directors Ray Kass (Department of Art and Art History and director of the Mountain Lake Workshop) and Peter Lau (School of Architecture + Design) traveled to Japan with a group of fifteen Virginia Tech students from various academic programs. Their project was centered in the Kansai region of Japan, which includes Kyoto, Nara, Osaka, and Kobe. Japan's most significant cultural sites and many of its designated National Treasures are to be found in the ancient capitals of Kyoto and Nara and the surrounding area. The two-week-long curriculum set for the students took them to expert lectures and tours of gardens, the workshop of *Noh* mask carvers and painters, and a textile-dyeing design studio, and introduced them to *karakami* (*fusuma* door woodblock printing) and professionals concerned with many aspects of traditional and contemporary Japanese architecture. Everywhere they visited they engaged in hands-on projects involving traditional Japanese arts and crafts, including techniques of wooden architecture and carpentry, *sumi-e* (ink) painting, lacquer work, fabric dyeing and design, *Noh* mask carving and painting, and garden design.

Kass and Lau continued the *Ki no Ichiku* program in the summer of 1998 at Virginia Tech to interact with on-campus coursework focused on Asian art and architecture techniques, a painting workshop with Kyoto-based artist Michael Hofmann, and a second Okura project. These *Ki no Ichiku* projects were sponsored by Virginia Tech's Honors Program and Design Consortium, College of Architecture and Urban Studies, and Department of Art and Art History.

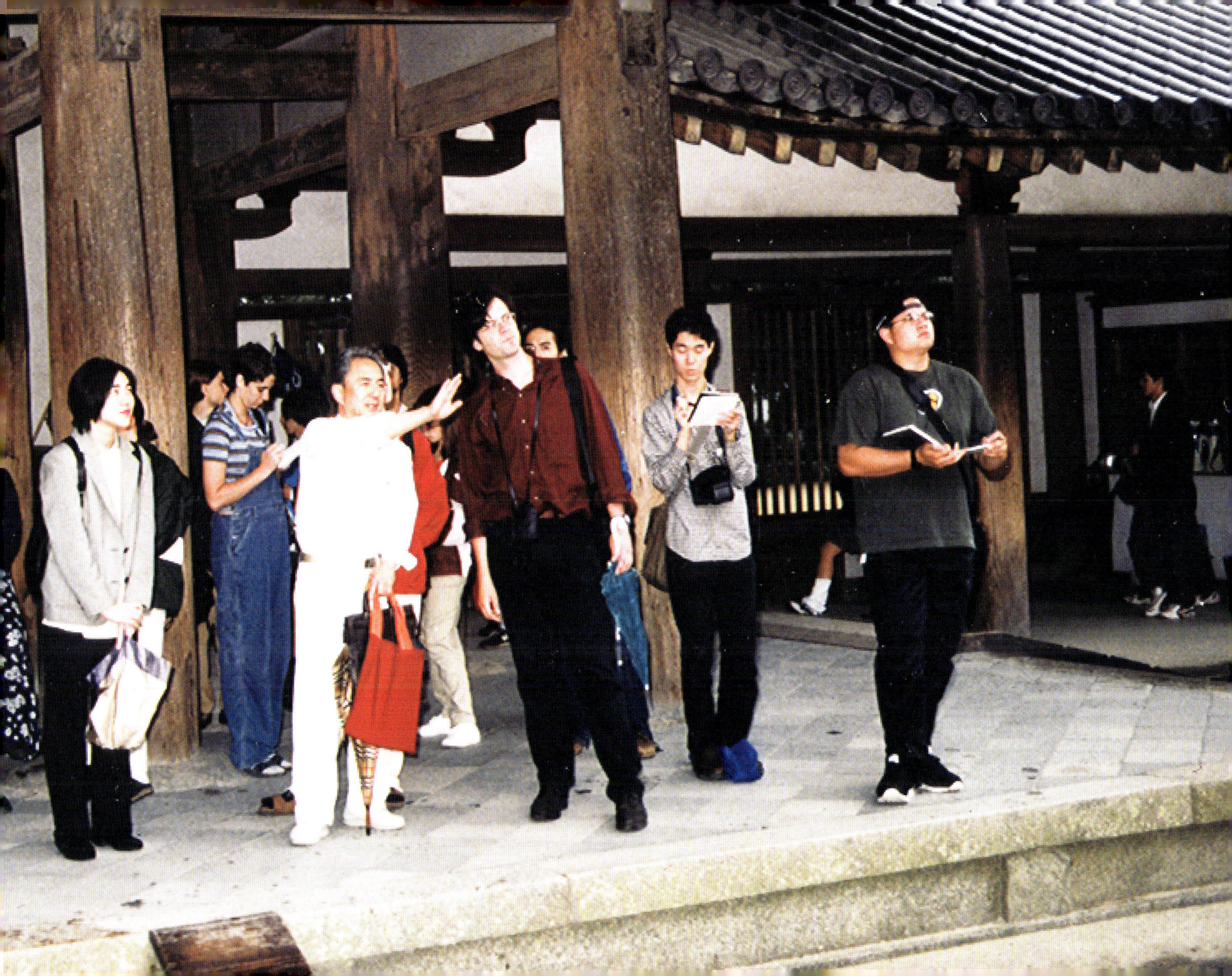

# THE *KI NO ICHIKU* PROJECT

**PETER LAU**

Mitsuo Ogawa, master carpenter, demonstrating the use of traditional Japanese hand tools at the Ikaruga Kosha Workshop in Nara Prefecture.
Photo Credit: Peter Laws

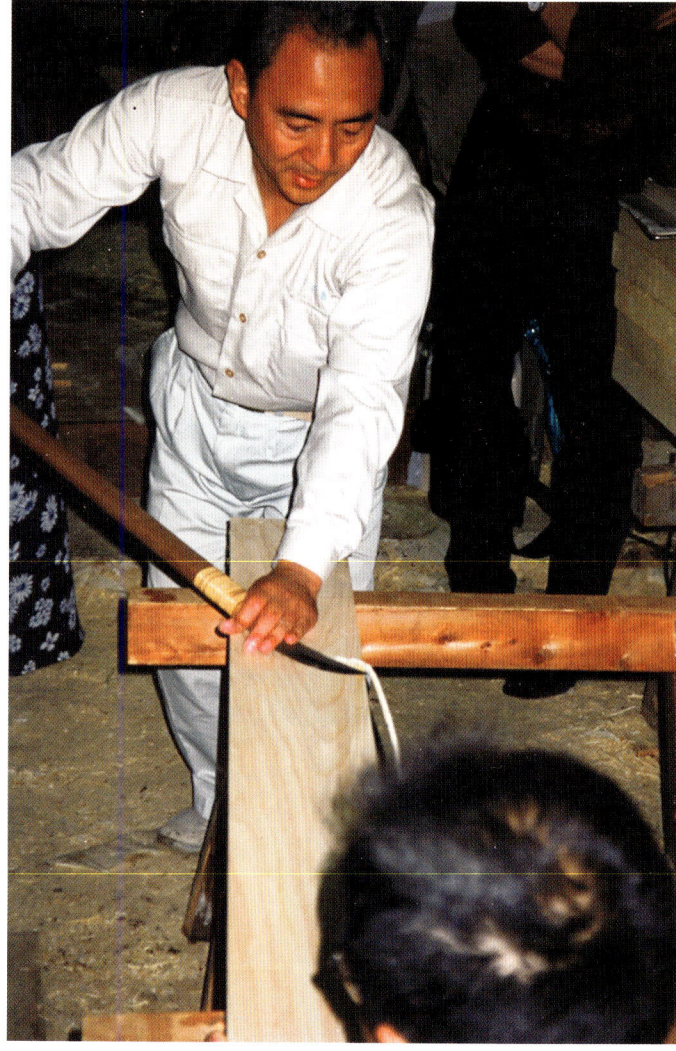

Following the tradition of the Mountain Lake Workshop, Ray Kass and I developed a program we called *Ki no Ichiku* ("Relocating the Tree") as a way to create meaningful experiences for students and members of the local community. Spanning a period between 1997 and 2000, *Ki no Ichiku* was intended to expose participants to art and design sensibilities found in Japanese culture. We started it as an interdisciplinary study-abroad program with a vision to expand into a full-fledged exchange program with academic institutions based in the U.S., Japan, and China. Though it never became a long-term exchange program, the collaborations it generated created bodies of work during the three years the program ran that now serve as part of the legacy of *Ki no Ichiku* and the Mountain Lake Workshop, namely the *Nisso Screen* (1997), the *Zen Garden Wall* and *Moon Viewing Pavilion* (1998), and *Souls on Garbage* (1998), a *sumi-e* painting workshop led by Michael Hofmann and Ray Kass on behalf of Kyoto artist Jiro Okura, who was unable to direct the project as planned.

My work on this Mountain Lake program grew from my own experiences as principal assistant to Ray Kass and the Mountain Lake Workshops from 1988 to 1990 (John Cage, 1988, 1989, and 1990; Howard Finster, 1989; and Jiro Okura, 1990) as well as my experiences in Japan, where I lived for seven years (1991–1998) after graduating in architecture from Virginia Tech. Working with Cage and Okura inspired me to move to Japan in the first place, and I spent most of my time in and around Kyoto as an apprentice to a master carpenter and later as a designer and carpenter for an architect specializing in traditional Japanese architecture. During my tenure in Japan, Kass and I began discussing the possibility of relocating

a historical building from Japan to the Virginia Tech campus. Out of that discussion we developed the idea to do a study-aboard program partnering with Kyoto University. The study-abroad idea, readily supported by Virginia Tech, created a framework for doing a workshop with Kyoto University students, all with the hope of building momentum for our relocation project.

I selected the Japanese title *Ki no Ichiku* ("Relocating the Tree"), because it conveyed an aspiration of the program not only to relocate a building, but also to create a cultural exchange through the transfer or "relocation" of knowledge and skills. *Ichiku* translates to "relocation," and *Ki* is "tree" or "wood." For the *Ki no Ichiku* program, *Ki* symbolized aspects of Japanese carpentry, arts and crafts, traditional architecture, and garden design that became a large part of the program content. *Ki* is also a motif found in Okura's work and the Mountain Lake workshops that he led.

*Ki no Ichiku* was cross cultural and interdisciplinary in nature in that participants hailed from several countries and had backgrounds in fields both design-related (e.g., art, architecture, landscape architecture, industrial design, and interior design) and non-design related (e.g. English, history, philosophy, engineering, and physics). We launched it in May and June of 1997 in the Kansai region of Japan and expanded it from a study-abroad program to an intensive, hands-on course at Virginia Tech in the summer of 1998. After another study-abroad program in 2000 (in Japan and China), *Ki no Ichiku* was ultimately intended to culminate with the seminal idea — the relocation of a salvaged historical building from Japan or China to the Virginia Tech campus for the purpose

of creating a focal point for an interdisciplinary academic curriculum for a broad range of students and the community.

The first study-abroad program (1997) spanned two weeks with the option of an additional week or two of self-directed study and featured key activities, typically twice a day, including workshops, demonstrations, lectures, and visits to several of Japan's great

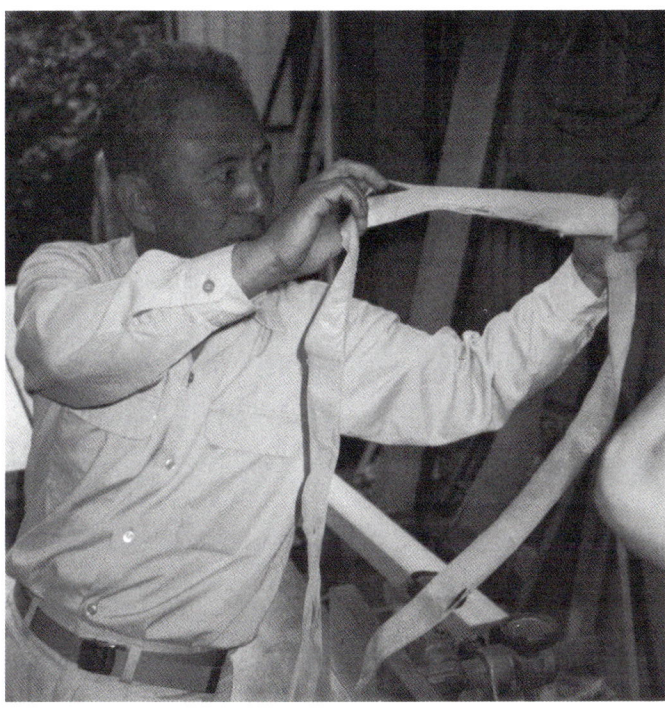

Mitsuo Ogawa shows
students micro-thin ribbon
of freshly planed wood.
Photo Credit: Peter Laws

Students visit Aizen Kobo,
the workshop of Kenichi
Utsuki, master indigo dyer.
Photo Credit: Peter Laws

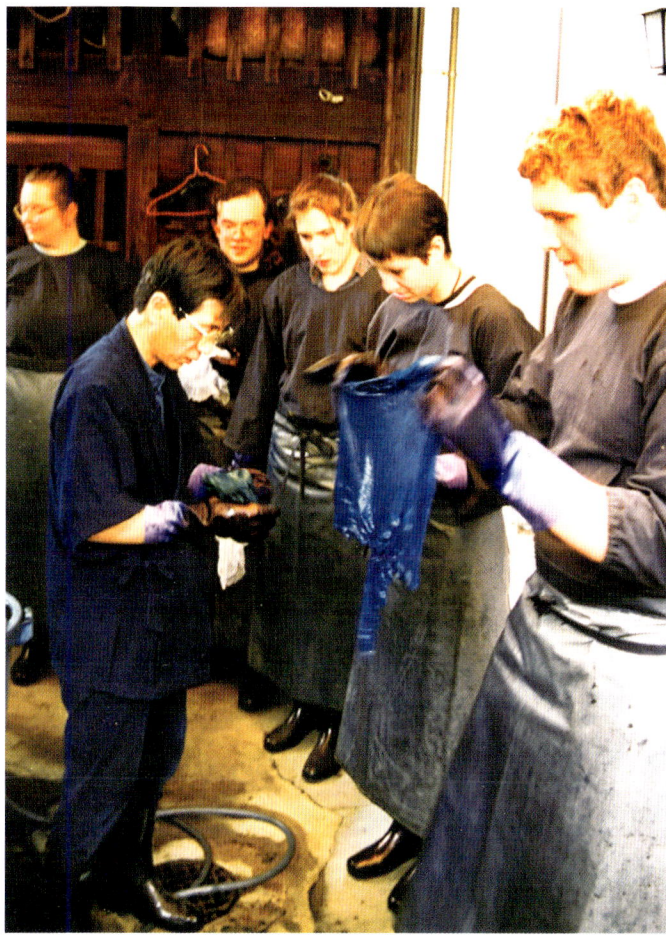

compound and his adjacent workshop, Ikaruga Kosha. In the workshop Ogawa explained Japan's long-standing tradition of master and apprentice, a process by which knowledge and skills are transferred through generations and an important reason many of the cultural traditions in Japan remain alive today. He demonstrated how to use several hand tools rarely found outside the world of traditional Japanese carpentry and at one point used a block plane to shave off several micro-thin ribbons of wood, each a couple inches wide and several yards long, from a timber column. Students carefully rolled up the nearly transparent ribbons for safekeeping as souvenirs.

The visits, like the one to Ikaruga Kosha, were behind-the-scenes explorations that revealed aspects of ancient arts and crafts not normally seen by outsiders. However, because these experts knew their worlds were threatened by modern culture, they were willing to open their workshops in hope of generating greater interest, building a wider audience, and keeping their respective traditions alive. Many such visits were featured during both the 1997 and 2000 study-abroad programs, including Karacho, a thirteenth-generation family of woodblock printers who produced the ancient patterns and geometries found on *fusuma* doors in places such as Shugaku-in and other historical buildings in Japan; Aizen Kobo, the indigo-dyeing workshop in Nishijin, Kyoto's famous textile district; Ryoichi Kinoshita, an architect and leader in the revitalization of Kyoto's traditional architecture; Marc Keane, landscape architect and author specializing in Japanese garden design; Ryosaku Takeda, master lacquerer and woodworker; Andrew Hare, an expert in the conservation of Japanese and Chinese paintings; Monica Bethe, an expert in *Noh* drama; Daniel Fagereng, artist and

*Noh* mask carver; and Julianne Fiore, a *shiatsu* specialist.

Embedded within the 1997 study-abroad program was a collaborative *sumi-e* painting workshop with Kyoto University that produced *Borrowed View: The Nisso Screen*. Led by Jiro Okura and sponsored by Nisso Industries, the workshop was co-produced by Ray Kass and me from Virginia Tech and Professor Shuji Funo and Mari Tanaka, a doctoral student, both of whom were at Kyoto University at the time. Similar to the Shisendo Garden Paintings workshops he did with Mountain Lake (1992 and 1993), Okura gave the brush to others to paint

temples, shrines, and gardens (e.g., Ryoan-ji, Shisendo, Honen-in, Fushimi-inari, Ryosen-an, Horyu-ji, Katsura Rikyu, and Shugaku-in among others). The program featured prominent master craftspeople, architects, artists, and academics. Big-name architects Tadao Ando and Shin Takamatsu were featured speakers who graciously opened their respective offices to talk to the group about design. Many of the participants still recall Tadao Ando's exuberant and self-aggrandizing explanation that all of his built work was based on the winning entries from inner-office design charrettes, which were held each time a new project came into the office. At the end of his explanation, he proudly pointed out he always won because his designs were the best. When quizzed by one of the students as to who determined this, Ando replied that he did, of course, because no one else in the office was qualified to judge the charrettes!

Perhaps more meaningful moments came from Mitsuo Ogawa — master carpenter of Horyu-ji, one of the world's oldest extant wooden buildings — who gave an in-depth tour of the temple

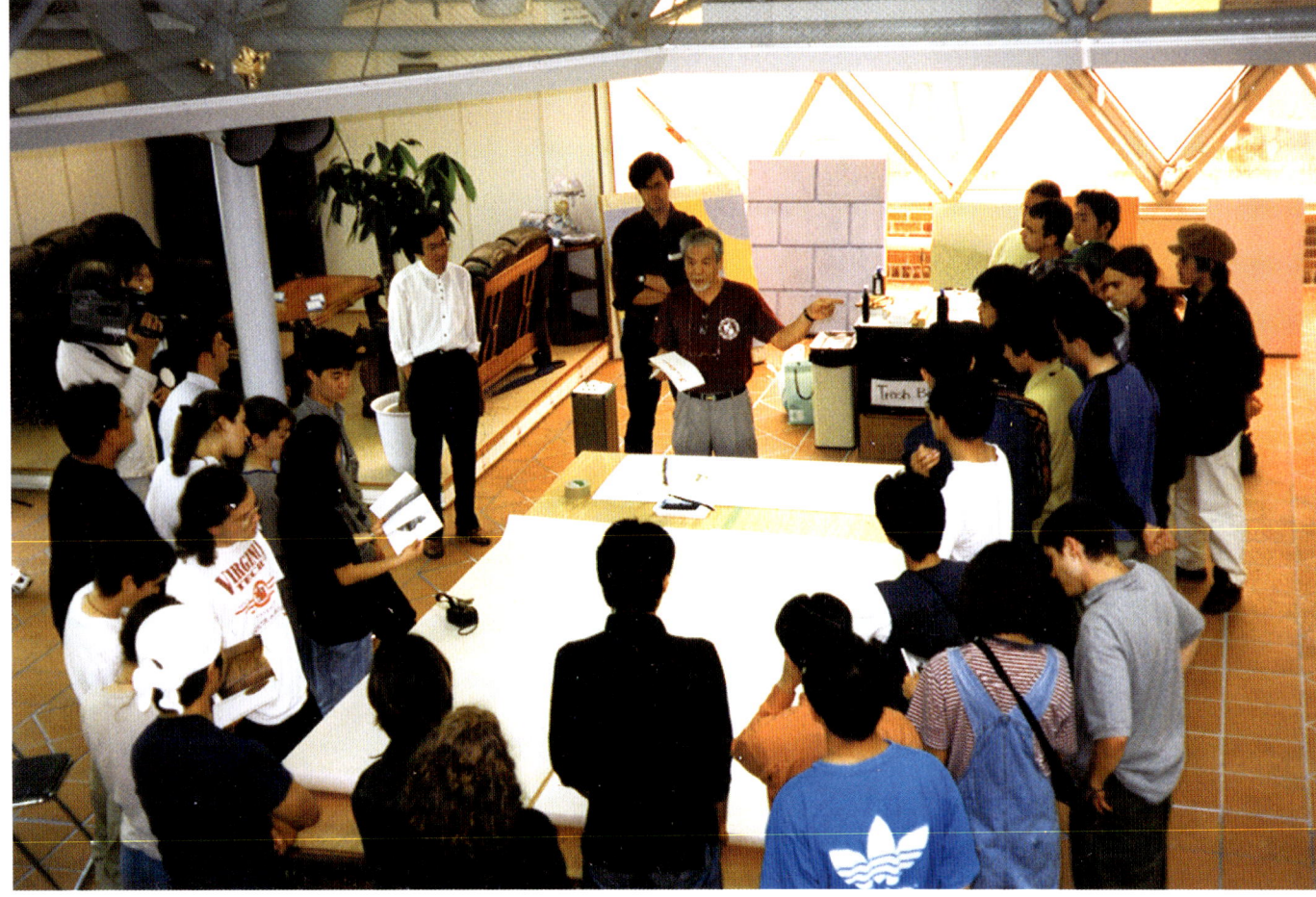

Participants gather inside Nisso Corporation's "Glass Pyramid" to listen to Jiro Okura explain the workshop activities.
Photo Credit: Peter Laws

technical exposure through hands-on, discipline-centered activities. I was lucky to have a great group of students and volunteers, including a teaching assistant and student who had been participants in the 1997 study-abroad program, students who enrolled in other summer classes, students who were not enrolled in classes but there for the summer, a high school student, alumni who lived in the area, alumni who came from out of town to help, and other volunteers from the community. They all came with enthusiasm, focus, and in some cases skills applicable to executing the *Moon Viewing Pavilion* and *Zen Garden Wall* in nearby Christiansburg.

The primary focus was hands-on activities centered around the two projects: crafting the pavilion utilizing 18-foot-long redwood staves, which the local timberwright supplied out of his inventory and which had been salvaged from old California wine barrels years before; and building a 4-foot-high, 26-foot-long rammed-earth garden wall using techniques over two thousand years old. We also spent time in the classroom where more conventional coursework included introductory lessons on Japanese architecture, carpentry, and garden design. Several Virginia Tech professors and local specialists generously offered their time and expertise as guest lecturers, speaking on topics relevant to the course. Short working sessions were held to familiarize the students with the hand tools in preparation for building the pavilion; shop fabrication of the pavilion got underway. Simultaneously, field tests were conducted and test blocks were made using local soil mixtures in order to determine the best blend of earth for building the garden wall. Thus began the process of wall building described in a later essay in this

the meditative line drawings instead of painting with just his own hand. Each person took turns carefully drawing one line at a time, finishing each line before the next line was started by another person. Line after line, this continued late into the afternoon until it became apparent that time was running out and we needed to pick up the pace in order to finish what we started before nightfall. At Professor Funo's suggestion, we shifted our approach, allowing participants to start a new line while the previous line was still being drawn, which essentially increased our pace twofold. Later that evening, Professor Funo

participated in a group toast; citing the belief that postwar Japan's economic leap forward was largely due to the adoption of U.S. manufacturing processes, he joked that it was only natural for him, as part of the postwar generation, to propose the time-saving idea that had saved the day, enabling us to complete 48 paintings!

The study-abroad programs were relatively short and required activities to fit nicely within day-long agendas. The 1998 summer curriculum at Virginia Tech, however, was planned within a six-week-long session, which allowed us to offer deeper

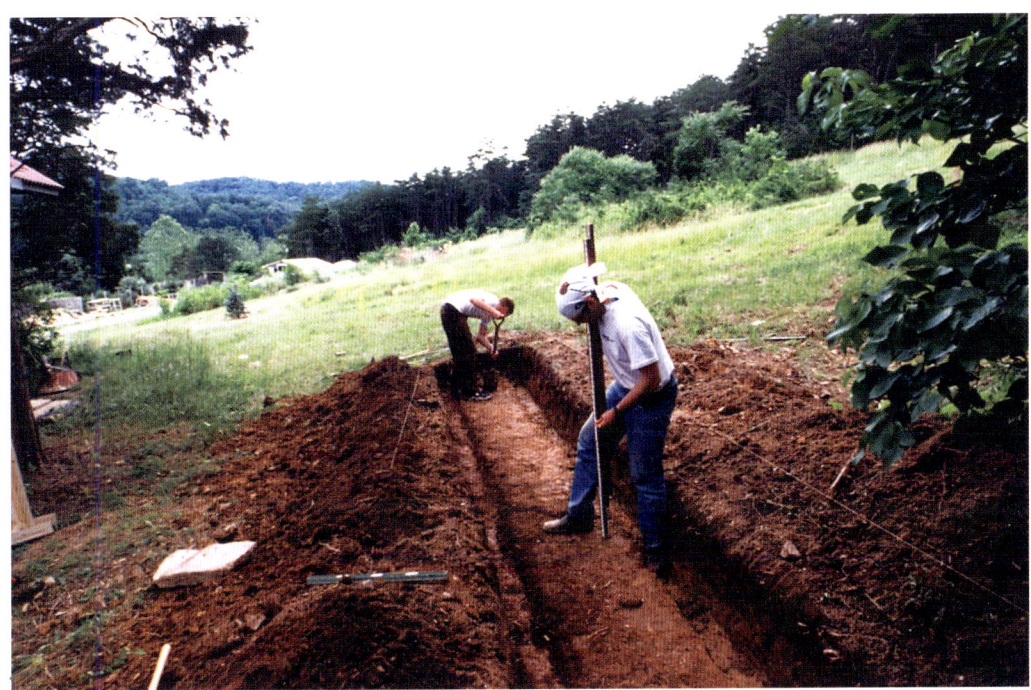

Students excavate for wall foundation and drainage. Photo Credit: Peter Lau

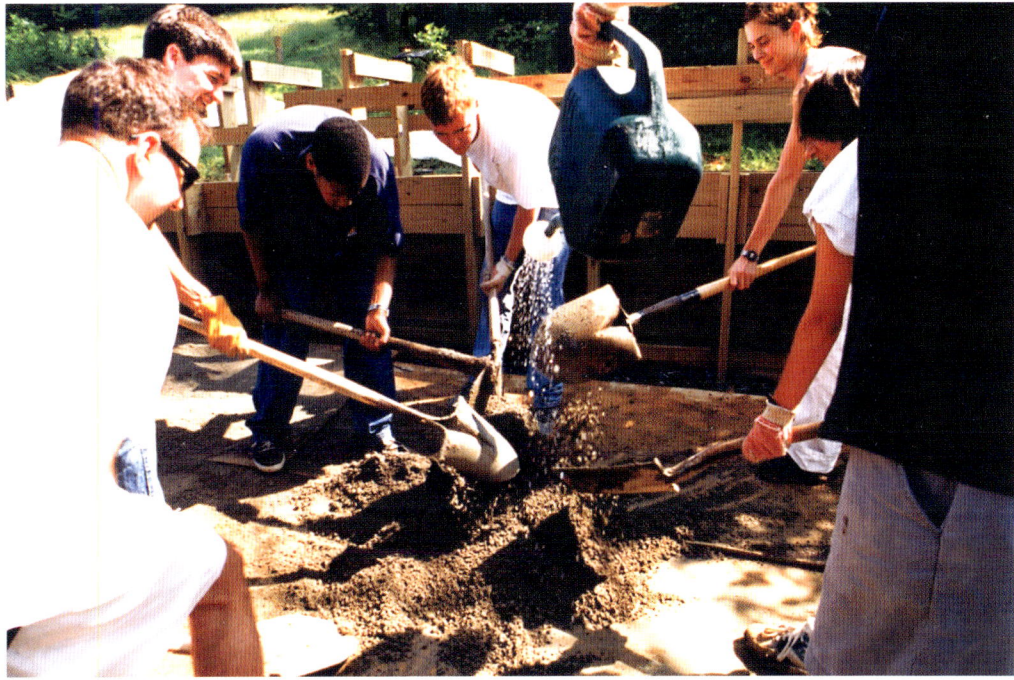

Participants prepare soil mixture. Photo Credit: Peter Lau

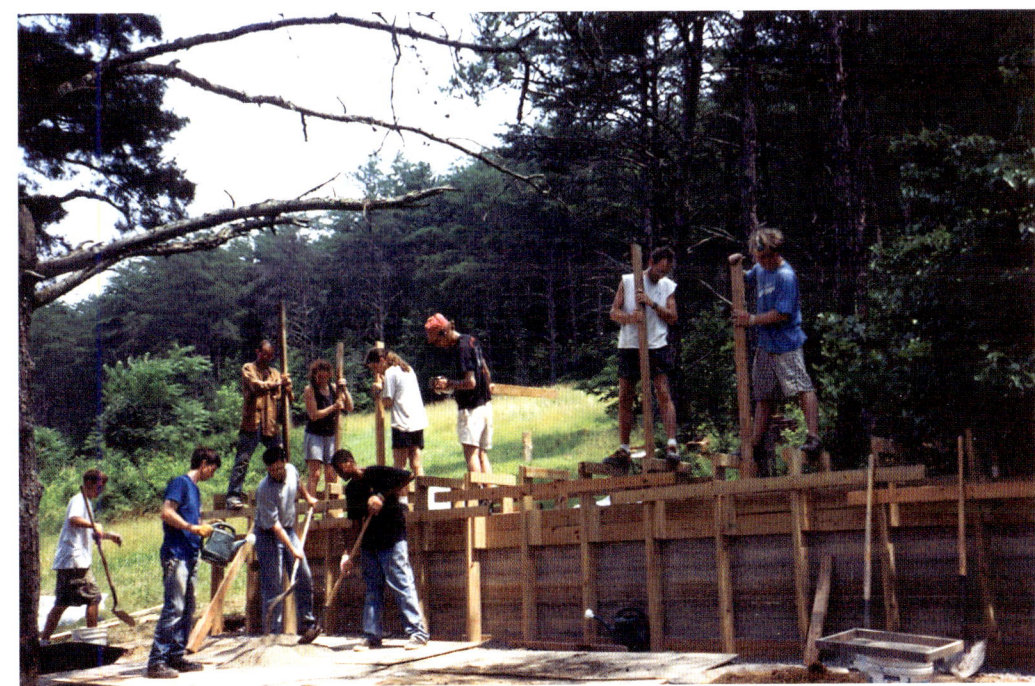

Participants tamp soil mixture in formwork. Photo Credit: Peter Lau

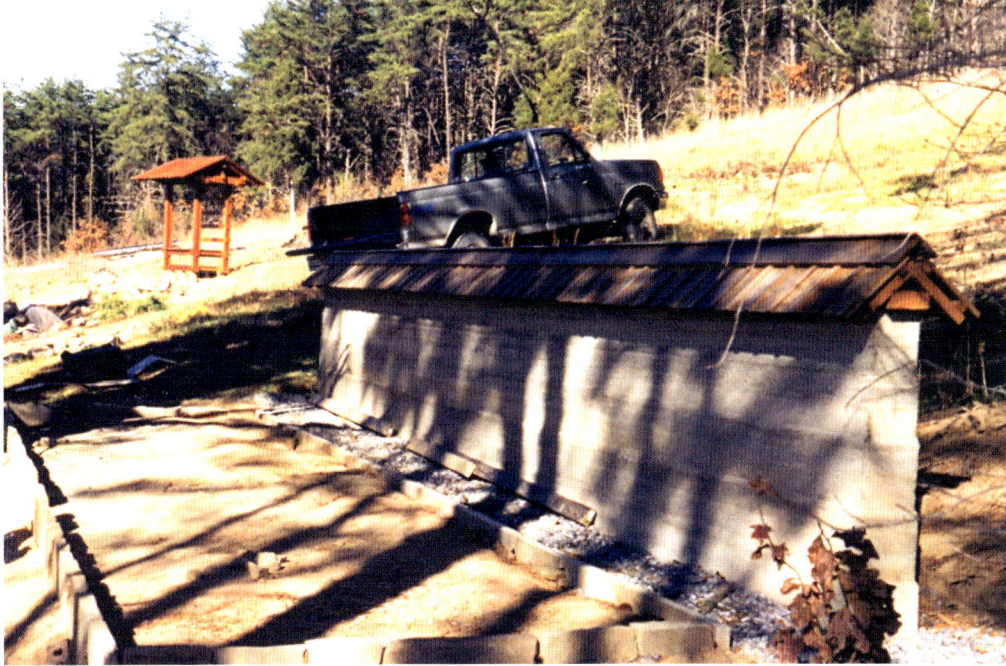

Rock garden under construction next to completed rammed-earth wall with Moon Viewing Pavilion visible in the background. Photo Credit: Peter Lau

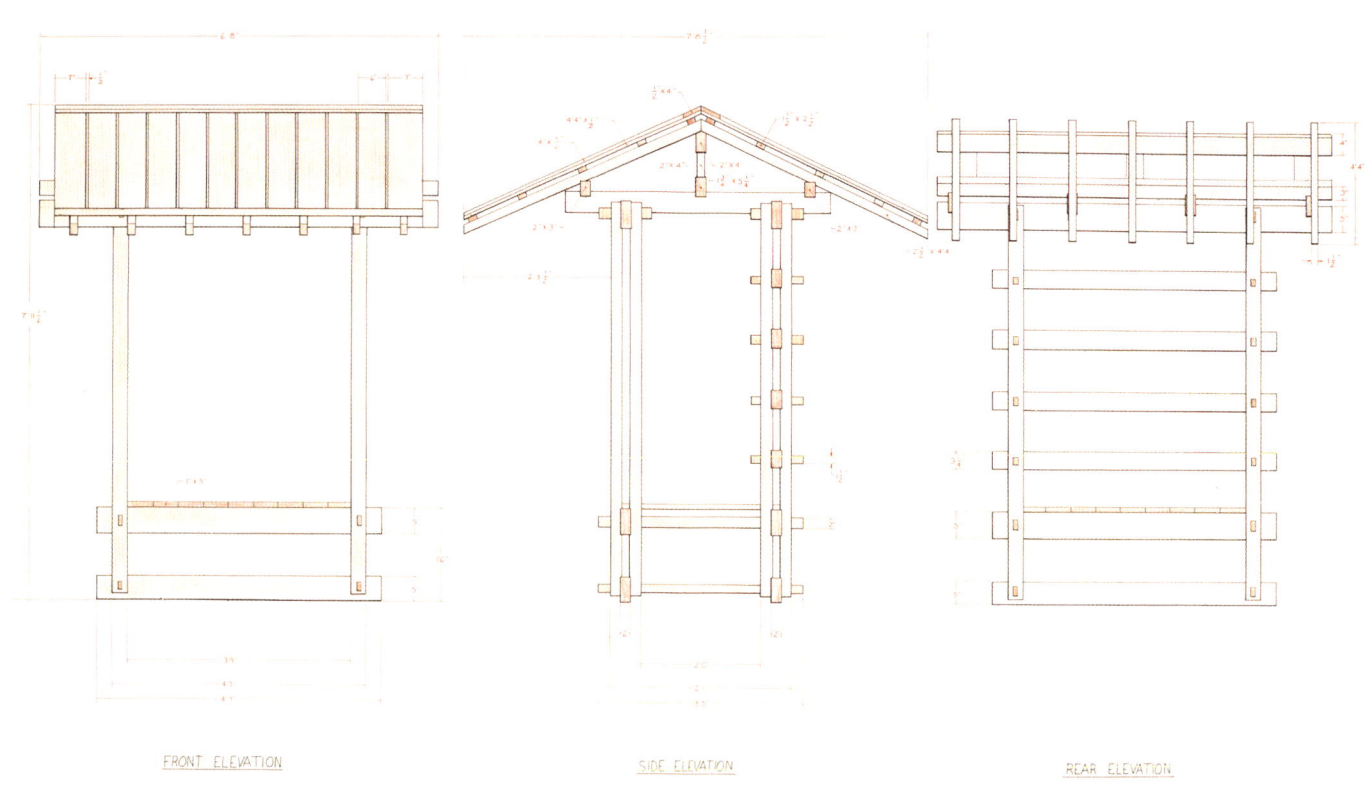

FRONT ELEVATION    SIDE ELEVATION    REAR ELEVATION

chapter, "Constructing a Rammed-Earth Wall for a Japanese Garden." The completed wall and pavilion are important components of the garden, which was laid out as part of the summer session and within about a decade had fully matured.

Building the pavilion and wall were steps to the larger-scale project of relocating the building to the Virginia Tech campus, and though it was never realized, we did lead another study-abroad program. In 2000 we traveled to Japan and China, splitting time between the Kansai region of Japan and Shanghai, Souzhou, and the Huangshan Mountains in China. The ancient gardens of Souzhou and quintessential imagery of Huangshan offered new and strong connections for the program which also helped create a deeper context for bridging the cultures.

Vital to the *Ki no Ichiku* project, as with other Mountain Lake workshops, was making a body of work as a means for creating meaningful experiences for participants and not just as an end in itself. Also important to the workshops is sharing with audiences how the work was made — the "making of" aspect. For many years the "making of" *Ki no Ichiku* was on display as an exhibition in the guesthouse adjacent to the Zen garden, a garden which, with other interconnected gardens, was developed over the years as part of the composition of the wall and pavilion.

Jerrie Pike, one of Kass' and my closest collaborators, wrote in an essay about one of the Mountain Lake workshops that "it is the custom of the Mountain Lake Workshop to adapt themes and methods from previous workshops and appropriately apply them to new endeavors." To me, *Ki no Ichiku* accomplished this along with creating meaningful experiences for all who put hand to brush, picked up a tool, or embraced the hot summer days in Japan, China, or western Virginia.

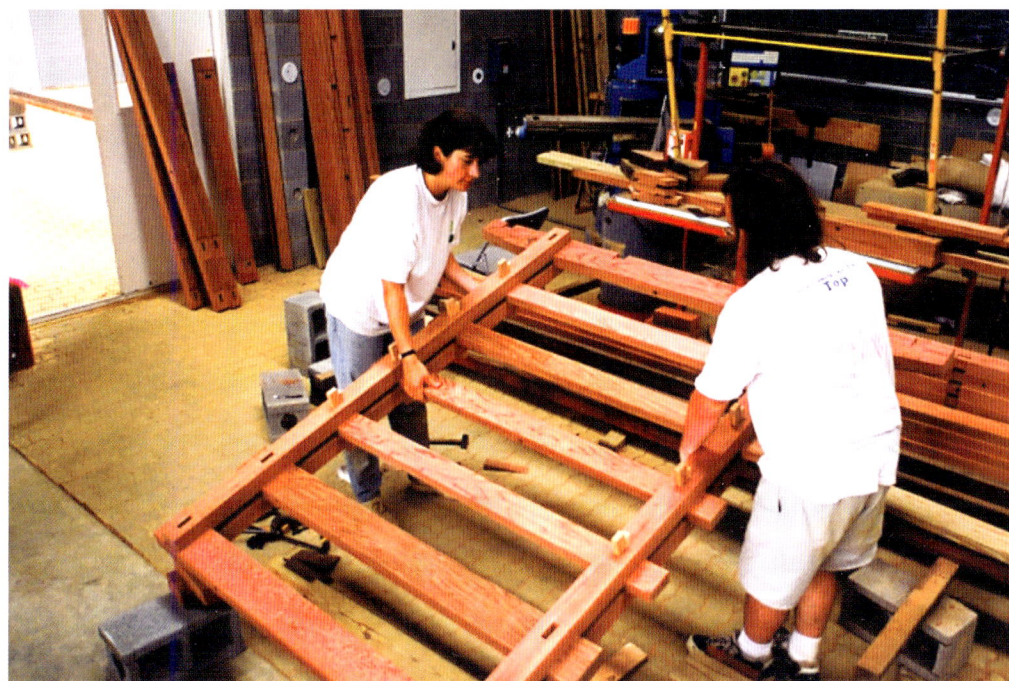

Students fabricate pavilion components. Photo Credit: Peter Lau

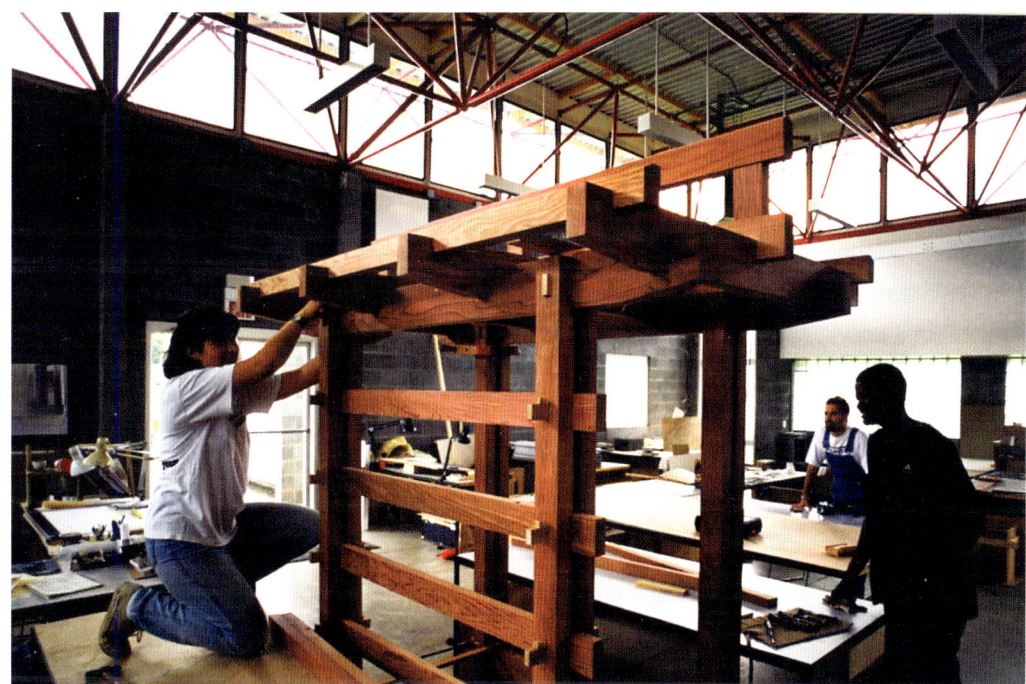

Students pre-assemble pavilion. Photo Credit: Peter Lau

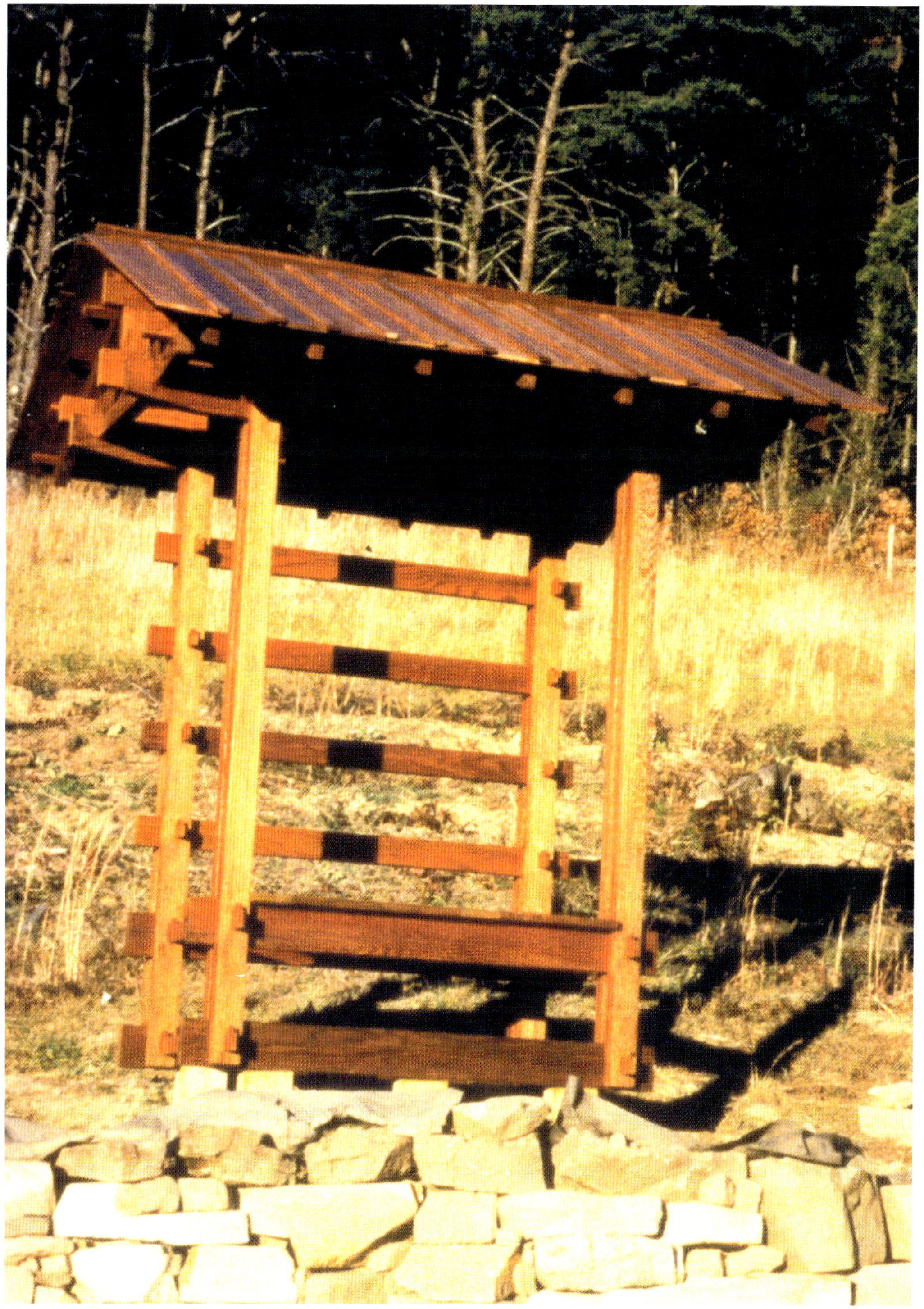

Assembled pavilion on site. Photo Credit: Peter Lau

# ANCIENT CAPITAL THROUGH THE EYES OF A NOT-SO-JAPANESE STUDENT

TARO HATANAKA

When I first learned about the *Ki no Ichiku* study-abroad program, I thought that it would be mostly visits to popular tourist destinations in the ancient capital of Japan. However, after attending several of the preparation meetings, I realized that this trip was going to be one of a kind and was going to be co-directed by two leaders with important connections in Japan who could arrange in-depth and otherwise inaccessible opportunities for us. We were a lucky group of fewer than twenty students whose common interests were generally related to art and design.

I am of Japanese descent and was born in Tokyo. However, by the time I enrolled in the College of Architecture and Urban Studies at Virginia Tech at the age of eighteen, I had spent more than one third of my life abroad in Europe, including six years at a private secondary school in Geneva, Switzerland. The foundation of how I thought and behaved was established during my adolescence in Europe. I had left Tokyo before I knew enough about Japanese culture to represent my country to the world.

At Virginia Tech my new American friends often asked me about many things related to Japan, but I felt that I had nothing much to offer. As I pursued my studies in design and architecture, I increasingly wanted to personally experience the depth and complexity of Japanese culture. The *Ki no Ichiku* program provided me with that special opportunity. Many of the personally fulfilling experiences that I had in Kyoto in 1997 left me with an unforgettable impression of the culture of the country of my birth.

The first event of the trip was a performance of a *Noh* play at the Nishi Hongan-ji temple complex. We were extremely fortunate because it is usually necessary to make reservations a year or more in advance. The May 21st event celebrates the birthday of Shin-Ran, founder of the Jodo Shinshu sect of Buddhism. Nishi Hongan-ji has the oldest existing *Noh* stage; on it the renowned actors/playwrights and developers of *Noh* Kan'ami and his son Zeami (1363–1443) performed. The stage is open for public viewing on this day and for only three other days of the year.

**Staying at a Buddhist temple:** Originally Buddhist temples offered accommodations for traveling monks and religious followers. Staying at Shukubo we slept on *tatami* mats, went to the local *sento* (public bath), and attended an early morning Zazen session (Zen-style seated meditation).

*Noh* **mask carving studio:** Daniel Fagereng, a young American apprentice, told us that the mask-carving craftsmen must first learn to make their own sharp tools and cannot progress toward mastery until they overcome their fear of them!

**Komorebi at Ginkaku-ji (Jisho-ji):** Kyoto has a large number of Buddhist temples, and we visited many, including Kinkaku-ji, the "Golden Pavilion;" Ryoan-ji, perhaps the most famous Zen rock garden in Japan; and Ginkaku-ji, the "Silver Pavilion" and garden, which had the greatest impact on me. It features an abstraction of Mt. Fuji, a mound of sand surrounded by an "ocean" of flowing linear patterns of carefully raked sand.

**Imperial Palace at Shugakuin:** The design of the temple pavilions and gardens is very simple, yet beautiful. The gardens often contain "borrowed views," miniature representations of certain landscape features or scenery of folktales.

**Are gaijin (foreigners) more Japanese?:** Why are we learning *shiatsu* massage from an American lady? There are many non-Japanese people living in Japan and learning more Japanese things than most Japanese people. Peter Lau is another one of them, as is Marc Peter Keane, an expert on Japanese gardens who gave us a lecture and tour of Honen-in temple and gardens.

**Pop culture of Japan:** Some students had developed interest in Japan from their passion for anime or manga comics which they purchased at the market.

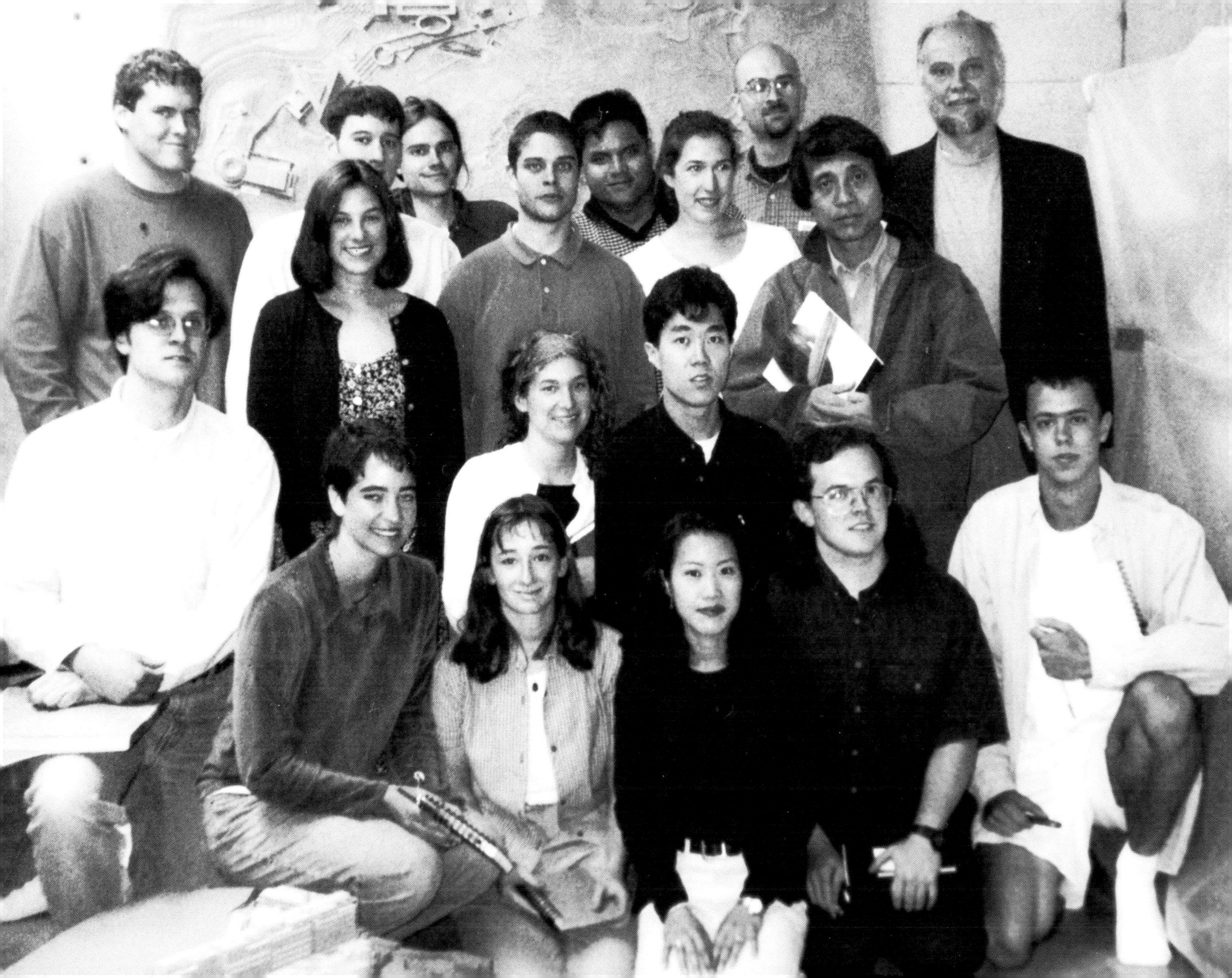

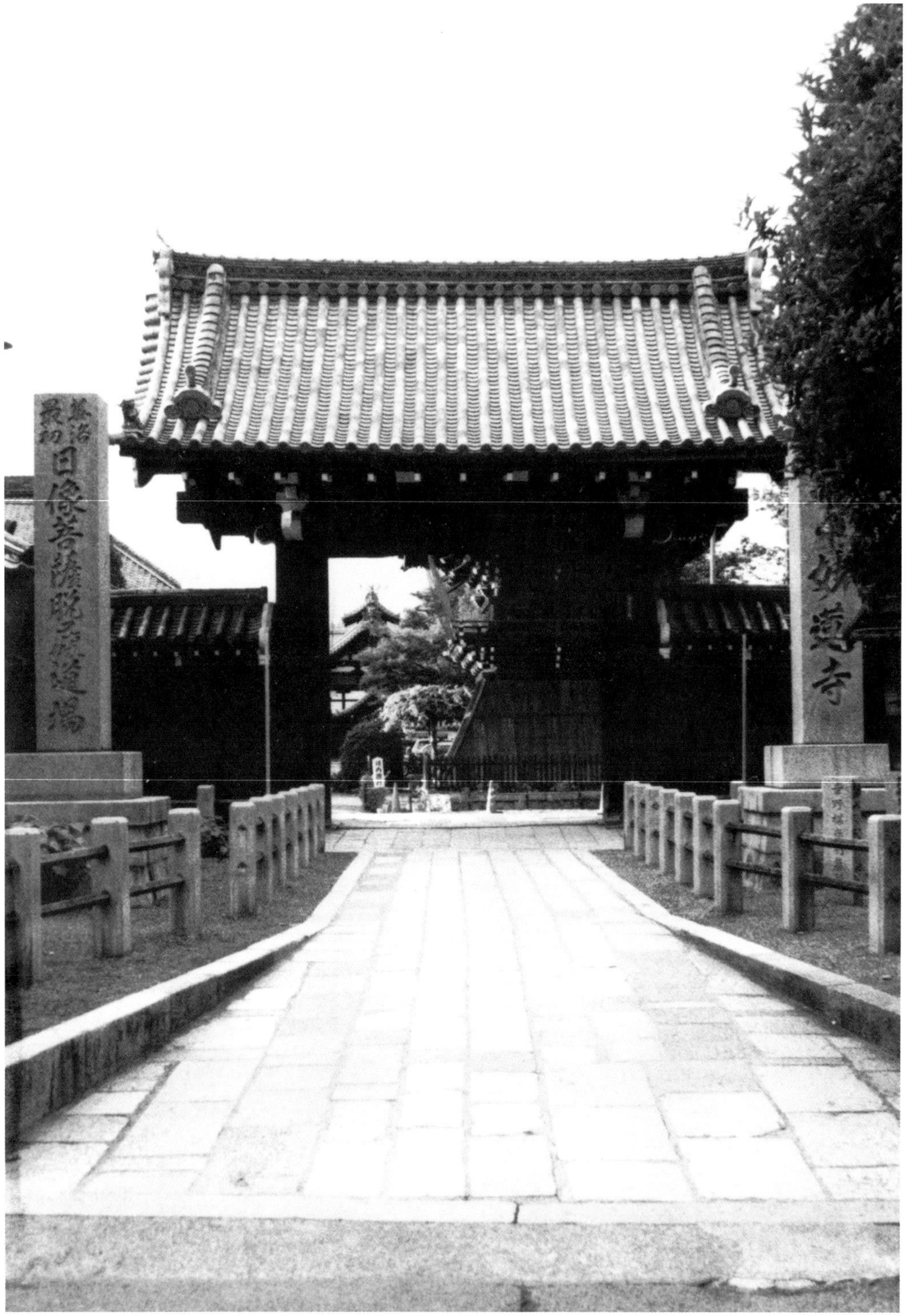

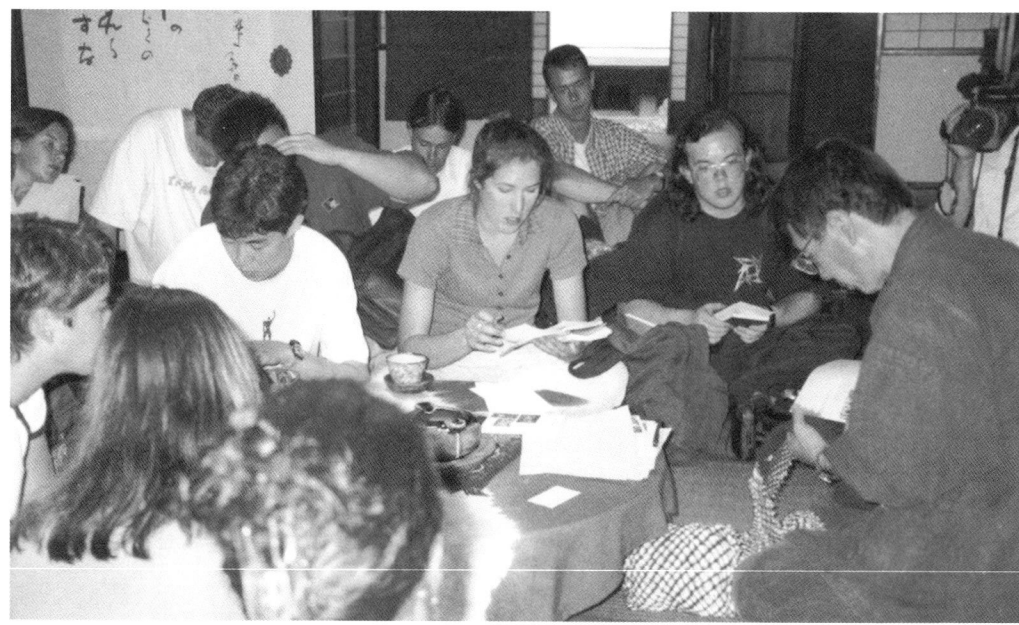

Aizen Kobo, indigo-dyeing workshop with master Kenichi Utsuki, Machiya shop showroom

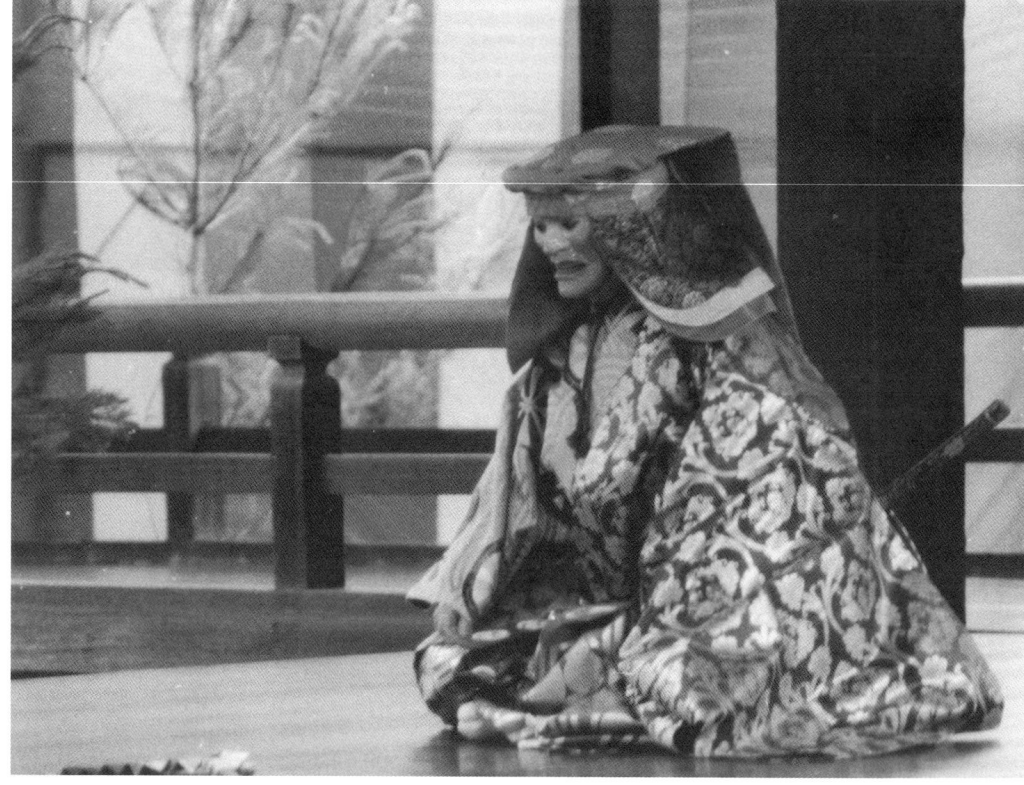

*Noh* actor in traditional costume on stage at Nishi Hongan-ji

Myoren-Ji, Kyoto (our home on our trips)

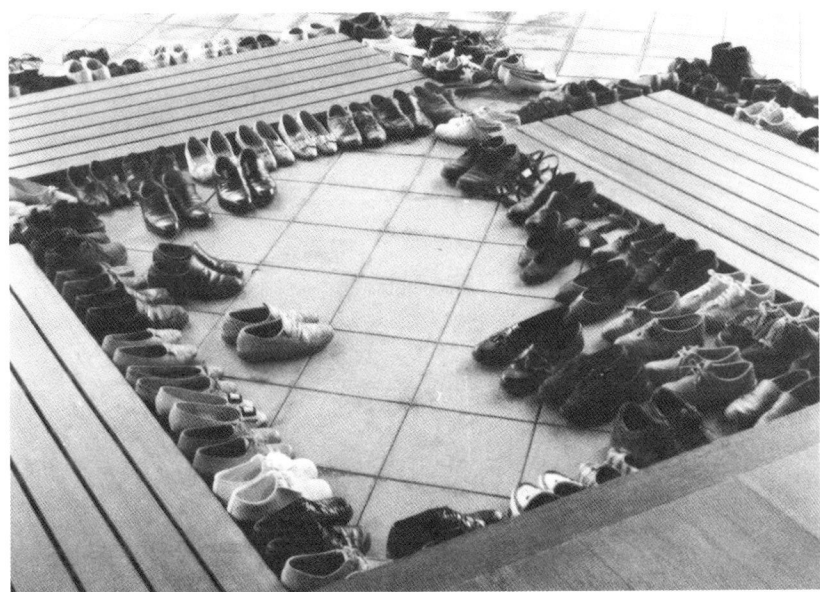

Students' and other patrons' shoes customarily organized and facing in the proper direction, waiting for their owners to exit after the play at Nishi Hongan-ji is finished

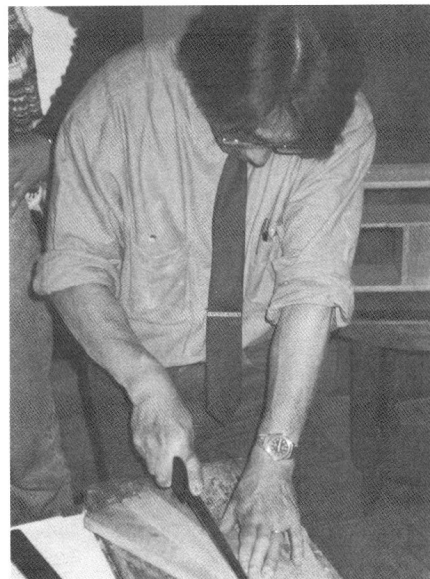

Ryosaku Takeda, master lacquerer and woodworker

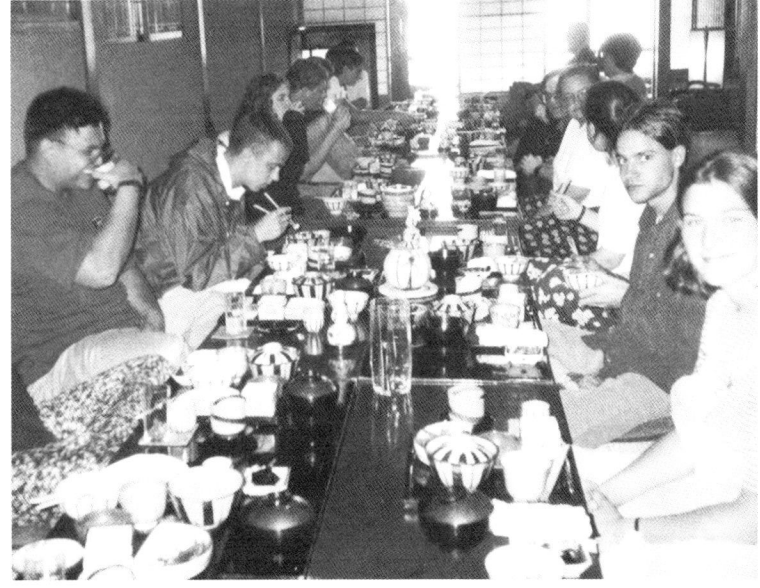

Students partaking in a traditional Japanese meal at Momochitaru-Kan, a shop and restaurant in a refurbished Kyoto townhouse

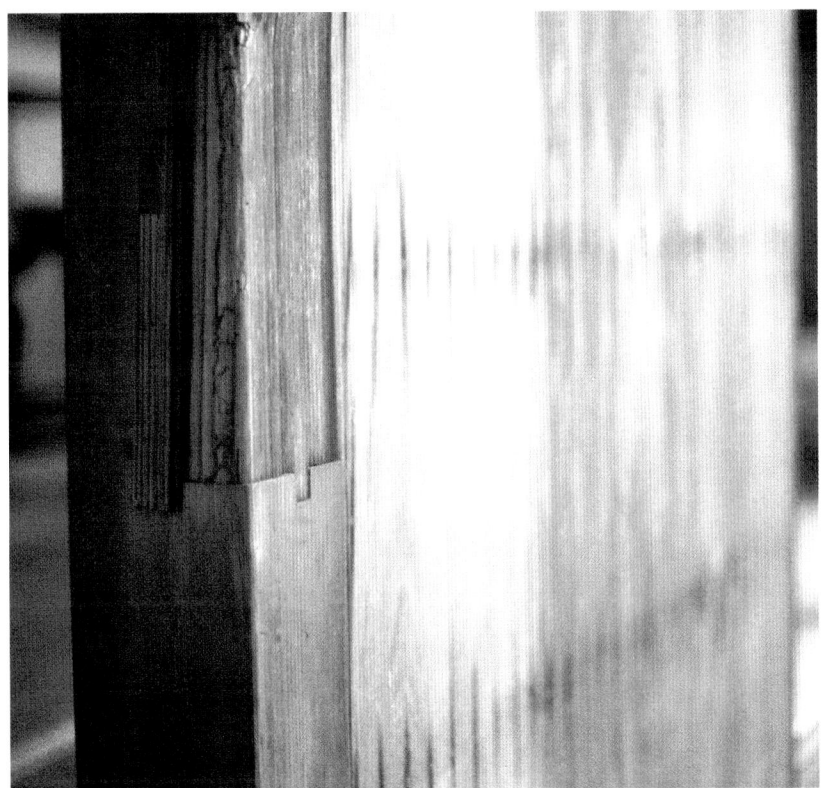

Master carpenter's repair of ancient wooden post using traditional joinery techniques

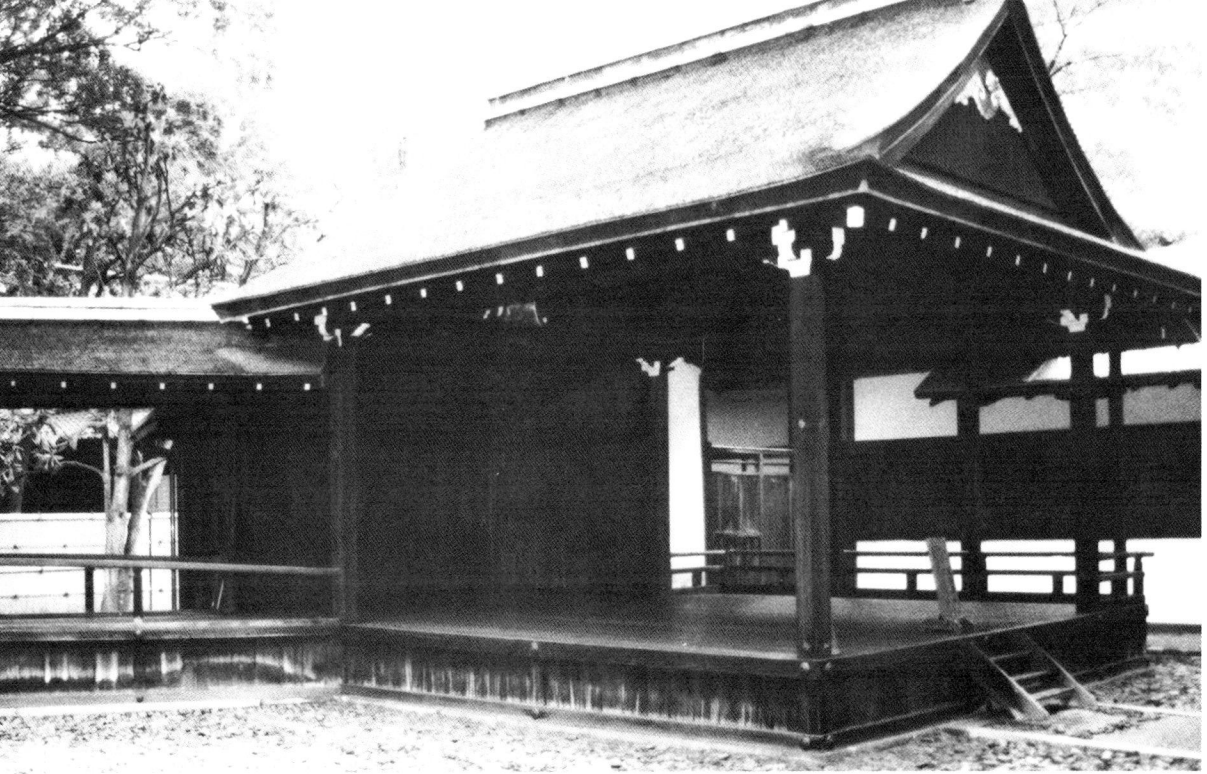

*Noh* stage, Nishi Hongan-ji, Kyoto, Japan

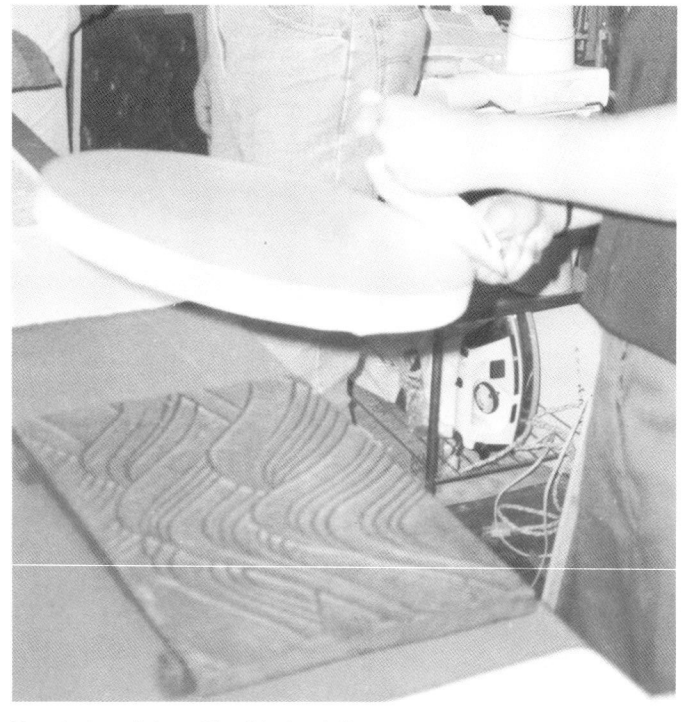

Karacho's workshop: Woodblock printing process

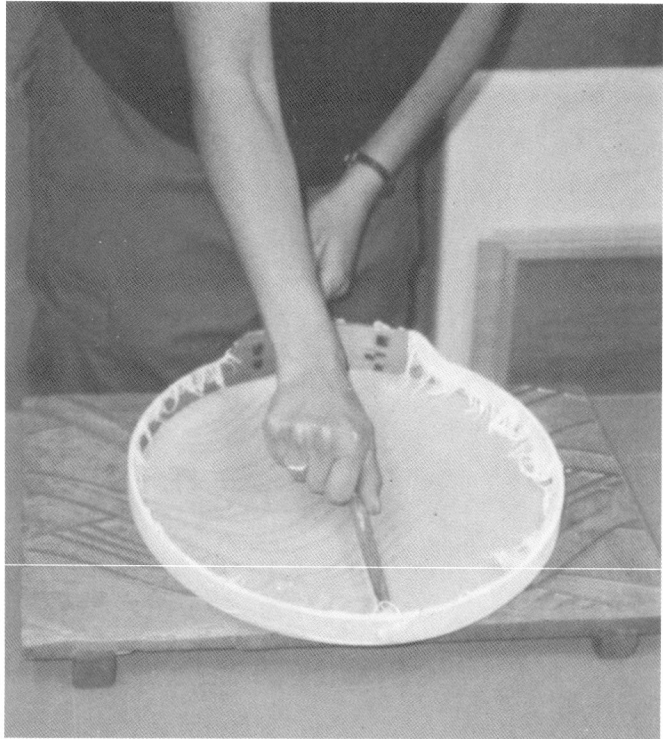

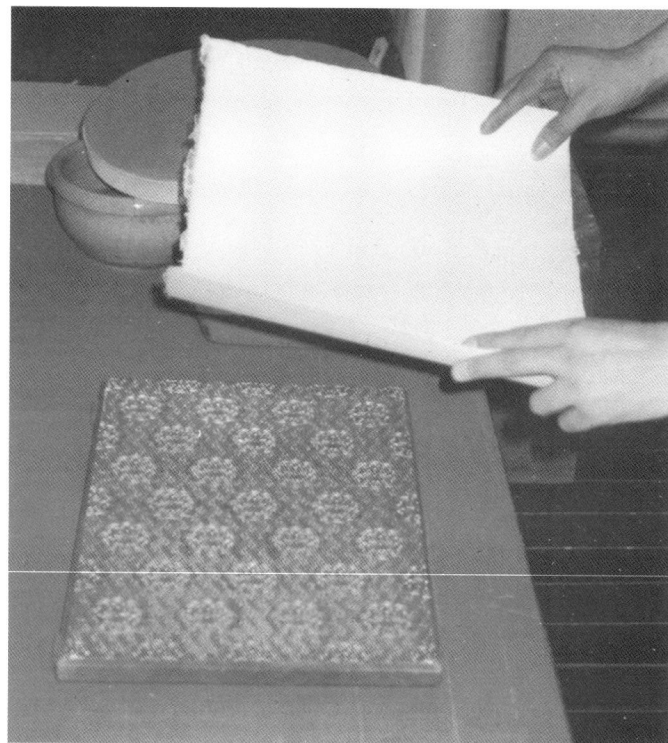

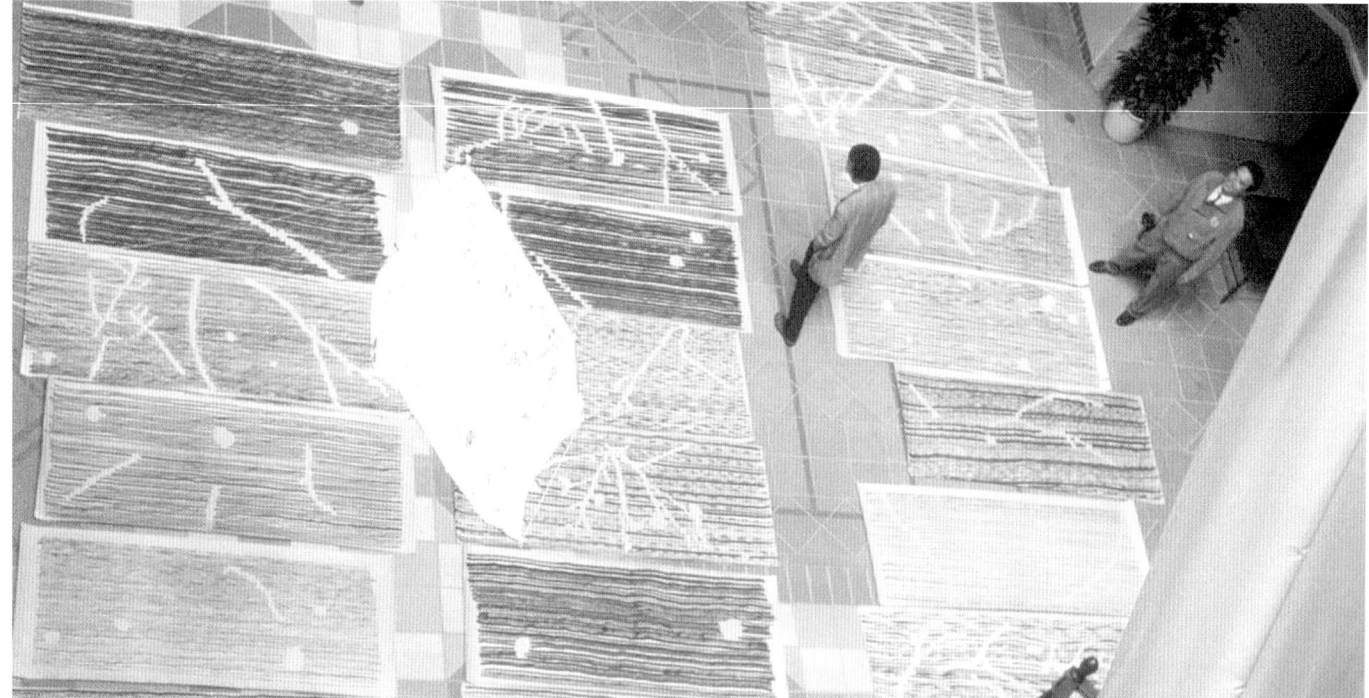

Kyoto University professor Shuji Funo (center) reviews the ink drawings made during an intensive day of activity for Jiro Okura's *Nisso Screen*

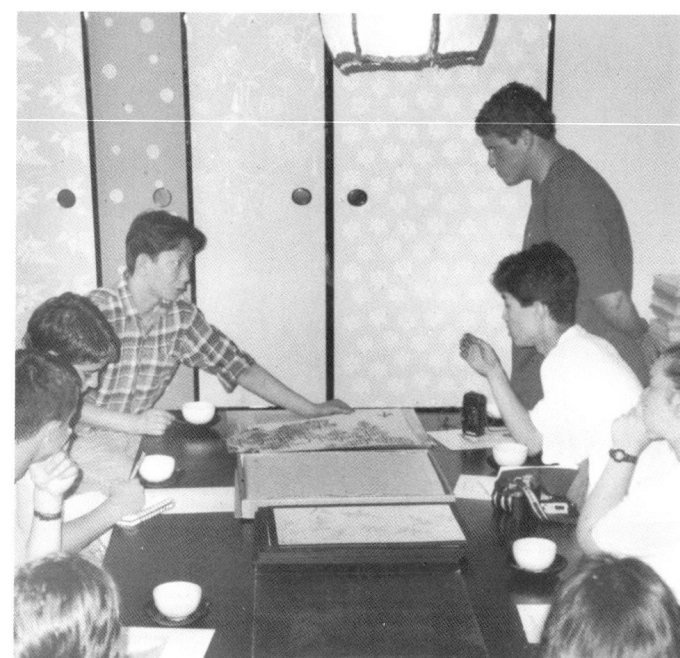

Students having tea with the Senda family in their Karacho workshop showroom while master printer Kenjichi Senda explains the history of the craft

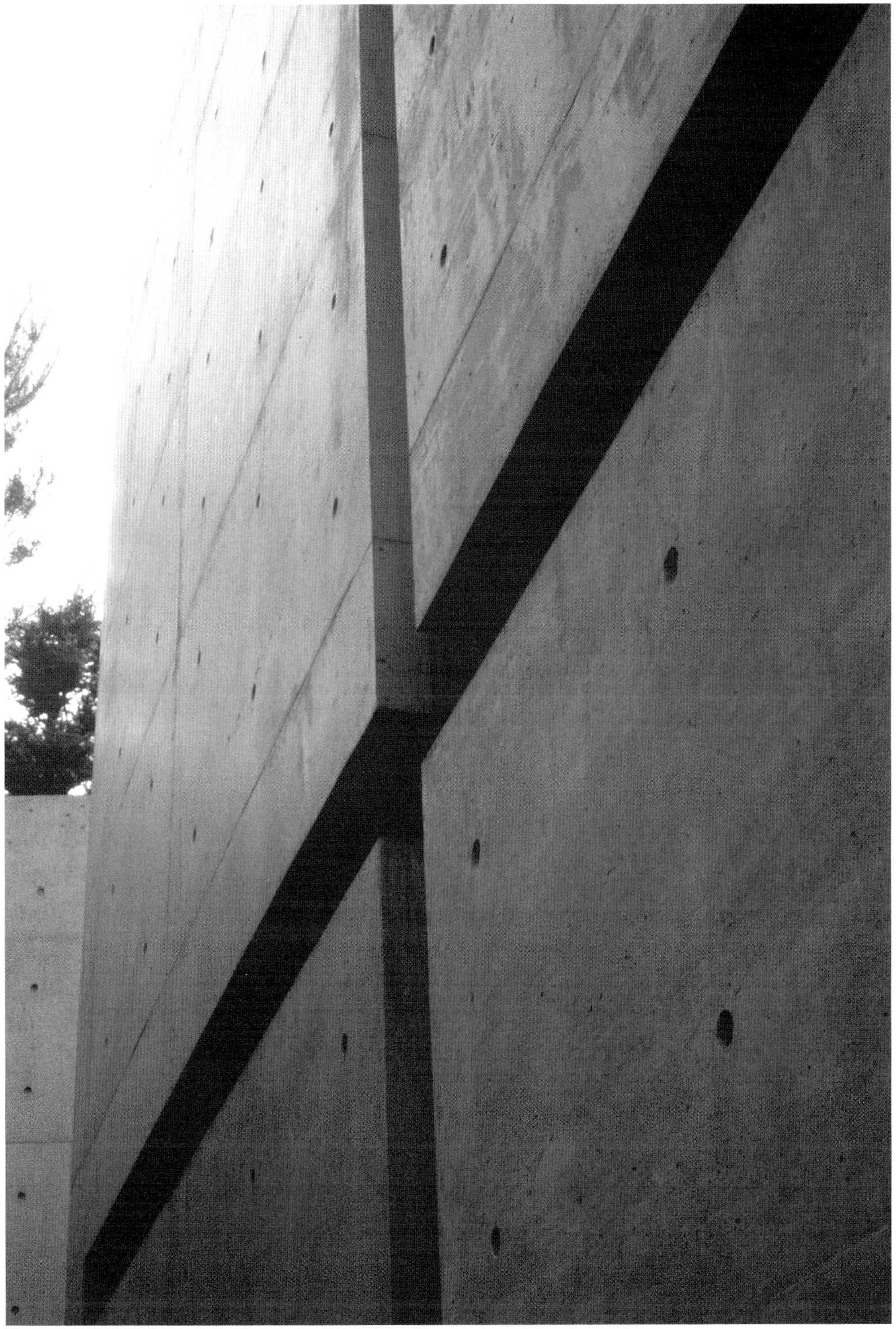

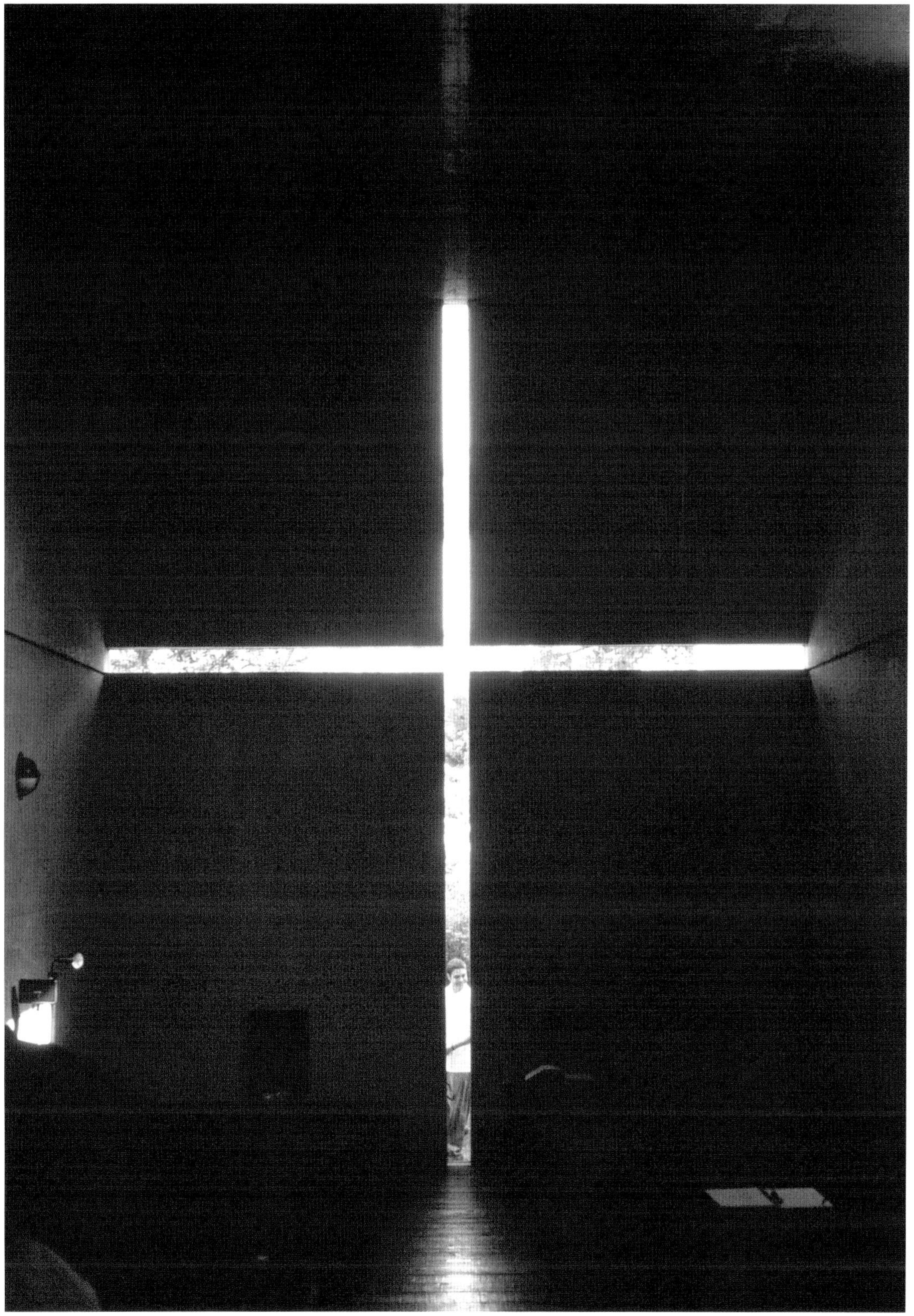

Tadao Ando's Church of Light, Ibaraki, City of Osaka

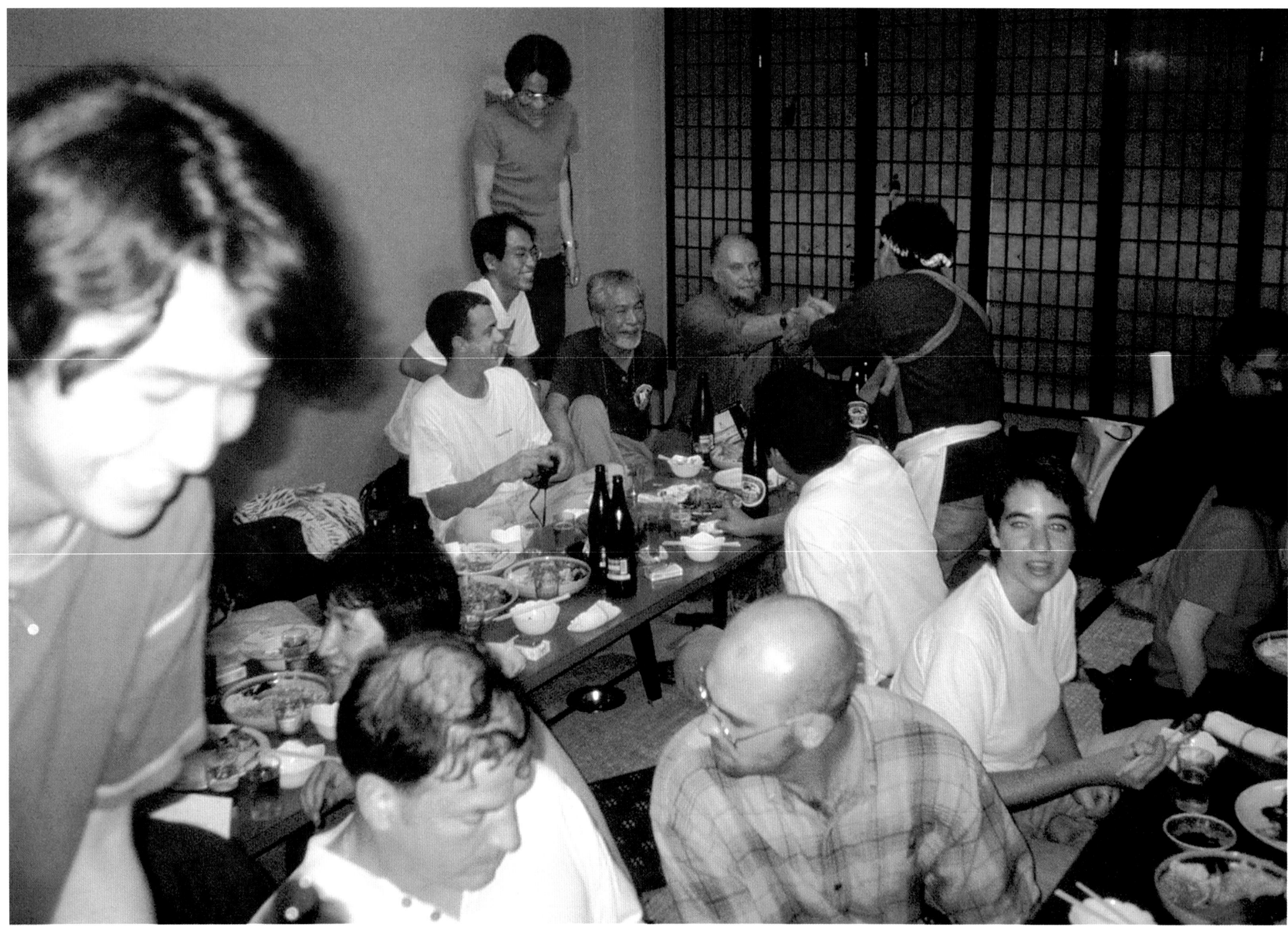

Celebratory drinking and dinner with Kyoto University students after finishing Jiro's workshop for *Nisso Screen*

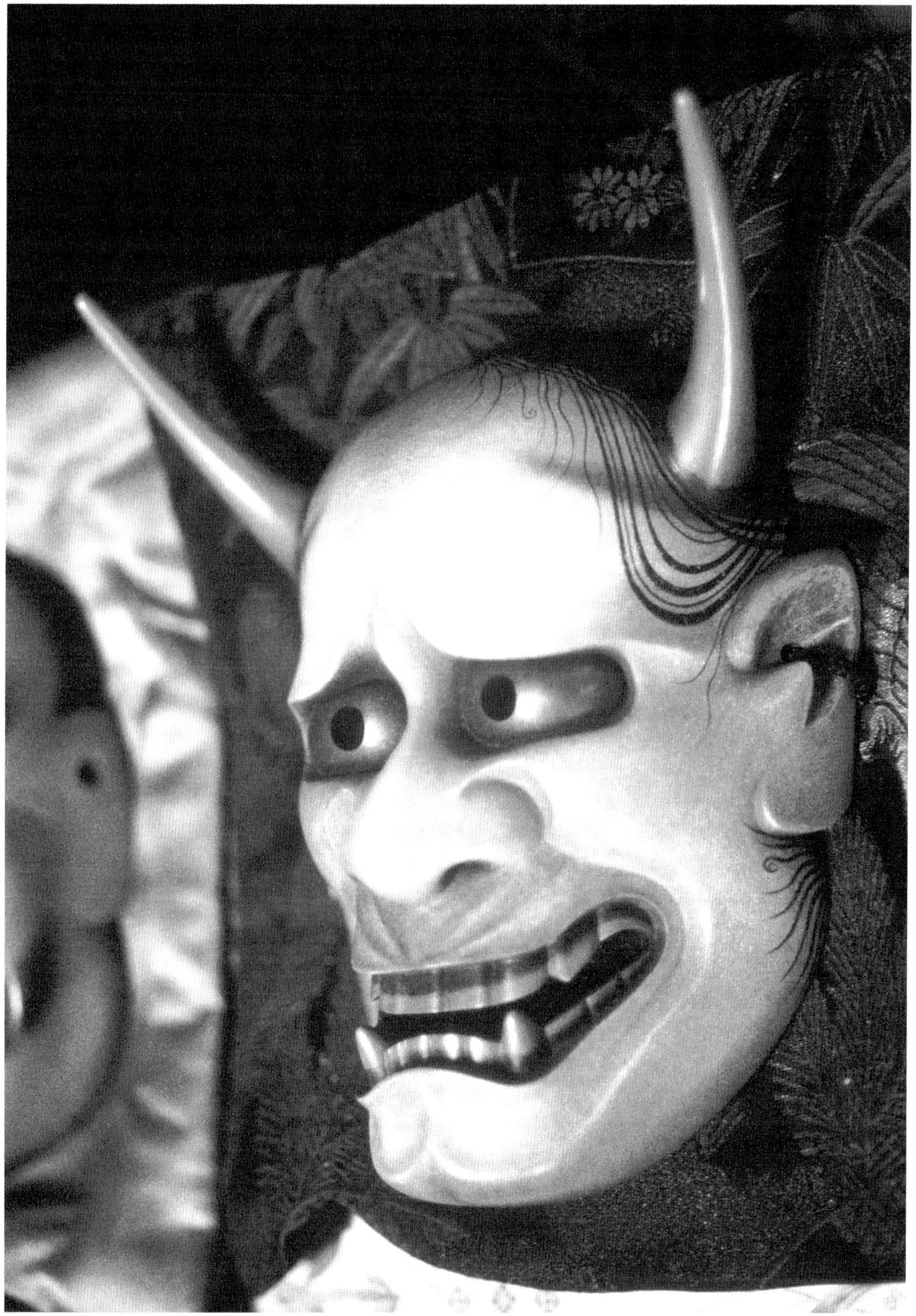

Traditional *Noh* mask

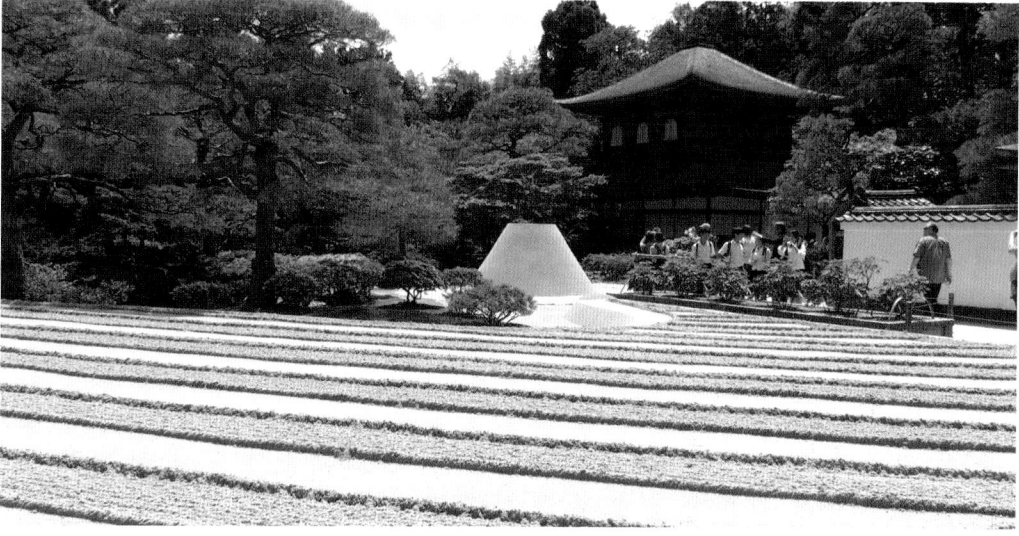

Sand mound symbolizing Mt. Fuji in Zen rock garden at Silver Pavilion (Ginkaku-ji)

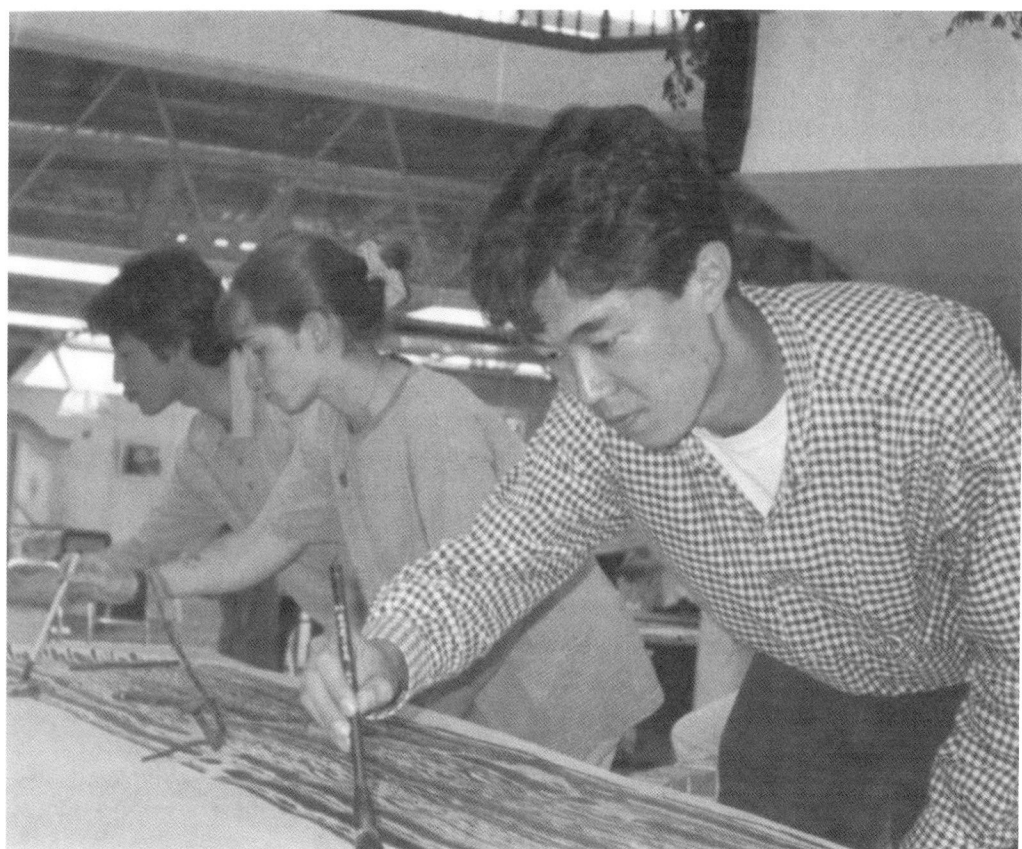

Painting lines on the *Nisso Screen* after professor Funo's suggestion to shift our approach and allow new lines to be started before previous lines finished. Taro Hatanaka on the right

# BORROWED VIEW: THE *NISSO SCREEN*, 1997

JERRIE PIKE

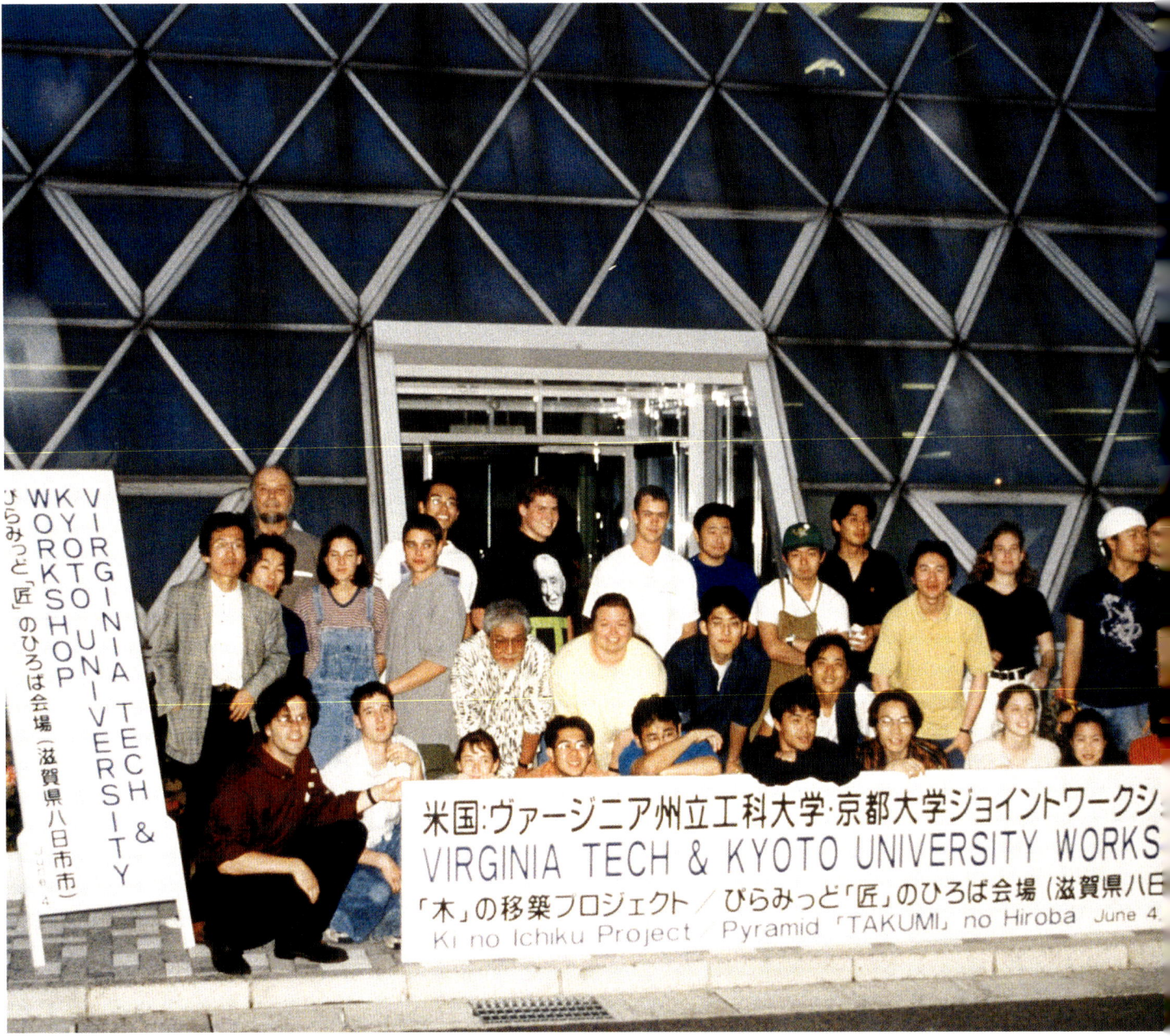

Jiro Okura's first Mountain Lake Workshop to be conducted in Japan was co-organized by Shuji Funo, Ray Kass, and Peter Lau and took place in a single day at the Nisso Corporation's "Glass Pyramid," a demonstration facility in Shiga Prefecture near Kyoto.[1] The workshop paintings were collaboratively executed by forty-two Japanese and American participants on forty-eight large sheets of industrial rag paper cut from a roll of Bee#844 rag paper that had been prepared earlier at Mountain Lake in Virginia to reflect appreciation for the light-loving qualities of traditional washi (Japanese paper); each sheet had been carefully glazed with nine coats of watercolor in alternating warm and cool hues with small amounts of metallic pigment added to create an off-white and luminous appearance.[2] The forty-eight paintings that were the result of the workshop were brought back to the United States and assembled on framed wooden panels (each 34 inches wide and between 88 inches and 98 inches tall) as a series of eight two-sided tripartite screens called *Borrowed View: The Nisso Screen*. The idea of a borrowed view is a concept specifically related to the Japanese garden aesthetic of designing small arrangements in a garden to reflect a distant view; since the experience of the *Nisso Screen* was taken home with us in the spirit of "relocating the tree" or the "borrowed view," it seemed very appropriate as a title element.

Exquisite lines are hallmarks of the *Nisso Screen*. They are based on controlled breathing and the Zen-like technical process used in black *sumi-e* (ink) calligraphy and painting. The forty-one American and Japanese participants (students, professors, corporate representatives, and community volunteers) were instructed by Okura, Kass, and Lau in

[1] The project was sponsored by the Nisso Industries Corporation Ltd., a prominent Japanese manufacturer of industrial scaffolding. Support also came from the following: Professor Shuji Funo, Department of Architecture and Urban Affairs, Kyoto University; The Blacksburg Summer Arts Festival '98 and '00; the Virginia Commission for the Arts in partnership with the National Endowment for the Arts; Jack Dudley, director, Virginia Tech Honors Program; the Department of Art and Art History, Armory Art Gallery, and College of Architecture and Urban Affairs at Virginia Tech University; the Art Museum of Western Virginia (the Taubman Museum), Roanoke, Virginia; the Horton Fund and the Mountain Lake Workshop of the Virginia Tech Foundation; Blue Ridge Timberwrights, Christiansburg, Virginia.; George Hutchins and the Hutchins Cabinet Shop.

[2] Workshop participants included Masato Ashida, Greg Bugtong, Mieko Cho, Tripp Cook, Yi Deng, Rebecca Fields, Shuji Funo, Jacque Gillentine, Mike Grant, Taro Hatanaka, Yasushi Iwasaki, Setu Kadota, Takuya Kamiyama, Ray Kass, Jin Kim, Shinichi Kitaoka, Peter Lau, Peter Laws, Dan Lehn, Ayako Mageshi, Monica Marino, Anne Miller, Kelley Monkevich, Gretchen Mourer, Yumiko Nakajima, TakasHi Oda, Jiro Okura, Ben Owen, Lara Pfadt, Shohei Saeki, Masayuki Sakamoyo, Keiichi Sato, Naomi Shinozaki, Kazuhiko Shiozaki, Michael Sonnichsen, Brian Spence, Hirohisa Tomiie, Kikuma Watanabe, Chris Wood, Akira Yamamoto, Ken Yokoi, and Shigehisa Yoshimura.

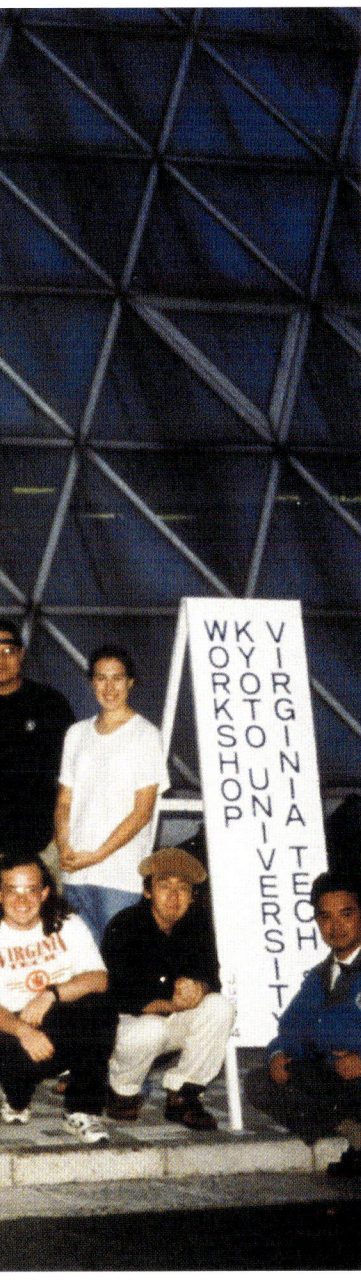

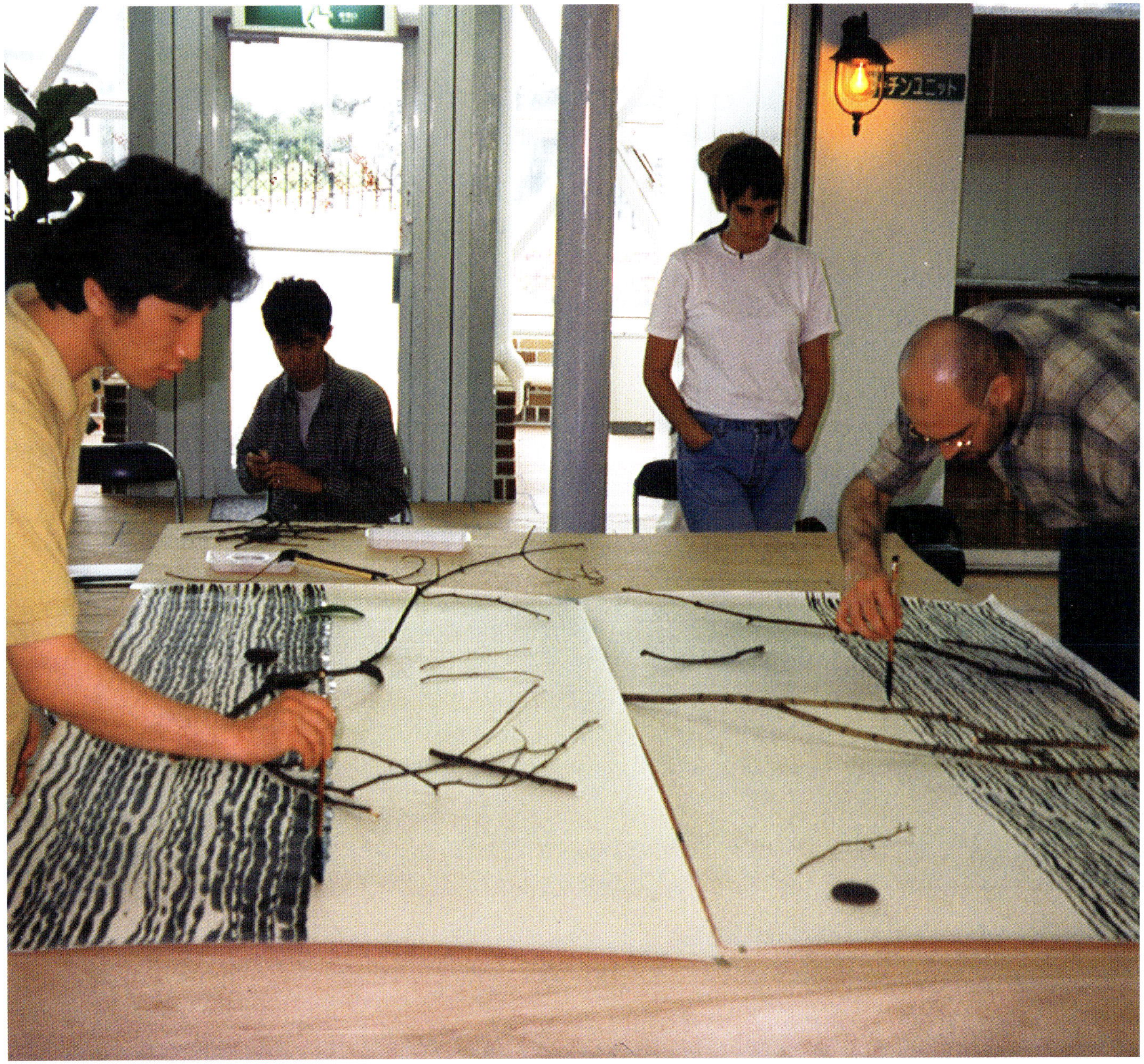

[1]This work recalls aspects of two of Okura's earlier workshops. The 1990 *Mountain Lake Screen Tachi*, the "movable wall" between Eastern and Western cultures, introduced workshop participants to Asian concepts of art and life, of which Okura emphasized the "pleasures" of process (i.e., carving, drilling, painting, and gilding). His concern with meditative process was again a working strategy of his Shisendo Garden *sumi-e* paintings executed at the Miles C. Horton studio at Mountain Lake in 1992 and again in 1993 at the Muscarelle Museum of the College of William and Mary in Williamsburg, Virginia. The Shisendo workshops were conducted in religious-like silence as some participants observed while others executed alternating thin and thick lines eventually covering a single very large sheet.

[2]Midway through the workshop it became apparent that the pace of the group activity must be accelerated in order to complete the work. At Shuji Funo's suggestion, participants modified the initial practice of executing only one-at-a-time sequential lines, to allow the next individual to begin his/her line as soon as the preceding participant had drawn approximately four linear feet of line.

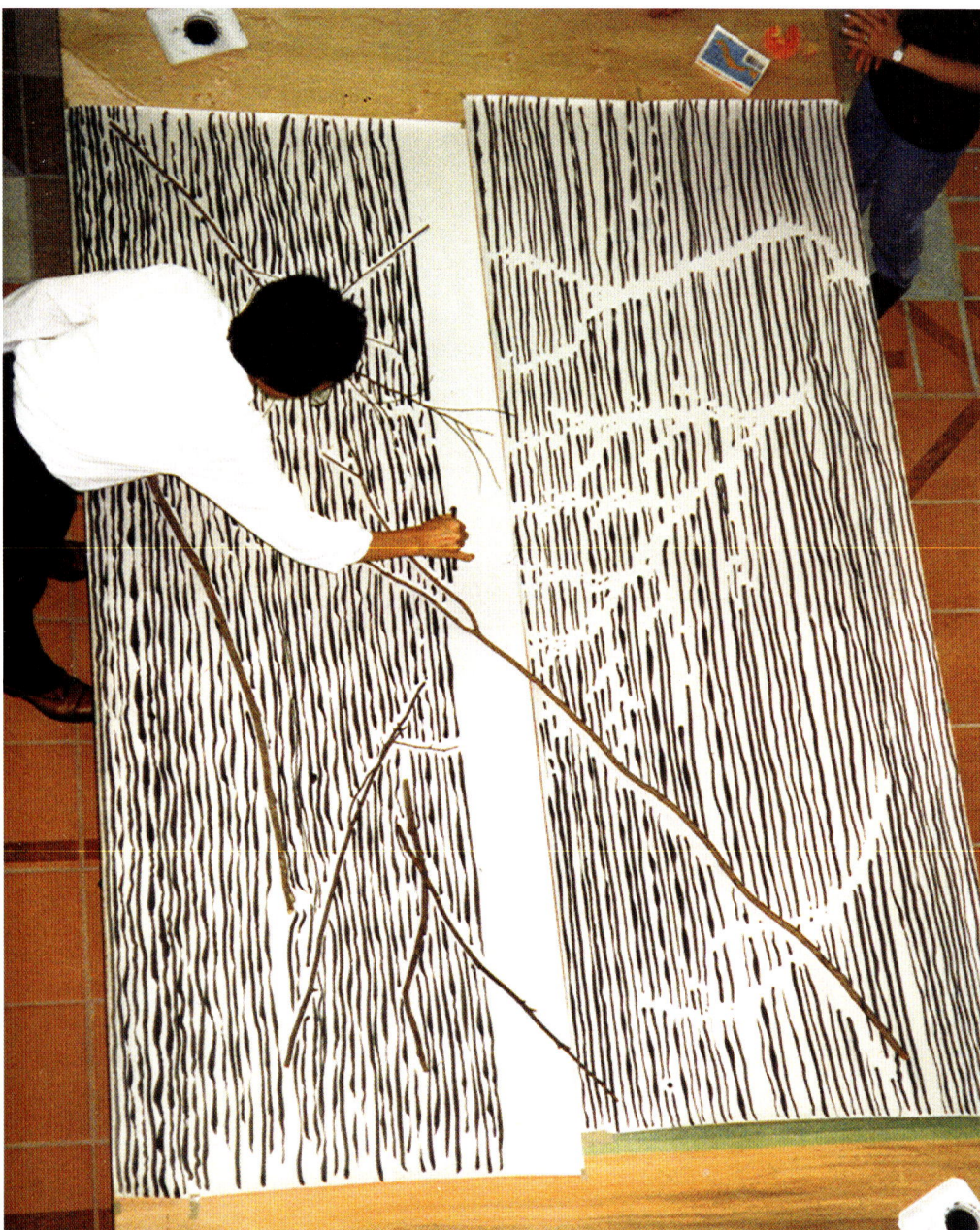

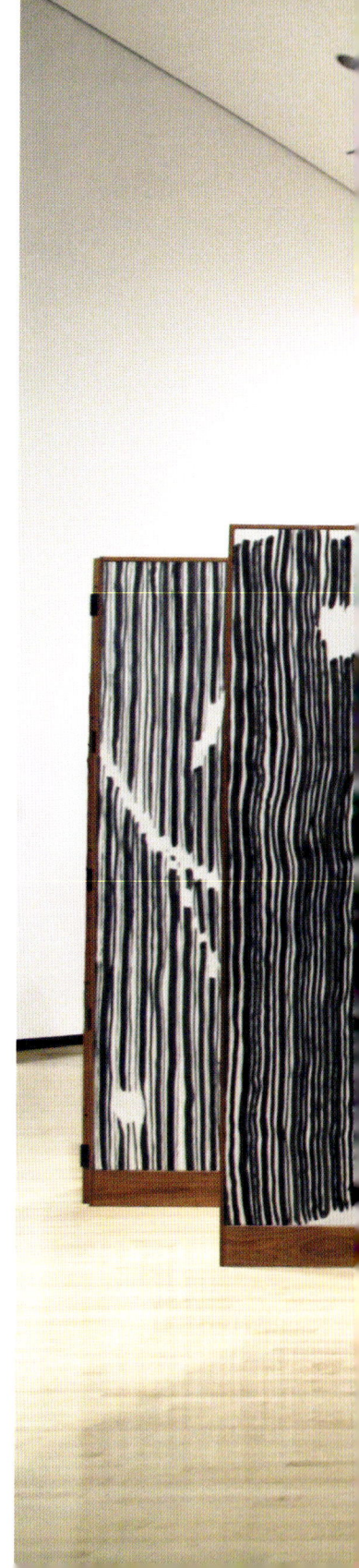

preparation for the final painting activity, in which, in a
continuous rotation, each participant solemnly executed
a single, long controlled line of alternating thin and thick
widths alongside the previous participant's line. Because of
the large size of the paper, participants took several turns
in the rotation before the paper was covered. The result is a
sequence of undulating "parallel" lines covering the paper.[3]

In the Zen-like spirit of the workshop, twigs gathered by students
at the Fushimi Inari Shinto shrine in Kyoto and stones gathered
from Virginia's ancient New River that had been used in earlier
workshops by American avant-garde composer and artist John
Cage were randomly placed, temporarily, on the paper. These
objects imposed interruptions of the painted lines that intersected
them, requiring each participant, in rendering a single line, to lift
the brush over them and then to continue painting.[4] In the finished
works these interruptions or "intersections with nature" left their
"negative imprints" on the paper like ghosts of natural forms.[5]

Each participant's painted lines possess individuality or
personality, while the overall work exhibits sufficient stylistic
unity to suggest that it could have been the product of a single
hand. An individual line was an exercise in concentration,
breathing, and control, and also a unique experience of the brush
and the ink. In many ways, these lines are related to *Zenga*, works
of calligraphy and drawing created by Zen monks as an aid to
meditation which quiets the mind, enhancing concentration.[6]

[3] It is the custom of the Mountain Lake Workshop to adapt themes and methods from previous workshops and appropriately
apply them to new endeavors. Just as Cage's work had earlier been an inspiration for Okura, in the manner of director Kass'
earlier projects the *Nisso Screen* paintings were covered with a thin layer of beeswax to create a reflective elegant surface.
Black walnut previously harvested for use in Okura's earlier sculpture workshop was selected for the screen frames.

[6] *Zenga* exhibits a quintessential style that creates a powerful visual impact principally through the boldness of black and
white rendered as dramatic and "spontaneous" brushwork which is, in fact, highly controlled through concentration. *Zenga*
brushwork (or "ink traces") manifests personality, not only of the artist but also of the intrinsic nature of the line itself. It is

an art that can be characterized by non-specificity of meaning, through which the
viewer can become an active "partner" in creating its significance. For more on
*Zenga* see Stephen Addiss, *The Art of Zen: Paintings and Calligraphy by Japanese
Monks 1600–1925* (New York: Harry N. Abrams, 1989), especially pp. 6–15.

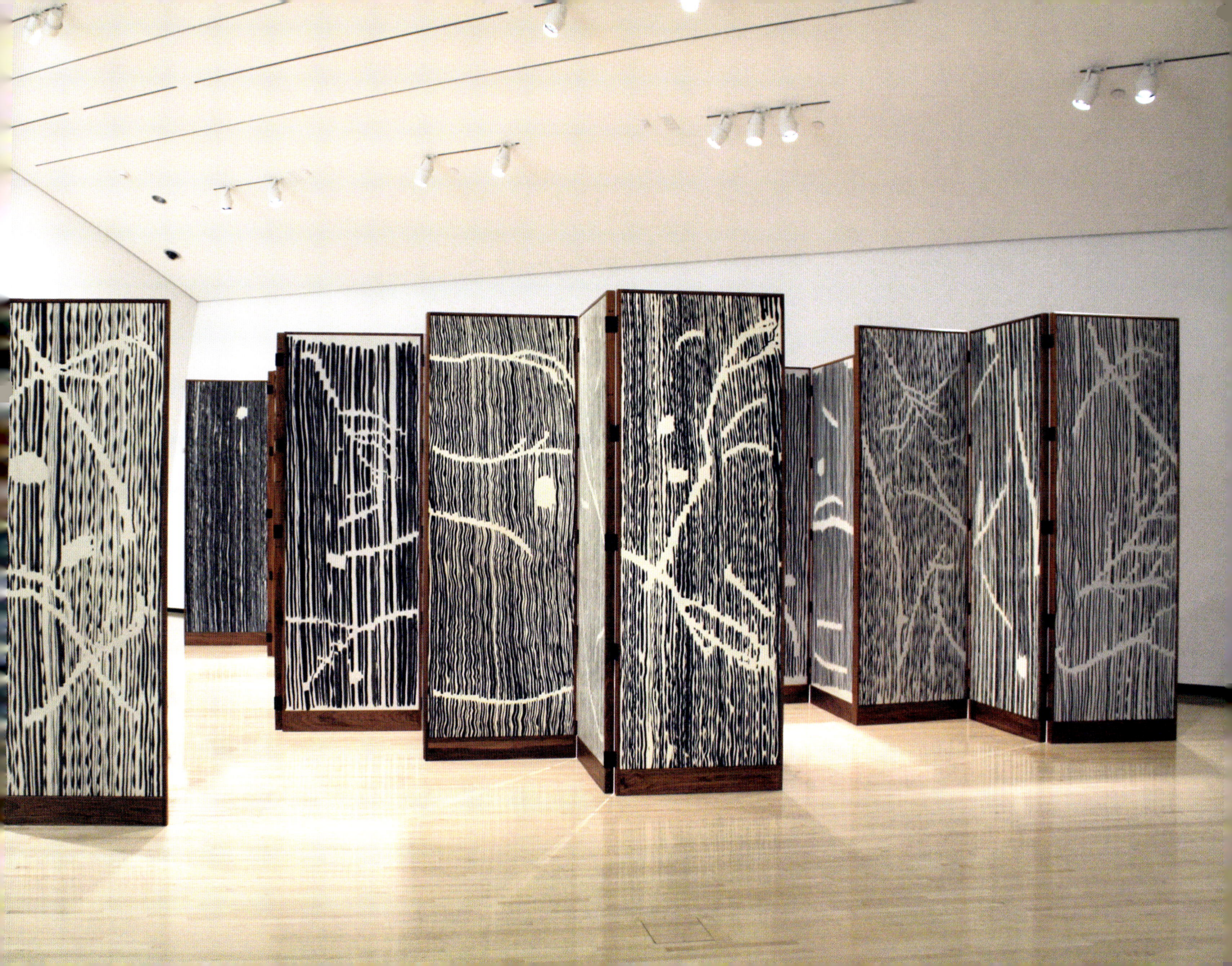

# JIRO OKURA: *SOULS ON GARBAGE*, 1998

JERRIE PIKE

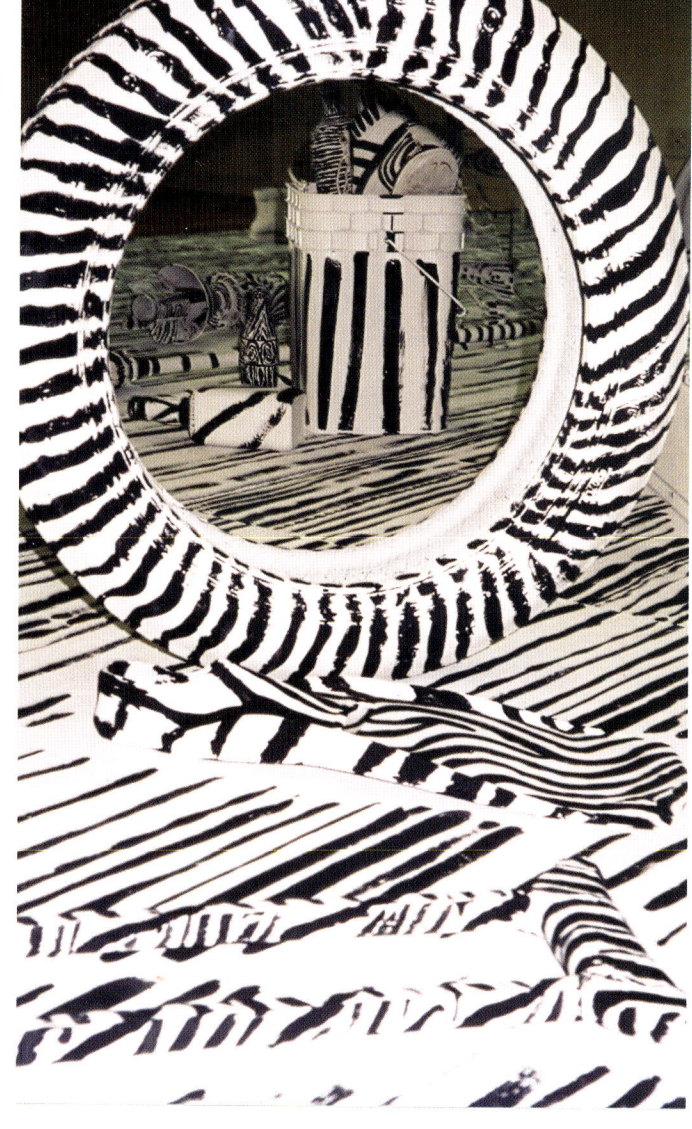

For June 1998, Jiro Okura designed a second workshop for the *Ki no Ichiku* program. The result of this workshop, conducted at the Miles C. Horton Center at Mountain Lake, was a three-dimensional installation which is a strategic and spatial variation of the *Nisso Screen* from the previous year. Okura titled it *Souls on Garbage*.[1]

In *Souls on Garbage*, the twigs and stones employed in Okura's earlier Mountain Lake painting workshops were replaced with items used and discarded by our consumer culture including a computer monitor, a broom, jars and various other containers, and a broken weed-eater, among other things. These objects were first "restored to tastefulness" with a coat of white latex paint. Most also received an ornamental coat of black latex lines applied so as to reinforce or enhance their three-dimensional shapes. This was done to prepare and emphasize each item of "garbage" to be included in the finished work as an actual object, rather than, as in the *Nisso Screen*, to have their forms "lifted over" by lines so they would remain in the finished work as mere "ghosts" of their real forms. These three-dimensional elements were then placed upon uniformly white platform panels which served as the "ground" for painted lines.

Using latex, the thirty-one participants then painted black lines on the white platforms, simultaneously introducing a new, intermittent method which resulted in new figural patterns in the work.[2] Some objects of garbage were transected with parallel lines rather than being lifted over, as in the *Nisso Screen*, by painters working on an essentially straight-line course. This variation adds considerable interest to the pattern of lines while still preserving the dramatic visual impact of each panel.

Stark, bold simplicity characterizes Okura's *Nisso Screen* and *Souls on Garbage*, both of which show minimal concern with composition but create a monumental visual impact with the greatest economy of means. Okura's concern is with the interaction between the artist's inner creative forces and the "universe outside," as he maintains that only "minimal control" is needed in the handling of materials. For Okura, minimal control signifies control over one's body — over breathing and the hand that holds the brush — while simultaneously allowing the materials to assert their own properties. His strategies embrace the belief that the artist can "paint without thinking," immersed in repetitive, nearly automatic movements of the brush which tend to purify the mind by eliminating superfluous thoughts, thereby inducing a meditative state.

The lines are "souls" (personal traces), as they have been in all of Okura's Mountain Lake workshop creations. They are traces of personality and products of concentration. The full effect of the assemblage and installation of the workshop pieces — dazzling patterns that achieve a coherent visual experience that is nevertheless possessed of an inherent sense of non-specific meaning — engages the viewer to participate in interpreting aspects of their significance.

[1] Okura independently developed this experimental workshop in Japan; it represents his response to the projects that engaged art-making with issues of microbiology and waste remediation that the Mountain Lake Workshops conducted with Mierle Laderman Ukeles, official artist-in-residence at the New York City Department of Sanitation, in 1994 and 1996. Because Okura was unable to attend, the workshop was actually carried out under the direction of Michael Hofmann, who said, "It was an honor and a pleasure working with Jiro Okura's installation, implementing his vision and then taking a little artistic license in its execution. The workshop created such a supportive and playful environment in which to work." Virginia Tech and the project directors wish to acknowledge the special support of Nisso Industries Co., Ltd., Tokyo and Osaka, Japan; Professor Shuji Funo, Department of Architecture and Urban Affairs, Kyoto University; the Blacksburg Summer Arts Festival '98; the Virginia Commission for the Arts; the Art Museum of Western Virginia; the Horton Fund and the Mountain Lake Workshop of the Virginia Tech Foundation; Blue Ridge Timberwrights, Christiansburg, VA; George Hutchins and the Hutchins Cabinet Shop, Floyd, VA; Jack Dudley, director, Virginia Tech Honors Program; and the VA Tech Department of Art and Art History, Armory Art Gallery, and College of Architecture and Urban Affairs.

[2] Technical assistants were Andrew Liss and Jason Barna; workshop participants were Unni An, Jason Barna, Jeff Benton, Steve Bickley, Patricia Brown, Greg Bryson, Truman Capone, Michael Grant, Julia Gunnels, Ngoc Ha, Taro Hatanaka, Christina Hister, David Huber, Ji Hae Kim, Yeonmi R. Kim, Daniel Lambert, Peter Lau, Candy Leslie, Andrew L. Lincicome, Andrew Liss, Heather Mann, Marek Materka, Ruby Moser, Ben Owen, Martin Palmez, Oudone Phouthakhanty, Jerrie Pike, Ridgely Schantz, Kun-Su You, and Samuel Taye.

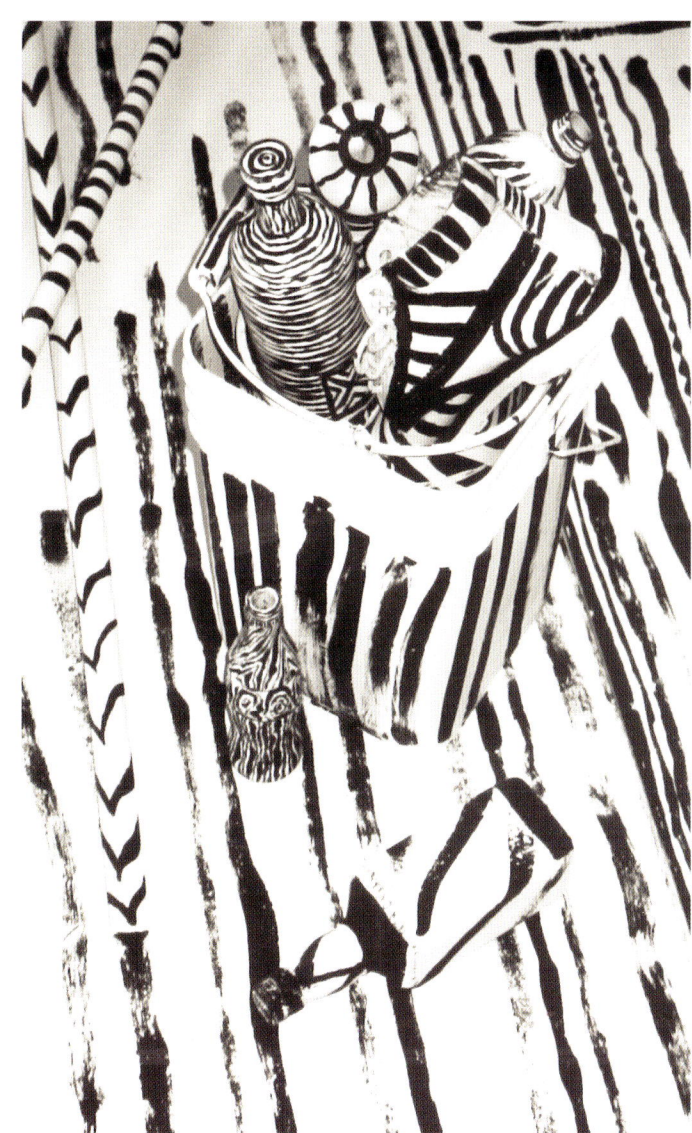
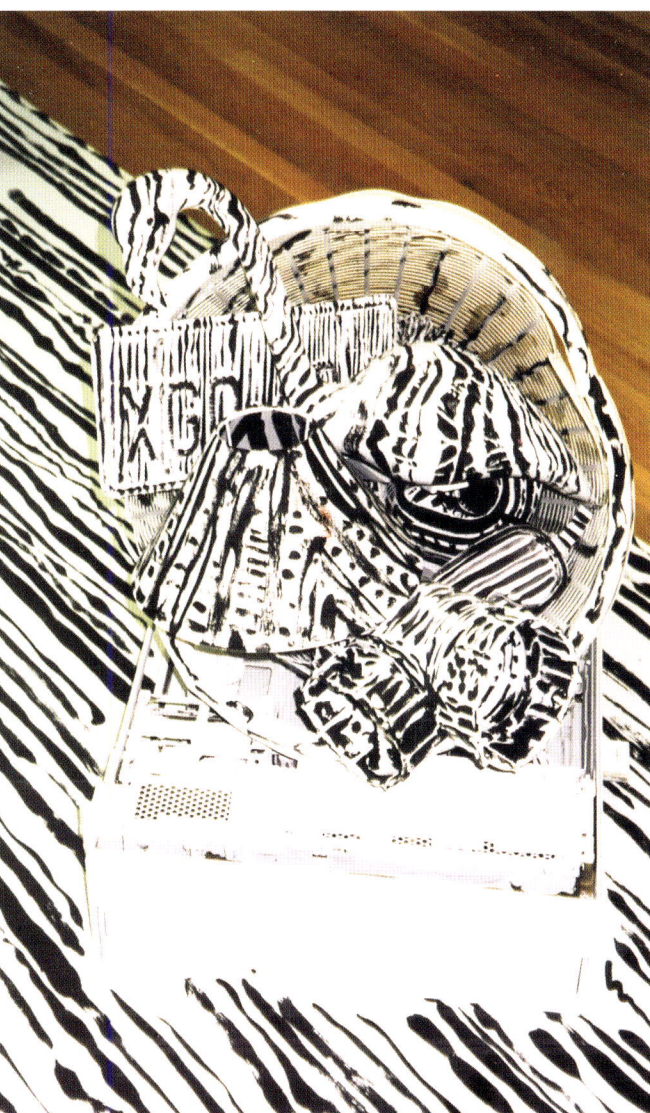
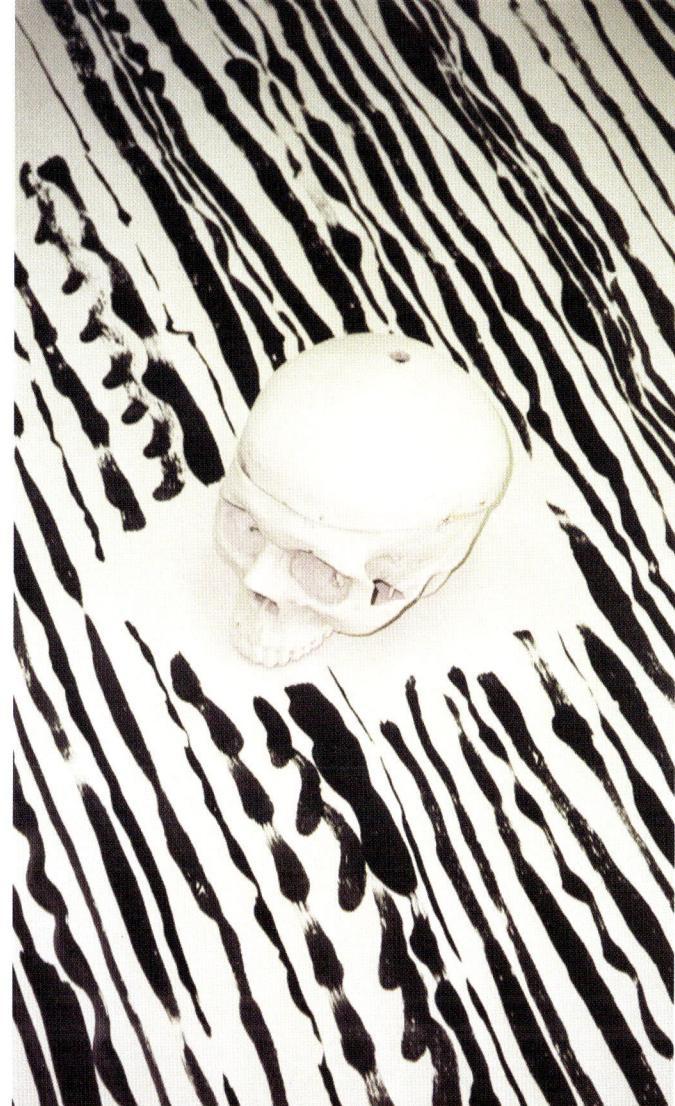

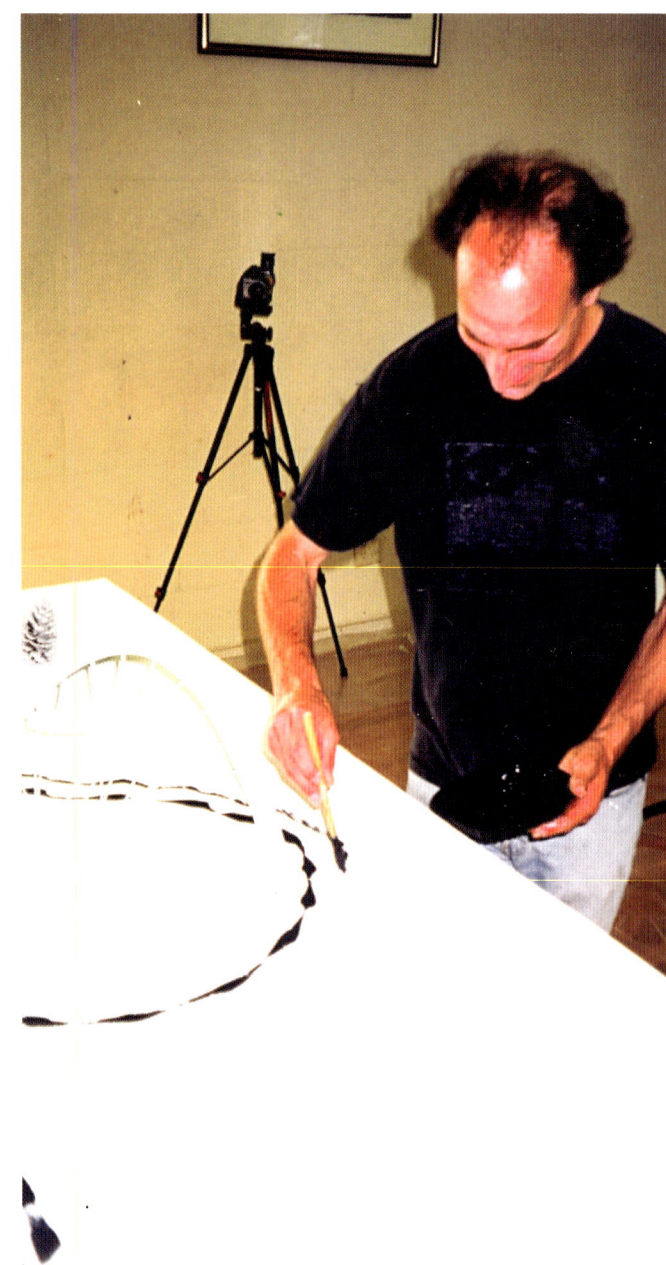

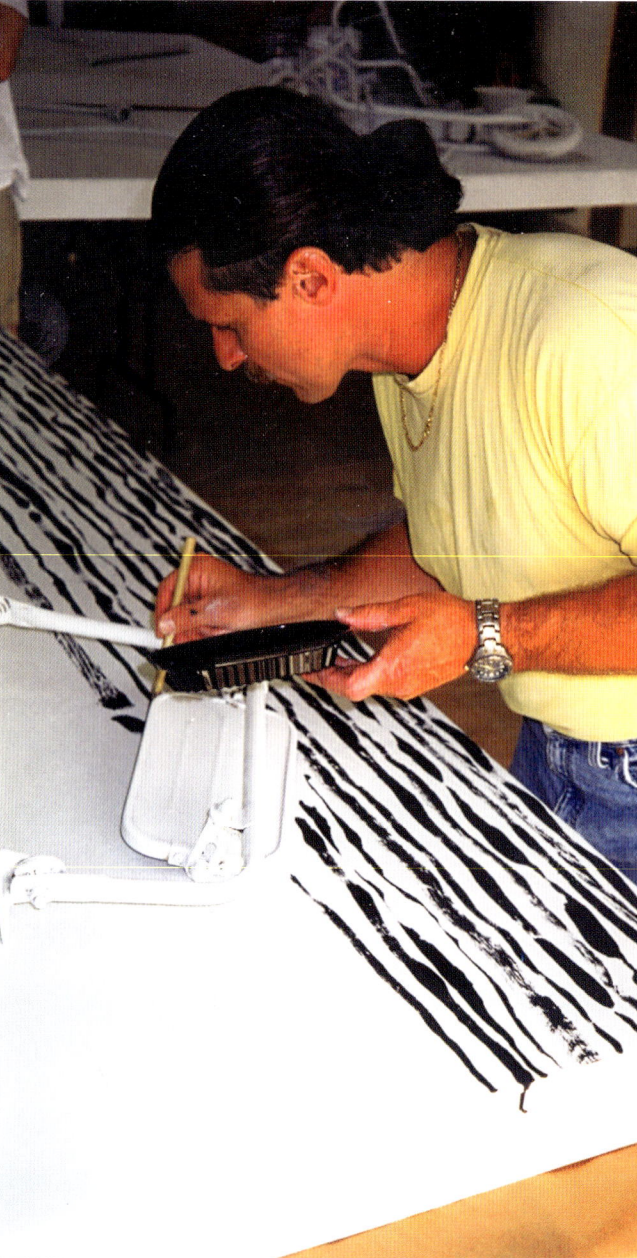

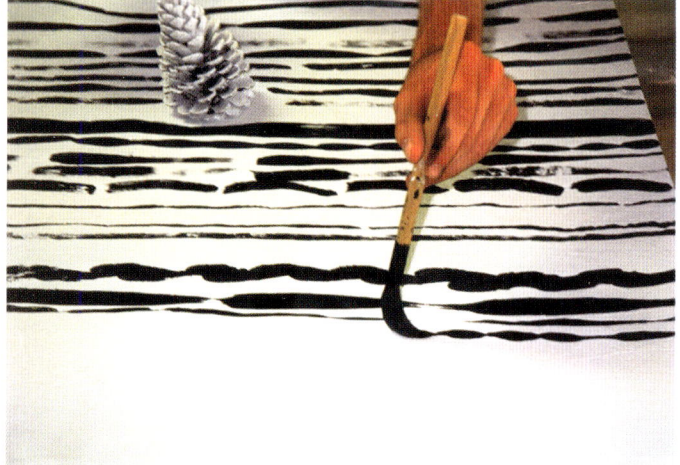

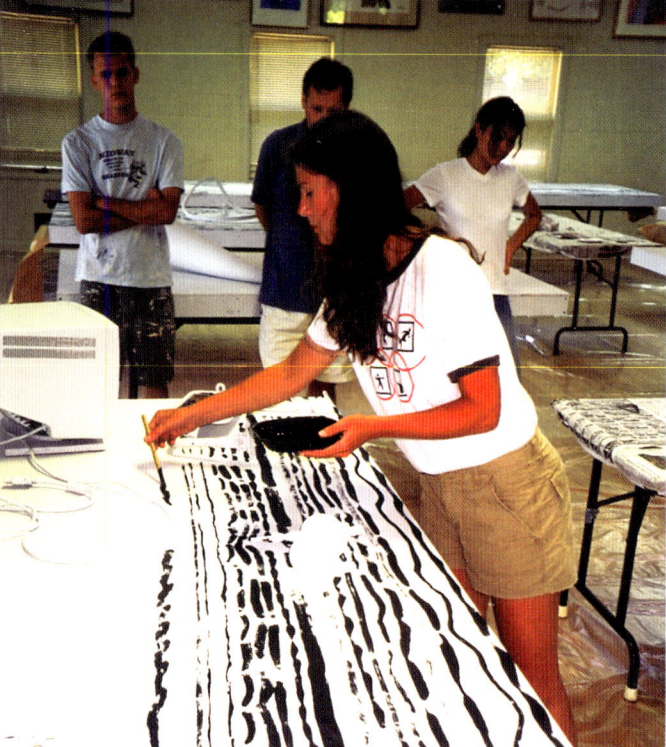

Michael Hofmann works on a
component of *Souls on Garbage*

Truman Capone creates "souls"

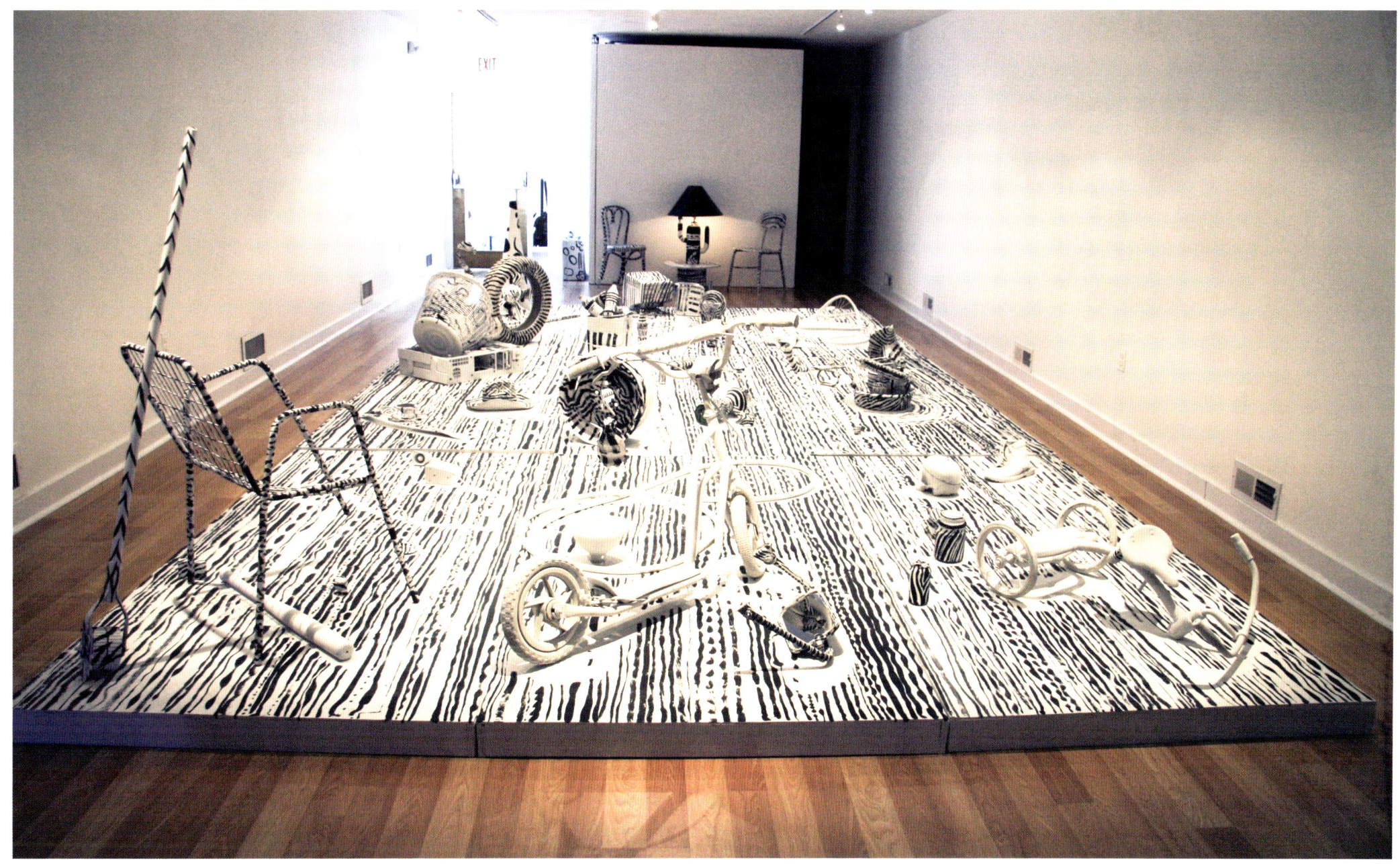

*Souls on Garbage*, 1998, painted wood platform with assorted painted "refuse" found objects, 144 x 288 x 4 in. (365.76 x 731.52 x 10.16 cm). Installed at Virginia Tech's Armory Art Gallery

# CONSTRUCTING A RAMMED-EARTH WALL FOR A JAPANESE GARDEN, 1998-2000

PETER LAU

One of the events of the special summer study in Asian art and design involved building a rammed-earth wall as a backdrop for an area intended to be developed into a Zen garden. In Asia rammed-earth construction has been used for over 2000 years, most commonly in the construction of houses in rural areas of China. It is done by packing layers of moistened soil into a wooden form. The soil, or mixture of soils, must be non-organic and have a clay content of 20 percent to 30 percent with the remainder being sand and fine aggregate. Hydrated lime and/or Portland cement is also added (about 10 percent of the overall volume of soil) as a stabilizer.

Our rammed-earth building process began with field tests of local soil mixtures. Several soil mixtures fit the basic criteria for suitable ratios of clay to aggregate, but actual test pieces had to be rammed before the ideal soil mix could be identified. To do this, large jars were filled with soil mixtures and water, shaken thoroughly, and allowed to sit overnight so that the particles in the mixtures could settle. The heavy particles — sand and gravel — quickly settled on the bottom of the jar, and the fine particles of clay and silt gradually settled above them. Separating the content of the soil and letting it settle provided a way to calculate the clay-to-aggregate ratio of the soil mixtures.

While tests of the most likely soil mixtures were being done, site preparation began along with fabrication of the wooden form that would contain the earth while it was being tamped. The rudimentary form comprised vertical pieces, or armatures, that held horizontal pieces, called form planks. The form planks were fixed to the armatures during the ramming process.

After each 10-inch-high level was packed with earth and the earth had dried overnight, the form planks were unfastened and slid up to the next level and secured once again.

Each time the form planks were slid up they were also "stepped-in" one-half inch, making an earthen wall that gradually got narrower as it got higher. The ziggurat-like form of the rammed-earth wall adds a dramatic dimension that allows light and shadows to cascade down the stepped surface into the raked sand of the Zen garden that was subsequently laid out beneath the wall.

Finally, the wall was capped with a small, gabled eave of redwood, which sheds water, protecting the wall from "spalling" (technically, spalling is damage caused by the freezing and thawing of water that has been absorbed into masonry surfaces). The finished wall is approximately 4 feet high and 26 feet long and is located in a Zen-style garden at Higo Garden Bonsai, a local business in Christiansburg, Virginia, that co-sponsored this project. The form planks now rest on the porch of an adjacent guesthouse, where they serve as benches for visitors who come to view the garden.

Rammed earth wall capped with reclaimed redwood "roof"

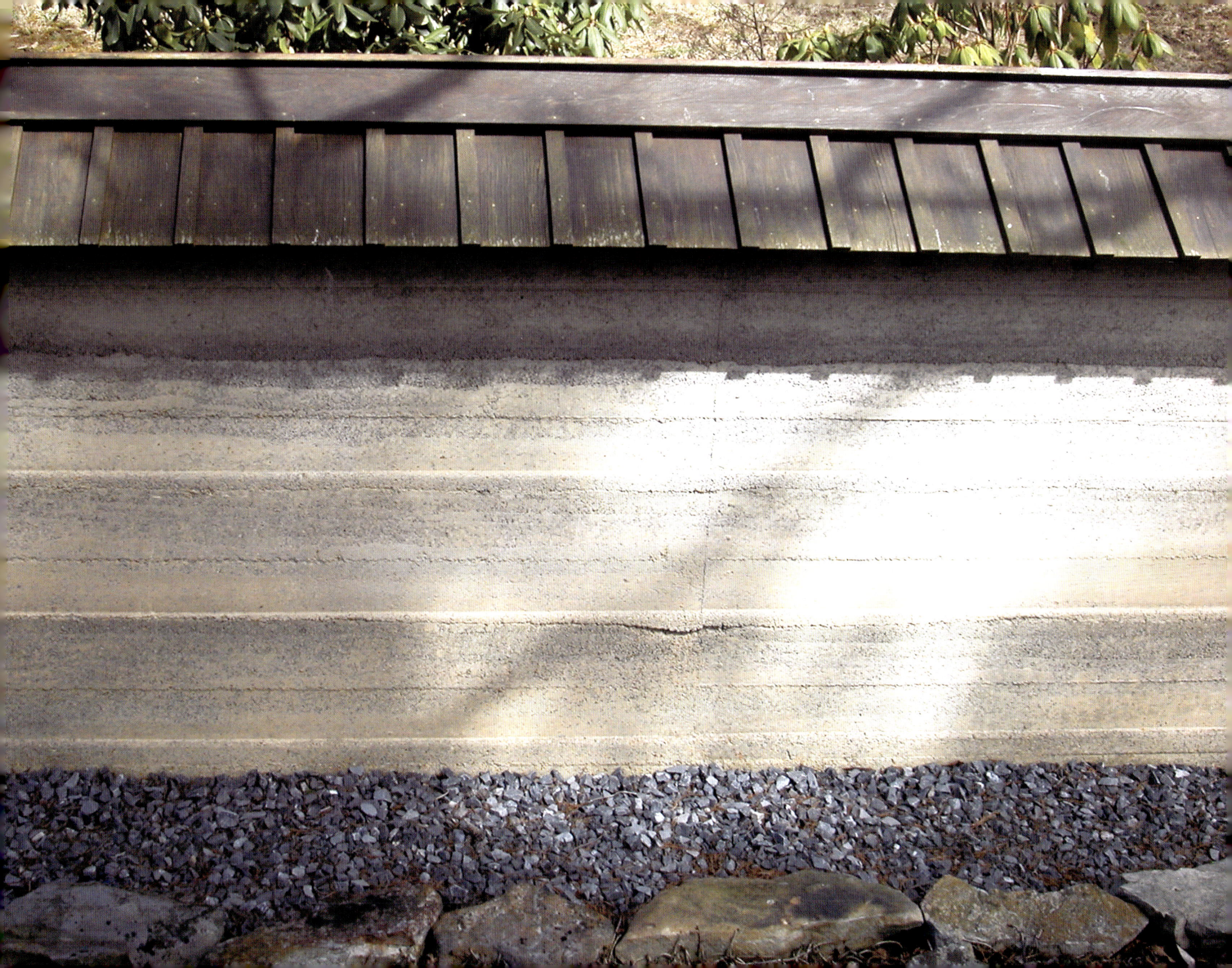

# MICHAEL HOFMANN: "SEEING THE DRAGON," 1998

RAY KASS

Michael Hofmann is an artist and teacher who paints in the manner of traditional ink and brush painting that has its origins in China. A San Francisco native, he lived in Kyoto, Japan, where he apprenticed for thirty-three years with the eminent *sumi-e* artist and Zen master Gyokusei Jikihara (1904–2005), regarded as one of the country's foremost *Nanga* painters.[1]

Mr. Hofmann's work draws inspiration from nature and Eastern philosophy, and displays warmth and vitality of spirit. In 1997 and 2000, he assisted us in *Ki no Ichiku*, our arts and crafts projects in Japan, and we invited him to come to Virginia in 1998 to lead a special Mountain Lake Workshop in *sumi-e* (ink) single brush *Nanga* painting.[2] (This was not Hofmann's only visit to Mountain Lake; also in the summer of 1998 he was guest director for Jiro Okura's first "Souls on Garbage" workshop when a schedule conflict prevented Jiro from attending.) He provided an introduction to the *Nanga* painting tradition and materials and a lesson in bamboo painting.

As a principal workshop contribution he gave a talk about the meaning of the dragon in traditional Asian culture, following it by painting *Under Mountain Lake Dragon* on four *fusuma*-size panels. The painting is today in the permanent collection of the Taubman Museum of Art.

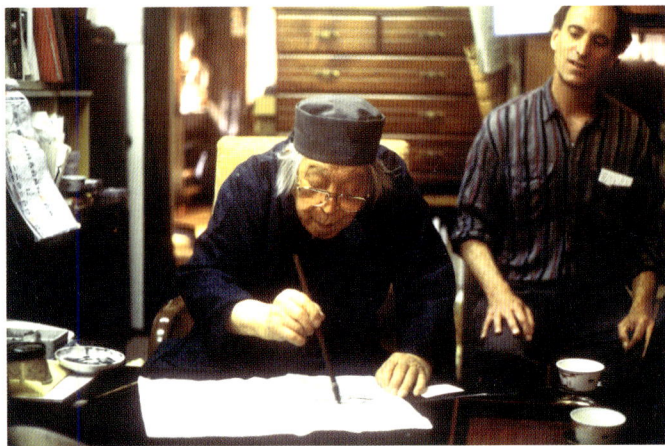

As Michael Hofmann looks on, Gyokusei Jikihara creates a painting

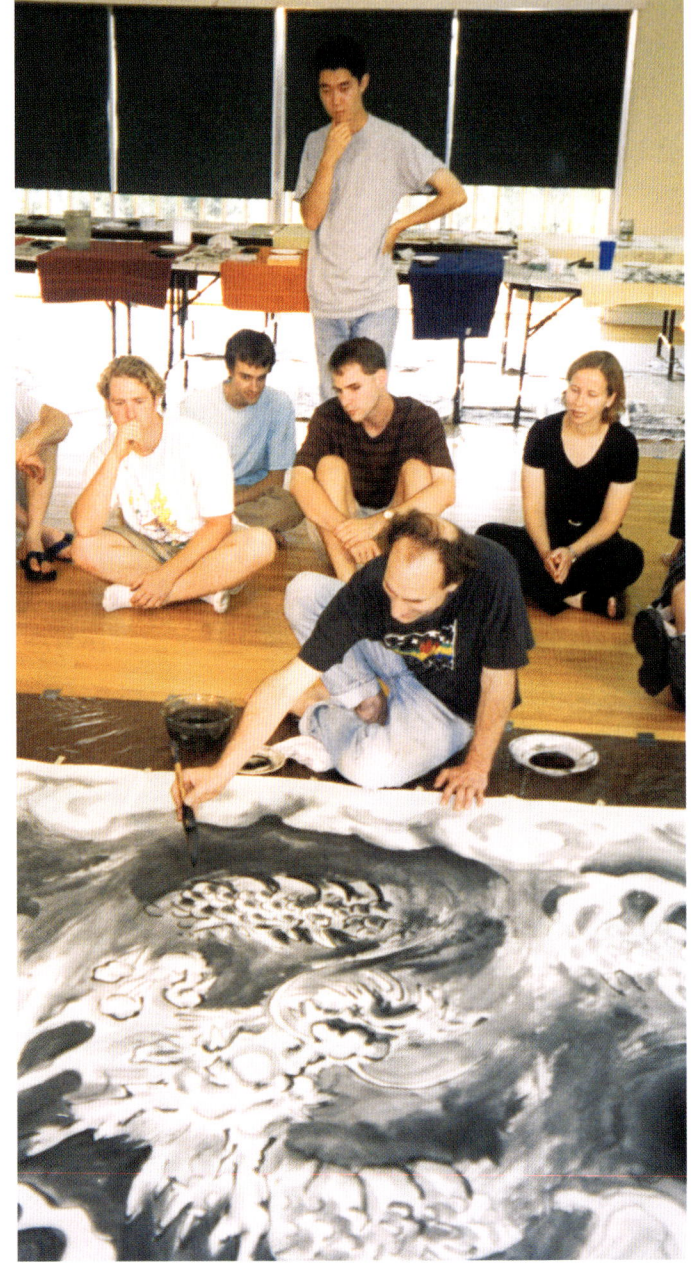

Michael Hofmann painting a dragon at the Horton Studio

[1] Gyokusei Jikihara was a Japanese master of calligraphy and a teacher in the Obaku School of Zen.

[2] *Nanga* is a school of Japanese painting adopted from the Southern style of China associated with the self-taught "literati," or intellectuals, and was strongly influenced by Zen Buddhism. During the 15th century, ink painting gained a more Japanese style of its own.

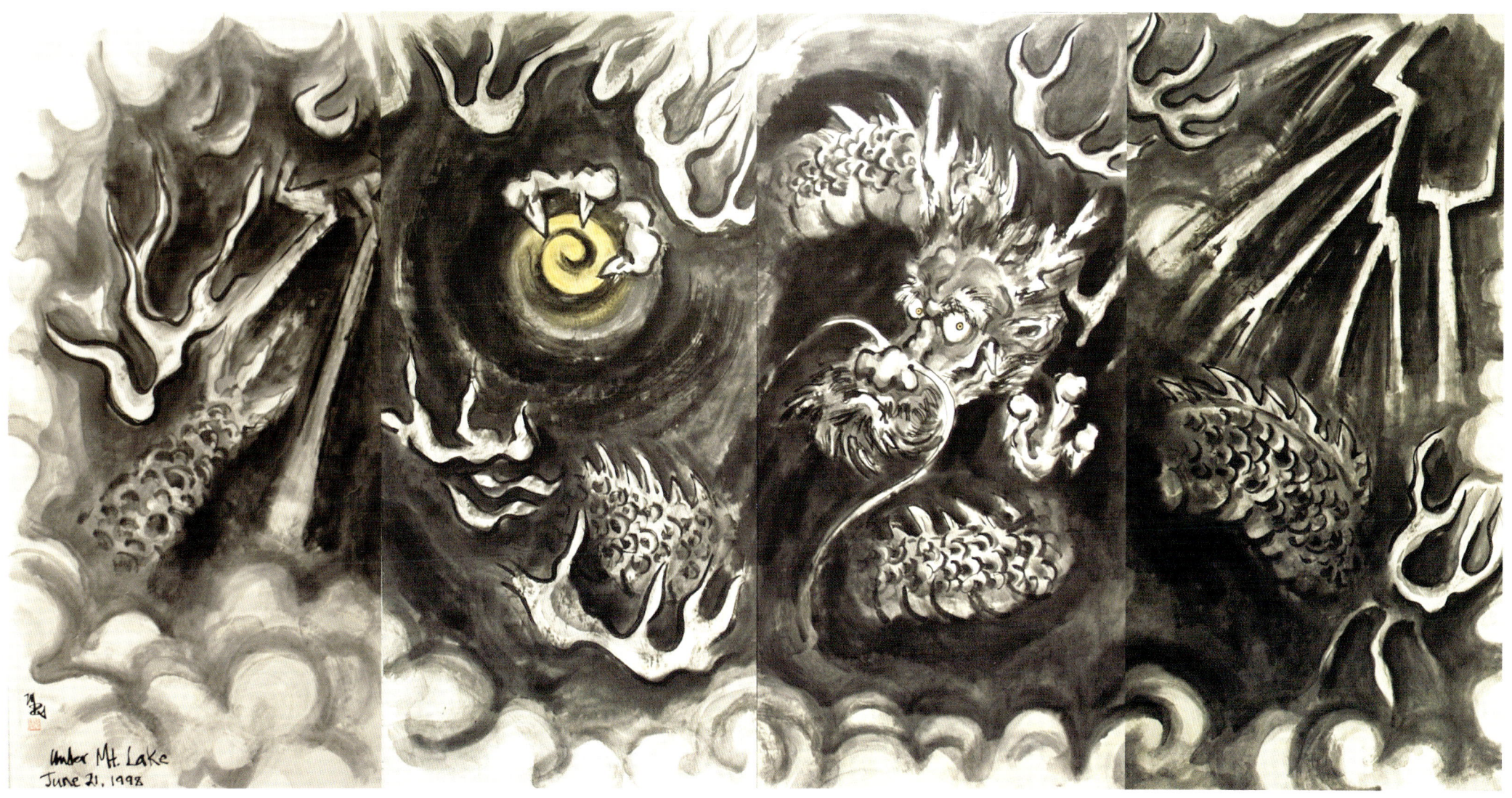

Michael Hofmann, *Under Mountain Lake Dragon*, 1998; *sumi-e*
brush painting on paper, wood, each panel 70 x 35 in. (177.8 x
88.9 cm) and overall 70 x 140 in. (177.8 x 355.6 cm).
Collection of the Taubman Museum of Art; gift of Ray Kass
and Jerrie Pike in honor of Ann Masters, 2005.032a-d.
Photo courtesy Taubman Museum of Art, Roanoke.

# XIAO YAN GAN: CHINESE SILK AND PAPER MOUNTING AND WATERCOLOR WORKSHOP, 2000

RAY KASS

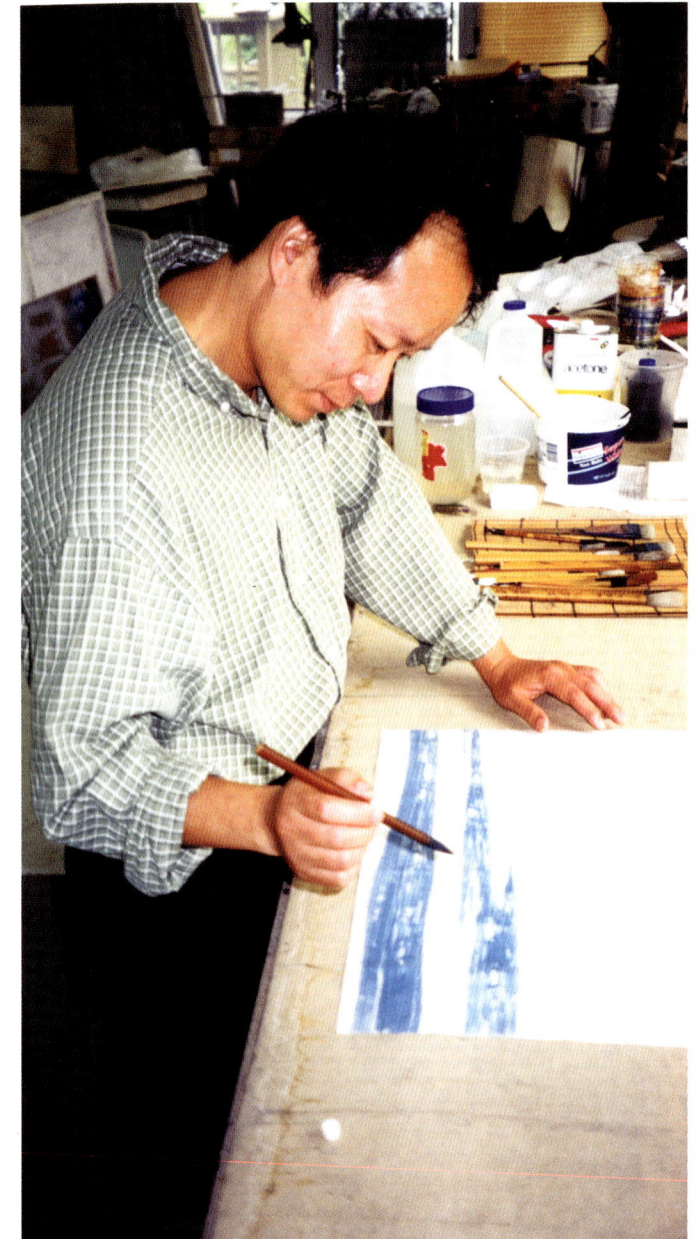

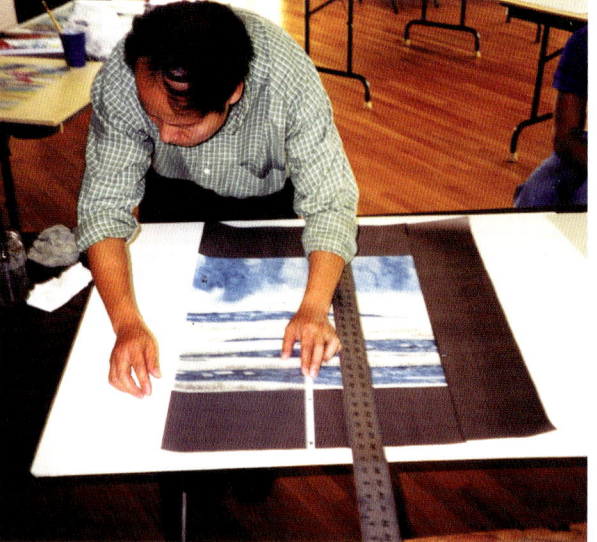

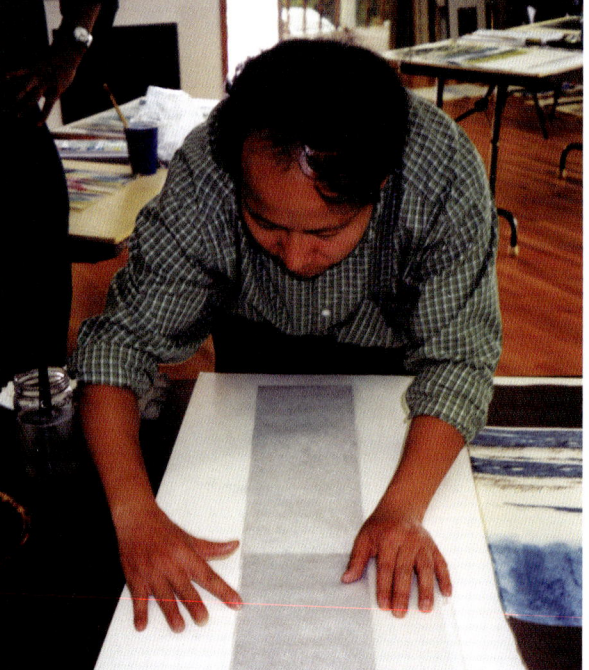

Xiao Yan Gan, a Shanghai artist whose work adapts traditional painting techniques to modern interpretations of the Chinese landscape, participated as a guest artist in Virginia Tech's art and design study-abroad programming in Shanghai, China, and Japan in May and June 2000. Mei Li Dong had introduced him to our group at a time when official hosts were often required to accompany groups on visits to significant cultural sites in and around Shanghai, and Xiao Yan Gan, who liked to be called "Sho-Sho" by friends, was an excellent host. Mei Li also arranged for her son Kalifa Dong-Ydeen, then fifteen years old, to accompany us on trips to Souchou and Anhui, and on our pilgrimage to the mythic Huangshan Mountains that every true artist is supposed to climb at least once in their lifetime.

To celebrate the "Year of the Dragon," we invited Sho-Sho to come to Virginia later that summer to have an exhibition and participate in a Mountain Lake Workshop. His workshop introduced community members and area students to both ink brush painting and traditional methods for mounting works done on somewhat fragile Asian paper or silk onto paper sheets or scrolls. The technique of Asian paper mounting became very important in future workshops, particularly for Jiro Okura's "Breathing Lines" workshops, the "Faces Off" exercise that we developed for James Donnelly and organized for the Nevada Museum of Art workshop in Reno in 2007, and Jacques Pourcher's "Atelier du Lac" experiment in my Virginia studio. The Asian paper and silk mounting technique also became especially important to me in my own developing work. When Morris Graves died in 2001, I made a group of layered paper and silk montages that were inspired by my impressions of his work.

[1] Huangshan Mountains, or the Yellow Mountains, are located in Anhui Province in eastern China. The mountains are not yellow, but were renamed in 747 AD after the legendary "Yellow Emperor" (Huang Di), the mythical ancestor of the Chinese, who is purported to have lived in the mountains and became a supernatural being. For more on this see: http://www.chinahighlights.com/huangshan/yellow-mountain/

[2] Xiao Yan Gan's exhibition was *Chinese Watercolor Scroll Paintings*, held at Armory Art Gallery, Virginia Tech, July 7–Sept. 1, 2000, with sponsorship from the Blacksburg Summer Arts Festival.

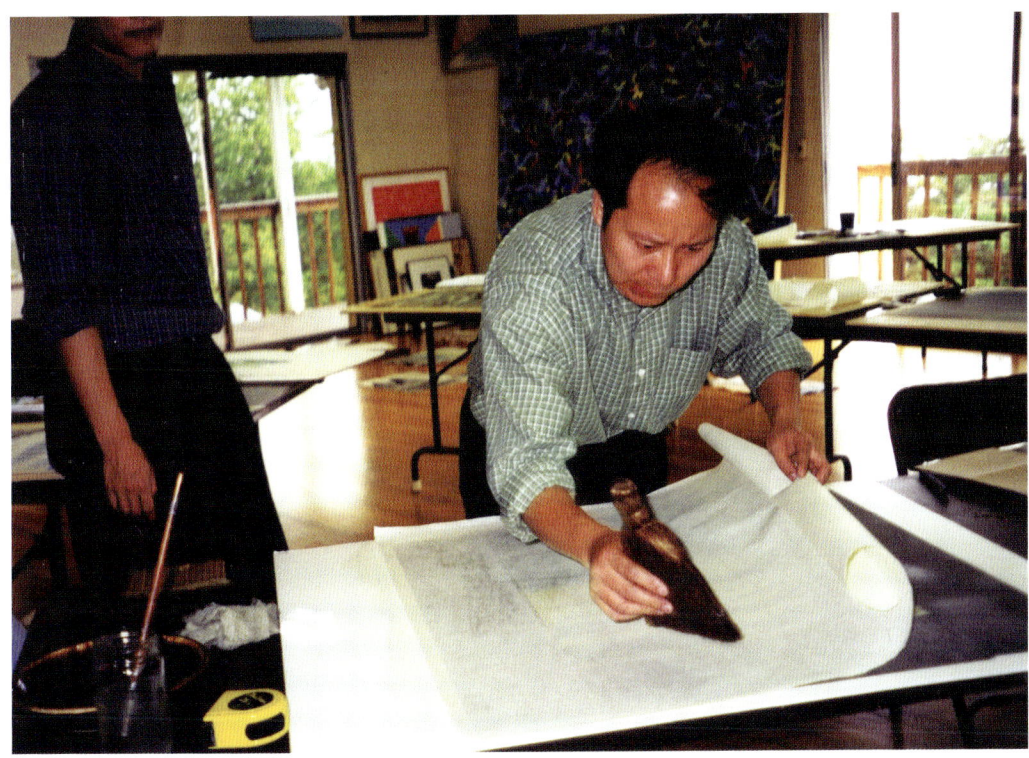

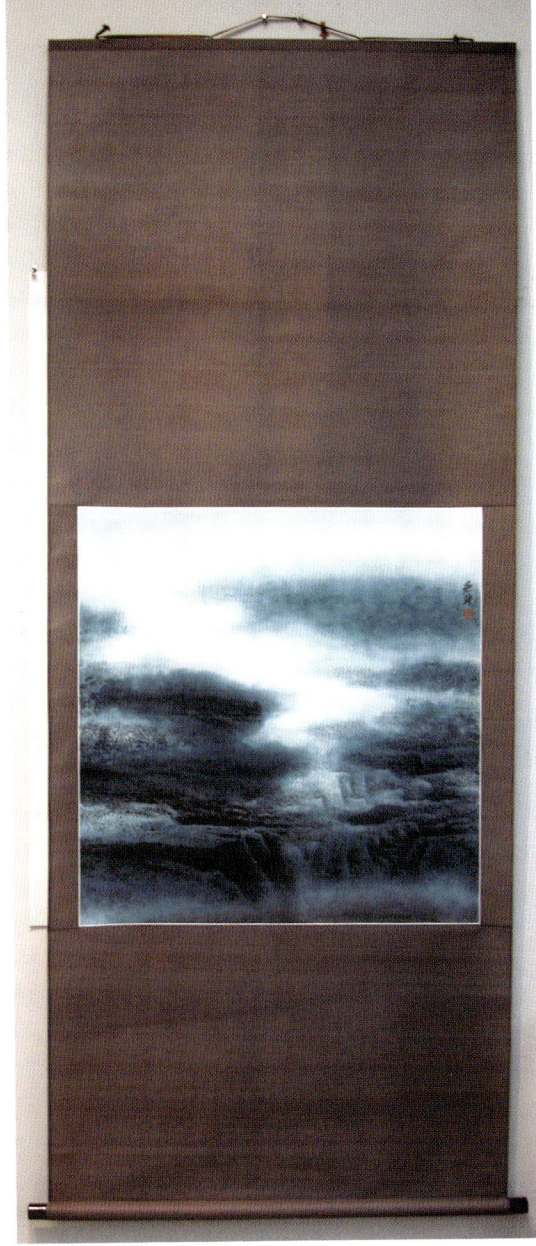

Xiao Yan Gan, *Untitled*, 2000 watercolor on mulberry paper, mounted as a scroll, bordered with silk, 27 x 27 in. (65.58 x 68.58 cm) image size; 77 x 34 in. (195.58 x 86.36 cm) scroll painting size

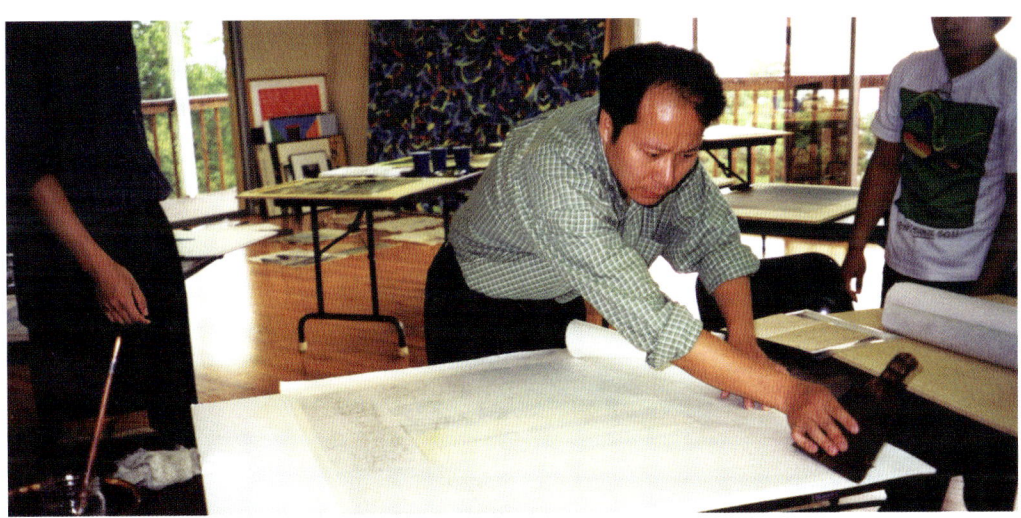

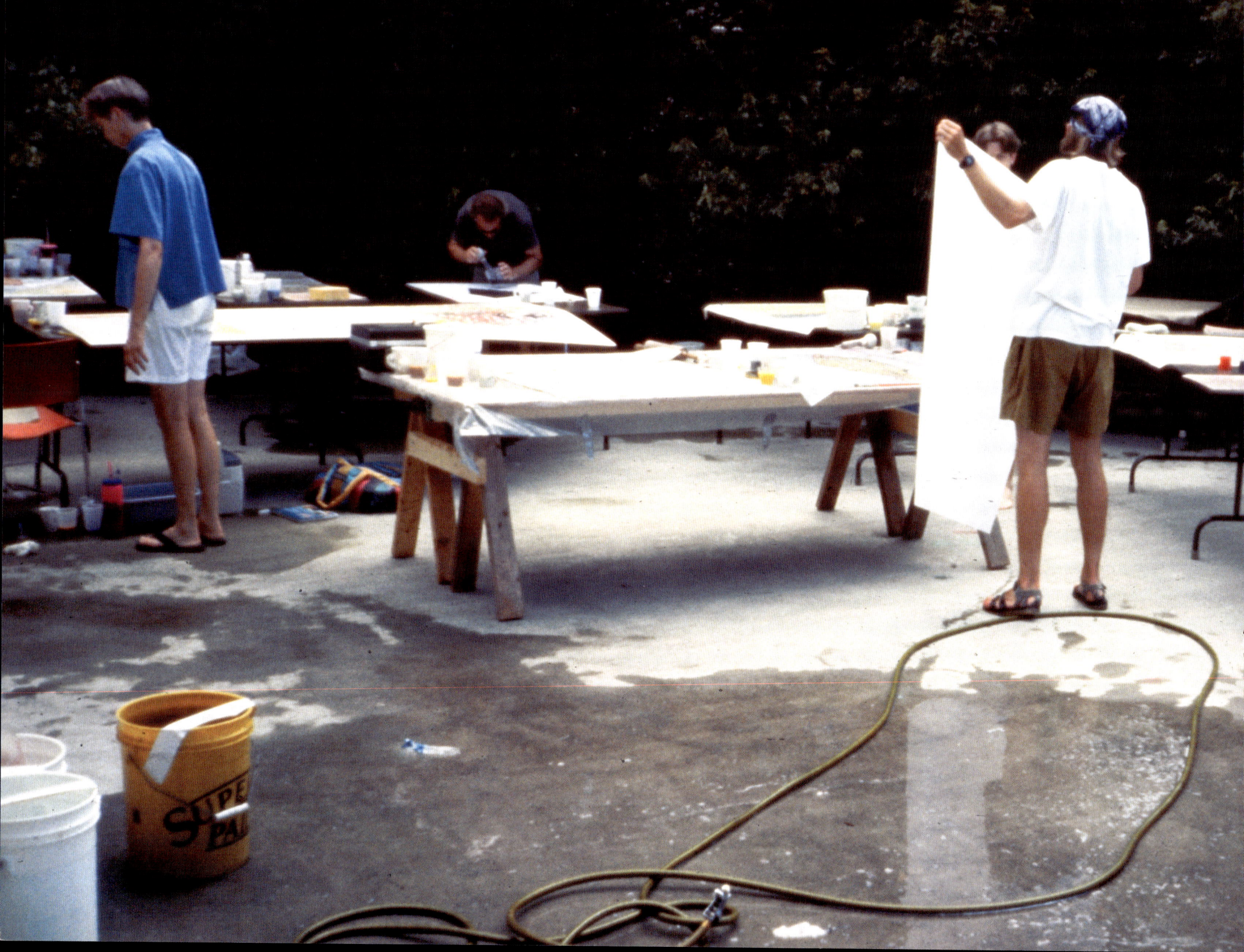

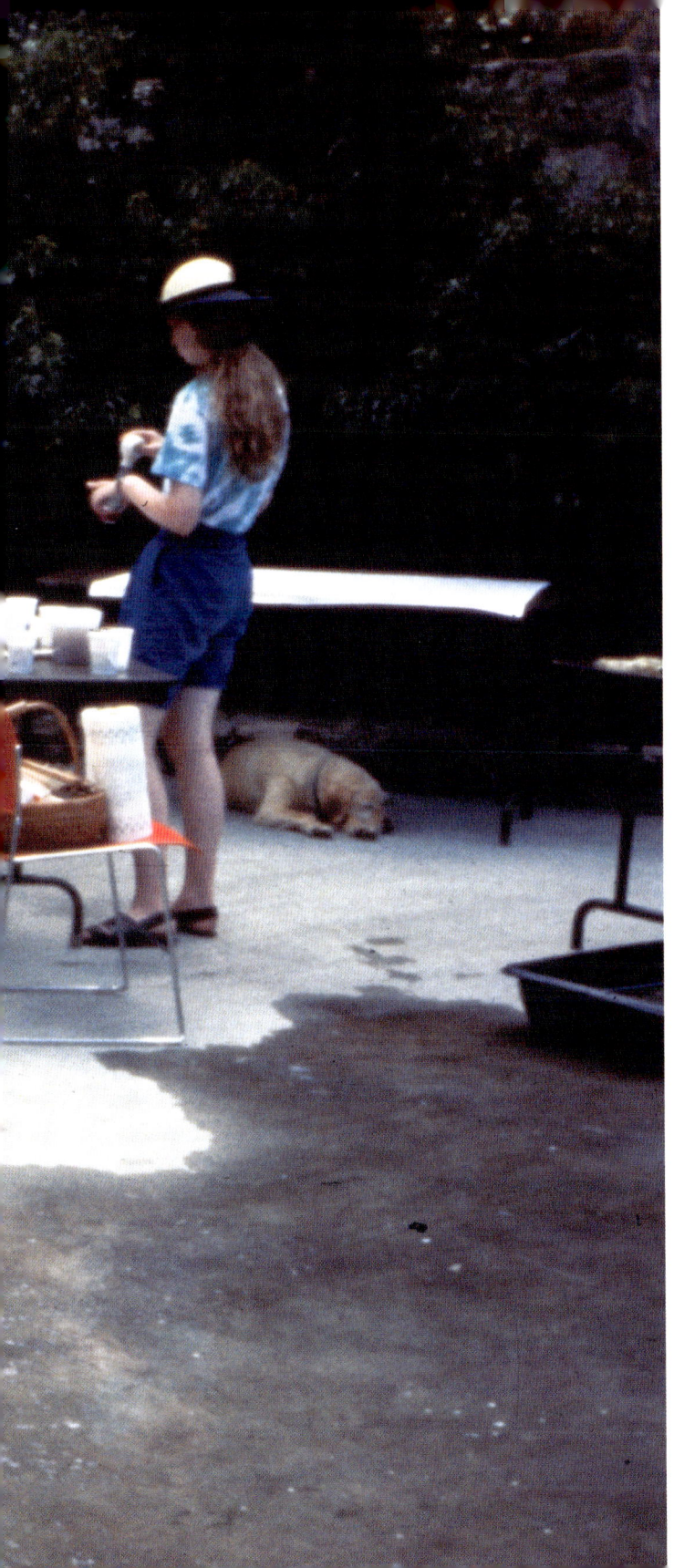

# VIII

## *The Mountain Lake Workshop: Collaborations with Traditional Processes and Materials*

# PYRAMID ATLANTIC AND HELEN FREDERICK: PAPERMAKING AT THE MOUNTAIN LAKE WORKSHOP

RAY KASS

In June 1993, Helen Frederick directed a week-long workshop at the Horton Center at Mountain Lake that engaged 32 community participants in making handmade Japanese-style vegetable-fiber papers. These extraordinarily strong long-fiber papers are usually derived from the inner bark of the mitsumata bush, gampi tree, and kozo (or mulberry) tree. However, we used a prepared abaca plant fiber from the Philippines, considered one of the strongest of the natural fibers, and neri, as a natural formation aid and viscous binder and a good deflocculant that slows drainage through the paper mold screens.[1]

In preparation for the workshop events, large papermaking molds were made in advance and covered with stretched synthetic silk in the manner of silkscreen frames; participants used these as forms to receive the carefully prepared solution of abaca fiber, water, neri, and cotton fiber. The pulp-filled molds were allowed to dry on tables placed outside in the sun. In similar but smaller molds, participants used the same solution to make smaller-scale works that used colored cotton pulp. The colored pulp allowed them to "paint" with colors that were actually embedded in the paper.

One extraordinary collaborative piece, titled *Mountain Lake Army Blanket*, was made by the small group of assistants in the workshop who ended every day by swimming across nearby Mountain Lake and gathering various bits of detritus, including an insect or two, from the lake bottom and subsequently embedding these finds in the paper pulp.

[1] Neri is made by pounding the roots of the tororo-aoi plant, a variety of the hibiscus tree. In the papermaking process, neri works to bind the fibers together, and, since it is not sticky, the individual layers of paper can be pulled apart during the drying process. A deflocculant is a material, usually an alkaline, added to a suspension to ionize all the particles in the suspension by introducing like electrical charges, thereby causing the particles to repel one another and remain in suspension.

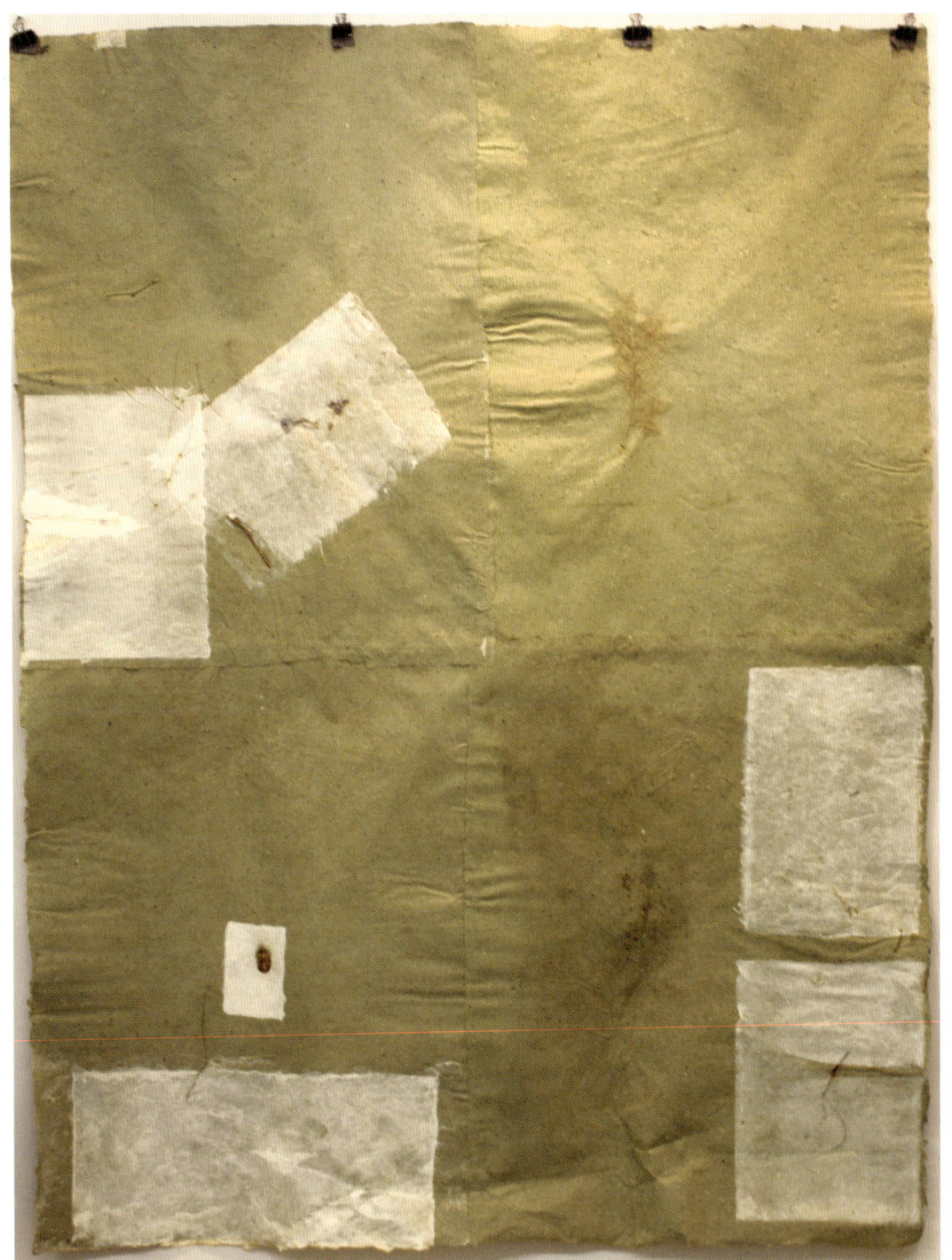

*Mountain Lake Army Blanket*, 1993, handmade paper infused with organic lake debris, 72 x 58.5 in. (182.88 x 148.59 cm)

# COLLECTIVELY SPEAKING

JANE M. FARMER

Ray Kass, *Untitled,* 1993, handmade Paper, 30.5 x 40.25 in. (77.47 x 102.24 cm), a piece made at Helen Frederick's Mountain Lake Workshop

Sure hands wield a vintage press. Others perform the ritual alchemy to transform fiber into paper. Elders record their stories while young people discover that they have stories to tell. A book, pages painstakingly stitched, is bound in leather and stamped with gold foil. Another is bound in a plain zip-lock bag. Incongruities? Unexpected convergences? Tradition and innovation, international dialogue and local community building, teaching and learning and making — all come together at Pyramid Atlantic Art Center in Silver Spring, Maryland, in a remarkable synergy.

Pyramid Atlantic, founded by Helen Frederick in 1980, is an advocate for a creativity-centered community. At the time of its founding, workshops were springing up all over the United States to perfect different media in order to establish their worthiness in the hierarchy of the art world. Frederick had a different agenda from the start. As an adolescent, she often visited the Marcel Duchamp collection at the Philadelphia Museum of Art. Immediately Frederick responded to the space for articulation and understanding provided by Duchamp's transformation of materials. Eventually she realized that the idea was as important as the object itself, that the object's not falling into our expected definition of beauty and art was what enabled the stimulation of our thinking and enabled us to accept our own answers about art.

Frederick's attendance at a musical performance by the innovative artist/musician John Cage was another revelation for a young student — a seminal experience she could fully appreciate only later. She then traveled to Ahmedabad, India, seeking more personal than artistic understanding. She was introduced to a papermaking community fostering communal/cooperative working. It was there that she experienced acceptance of the abilities and contributions of all, even including the street children. Frederick's arrival followed a visit by the American artist Robert Rauschenberg, an inveterate collaborator within disciplines, media, and materials and a longtime friend of Cage. The Ahmedabad community was sensitized by his intermixing of traditional materials, local culture, and observational statements, and welcomed Frederick as another American who wanted to learn and interact with handmade paper. Thus the experience was pivotal in her work and development as a collaborator.

The collaborative workshop Frederick founded was named "Pyramid Prints and Paperworks" for the large graphic mural that was a defining landmark on Pyramid's block in the warehouse district, not far from the Maryland Institute College of Art and Design. Pyramid quickly became known as an experimental center for innovation, technical support, and the combination of printmaking and papermaking.

In Pyramid's work with members, artists-in-residence, and students, the most important goal has been to provide a place of neutrality, safety, support, and technical expertise. This environment frees the artists from many restrictions: the expectations of professors, teachers, galleries, museums, and critics. Frederick had witnessed this freedom in the work of Duchamp, the musical collaboration of Cage, the experimentations of German-Swiss artist Dieter Roth, and the collaboration of Rauschenberg's printmaking and papermaking.

Helen Frederick has continued to explore the nature of collaboration and creativity and to provide this open-ended yet supportive environment for artists of all ages, experience, and reputation.

This essay is excerpted from the catalog *Collaboration as a Medium, 25 Years of Pyramid Atlantic* (Silver Spring, MD: Pyramid Atlantic Art Center, 2005)

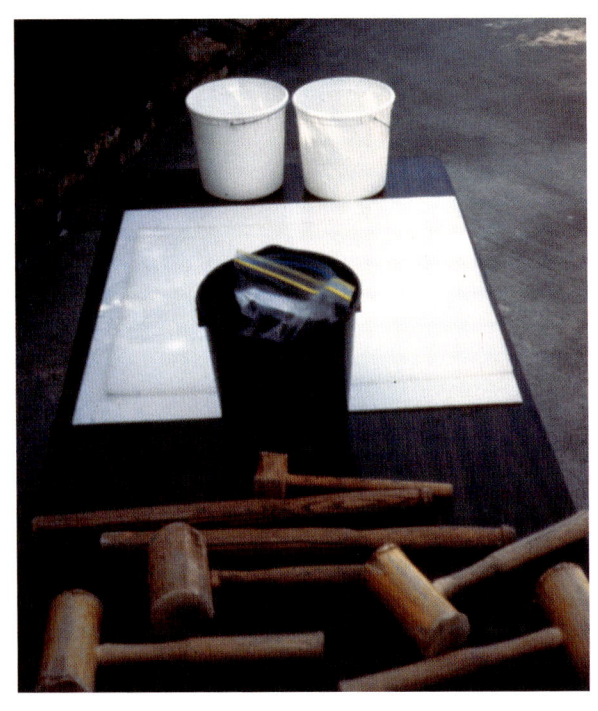 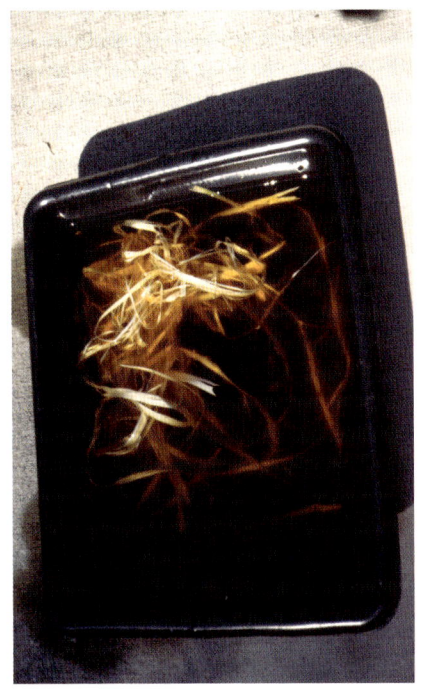 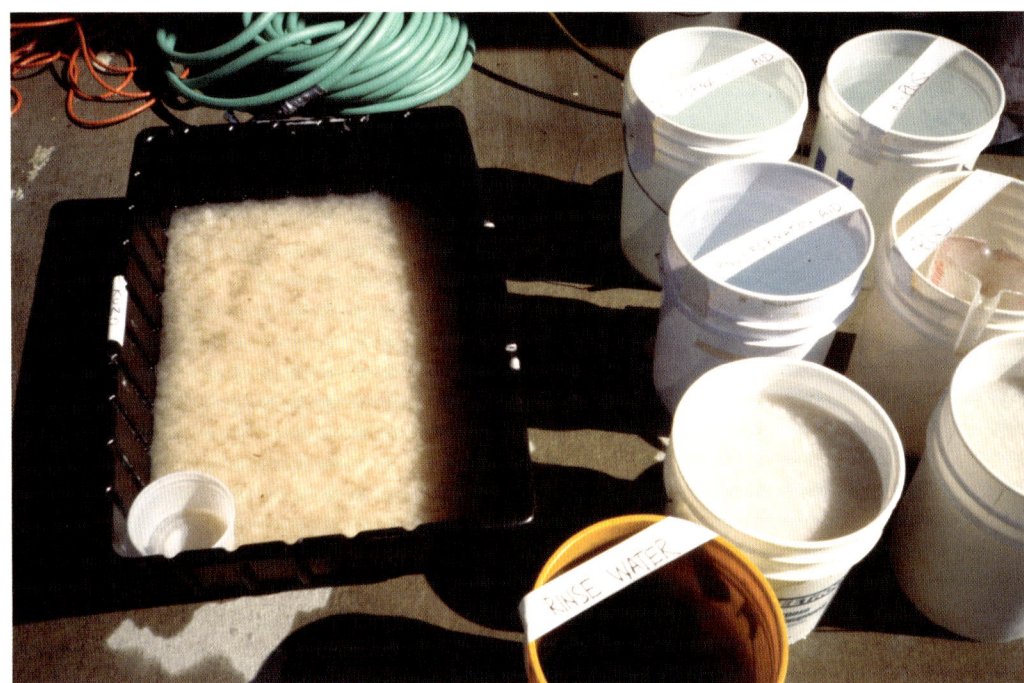

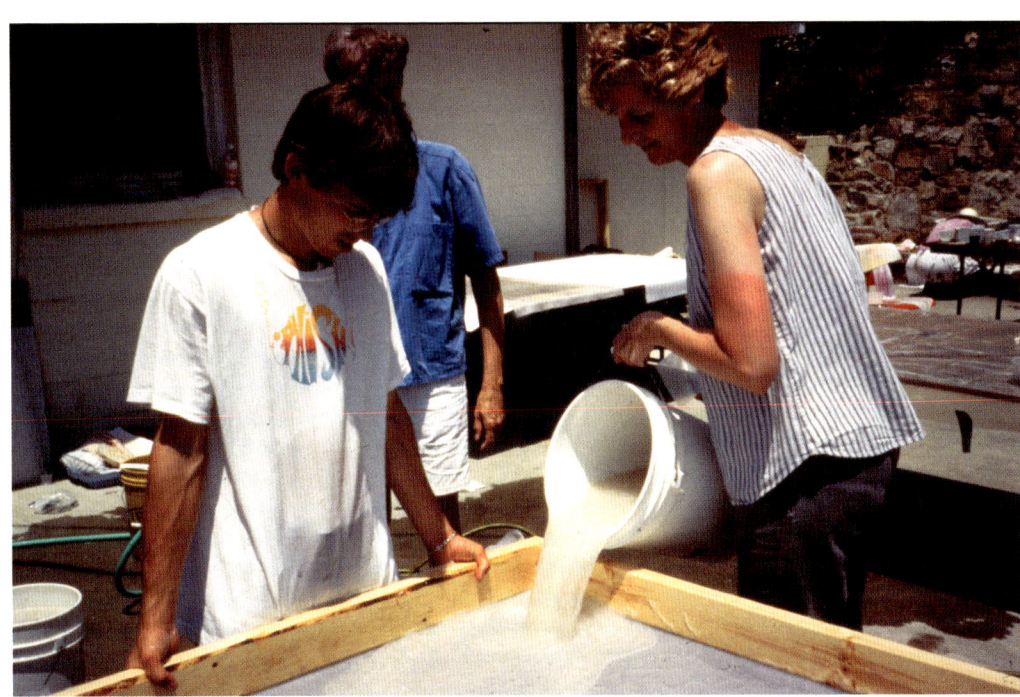 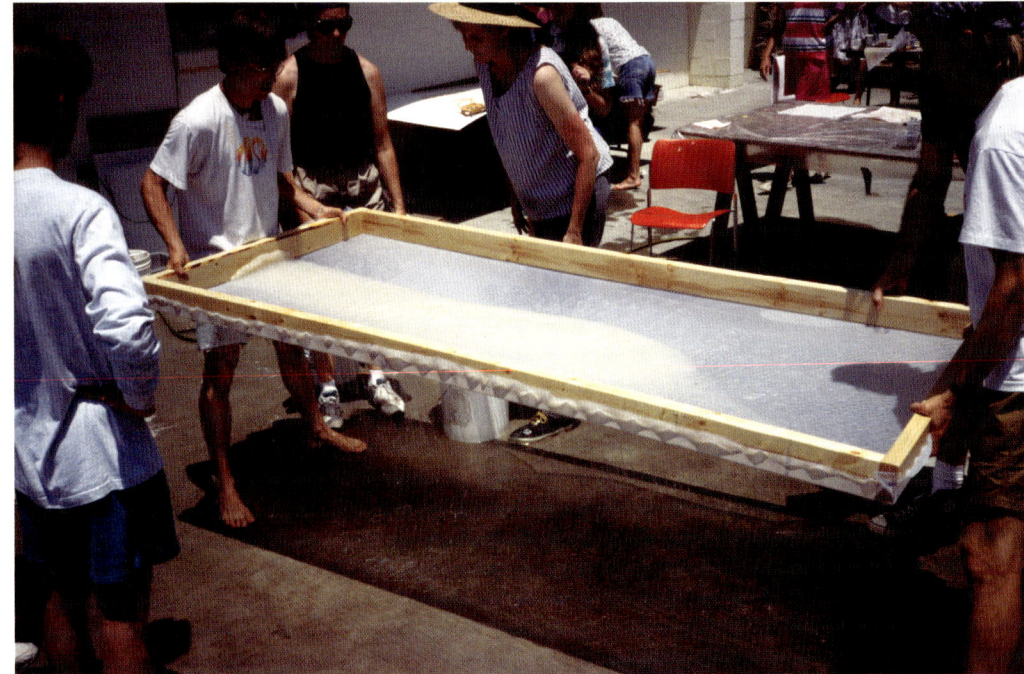

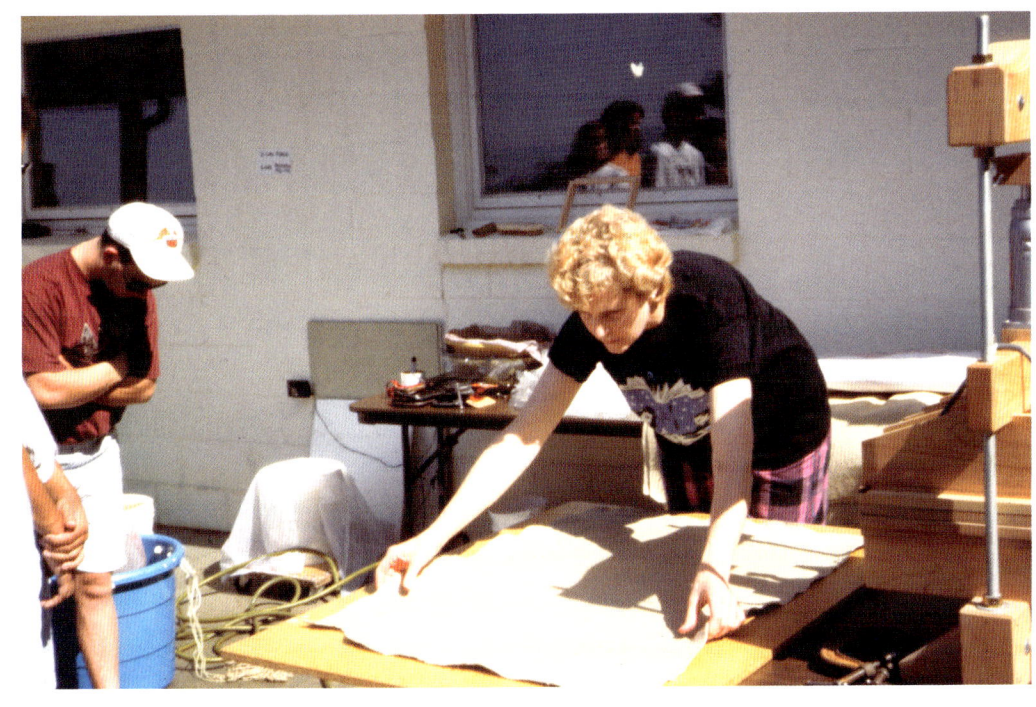
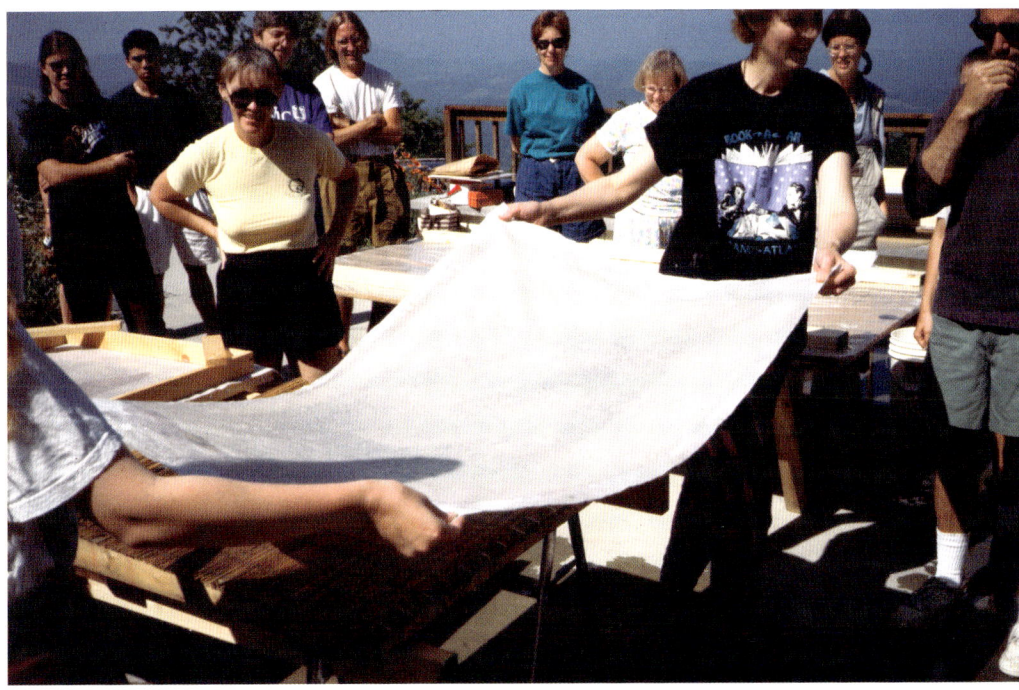
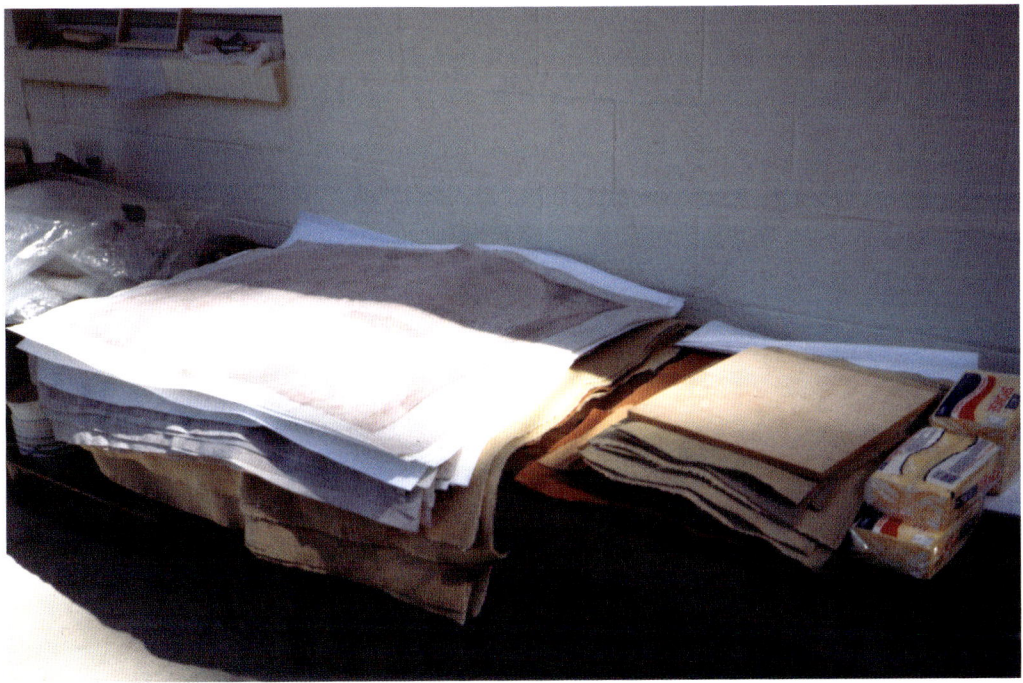
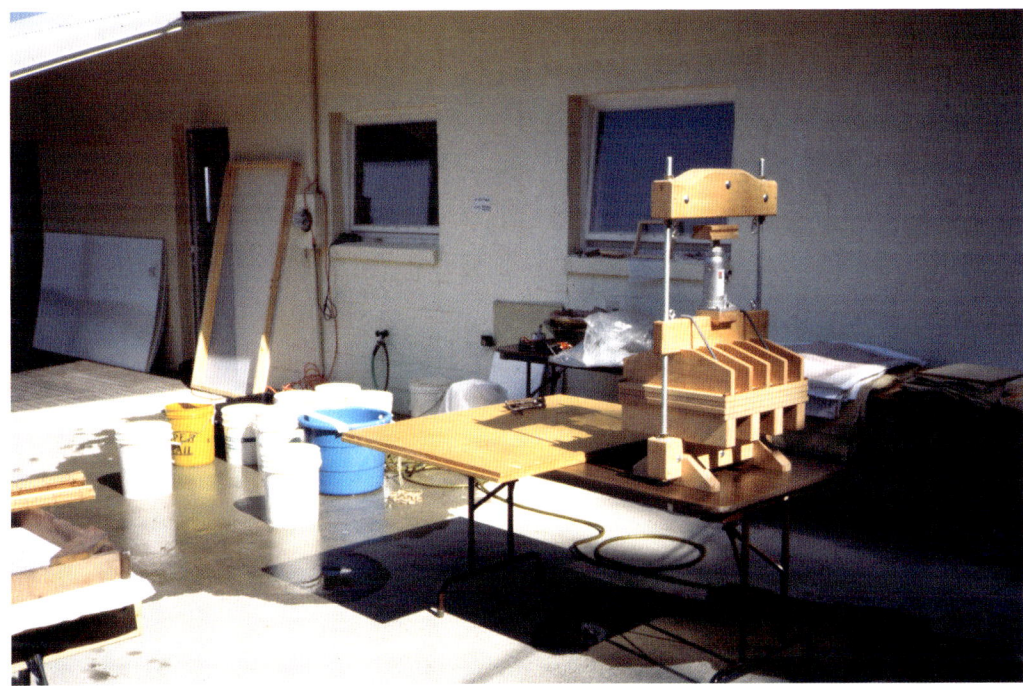

# PAPERMAKING AT THE MOUNTAIN LAKE WORKSHOP WITH HELEN FREDERICK AND MIERLE LADERMAN UKELES

KATHY PINKERTON

From the mid-1980s to 1990s I worked exclusively in handmade paper. I learned to make large-scale handmade paper by taking workshops at Penland School of Crafts in North Carolina and with Helen Frederick at Pyramid Atlantic in Maryland; this was in the mid-to-late '80s. In preparation for Helen's workshop at Mountain Lake, we made several giant molds in my Blacksburg studio using two by fours and fine mosquito netting that was similar to a silk screen but not as fine so as to allow the water in which the paper pulp mixture was suspended to drain through. Helen used long-fibered kozo at Mountain Lake, which is very labor-intensive to prepare because it must be beaten by hand. The abaca fiber which I prefer to use, and which most workshop participants used as well, can be machine pulped and purchased pre-beaten to your specifications.

My work was done on a large vacuum table, and my pieces were "drawn" with pigmented pulps into a base of floating pulp fiber. The images were not applied to a surface in the manner of painting or drawing; rather, the images *were* the surface. The process is somewhat similar to weaving; but unlike the warp and weft threads on a loom, my fibers floated in water as I created a design. I used pigmented cotton and abaca for my large-scale pieces. The table, which was 4 feet by 8 feet, enabled me to work on a large scale.

The focus of Mierle Laderman Ukeles' Methanogenesis workshop with Ray Kass was on the biodegradation of organic material in anaerobic systems, usually in swampy areas. One day participants in the Methanogenesis workshop came to my Blacksburg studio to work on the large vacuum table. Since papermaking on a vacuum table also has an anaerobic

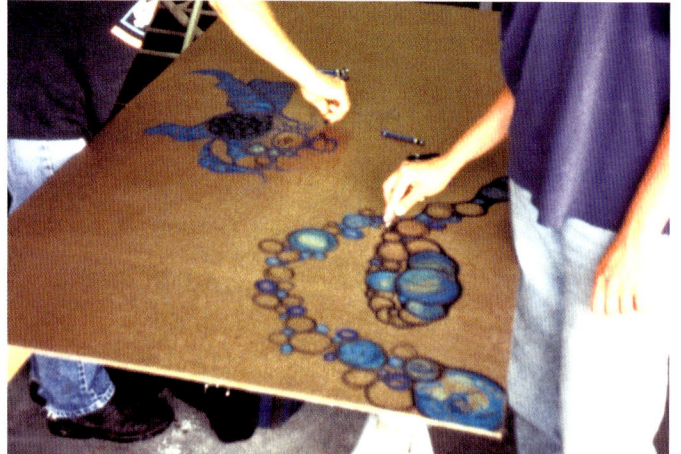

quality to it (i.e., air is drawn through the slurry of pulp, creating a partial vacuum), this seemed like a perfect complementary component to the Methanogenesis workshop. Actually, from the moment papermaking pulp is suspended in water, even without a vacuum process, a swampy environment begins to evolve, and one must work quickly before the slurry ferments. Our group made a multitude of small, blue sheets. The pulp was a combination of cotton and abaca that was pigmented a rich ultramarine blue. We dried each sheet on a smooth plastic surface. This gave the paper a shiny, almost plastic feel since paper in its wet stage will take on the texture of anything it is placed on.

Participants then made abstract drawings with water-soluble

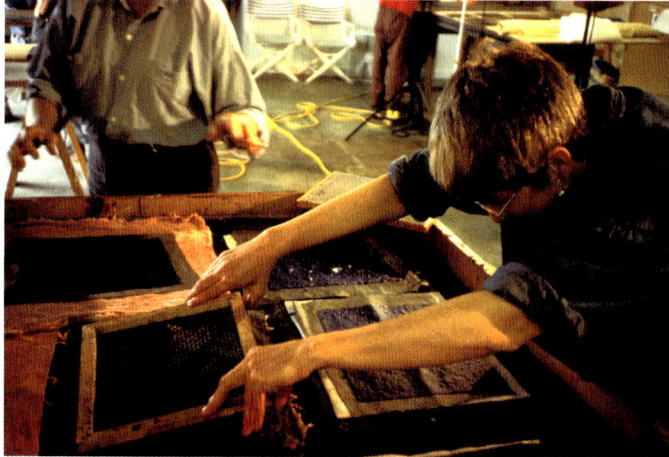

crayons on rectangles of Masonite that were sized to match the sheets of blue paper. These drawings, intended to be meditational images representing methanogens (anaerobic microbes) essential to the methanogenesis process, were then transferred, or imprinted, onto the "blue leaves" using the vacuum table. Several participants worked together making a number of large meditational drawings in which each individual started from a different corner of the Masonite surface and then drew toward the center. These large, group drawings developed an extraordinary intuitive harmony as the participants worked in unison.

I produced handmade paper works on a large scale and exhibited them for nearly fifteen years.

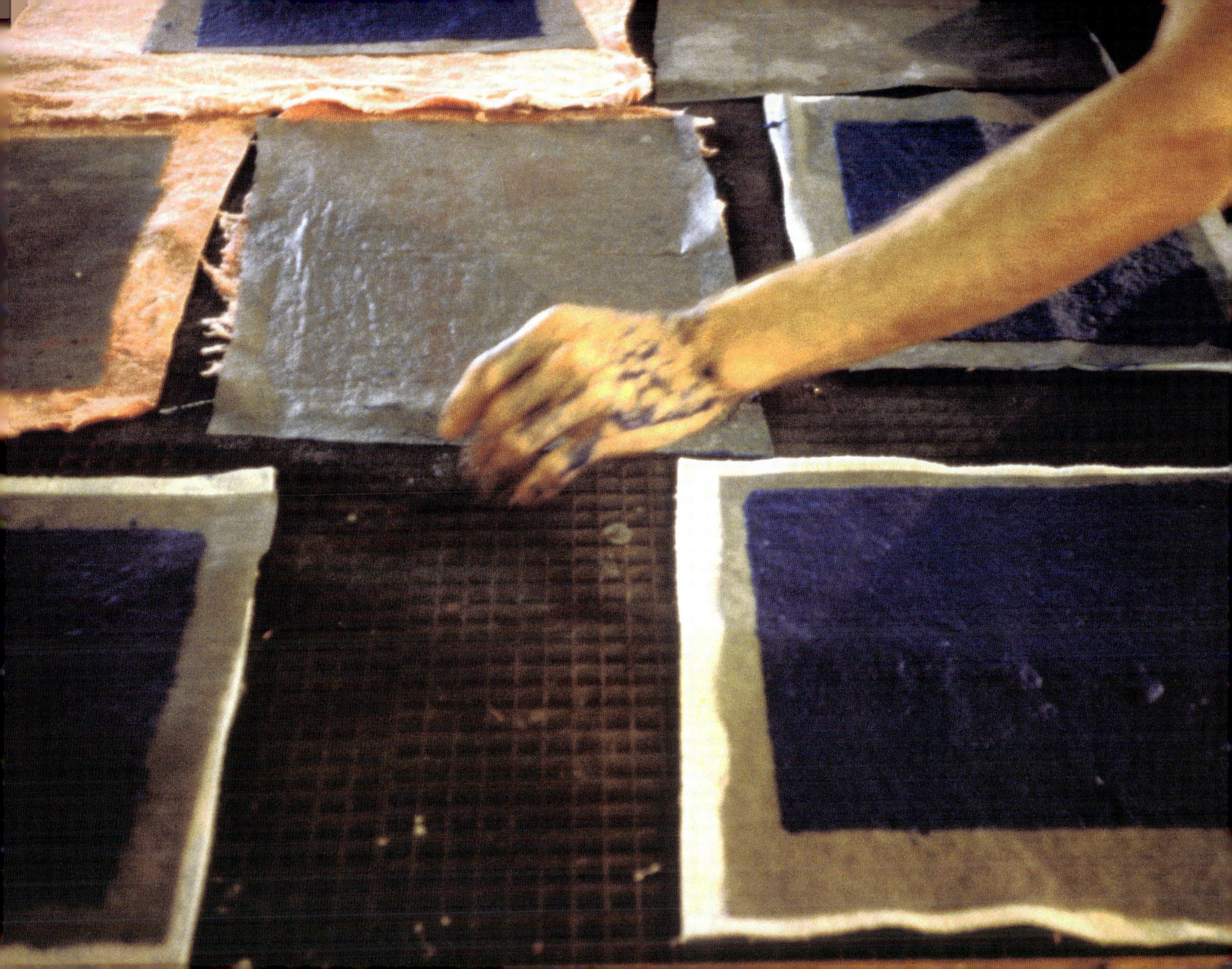

# FRESCO WORKSHOP, 1989

## ALSTON (STONEY) CONLEY

Alston (Stoney) Conley, *Shrine*, 33, June 1980, fresco on panel, x 21 x 1 in. (83.2 x 53.4 x 2.54 cm).

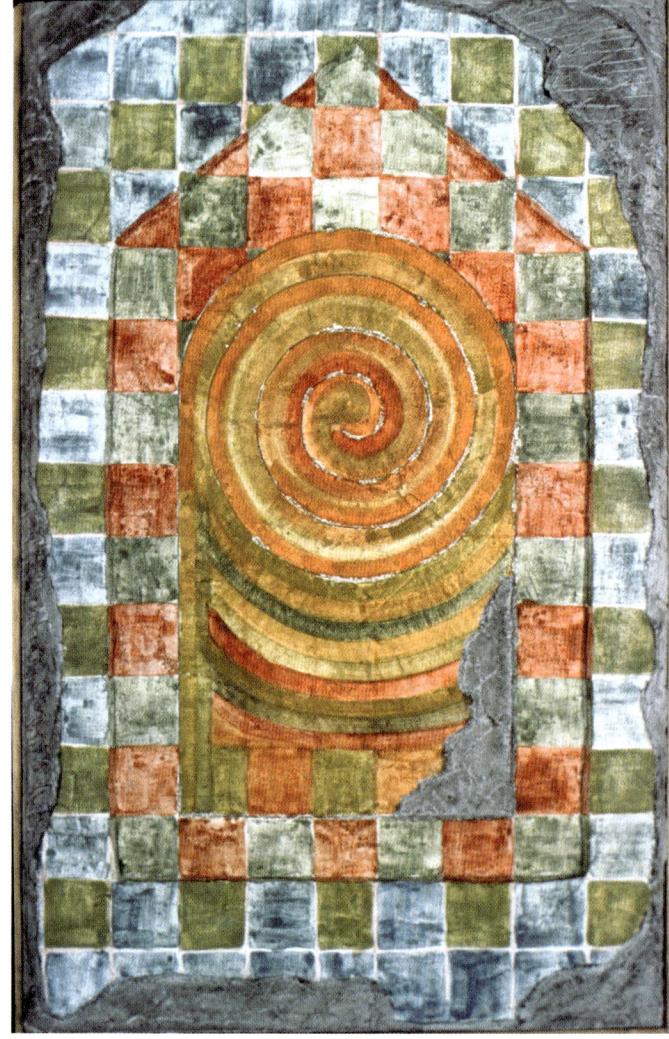

*Alston Conley came to Mountain Lake in 1989 to give a workshop on fresco painting so we could learn skills that we anticipated using for another John Cage workshop, which, unfortunately, he did not live to do. In the text below, Conley describes the process by which he became an "itinerant fresco teacher," able to pick up the tools of his trade and travel to the Virginia mountains.*

I discovered fresco as a student at the Skowhegan School of Painting and Sculpture in 1977. I had been making fragments of contemporary walls in building plasters and paint. At Skowhegan I noticed how brilliant the colors were and how the pigments bonded to the plaster surface. Wanting to learn more about the technique, I read the chapter on fresco in Ralph Mayer's *The Artist's Handbook* and started gathering materials.[1] The plaster, slaked fresco lime, was the hardest thing to find; no art store sold the material. I found a source in western Massachusetts for quick lime, the calcium oxide powder used to make fresco lime by the process known as "slaking" — i.e., mixing water with quick lime plaster to create calcium hydroxide (the desired slaked fresco lime) and then aging the resulting plaster. Mixing quick lime with water during slaking produces lots of heat, steaming off some of the water and creating the possibility of an explosion because of the chemical reaction $CaO + H_2O = Ca(OH)_2 + Heat$.

Armed with appropriate fresco-making materials, I used two fellowships at the Fine Arts Work Center in Provincetown in the winters of 1978 and 1979 to make a series of true fresco panels with actual slaked lime, shaped as fragments of walls from imaginary civilizations. Then in the summer of 1980 I worked at the Skowhegan School of Painting and Sculpture as the co-dean of students with my wife Mary Armstrong. George Schneeman taught fresco that summer and it was our first meeting.[2] Best known for his collaborations with poets, Schneeman made small frescoes on cast cement forms, often circular shapes (cast in garbage can lids) one inch or more thick, upon which he would apply his top intonaco painting surface. I was still making my wall fragments with wood lathing and the traditional three layers of plaster. I added white cement and horsehair to the first coat that was then pressed through the openings between the wood laths so that the plaster, squeezing around the inner sides of the laths, would hang securely in place. I needed a strong structural first layer, and the additives provided that.

I spent the 1981–82 academic year on a Fulbright grant in Florence, where I finally got to see the Italian masters' frescoes and visit behind-the-scenes at the Sistine Chapel during its historic restoration.[3] Frescoes aren't known for being portable, so I borrowed Schneeman's technique of casting small, round cement "tondos" as well as trying fresco on Masonite panels. When I returned to the U.S., I started making icon-shaped panels of polystyrene, which was readily available as insulation panels. I discovered a new cement product called Conproco Structural Skin; it contained small plastic fibers, an alternative to horsehair, which added strength. I also used the material Acrylic 60, which when mixed with the Conproco increased its ability to stick to a nonporous material like the polystyrene panels. These materials allowed me to become an itinerant fresco teacher as they were much more portable.

[1] Ralph Mayer, *The Artist's Handbook of Materials and Techniques*, first edition (New York: The Viking Press; 1940) 5th edition revised and updated with Steven Sheehan (New York: Viking Penguin; 1991).

[2] Schneeman (March 11, 1934 — January 27, 2009), who was born in Minnesota, was largely a self-taught artist influenced by Italian Renaissance painting. He worked in various media including collage, egg tempra, and fresco and was especially well known for his collaborations with New York poets including Peter Schjeldahl, Anne Waldman, Larry Fagin, and Ted Berrigan. He exhibited at Holly Solomon Gallery in Soho during the 1970s and early 80s.

[3] My experience with the Sistine Chapel started at Skowhegan when I gave a fresco demonstration to visiting lecturer Leo Steinberg, a well-known Modern Art critic and art historian with particular expertise in the Italian Renaissance. Steinberg suggested I visit the Sistine Chapel and get up on the scaffolding while the current, somewhat controversial restoration was in progress. He wrote me a letter of introduction. On weekends the Vatican was letting those in the field onto the scaffolding to see the restoration work. When Mary and I went to Rome we were given a tour of the conservation process, which had reached the middle of the ceiling. They were cleaning Adam and Eve and the Serpent, and on one side was the fresh, bright color of the clean surface and on the other the dirty painting. In the middle of the Michelangelo-designed scaffolding was a dentist-office-like chair that leaned back and was equipped with a light with a magnifying glass. Here the conservators

# FRESCO PREPARATION & PROCESS

Roger Hedgepath, *Untitled (Fresco for John Cage)*, 1989, pigment on true fresco, 15.75 x 12.25 in. (40 x 31.12 cm), Made using one of the rocks from John Cage's 1988 workshop

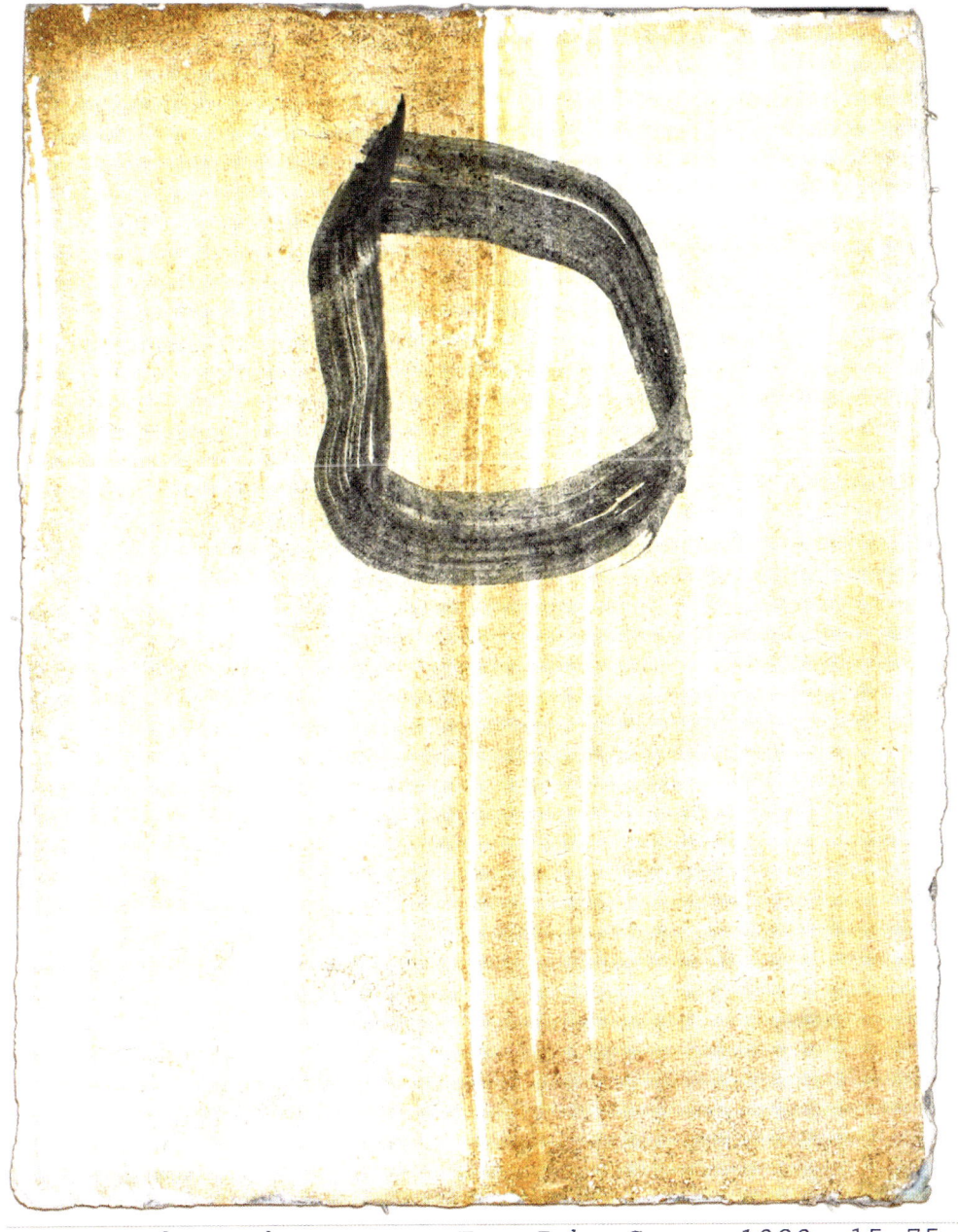

Prep 2-inch-thick polystyrene insulation panels by roughing the surface and then applying Conproco and Acrylic 60 mixture. After they've dried, mix aged lime plaster with a fine sand in a ratio of 1 to 1 and apply a 1/8- to ¼-inch-thick layer; this is the *intonaco* painting surface. Let it set up for 30–60 minutes while grinding pigments in water with a muller; then start painting. Usually you can paint for 6–8 hours before the *intonaco* surface will no longer bind with the pigment.

**Materials list:**

*Fresco lime

*Fine sand

*2-inch-thick, stiff foam insulation with roughened surface cut into workable sizes (12 in. x 16 in. or 16 in. x 24 in.)

*Conproco Structural Skin — 1/2 bag will cover two, 2 ft. x 8 ft. panels

*Acrylic 60 — additive for cement products to increase adhesion on nonporous materials

*Tables to work on covered with plastic

*Glass palettes for mixing pigments

*Sand trowels

*Powder pigments

reclined while they applied a mild water-based cleaner with a cotton swab and then rinsed off the surface with another. I came away impressed with their process and how delicate they were in cleaning the ceiling. They knew what they were doing. Backed with historical data and research, they knew how many times the ceiling had been given coats of animal skin glue as a varnish in an attempt to brighten the colors. Unfortunately, all that these applications of glue accomplished was to repeatedly seal in the dirt created in part by the smoke from candles and incense that had risen to the ceiling over the centuries.

# M.C. RICHARDS AND THE MOUNTAIN LAKE WORKSHOPS: COSMOS AND CREATION IN CLAY, COLOR, AND WORDS, 1997

RAY KASS

M.C. Richards' long commitment to building a strong sense of community in art and life had its origins in her experience teaching at Black Mountain College in the late 1940s. At Black Mountain she came to "think of her work as integrating the soul, the mind, and the muscle"— a philosophical overview essential to the interdisciplinary scope of her work in various mediums; her pottery became the inspiration for her poetry, her poetry found shape in her pots and paintings, and all were united by a unique spirit of ceremonial ritual. Perhaps the clearest expression of these principles is set out in her landmark 1962 book *Centering: In Pottery, Poetry, and the Person*, which has become a foundation classic of "New Age" literature. "I move," she wrote, "from the silhouette the surface the shape to the invisible space within, without which the pot would still be a lump of clay."[1]

I first met M.C. (short for Mary Caroline) Richards in 1995 when she was visiting at Suzi Gablik's country house near Blacksburg, Virginia. I had owned a copy of *Centering* since the mid-1960s and often heard mention of its author at board meetings of the Jargon Society (a press founded by poet Jonathan Williams that grew out of his Black Mountain College years) and in conversation with my friends John Cage and Merce Cunningham. Suzi took us into town to have dinner, and a discussion about a possible future workshop with M.C. came up almost immediately; it would incorporate drawing, ceramics, writing, and book-making with an autobiographical and community focus.

I subsequently made several trips to visit M.C. in Kimberton, Pennsylvania, at Camphill Village, where she had lived since 1984. Camphill is a dynamic farming, gardening, and

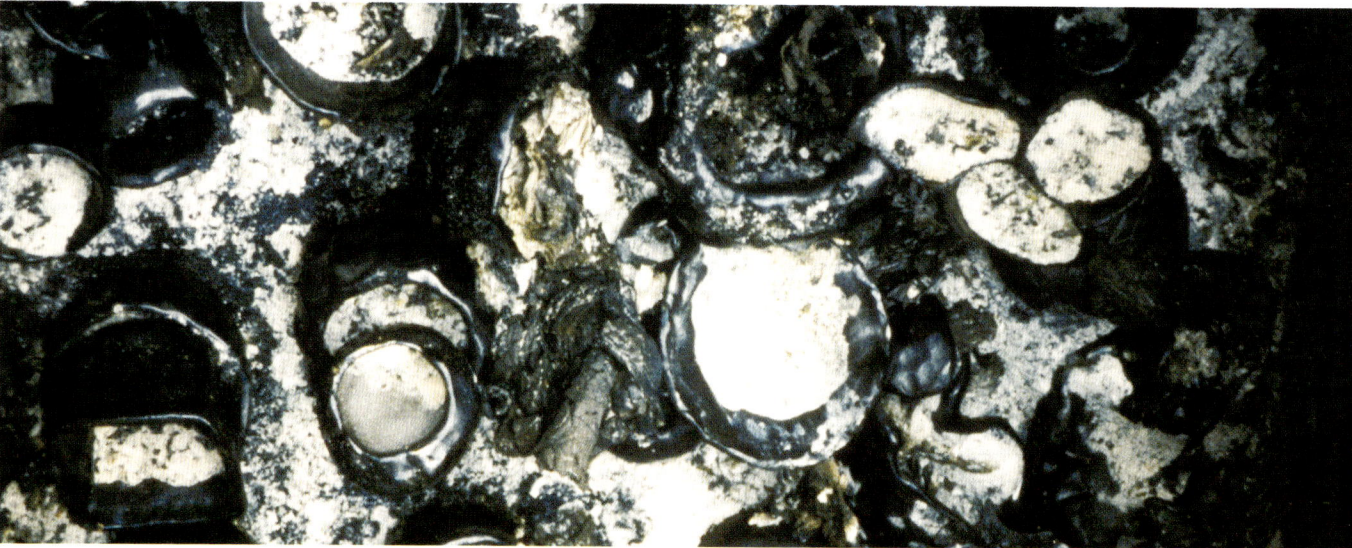

handcrafting community of more than 100 people of all ages where M.C. cared for residents with various developmental disabilities. The community is grounded in the anthroposophical principles of Rudolf Steiner, whose educational philosophy had inspired the Waldorf Schools, also known as Steiner Schools, which encourage individual imagination and incorporate the arts in all aspects of academic study. M.C. maintained a small painting and pottery studio at Camphill and often cooked breakfast for thirty or more of the residents.

On one memorable visit with M.C. and my graduate intern, Andy Liss, we drove into New York City to see a special gallery exhibition of Morris Graves' flower paintings. Their radiant colors thoroughly delighted her — expression through the transformative experience of color has a special place in anthroposophical philosophy. Afterwards we took her downtown for dinner at Merce Cunningham's apartment.

[1] M. C. Richards, *Centering: In Pottery, Poetry, and the Person* (Hanover, NH.: Wesleyan University Press, 1962), p. 64.

# COSMOS AND CREATION IN CLAY, COLOR, AND WORDS WITH MARY CAROLINE RICHARDS

ALWYN MOSS

What I remember most about those October days in 1997 in the Mountain Lake workshop is how M.C. Richards' faith in "creating out of nothingness" or "fecund emptiness" affected all that we did there and how we did it. For my own work, at least, the experience has been a lasting legacy, as were my times with M.C. herself, whom I had known for a number of years. While I was studying to be a Waldorf teacher, we were often involved in the same anthroposophical (Steiner) events and schools.

We gathered on the first day of the workshop in the large, light-filled studio room of the Horton Center at Mountain Lake, surrounded by mountain views aglow with autumn foliage. There were eighteen or more of us, some local, others from farther away, several I had known before. Although the workshop was free of charge, it did request that participants be willing to spend several days with M.C., something that did not seem to be a problem for anyone involved. Standing there around the big table we were, I felt, already *community*. The word *community* came naturally to me because I knew from M.C.'s writings and history that community was a core mission of her life, even before her years at Black Mountain College; that the making and sharing of art was not only a primary aspect of creating community but her life's work.

Now the *doing* of it would begin. But while the making of art was central to the workshop, the words she spoke (always the poet) were transformative in themselves. We were asked to "let go of thought," to "trust in the invisible, and in our intuition"— and in that way let the work flow freely out as gifts. Standing in her place at the table now, tall, strong, and serene, M.C. focused her attention on the large,

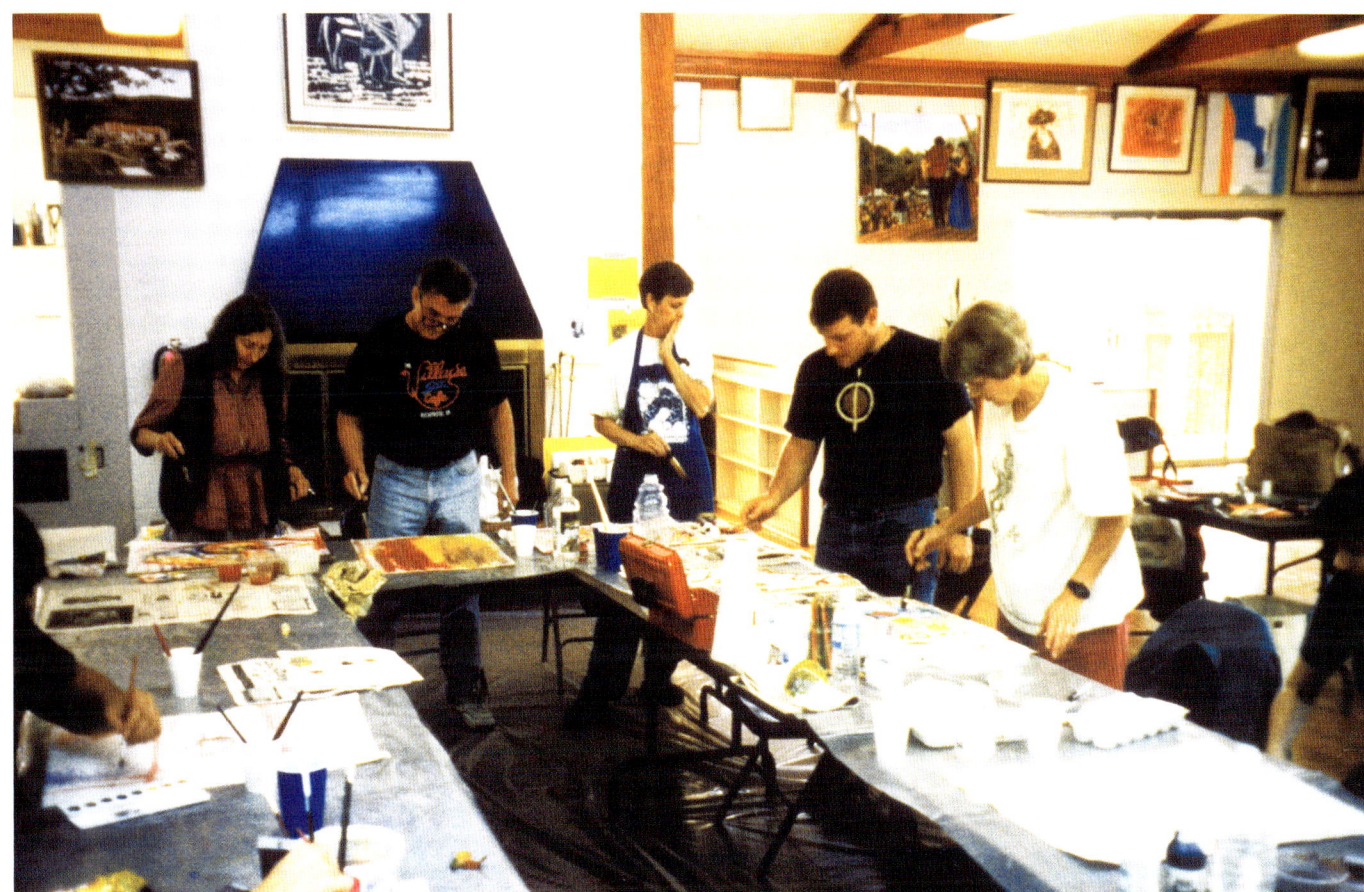

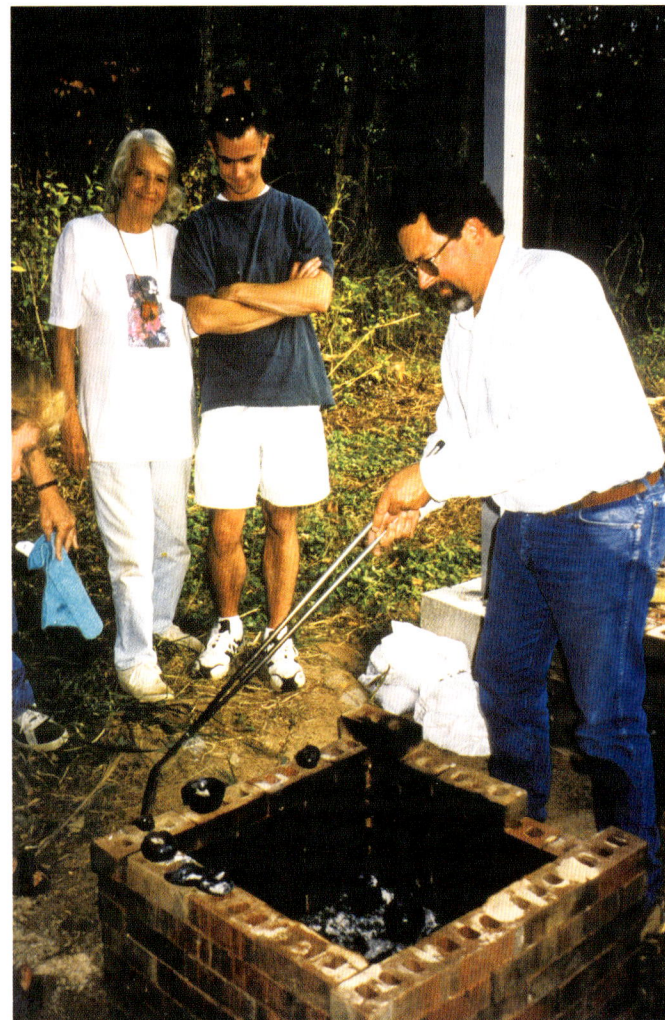

M.C. Richards and Chris Wood look on as David Crane empties the kiln

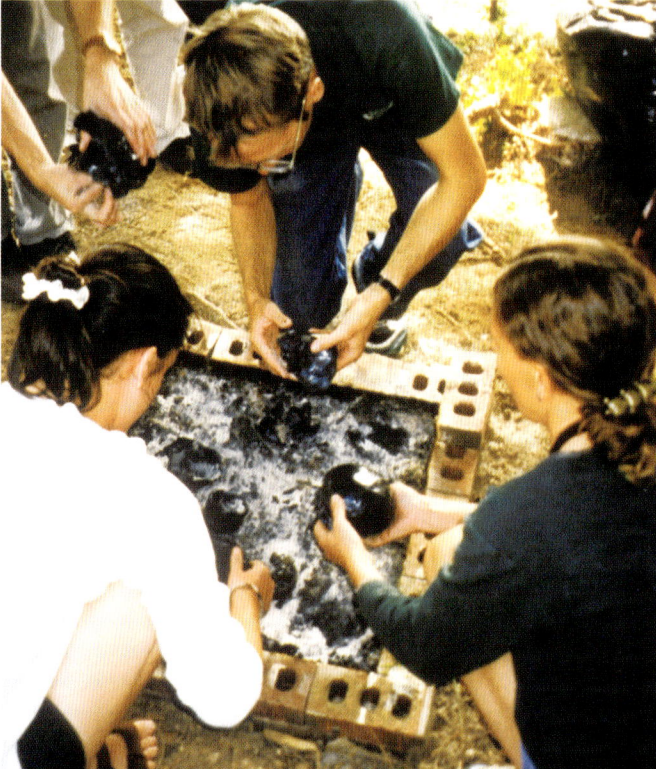

Workshop participants remove low-fire black pots from the kiln

fat coil of clay she had circled around the entire table, from which she indicated we were to each take our portion.

"Use your part as a doodle," she said, and while doing that, if we wished, we could introduce ourselves to each other in any way we chose. So there we were, listening to each other, our hands and fingers freely manipulating the soft, slightly wet gray matter with as little conscious intentionality as possible. "Take the clay, and feel your fear into it." This helped me, as I was always a little timid about clay. "Working from Source," as M.C. put it, "uninvolved with reasons *why* and all the flimsy fabric of *mentation*," we are free and brave enough to do what we do even if we do not know what we are doing. No judgment or opinions came from our guide, which helped us not to judge our own work or ourselves.

We later fired the pinch pots and some delicate, leaf-like creations that M.C. guided us in making. The firing was done with the help of the ceramic artist and Virginia Tech professor David Crane at a kiln that M.C. built with the help of some of the workshop participants at an off-site location.

The clay that we used was a terra cotta or earthenware, and the kiln was of a "loose-stack" brick construction that allowed for plenty of air to enter through the sides during the firing. We burnished our pots and then carefully layered them, allowing a little space between each, in a dense medium of fine sawdust (donated by a local cabinet shop) that filled the kiln. The kiln was lit with some leaves at the top of the heap, then a metal cover was placed over it and it was allowed to smolder for a day or more.

A "sawdust fire" process is somewhat like that of low-fire raku, with one major difference. In raku firing, the clay objects are removed while still red-hot and then immediately subjected to a post-firing reduction in a pit or container of combustible materials that contribute unpredictable qualities to their glaze. The pots that came out of our kiln, by contrast, were all intensely black!

For the "Color and Words" aspect of the workshop, we made little books — an experience of combining visual imagery with words. We were asked to take a large piece of newsprint (18 inches x 22 inches) and color both sides using crayons, colored pencils, or paint or all three. I used mostly watercolor paint. Many of us had folded our newsprint into book size; this made it possible to relate to the sizes and foresee, at least a little, what we were doing. Then we folded the full sheet three times (up from the bottom, the side, and then the bottom again), which made a book about 6 x 10 inches. "Cut the pages and sew them together" M.C. said, helpfully doing it herself so we could follow instructions.

In regard to words in response to colors M.C. said: "Don't try to make the words belong"; so I didn't. On one page blue, yellow, purple, and black had created a huge triangular form coming up

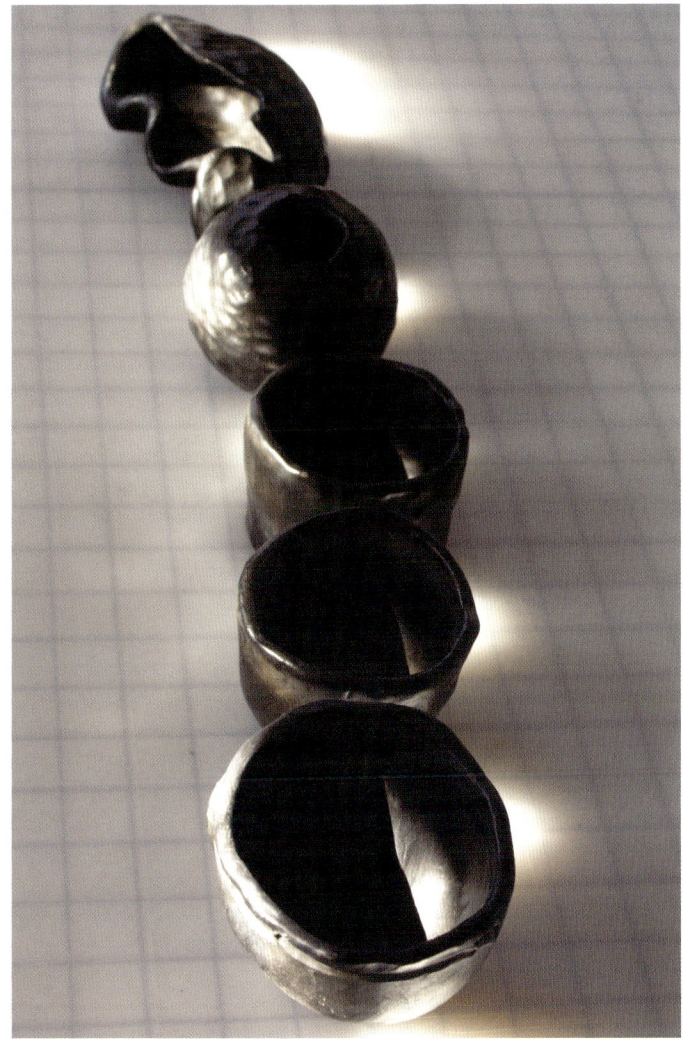

M.C. Richards' exhibition in Virginia Tech's Armory Art Gallery

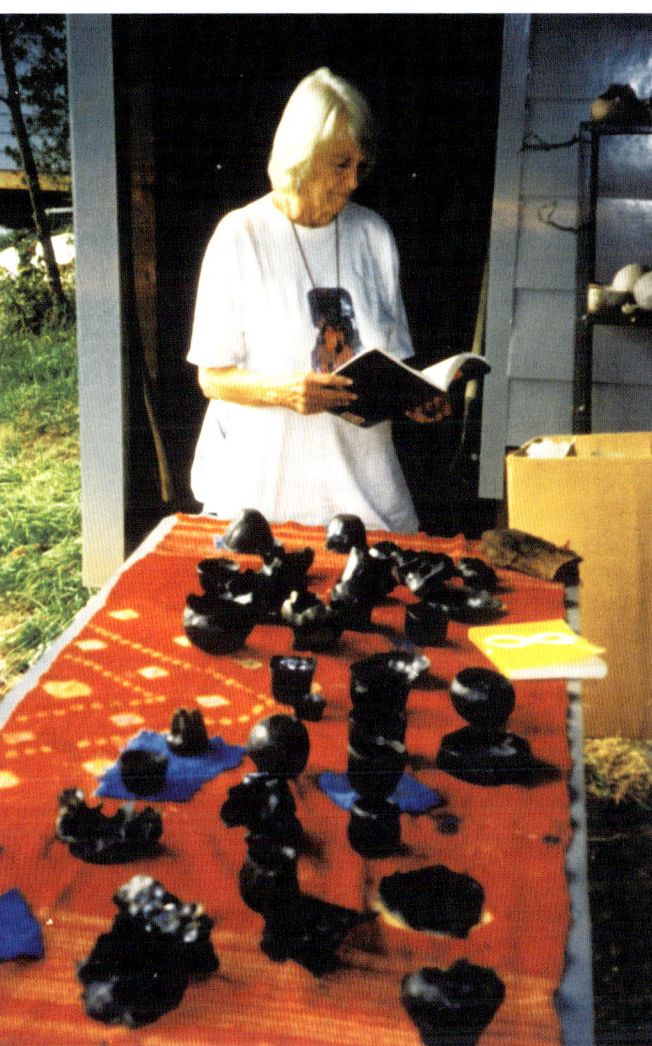

M.C. reading her poetry at the kiln ceremony

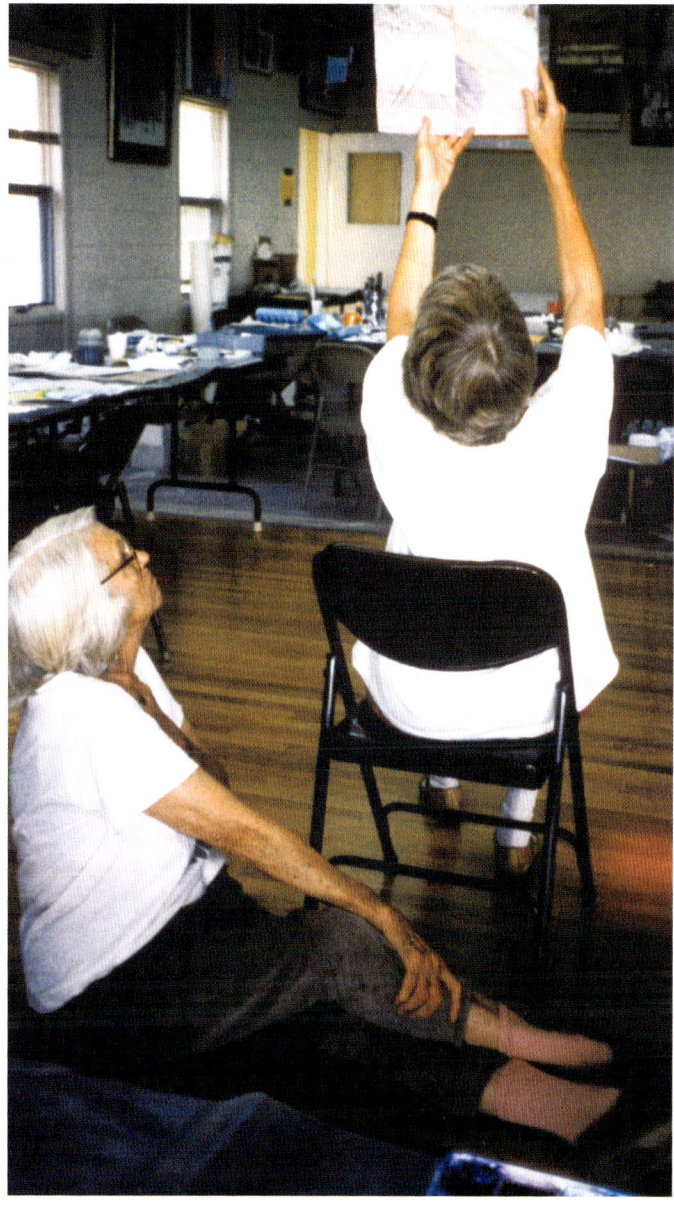

M.C. listening to Matt Belay as he holds his handmade book overhead at the reading ceremony

from the bottom. I wrote, *Now at last we are moving — Where?* Many years later I don't know where my clay piece is, though I liked it, but I have the book — and words of M.C. that live on in her many books and in me. Imagine, as she would and did say, "Creating out of Nothingness: the path of Evolution."

Each participant then took a turn sitting in a chair at the center of our group and, holding their book up over their head, ceremoniously read their illusively constructed and illustrated poetry, while M.C. sat on the floor behind them gazing up at their evocative creations.

# LYNNE HULL AND THE MOUNTAIN LAKE WORKSHOP: RELIC HABITATS, SEPTEMBER 1999

RAY KASS

Internationally recognized Colorado eco-artist Lynne Hull conducted a series of week-long collaborative workshops sponsored by Virginia Tech's Department of Art and Art History, the Wilderness Conservancy at Mountain Lake, and the Virginia Commission for the Arts. A sculptor and installation-artist, Hull specializes in constructing site-specific habitats for wildlife. For "Relic Habitats," her multi-faceted workshop, students and community members gathered specific materials and wove and carved them to create grounded structures and organic flotation devices. Natural materials and found objects were used to create (or simulate) natural animal habitats in order to promote a greater awareness of the sensitive conditions of the natural environment. Her workshop created three public artworks in rural and urban settings: the accessible lakeside trail in the wilderness area of Mt. Lake; several sites along Stroubles Creek and the Virginia Tech Duckpond in downtown Blacksburg; and at Virginia Tech's landfill. All three locations support wildlife — although one location is almost pristine in nature, the others are deeply afflicted by urban contamination. The artworks were non-permanent, biodegradable structures. A list of species and flora prevalent at all three sites was researched and distributed to participants before the workshops began.

The Mountain Lake site project called attention to the hemlock crisis. Based on the idea that art can reveal "the invisible" and on the work of *Common Ground*, a project to re-vitalize the tradition of "Tree Dressing Day" in Great Britain, Hull worked with participants to "dress" (decorate) a hemlock tree near the Mountain Lake lodge with images of all the biotic species associated with native hemlocks; all the species identified are at risk of disappearing with the loss of hemlocks to the deadly "Wooly Adelgid" (aphid) infestation that has afflicted the southeastern United States.

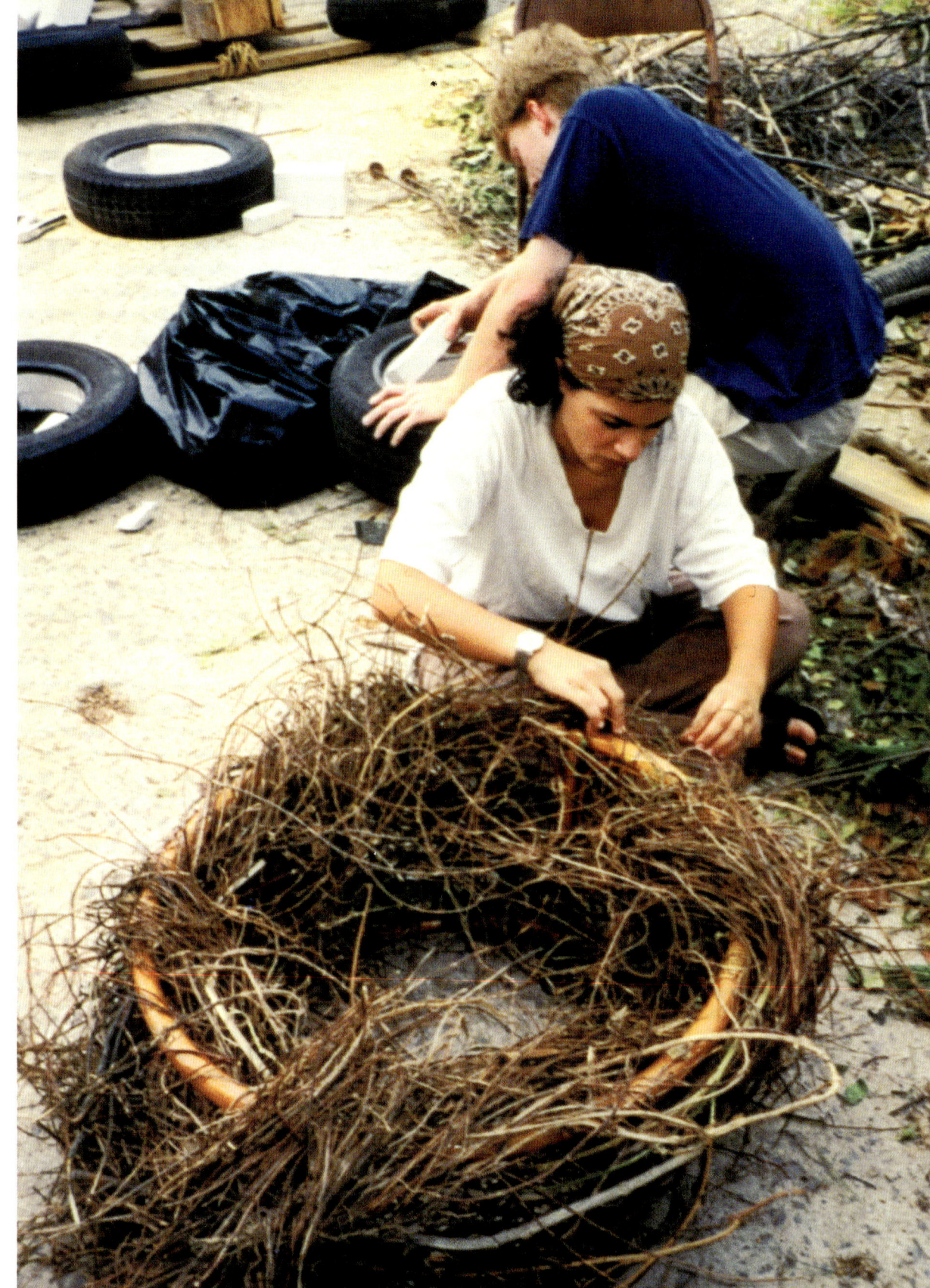

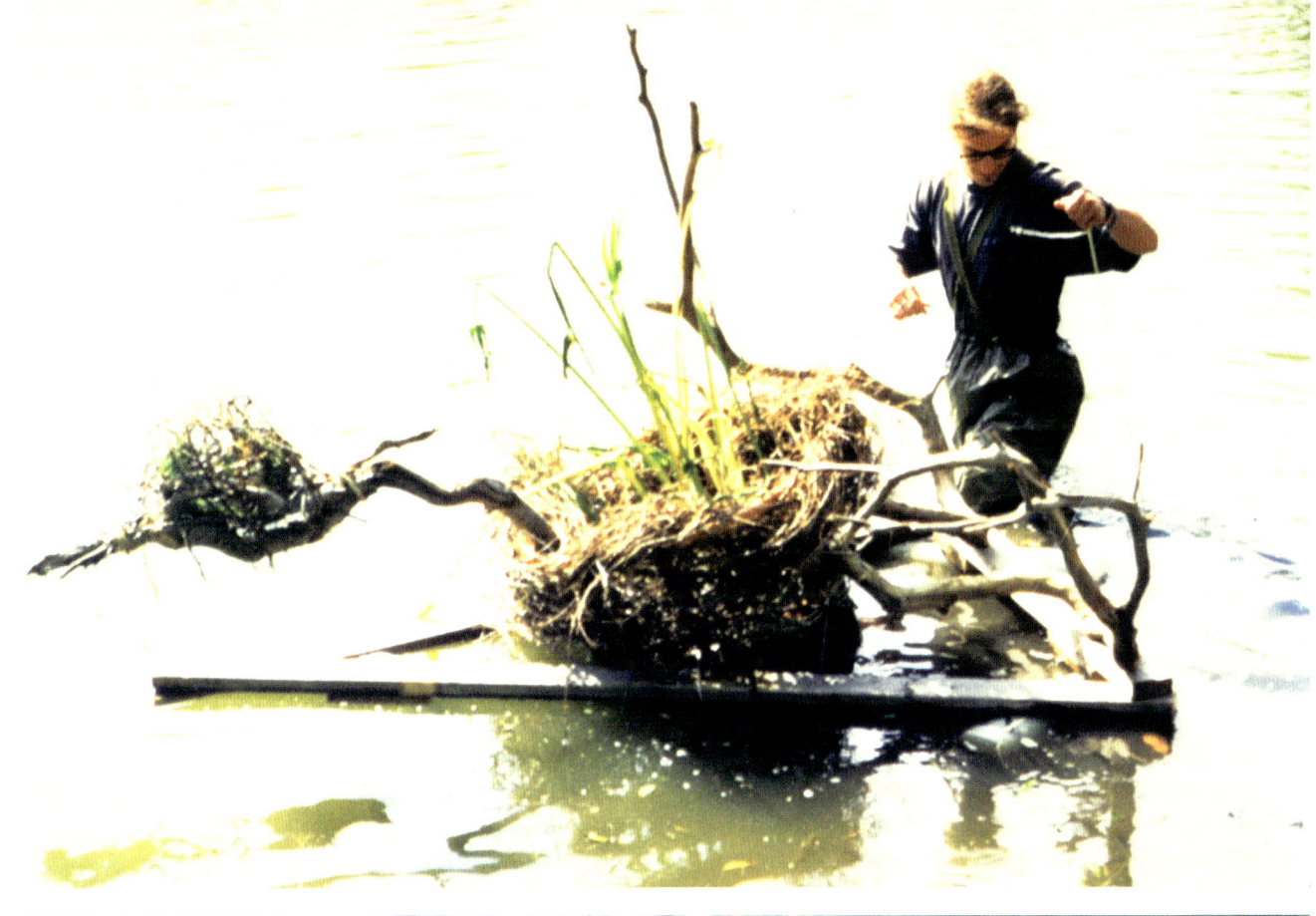

The group also dressed other trees with draped "hammocks" of inscribed cloth designed to collect seeds to be stored at the seed bank in Colorado.

A floating aquatic "eco-sculpture" was built and launched in a small pond beside the lake that was intended to offer habitat for aquatic creatures developing in the pond as well as assist in filtering and cleaning the water. It was a symbolic "life raft" for creatures of the natural habitat.

A "Hemlock Celebration" day was convened at Mountain Lake and a large audience came to admire and celebrate the living hemlock trees, view the "dressed" trees, participate in the seed collecting process, and enjoy music and poetry readings that accompanied the "art opening." Graphic design students in the workshop designed a pamphlet illustrating the hemlock / aphid situation; it was distributed to visitors and displayed as a larger panel in the museum / nature center at Mountain Lake lodge. At the same time, Arts Administration graduate students identified an audience for a public information campaign.

At the Virginia Tech landfill site workshop participants constructed another "life raft / floating island" of boards, branches, old tires, PVC pipe (materials typically found in landfills) and then planted it with aquatic filtration plants to help clean the water in the little runoff pond; "life raft / floating island" also functioned as a sundeck for turtles and waterfowl and as an underwater shelter for aquatic life while its extended branches acted as perches for songbirds. Created in segments, it was installed for a week in the Duck Pond on the Virginia Tech campus as a statement of conditions there and was then moved to the landfill site.

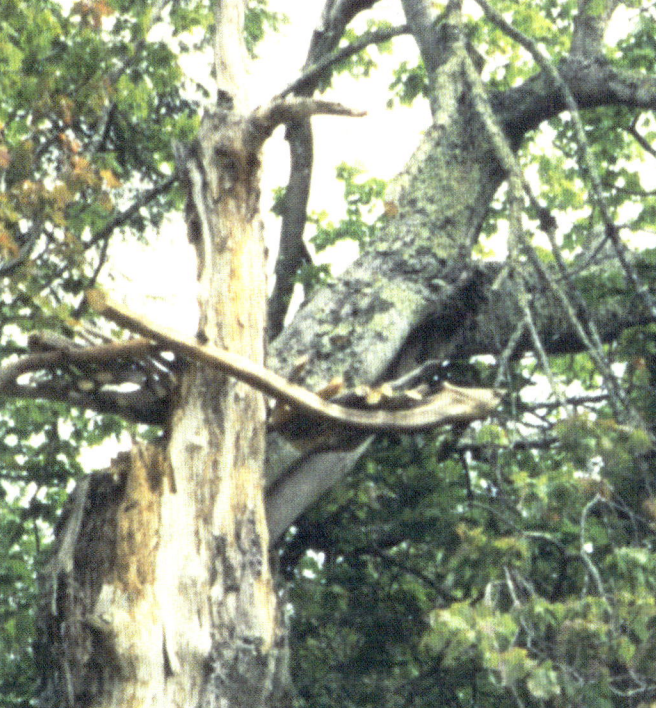

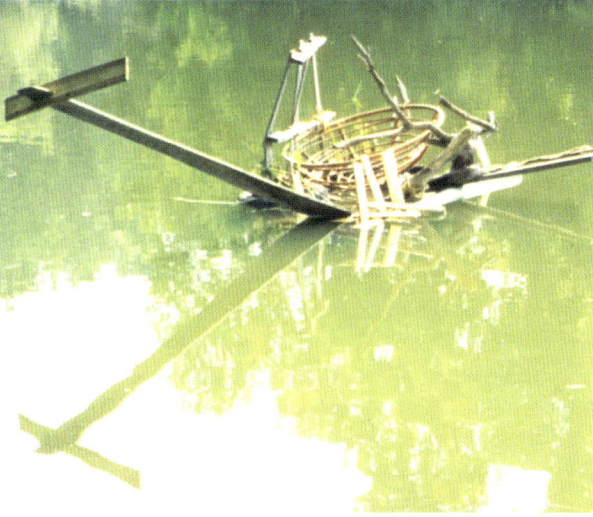

Workshop Volunteers: Ryan Snyder, Brian Emery, Travis Hanks, Elizabeth Janka, Jeremy Rueger, Anna Gianakos, Rex Hartson, Jennifer Otey, Caroline Meredeth, Sara Wardell, Antoinette DiVittorio, S.L. Rosa, Amy Winat, Pam McGraw

# LEE SAUDER, PYROMANCY: IRON SMELTING AND FORGING WORKSHOP, 2001

RAY KASS

(right) Steven Bickley
tending the "bloomery"

(below) Lee Sauder, *Untitled
(Aristotle's Sword)*, 2002, forged
iron, 12 x 48 x 8 in. (30.5 x
121.9 x 20.3 cm). Collection of
the Taubman Museum of Art,
Gift of Ray Kass, 2003.015

In 2000, sculptor and art professor Steve Bickley was working collaboratively with Bill Reynolds, professor of material science and engineering at Virginia Tech. Their work was part of the innovative interdisciplinary programs that Tech's Art and Art History Department was advancing in the Science and Technology Colleges. Aware of the interdepartmental work going on at Tech, I simultaneously — and fortuitously — learned of Lee Sauder's artwork when I saw one of his "burn"-imprinted framed works on paper in a Lexington art gallery and asked the owner how I could meet the artist. As it turned out, Sauder worked very close to other Lexington friends. He had taken over Larry Mann's blacksmith shop on McLaughlin Street — which earlier had been one of Cy Twombly's studios — and was making custom forged wrought iron gates and railings. When I visited him in 2001, he was working at the forge. It struck me that the process of working forged iron not only was vividly beautiful but had a special cultural legacy in rural America and the Appalachian region in particular. Sauder had, in fact, written an informative narrative about the technical elements of "bloomery" iron forging as well as its local cultural relevance.[1]

I was delighted to learn that Lee had made a portable "bloomery" (a furnace for producing iron) that fit into his pickup truck along with his forging tools. I was planning an exhibition of his artwork for Virginia Tech's Armory Art Gallery when it occurred to Steve Bickley and me that we could do an iron-forging workshop as a related program.[2] Using Sauder's portable bloomery, iron was forged on the Tech campus to an enthusiastic audience of students and community participants. We then took a smaller

group of volunteers to Sauder's Woods Creek Forge in Lexington, where he and Bickley engaged the volunteers in the labor-intensive hammering of red-hot iron on a huge anvil to pound it into a formed object.[3] The workshop's group efforts resulted in a beautiful sculpture titled *Aristotle's Sword* that is in the permanent collection of the Taubman Museum of Art in Roanoke, Virginia.

Cy Twombly lived just a block away from Sauder's studio and visited one evening to watch the forging process. I think that his visit that evening may have brought Cy closer to his decision to work with Steve Bickley on casting bronzes, a two-person collaboration using traditional processes for a distinctively contemporary result that I describe later in this chapter, in "Cy Twombly: Foundry Sculpture."

---

[1] Excerpts of Sauder's article, which originally appeared in the July 1999 issue of *The Anvil's Ring* (the quarterly of the Artist Blacksmith Association of North America), have been revised and included here as Appendix B, "The Basics of Bloomery Smelting."

[2] *Fiber and Form / Iron and Paper*, an exhibition of forged iron sculpture and "pyroprint" iron-burn drawings by Lee Sauder, was curated by Francis Thompson and shown at the Armory Art Gallery from October 4 to October 26, 2001, to coincide with his on-campus "bloomery" demonstration workshop.

[3] The three-day iron forging workshop in early October was directed by Sauder and Bickley, with contributions from Professor Bill Reynolds, College of Engineering. I was a project coordinator along with Francis Thompson, graduate assistant in arts administration at Tech. This project received grant funding from the Virginia Commission for the Arts of the National Endowment for the Arts.

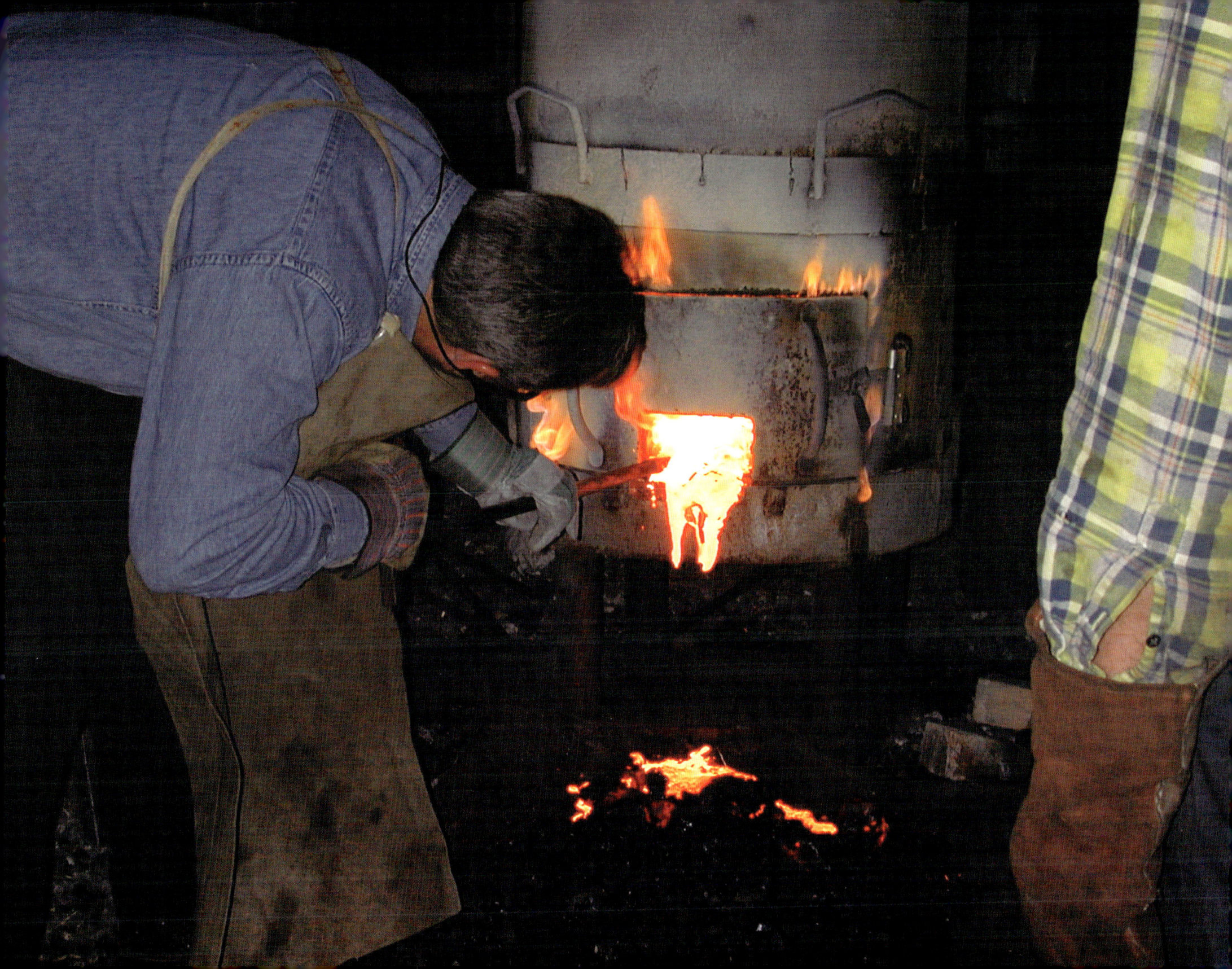

# JAMES DE LA VEGA: TALKING WALLS AND SIDEWALKS

RAY KASS

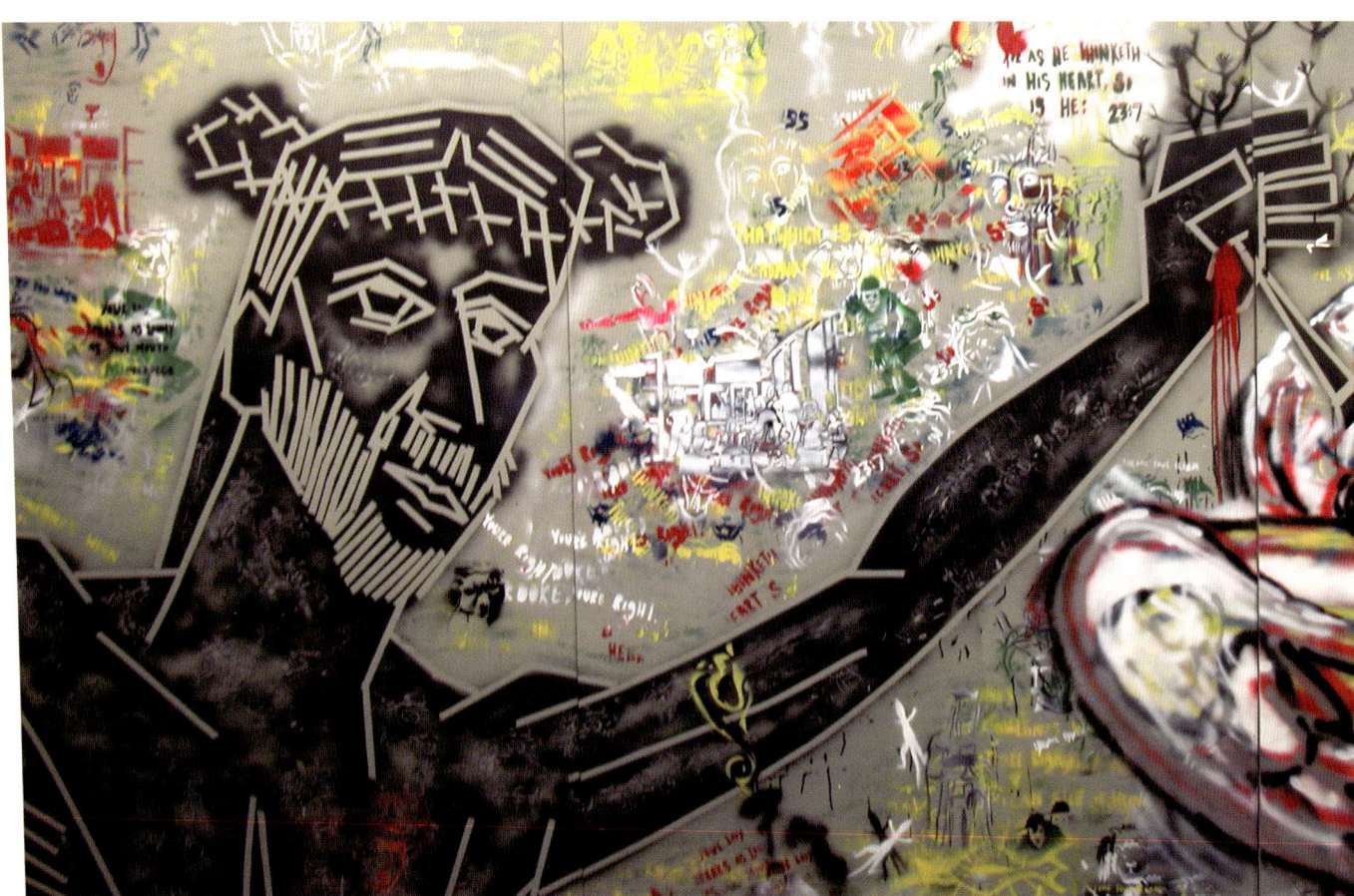

James De La Vega converts the walls of East Harlem into an open air canvas documenting New York's Barrio culture. The walk up Lexington Ave. to 106th St. is punctuated by his various murals portraying an eclectic combination of subjects including Picasso's "Guernica," dead hip-hop stars, and religious icons, all illustrating the hybrids of Harlem's Caribbean, African, Latin and American cultures.

De La Vega claims public space with the speed and ferocity of his neighborhood's graffiti artists (at times collaborating with them), transforming the barren walls of his surroundings into life-infused pieces with a distinct agenda. His work has trickled throughout the city, appearing on sidewalks in the form of painted cigarette butts (to trick the viewer) and inspiring "street philosophy" chalk drawings, spray-paint silhouettes, and masking-tape outlines. De La Vega's signature spray paint and masking tape technique is used to depict Christ and the Last Supper with accompanying commentary on the conditions plaguing the city's people.[1]

[1] Anonymous, *Flyer*, #29 (Dec. 2000), p. 25.

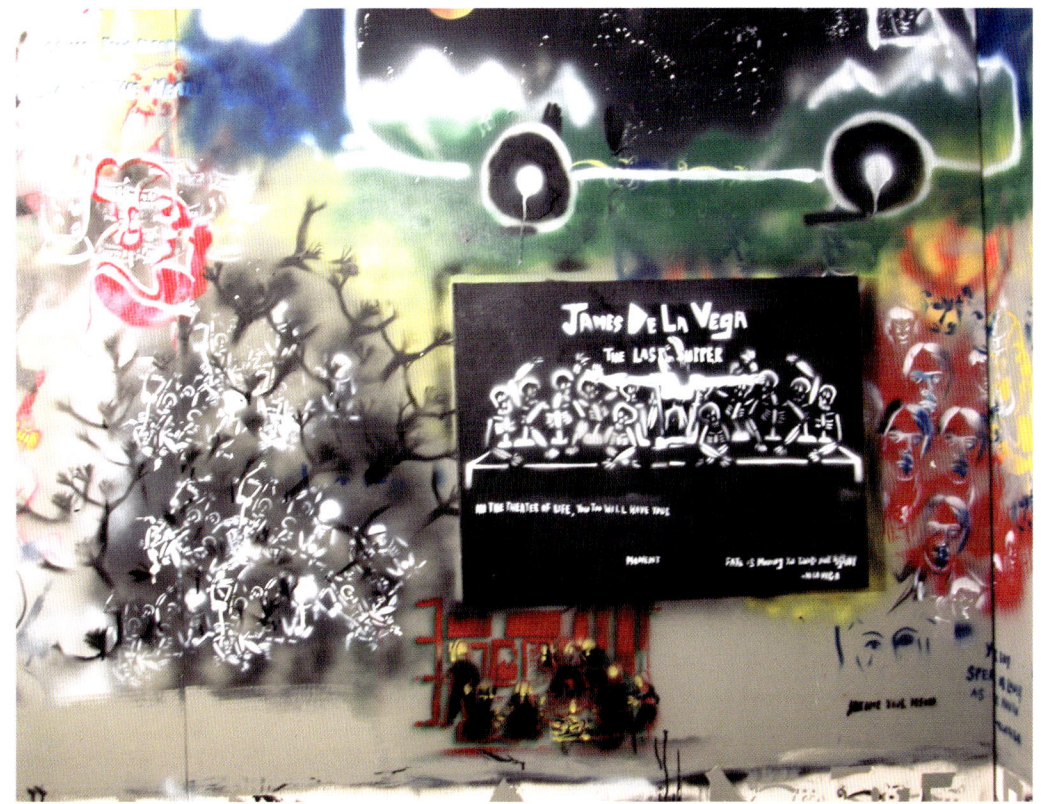

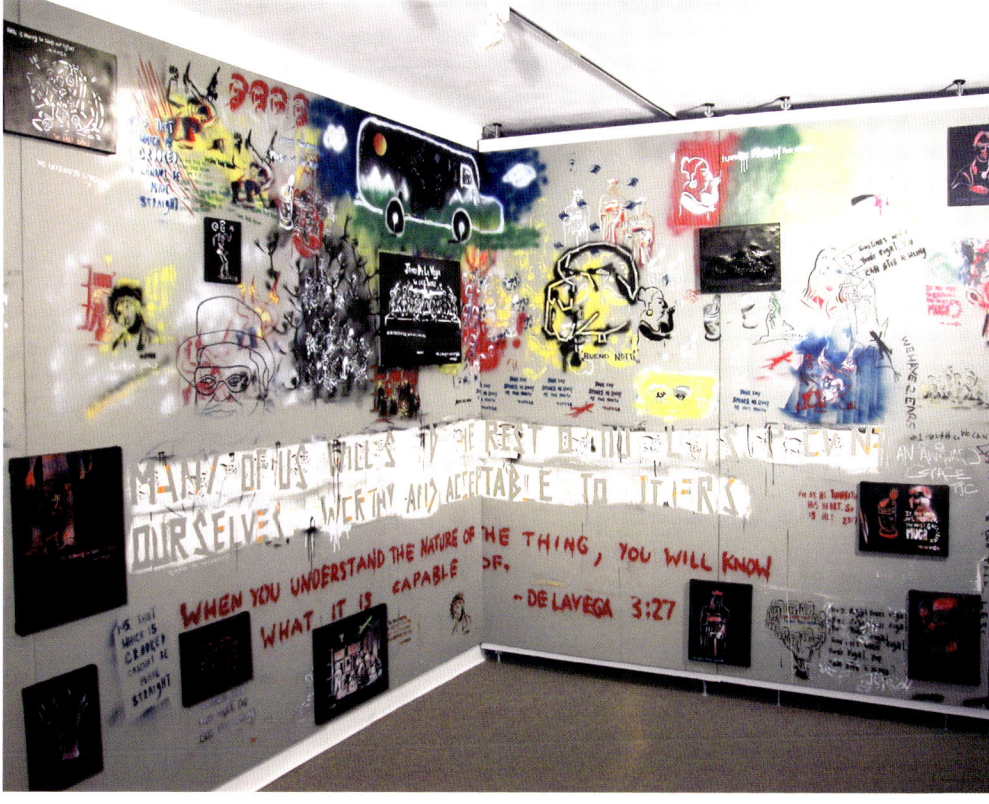

A long-time neighbor of mine in East Harlem, James De La Vega began making his reputation as a street artist in the mid 1980s. His wall-mural portraits and street inscriptions were unique and unlike the highly stylized script-like graffiti that adorned the New York City subways at the time. The spray-painted subways were transformative images of sacred terror that roared downtown from and disturbed the complacent consciences of the establishment. The anthropomorphized presence of the serpent-like trains gave presence and voice to the disenfranchised minorities in the South Bronx who created them in the night-time train yards. I thought that they were beautiful and scary, but most of the downtown public just saw the scary part; since the crack-down and clean-up, subway trains have never looked so good again.

De La Vega's figurative mural works usually paid homage to Barrio legends and were eloquent, poetic evocations of Puerto Rican culture. His chalk and masking tape sidewalk inscriptions were uplifting and intended to inspire people underserved by the society that surrounded their ghetto. His sense of purpose to my mind elevated him to an artist of stature who could take a seat beside other community leaders. His high-mindedness did not prevent him from being arrested, along with many of the graffiti artists, during the "Broken Windows" policing policy, a crackdown on misdemeanors that occurred during Mayor Giuliani's administration.

In 2000 I invited James De La Vega to Blacksburg, Virginia, to conduct a week-long Mountain Lake workshop combining all of his various image-making techniques in a large, narrative

mural to be created collaboratively with students from Virginia Tech and community members. As I had done for Howard Finster's Mountain Lake "workout" in 1985, I prepared for De La Vega's workshop by having plenty of regular paint, spray paint, many different color chalks and masking tapes, canvases, and sixteen reinforced 4 by 8 feet. grey-painted plywood panels that were hung on panel clips on Tech's Armory Art Gallery walls. De La Vega arrived with many stencils and cut many more during the workshop. It was amazing to watch him draw his elegant forms with a box cutter knife with such ease. It was equally amazing to watch him when he went out on campus and used masking tape to "draw" a huge image of Christ on the cross on a campus plaza with no preparation other than his innate sense of scale and proportion.

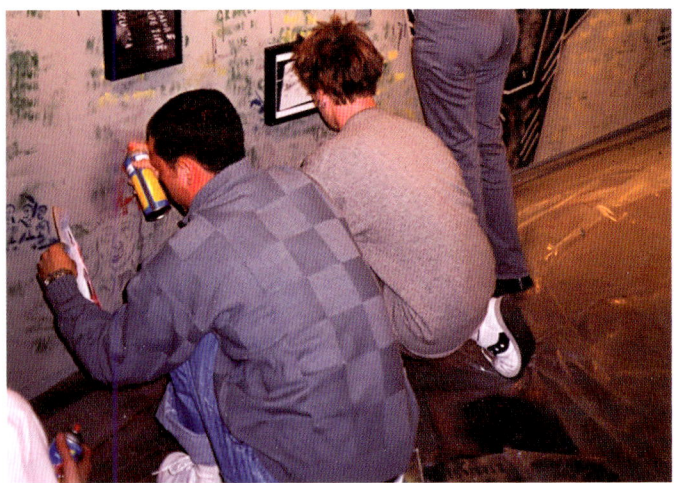
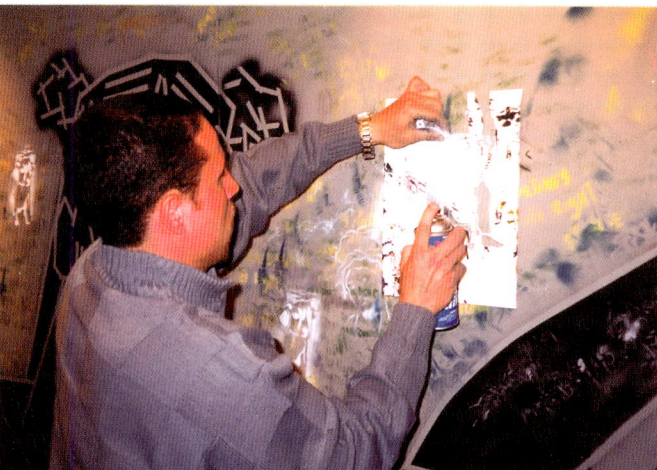
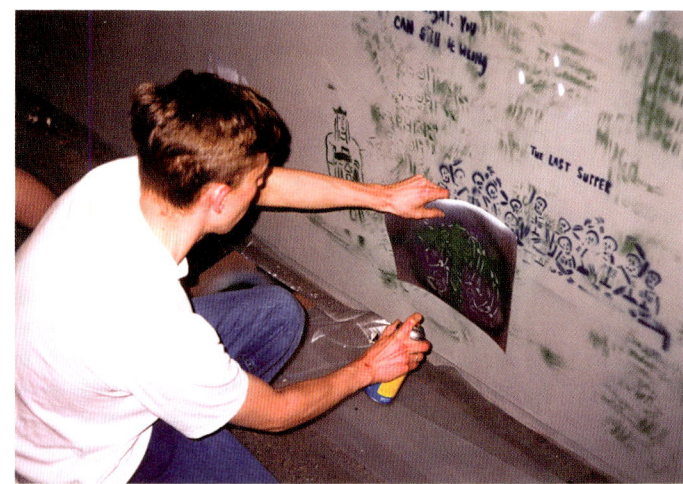
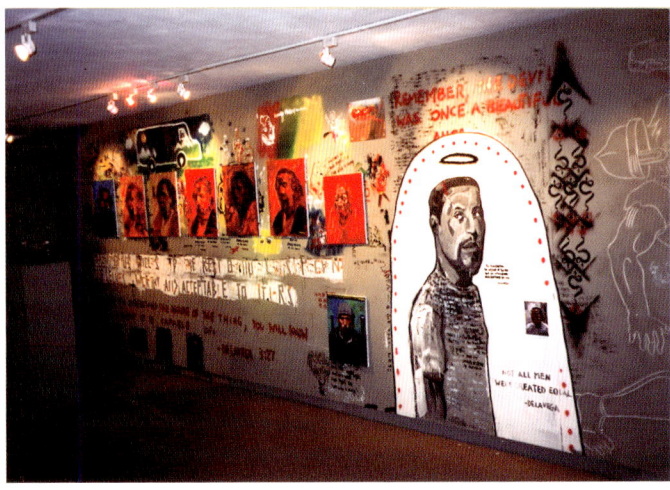

James gave a well-attended slide lecture that emphasized his ideas about the positive role that public art can play in uplifting the community. After the collaborative gallery installation was completed, he led workshop participants in making sidewalk inscriptions all over the campus and downtown Blacksburg. I jumped through quite a few hoops to get administrative approval for these activities — but most of them were removed in a day or two anyway.

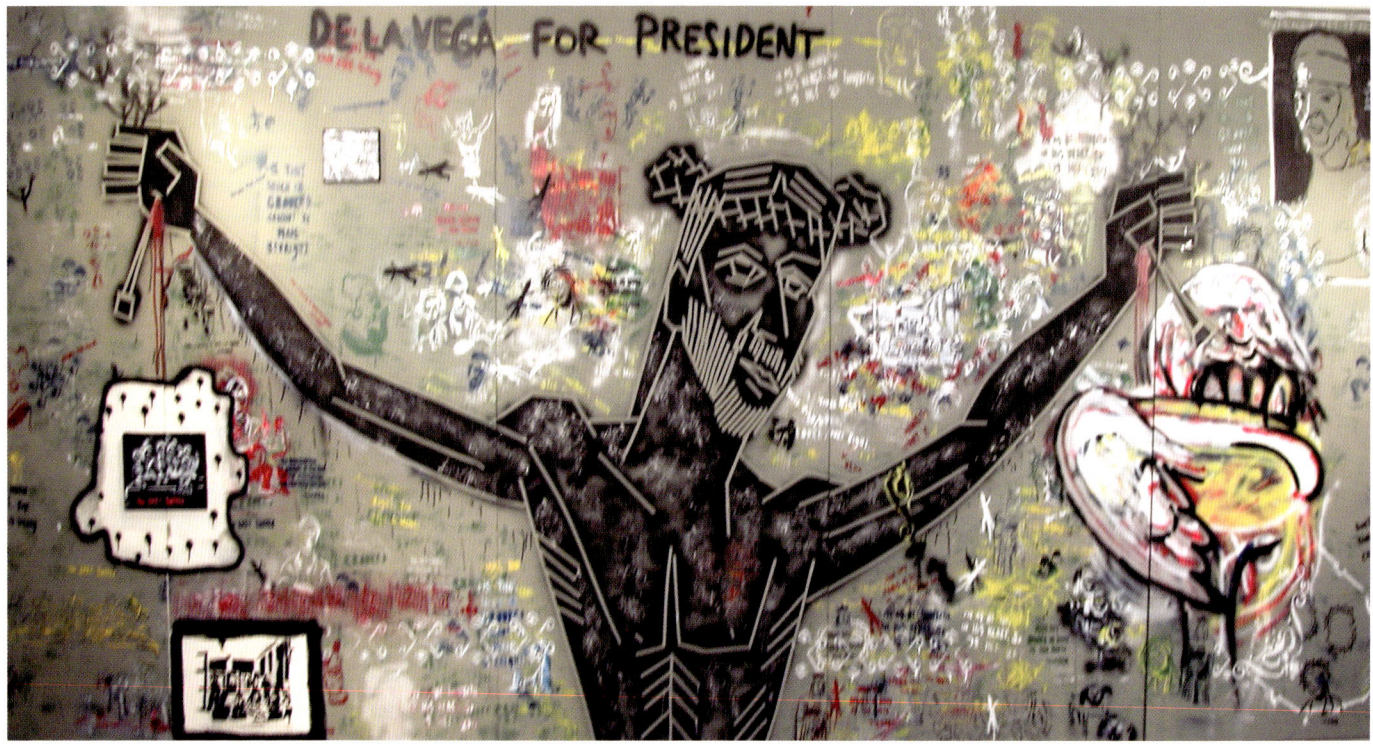

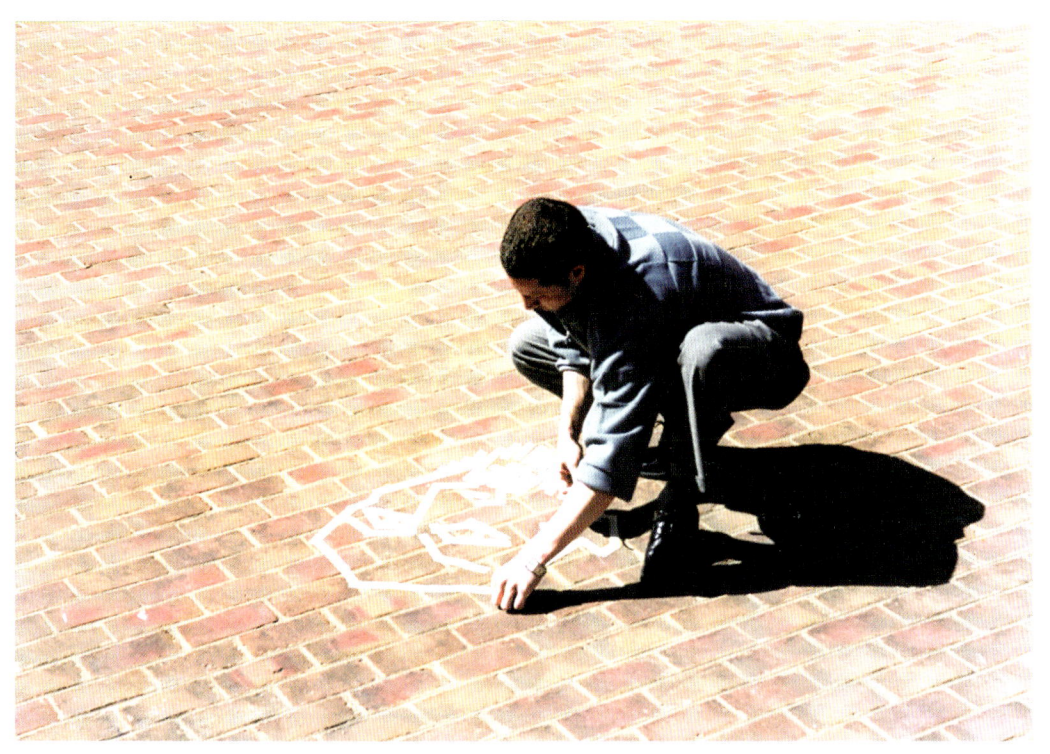
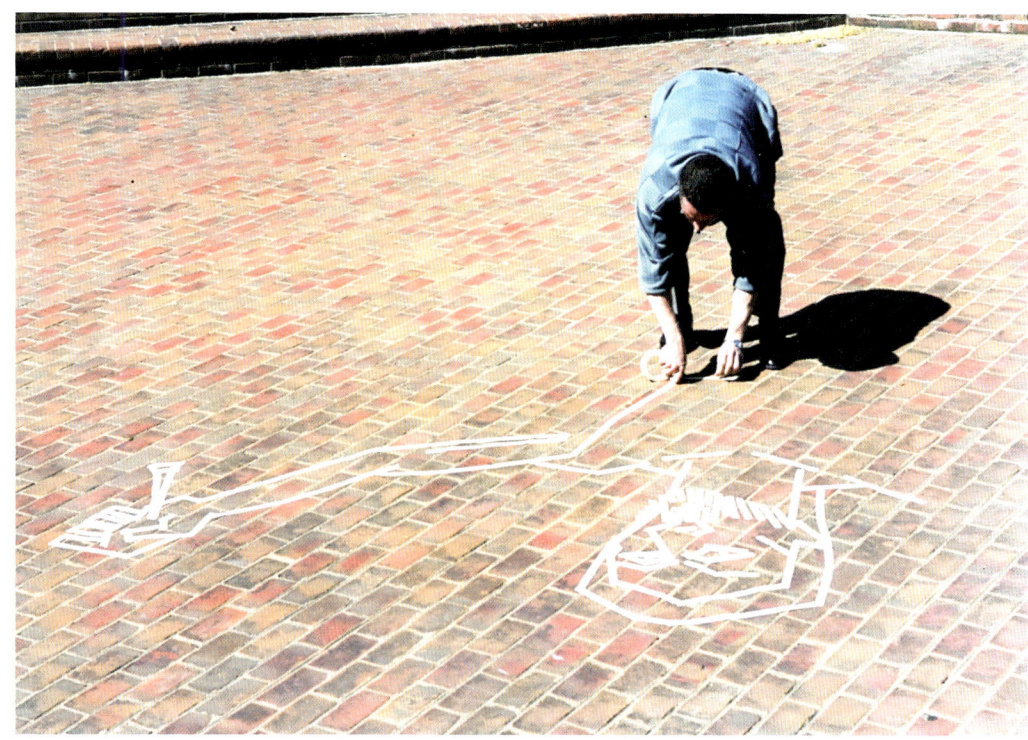
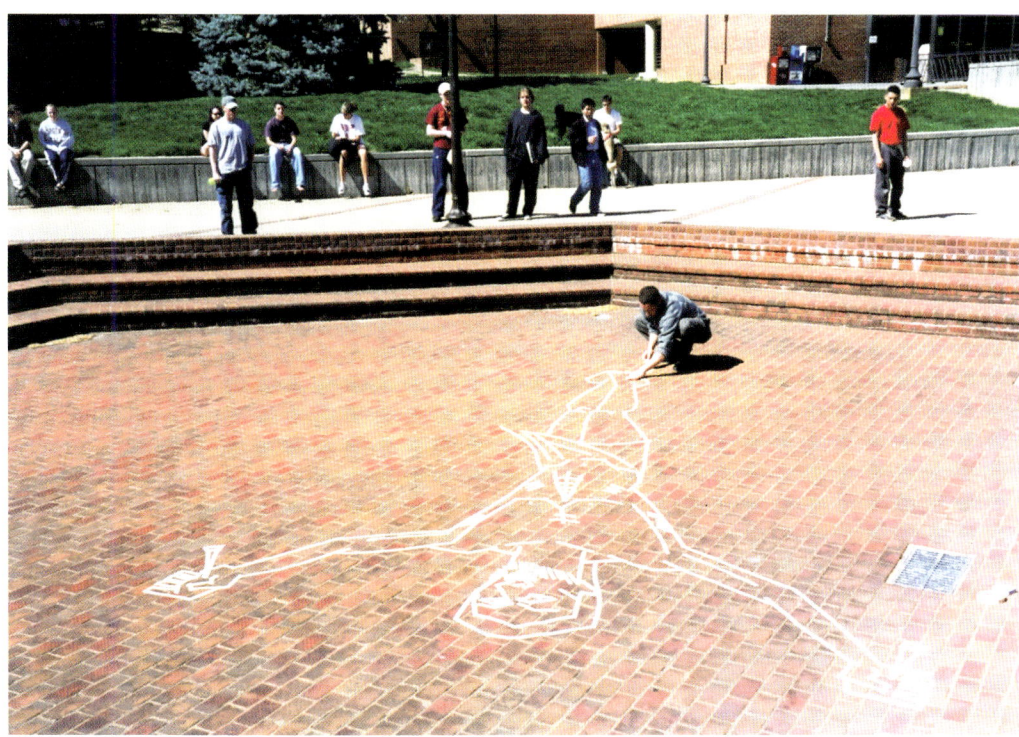
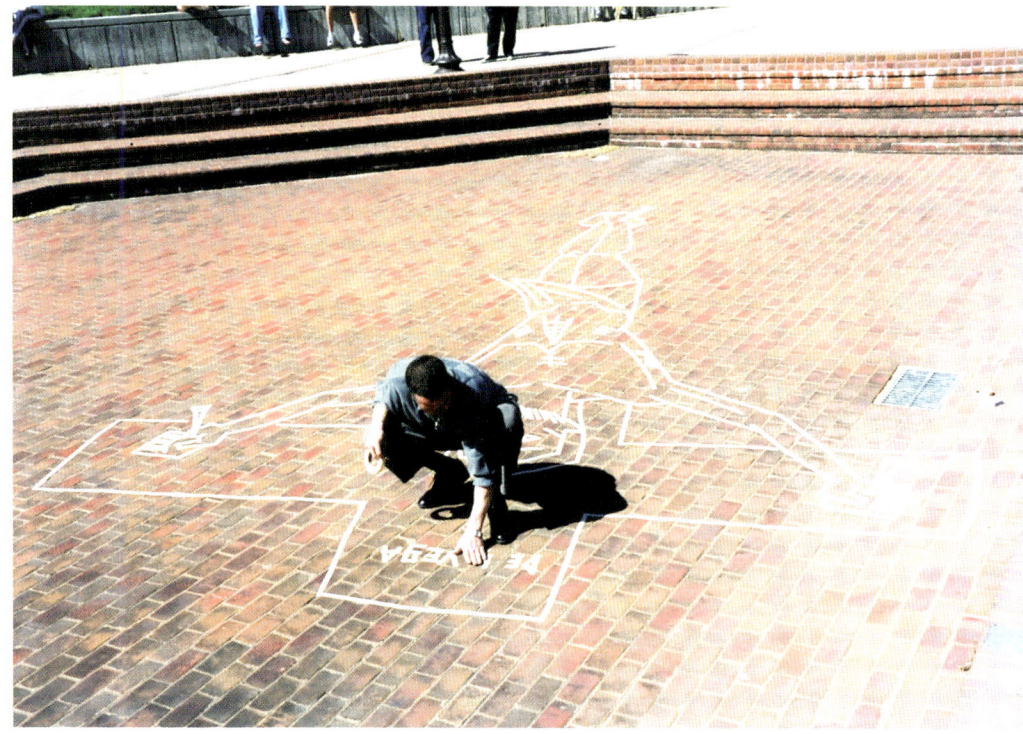

191

# JAMES DONNELLY: *"FACES FIGURE"* AND *"FACES OFF,"* 2003

RAY KASS with an endword by JAMES DONNELLY

In 2002 Mei Li Dong, who had hosted our *Ki no Ichiku* group in Shanghai, China, in 2000, invited me to visit Edinburgh, Scotland, and see the new house that she and her husband, Peter Ydeen, had acquired for their daughter, Ati Dong, who was a student at the Edinburgh College of Art. While I was there, Mei Li and Peter introduced me to the work of a young Edinburgh artist, James Donnelly, and Ati arranged a studio visit. James was painting vivid, small portraits in oil and beautifully patterned animal skins on white acrylic surfaces, for display purposes mounting both types flush on the projecting surface of deep boxes. He had recently installed his graduation exhibition and presented his portraits in interesting juxtapositions on an overall floor-to-ceiling pattern of his design that covered the gallery walls. I thought that the geometric patterns on the walls and the shadow patterns cast by the three-dimensional boxes upon which the paintings were mounted worked together in an extraordinary way. I wondered where he might go next in integrating his painting experience with a gallery installation and invited him to create a gallery installation at Virginia Tech's Armory Art Gallery. We sent him photographs of local people from the New River Valley to work from, and he combined their portraits with sensuously painted images of animal skins.

Donnelly's visit, which involved participants in several activities, was the occasion of building on and expanding techniques employed in earlier Mountain Lake workshops. His project and methodology, which we named "Faces Off," involved first of all the use of viewfinders, which had been a practical way of engaging novices in making quick sketches as part of Joe Kelley's *Appalachian Trail Frieze* workshop.[1] It now was

adapted to engage participants in making close-up portraits of each other in water-soluble color crayons directly on the acrylic surfaces of the small viewfinders. The colorful tracery that resulted was then applied to paper in the manner of the image-transfer strategy that Kathy Pinkerton had introduced in the paper-making project that we later titled "Blue Leaves." This project, which occurred during Mierle Laderman Ukeles' 1994 Methanogenesis workshop, utilized the paper-mounting techniques that we had learned from Xiao Yan Gan.

The small portraits in water-soluble crayon transferred easily onto individual rectangles of mulberry paper that were then mounted on plywood panels in the Asian manner learned from Gan and allowed to dry and stretch flat overnight. Then the next day the drawings were cut off of the plywood panels and re-mounted together on larger pieces of mulberry paper. The final Asian paper mounting contributes an extraordinary finish and continuity to the portraits by which accidents and a wide range of stylistic differences achieve a remarkable unity.

"Faces Off" became one of Mountain Lake's "run-out" workshops, joining Jiro Okura's "Breathing Lines," *John Cage's STEPS: A Composition for a Painting to be Performed by Individuals and Groups*, and the "Paper Smoking" and "Asian Paper Mounting" workshops as offerings that we take on the road to schools and community art centers. The "Faces Off" workshop is the perfect complement to the Asian Paper Mounting, and those two activities were the centerpiece of a five-day visit to the Nevada Museum of Art in Reno when my painting *Broad Channel* was being installed there in 2007.

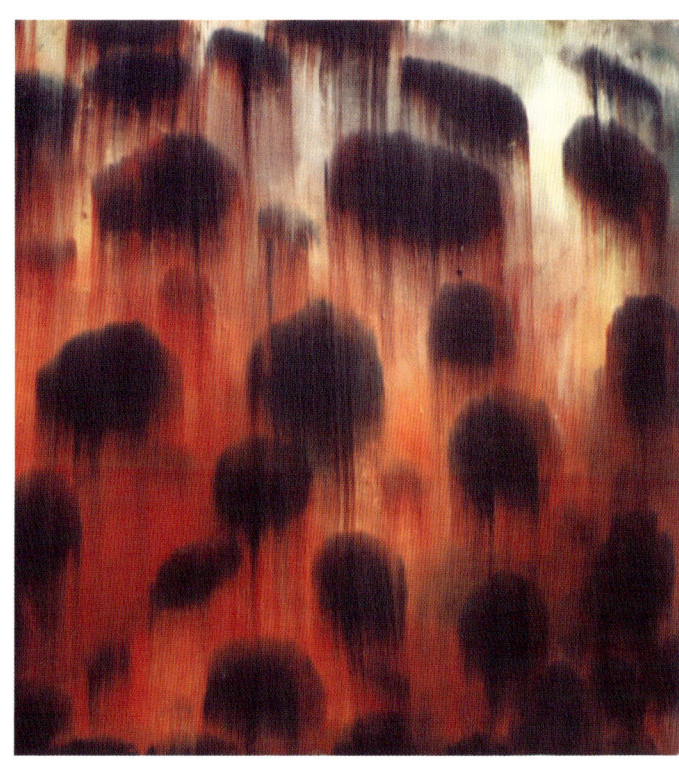

James Donnelly, *Spotted Leopard Fur*, 2000–2001, oil on acrylic, 12 x 10 x 4 in. (25.4 x 30.48 x 10.16 cm)

[1] See p. 8

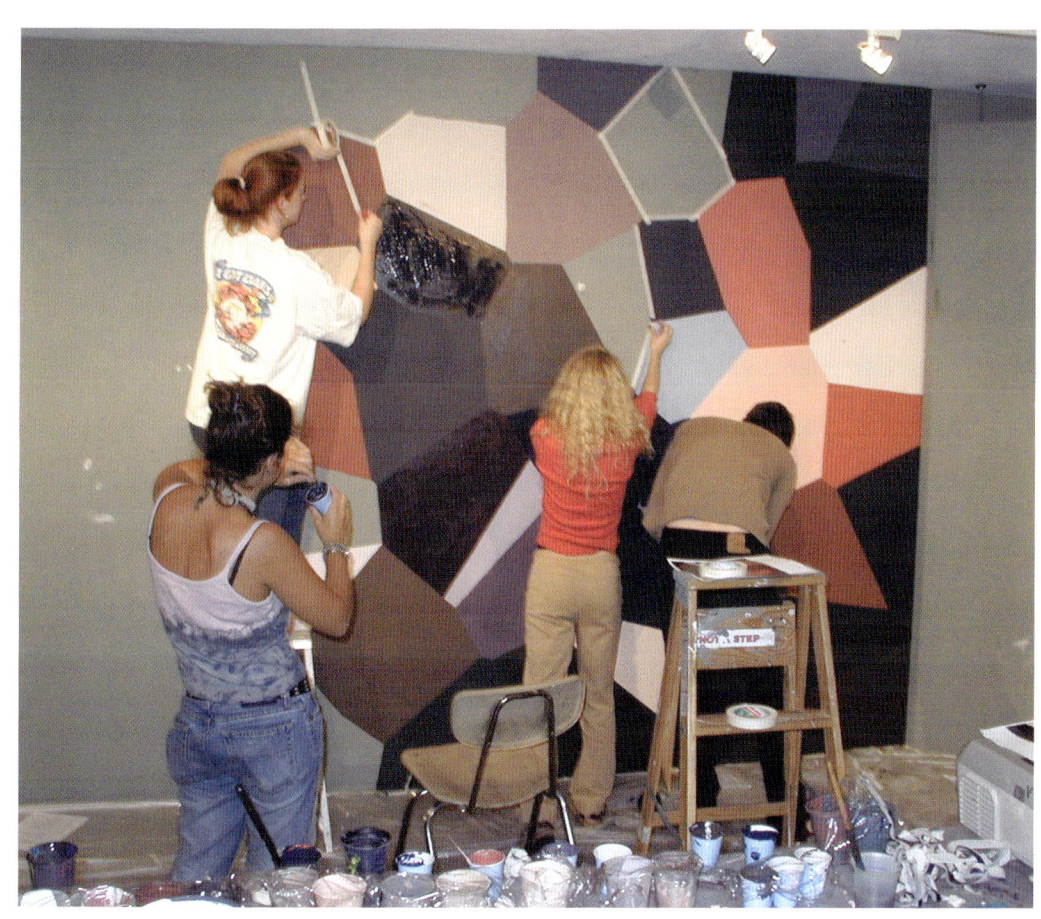

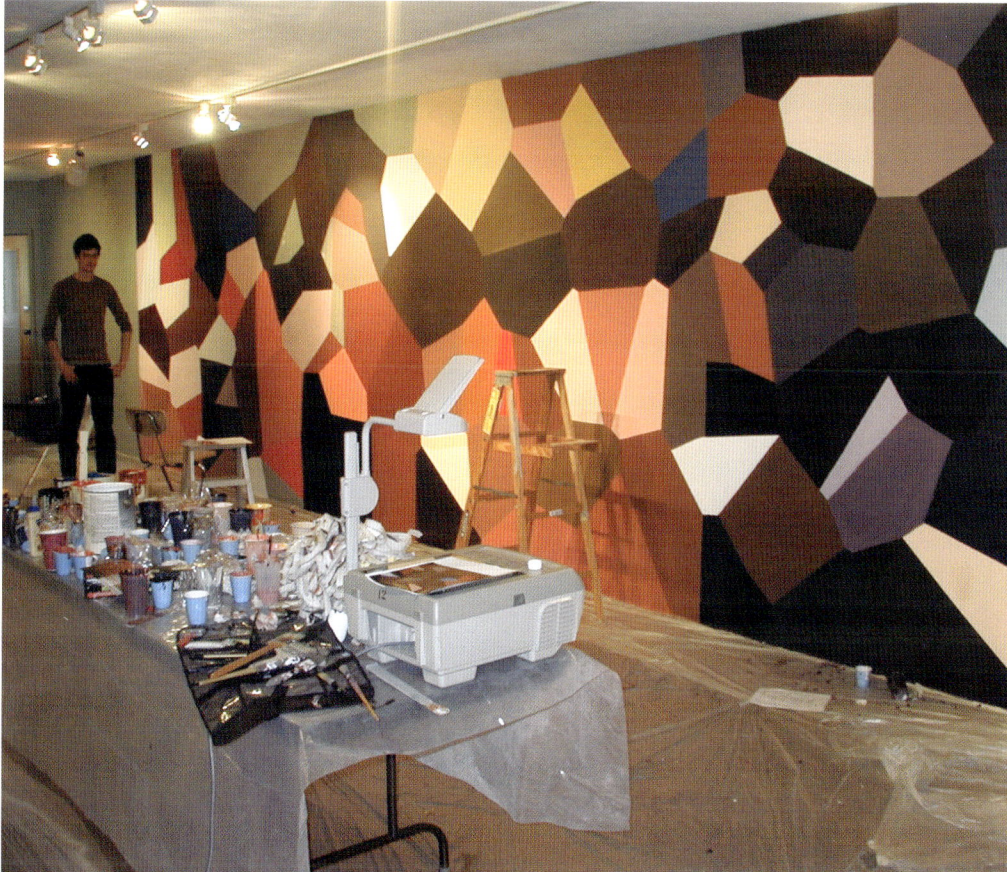

(Above) workshop participants preparing a gallery wall, *Spotted Leopard Fur*, 2000–2001, oil on acrylic, 10 x 12 x 4 in. (25.4 x 30.48 x 10.16 cm); (right) James Donnelly standing beside a wall that he designed for the *Faces Figure* exhibition at the Armory Art Gallery

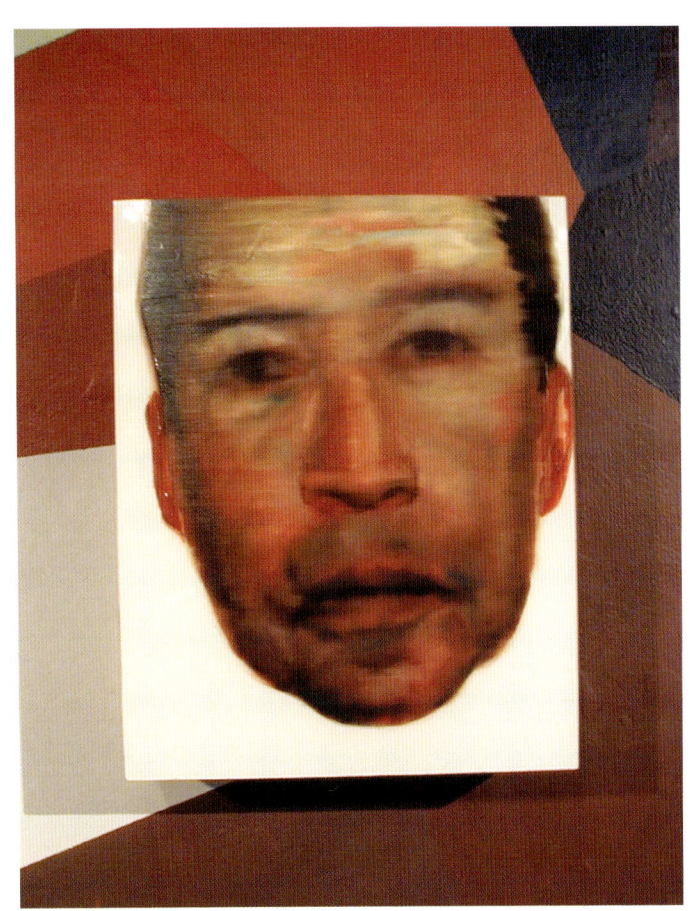

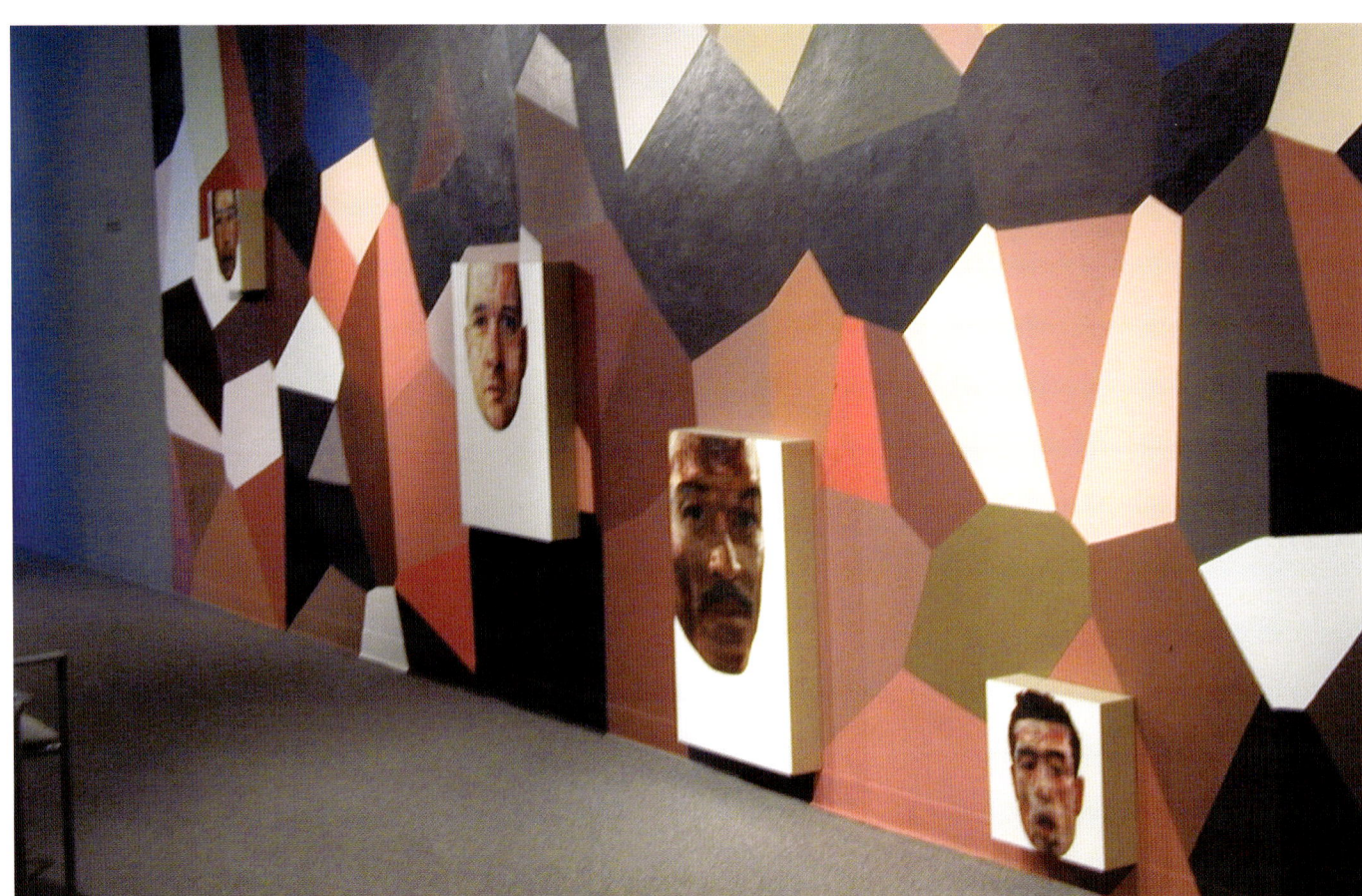

James Donnelly, *Dr. Wallace Huff*, 2003, 16 x 12 x 4 in. (40.64 x 30.48 x 10.16 cm), oil on plastic

# THE SKINS OF OURSELVES

JAMES DONNELLY, DECEMBER 2001

Our Skins, our faces, our identity. Unique?

As unique as the spots on a leopard, as the stripes on a zebra? Yes.

Instantly recognizable.

Examine, pare down to fundamentals. What's so unique?

To non-human eyes we must surely appear
different, but (equally) identical.

Can you reduce to the basic human?
No, but it is a worthwhile exercise.

The non-portrait.

Nothing to do with individual ego or identity. Everything to do
with humanity. What it is to be human? It's all in the face.
Everything else is a distraction.

I paint. I like to make interesting marks. I want people to *want
to* look at my work. To feel it has worth. The only way I know
how to do this is to put worth into the painting. If I feel it has
worth (worthy) someone else will. I am human not unique.
I love oil paint, its smell and texture. My work is just a skin
of oil paint.

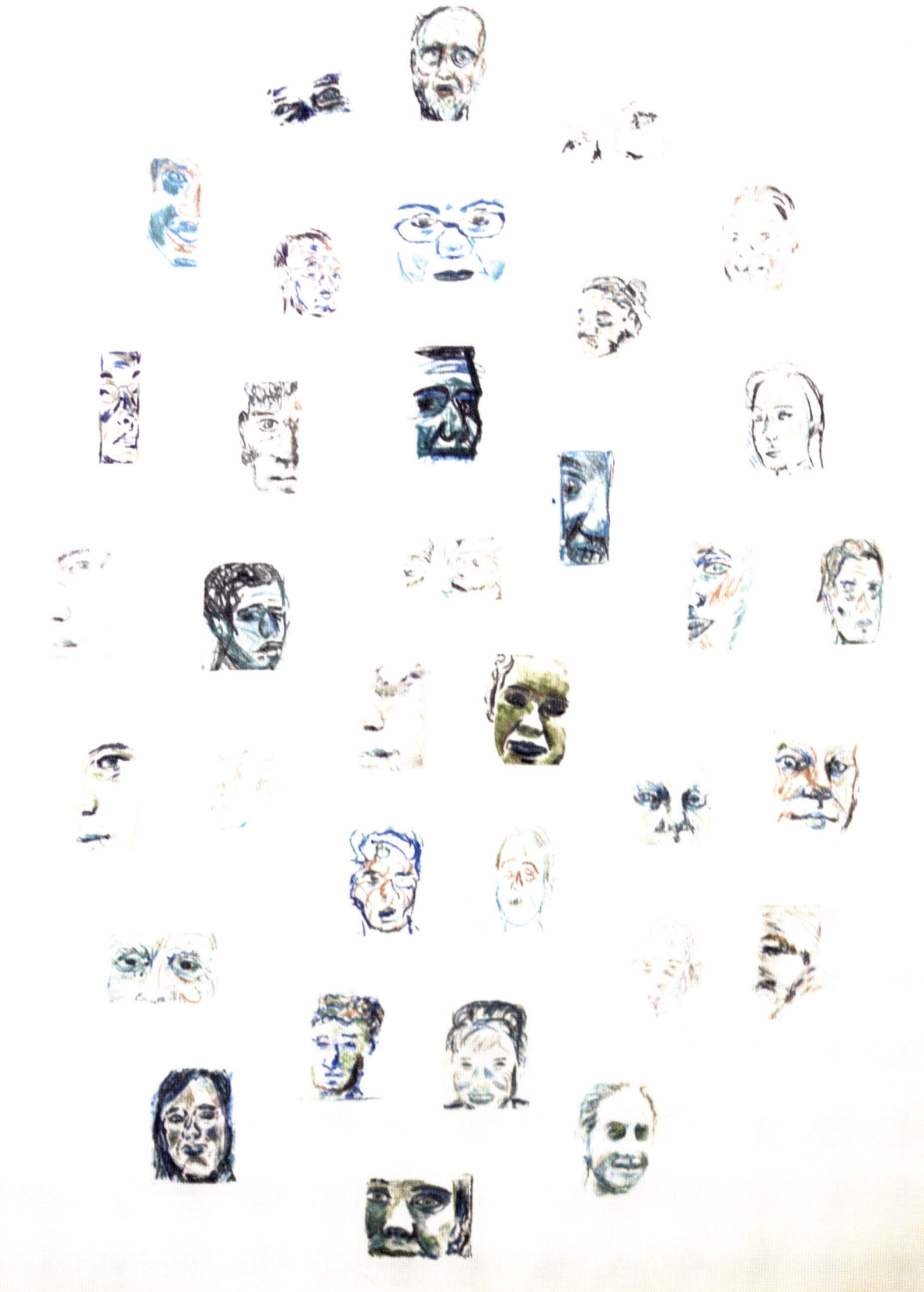

# CY TWOMBLY: FOUNDRY SCULPTURE, 2002

RAY KASS with STEVEN BICKLEY

I met Cy Twombly at Sally and Larry Manns' Lexington home on McLaughlin Street sometime in the mid 1990s. Even before our introduction, a work of art that crossed my path seemed to be leading me toward a meeting with this western Virginia artist. Around 1990 an array of personal objects and works of art that seemed evidently connected to him began showing up at antique shops and flea markets in Roanoke.[1] One day while visiting Ed Bordett's Art Images silkscreen studio in Roanoke, where Brian Sieveking was producing the Mountain Lake Workshop silkscreen prints by Howard Finster, I noticed a small, unsigned painting on canvas mounted on wood (about 6 inches square) that had consecutive, horizontally scribbled pencil lines crossing the lower half. I asked Bordett what he knew about it. He told me that he had bought it at Bob Beard's antique store on the Roanoke Market for $2. When I admired it, he offered to sell it to me; I was tempted but, as a professor at a Virginia land grant university, I chose to comply with the unspoken ethical mandate expected of a public service employee and told him that I thought it could be an early work by Cy Twombly. I persuaded him to keep it and give me time to do some research on it. He later consigned it to an art associate of mine in Paris who had the painting authenticated and eventually signed by Twombly.[2]

A decade or so later, after my introduction to Cy, a second significant object took our relationship in a very positive direction. Any vintage Louisville Slugger baseball bat is a beautiful object, and I was delighted when Brian Sieveking showed me two that he had purchased for his personal collection. The bats were embossed with the signature of Twombly's father, Edwin Parker "Cy" Twombly, who had pitched for the

Chicago White Sox for one season of Major League baseball before quitting to play in the more lucrative Minor League.[3] Sally Mann had mentioned to me that Cy was upset that so many items of personal importance to him had been liquidated during the estate sale of his mother's house that had been arranged, unbeknownst to him, by his sister.[4] I asked Brian if he would sell me one of the bats so I could return it to Cy.

When I visited Cy at his home in Lexington later in 2001 to give him the bat, he was visibly moved. He asked me what I wanted for it in exchange, and I said that it was a gift but I'd like to work on a project with him. He did not know much about the collaborations of the Mountain Lake Workshop, but at the Menil Collection in Houston he had seen John Cage's big *New River Rocks and Smoke*, a watercolor made by Cage in 1990 at the Mountain Lake Workshop, and had liked it very much. Given Cy's private nature, it seemed unlikely that such a project was possible, but then he asked me if I knew a foundry specialist he could work with who would be able to give him more control over color and patinas of cast bronze and assist him in chipping off elements of the investment.[5] He mentioned that he was not satisfied with the work of a local Virginia foundry. He wanted to begin a new group of smaller foundry pieces inspired by small, hand-squeezed clay sculptures by the late Willem de Kooning that he admired.[6]

The following week I brought Steve Bickley, a sculpture professor at Virginia Tech and a foundry expert, to Lexington to meet with Cy at his home. Cy's subsequent project with Bickley is unique in our Mountain Lake experience in that it had no public participation beyond the two of them. In spring of 2002,

a private studio in one of the College of Architecture facilities off Prices Fork Road in Blacksburg was arranged for them to use. Cy would visit periodically, staying for as long as a week in a B&B just off-campus. Working alone in a room adjoining Bickley's studio, he made pieces in a white stone clay body, in a couple of cases incorporating found materials (for example, a wooden box that he used as a base in a piece that he referred to as "The Bone Yard"; Cy thought it resembled a work that he had just done for the Menil Collection) and in other instances simply assembling found objects — an actual pumpkin topped with a round metal candy box topped by a small toy reindeer and finally a wooden African spoon balanced atop the reindeer's antlers; although a mold was made, this piece was never cast. Cy did all of the clay work and Bickley made the rubber molds and oversaw the casting at a foundry in Tennessee; they both worked together removing elements of the investment wherever Cy wanted it removed.

As Bickley noted,

*Cy wanted to work directly in clay, squeezing and shaping about 16 new works. I then made castings of 12 of these, some in multiples. However some we did not cast but left in wax. In total we made 20 castings and he would chisel and paint, wanting to keep the works darker in color than his usual applied white finish.*

Of the clay and assemblage pieces, fifteen were cast in bronze. They'd been initialed "CT" in the molds, initials that Cy personalized with a "hot stick" (a hot poker) when they came out of their casts.[7] In a few cases, such as the so-called "Bone Yard," two or more casts were made. Most of the pieces were left untitled

[1] In 1988 personal items belonging to Cy Twombly, including early art works and photographs, were liquidated at an estate sale of the contents of his mother's house in Lexington, Virginia.

[2] Bordett sent the piece to Barbara Divver, a very reliable art associate in Paris, to be evaluated. Divver contacted Twombly's son Alessandro, and the piece was indeed authenticated and subsequently signed.

[3] Edwin Parker "Cy" Twombly (June 15, 1897 – Dec. 3, 1974) was an American right-handed pitcher in Major League baseball who appeared in seven games for the 1921 Chicago White Sox. He eventually became the athletic director at Washington and Lee University where the school's swimming pool is named for him.

[4] Sally Mann wrote about the sale in her memoir, *Hold Still* (New York, Boston, London: Little Brown & Company, 2015), pp. 73–74.

[5] As part of the casting process the wax forms of sculptures get dipped in a liquid ceramic investment before they are cast; after casting some of ceramic investment sticks to the bronze.

Cy Twombly, *Untitled*, ca.
2004, Bronze, 13 x 9 x
6.25 in. (33 x 29.9 x 15.9
cm). The Menil Collection,
Houston, gift of the artist

and identified by measurements, though two had nicknames — besides "The Bone Yard," there is another piece that has an uncanny resemblance to a loaf of bread; on it Cy wrote "Slice of Life" and mused, "the art historians will have fun with this."[8]

The pieces were taken to Cy and he kept some of them on the windowsill of his storefront studio in downtown Lexington. Cy personally designed a "PF" metal stamp (standing for "Price's Fork" where Bickley lives) and was present when each of the sculptures was embossed with this seal.

Cy Twombly had exacting personal standards and he was never completely resolved about the scale of some of the pieces; although signed, some of the pieces may have remained "unfinished" in his estimation.

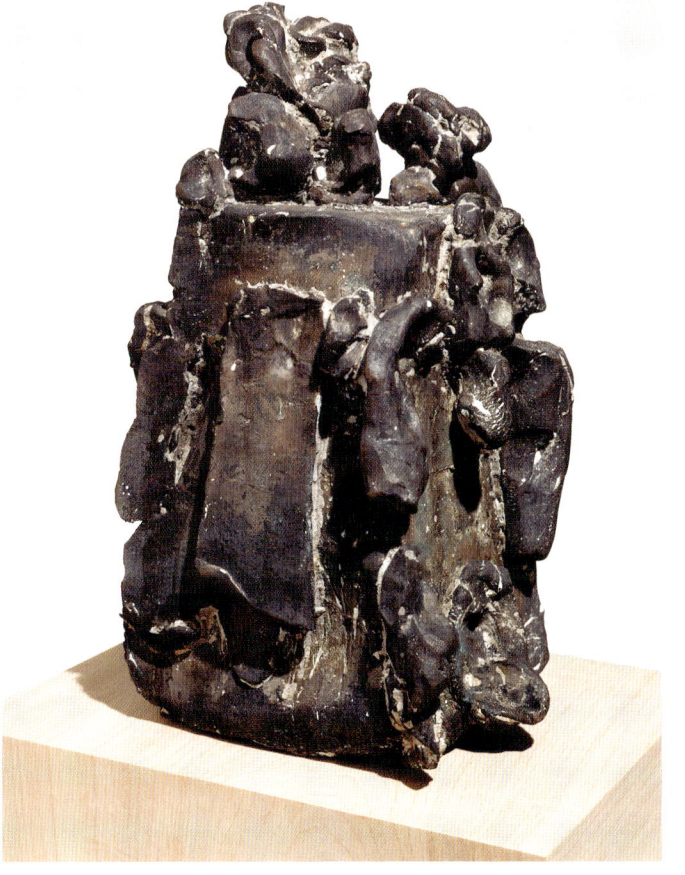
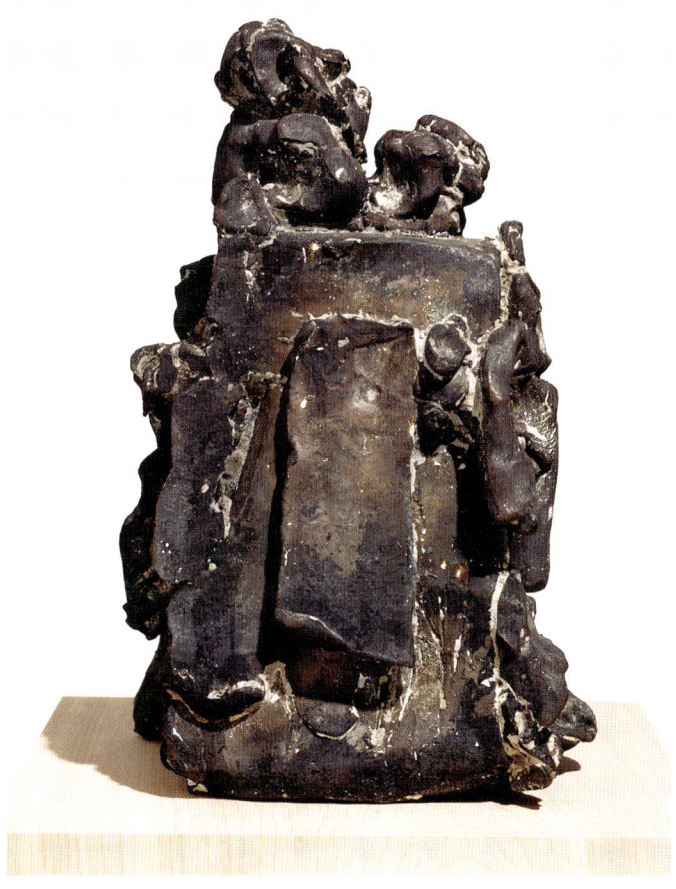

"Cy and I had a discussion about these particular works by de Kooning. I visited de Kooning periodically in the late 1960s and '70s at his Long Island studio, and he had shown me some new hand-sized bronze castings that he kept in a box under a window bench seat. He told me that he enjoyed their small scale and that they were highly personal to him and he did not want to give them to his gallerist, Xavier Fourcade, to be exhibited. However, they were exhibited soon afterwards. I have often wondered what he thought of the enlarged versions that were later made of them—I recall one in which you can see an enlarged thumb print.

As Bickley recalled, molds were made for everything but not all were cast. Three casts were made of "The Bone Yard," which included eight small pieces that can be arranged on their cast box. The pieces were very heavy and Cy had an additional

group of the eight pieces that went on "The Bone Yard" cast so he could make different arrangements of them on the original wood box in his studio in Lexington; the bronze cast of the wooden box would have been too heavy for him to easily lift.

According to Bickley, "only two works that he made in our workshop referenced his earlier 'white' work. One of these [was the piece] that he called 'The Bone Yard'. The other, that he called 'Slice of Life,' was the only piece that his classic writing appears on, other than his signature initials."

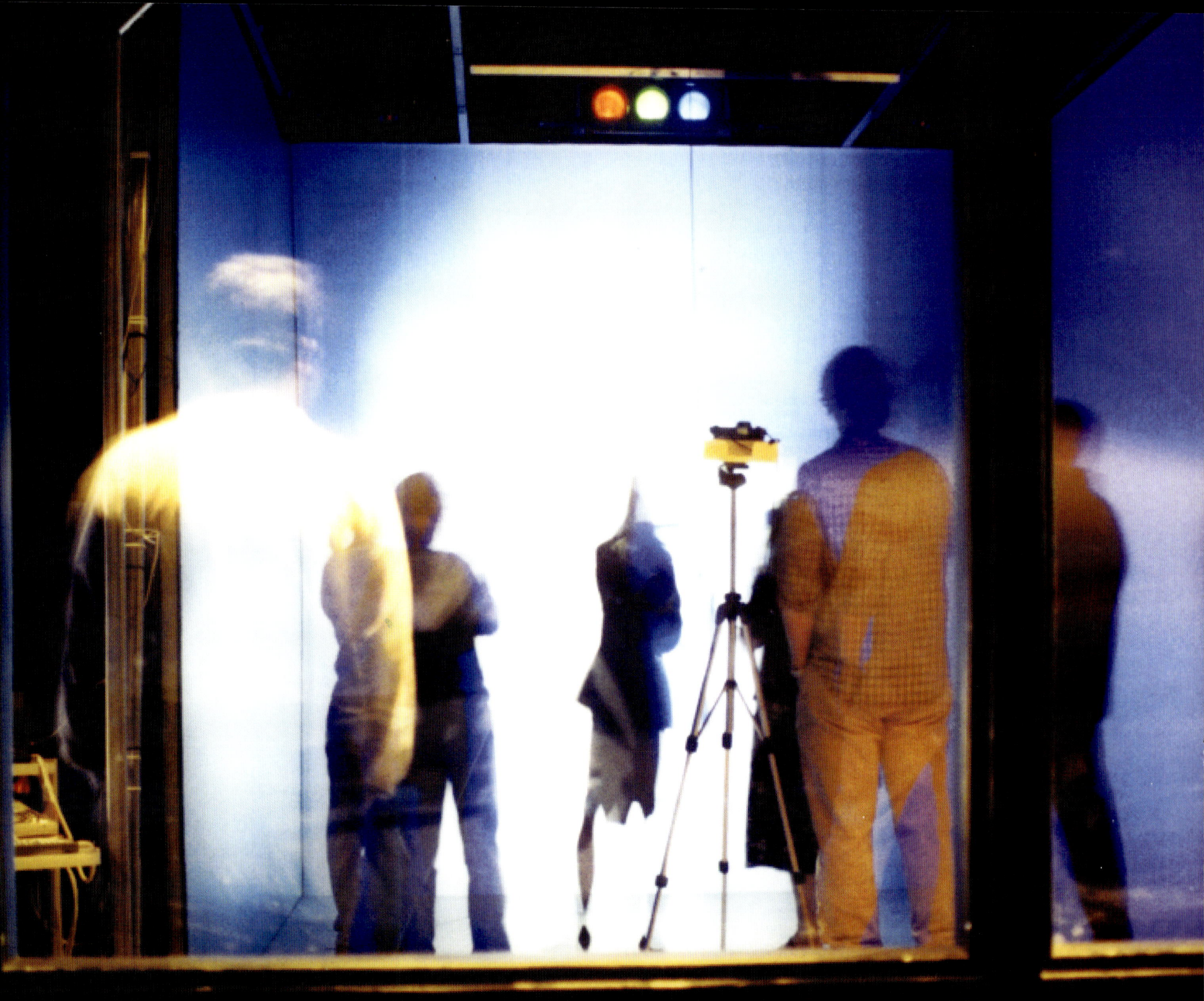

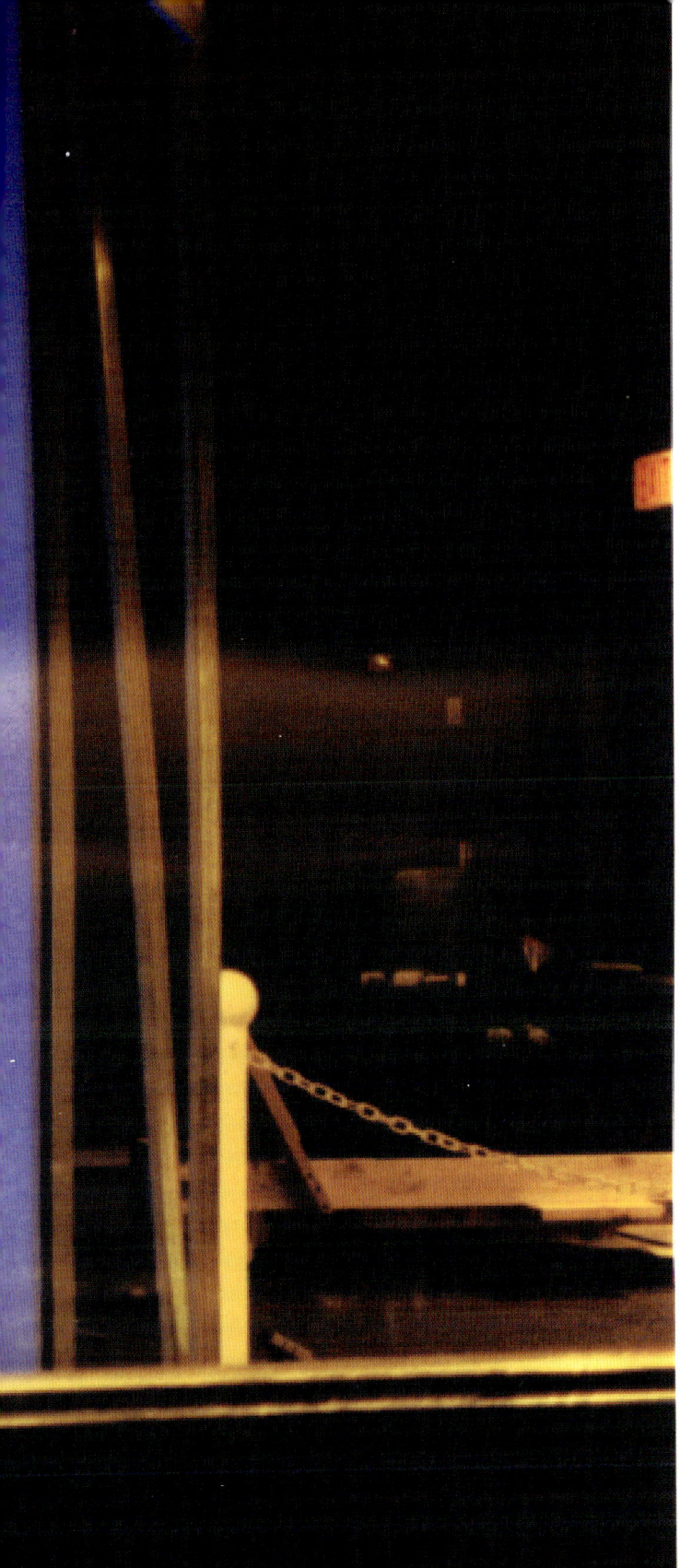

# IX

*The Mountain Lake Workshop: Collaborations with Tradition and Technology*

# METHANOGENESIS WORKSHOP: MIERLE LADERMAN UKELES, 1994

HOWARD RISATTI

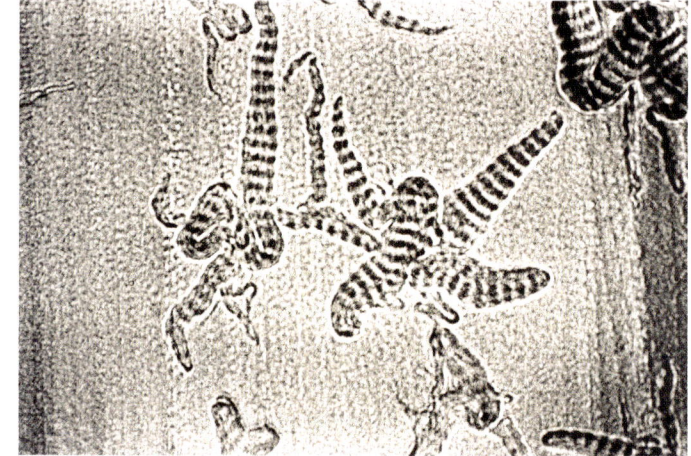

Microscopic image of "Dancing Methanogens" Photo: Dr. Greg Ferry

The exploration of the roles and images of micro-organisms in nature that Kass had undertaken in his 1991 vorticella workshops was further developed when Mierle Laderman Ukeles came to Mountain Lake in the late spring of 1994. At that time the social aspects of her art, which concerned garbage collection and waste disposal, gave it importance for the issue of a "context for art."

The creation of a "context for art," a way of locating art meaningfully within the larger cultural and social complex, had been a driving force behind the Mountain Lake programs, both workshops and symposia. For example, "Artists' Intentions: Enduring Values/Discounted Goods," the critical theory symposium of fall 1989, featured several panelists who raised provocative criticisms about the hermetic nature of so much contemporary art. Critic Suzi Gablik, for example, questioned its "art for art's sake" values because, as she argued, it resulted in aesthetic objects that were disengaged from any meaningful context. She urged artists to reconsider their attitudes and to "make art as if the world mattered."[1]

The symposium of 1990, "Decadence and Conscience: What Is Art Doing?" raised issues related to those of the 1989 symposium. Ukeles, who was one of the panelists, echoed the concerns raised by Gablik the previous year when she questioned the value of the "minimalist and process art of the '60s" because, as she said, it seemed to be "unconnected to the human labor, processes, and industrial systems out of which the ordering and procedures of such art sprang."[2]

Concern with garbage and waste disposal is part of Ukeles' larger philosophical interest in maintenance of finite systems,

of which sanitation is a pure example. Her work in this area became a highly visible public issue when headlines described barges searching for places to dump New York City's garbage after incidents in which ocean-dumped medical waste began to litter public beaches. A law passed many years earlier forbidding New York to ship its waste beyond its city limits had forced the city to turn its attention to developing a sophisticated system of waste disposal and bio-remediation. Such a system can be seen, as Roanoke curator Mark Scala has pointed out, as a "perfect metaphor for the closed system that is, ultimately, the planet itself."[3]

Ukeles, who has been the official (unsalaried) "artist-in-residence" at the New York City Department of Sanitation since 1977, spent one and one half years traveling around the city talking to sanitation workers and officials. After this, she did an eleven-month performance piece called *Touch Sanitation* in which she went to the five boroughs of New York and personally shook the hand of every one of the city's 8,500 sanitation workers, thanking each "for keeping New York City alive."[4] This was an effort to encourage a greater understanding of the importance of the work done by workers whom Scala refers to as the "'untouchables' of metropolitan culture."[5]

Later in New York City Ukeles choreographed a work called *Ballet Mécanique*, a "ballet" of six street-sweeping vehicles that was part of the New York City Art Parade of 1983. She also has made a "contextual sculpture" for the Department of Sanitation called *The Social Mirror* by covering a garbage truck with hand-tempered mirrors so people would be confronted with their own images, making clear their roles in the creation of waste.

Other works include sculptures made from landfill materials, waste-hauling vehicles, and disused equipment from the sanitation department. At New York City's 59th Street Marine Transfer Station, where at one time 3,000 tons of garbage was loaded daily on barges for transport to the Fresh Kills Landfill in Staten Island, she is working on a massive long-term project called *Flow City*. As a model for this project, she created *Re-entry*, a 90-foot-long "viewing corridor," a kind of "ramp-tunnel" through 20 tons of recyclables. This "Passage Ramp" leads to the "Glass Bridge" and "Media Flow Wall," where visitors can see what happens to some of the 26,000 tons of garbage generated by the city every day.[6]

Because of the way such activities used art as a means to make visible the "underbelly" of urban culture, to place in context the full scope of the material waste of modern urban life, Ukeles' work and ideas were of special interest to Mountain Lake. After about four years of discussion and planning, Ukeles agreed to do an interdisciplinary, collaborative workshop. But considering the huge scale and urban nature of her previous work, it was unlikely that such performances, if they could even be repeated or re-created at Mountain Lake, would be meaningful to a small, rural community.

However, with Cage's interest in fungi and Kass' interest in single-celled organisms like the vorticella, discussions during the planning stages of the workshop eventually led to the idea that an art and science interface could be done involving waste

[1] Suzi Gablik, "Deconstructing Aesthetics," *New Art Examiner* (Jan. 1989), p. 32. For more on Gablik's position see her book *The Reenchantment of Art* (New York: Thames and Hudson, 1991).

[2] Ukeles in personal correspondence with the author, 16 July 1996. Ukeles quoted in Suzi Gablik, "Art and Audience in a Model Partnership," *New Art Examiner* (Jan. 1989), p. 33.

[3] See Mark Scala's essay for the exhibition *Methanogenesis: Mierle Laderman Ukeles and the Mountain Lake Workshop* which he curated at the Art Museum of Western Virginia, 5 May–20 Aug. 1995, n.p.

[4] See Gablik, "Art and Audience," p. 33.

[5] See Scala, Mierle Laderman Ukeles exhibition essay, n.p.

[6] Altogether, she has done five "work-ballets," two in New York City and one each in Rotterdam, Pittsburgh, and France. Several years ago she received a grant to create art for New York City's Fresh Kills Landfill, the nation's largest. Her intention is to create a work that will help make people aware of the problems involved in disposing of waste material. (Correspondence with the author, 16 and 26 July 1996.) For more on these projects, see Mierle Laderman Ukeles, "A Journey: Earth/City/

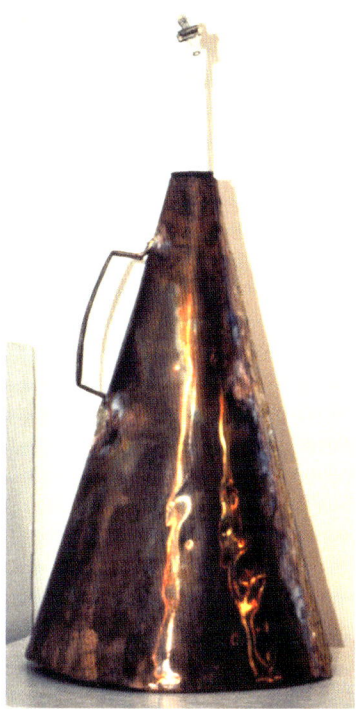

Copper funnel made for the re-enactment of Count Alessandro Volta's 1776 lakeside experiment and the discovery of methane gas and anaerobic bacterica, 38" high x 12" diameter, 1994

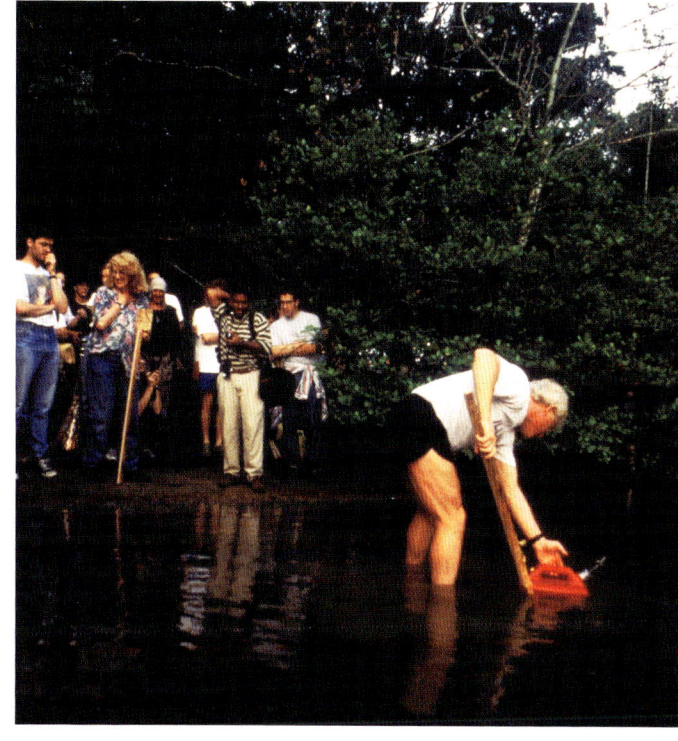

Dr. Greg Ferry performs a re-enactment of Count Alessandro Volta's 1776 experiment that resulted in the discovery of methane gas and living anaerobic microbes in previously thought-to-be dead underwater lake detritus, establishing the basis for modern microbiology.

at a fundamentally organic level. This would be a way to make people aware of the problems of waste "management" at a level other than the equipment involved in the removal of garbage. For a possible workshop, the idea evolved that Ukeles might consider doing something with micro-organisms, micro-organisms as they relate to waste at the level of natural biodegradation and bio-remediation systems. This would be a genuine cross-disciplinary project that involved art and science, something that Kass had originally wanted to explore with Cage via mycology as a way to use the resources of the university community as well as the local community.

With this in mind, and after a year of meetings between Kass and members of Virginia Tech's Anaerobic Laboratory where anaerobes (micro-organisms that live in oxygen-free environments) are studied, Kass suggested that Ukeles might do something based on the behavioral activities of anaerobes. When Dr. James G. Ferry, professor of microbiology, agreed to participate in such a project, Kass organized an interdisciplinary collaborative experiment in June of 1994 that involved Ukeles, Ferry, and local participants. As part of the preparation for the workshop, Ferry informed participants about the principles of methanogenesis, the creation of methane gas as a by-product of the anaerobic bacterial decomposition of organic matter.

He also explained the role of marshes in the global carbon cycle and referred to the important discovery of methane gas in 1776 by Count Alessandro Volta. This discovery, which is generally recognized as formative to the foundation of modern microbiology, led to the idea that, as in the Shinto ceremony that began Okura's 1990 workshop, a "performance" of sorts could be organized to begin Ukeles' workshop.

At Pandapas Pond near Blacksburg, Ferry and other participants did a performance in which they repeated Volta's experiment which had resulted in his discovery of methane gas. Wading into shallow water and holding inverted funnels over the water as Volta had done, participants stirred the pond's muddy bottom, releasing the methane trapped in its anaerobic sediments. Because methane gas is lighter than air, it was captured at the top of the inverted funnels. Then, because it also is a colorless and odorless gas, to prove its existence it was ignited as it rose through the top of the funnels.

What the experiment demonstrated was that here, in this pond, and in wetlands all over the world, bacterial life exists. The activity of this bacterial life breaks down organic matter and frees the carbon trapped in this matter so it can be re-used by plants through photosynthesis. Bacteria do this as they nourish themselves (i.e., "eat" organic matter), producing the by-product compound methane gas. One of the essential building blocks of the carbon-based cycle of life, methane is as invisible as are the bacteria that produce it. Comprising 50 percent of the world's life, bacteria cannot be grasped visually with the naked eye, only indirectly by the indexical signs of their presence. As in the earlier workshops, especially Kass' vorticella

experiments, the idea that all of nature can be understood simply through direct visual observation had to give way to the realization that certain fundamental aspects of nature can be understood, in any profound sense, only at a conceptual level. And, as a consequence for the artist, fundamental aspects of nature such as these can only be represented in visual form symbolically and metaphorically, not pictured "realistically."

Ukeles conceived of the workshop as an attempt to pierce through the psychological and physical barrier to the unseen world of micro-organisms through the use of imagination, that is to say, through art. As she has said, "our imagination, our creative ability, is the most important thing that we bring to the world."[7] The re-creation of the Volta experiment was important, not for nostalgia's sake (neither Ferry nor Ukeles is interested in that), but because it showed Volta's search for something he did not understand, his discovery of something (methane gas), and his recognition of the importance of this discovery (that the

Flow," *Art Journal* (Summer 1992), pp.12–14, and Gablik, *The Reenchantment of Art*, especially pp. 69–75. The landfill closed in March of 2001 but was temporarily reopened after 9/11. Ukeles' Fresh Kills project, titled *Reconnaissance*, is ongoing and is to include a Landing: Cantilevered Overlook. For more on the current status of the project see Donald Goddard, "Mierle Laderman Ukeles: Penetration and Transparency: Morphed (with videographers Kathy Brew and Robert Guerra)," *New York Art World*, http://www.newyorkartworld.com/reviews/ukeles.html. Also see *Mierle Laderman Ukeles: Maintenance Art*, retrospective exhibition catalogue, Queens Museum (Munich, New York, London: Prestel, 2016).

7 Quote taken from *Methanogenesis*, a video tape of Ukeles at Mountain Lake in 1994.

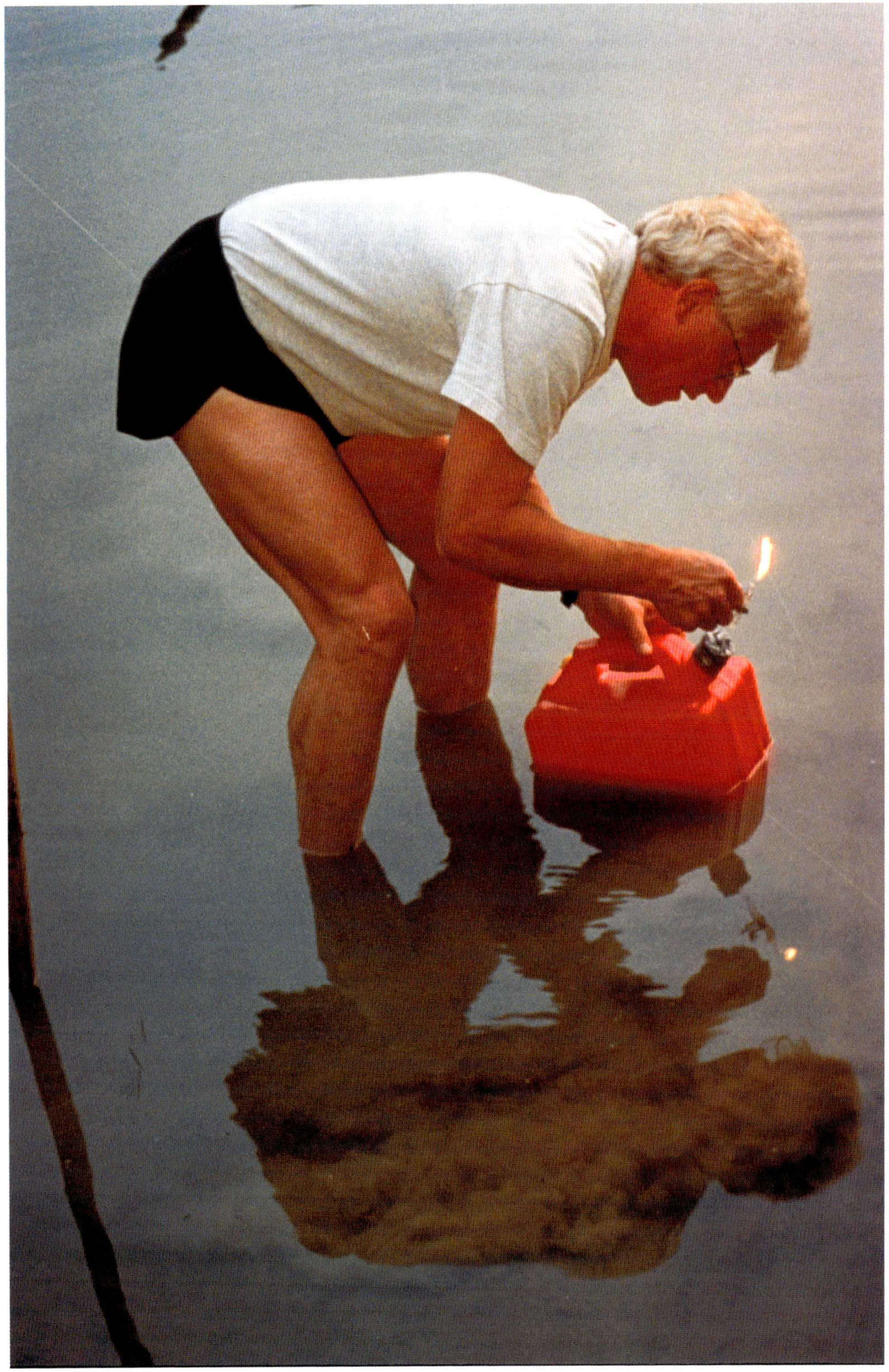

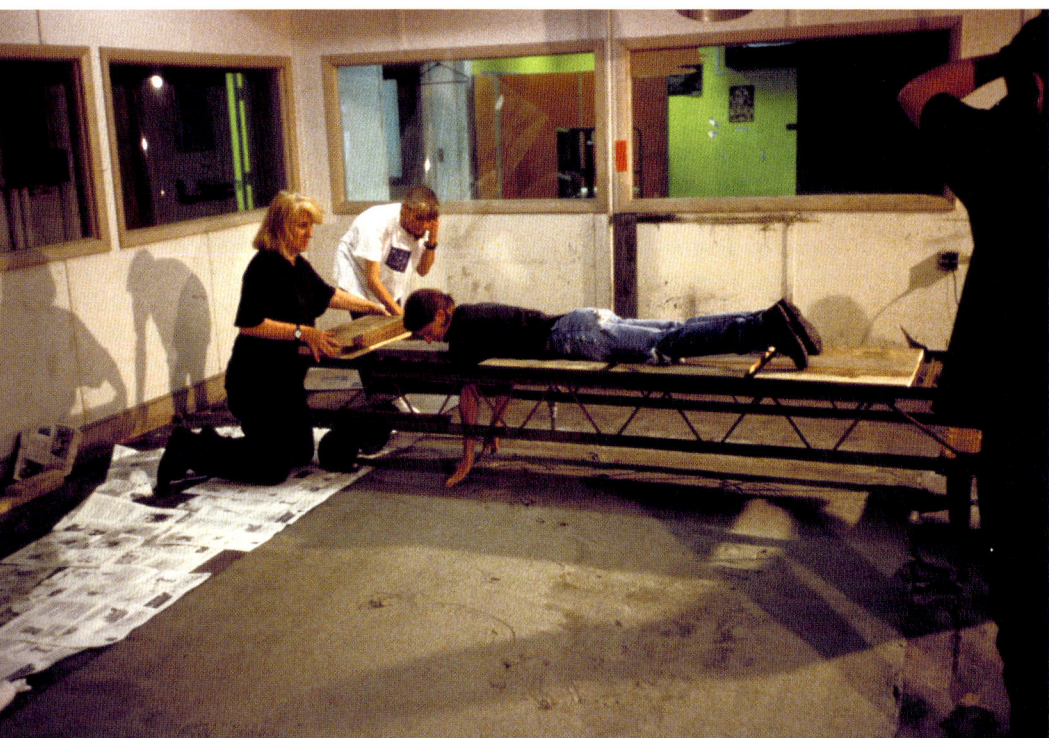

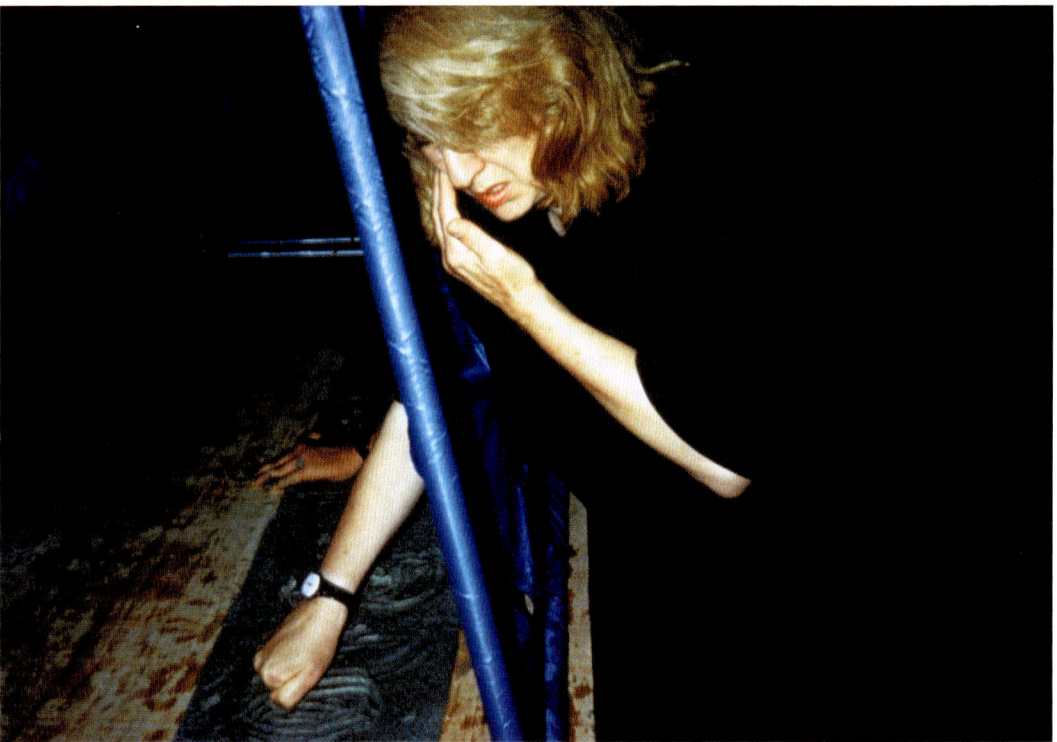

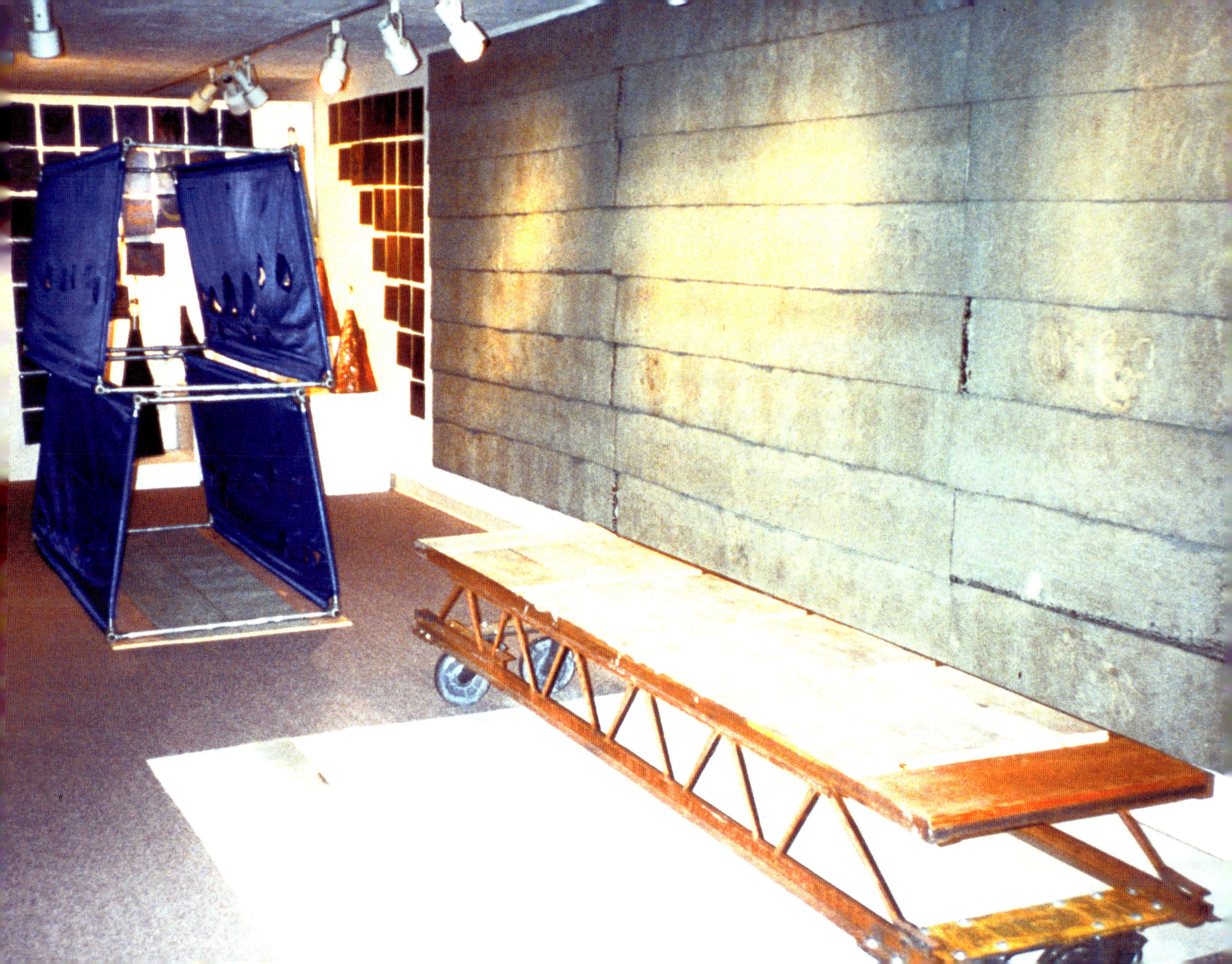

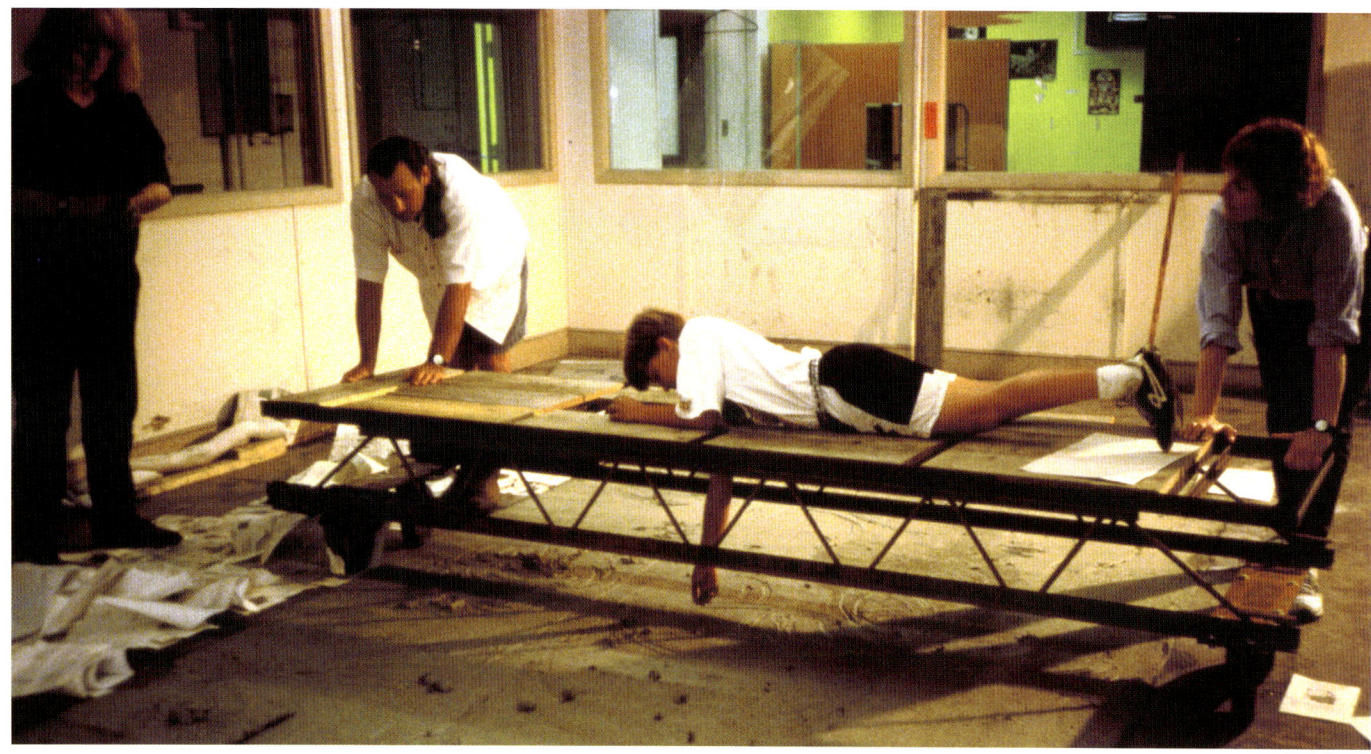

production of methane by bacteria is an essential part of the life cycle). For Ukeles, these three actions are things that science shares with the artistic imagination, for the artist also reaches into the unknown to wonder, to discover, to understand, and to make connections between the self and the larger world. Connections that can be made with the invisible world of bacteria, according to Ukeles, offer an important survival strategy for today's world.

Workshop participants were taught something of the biochemistry of organic degradation to help them understand not only the science behind Ukeles' work but also the uniqueness of her approach. Then, to further help them overcome any squeamishness they may have had about the idea of bacteria, waste disposal, and remediation, Ukeles designed a special hand-washing ritual and various studio exercises. She calls this squeamishness a "shudder response," and believes that it comes from millennia of avoiding decaying material for fear of disease.

Now, however, she argues that we must overcome this often involuntary negative response to achieve a wiser, more enlightened understanding of microbial activity and to see it as an essential part of the cycle of life.[8] To achieve this, she asked participants to do a "face and stomach touching" exercise so they could recognize how these parts of the body connect with the world of micro-organisms and with the digestive process, how nourishment and also waste generation are interrelated. It was important for participants to understand that bacteria break down organic matter while nourishing themselves and, at the same time, release carbon back into the life cycle so that life itself can be sustained.

For the workshop participants Ukeles devised an exercise which utilized a material called Gundseal.™ Even before the workshop, Ukeles had been working with Gundseal, a brand name of bentonite-lined vinyl landfill liners.[9] Bentonite is a type of clay that becomes impermeable when wet; thus it is reputedly an

excellent landfill liner and cap that will prevent seepage of toxic liquids into ground water. Using this Gundseal liner as a kind of sediment layer — the bentonite has a smooth, almost oozy consistency — participants were asked to think of one of their hands as related to life and the other to art. (The "art hand" was regarded as a movement towards connection to the larger world.) While touching their faces (i.e., the self) with the "life hand," participants were asked to make similar marks on the bentonite with the "art hand" (the reaching-out or feeling hand). Each "life touch" had a corresponding "art mark." Each mark was considered as expressing, even asserting, the individuated self, but in such a way that the conceptualizing, abstracting mind would be overridden by the feeling hand. Then, while touching their stomachs, the very place where major unseen anaerobic activity takes place within the body, participants were asked to make more repetitive, interconnecting marks on the Gundseal that would represent the cyclical life functions that the bacteria carried out.

Using hands and sticks, participants drew into the bentonite, making their own unique curvilinear marks. In a kind of automatist ritual symbolically mimicking the invisible nature of bacterial activity, they made these marks "blind" (i.e., without actually seeing what they were doing). To allow this, two procedures were developed. In one, "blind drawings" were made using a method that entailed a "blind drawing screen," a 16-foot-long tent-like structure with a series of armholes on both sides. By placing an arm through the holes in the blind drawing screen, participants could make drawings with their hands on unseen 1 x 8 foot bentonite panels that had been placed inside on planks.

[8] This was similar to Cage's attitude towards mushrooms even though (as he noted) some people think they are "creepy." Cage tried to cultivate an equanimity about things in the world, including things like unusual sounds, noises, and even fungi. He did this in order to recognize them as part of the world, part of the larger cycle of nature, and to point out that our predilections or attitudes about them often have little to do with what they actually are or how they actually function in the larger world. This is akin to Tobey's "seeing a thing without prejudice" and is also related to Greenberg's idea that art is like nature itself, not a picture of nature; it is also connected to Heidegger's phenomenology and the return to "things" themselves.

[9] Ukeles first worked with methanogens in a workshop/performance done with Suzanne Lacy at the California College of Arts and Crafts in Oakland in 1989; the work was called *Making a Landfill*. Correspondence with the author, 16 July 1996.

[10] Other activities of the workshop involved papermaking with artist Kathy Pinkerton in which participants made small drawings with water-soluble crayons on Masonite panels. The images, inspired by the forms of methane-producing anaerobic bacteria, were then transferred onto handmade paper using a specially built vacuum table. Even though Ferry and Kass were quite interested in works produced in the other activities of this workshop, these paper "leaves" and panels were not chosen to be included in the public exhibition at the end of the workshop because Ukeles felt they did not express her sense of the invisible and abstract nature of microbial activity. To her, they seemed visually too literal and not abstract enough. It was a rule at Mountain Lake that guest artists had to feel comfortable with the outcome of their workshops, something Ukeles clearly did not with the handmade paper works. Cage also had rejected several paintings from his workshops for the same reason.

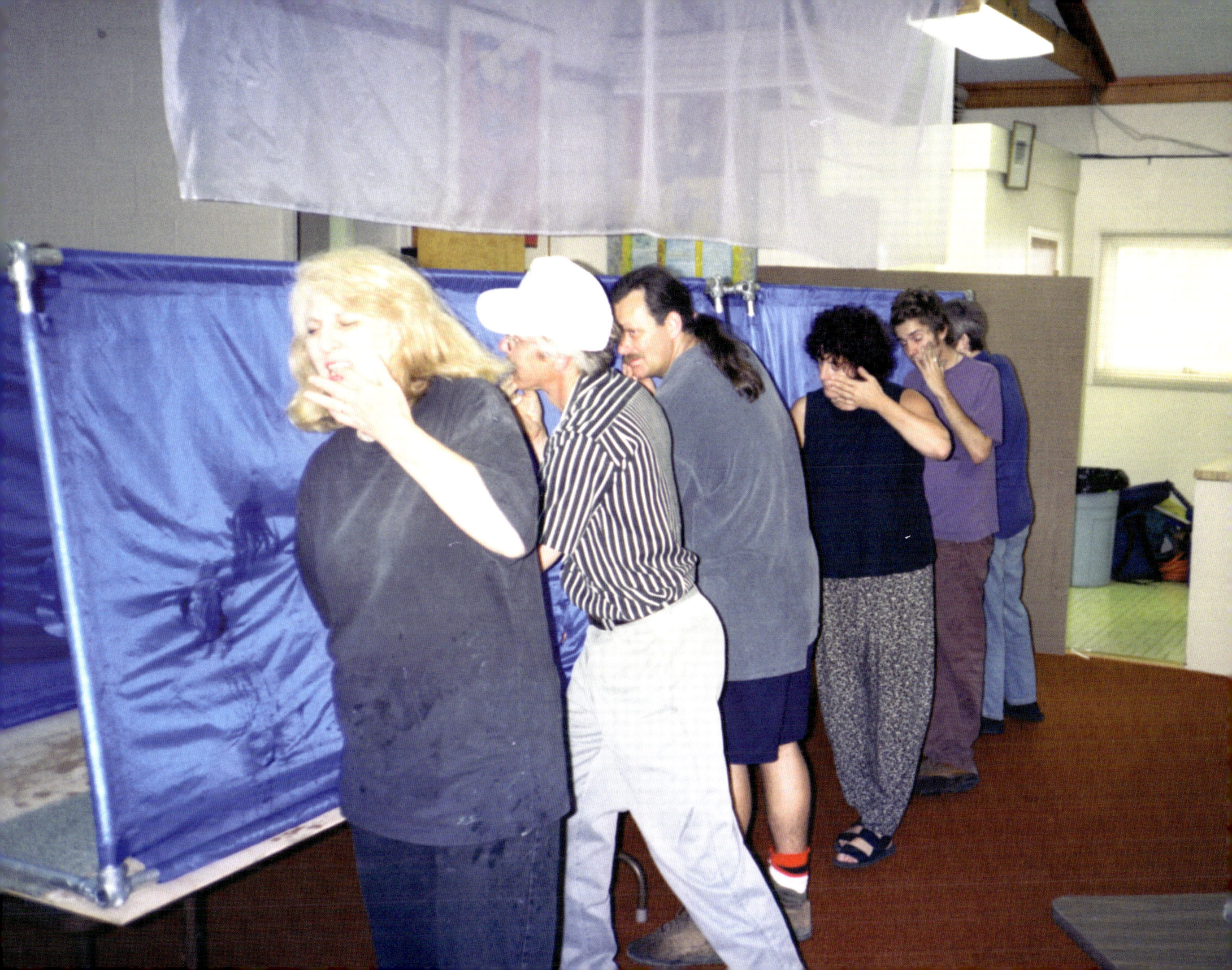

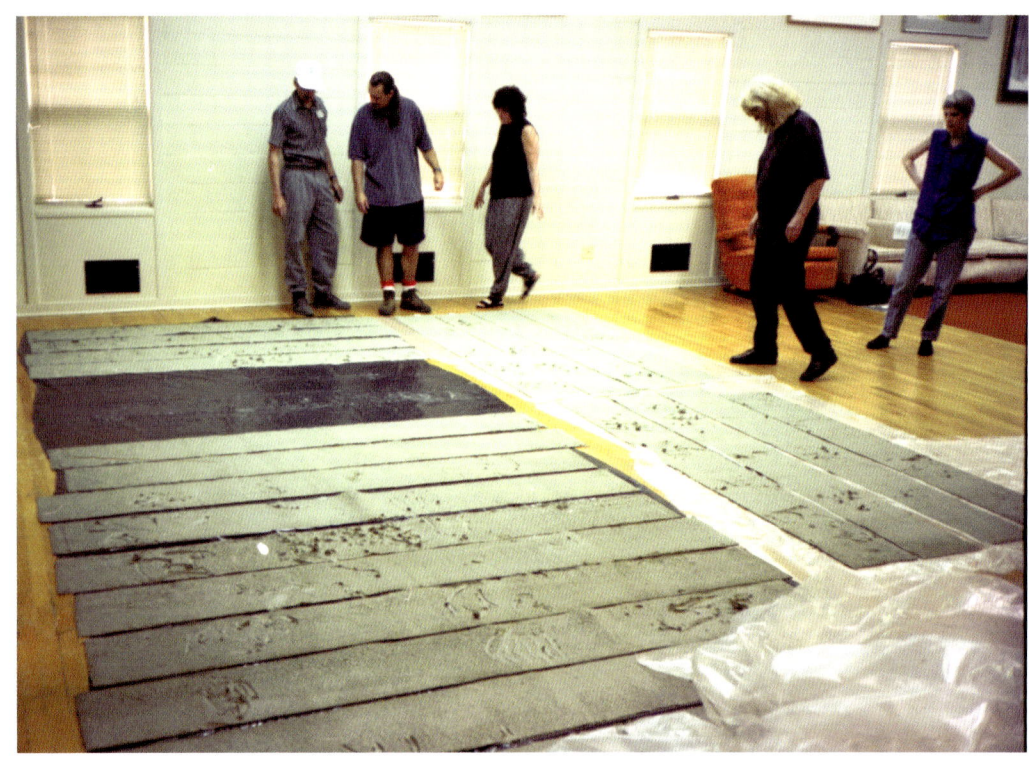

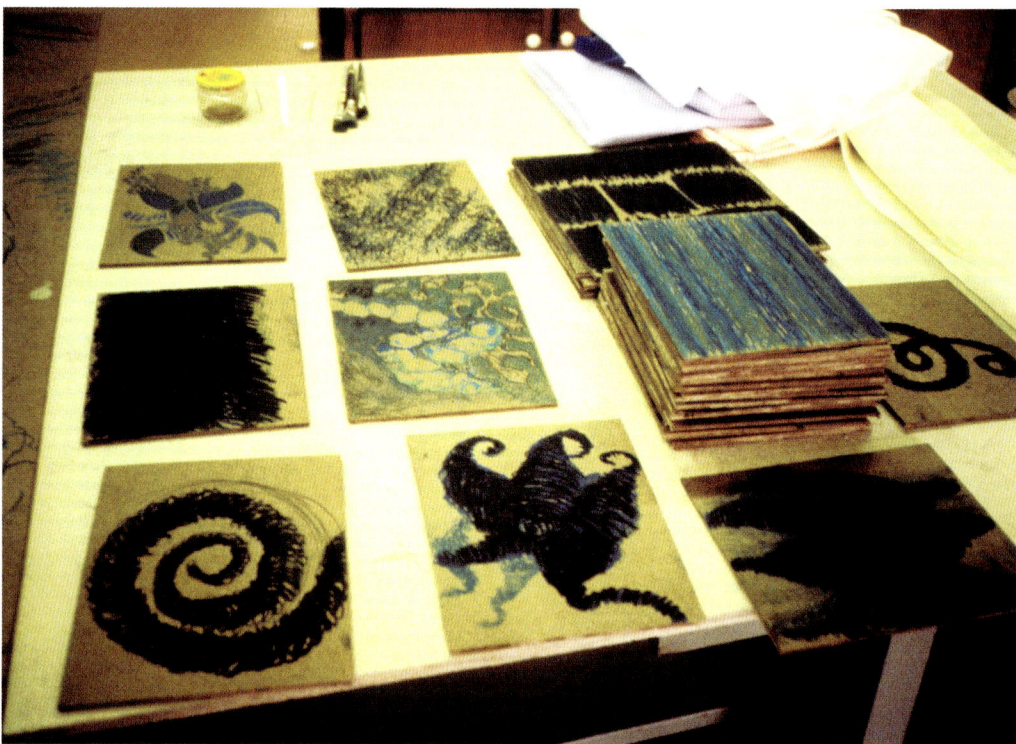

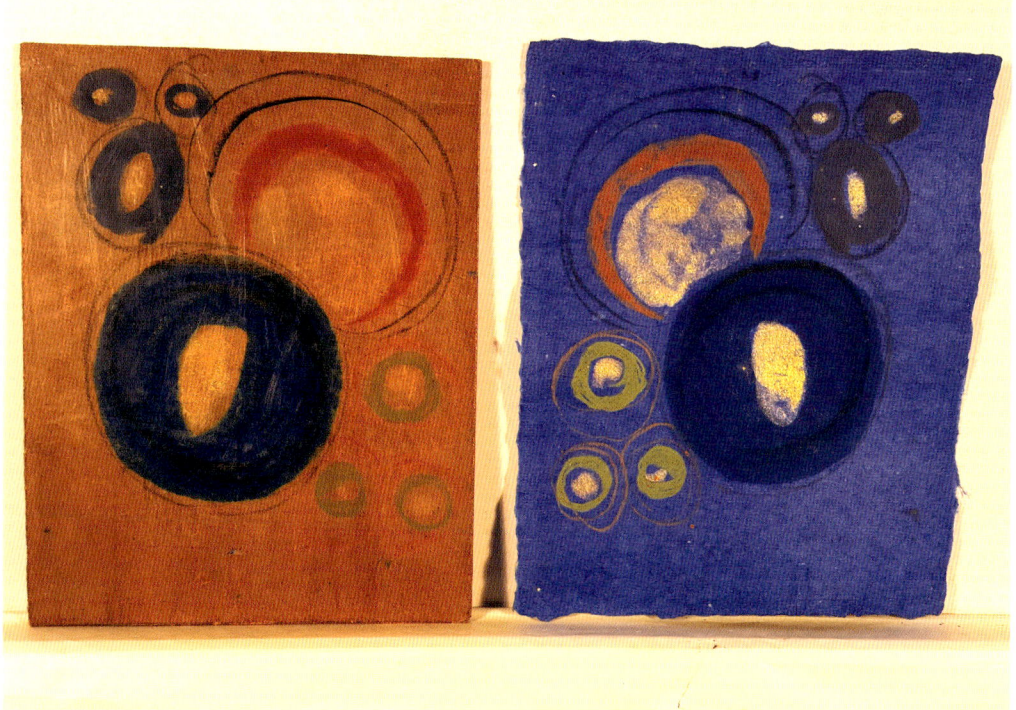

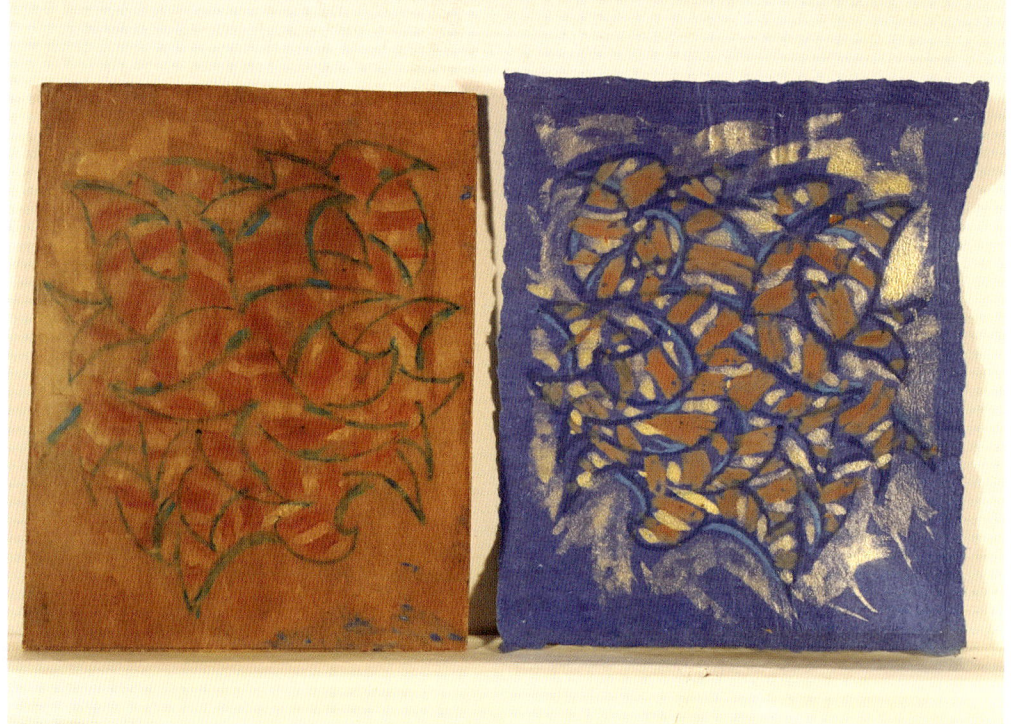

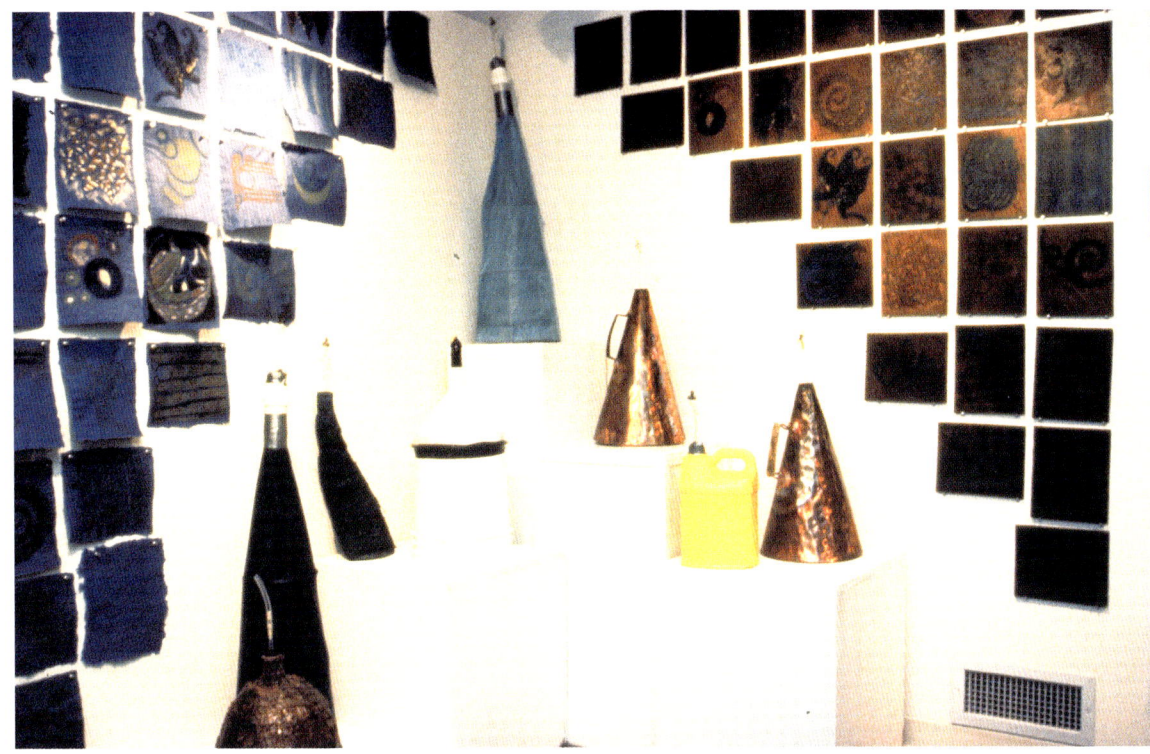

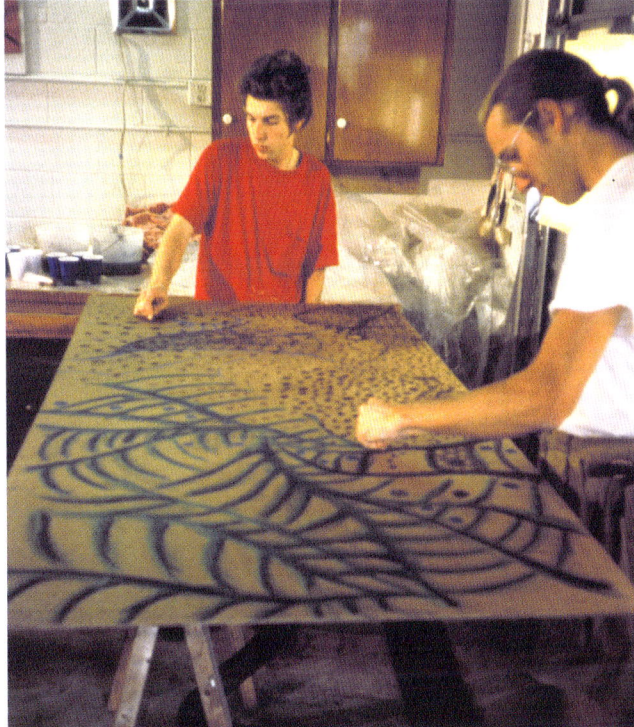

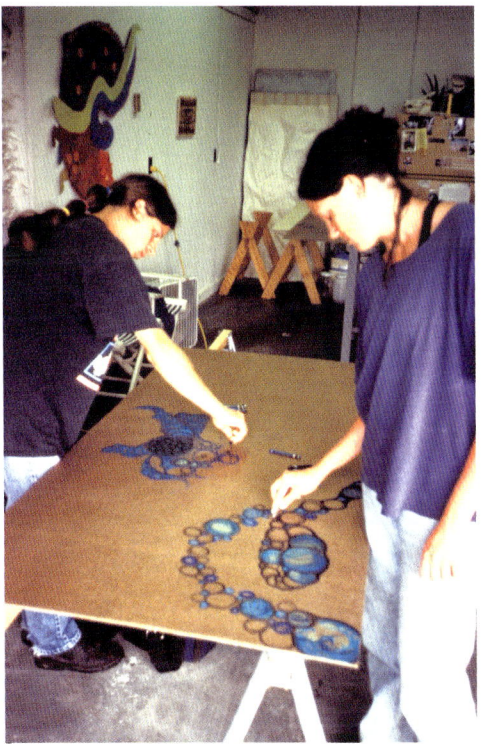

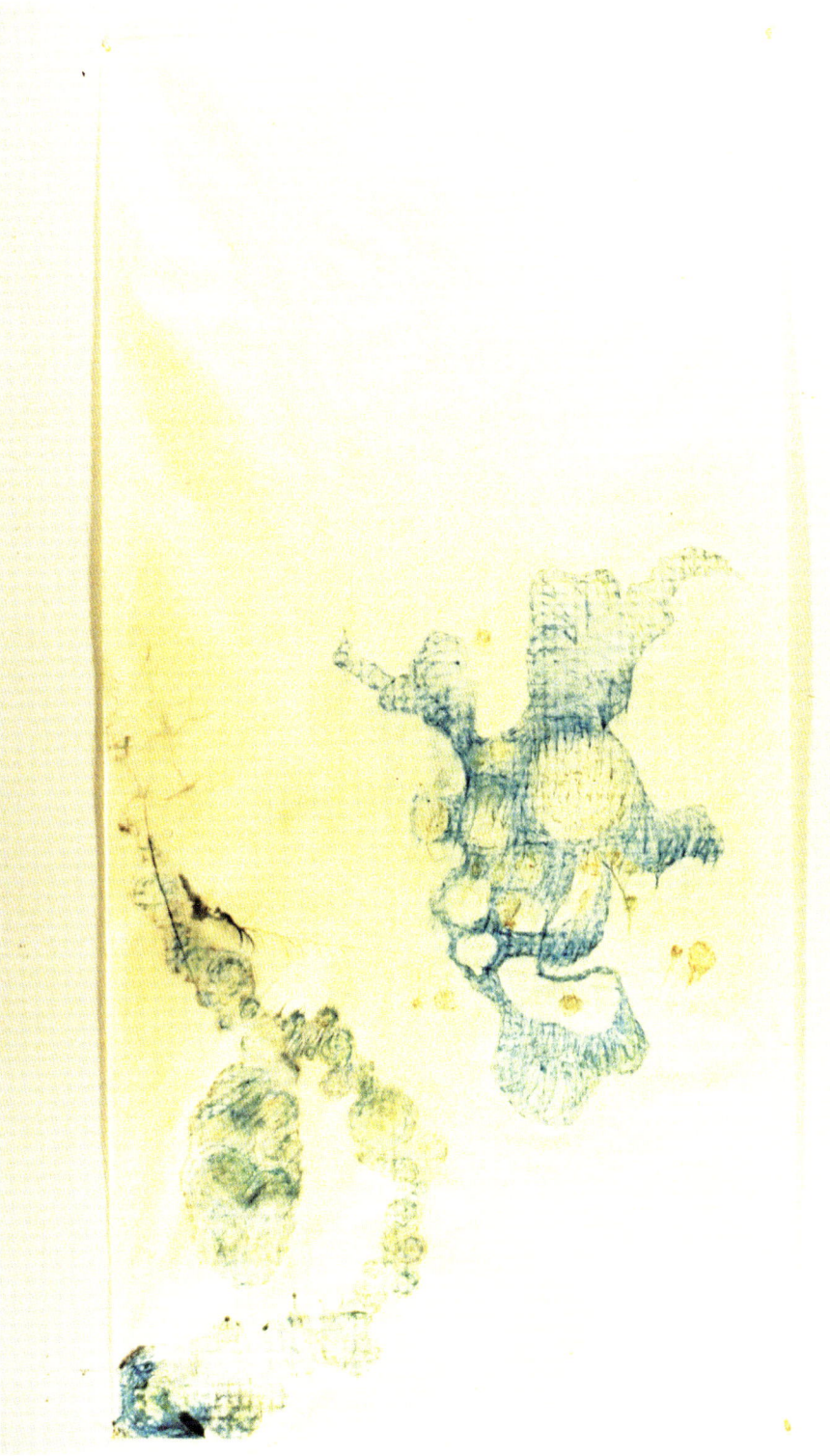

A second method utilized a cart made of used materials; similarly, it came to be called the "blind cart" because it allowed participants to lie on it and be rolled above 8 x 72 foot lengths of the bentonite liner without touching the liner. Reaching through an opening in the bottom of the cart, a participant could draw without seeing what he or she was drawing. Because they could not see their own "blind drawings," their activities symbolically connected them to the invisible world of bacteria and micro-organisms which sustain the visible world we see even though they are hidden.[10]

The "blind drawing" techniques which derived from the touching exercise are related to Surrealist devices such as automatic drawing in that they were intended to open a passage into the unconscious mind, in this case into the area of the "shudder response" as a way to the world of micro-organisms. The touching exercises and the use of bentonite also were ways of anchoring the artworks to waste, bio-remediation, and the self so that the meaning of their forms could not be misconstrued as free-floating and purely abstract signs. Just as in all the workshops at Mountain Lake, the processes, the activities, and the materials used (whether they be "dementions," stones, wood, twigs, or vorticella) framed the range of possible metaphorical interpretations that could logically be created around the art.

When these "blind drawings" are exhibited as a corridor through which one can walk, they simulate Ukeles' earlier ramp-tunnel, a construction that actually went through recyclable materials, as well as passage through a landfill with liners for sides. When they are hung in layered panels on the wall, they suggest the stratigraphical layers of bacterial activity. In each manner

of presentation, they are powerful metaphors for the hidden presence of life-sustaining activities essential to the earth itself. Wet, the bentonite is soft, smooth, and impressionable, receptive to the touch of the participants just as the earth is sensitive to the activities of humans. However, when the bentonite dries like a drained wetland, it hardens, cracks, and peels, turning into a light gray desert-like surface, desiccated and barren of life. Carrying the haunting traces on its surface like scars of life that once was, it hangs like a carcass of flayed earth before the spectator.

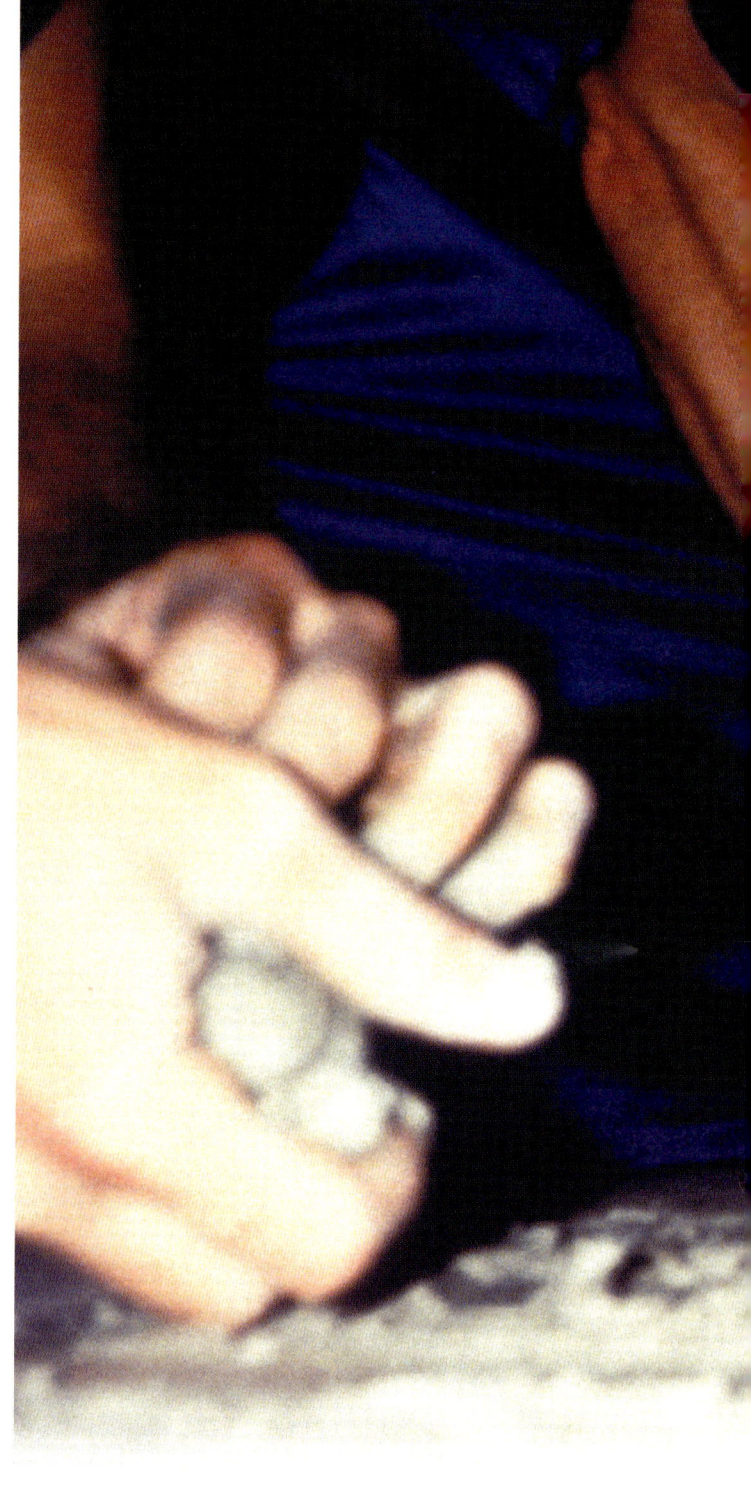

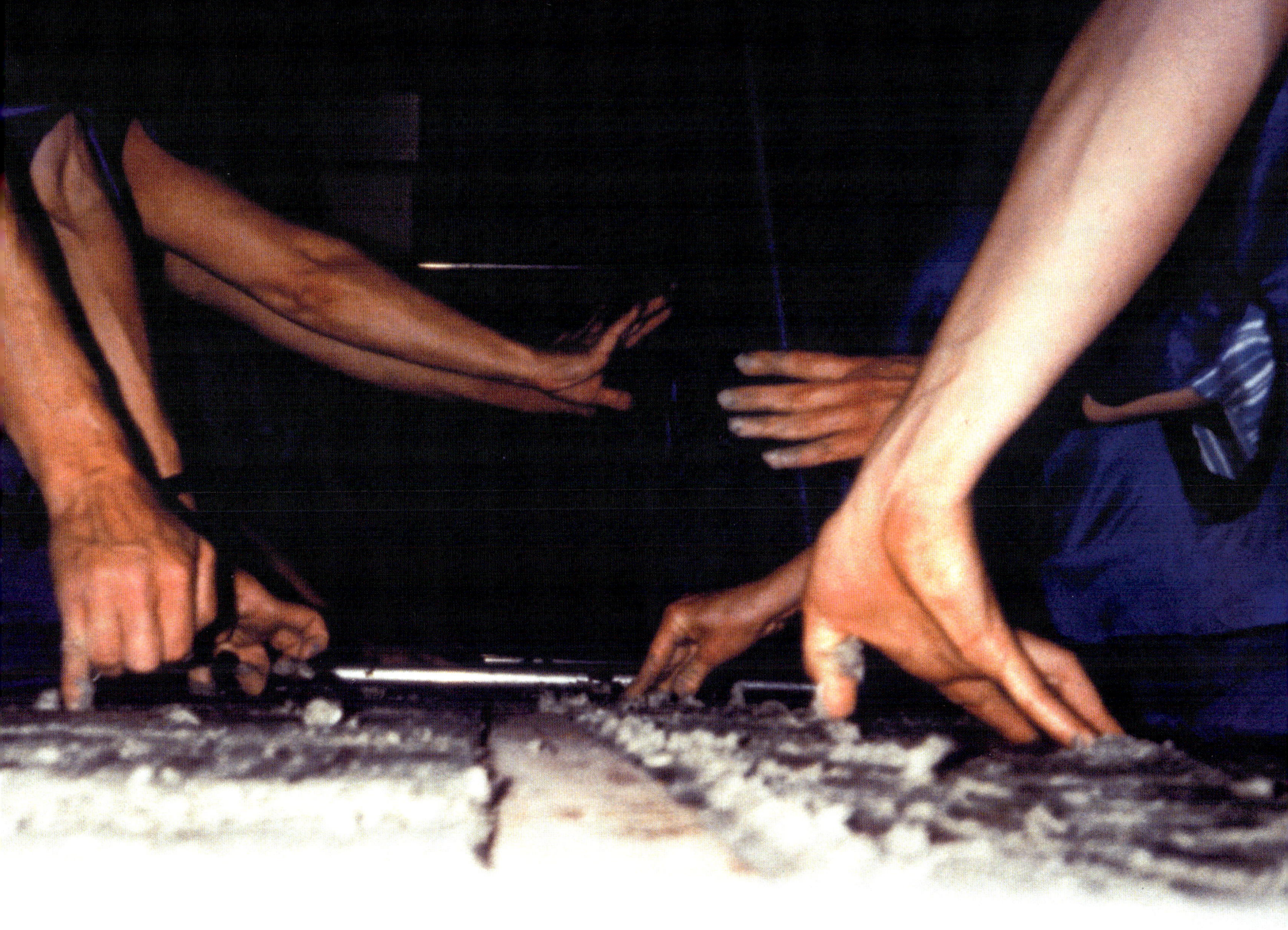

# ART VOLANT: JACKIE MATISSE'S COLLABORATIONS IN ART AND SCIENCE

HOWARD RISATTI

New York and Paris-based artist Jackie Matisse (granddaughter of Henri Matisse) has been making and flying long-tailed, Asian-style kites for decades. Her interest in kites began around 1962, inspired by two events. One was seeing a solitary kite flying in an empty sky over Harlem while she was on her way to La Guardia airport. The second was her purchase of a Thai "serpent" kite she saw displayed in a tiny box in a store window. Advertised to be 22 feet long, to her surprise it actually was, and, as she said, it "flew with unbelievable ease."[1] This kite and the image of that lonely kite in Harlem got her to thinking about kites as a means of artistic expression, as a way of sculpting the air and drawing in space with both line and color. Soon she began making kites with tails as long as 35 or 40 feet. She also began adding various colorful abstract designs to their tails and heads.

As a young person Jackie Matisse lived in Paris and New York and early on met many artists including the Surrealists as well as Fernand Léger, Piet Mondrian, and Jean Dubuffet. Her openness to kites certainly shows an artistic sympathy to the Surrealists, who flouted conventions and admired both naïve and children's art. Like the Surrealists, Dubuffet, who took it upon himself to instruct her about art when she was a young girl in Paris, also had an interest in the art of children and the insane.[2] And there was Alexander Calder, an artist of whom she was personally very fond, as she was of Joan Miró. Her kites echo Calder's interest in a sculpture based on movement and change, just as they reflect Miró's almost naïve, childlike isolation of colorful forms against a simple background.[3]

When, in 1999, Ray Kass saw photographs and a video of Jackie Matisse's kites "flying" underwater, he was immediately struck by their ethereal, otherworldly forms, and he extended an exploratory invitation to her to participate in a Mountain Lake Workshop project. She agreed, and — caught up in the spirit of Mountain Lake — in the spring of 2002 she became involved in a radically new and technologically ground-breaking project, a collaboration with supercomputer scientists to create simulated kites to fly in virtual space. Tom Coffin of the University of Illinois' National Center for Supercomputing Applications (NCSA) in Arlington, Virginia, endorsed the project. An artist himself, Coffin proposed it to the University of Illinois' Electronic Visualization Laboratory (EVL) in Chicago, where it was accepted. Former graduate student Shalini Venkataraman then wrote a computer program so that the virtual kites would "fly" in space like real kites, pulling, stretching, and swirling in the wind.

As part of her project Jackie Matisse also did a workshop with students and other members of the Mountain Lake community making and painting kite tails. Some of her kite tails were then exhibited at Virginia Tech's Perspective Gallery in April/May of 2002 at the same time that the first showing of *Art Flying In and Out of Space* took place Virginia Tech's Virtual Reality Cave.

The result of the Mountain Lake collaborative project, *Kites Flying In and Out of Space*, is the first virtual reality (VR) art piece ever created to use big broadband "grid" computing full-immersion techniques. When it was shown in the fall in Amsterdam at the iGRID 2002 Conference sponsored by science and technology center SARA (Stichting Academisch Rekencentrum Amsterdam), Scott Bradner of *Network World* called it the "most emblematic demonstration of a real-time interactive, 3-D work of art" and "a beautiful personification of distributed computing."[4]

Among the features that made *Kites* so compelling was the way it exploited the CAVE™ at SARA to set three-dimensional form in motion. A CAVE is a 10 foot x 10 foot structure in which computer-generated images are rear-projected onto walls and floor so that a person standing in the CAVE is completely surrounded by (i.e., fully immersed in) stereoscopic computer graphics.[5] To appear as three-dimensional forms in space, these graphics must correspond perspectively to a viewer's location in the CAVE. This is done by having a computer track the viewer's position and movements in real time. With *Kites* a participant wears special glasses and holds a wand with a virtual kite string attached to control the kites' movements and to inject wind into the scene. The glasses, tracked using magnetic sensors, feed data to a computer that continually recalculates the kite forms (~ 30 frames/second) and projects them back into the CAVE.

This ensures kite movements appear perspectively correct even when the viewer moves or turns his or her head. In part because they are not stationary forms, each of the twelve kites in the piece is so complex to simulate (each utilizes up to 15 megabits/second) that a distributed computational model using processors on multiple machines is needed. At SARA servers distributed across the globe (Chicago, Canada, Japan, Singapore, and Virginia) were enlisted to calculate kite forms, each server streaming a single kite into the CAVE. In the international scope of its collaboration *Kites Flying In and Out of Space* was a wonderful example of network performance and a visual metaphor of the

---

[1] All quotes, unless otherwise noted, come from interviews that the author conducted with Jackie Matisse over several years.

[2] According to Jackie Matisse in conversation with the author, Dubuffet and his wife invited her to dinner once a week where they talked about art.

[3] For more on Matisse's background, see Jill Johnson, "Airborne Abstraction," *Art in America* (December 2005), p.131. Some of this information also comes from the author's interviews with the artist.

[4] Scott Bradner, *Network World* (14 October 2002).

[5] CAVE™ is a registered trademark of the University of Illinois where the concept and technology were developed at its Electronic Visualization Laboratory (EVL) in Chicago. The project would not have happened without Coffin, who not only endorsed the project, but organized technical support. Venkataraman worked under Dr. Jason Leigh at EVL while writing the program. Dr. Paul Weilinga, Director of SARA, also gave support.

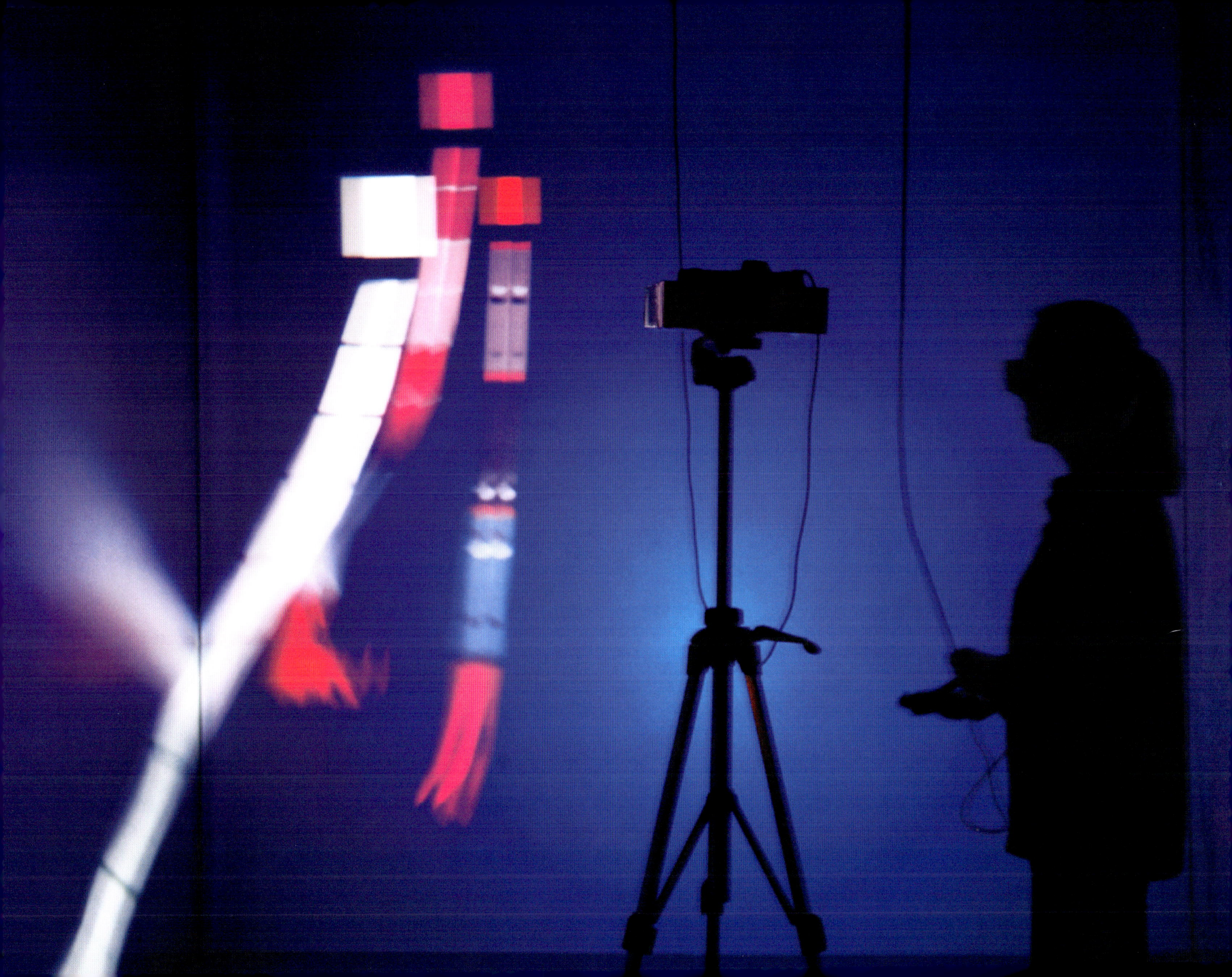

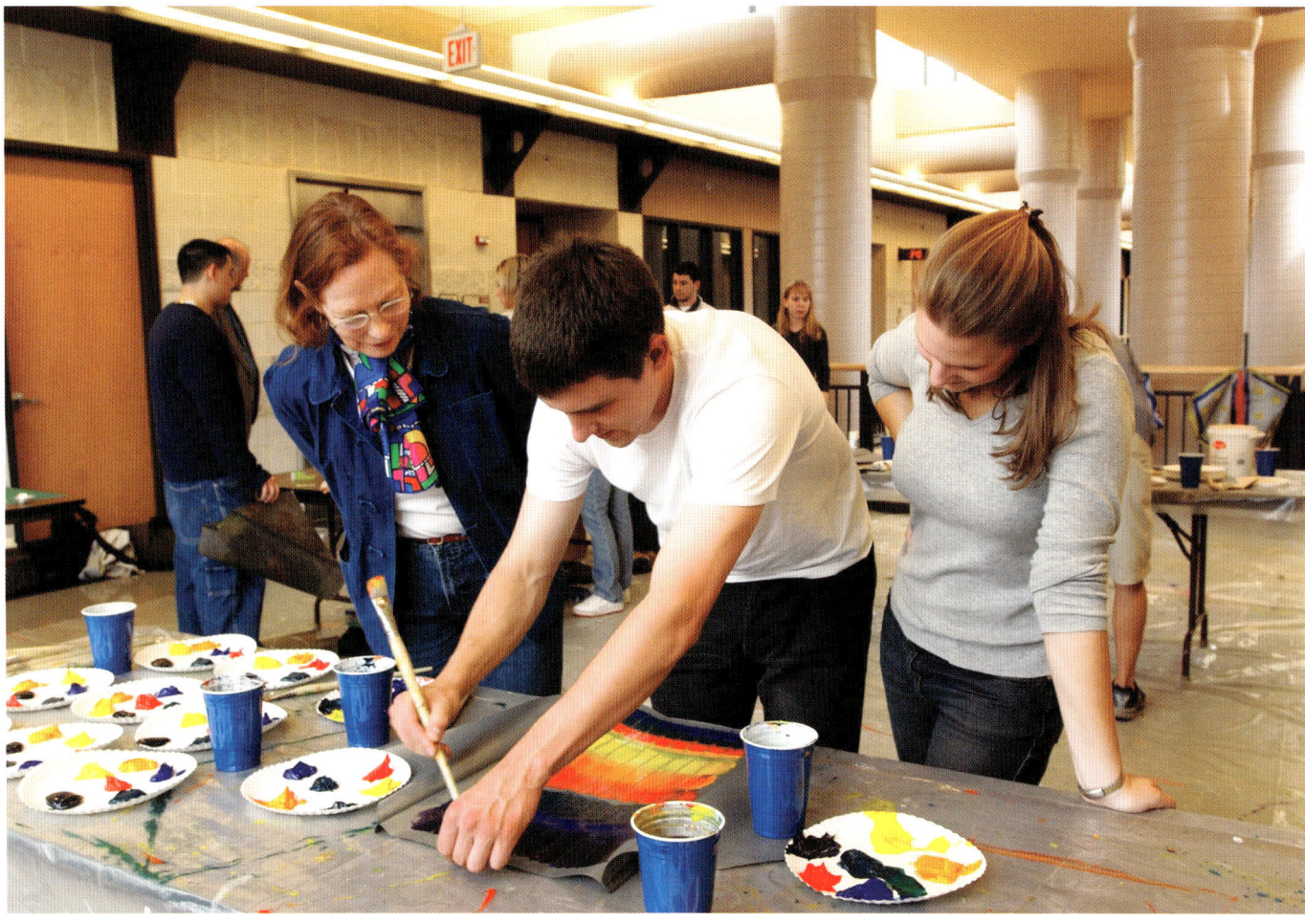

metaphor from the invisible grid network used three years earlier in the CAVE at SARA in Amsterdam to the virtual space visible in front of the screen. Through the international grid kite flyers also could have interacted from distant sites, thereby giving a global dimension to the metaphor of global interaction.

To go from flying real-world kites to collaborating with scientist/engineers to fly virtual kites seems for Jackie Matisse a radical transformation of both means and ends. I say radical because collaboration challenges the art world's insistence on the singularity of artistic production and because computer imaging challenges the art world's belief in "personal touch" as a sign of creative individuality.[7] Collaboration also is a risky move for the artist as well because, when genuine, it means giving up a degree of artistic control and putting personal identity in jeopardy. But making and flying kites as art is already a departure from mainstream art practice, so much so that the artist risks not being taken seriously.

Moreover, for Jackie Matisse, who had no formal art training, artistic endeavors with kites posed both a practical and a psychological challenge. Here the influence of Marcel Duchamp was instrumental in shaping her thinking by offering an example of a non-conventional artist, something reflected in his "ready-mades" and his fascination with chance, science, and Alfred Jarry's "pataphysics."[8] That Jackie Matisse developed her own fascination with Jarry was evident as she exhibited eleven kite tails under the title *Pour le Vacuovélodrome of Alfred Jarry* in November of 2003 at the Nicéphore Days Conference in Chalon-sur-Saône, France, sponsored by the Ecole Nationale

possibilities of global cooperation through art and technology.

A version of Kites was shown in May of 2005 at Zone: Chelsea Center for the Arts in New York. Titled *Art Flying In and Out of Space*, it was a flat-screen, interactive stereoscopic installation. Similar to 3-D movies, this technology uses polarized stereoscopy: two projectors with different polarizing filters display differing images (one for each eye); when viewers wear matching polarized glasses they see the separate images and experience a 3-D effect similar to that of 19th-century stereoscope photographs.

To simplify computer computations, in this version feedback from a hand-held tracking mouse with a virtual string attached was fixed to a stationary point in front of the screen, not to a mobile viewer as in the CAVE.[6] Rear-projection allowed viewers to stand close to the 8 foot x 10 foot screen without casting shadows so the screen completely filled their field of vision and any perspective discrepancies became imperceptible. Up to five participants with 3-D glasses and a hand-held mouse could each fly their own kite and interact with each others' kites. This multi-participant feature extended the collaboration

[6] Artist-programmer David Pape, Department of Media Study, University of Buffalo, developed the mouse and adapted the VR CAVE program for other platforms so it could be used in a gallery situation.

[7] For more on these issues see Holland Carter, "The Collective Conscious," *The New York Times* (5 March 2006), sec. 2, pp. 1, 29.

[8] Duchamp became Jackie Matisse's step-father when her mother married him in 1954. She grew very fond of him and gained invaluable artistic experience working with him from 1959 until his death in 1968 helping him assemble his *Boîte-en-Valise*

(portable museum). Pataphysics was invented by Jarry around 1898 as a mixture of science, theology, art, and the absurd. For Duchamp's interest in Jarry see Dawn Ades, David Hopkins, and Neil Cox, *Marcel Duchamp* (New York: Thames & Hudson, Inc.; 1999), pp. 78-79.

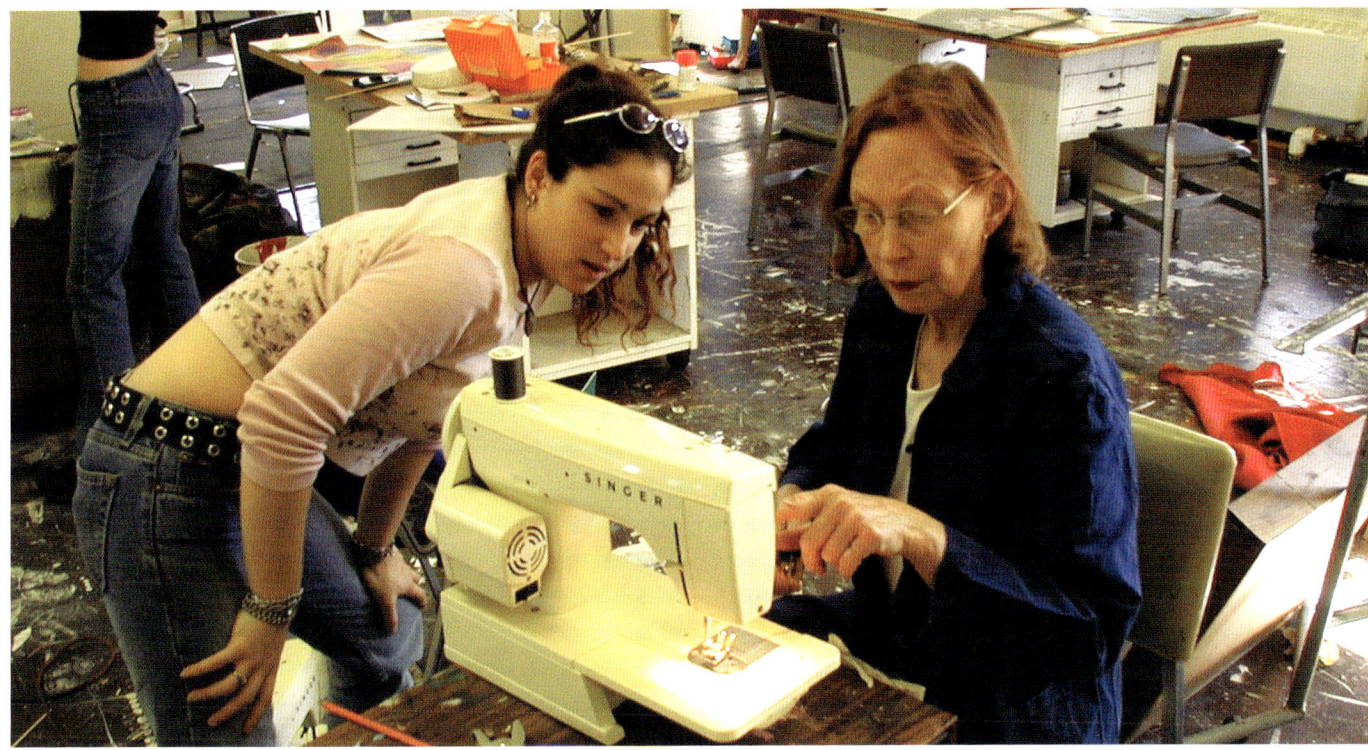
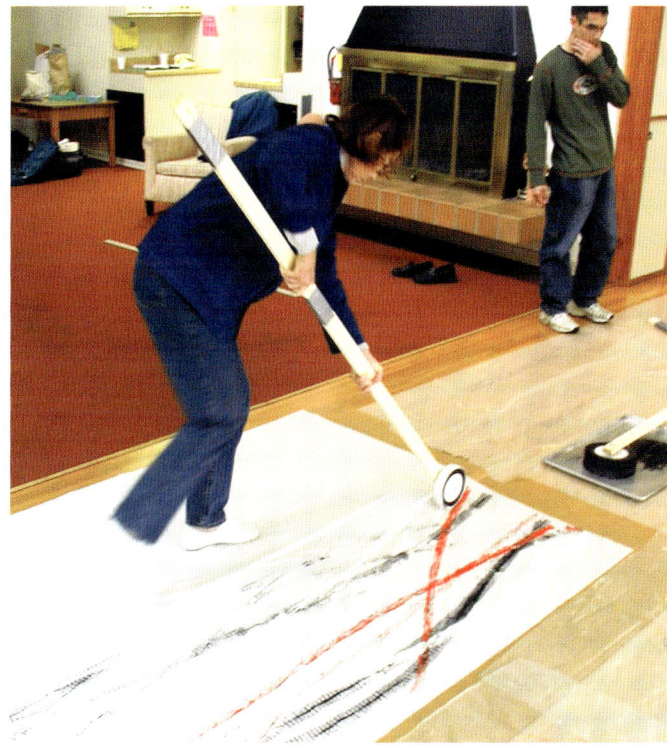

Supérieure d'Arts et Métiers (ENSAM). At Nicéphore Days she also exhibited *Art Volant dans l'espace et ailleurs*, a version of her Mountain Lake collaborative project of kites flying in virtual reality with interactive sound by composer Tom Johnson.[9]

To most people flying kites seems akin to children's play or simply an attempt to recapture innocence lost. For Jackie Matisse, however, it moves beyond simple adult desires for innocence and purity. Her kites with their colorful tails take Calder's conception of sculpture as movement and change (rather than mass in place) and infuse it with an animating spirit. That's why in the early 1970s she and six other artists including Tal Streeter, Curt Asker, and Istvân Bodoczky signed the *Art Volant Manifesto* (*Flying Art Manifesto*) declaring that the kite is "a vehicle joining the spirit and the physical … , the kite's flying line connects the human hand and mind with the elements."

For Jackie Matisse, kites are a vehicle that enables one to play with color, to "draw" lines in the sky, and to sculpt the air. As she has said, "my kites play games with the light, hide and seek with the clouds." The term "play," however, should be understood more in the philosophical sense of an inventive interaction of creative possibilities through chance and a loosening of personal control. This openness to chance as a genuinely collaborative force in her work has its roots in the1950s and '60s, especially in Gesture painting, Earth and Conceptual/Process art, and the ideas of John Cage.

In Gesture painting, including both French *Tâchisme* and American Abstract Expressionism, the mark left on the canvas is a physical manifestation of an action, a two-dimensional trace in paint declaring the artist's presence in the world. Such works were not pre-planned but the result of "situations" organized to open the artist to the unexpected so that painting would become

a path to the new and to self-discovery. Jackie Matisse shares with the *Tâchistes* and the Abstract Expressionist Gesture painters their openness to chance and the idea of art as a performative act. However, her kite drawings are three-dimensional and made, literally, in the vastness of empty space. They leave no physical trace because their lines are not material manifested on a ground, but lines only in the sense in which we would speak of a "bee" line, a direction or motion of an object — real or imagined — in and through space. Thus, the sculptural forms her kites locate in space are unstable and transitory, continually coming into being and, at the same time, continually disappearing into nothingness. If they are to be understood as betraying the artist's existential presence, it is at best a fleeting, transitory presence existing only as long as the mind can embrace them as object and concept.

In their conceptual and environmental aspects her works have strong affinities to Earth and Conceptual/Process Art of the

° The Chalon-sur-Saône exhibition was at the Espace des Arts Gallery in connection with the New Technologies in Contemporary Art Conference/Nicephore Days Conference of New Technologies at ENSAM, where the author spoke about Matisse's work in the symposium. In 2004 Matisse's kite tails also became stage sets for a Merce Cunningham Dance Company performance at the Joyce Theater in New York City. The most recent exhibition of her kites, *Jackie Matisse: Jeux d'espace*, was at the Musée Matisse, Le Cateau-Cambrésis, France, 6 July–22 Sept. 2013; the museum was founded by her grandfather Henri.

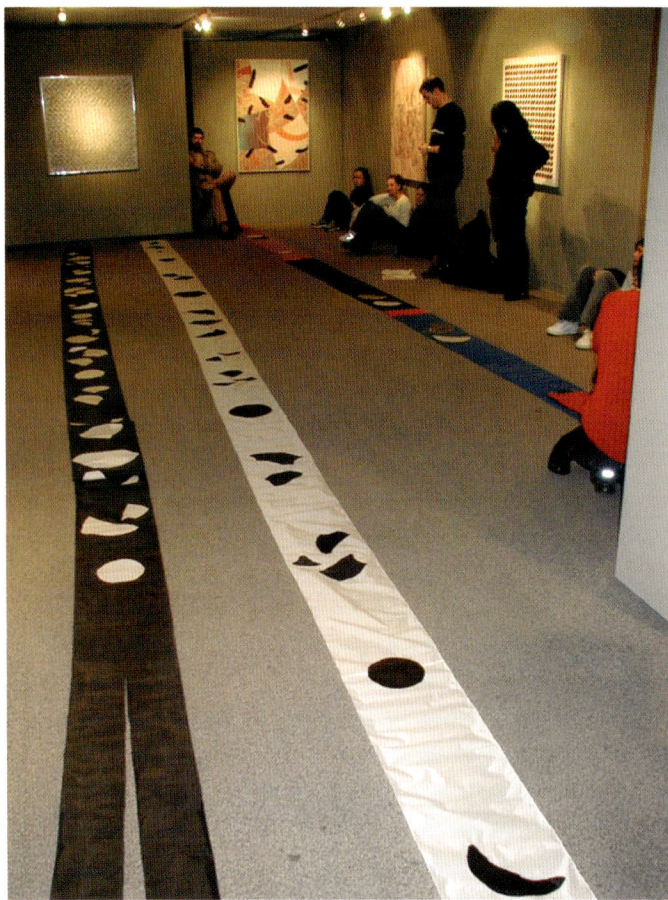

Students attend the opening of
Jackie Matisse's exhibition in
Virginia Tech's Perspective Gallery

1960s, for example, Michael Heizer's motorcycle drawings in the Nevada desert, the airborne sculpture of Otto Piene and Group Zero in Düsseldorf, and the work of Hans Haacke, specifically his 1967 *Sky Line*. *Sky Line* was a series of helium-filled balloons strung on a line like pearls; when it was released in Central Park it floated upwards, creating an actual, physical line in the sky whose shape was determined by chance by the breeze, thus diminishing the role of the artist in the work's final actualization.

This de-centralization of the artistic presence in *Sky Line* reflects the ideas of Cage who, already in the 1950s, tried

to free art from individual taste and ego by using chance methods derived from the *I Ching* to compose music. His solo piano composition *4'33"* (sometimes referred to as *Silence*) has no notes, so when pianist David Tudor premiered it in 1954, only the ambient sounds of nature were heard in the open-air concert hall. Cage extended his chance experiments to printmaking at Crown Point Press beginning in 1978 and to watercolors at Mountain Lake beginning in 1983.[10]

Jackie Matisse's work, even more than Haacke's *Sky Line*, is influenced by Cage, with whom she developed a close friendship through her stepfather, Marcel Duchamp. Nevertheless, her work remains independently her own because, unlike Haacke or Cage, she never tries to completely relinquish control. Instead, she actively flies her kites and in doing so draws sculptural forms in space that can be seen as extensions of her presence in the world and reflections of her "wishes and desires." On the other hand, the movements of her kites are only prompted by her actions, not completely controlled by them — air currents, air resistance, gravity, aerodynamics all play their part in flying her kites with her. In a kind of mutual action and interaction, the slightest of hand gestures are magnified but they are also altered by the forces of nature acting upon the kite. What results is a "give and take" between her hand and the forces of nature, and the resistance felt, as French philosopher Mikel Dufrenne would argue, is nature tugging back.[11] As Jackie Matisse has said,

*My kites push and pull on the wind. ... My hand grows longer and longer until I feel I am somehow in contact with that immensity into and out of which all things come and go.*

In a sense this is a post-Cagean sensibility because, in giving oneself over to the process of flying, one is neither the sole agent nor a passive witness, but a genuine collaborator with and in nature. This makes the sky an arena in which to both act and be acted upon, not only to allow, but to prompt the unexpected into being.

On a philosophical level Jackie Matisse's art is a reminder that we are not alone in the world, but a part of it, that our actions reverberate beyond ourselves. This gives her work a certain resonance with the environmental movement and the existential belief in personal responsibility. It also challenges Post-Structuralist claims that signs lack presence, that they no longer directly connect to lived experience, only to other signs. As Dufrenne would argue, encountering nature through the kite is a direct, lived experience, one that helps situate humankind in that larger world extending beyond the self — after all, when the artist tugs on the kite line, it is nature, in its fullness, that tugs back.[12] This situating of humans in the world through direct experience, it seems to me, is the intellectual underpinning of flying kites as an artistic endeavor.

Not surprisingly, in 1979, when one of her kites accidentally fell into the sea, Jackie Matisse got the idea of "flying" kites underwater. This led to collaborations with composer David Tudor and filmmaker Molly Davies in the creation of *Sea Tails*, a six-monitor, six-channel video installation with electronic score by Tudor. *Sea Tails* was shown at the Pompidou Center in 1983 and another version, titled *Sound Totem, 9 Lines*, was performed in the Whitney Museum Sculpture Court in

[10] From 1987 until his death in 1992, Cage annually made prints with Kathan Brown at Crown Point Press in Oakland, CA using chance procedures. Cage's Mountain Lake Workshops were in 1983, '88, '89, and '90.

[11] Mikel Dufrenne, *In the Presence of the Sensuous: Essays in Aesthetics*, edited and translated by Mark S. Roberts and Dennis Gallagher (NJ: Humanities Press International, Inc.; 1987), p. 132.

[12] Dufrenne, p. 132.

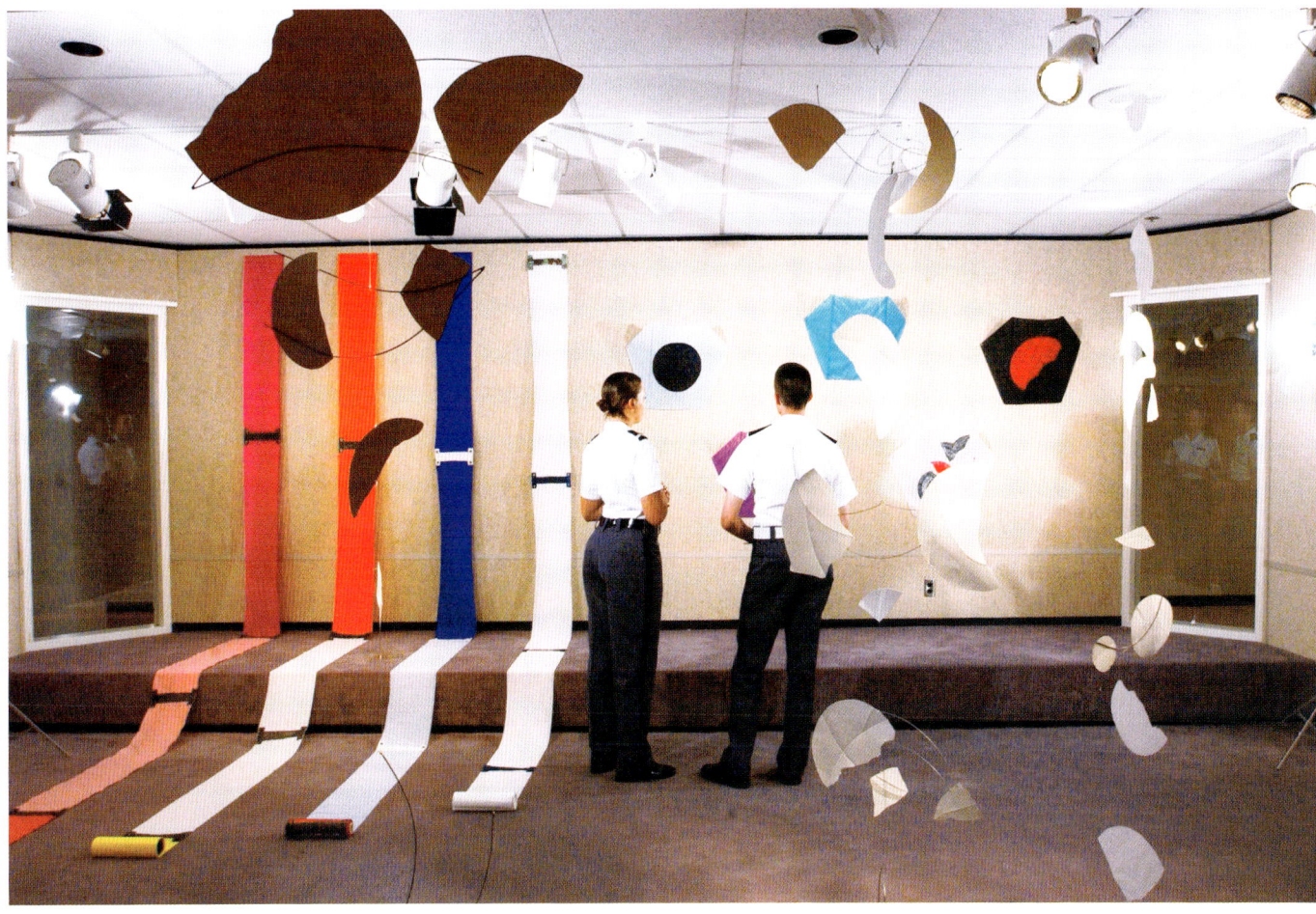

1986.[13] In a way these collaborations, which were radically different because now the artist was sharing control not only with nature but with two other artistic personalities, eventually led to her Mountain Lake Workshop project.

While the focus of the Mountain Lake Workshop has always been collaboration, over the years the collaborations have increasingly involved art and science, including Cage and mycologist Orson Miller; Kyoto minimalist Jiro Okura and the Brooks Wood Research Center; and NYC Department of Sanitation "artist-in-residence" Mierle Laderman Ukeles and microbiologist James Ferry. When Ray Kass happened to see photographs of Jackie Matisse's kites and a video of *Sea Tails*, there was no question in his mind: To "fly" those kites in virtual space at Mountain Lake seemed appropriate both to the artist's own experimentations and to the direction the Workshop had been going.

Thus began Jackie Matisse's virtual reality collaboration, one which furthered a shift in the dialogue in her art from nature to science/technology, two of her long-standing interests. From early on her kites have featured a black square on their heads as an homage to Malevich (1878–1935), the Russian Suprematist painter who related art to the very new technology of aviation — he often wrote of Suprematism as "aeronautical" and tried to express pure feelings unencumbered by physical material.[14] But Malevich never actually employed modern technology in his work, so his example remained abstract and imaginary. Matisse's first-hand experience of artistic and technological collaboration began in the 1960s when, through Niki de Saint Phalle, she met Jean Tinguely and Billy Klüver. Klüver,

an engineer for Bell Laboratories and a founding member of E.A.T. (Experiments in Art and Technology), collaborated with Tinguely on his *Homage to New York*, that animated sculptural machine which self-destructed in the MoMA Sculpture Garden in 1960. Klüver also assisted Robert Rauschenberg with his 1963 sculpture Oracle and was instrumental in the 1966 collaboration 9 *Evenings: Theatre and Engineering*, in which Rauschenberg and Tudor both participated.[15]

With this background plus Matisse's work with Tudor and

Davies, a supercomputing collaboration seems a logical extension of her ideas. Flying virtual kites, in one sense, realized both her and Malevich's ambitions towards creation of physically unencumbered form; they are, after all, pure gossamer veils of light, ghostly forms that can be wrapped around a person but cannot be touched. Trying to hold them is, as she has said, "like trying to hold onto a rainbow." But in another sense, her engagement with technology is more than a dematerialization of the art object as Malevich wished. It is an attempt to extend art's social dimension into the world of cutting-edge technology by

[13] *Sea Tails* was filmed over eight days in Nassau in the Bahamas where Matisse flew the kites, Davies filmed, and Tudor recorded sea sounds for his electronic score. *Sea Tails* is now in the Modern and New Media Collections, Getty Research Institute. In its title, *Sound Totem* recalls John Cage's 1943 musical composition *Totem Ancestor* and Jackson Pollock's early Abstract Expressionist paintings *Totem Lesson I* (1944) and *Totem Lesson II* (1945).

[14] See Herschel B. Chipp, "Kasimir Malevich, 'Suprematism'," *Theories of Modern Art: A Source Book by Artists and Critics* (Berkeley & London: University of California Press, 1968), pp. 341–346, esp. 343.

[15] In December of 1966 Klüver helped establish E.A.T. which was later engaged by Pepsi-Cola International to create the Pepsi Pavilion at the 1970 Osaka World's Fair, to date the most ambitious art and science/technology collaboration.

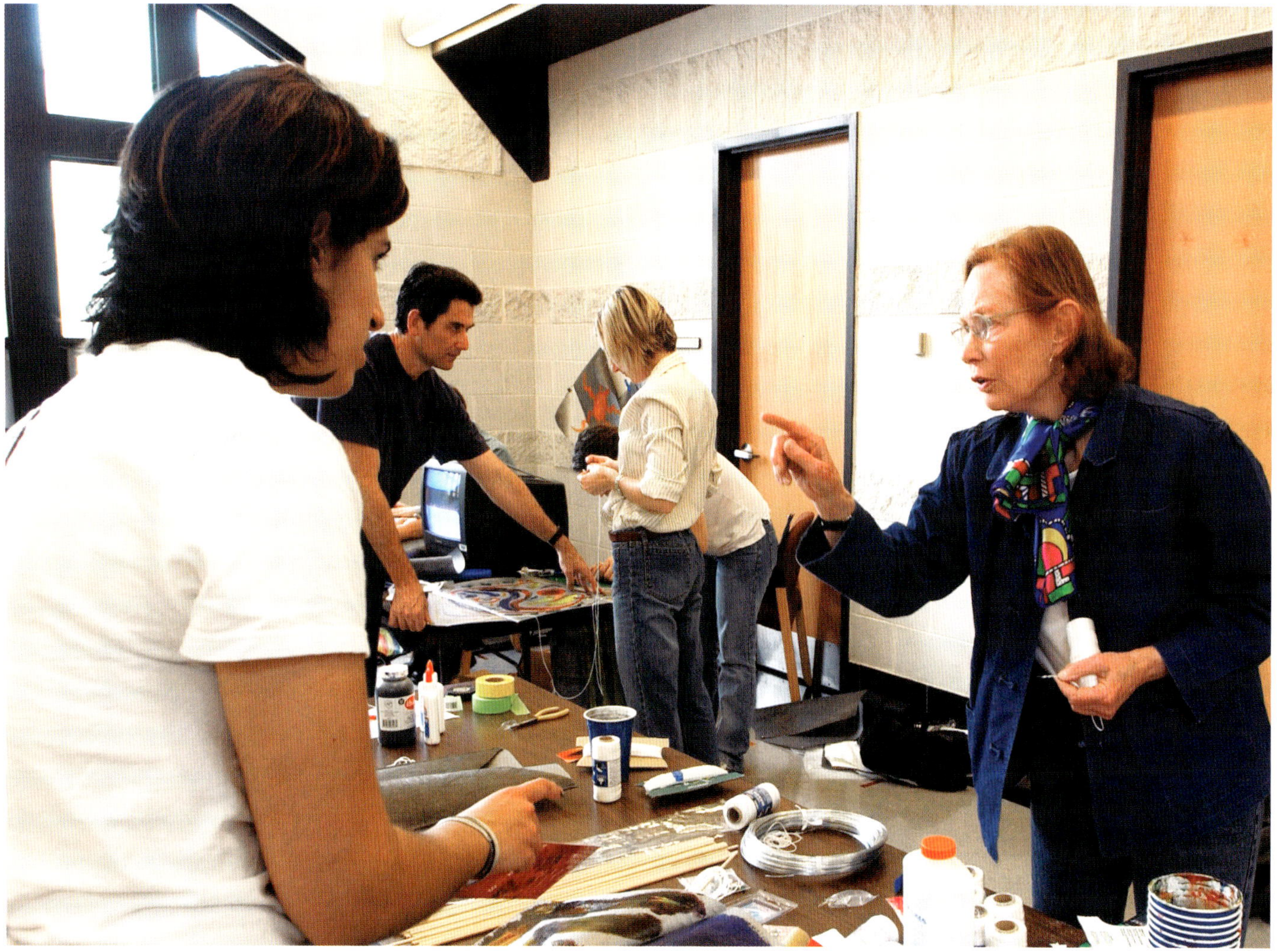

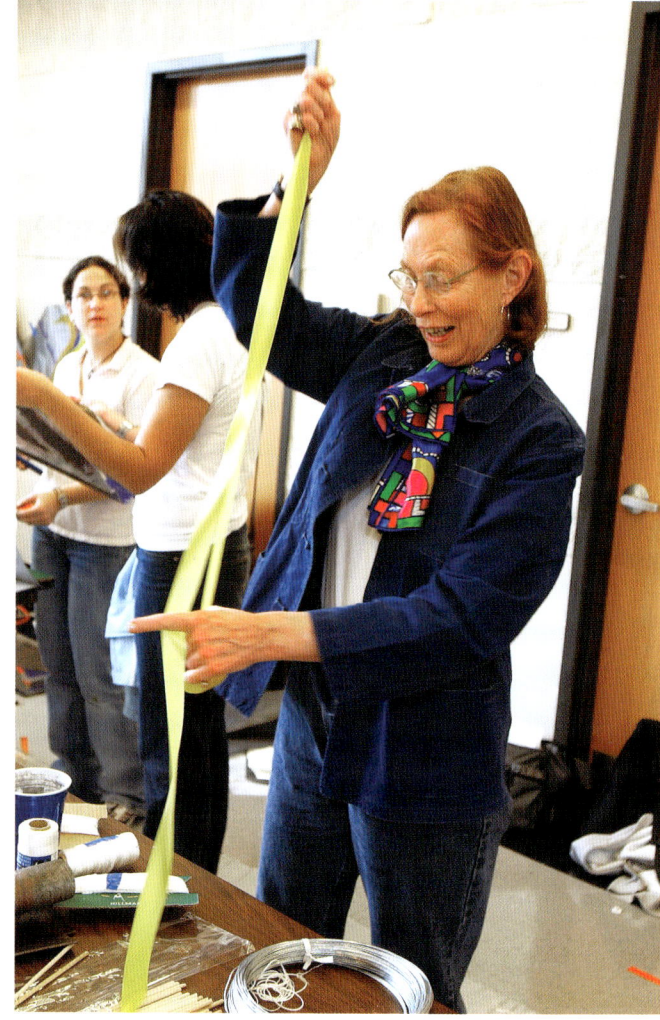

collaborating with that technology so the creative spirit of art and science can come together. This collaboration, at the level of code writing and performative interaction, transforms virtual space from a purely technological site, a locus of scientific innovation, into a metaphorical arena for art's social engagement with science and technology and the world at large. This collaboration is an attempt to work from inside science to integrate art and technology, to get artists and scientists to collaborate — without instrumental and economic imperatives driving their work.

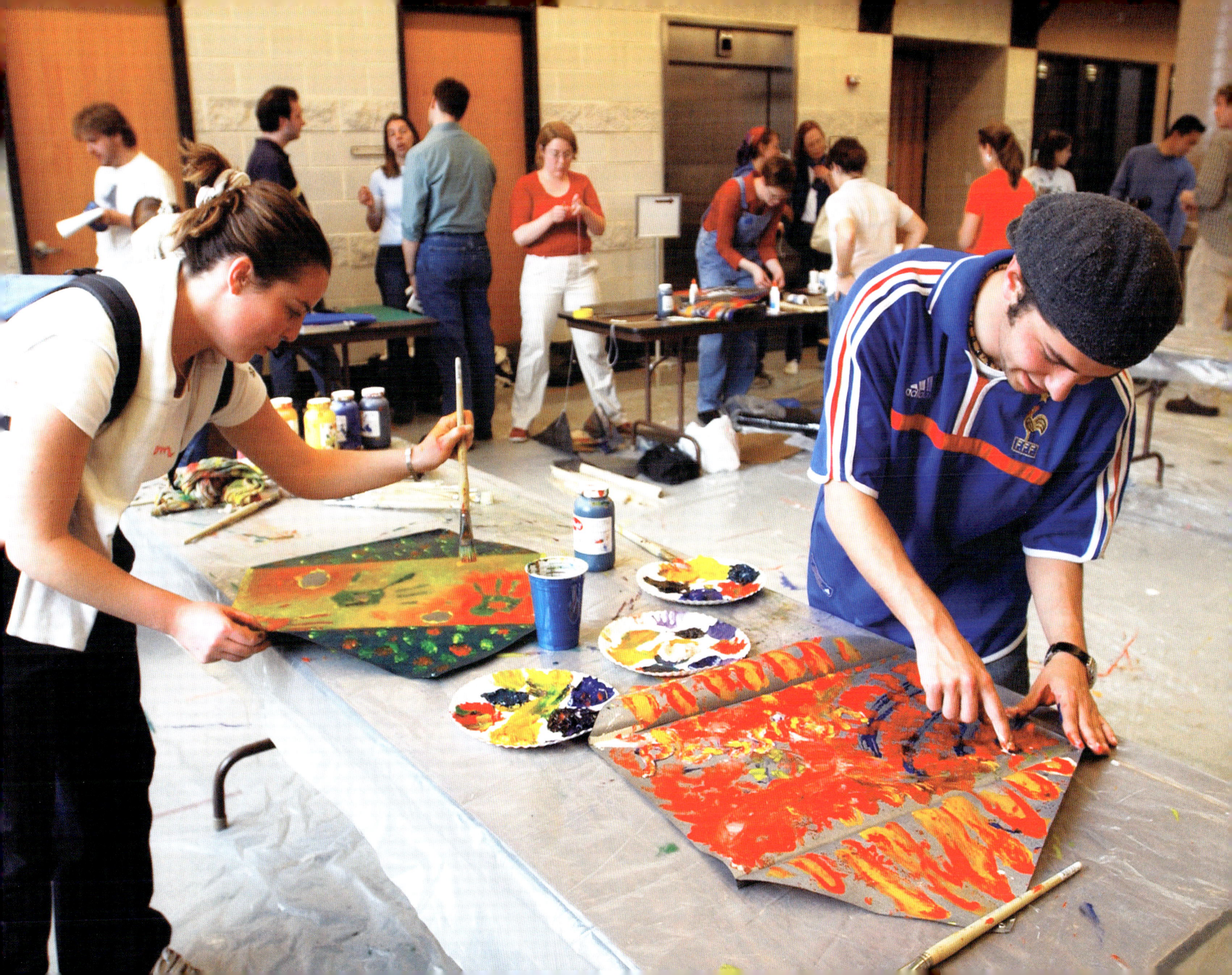

# KITES FLYING IN AND OUT OF SPACE AT iGRID 2002

TOM COFFIN in consultation with
RAY KASS and FRANCIS THOMPSON

(right) View of Matisses' kites flying underwater in Molly Davies' 1983 video *Sea Tails,* music by David Tudor

(far right) View of CAVE

(below) Jackie Matisse flying kites in the CAVE

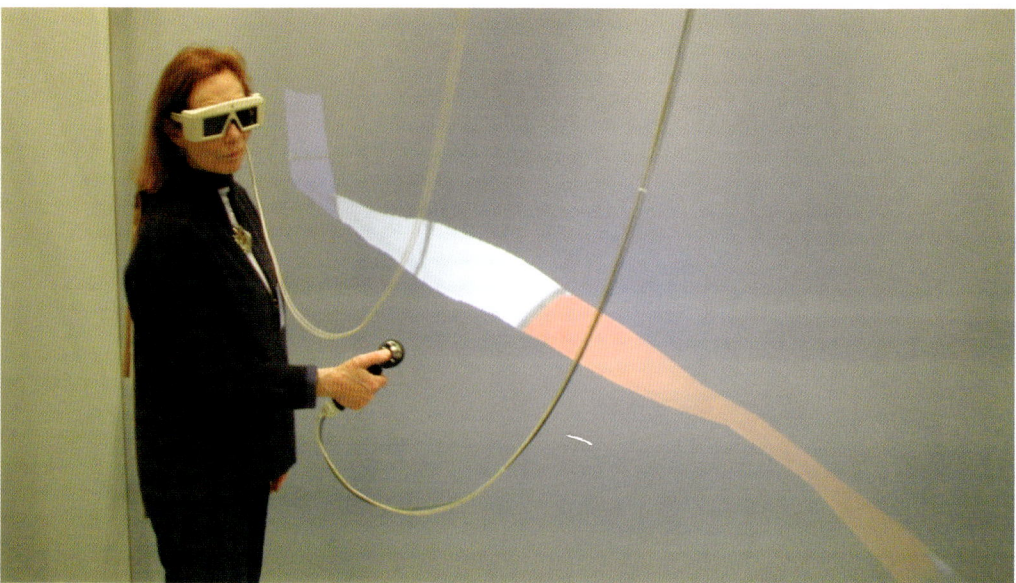

Jackie Matisse's *Kites Flying In and Out of Space* is the first high-bandwidth art piece ever created.[1] Exhibited in a CAVE at the iGRID 2002 Conference hosted by SARA in Amsterdam, the Netherlands, September 23–26, 2002, *Kites Flying In and Out of Space* utilizes a "grid" model for real-time steering of calculations on computers distributed over high-speed networks.[2] Each of the twelve kites appearing in the piece utilizes up to 15 megabits per second. This art piece uses a total of approximately 180 megabits per second in calculating the forms and theoretically could utilize even more. CAVEs around the world could potentially view this application through a connection to the Starlight high-speed networking program. The kite structures are so complex to simulate that a distributed computational model using processors on multiple machines is needed. *Kites Flying In and Out of Space* enlists servers distributed across the globe in Chicago, Canada, Japan, Singapore, and Virginia to calculate its forms. Each of these servers "streams" a single kite to SARA in Amsterdam, where the kites are then displayed in the CAVE™.[3]

A participant in the CAVE presentation can manipulate the kites and control the wind. When a person injects wind into the scene, messages are sent to all the servers. These messages contain information regarding wind direction and strength. The servers then calculate the resulting modifications to their individual kite structures. That information is then streamed back into the CAVE. This process is called real-time simulator steering, and it is the basis for the steering of high-performance calculations on supercomputers distributed over a high-speed network. This "grid" model has never been used for art prior to *Kites Flying In and Out of Space*. It is an example of "grid" computing resulting in an original work of art.

*Kites Flying In and Out of Space* is a collaborative art piece initiated by the Mountain Lake Workshop of the Virginia Tech Foundation in 1999. Jackie Matisse was invited to participate in an experiment in virtual reality using her imagery.

Jackie Matisse speaks of the piece: "These kites are evolved from my use of the sky as a canvas and from my need to use movement in my work. The square head is an homage to Malevich, the Russian Suprematist painter of the black square. The kites have very long tails, which are derived from a Thai serpent kite which I lost over a forest and which flew with unbelievable ease. It had such lift and in my mind it became a flying carpet and with it I could travel in the air. I began making [kite] tails and this enabled me to put color and line into the sky. I have always been interested in the connection between art and science. Since my kites were very hard to fly in all conditions, I experimented with alternative spaces such as underwater, video, and now virtual reality. The networking has enabled me to compose and fly many more kites than I would have been able to fly in real space."

The movement of the kites uses a physically based simulation technique called "mass spring" model. A mesh of approximately 250 points constructs each kite. The movement of the mesh translates to the movement of the kites.

*Kites Flying In and Out of Space* is scalable computationally as well as geographically. It is a very good test of high-speed networking because the application requires a multicast enabled network to accomplish communications. The kites have become a visual metaphor for network performance.

[1] By Jackie Matisse, in collaboration with: Tom Coffin, Ray Kass, Ulrike Kasper, Jason Leigh, Francis Thompson, Shalini Venkataraman, and Paul Weilinga. With special thanks to the following institutions: The Mountain Lake Workshop of the Virginia Tech Foundation, SARA (Amsterdam, Netherlands), Electronic Visualization Laboratory at the University of Illinois at Chicago, National Center for Supercomputing Applications at the University of Illinois Urbana-Champaign, Alliance Center for Collaboration, Education, Science, and Software (Arlington, Virginia), Sorbonne and La Cité de la Musique (Paris, France), New Media Innovation Center (Vancouver, British Columbia), Virtual Reality Development and Research Laboratory, Tohwa University (Fukuoka, Japan), Institute for High Performance Computing (Singapore), and Starlight (Chicago).

[2] A detailed paper describing the program for *Kites Flying In and Out of Space* is online at http://calder.ncsa.uiuc.edu/ART/MATISSE/

[3] CAVE™ is a copyright of the University of Illinois.

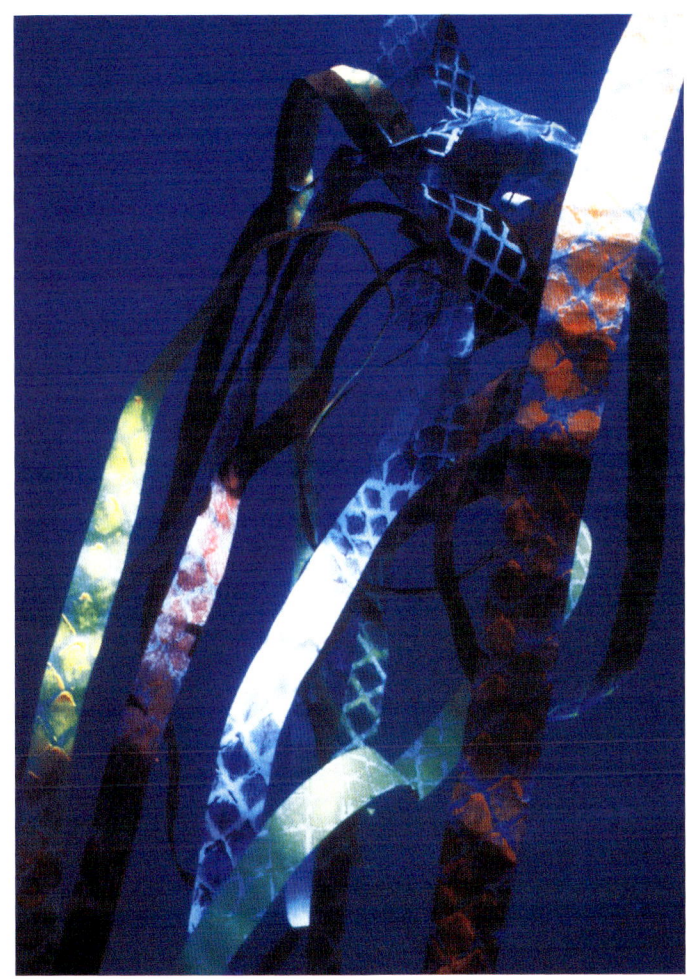

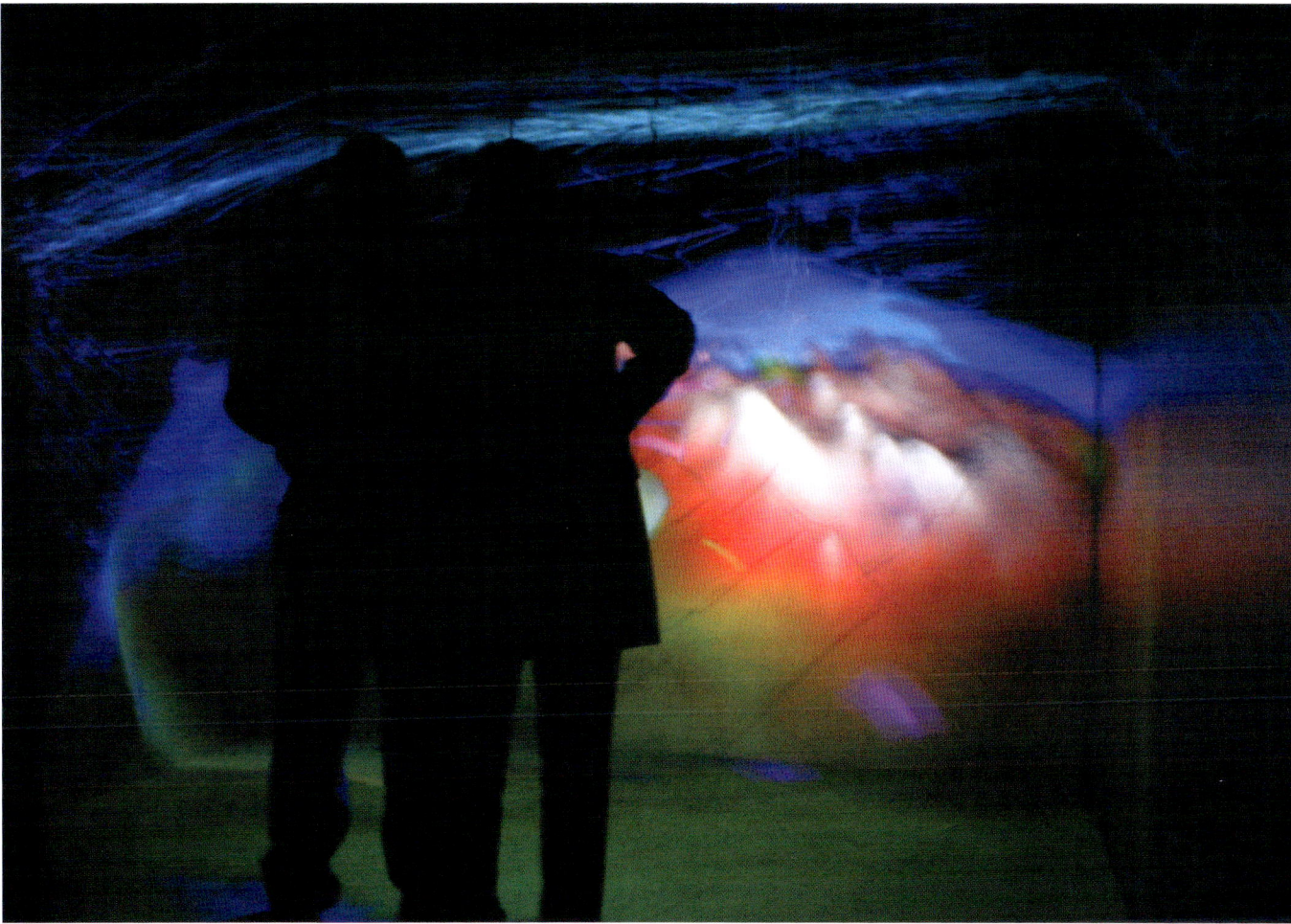

The kites have different sections, and the movement of these sections indicates the size and latency of the network data. A fast and smooth-moving kite represents a good connection. A slow and jerkily moving kite indicates a network connection with a problem. In this way, network performance can be visualized.

# BRUCE McCLURE:
## *ROTO-OPTICS* AND BEYOND

RAY KASS

Bruce McClure was a regular participant in the Mountain Lake Workshop in the 1980s and had the opportunity to work closely with composer John Cage (1912–1992) in two extensive workshops in which he assisted Cage and kept a diary of the workshop activities. Later, in New York City, he pursued an active acquaintance with Cage, who I believe exercised an encouraging influence on Bruce's developing artwork.

In the summer of 1995 McClure conducted the first Mountain Lake Workshop of his own devising. "Roto-Optics," as it was named, focused on the retinal experiments of Marcel Duchamp as seen first in his 1920 work *Revolving Glass Machine/Rotary Glass Plates (Precision Optics)* made with the aid of Man Ray; and then in his film *Anémic-Cinéma* (1926), done in collaboration with Man Ray and Marc Allegret. Using these early Duchamp works as a resource, McClure collaborated with community participants who individually painted disks that could be spun on fan motors. The *Roto-Optics* exhibition installed at the Armory Art Gallery as part of the summer Arts Festival transformed these colorfully painted spinning disks into a spectacular, almost hallucinatory, strobe-light-assisted installation. During the installation, gallery viewers could actually choose, from a selection of rotary discs, those they wanted to "play" and thus create their own personal art experience.

McClure's second workshop, "Microcinema/Filmstreams," put cameras in participants' hands and led them on an investigatory journey exploring the surface of media imagery as it transitions between film, video, and digital realizations.

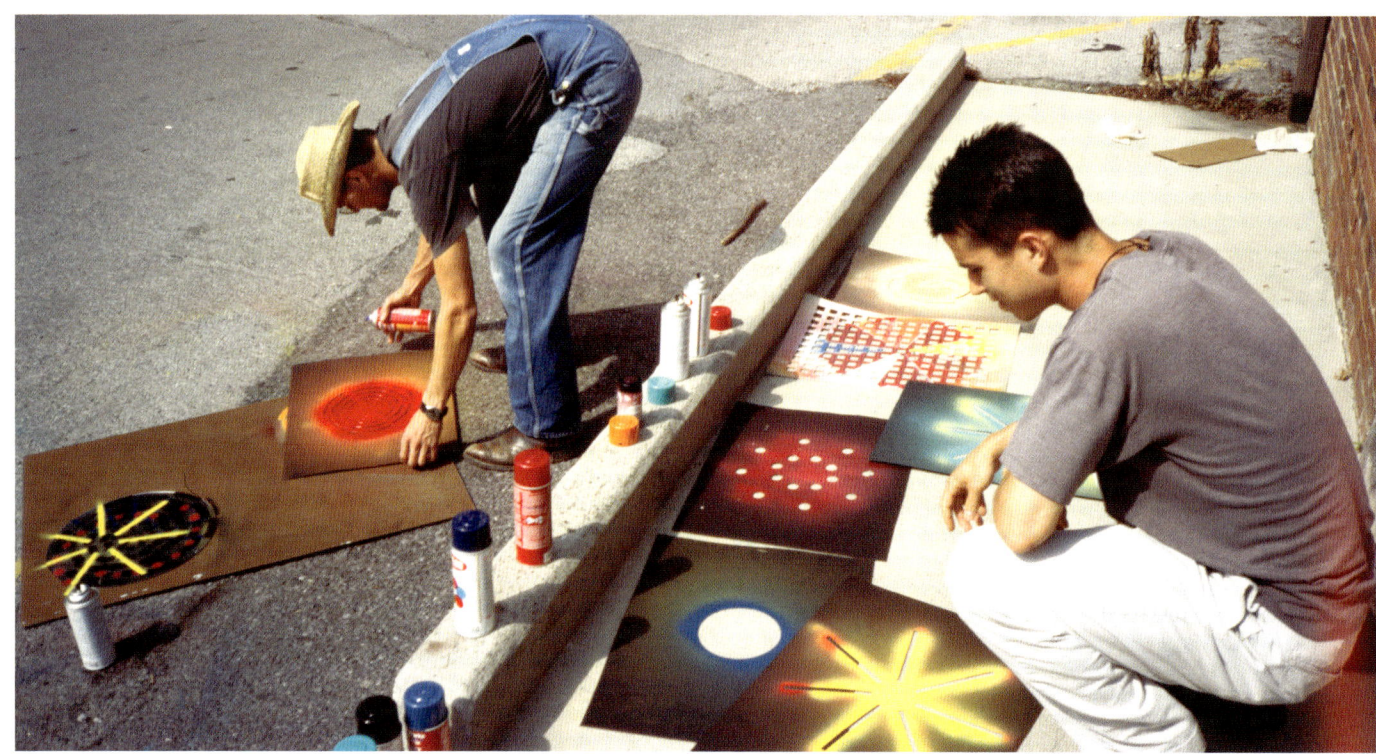

More recently he has developed a special interest in deconstructing the elements of film projection and imagery and combining them with "painterly" and performance impulses in the manner of improvisational theater. In his current work — which engages illusionist issues, three-dimensional elements, and projected surfaces of organic patterns — he relates an imagery of substance and shadow that transforms his pieces essentially into environmental works of performance art.

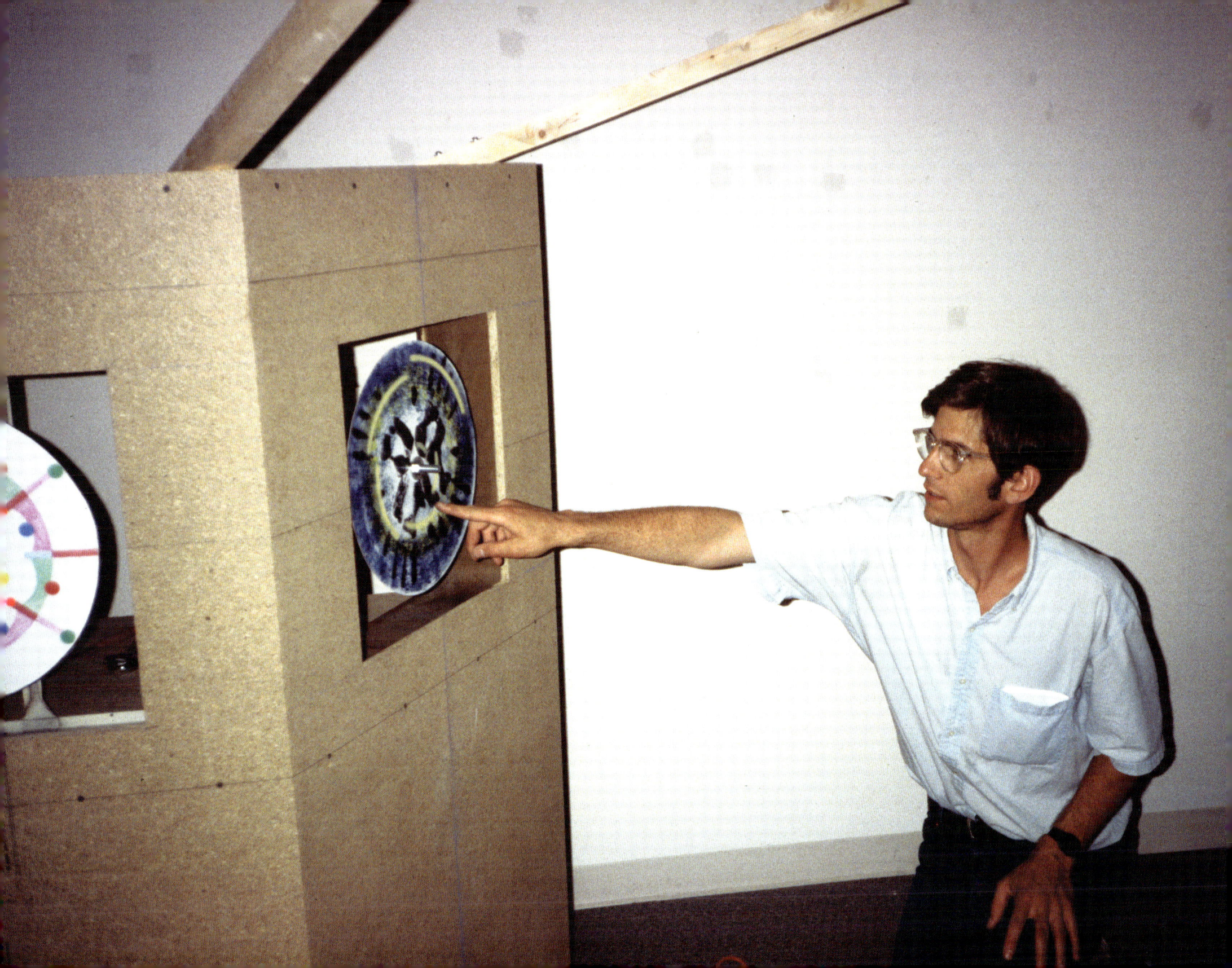

# MICROCINEMA/FILMSTREAMS, 2002

BRUCE McCLURE

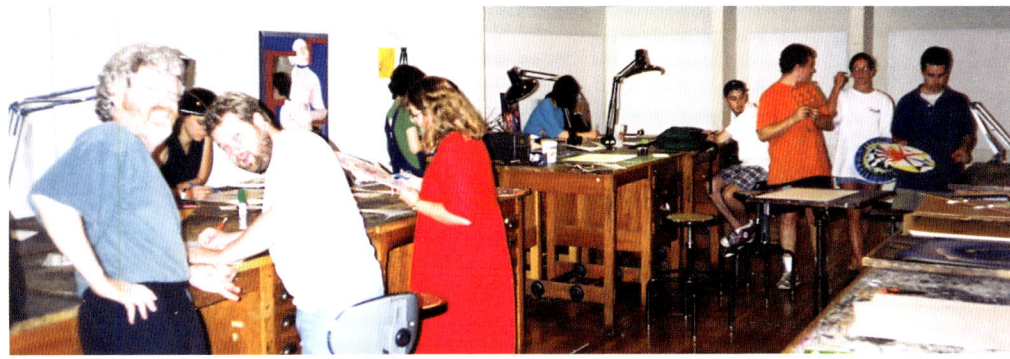

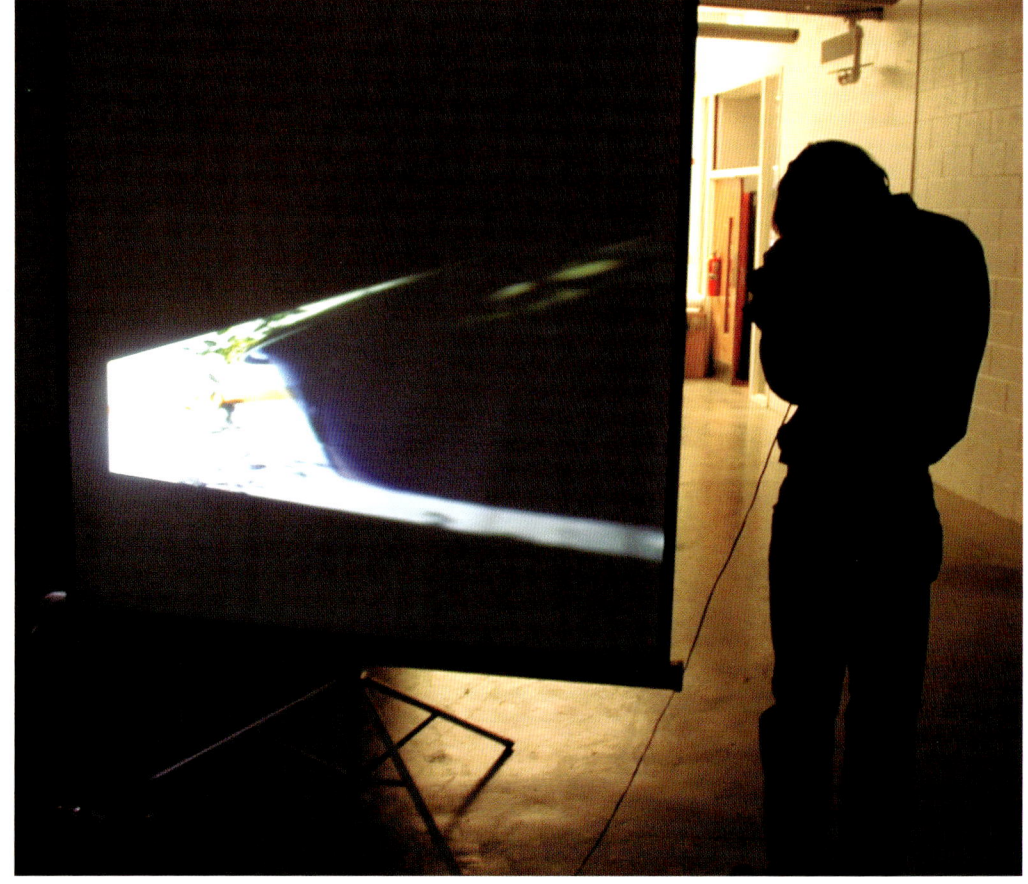

My Microcinema/Filmstreams workshop is about the experience of documenting film works in video and in digital media. Using a video camera, I seek to find an equivalence of projected light as seen on a movie screen. Of course, the resultant imagery necessarily amounts to a parting of the ways — twins separated at birth — because the narrative content of the imagery and the physical sensation of the two media platforms (film and video) are utterly different sensory experiences.

The workshop will seek to reintroduce participants to the light of the projector and how it is modified by film material which will, in turn, serve as the subject for the video camera. The film surface projected and reflected spins out as staccato gestures in time that will be subjected to a new rendering when seen as scanning video light from a television monitor or video projection system.

My projector performances contrast radically with assumptions most have about the "movies," subverting camera hegemony and tracing an open curve for film that approaches zero. The incandescent light staged in my cinematic hardware is preserved while at the same time I renounce the normative implementation of technology. Cinematic acts that I publically commission as performances are not virtual reality but a metaphor for consciousness itself and must be claimed, the terms negotiated and insisted upon.

# METEMPSYCHOSIS: "MET HIM WHAT?"

RAY KASS

(L-R) Sally Mann, Jessie
Mann, and Ray Kass.
Photo: Luke Demarest

*Metempsychosis*: I first encountered this marvelous word in a modern literary masterpiece, James Joyce's *Ulysses*; Joyce's terse definition follows on an inquiry by Molly Bloom to Leopold Bloom:

*She swallowed a draught of tea from her cup held by not-handle and, having wiped her fingertips smartly on the blanket, began to search the text with the hairpin till she reached the word.*
  *– Met him what? he added.*
  *– Here, she said. What does that mean?*
  *He leaned downward and read near her polished thumbnail.*
  *– Metempsychosis?*
  *– Yes. Who's he when he's at home?*
  *– Metempsychosis, he said, frowning. It's Greek: from the Greek. That means the transmigration of souls.*
  *– O, rocks! she said. Tell us in plain words.*[1]

The "transmigration of souls," and the sense of random searching, if not adventure, inspired by Joyce's reinvention of an ancient tale as a modern classic, guided me in organizing a collaborative Mountain Lake Workshop in which Sally and Jessie Mann (mother and daughter) and laser artist Liz Liguori made paintings on laser-exposed photographic paper, and then literally painted over a selection Sally Mann's famous landscape photographs. The works are diptychs that announce a new collaborative identity and a cosmological universe that the artists declare as their world.

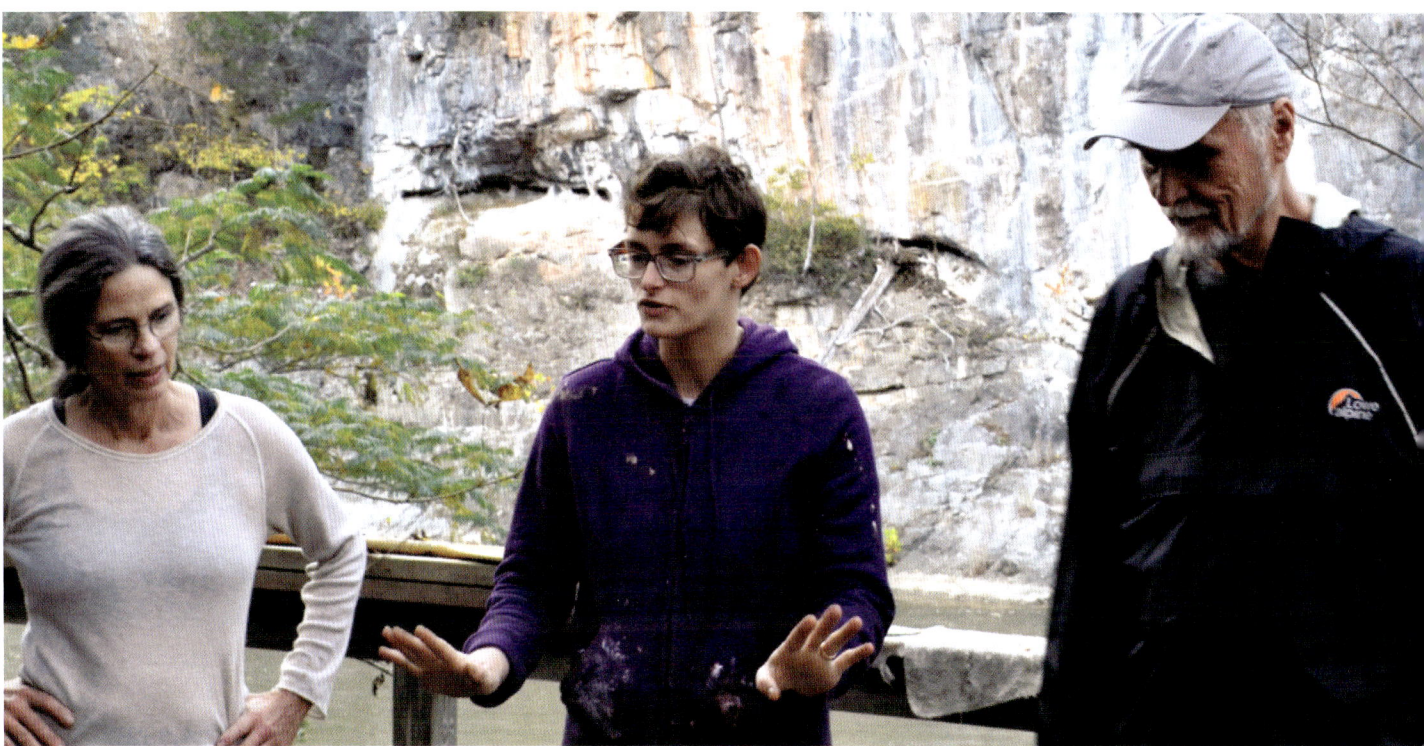

[1] James Joyce, *Ulysses* (New York: The Modern Library, Random House, 1934), pp. 64–65

# THE METEMPSYCHOSIS AND THREE GRACES WORKSHOPS: TAKING PHOTOGRAPHY IN NEW DIRECTIONS THROUGH COLLABORATION

JESSIE MANN

By reaching across disciplines and communities of practice, ideas gain in relevance and translational traction. The Mountain Lake Workshop is a wonderful way to make this sort of collaboration and translation possible, not only between artists, but also between artists and communities. The "Metempsychosis" and "Three Graces"[1] workshops brought together people from amazingly diverse backgrounds — artists working in different types of media including photography as well as non-artists. The work that came of these workshops would not have been possible without this collaborative opportunity. On a very basic, functional level, the work is large and the process to produce it requires many hands and coordinated cooperation, something that would not have been possible without a mechanism to support this level of group activity. On a more ephemeral level, the work wouldn't be what it is without the psychic contributions of the diverse team that brought it to fruition. Furthermore, the work would be impoverished in meaning without the involvement of the community at large. With sharing of the inspirational process across communities and between people, the meaning and purpose of this work, and of artwork in general, become enriched.

The work that came from these workshops is an effort at combination and transmutation. The process that was explored brings many of the principles of American Abstract Expressionist painting into the realm of photography. Art critic Clement Greenberg outlined the hallmarks of Abstract Expressionism saying "if the label 'Abstract Expressionism' means anything, it means painterliness: loose, rapid handling , or the look of it; masses that blotted and fused instead of shapes that stayed distinct; large and conspicuous rhythms; broken color; uneven saturations … ; exhibited brush, knife, or finger marks. …"[2]

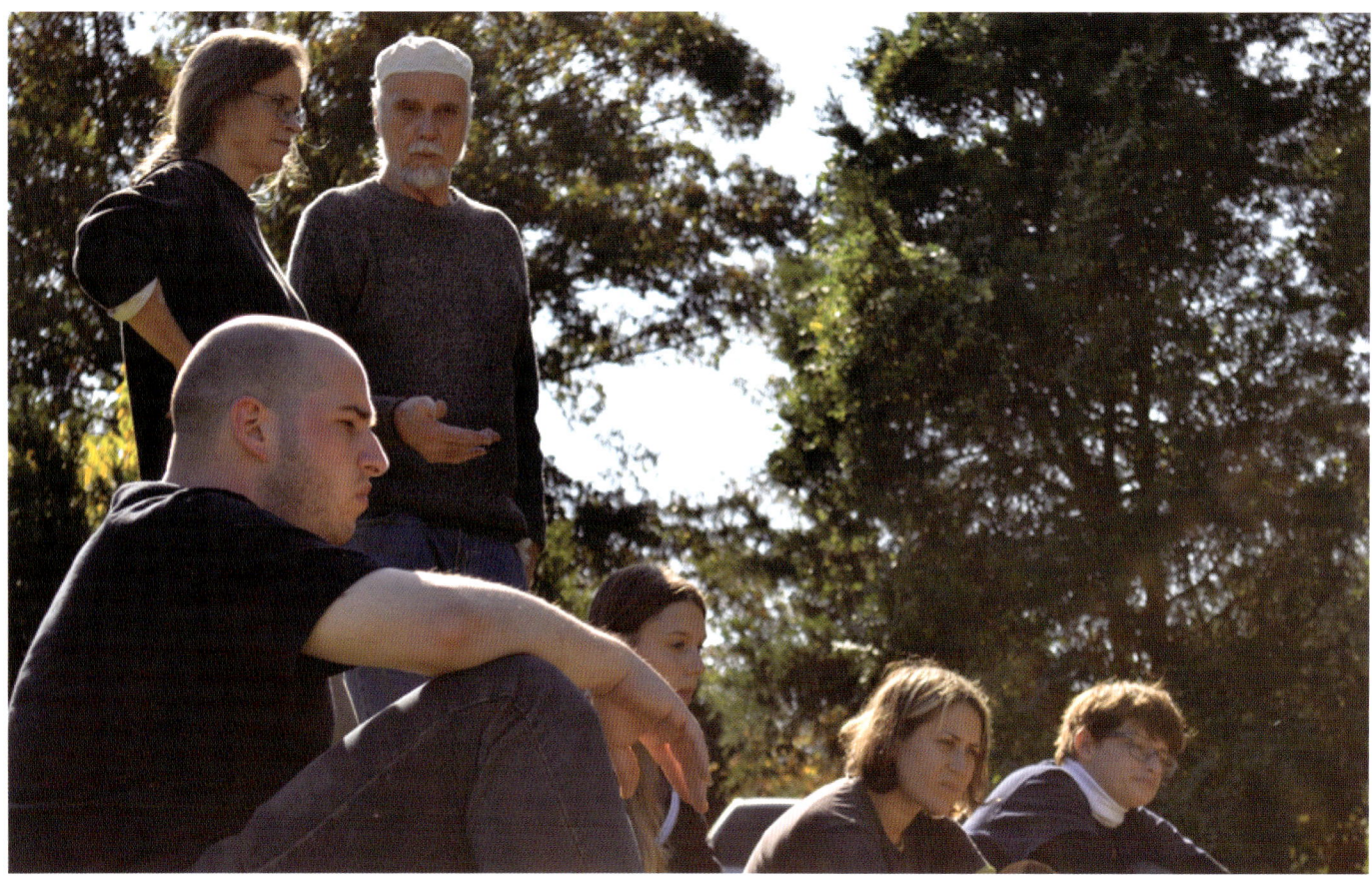

(above, L-R) Justin Nissley, Sally Mann, Ray Kass, Caitlin Mann, Liz Liguori, and Jessie Mann.
Photo: Luke Demarest

The work executed in the workshops is an attempt to re-create these elements but with photographic processes rather than paint. It is a rediscovery of the elements of photography, employed toward an "abstract expressionist" end. In the groundbreaking abstract images of Aaron Siskind (1903–1991), photography was reborn as an abstract medium. The photographic images that came out of these two Mountain Lake workshops, but especially the "electromagnetograms" (as we have come to call them) that came out of the Metempsychosis workshop, expand upon some of the same methods Siskind introduced in his own work in an effort to explore the essence of the medium of photography independent of realistic narrative, in the same way the Abstract Expressionist artists explored the essence of painting free of realistic narrative.[3] The electromagnetogram is an effort at isolating light, surface, saturation, and rhythm in the manner of Abstract Expressionism. In this case, we are using photo chemicals and lasers as a means to paint with light instead of pigment.

Collaboration with my mother, Sally Mann, on this project using the abstract expressionist nature of the electromagnetograms allowed us to explore a latent and, I feel, an often overlooked expressionism in her work. I have long believed she has taken

---

[1] The latter is described in Sam Krisch's essay in this chapter, "Three Graces in Public: Digital Montages."

[2] Clement Greenberg, "After Abstract Expressionism," in *Clement Greenberg, The Collected Essays and Criticism*, Vol. 4, *Modernism with a Vengeance, 1957–1969*, edited by John O'Brian (Chicago and London: University of Chicago Press, 1993), p. 123.

[3] The term *metempsychosis* comes from the Ancient Greek and refers to the transmigration of souls and rebirth.

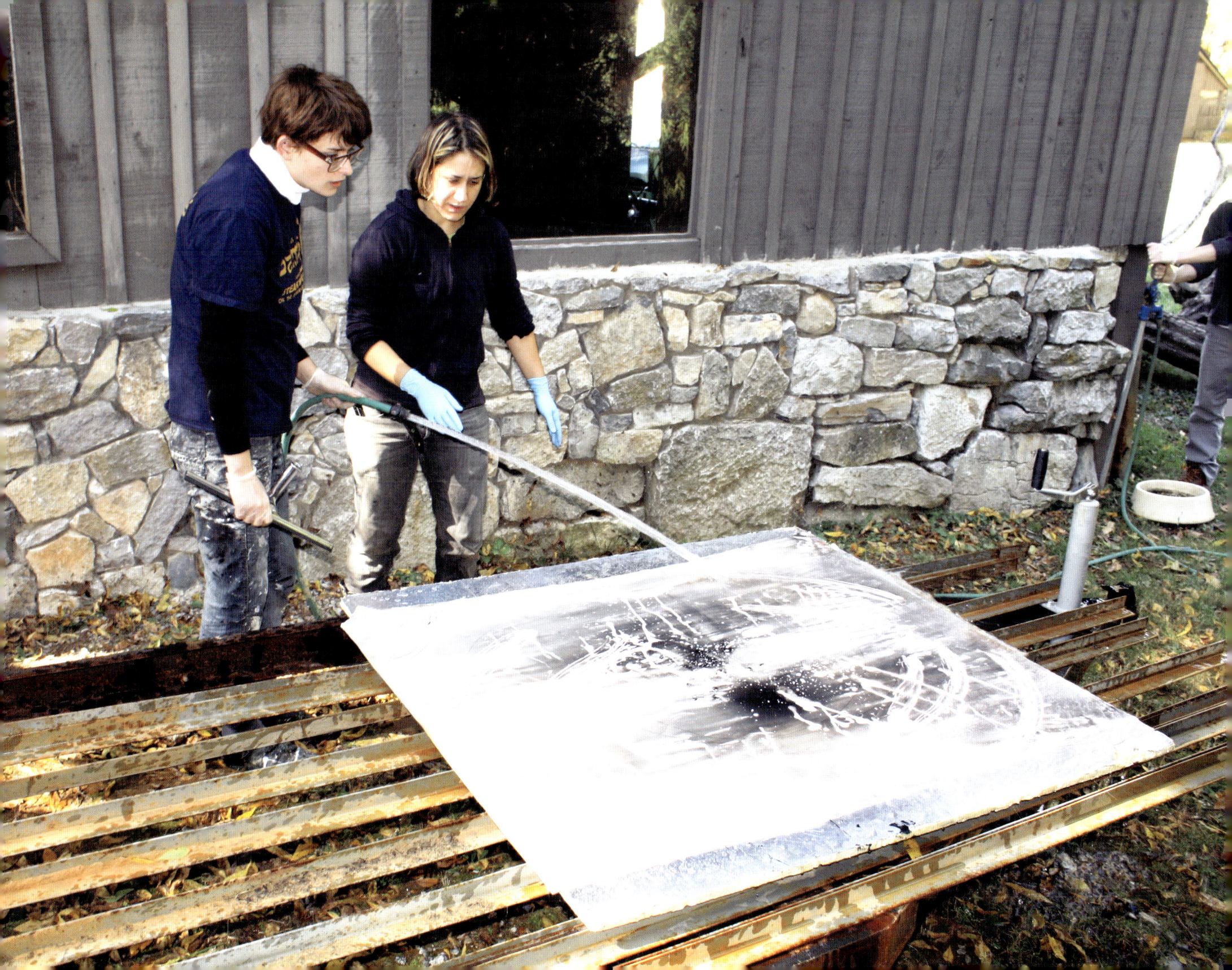

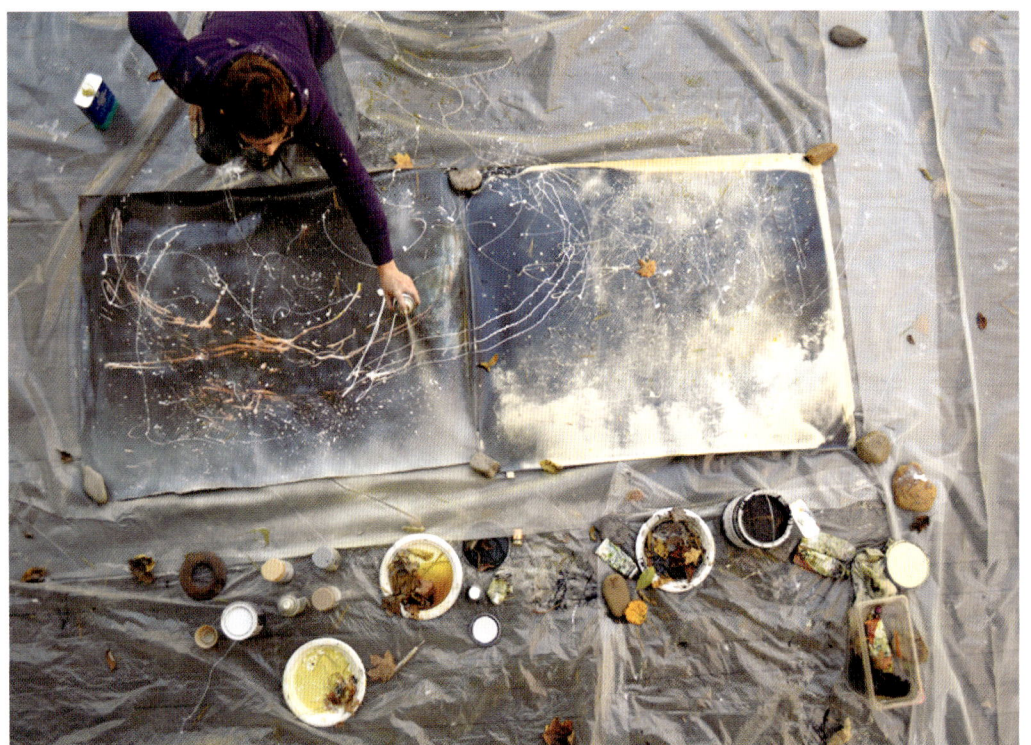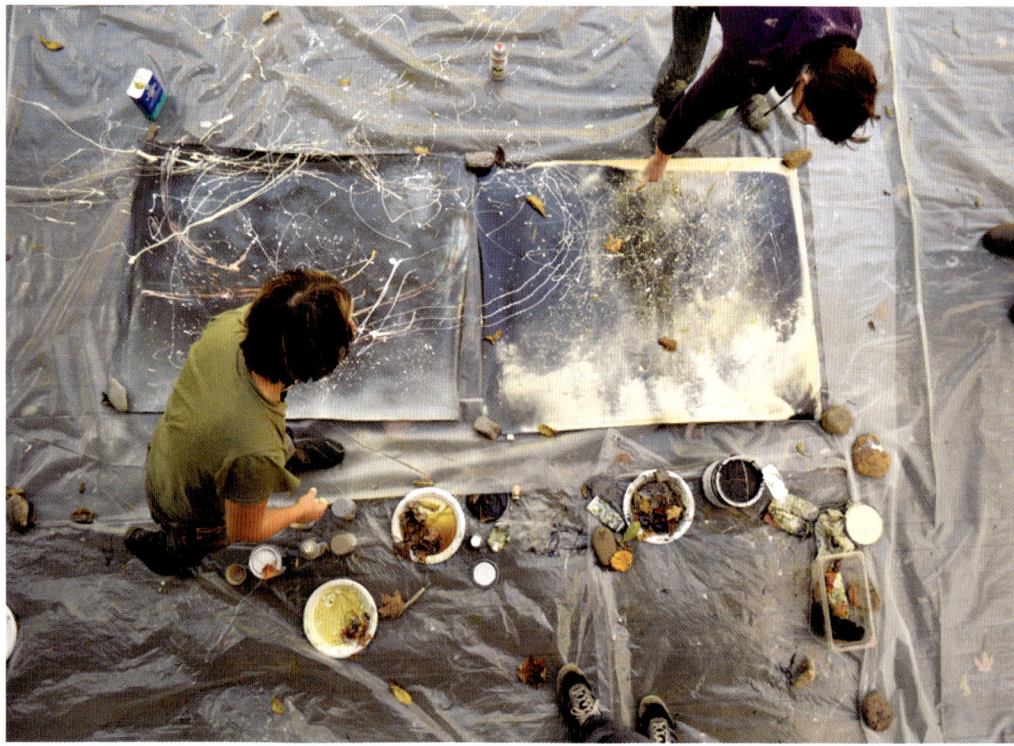

photography into the realm of Abstract Expressionism by emphasizing the surface, the mark, and the accident in her work.

Our collaboration allowed me to explore the overlap between photography and painting, so often held up as contrasts to each other. My mother's work has always been defined by the photographic printing process and, like abstract painting, addresses process as much as, if not more than, representation. And more generally, photography, particularly non-digital photography, is increasingly playing with chance effects, distressed surfaces, texture, and the "exhibited finger mark." This collaboration became a wonderful way to make that shift from photograph-as-representation-of-reality to photograph-as-signifier-of-process explicit, to directly address the meaning afforded the photographic process now that digital photography has taken over historical and documentary functions, the very functions traditional "wet" photography

once wrested from painting. By using photo chemicals as paint, by deconstructing the photographic process, and by using light and chance in new ways, it was possible to address directly the abstraction that my mother's work so brilliantly flirts with.

Furthermore, in terms of collaborations, in the same way that some of the most important scientific discoveries come from collaborations across disciplines, so too for art. It can take a lifetime of steady work to master one medium or area of study, and to bring together diverse practitioners, each with years of practice and focus, creates a synergy the result of which is much greater than the sum of the parts that compose it. The national scientific grant structure is increasingly favoring trans-disciplinary proposals, and the Mountain Lake Workshop is the artistic equivalent of this effort, but one which has been in existence, well ahead of the intellectual curve, for decades. Without these efforts and the support this workshop provides,

it is hard to even contemplate the intellectual impoverishment we would suffer. It was a great honor to be involved in such an extraordinary and prescient support structure, and I, for one, look forward with great anticipation to the synergies and collaborations that will come of it in the years to come.

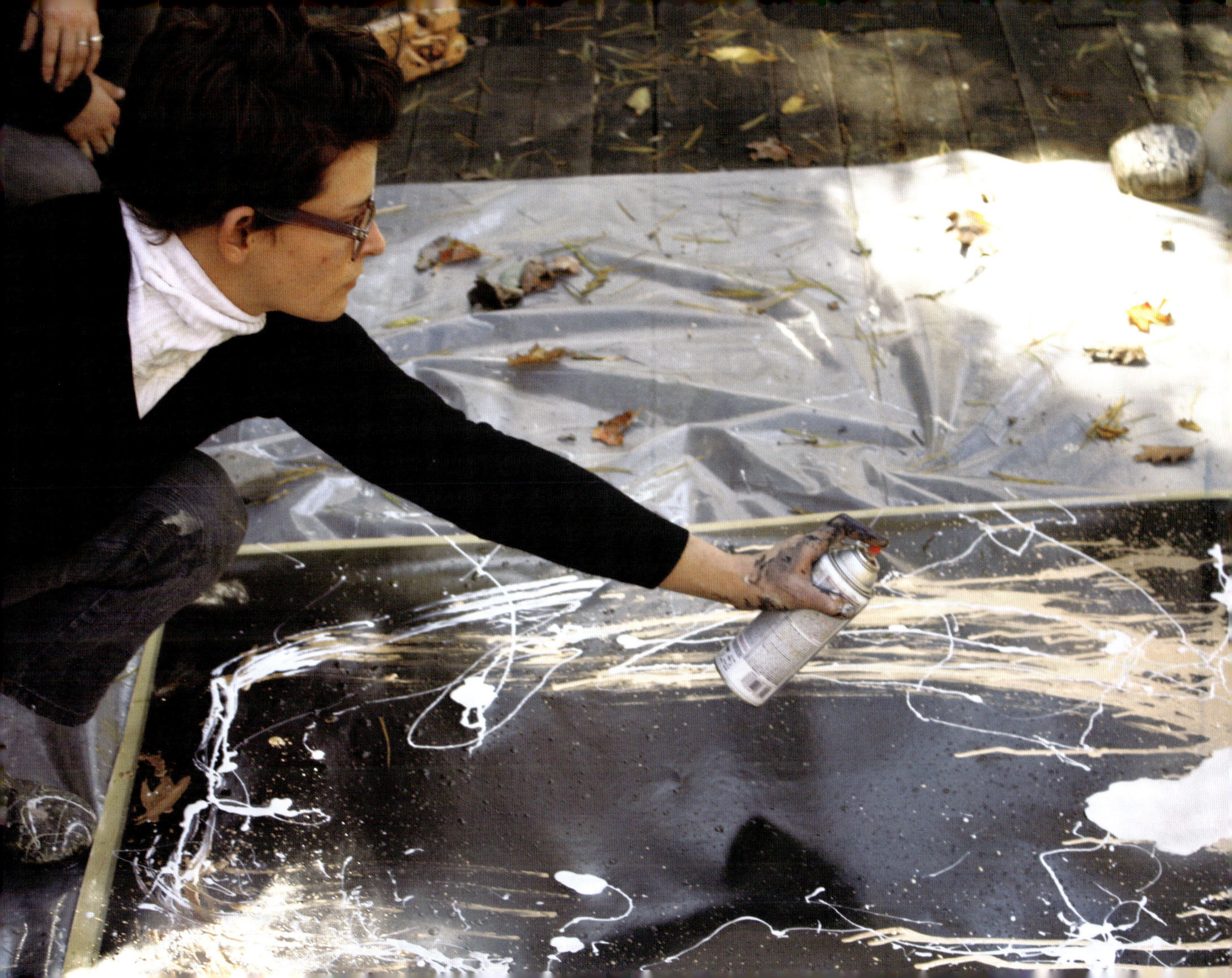

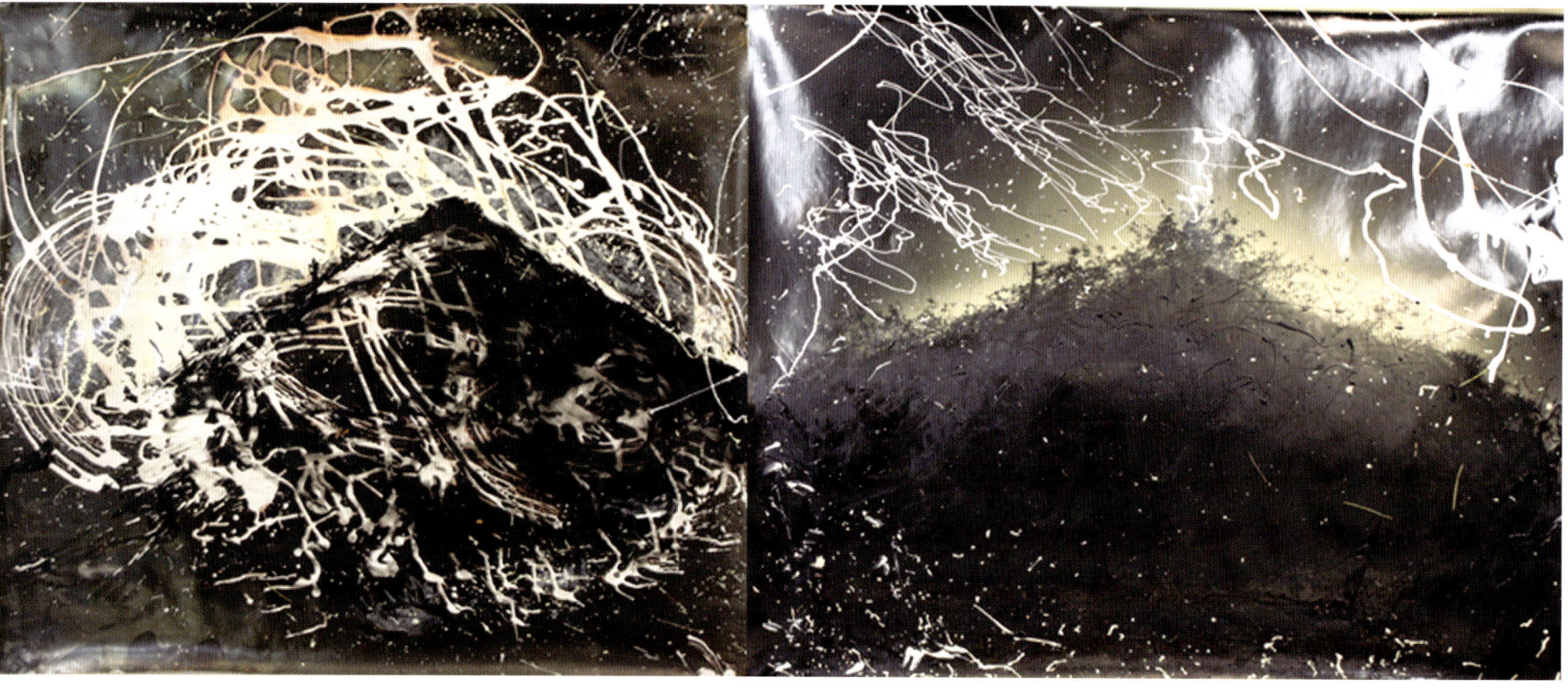

Sally and Jesse Mann with Liz Liguori and The Mountain Lake Workshop, *Metempsychosis Diptych #1*, 2011, enamel oil paint, developer, photography and and laser imagery on photographic paper, 40 x 100 in. (101.6 x 254 cm)

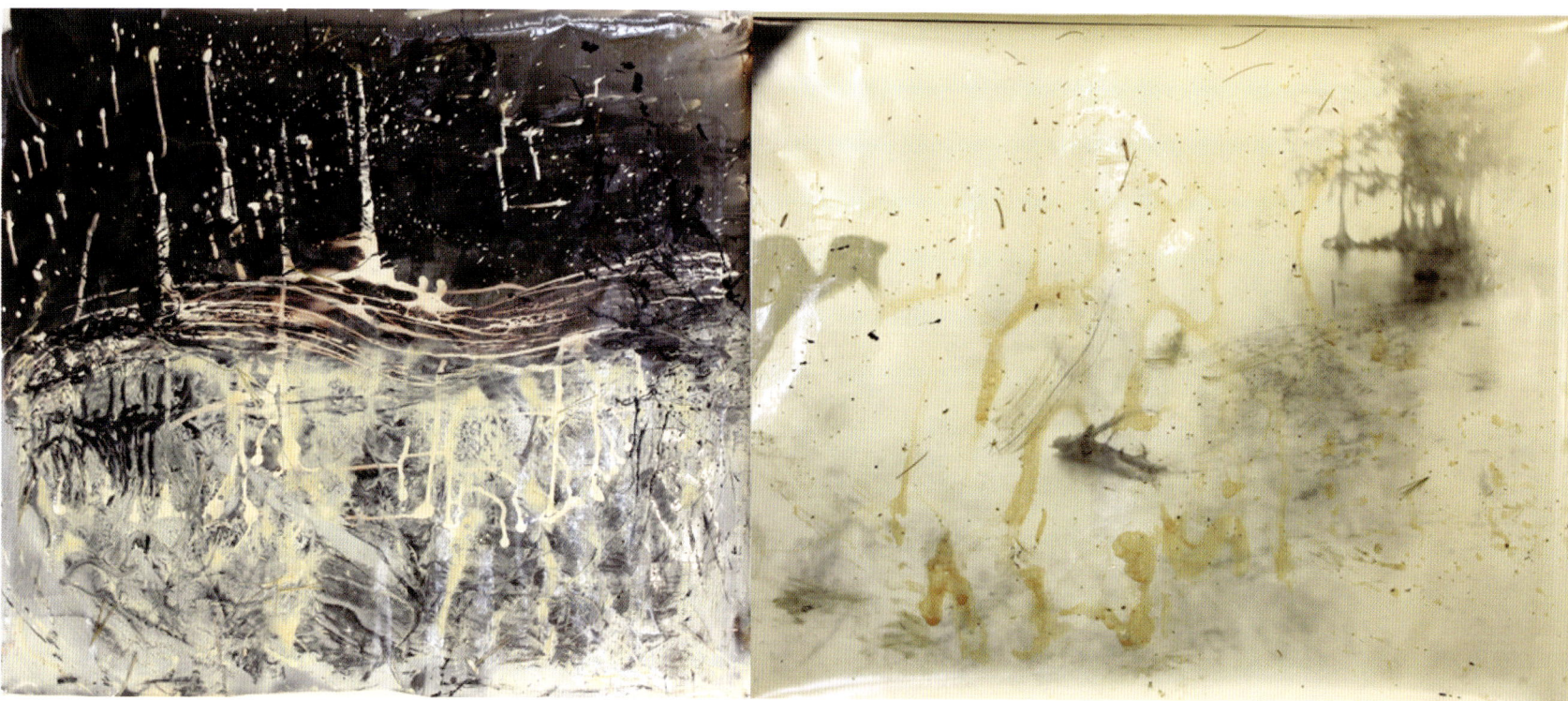

Sally and Jesse Mann with Liz Liguori and The Mountain Lake Workshop, *Metempsychosis Diptych #3*, 2011, enamel oil paint, developer, photography and and laser imagery on photographic paper, 40 x 100 in. (101.6 x 254 cm),

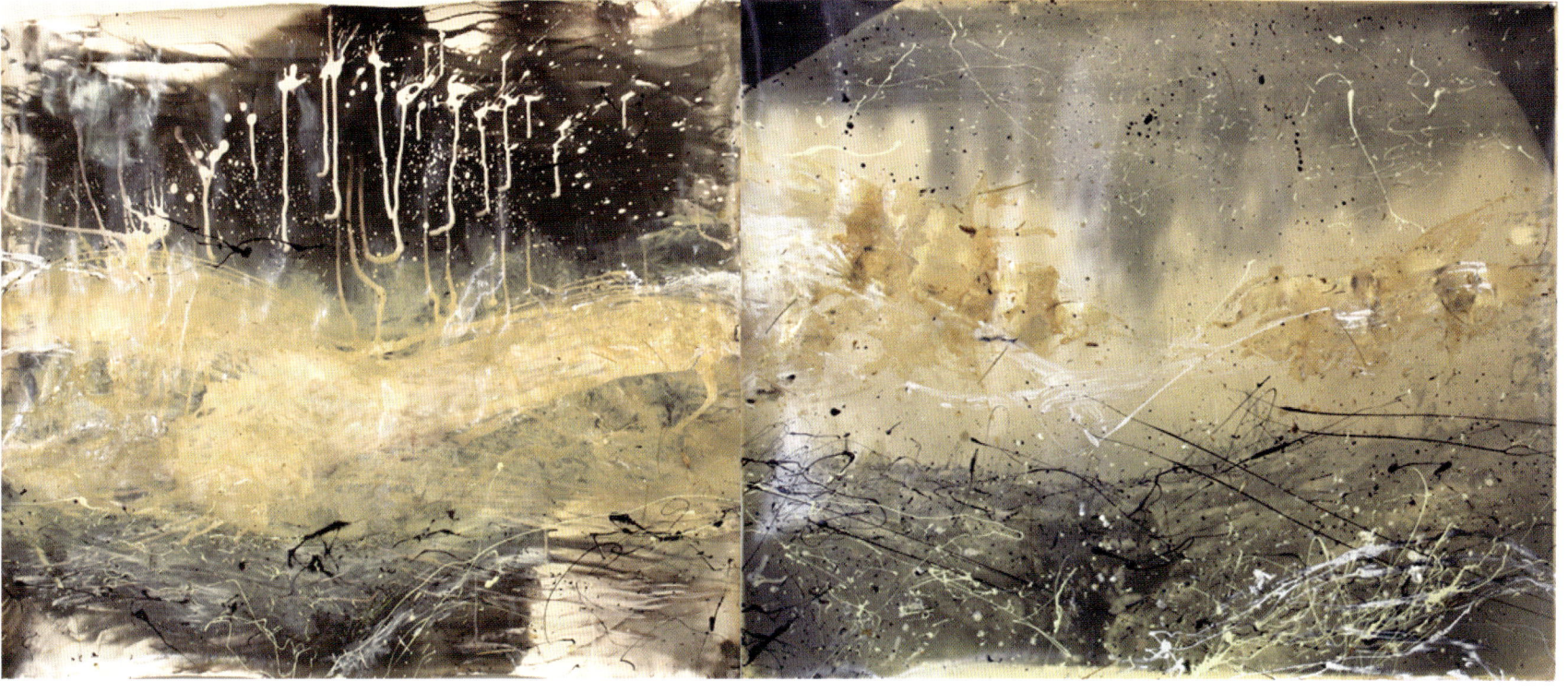

Sally and Jesse Mann with Liz Liguori and The Mountain Lake Workshop, *Metempsychosis Diptych #4*, 2011, enamel oil paint, developer, photography and and laser imagery on photographic paper, 40 x 100 in. (101.6 x 254 cm)

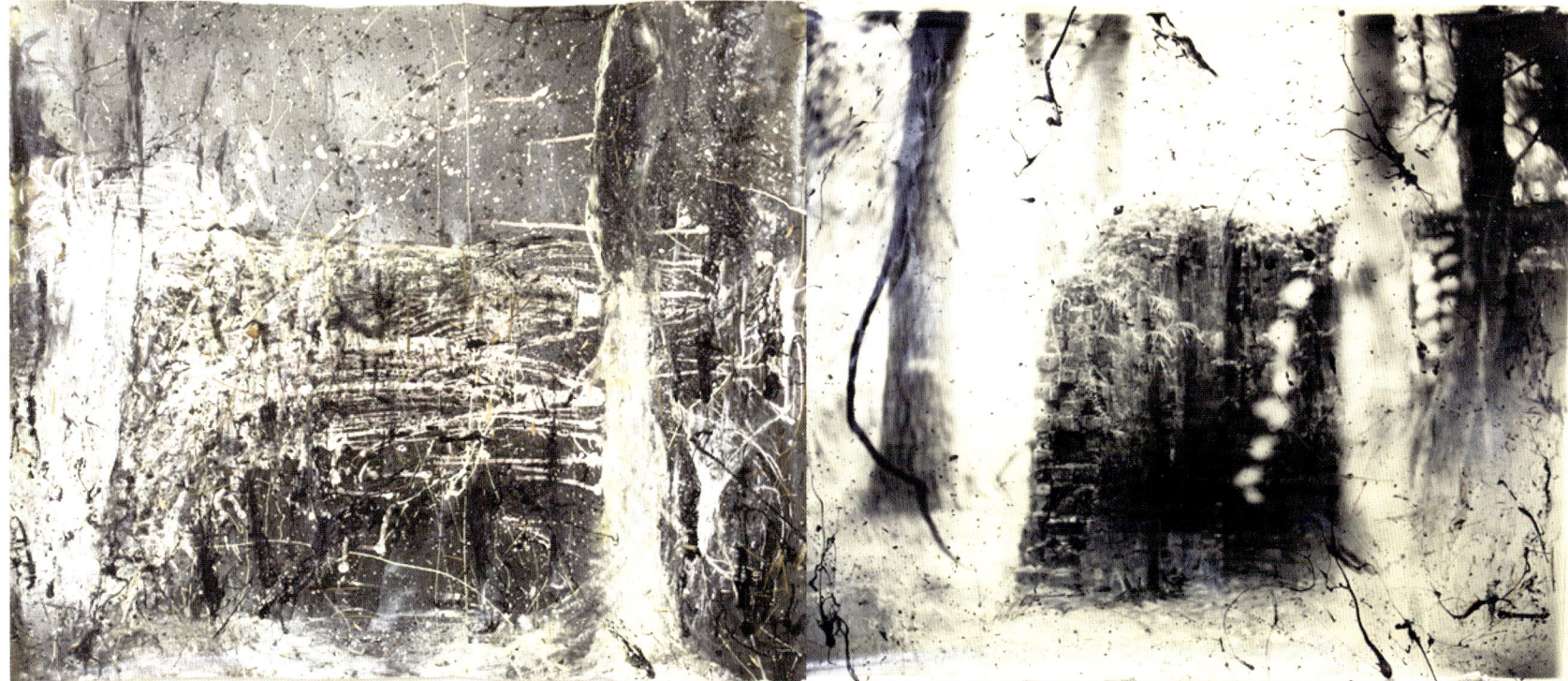

Sally and Jesse Mann with Liz Liguori and The Mountain Lake Workshop, *Metempsychosis Diptych #2*, 2011, enamel oil paint, developer, photography and and laser imagery on photographic paper, 40 x 100 in. (101.6 x 254 cm)

Sally and Jesse Mann, with Liz Liguori and The Mountain Lake Workshop, *Three Graces Diptych #1*, 2013, enamel oil paint, developer, photography and laser imagery on photographic paper, 40 x 100 in. (101.6 x 254 cm)

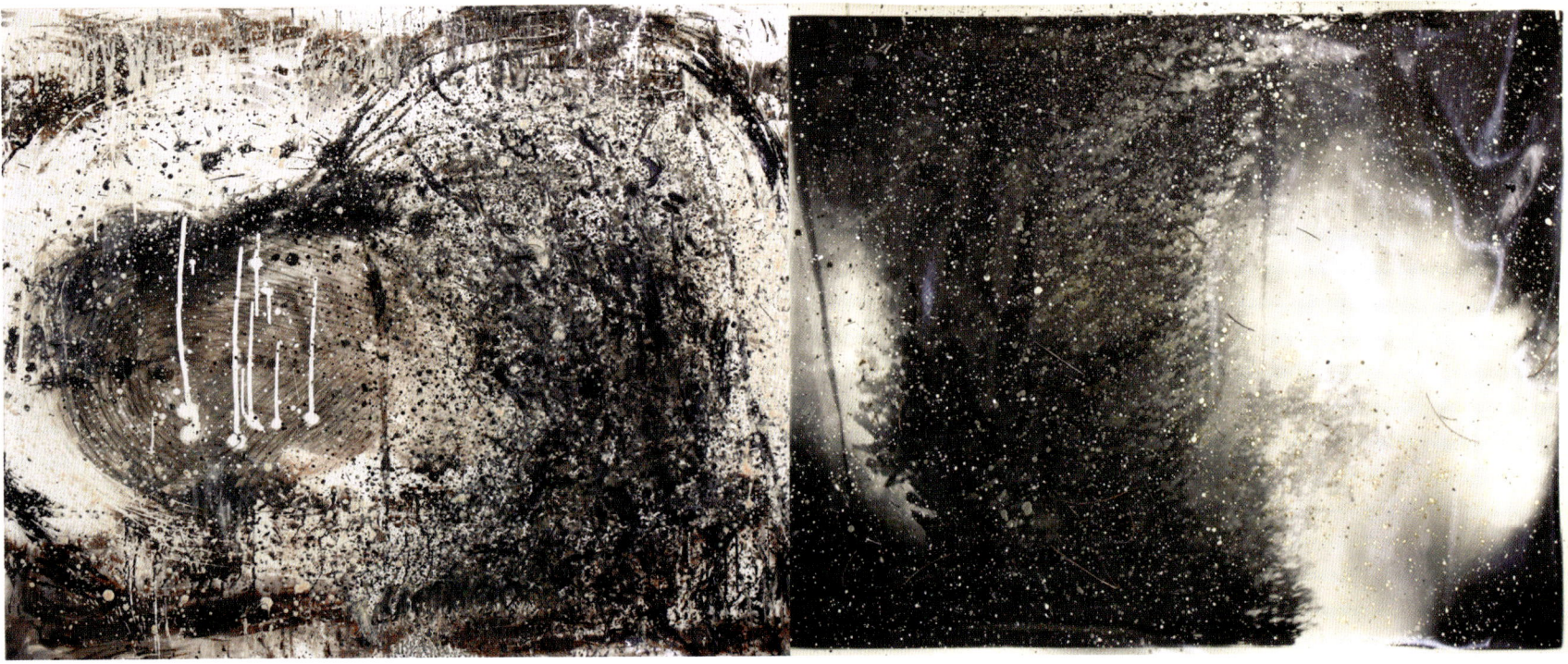

Sally and Jesse Mann, with Liz Liguori and The Mountain Lake Workshop, *Three Graces Diptych #2*, 2013, enamel oil paint, developer, photography and laser imagery on photographic paper, 40 x 100 in. (101.6 x 254 cm)

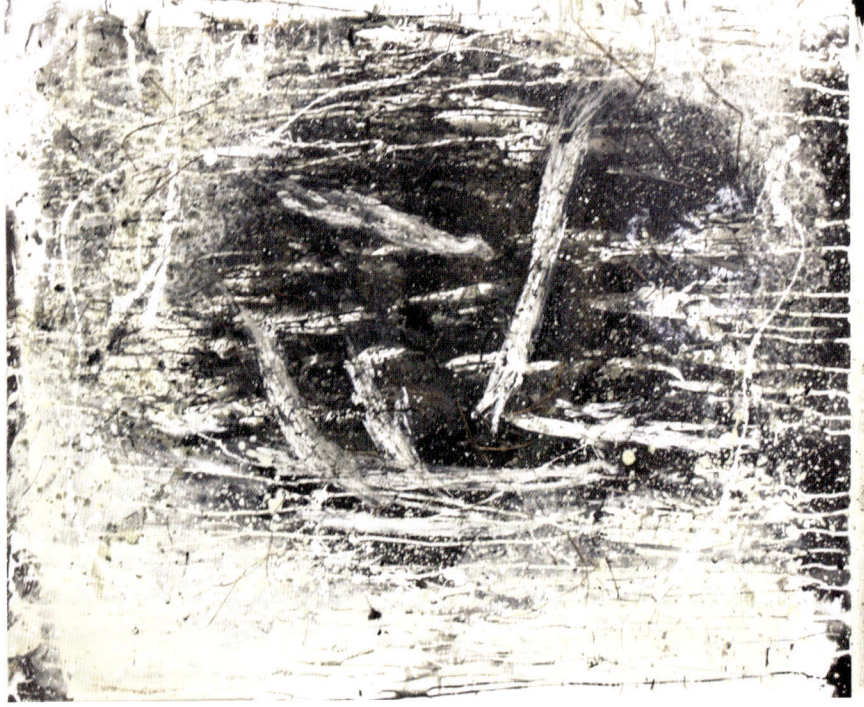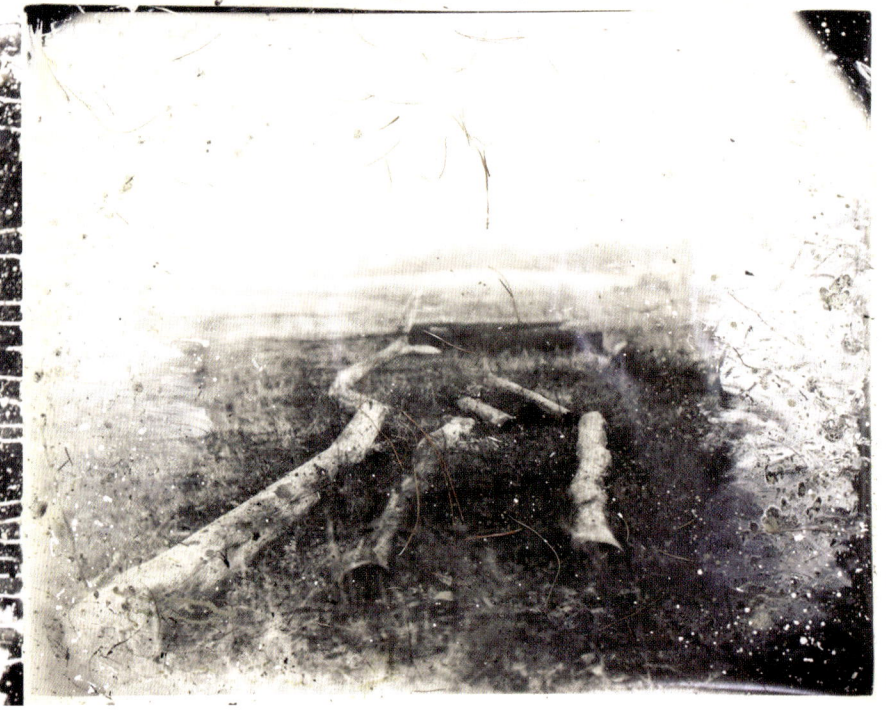

# THE MOUNTAIN LAKE WORKSHOP AND DEVELOPMENT OF THE ELECTROMAGNETOGRAM PROCESS

LIZ LIGUORI

An "electromagnetogram" is a photographic print made without a camera, using a method which combines aspects of photography, lighting, and painting. The name is derived from the use of a laser (light amplification by stimulated electromagnetic radiation) to expose photographic paper. This process was developed for the Mountain Lake Workshop by my collaborator, Jessie Mann, and myself as a creative solution to combine Mann's practice as a painter and my own practice as a lighting and multimedia artist. We used the electromagnetogram process to co-direct the "Metempsychosis" and the "Three Graces" workshops that included photographs by Jessie's mother, photographer Sally Mann, and a darkroom performance of John Cage's *STEPS*.

In the electromagnetogram process unexposed photographic paper is laid out under the safe light of the darkroom. The process begins with Jessie Mann applying fixer — the chemical used in the typical development process for "fixing" a photographic image, making it insensitive to further action by light. She does this with her hand, with a flick of fingers creating a gestural splatter very much in her style as a painter. I watch her movements and sense the approximate placement of the colorless chemistry (which is indiscernible on the surface in low-light conditions), and respond with gestures of light refracted and diffracted from a beam of coherent monochromatic light — a laser. The laser allows me to "paint" with light by exposing areas of the paper surface that remain photosensitive (have not been spattered with fixer). Combining the use of prisms, refraction and diffraction techniques, and filters allows for overall control of the tones and saturation. The final print then becomes a record of both painterly effects and the movement of the light across the surface.

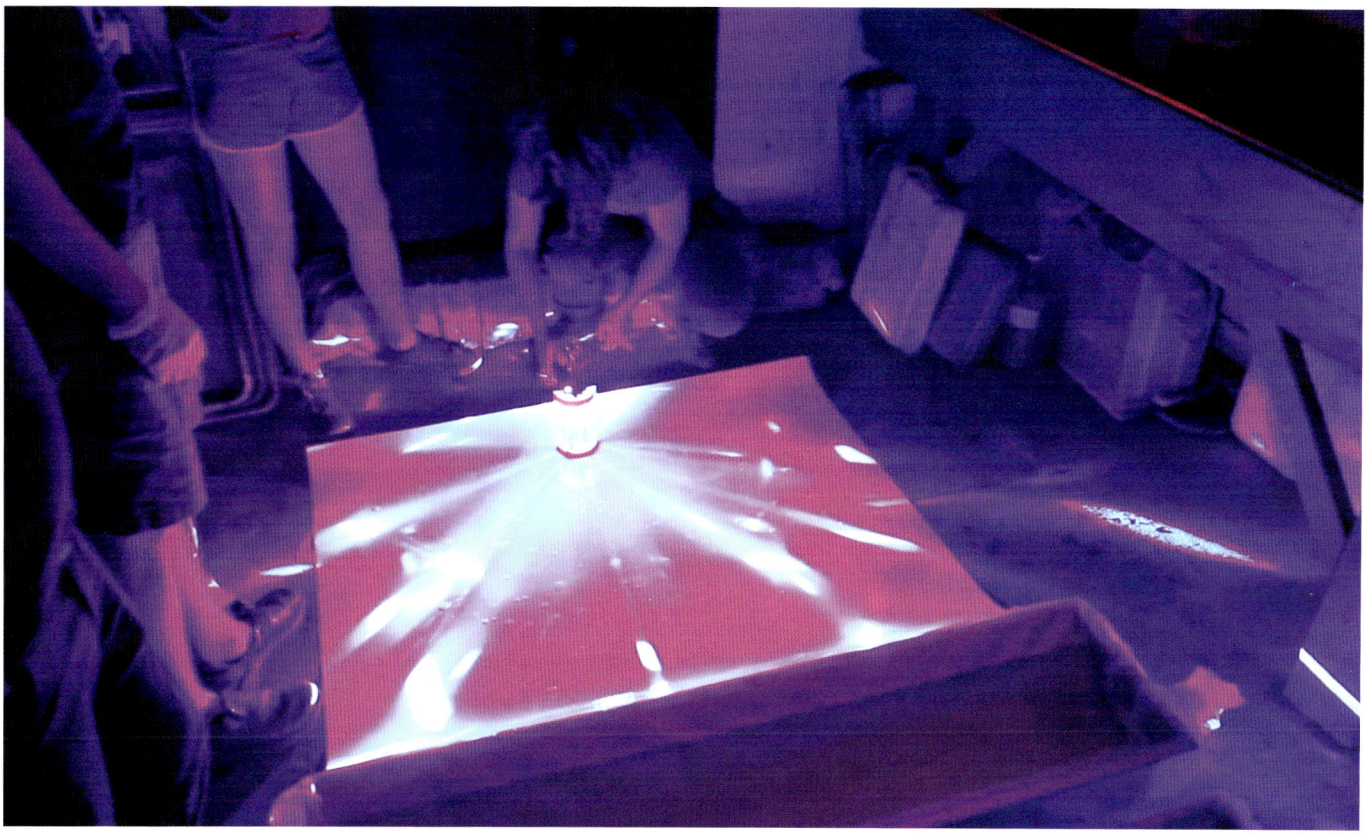

Liz Liguori, crouched on the darkroom floor, exposes photographic paper to blue laser light through a prism array

With a few exceptions, the rest of the process is much like the black and white darkroom process. The developer and the stop bath (fixer) usually are applied by submerging the paper in a bath in a large tray. Initially we used the same 60-inch-long wooden trough that was originally built for John Cage's *STEPS* performance as a "tray" for our photo bath. With the help of five or six pairs of hands, the large sheet was fed through the trough of chemicals in a kind of rolling submersion. Then we realized we could also use the development process in a painterly way to better control the tone and saturation of each print while still leaving the paper surface open to last-minute opportunities for unanticipated effects. From that point on,

we began applying all the chemistry by hand except for the final fixer bath that stops further development of the image.

This process thus was both an artistic choice and our practical solution to developing the very large prints for the *STEPS* performance workshop in Sally Mann's modest-sized wet plate colloidal darkroom without having custom-built trays.

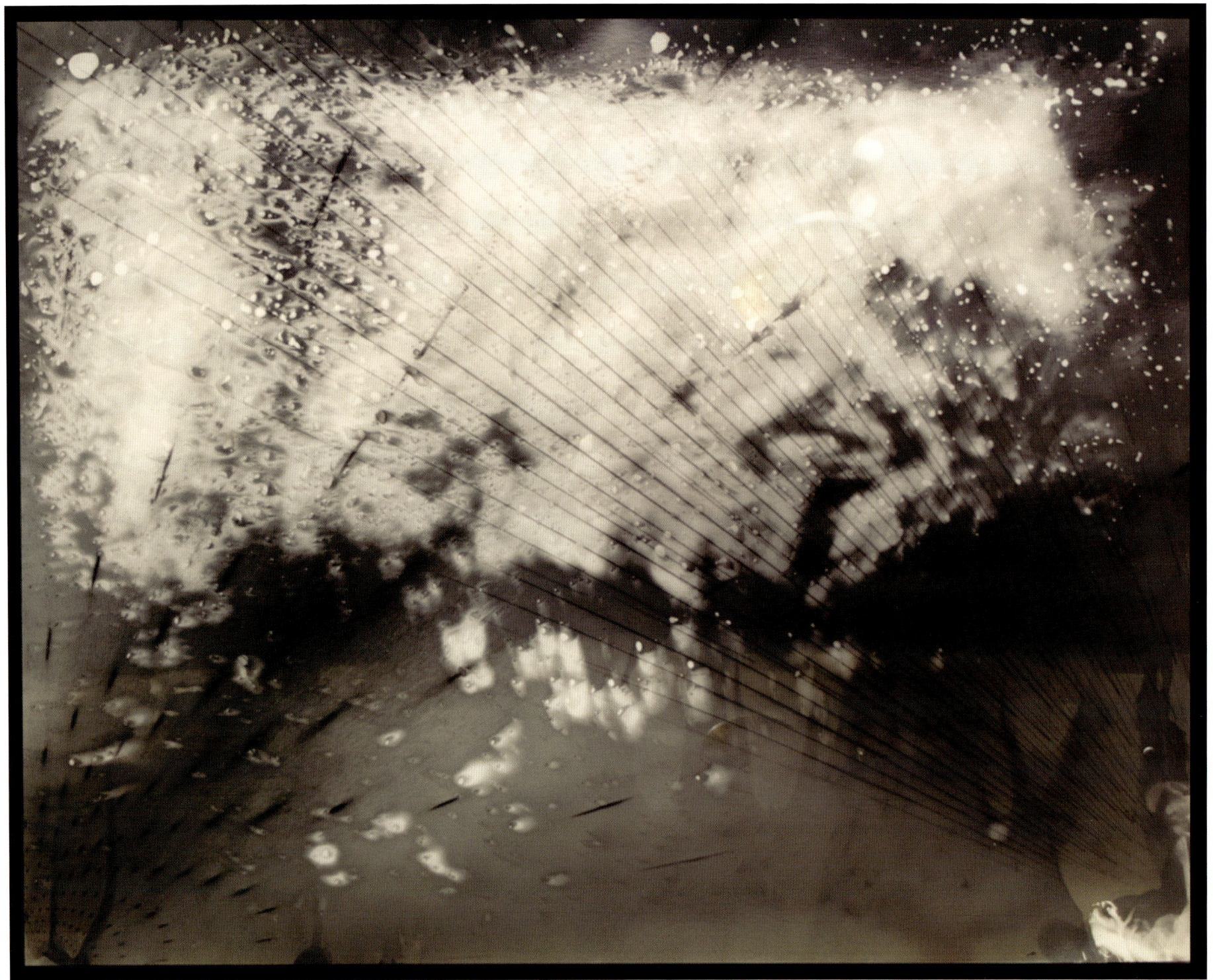

Liz Liguori and Jessie Mann, *Rise Over Run*, Electromagnetogram on photo paper, 40 x 60 in. (101.6 x 152.4 cm)

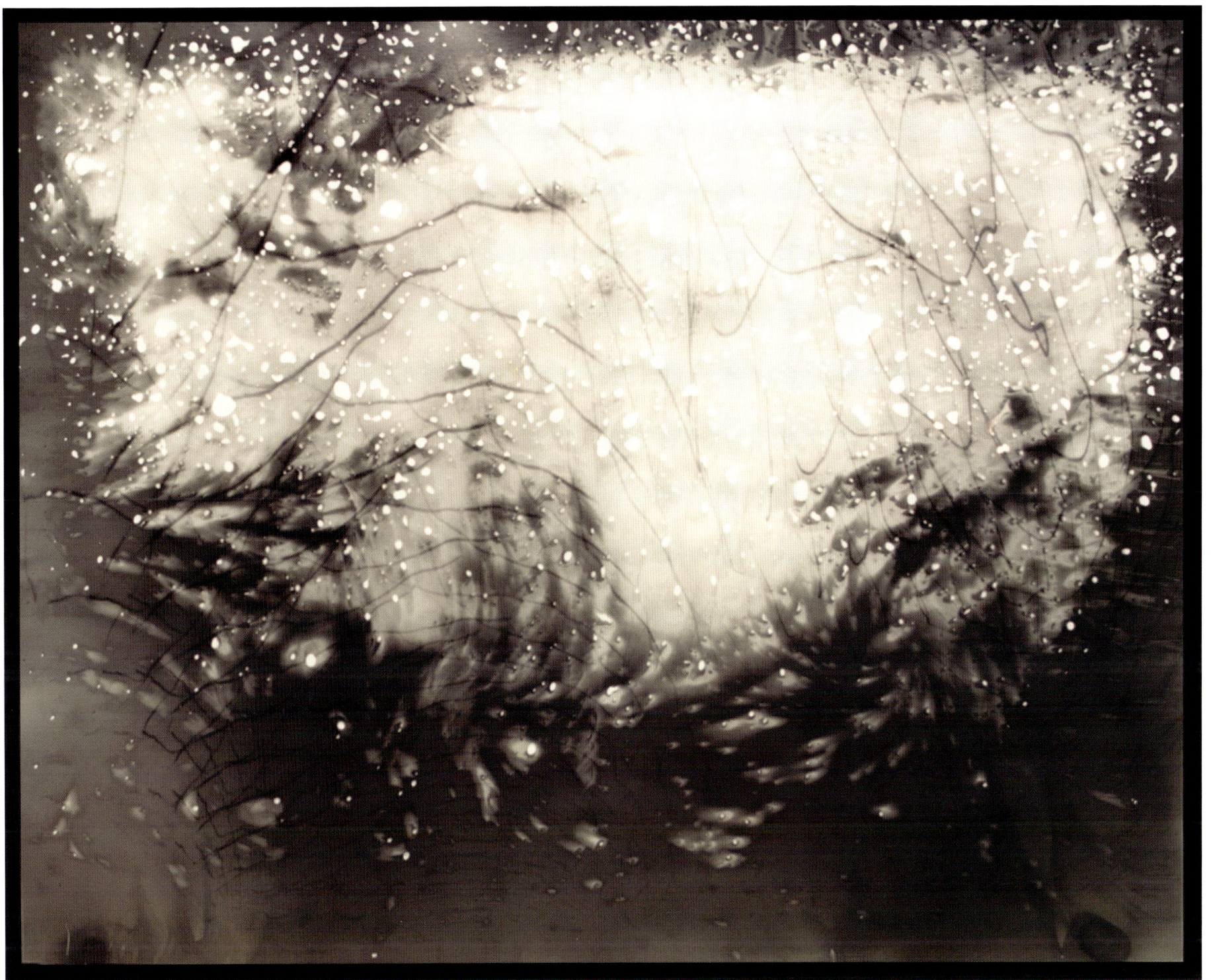

Liz Liguori and Jessie Mann, *Wash Cycle*, Electromagnetogram on photo paper , 40 x 60 in. (101.6 x 152.4 cm)

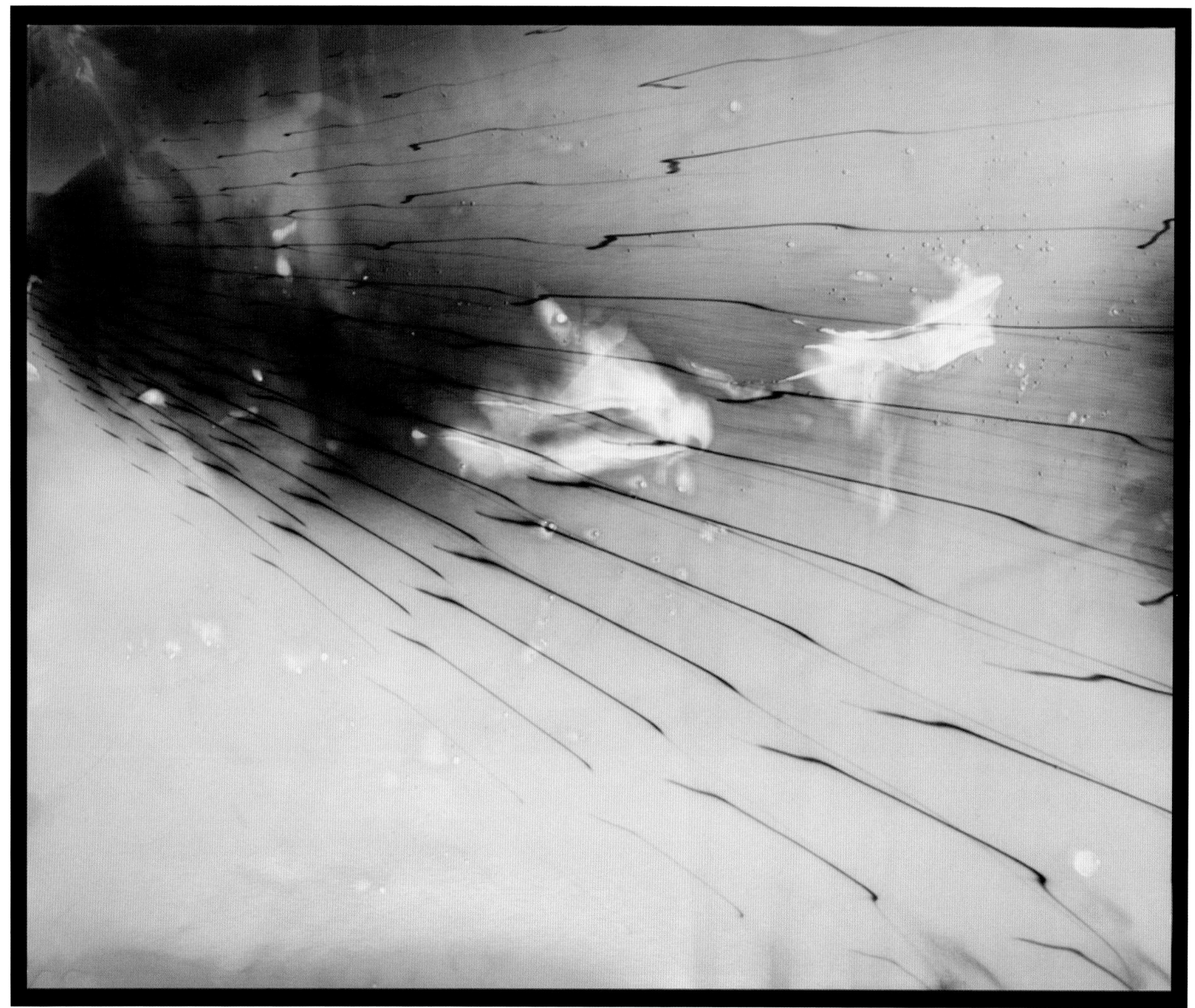

Liz Liguori and Jessie Mann, *Solar Wind*, Electromagnetogram on photo paper, 40 x 60 in. (101.6 x 152.4 cm)

# THREE GRACES IN PUBLIC: DIGITAL MONTAGES

SAM KRISCH

On a Sunday afternoon, May 11, 2013, a group of artists and Mountain Lake Workshop participants gathered at Three Graces, the Mann family farm near Lexington, Virginia. Ray Kass (workshop co-creative director) and I (a digital artist and photographer) directed the day's activities. Our request was quite simple. All artists and participants were asked to spend time walking the property photographing with their cell phones or digital cameras whatever they saw that interested them. The idea was to capture in visual form something of the individual character of each artist and participant.[1]

For two hours they went at their own pace capturing images of various scenes, doing casual portraits, and photographing signs on the farm and other objects that caught their eye. They had been encouraged to use smart phone apps, but "straight" images from phones, tablets, and digital cameras were also welcome for submission. The ultimate goal of the project was to assemble a collection of images, however disparate, highlighting participants' personal styles, and use them for crowd-sourced artistry.

The result of their efforts was a pool of over 1,400 images drawn from the natural surroundings and farm and studio structures which were then combined with various images documenting "Metempsychosis," an earlier workshop convened at "Three Graces" in 2011. During the summer of 2013, Ray Kass and I assembled the digital composite collages with assistance from Ryan Broughman. We selected images using Adobe Photoshop Lightroom and assembled them using Adobe Photoshop. The assembled images were superimposed at various levels of transparency and in various sizes and then re-combined by again overlaying, in part or whole, at various scales in the manner of the Mountain Lake Workshop's earlier "Appalachian Trail Frieze" and "Virginia Pathways" projects.

Each of the resulting works, five in all, possesses a uniquely whimsical personality inspired by the workshop's atmosphere of group collaboration and synergistic creativity.[2] All five have common elements from the natural surroundings. For example, one titled *Martians* emphasizes textures such as wood, metal, rock, even snakeskin, and features vertical elements such as trees and a group of figures. Its colors include a mix of green, gold, and blue. Another, titled *Snail Darter*, has more horizontal elements including anthropomorphic shadows and logs, a tree branch that evokes a serpent's head, another that resembles a fawn, and a grove of vertical vegetation. It has a bit of red and is layered over a black-and-white background of bubbling water. In the work titled *Eno End*, lettering from objects and signs on the property is used in combination with natural elements; with the exception of some of the letters, it has less color than the other works. More human and animal images appear in the work titled *Graces' Faces*, including images of artists Sally Mann and Ray Kass in the lower right-hand corner, Jessie Mann in the upper right-hand corner, a faint Liz Liguori layered on the right-hand edge, and me, Sam Krisch, in the upper right corner being watched over by a pair of masks. Here many of the common elements are layered: textures, type, snakeskin, rock, and wood, along with artworks by Sally Mann, Jessie Mann, and Liz Liguori that were created in the "Three Graces" workshop and the earlier "Metempsychosis" workshop. The final image, titled *Three Graces*, is a black-and-white composition using signage and place elements.

[1] This project was made possible in part by generous donations of paper and ink from Epson America Inc. and by the Virginia Commission for the Arts and the National Endowment for the Arts.

[2] The five large, digital composite images were printed on an Epson 9900 large format inkjet printer using archival digital pigment inks on matte Epson Ultra Smooth Fine Art Paper.

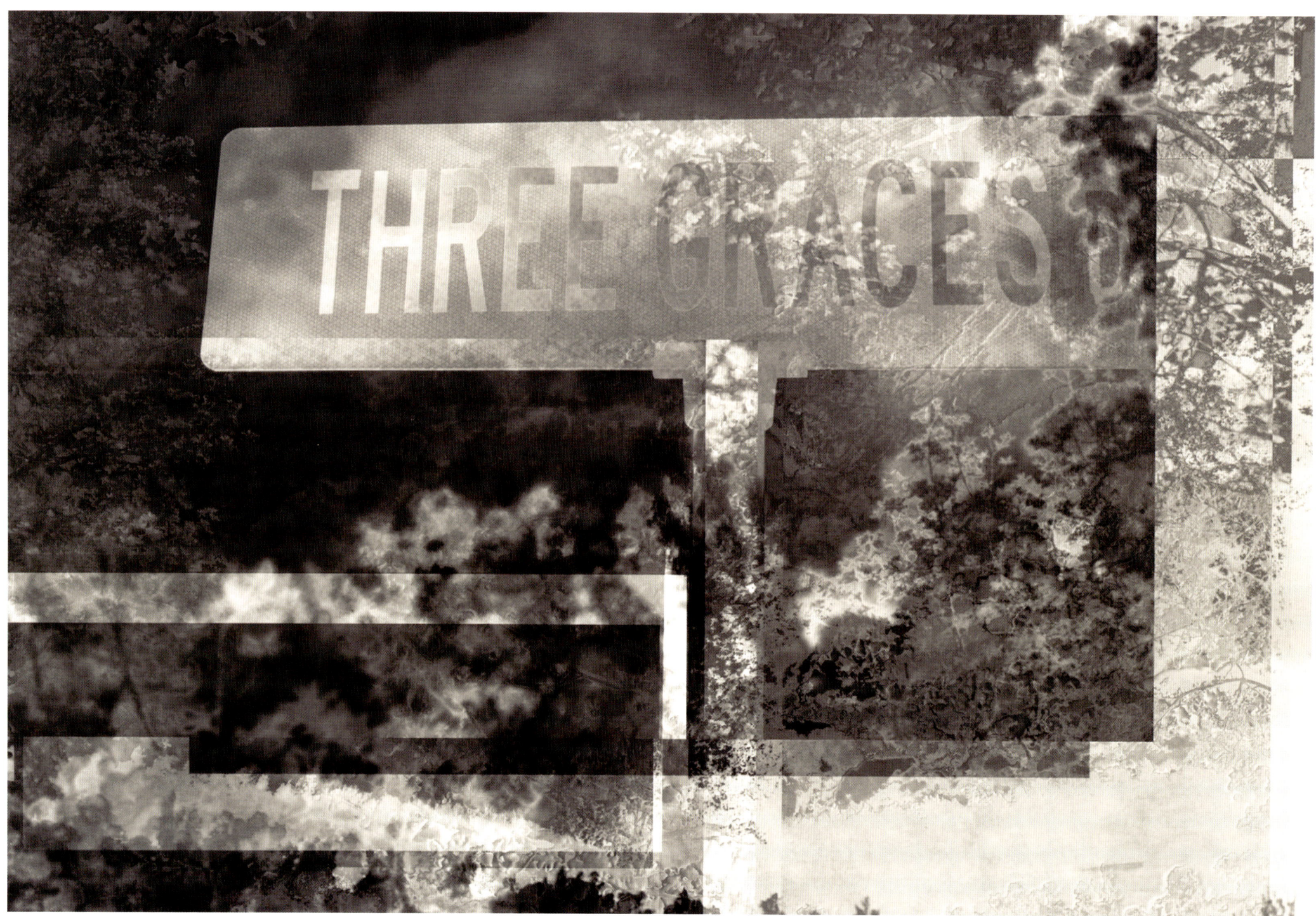

Sam Krisch and the Mountain Lake Workshop with Ryan Broughman, *Three Graces #5 – Three Graces*
(Title Image), 2013, digital print on paper, 36 x 48.625 in. (frame size) (91.44 x 121.92 cm)

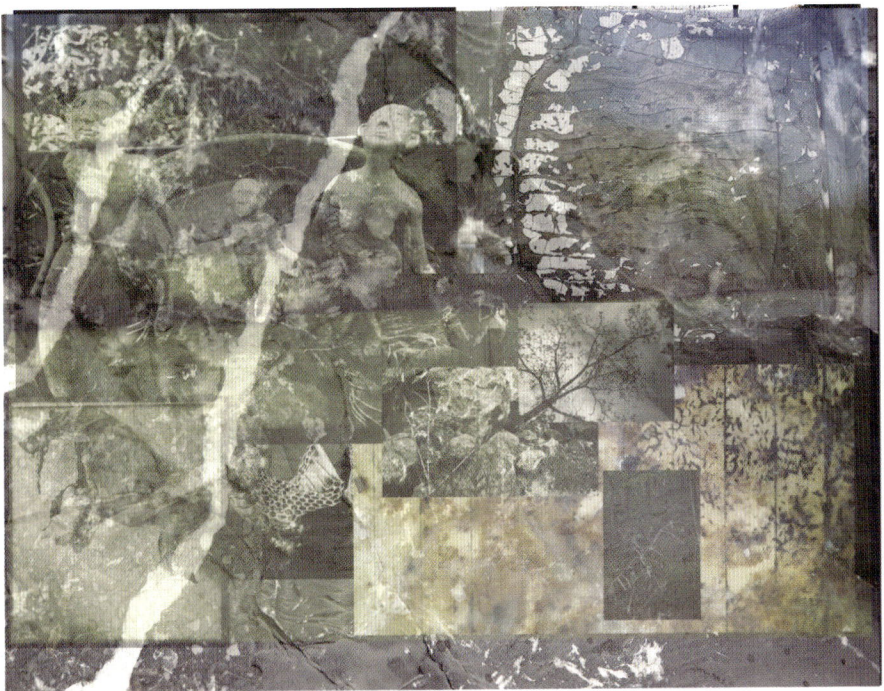

Sam Krisch and the Mountain Lake Workshop with Ray Kass and Ryan Broughman, *Three Graces #1 – Martians*, 2013, digital print on paper, 48.875 x 65.625 in. (frame size) (121.92 x 165.1 cm)

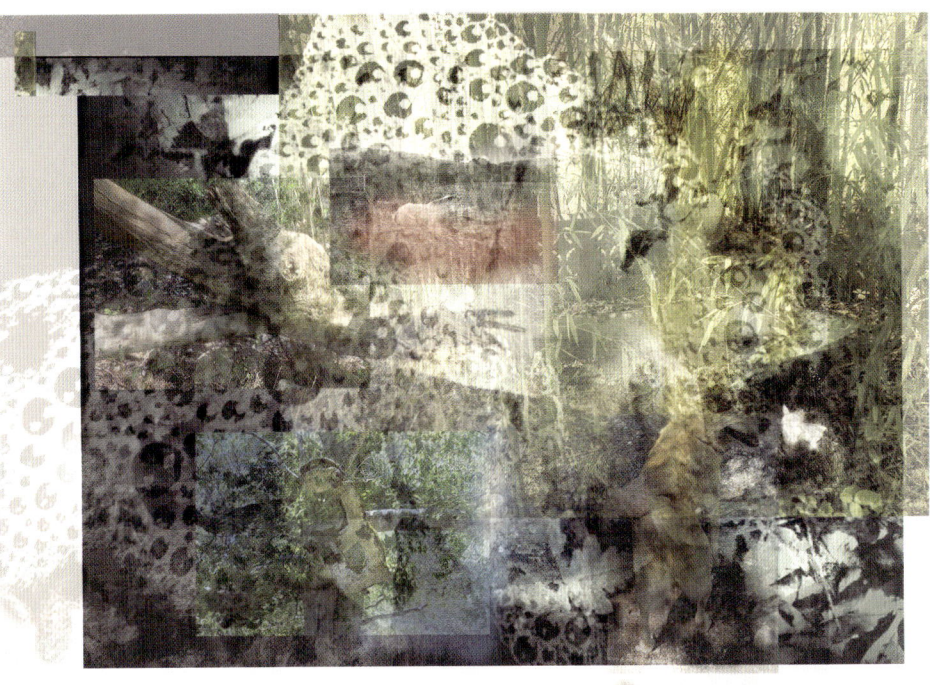

Sam Krisch and the Mountain Lake Workshop, *Three Graces #3 – Snail Darter*, 2013, digital print on paper 48.875 x 65.625 in. (frame size) (121.92 x 165.1 cm)

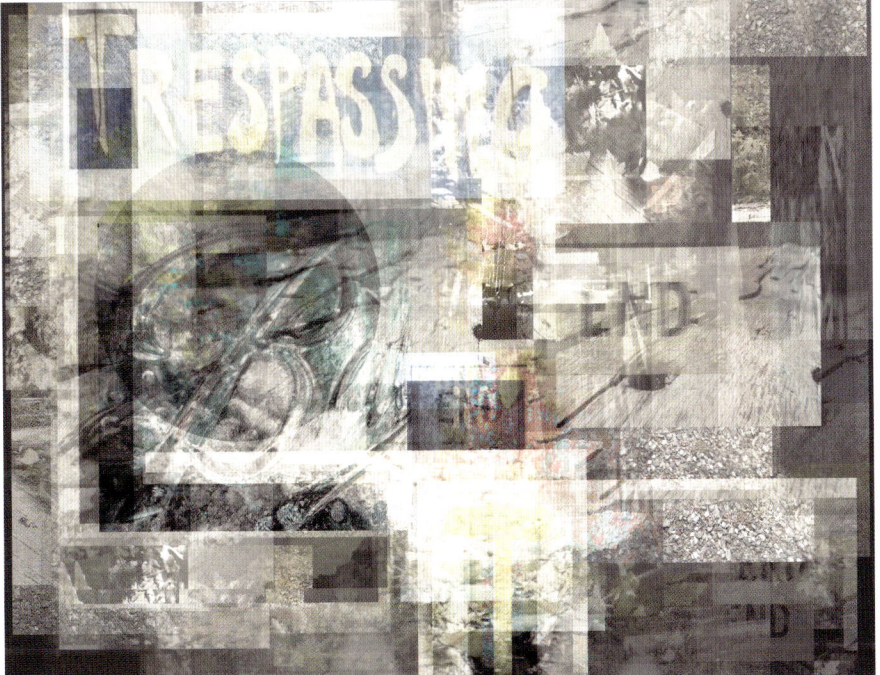

Sam Krisch and the Mountain Lake Workshop with Ryan Broughman, *Three Graces #2 – Eno End*, 2013, digital print on paper, 48.875 x 65.625 in. (frame size) (121.92 x 165.1 cm)

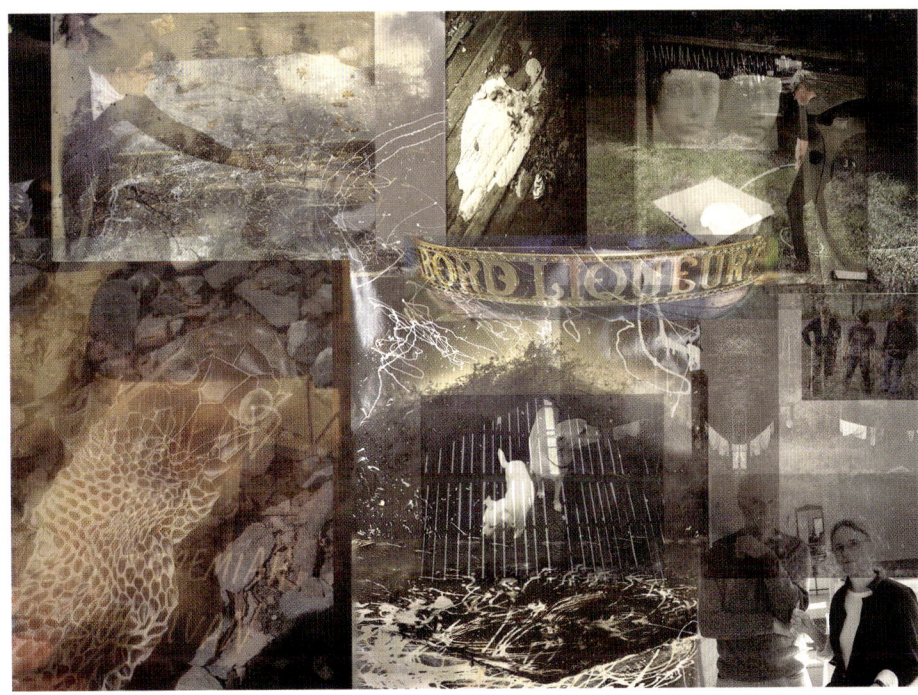

Sam Krisch and the Mountain Lake Workshop with Ray Kass and Ryan Broughman, *Three Graces #4 – Graces' Faces*, 2013, digital print on paper, 48.875 x 65.625 in. (frame size) (121.92 x 165.1 cm)

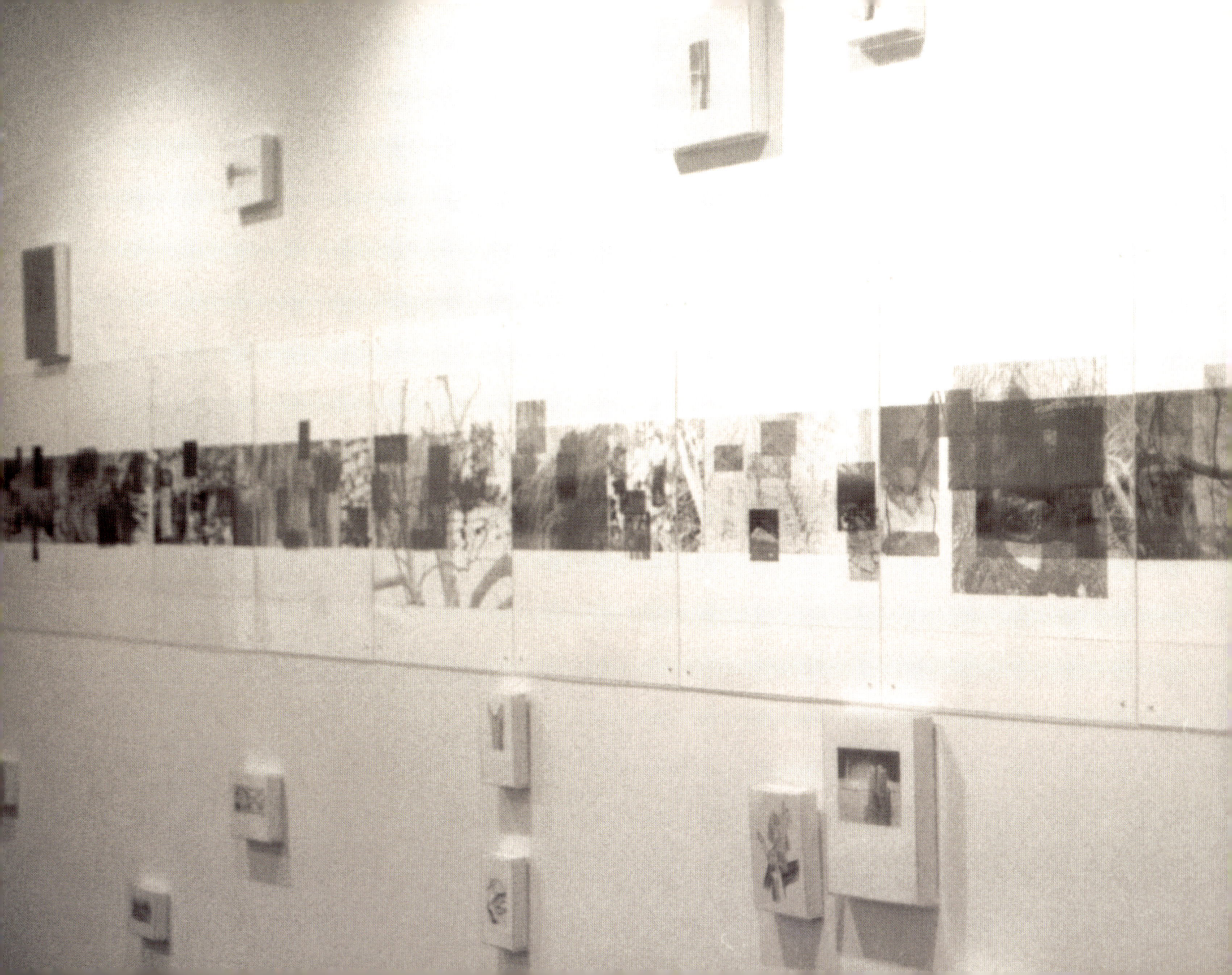

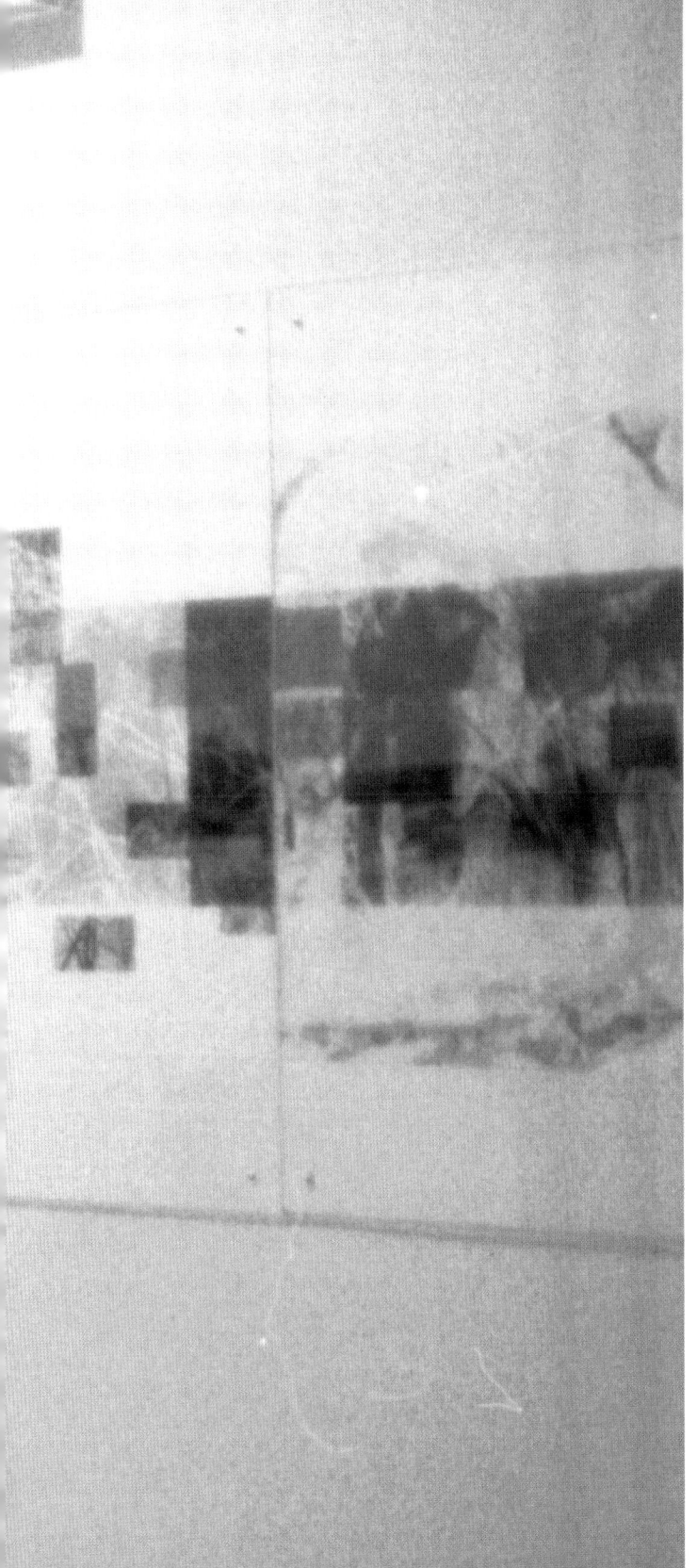

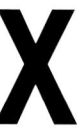

# *Extended Sensibilities*

# PATHWAYS: *APPALACHIAN TRAIL FRIEZE* WORKSHOP

**HOWARD RISATTI**

Joe Kelley and the Mountain Lake Workshop with assistance from Stefan Gibson, *Pathways: The Appalachian Trail Frieze*, 1994: gallery installation (below); detail (right)

In the way it uses chance imagery, the "Appalachian Trail Frieze" workshop, begun in 1994, is similar in design to John Cage's 1988 and 1990 workshops and to Ray Kass' 1991 and 1993 workshops. Conceived as an ongoing collaborative project, the workshop was conducted in the Jefferson National Forest by former workshop assistant Joe Kelley in conjunction with the U.S. Forest Service.[1] Inspiration for the project came from an earlier activity, that of photographing the Ripplemead site on the New River, known fondly as "John's Place," where Cage acquired most of the rocks he later used in his two painting workshops at Mountain Lake.

From this project came the idea of giving participants paper and drawing implements or film and asking them to draw or photograph places of interest to them while hiking on and near the Appalachian Trail in the area around Mountain Lake.[2] The photographs, which are personal records of individual participants' visual experiences of both physical places and seasonal changes, were collaged together using chance procedures to create a long frieze. The frieze has a narrative quality in the way it unfolds in time as viewers move through the installation, thereby creating something akin to the experience of walking along an actual forest trail. The drawings, installed in different size plastic box-like frames and randomly placed above and below the frieze, punctuate the viewer's passage along the frieze, imitating encounters with unexpected details seen along the trail.

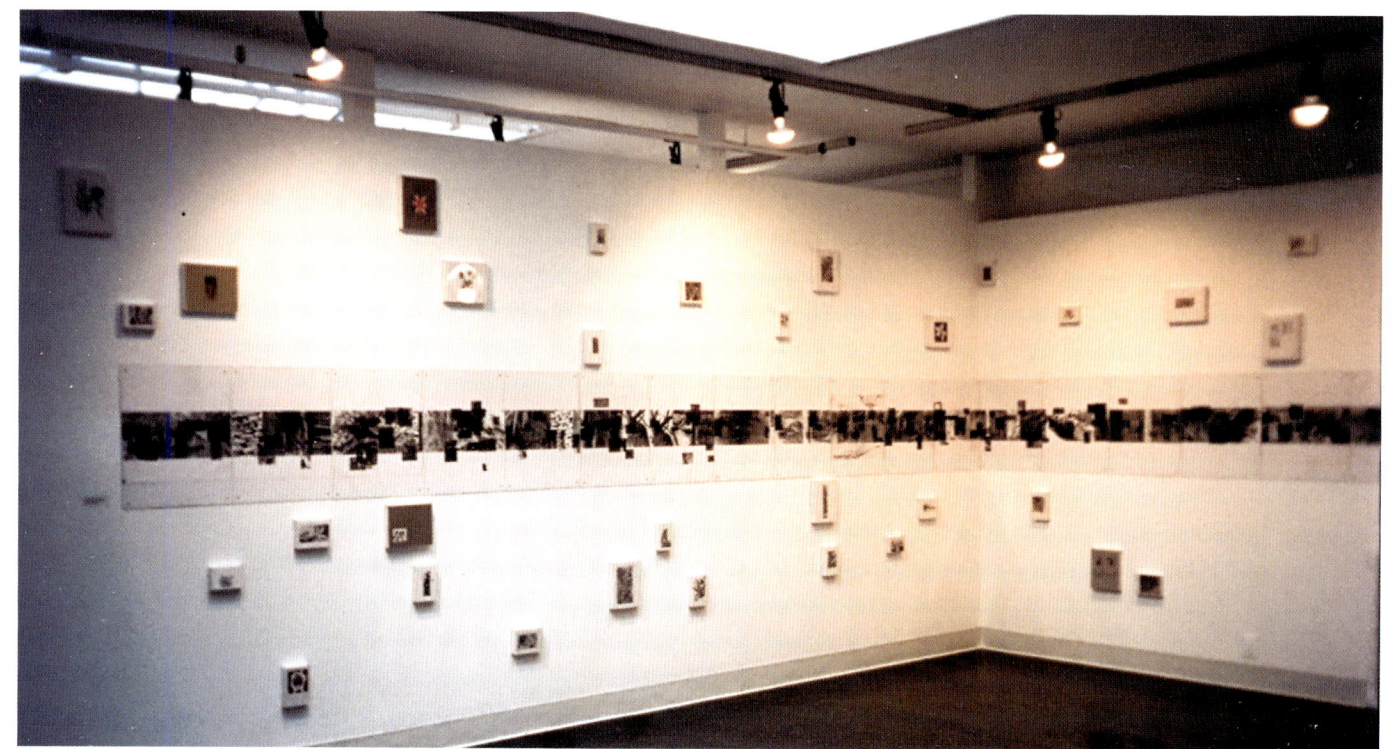

[1] In 1990 Kass, who had become a Shinto priest, blessed eight black walnut trees in the Jefferson National Forest that had been selected for Jiro Okura for his *Mountain Lake Screen Tachi* workshop. This ceremony was also conducted in conjunction with the U.S. Forest Service.

[2] The "Appalachian Trail Frieze" project also influenced the 2013 Mountain Lake Workshop titled "Three Graces in Public: Digital Montages." Named after the Mann family farm near Lexington, Virginia, where it occurred, it also was a collaborative project; however, it was carried out using digital technology (cameras and cell phones) as opposed to wet film.

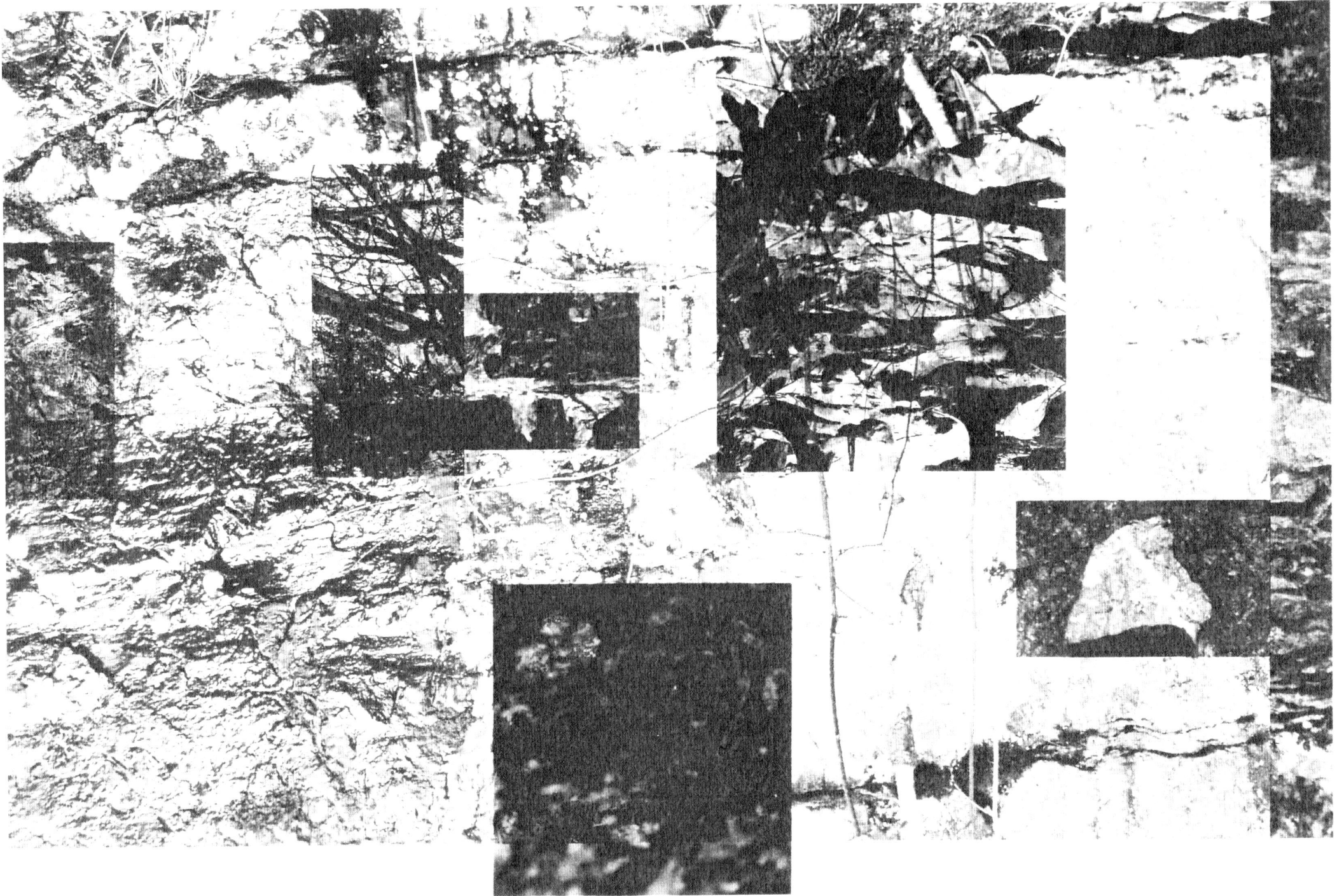

# THE APPALACHIAN TRAIL FRIEZE:
# A PHOTOGRAPHIC MONTAGE

## JOE KELLEY

Ray Kass with Stefan Gibson,
*John's Place at Ripplemead I*
1993, halftone photograph,
15.125 x 14.25 in.
(38.47 x 36.20 cm)

*The Appalachian Trail Frieze* was a Mountain Lake Workshop project I proposed to Ray Kass in the fall of 1993. Sponsored by the U.S. Forest Service, the workshop was conceived to be about the experience of walking on the Appalachian Trail and originally, at Ray Kass' suggestion, was to have a parallel component about modern forms of human transportation. I had worked with Ray Kass on the second John Cage workshop, "New River Rocks" and "Watercolors" (1988), so I was familiar with Mr. Cage's method of composition using chance operations. In the summer of 1993 I was working as a Ridge Runner for the Roanoke Appalachian Trail Club, and it was during this time on many work hikes that I put together the idea of using chance operations to compose photographic montages using photos and drawings done by several anonymous participants. Using chance operations was an appropriate tool because it eliminated both individual authorship and hierarchical ordering of images, thereby emphasizing communal experience over that of the individual.

On several hikes during the fall and winter of 1993, and then again in the spring of 1994, workshop participants took to the trail to take photographs and make drawings of close-up views and details of natural elements that interested them as they walked along the trail; they were discouraged from attempting "artistic" compositions or capturing scenic views or panoramas. The drawing activity was governed by a few specifications. Each drawing was to be made on a small piece of pastel-colored paper (there were four different colors) pre-cut to fit one of four different size plastic frames that looked like shallow boxes. Participants were also given pieces of construction paper/mat board that not only had been pre-cut to fit one of plastic frames but also had a small rectangular window (sizes varied) cut out of it. Participants were to use these windows as view finders in

order to isolate small details that they observed in nature. Using Conté crayons and pencil, they were to draw these details, placing the mat board with the window onto the pastel sheet so as to mask most of the sheet, allowing the image to float on the paper. This method successfully formatted the presentation of the drawings in an interesting manner that brought a kind of unity to a display of works by many different hands. The same view-finder technique was to be used when taking photographs so as to direct focus on details and not larger scenes or panoramic vistas.

An overall sense of unified presence was furthered when the drawings, each placed in the correct size plastic frame, were randomly arranged on a wall above and below a running photomontage composed of layered fragments of the participants' photographs. Emphasis was not on landscape photography and drawing in a traditional sense but more on what a person saw and thought memorable at the time.[1]

Ray Kass and Stefan Gibson, his studio assistant at the time, had been working on a series of photomontages titled *John's Place at Ripplemead*. The polygonal montages, composed of layered images of portions of Ray's photographs, were made for a German magazine, *MusikTexte*, as homage to John Cage, who had recently died.[2] Kass' photos were of a place called Ripplemead

on the New River where he and Cage had gathered the stones for Cage's watercolor workshops. I very much liked these images and used the same montage-masking technique to make the *Appalachian Trail Frieze*. Along with Ray Kass, Stefan Gibson became the most important collaborator on the photographic montage part of the project, spending many hours in the darkroom with me printing the images for the photomontage. The *Appalachian Trail Frieze* was designed to be installed using chance operations to arrange the montages and drawings specifically for each exhibition space. First shown in the late

[1] At the time I was working as part of a small team to photograph major roads in the area. The photos the team took were not used in the final compositions, mostly because I decided to focus on the Appalachian Trail as the main image source. I intended to continue the project, focusing on other corridors of transportation in the future.

[2] Cage died in August of 1992. Ray Kass, "John's Place at Ripplemead," *MusikTexte*, 46/47 (Dec. 1992).

[3] Virginia Pathways was sponsored by the National Linear Parks annual conference and the Virginia Tech Design Consortium and was planned to coincide with Carlton Abbott's exhibition *Parts and Pieces* at Virginia Tech's Armory Art Gallery.

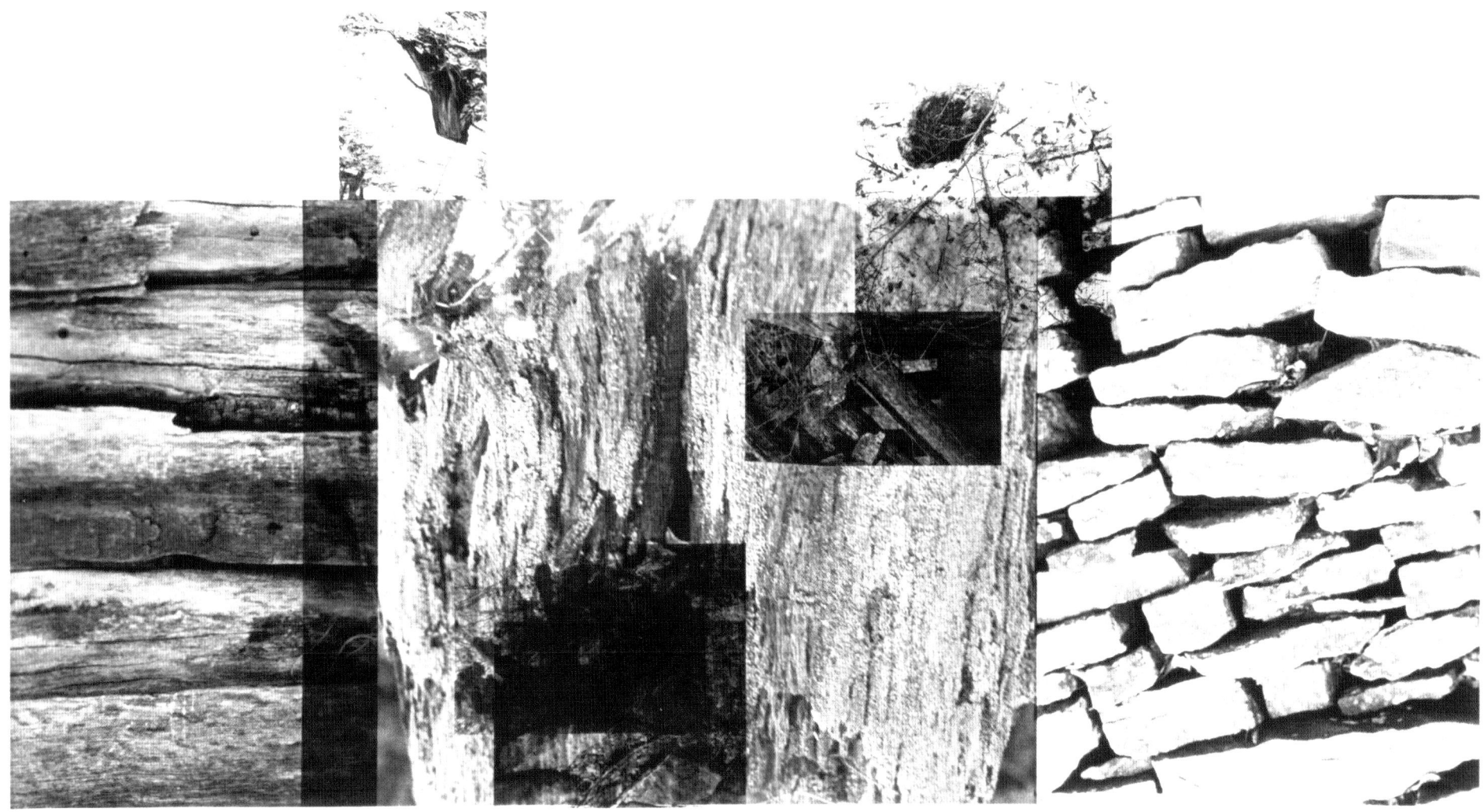

summer of 1994 at the Armory Art Gallery at Virginia Tech, it was always intended that the project continue on, to include experiences of environment, travel, and movement from the perspectives of many people from around the world.

During the fall of the following year (1995), Ray Kass and I organized a similar drawing and photography experience with landscape architect Carlton Sturges Abbott.[3] Conceived as an extension of the "Pathways: Appalachian Trail Frieze" workshop, we called it "Virginia Pathways." This time we went to Rocky Knob and places along the Blue Ridge Parkway, which

intersects the Appalachian Trail. Most notably the group hiked to a small shelter originally built by the Civilian Conservation Corps (CCC) in the 1930s and did photographs and drawings with Mr. Abbott, whose father, Stanley Abbott, had been the head designer of the Blue Ridge Parkway. It was very relevant to the project that he be involved and talk about the history of the parkway and landscape design and his experience in general.

Computer imaging and digital graphics programs have made it much easier to produce the photomontages and make the irksome task of spending long hours in a darkroom with

photo chemicals unnecessary. We all saw the potential of what the computer could bring to such a project: a vision of many people making a record of their combined experience of their environment from around the world. In this sense, the project was never intended as something closed-ended, or as something to be complete, but always continuing.

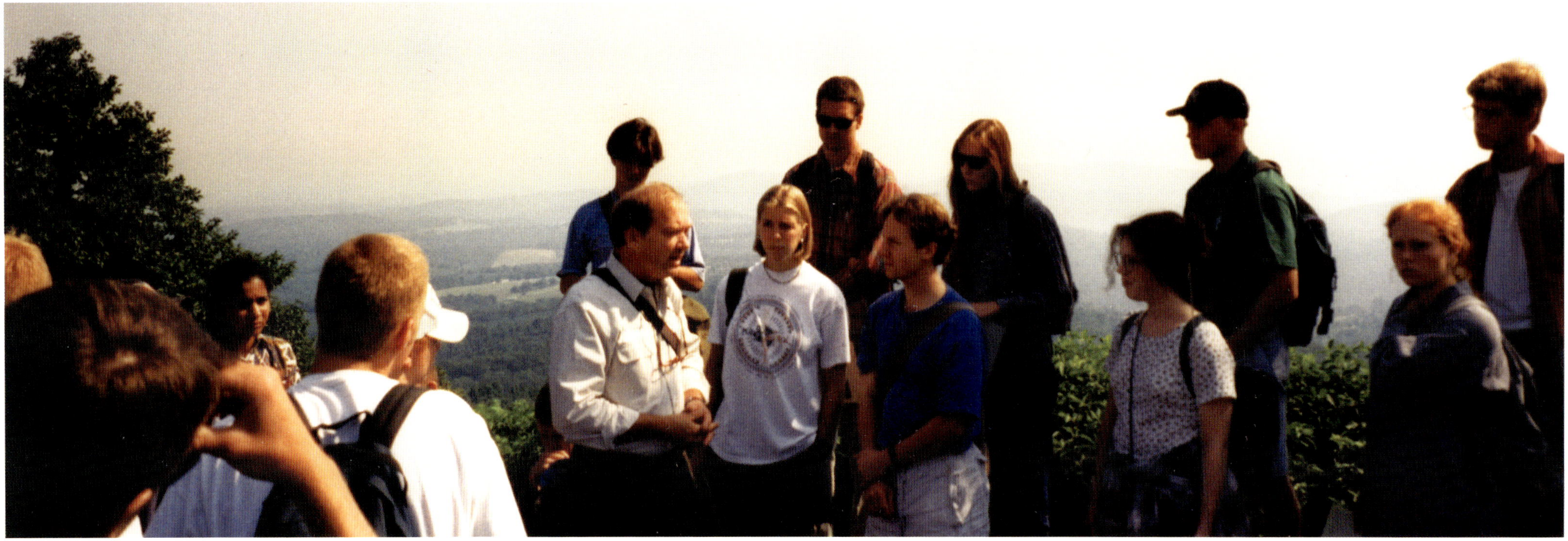

Carlton Abbott (center-left) with our group at Rocky Knob, Virginia

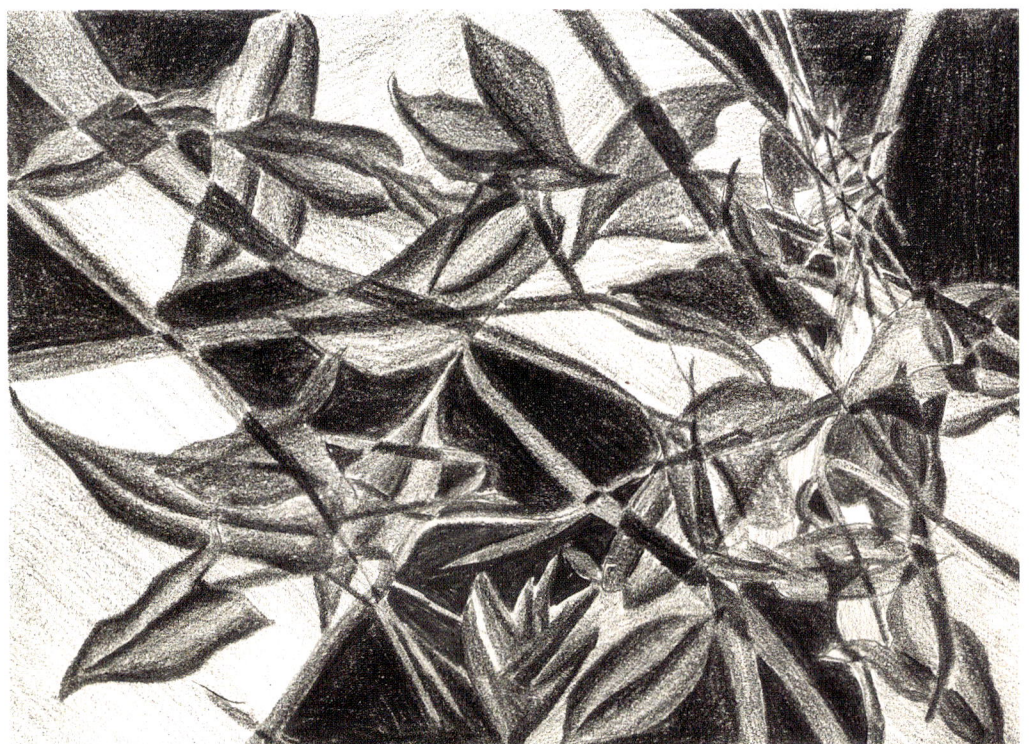

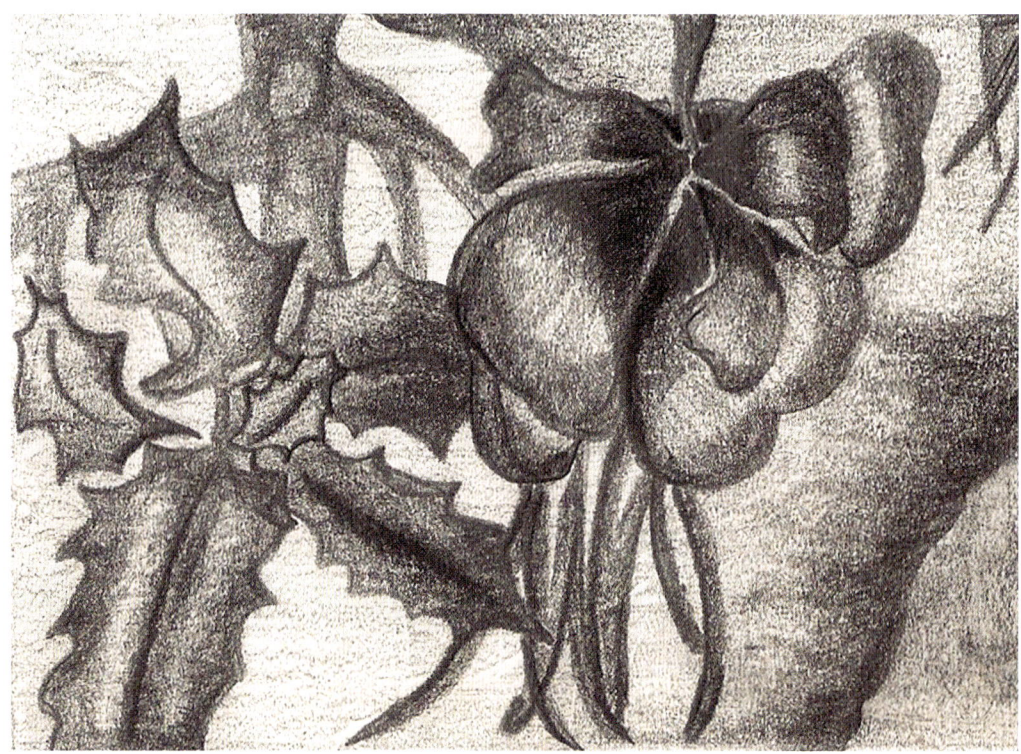

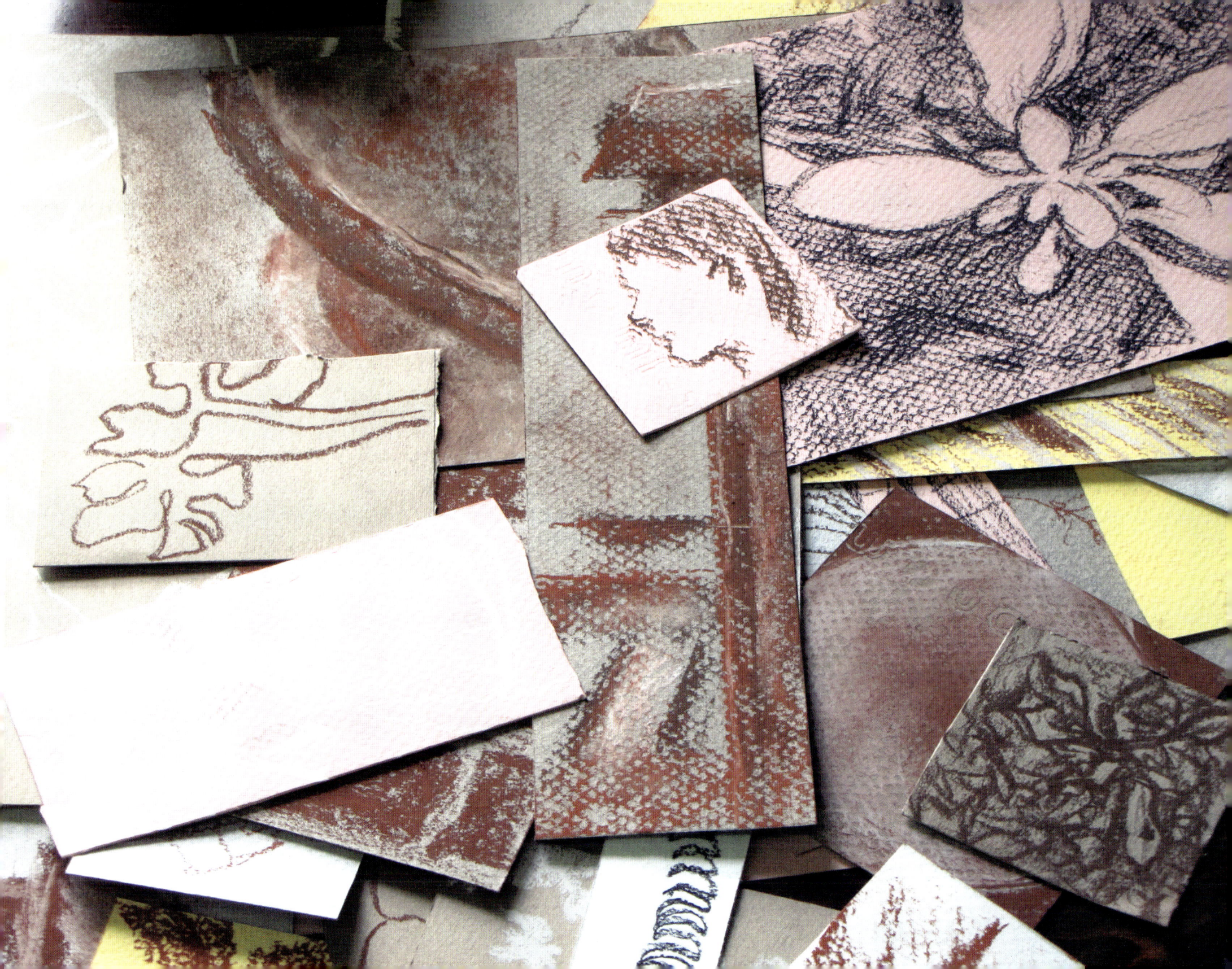

# SOUND VISIONS:
# JACQUES POURCHER

ULRIKE KASPER

The French artist Jacques Pourcher, who lives and works in Chamalières, France, where he was born in 1950, has transferred the musical concepts of John Cage into visual arts. In his minimal paintings on oriental handmade paper, Pourcher searches for a sensitive sphere, where color and sound become equal. The rhythm of sounds and silences found in his work is drawn with almost invisible fields of pale colors. In Pourcher's paintings, the variation of colors and movement has no beginning and no end. Every painting is like a fragment, a part of a whole. His work — inspired not only by Cage but also by other composers of the New York School, such as Morton Feldman or Christian Wolff — can almost be read as a score. Thin lines in clear tones seem to disappear in a white space, like sound disappearing in silence. He is creating an interplay of the senses. His intention is not to describe or illustrate what he is listening to, but to evoke it. In this sense the paintings of Pourcher can be considered a landscape of meditation.

They are abstract but can allude to a specific content. *Ocean/ Zürich/Joyce* represents a map of Zurich depicted as overlapping circles the intersections of which locate places frequented by James Joyce in Zurich.[1] For the exhibition *Sound Visions*, Pourcher painted four series of works.[2] Ray Kass thought that one series, titled *One: Variations*, suggested the possibility for a new Mountain Lake Workshop collaborative project.[3] During our visit to Blacksburg Jacques Pourcher and I met with Kass at his studio to create a project for the Mountain Lake Workshop. Kass had been making montages of layered mulberry papers and silk as an homage to one of his recently deceased mentors, Morris Graves, the eminent Pacific Northwest mystic artist who had been a close

friend of Cage. Kass was utilizing the Asian paper-mounting technique that he had recently learned from Xaio Yan Gan. In the course of repeatedly mounting the silk and paper elements, he had saved all of the mulberry-paper strips that remained after cutting the compositions off of the mounting boards. Taking these strips, we painted random white lines of varying width on them with no particular order or intention.

Then Pourcher and Kass mounted many of the strips, overlapping them in a white-on-off-white *mélange* of vertical and horizontal stripes that had an uncanny relationship to Jacques' work.

[1] *Ocean/Zürich/Joyce*, 2002. Collection of the Taubman Museum of Art, Roanoke, Virginia.

[2] *Sound Visions: Paintings by John Cage and Jacques Pourcher*, curated by Ray Kass and Ulrike Kasper, Armory Art Gallery, Virginia Tech, Blacksburg, Virginia, Summer Arts Festival, 2003.

[3] *One: Variations* (a series of five paintings), October 2002 (25 cm x 25 cm), watercolor on paper.

Jacques Pourcher with Ray Kass and
Dr. Ulrike Kasper, *Atelier du Lac*, 2003,
watermedia montage of layered paper strips,
33.75 x 33.75 in. (85.73 x 85.73 cm)

# COMMENTARY ON
# THE *PEN WIPER PIECE*

RAY KASS

In writing his beautifully crafted music with fountain pen and ink, John Cage was always wiping the tip of his pen, and a sheet of pen-wipes that John's friend, the eminent composer Earle Brown, picked out of a wastebasket one day is a remarkably beautiful piece in its own right. Cage gave it to him, insisting it "is not a drawing"— an interesting commentary coming from the man who made non-intention his primary creative motive.

When Cage became more deeply involved with the mixing of his watercolors at the Mountain Lake Workshop, he often used "try-out" sheets to gauge the weight of the color and wetness on the sheet (usually seeking a lighter intensity in both qualities). When he suggested that I "make a piece" out of the beautiful paper towels that were try-outs from his painting *New River Watercolors, Series IV, #1*, I felt that his goal of non-intention should find further fruition. Twenty years later, as a result of a workshop with the artist and scholar of Zen Stephen Addiss, the by-products of the work of Cage's own hand and eye were made into five sets of "John Cage's Zen Ox-Herding Pictures."

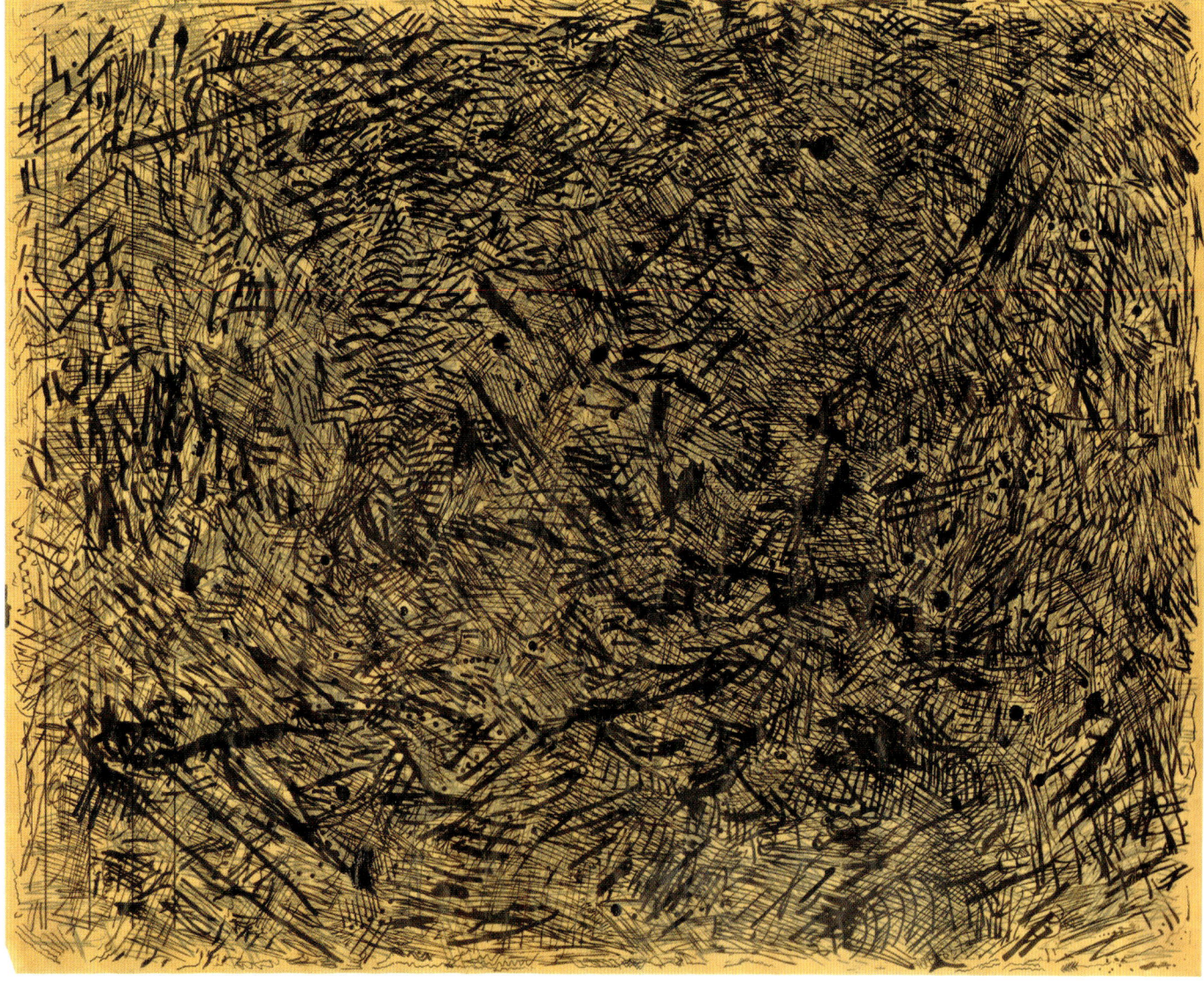

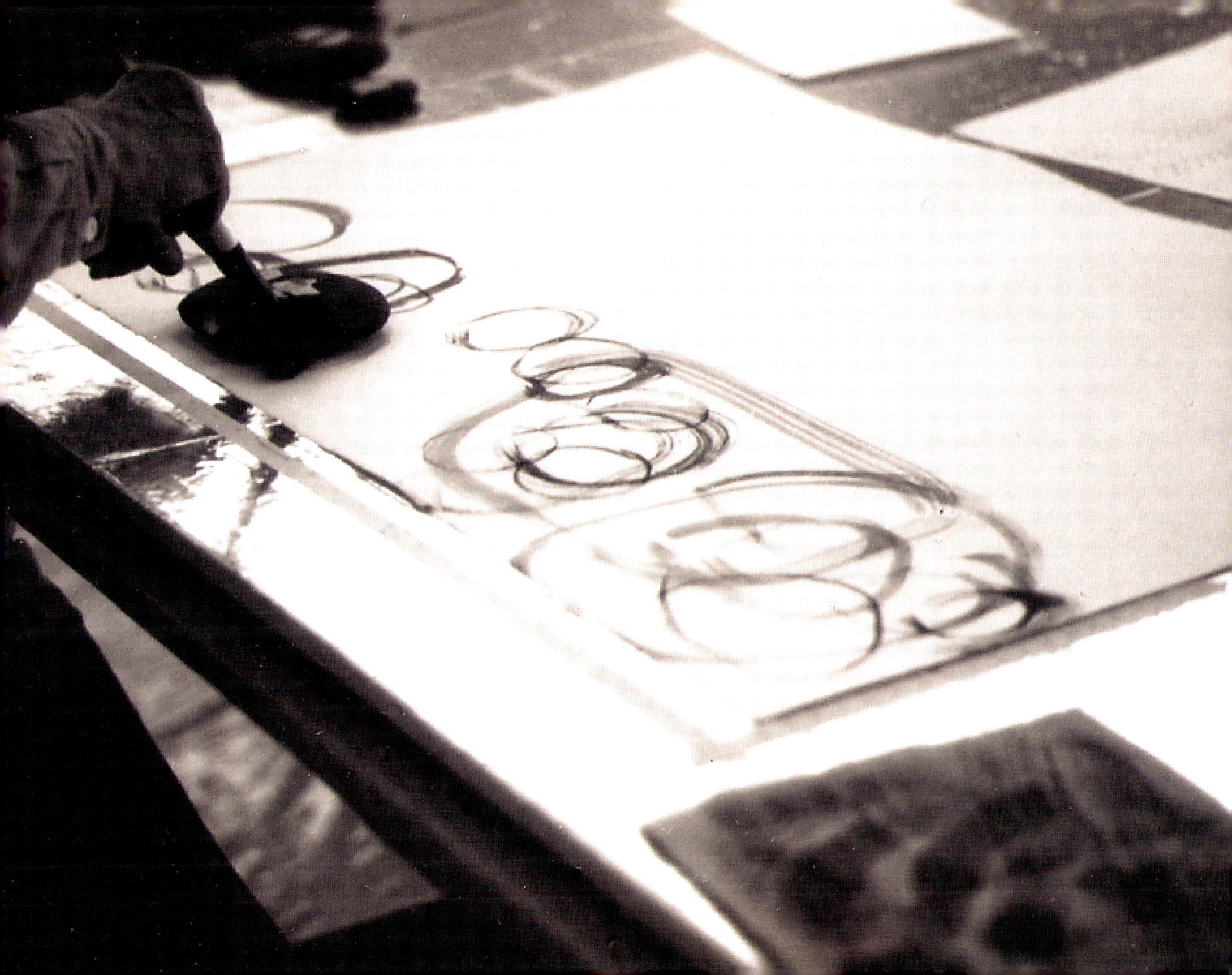

# STEPHEN ADDISS AND THE MOUNTAIN LAKE WORKSHOP: *JOHN CAGE'S ZEN OX-HERDING PICTURES*

RAY KASS

The project of creating a new rendition of Zen Buddhism's "Ten Ox-Herding Pictures" that Stephen Addiss undertook in collaboration with the Mountain Lake Workshop began with his response to a group of paper towels that had been painted on with watercolor by John Cage nineteen years earlier during a Mountain Lake workshop in Virginia in 1988. The paper towels were a by-product of Cage's serious engagement with watercolor painting and were among the many and varied practice sheets that Cage generated as a consequence of his experimenting with applying paint to paper by hand. He was "practicing" in order to gain understanding of and skilled performance (according to his own standards) with the new materials that would generate essential "choices" that would be subjected to his use of "chance operations" to determine the composition of each of his *New River Watercolors*.[1]

While painting the contours of the stones for the eight works comprising a specific series, *New River Watercolors, Series IV* (1988), Cage tried out his brush, often repeatedly, on fifty-four paper towels. This group of "try-out" paintings were particularly appealing to me, and I frequently admired them and said so to Cage as I removed and refreshed the paper towels beside him on the painting table. I thought that many of his "practice sheets" were simply beautiful because of their fresh, unselfconscious character — but together as a group, I thought that the paper towel studies were an extraordinary collection. At one point I said that I thought they were a wonderful group of paintings and that perhaps we should do something with them, and Cage (who also admired them) responded that I should "make a piece out of them ... [in the future]."

I set them aside in the workshop archival collection and periodically showed them to visitors. For many years I thought about what kind of project could bring them together as a meaningful "piece."

The special opportunity for a new collaboration that could utilize Cage's paper towel "try-out" paintings occurred nineteen years later, a couple years after I had begun working on Mountain Lake projects with composer, musician, poet, painter, and Japanese Zen art historian Dr. Stephen Addiss. I knew that Cage had liked Addiss personally and admired his published scholarship on Zen Buddhist art. A favorite book that Cage had shown me on a visit in New York years earlier was Addiss' *The Art of Zen: Painting and Calligraphy by Japanese Monks 1600–1925*.[2] We always had a copy of this book at the workshop when Cage was painting.

Addiss studied with Cage in his famous classes in composition at the New School for Social Research in the late 1950s/early 1960s, occasionally functioning as a teaching assistant. I had met Addiss on several occasions and known of his scholarly writing and artwork for more than twenty years when I began actively working with him in 2005. At first I "smoked" paper in the manner that I had developed for Cage for Addiss to use for his own excellent *sumi-e* painting. The following year, 2006, we worked together in organizing a Mountain Lake workshop in paper-smoking at the University of Richmond, as well as a related exhibition including paintings by Cage on "smoked paper."

In November 2007, I invited Addiss to give a lecture at Virginia Tech on the development of Asian scripts and to conduct a "paper-smoking" workshop. That is when I showed him the paper towels that Cage had painted on in 1988 — and spontaneously suggested that he select ten from the group that he felt bore a correspondence to traditional Buddhist ox-herding pictures. Backing off a bit from my initial enthusiasm, I asked him respectfully if he thought that the paper towels and their wholly abstract imagery might work as visual signifiers in that context. He did! I'm sure that the idea occurred to me only because Addiss' expertise in Zen Buddhist art and his personal understanding of the work of Cage made it obvious to me that I should invite him to collaborate on a new piece — the "piece" that Cage had proposed nearly twenty years earlier.

Addiss selected the first set of ten of the images from the fifty-four painted paper towels, and I encouraged him to select two additional sets of ten. Then we decided to use "chance operations" based on Cage's own computer-generated pages of *I Ching*–derived random numbers from his watercolor workshops to select a fourth set of ten. Then, with Addiss' encouragement, I chose a fifth and final set of ten images from the fourteen remaining paper towels.

After completing the selection of five sets of ten images, we decided not to reveal the order or origins of the selection of the four sets subsequent to Addiss' first selection. It seemed unessential to the authenticity of the collaboration and introduced an element of appropriate ambiguity.

Traditional presentations of ox-herding pictures (usually in sets of ten) always include poems accompanying each painting. Over a period of eight months, Addiss selected the text/poems

[1] For more on this see Ray Kass, "John Cage Wipes His Brush: The Mountain Lake Workshop Legacy," in Stephen Addiss and Ray Kass, *John Cage: Zen Ox-Herding Pictures* (New York: George Braziller Publishers, 2009), pp. 8–11.

[2] *The Art of Zen* was published by Harry N. Abrams in New York in 1989.

[3] Images and poem/texts are reproduced in Addiss and Kass, *John Cage: Zen Ox-Herding Pictures*, pp. 24–123.

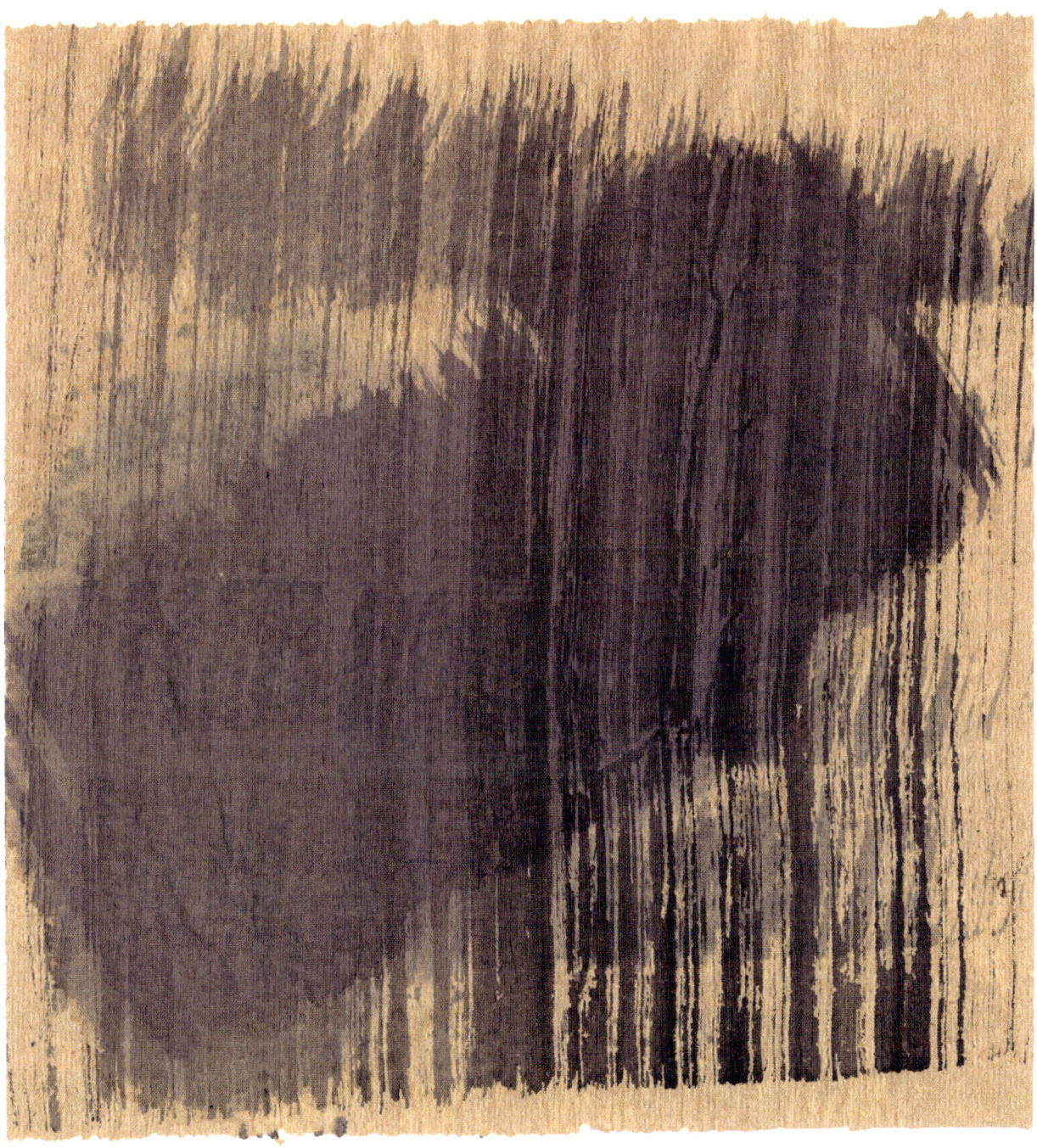

to accompany each of the fifty images from Cage's own published writings.[1] I think that his sensitive selection of the fifty texts breathes additional vigorous life into the project. Passages in Cage's writings touch many thoughts and feelings that are correspondent to those that customarily accompany the ten ox-herding pictures. Also, there is another precedent for Addiss' selection of the texts from Cage's writings through the use of chance: in Cage's own strategic rendering (using chance) of texts by James Joyce and Ezra Pound (and others), such as his *Writing for the Fourth Time Through Finnegans Wake* or *Writing Through the Cantos*, meant to offer new meaningful experiences for the reader. Addiss is offering a new experience of the traditional ten ox-herding pictures to the viewer and the reader.

By placing the paper towel images painted by Cage in the context of the traditional Buddhist ten ox-herding pictures, I hope that we have made a contribution to the ongoing collaborative spirit of "indeterminacy" that Cage's work represents for the past, present, and future of art.

# JOHN CAGE AND THE HISTORY OF *ZEN OX–HERDING PICTURES AND POEMS*

STEPHEN ADDISS

Ox-herding poems and paintings have a long history in Zen, being utilized by Masters over the centuries as teachings that could be readily understood by people at all levels of society. While the ox has long been a symbol of fertility in China, in Zen it also represents the heart-mind (in Chinese and Japanese the same character has both meanings), so "searching for the ox" can be understood as searching for one's own true self. As a metaphor for the path to enlightenment, ox-herding poems and paintings form a spiritual narrative. In this way they join a much larger tradition, the journey outwards that leads to a journey inwards. However, the basic structure of these narratives — searching, finding, and returning — informs only the first six of the usual ten ox-herding pictures. Now, after the return, there is "transcending the ox," going back to the origin, and finally re-entering the village bearing gifts. This corresponds to Zen training, in which one grapples with the question of self, reaches enlightenment, and then returns to the world with compassion for all creatures.

There are several early Zen texts that refer to the ox as one's own Buddha-nature. For example, a disciple asked the Master Pai-cheng (720–814) how to search for the Buddha without knowing the way. Pai-cheng answered, "It's like looking for the ox on which you're riding." The disciple then asked what to do when conscious of the truth, and Pai-cheng replied, "It's like returning home on the back of an ox."

Ox-herding pictures have been created many times over the centuries. Some sets end with the eighth image, the empty circle. But as John Cage frequently noted, the final two pictures are also important because after enlightenment, one comes back to the world — both for one's own continuing practice, and to help all others.

While there have been many sets of paintings of the ox-herding series created in Japan, they almost always conform quite closely to the K'uo-an and Shûbun prototypes, with literal images when possible for the narrative. The five sets of John Cage abstract paintings that comprise *John Cage's Zen Ox-Herding Pictures* created by Ray Kass and myself in 2008 from densely marked paper towels that Cage used to wipe his brush offer a different potential connection between text and image in which you, the viewers, are invited to make your own correlations and interactions. The artist's freedom from intention, often celebrated by Cage in his music, poetry, and visual art, is here extended to a major Zen theme; Ray Kass and I welcome your participation in this ongoing process.

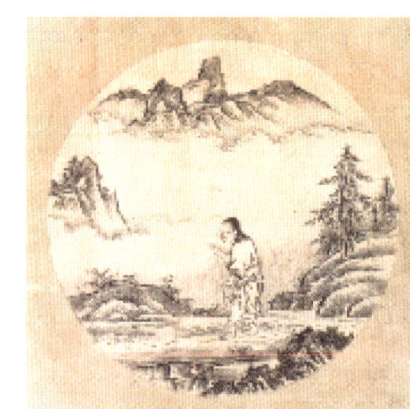

### 2. Finding the Ox

Along the river,
under trees —
jumbled tracks!
Thick fragrant woods,
is this the way?
Though the ox wanders
far in the hills
His nose touches the sky.
He cannot hide

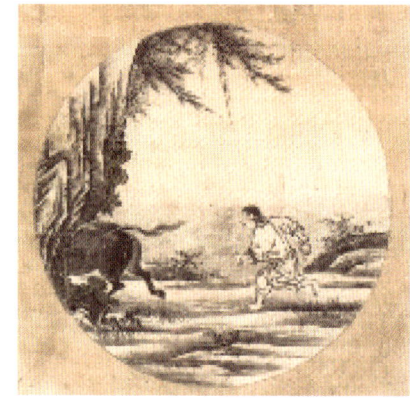

### 3. Seeing the Ox

Oriole on a branch
chirps and chirps,
Sun warm, breeze through
the willows.
There is the ox,
cornered, alone.
That head, the horns!
Who could paint them?

The examples of the *Ten Ox-Herding Pictures* come from *Kyoto Gozan Zen no Bunka* (*Zen Treasures from Kyoto Gozan Temples*) Translations from K'uo-an's poems are provided courtesy of Stanley Lombardo

This text is excerpted from Stephen Addiss, "The History of Zen Ox-herding Poems and Paintings," in Stephen Addiss and Ray Kass, *John Cage: Zen Ox-Herding Pictures* (New York: George Braziller Publishers, Inc., 2009), pp. 16–21.

# JOHN CAGE'S OX-HERDING
# PICTURES & POEMS (SET #1)

images and text by JOHN CAGE;
selected and arranged by STEPHEN ADDISS

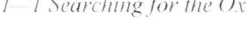

*I—1 Searching for the Ox*

feelings

empty

being lost

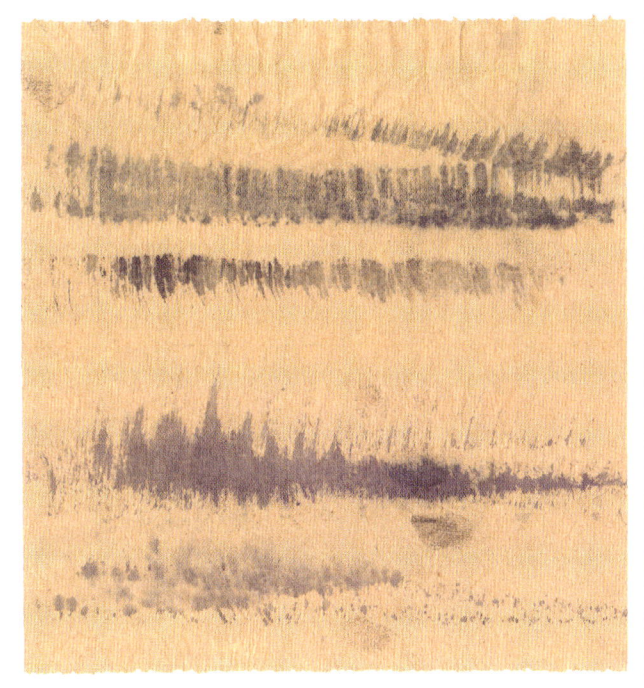

*I—2 Finding its Traces*

more space

to feel with my feet the faint tracks

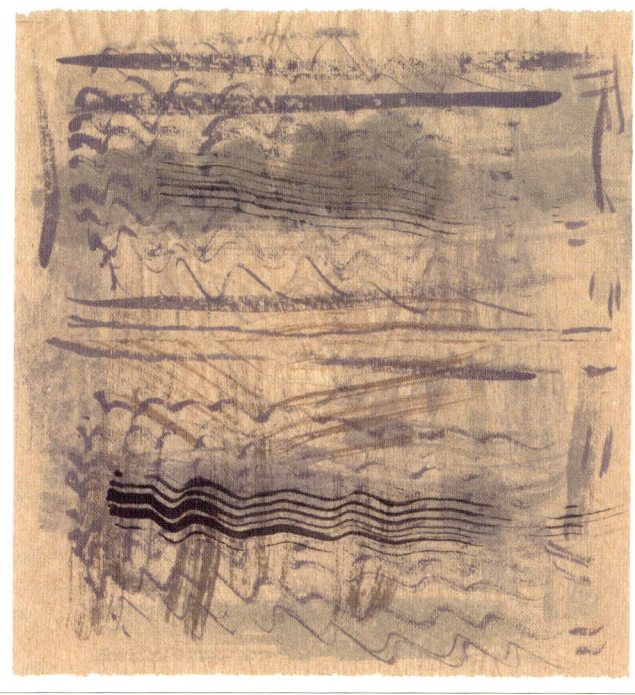

*I—3 Seeing the Ox*

It was a juncture

to go that way or this

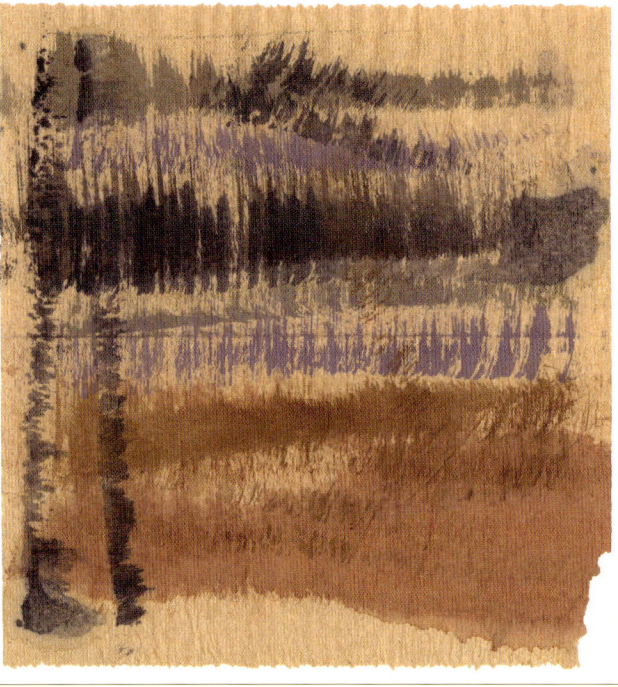

*I—4 Catching the Ox*

Arriving, realizing we

never departed.

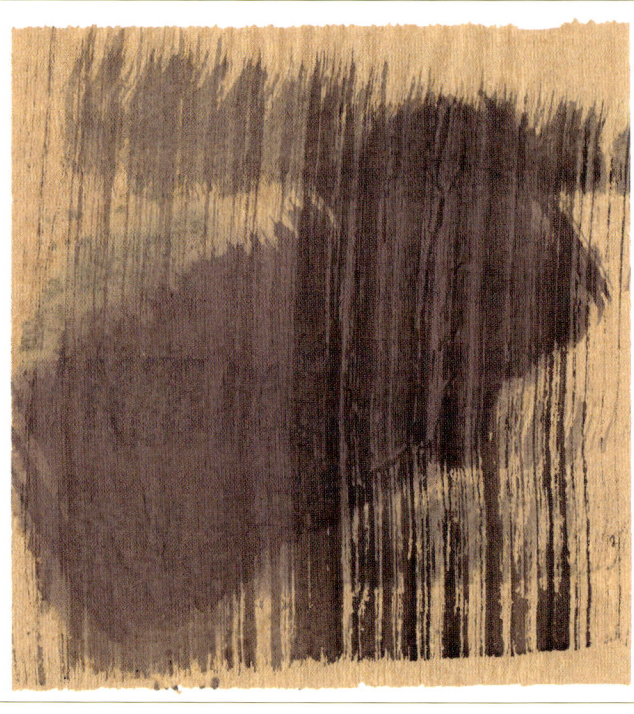

*I—5 Taming the Ox*

the dance

the magic

in some way

the contours

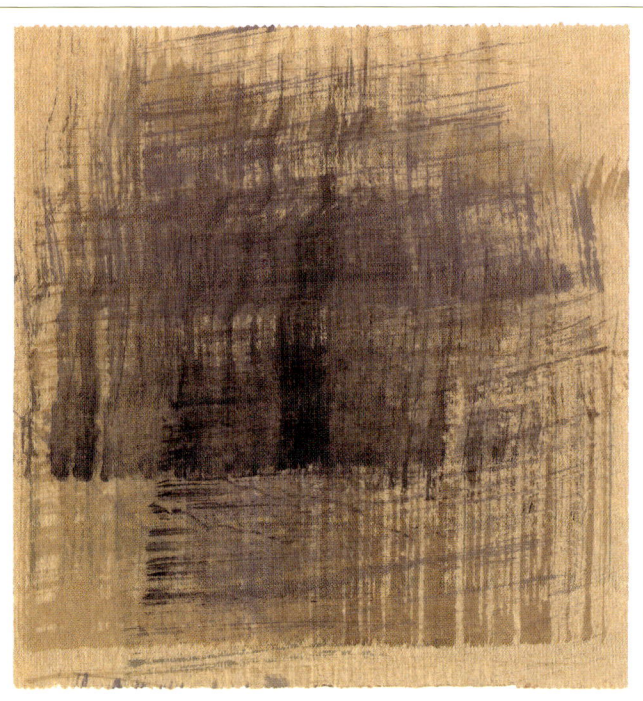

*I—6 Riding the Ox Home*

let it dance

between mind

moving and not moving

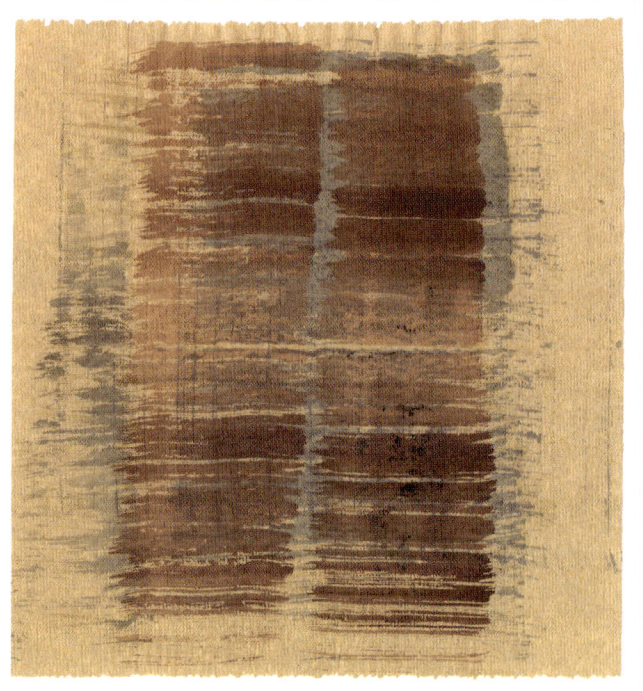

*I—7 Forgetting the Ox*

Multiplicity

ran

no play of power

dancing

free

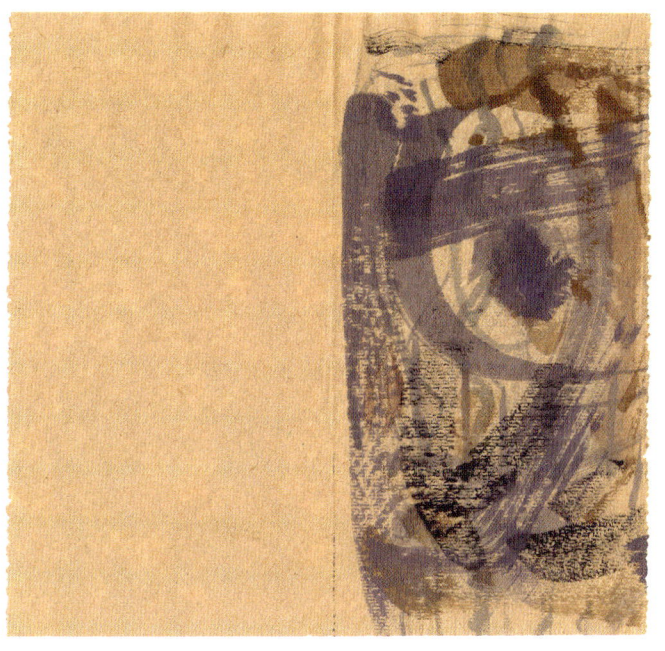

*I—8 Transcending the Ox*

actions move from zero

began

a center

*I—9 Returning to the Source*

nothing's changed yet

something immense

that adds up

to zero

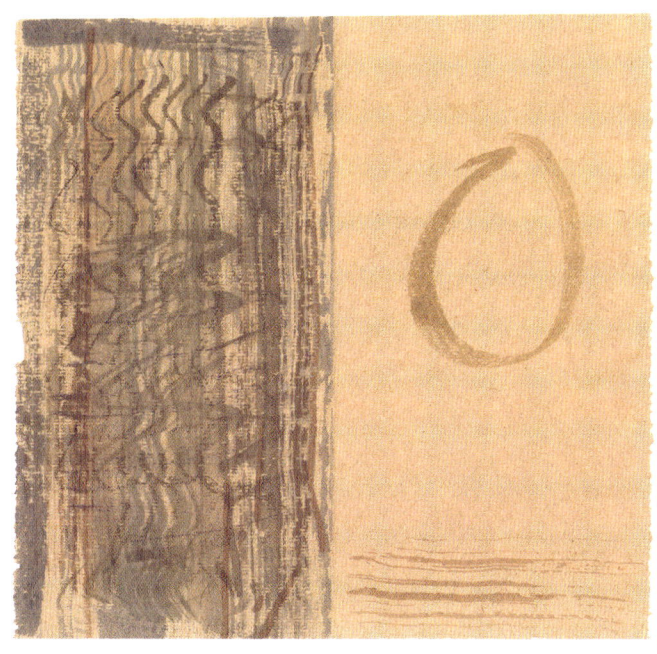

*I—10 Entering the Marketplace*

liberation

the flower the smile

the return bearing gifts to the village

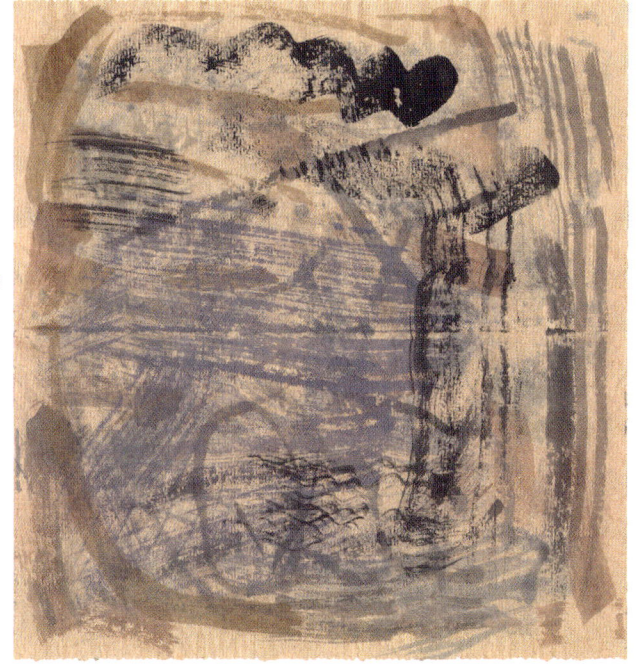

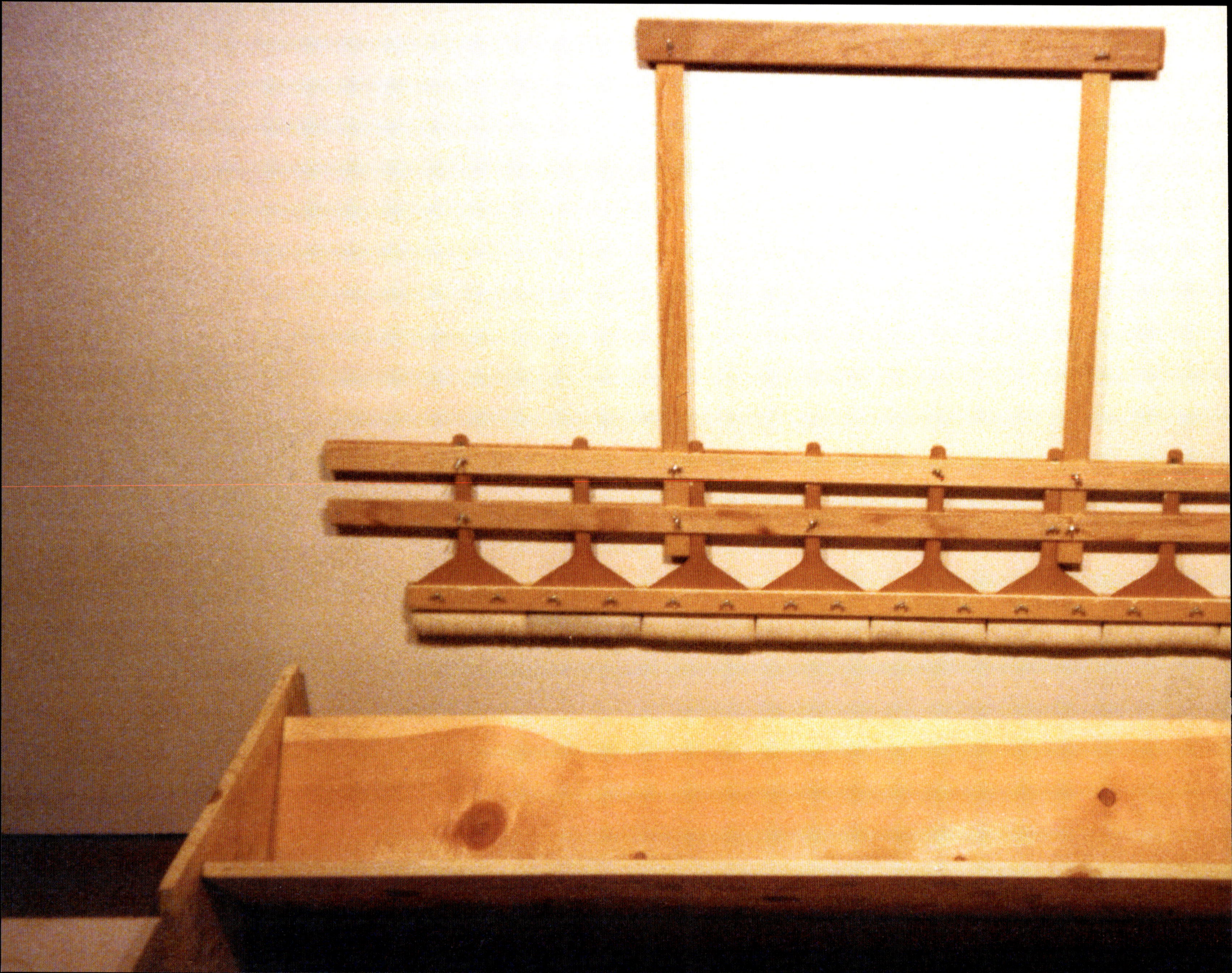

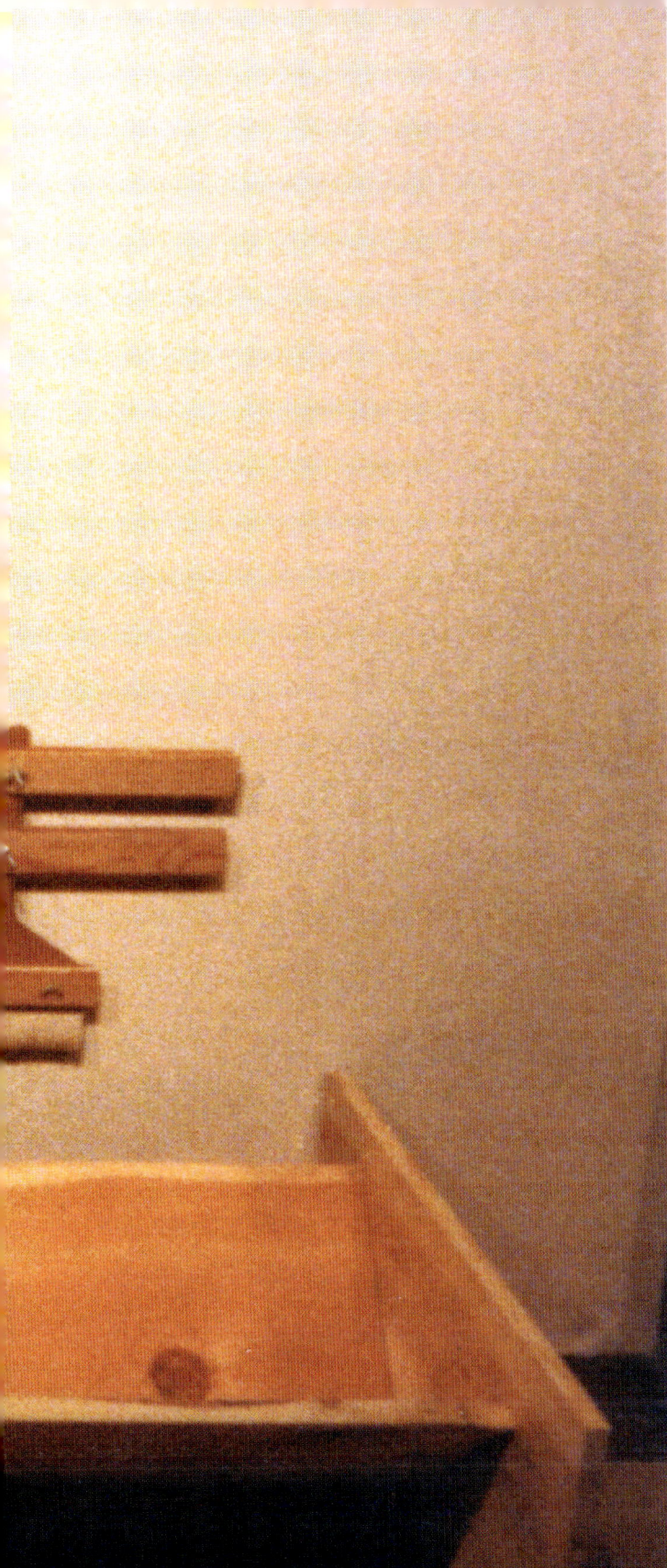

# XI

## *Performing John Cage's STEPS*

56-inch-wide brush and 60-inch-wide wooden trough that John Cage used to perform *STEPS: A Composition for a Painting*, 1989

# ONGOING PERFORMANCES OF *JOHN CAGE'S STEPS:* *A COMPOSITION FOR A PAINTING*

RAY KASS

When I wrote the notation for John Cage's original performance of *STEPS* for the John Cage Trust in 2006, Howard Risatti suggested that I discuss the possibility of ongoing performances of the piece with the trust's director, Laura Kuhn. She suggested that I write two variations of the notation — the first, *John Cage's STEPS: A Composition for a Painting*, describing exactly what Cage did when he performed the piece in my studio and the materials he used; and the second, *John Cage's STEPS: A Composition for a Painting to Be Performed by Individuals or Groups*, that would allow for a wide range of interpretation and require that the performer(s) give the resultant painting a new name. We referred to the latter as "the second notation."[1]

The first two performances of *STEPS* by an individual were done by Stephen Addiss in 2006 at the Capital One West Creek Campus in Richmond as part of their art program. He worked with the same materials and on paper of the same size as Cage had used; Addiss named his two versions *Sumi-e I* and *Sumi-e II*.

I began discussing the piece and the possibility of a performance with Merce Cunningham, who at that time was wheelchair-bound but still actively choreographing for his dance company. I acquired a wheelchair from the local Goodwill store in Salem, Virginia, and applied ink to the wheels and performed *STEPS* on a piece of fabric for an exhibition in Taiwan.[2] I named the piece *John Cage's STEPS – for Merce*, to encourage Merce to perform this second notation along with his dancers. On October 23, 2008, Merce choreographed three performances of the piece at the Cunningham Dance Studio on Bethune Street in New York City's Greenwich Village. *Dancers I* and *Dancers II*

were choreographed by Merce for four dancers.[3] However, for *Dancers III*, Merce agreed to perform it under his own power; Risatti and I, with the help of workshop assistants, inked the wheels of his wheelchair every 20–30 seconds as he performed, creating graceful arcs across fabric taped to the studio floor. Afterwards, Merce choreographed the dancers as they applied washes with the big brushes. I believe that it was very likely his last live performance and I am grateful that we had the opportunity to make a video documentary of his performance.

In 2009, I created two more performances of *STEPS*, *Current I* and *Current II*, one of which was exhibited in May 2009, along with the Merce Cunningham pieces, at the Museo Nacional Centro de Arte Reina Sofía in Madrid, as décor for the dance company's dance performance.

In subsequent years, individuals and groups in Vienna, Salzburg, Washington, D.C., New York, Seattle, and Roanoke have performed the "second notation" in a variety of ways. The portfolio that follows documents aspects of these performances.

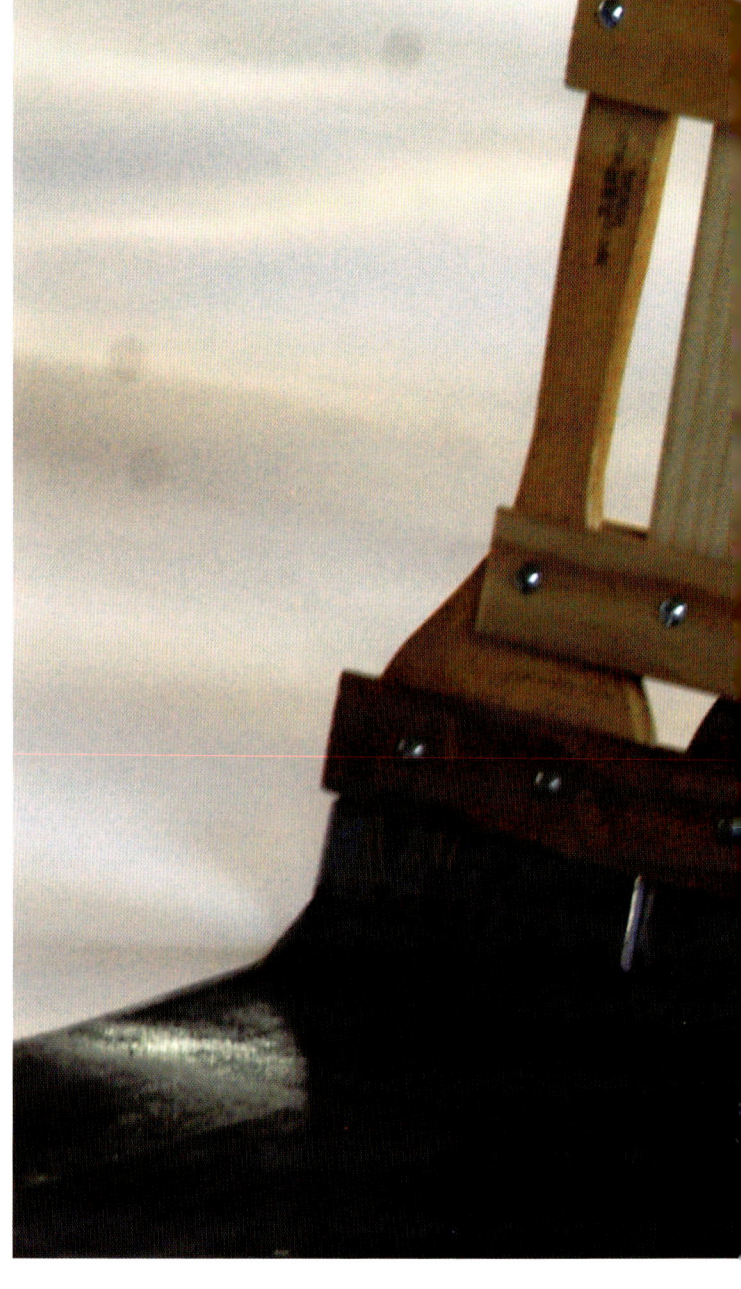

[1] The notation, which may be performed by individuals or groups, is available from Edition Peters. http://edition-peters.com/

[2] Tsai-Mo "Tu Yia" painting exhibition, the 8th Tsai-MoArt Festival in Taichung (Taiwan), Sept. 2009, Da Dun Gallery, Taichung Cultural Center.

[3] They were Jamie Scott, Dylan Crossman, Krista Nelson, and John Hinrichs; they performed *Dancers I* and *II* and applied the washes for Merce for his solo performance, *Dancers III*. At the time they were members of the "RUGS," or Repertory Understudy Dance Group; all became regular members of the Merce Cunningham Dance Company within the year.

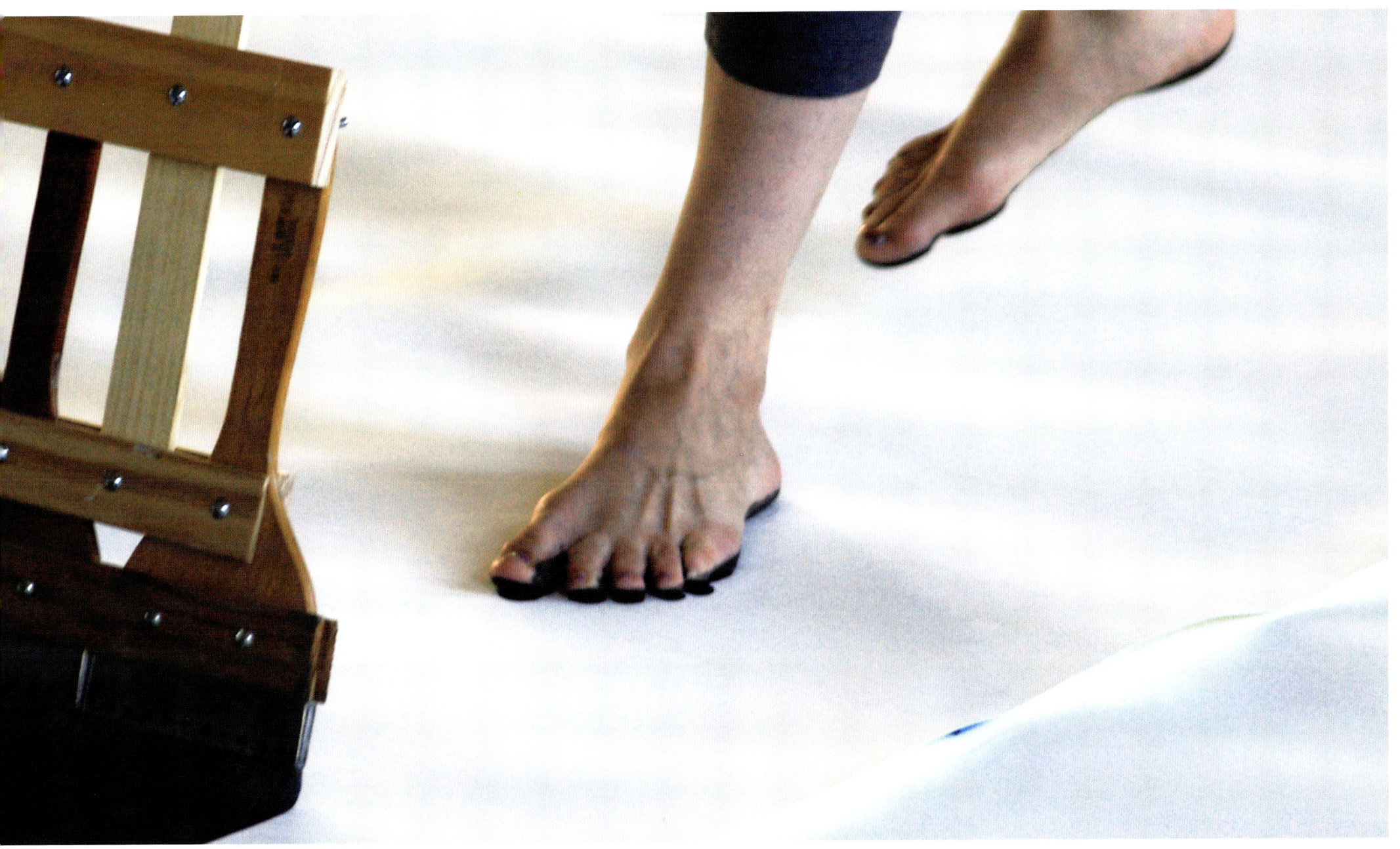

# STEPHEN ADDISS:
## *SUMI-E*, 2006

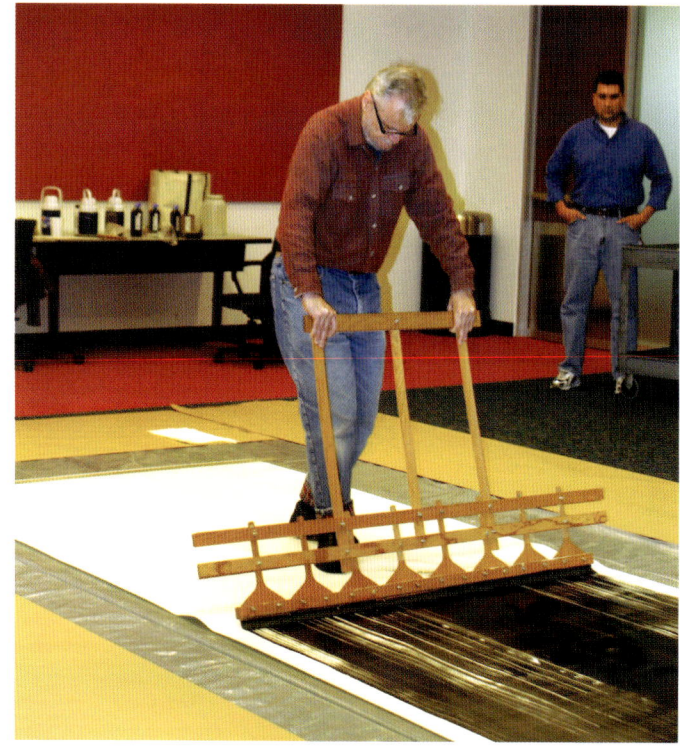

Stephen Addiss performs
*STEPS*, 2006,
Capital One Financial Corporation, West Creek Campus, Richmond, VA,
Photo: Audrey Seo

Stephen Addiss, *Sumi-e I*, 2006, ink and watercolor
on rag paper, 72 x 207 in. (182 x 525.78 cm)

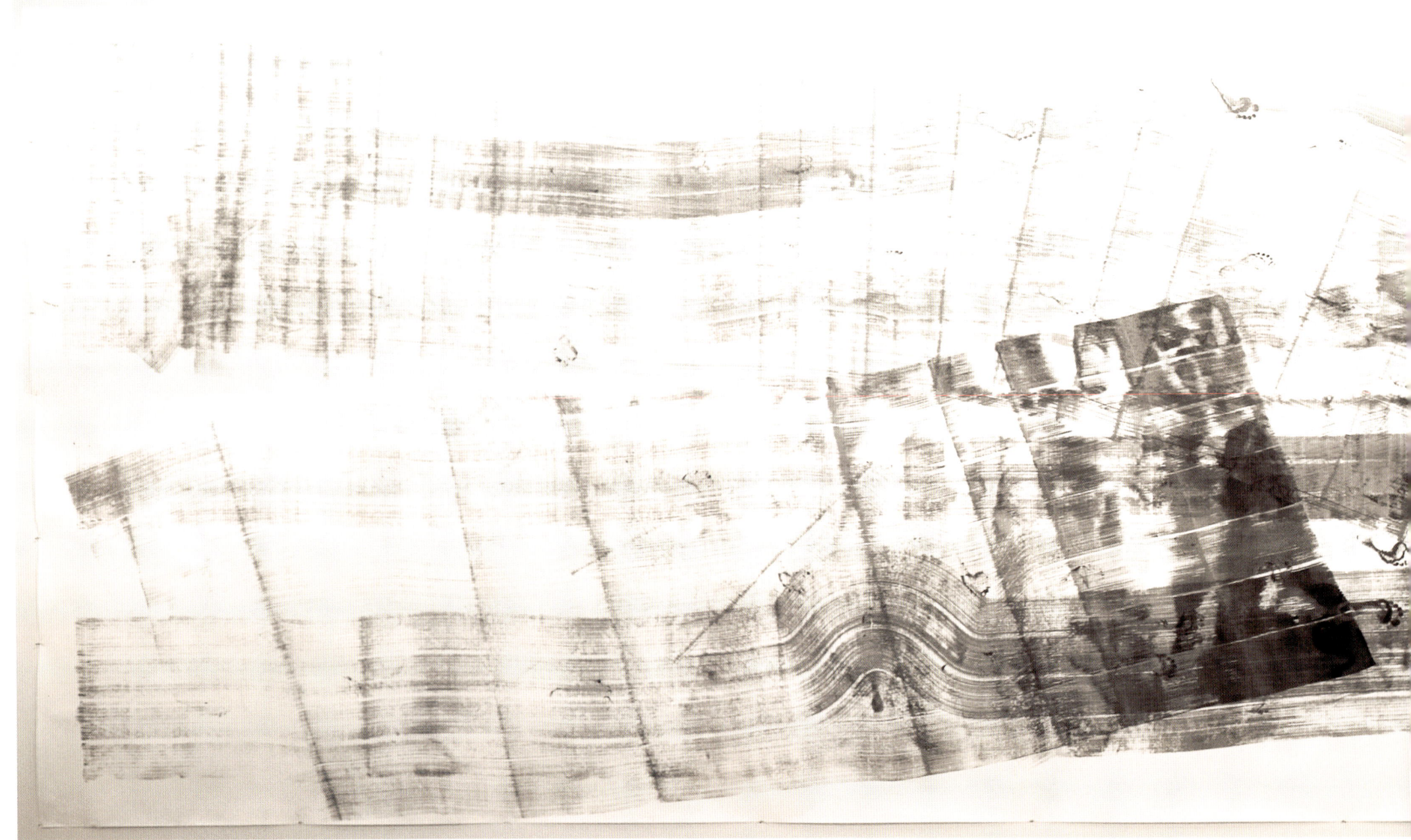

Merce Cunningham and the Repertory Understudy Dance Group with the Mountain Lake Workshop, *Dancers I*, 2008, a performance of J*ohn Cage's STEPS: A Composition for a Painting*, water media on rag paper, 141 x 360 in. (358.14 x 863.6 cm)

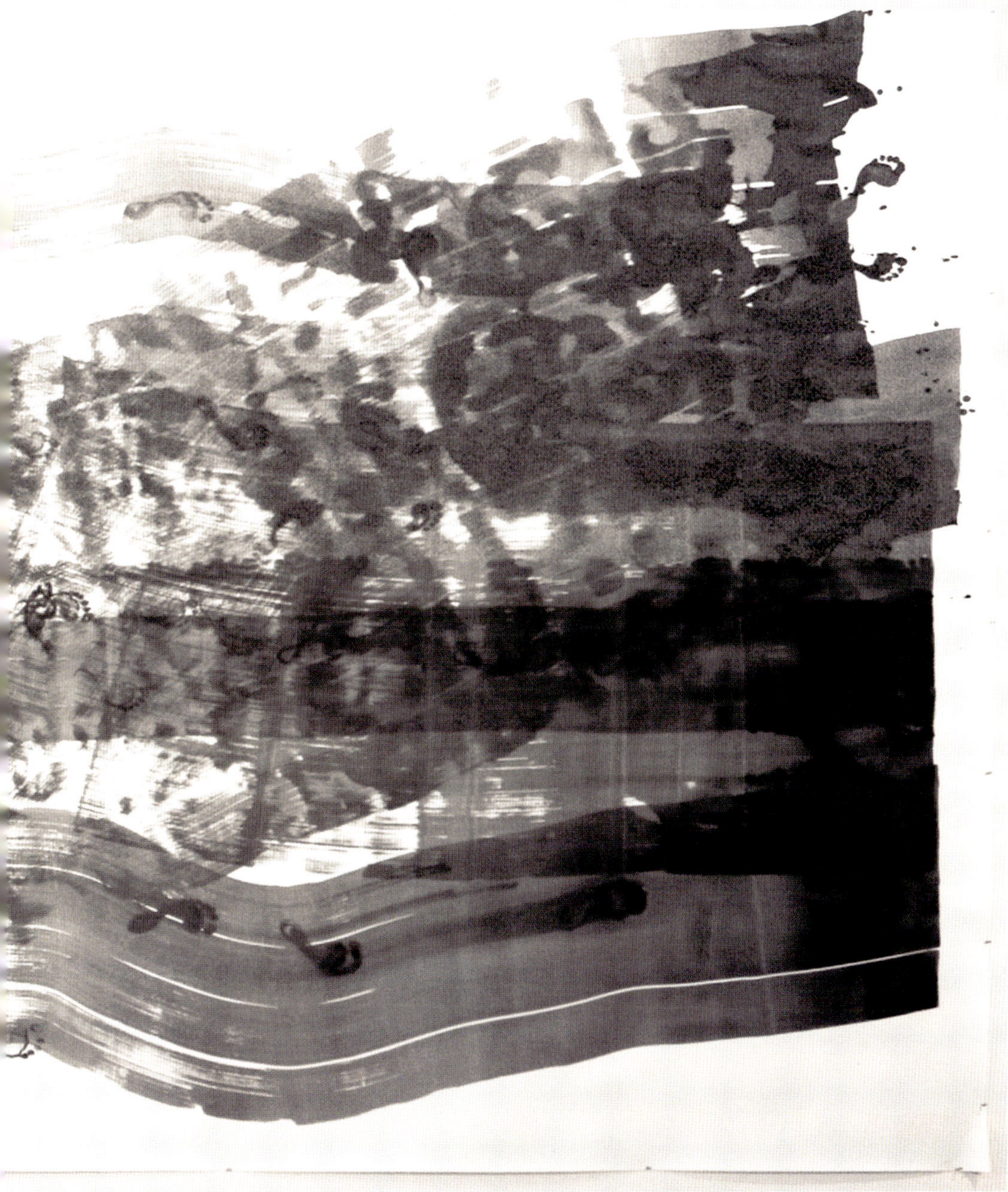

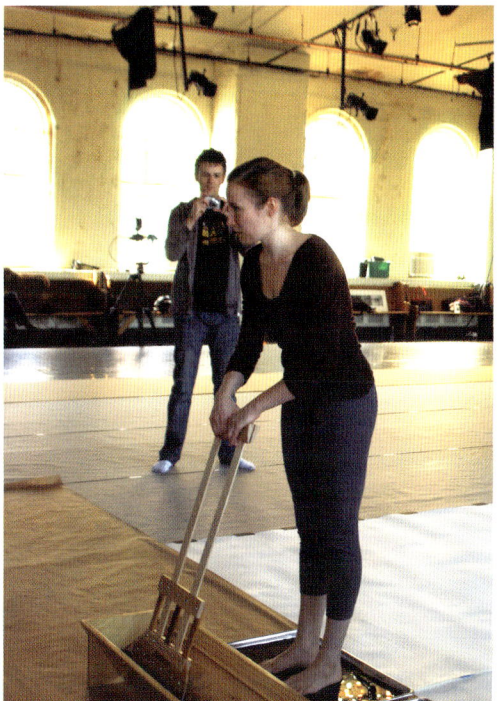

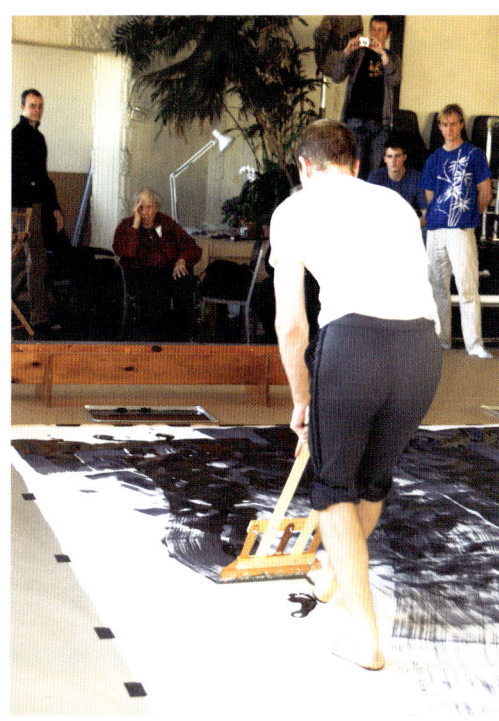

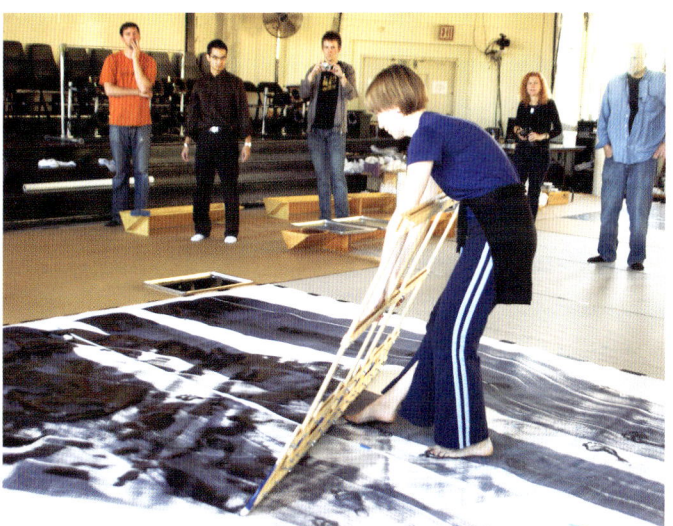

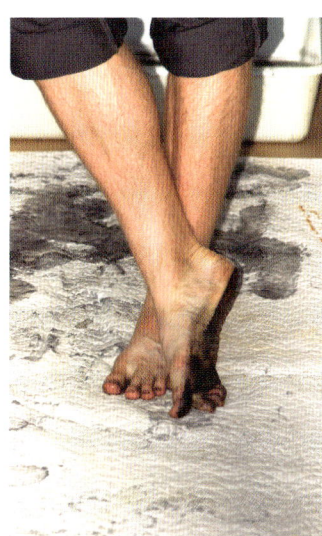

Clockwise from top left: Krista Nelson, John Hinrich, John Hinrich's feet, Jamie Scott.
All photos: Audrey Seo

263

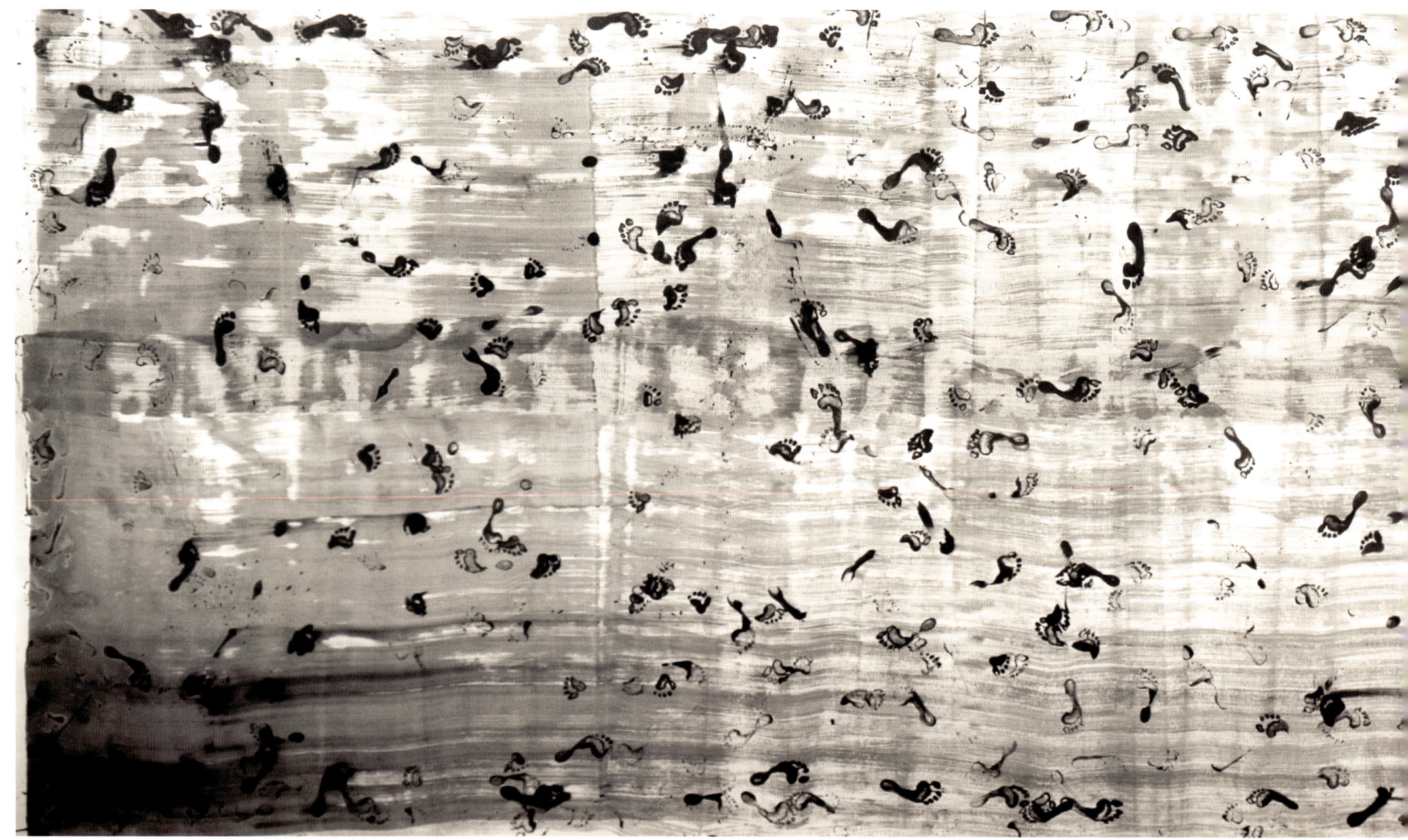

Merce Cunningham and the Repertory Understudy Dance Group with the Mountain Lake Workshop, *Dancers II*, 2008, a performance of J*ohn Cage's STEPS: A Composition for a Painting*, water media on rag paper, 141 x 360 in. (358.14 x 863.6 cm),

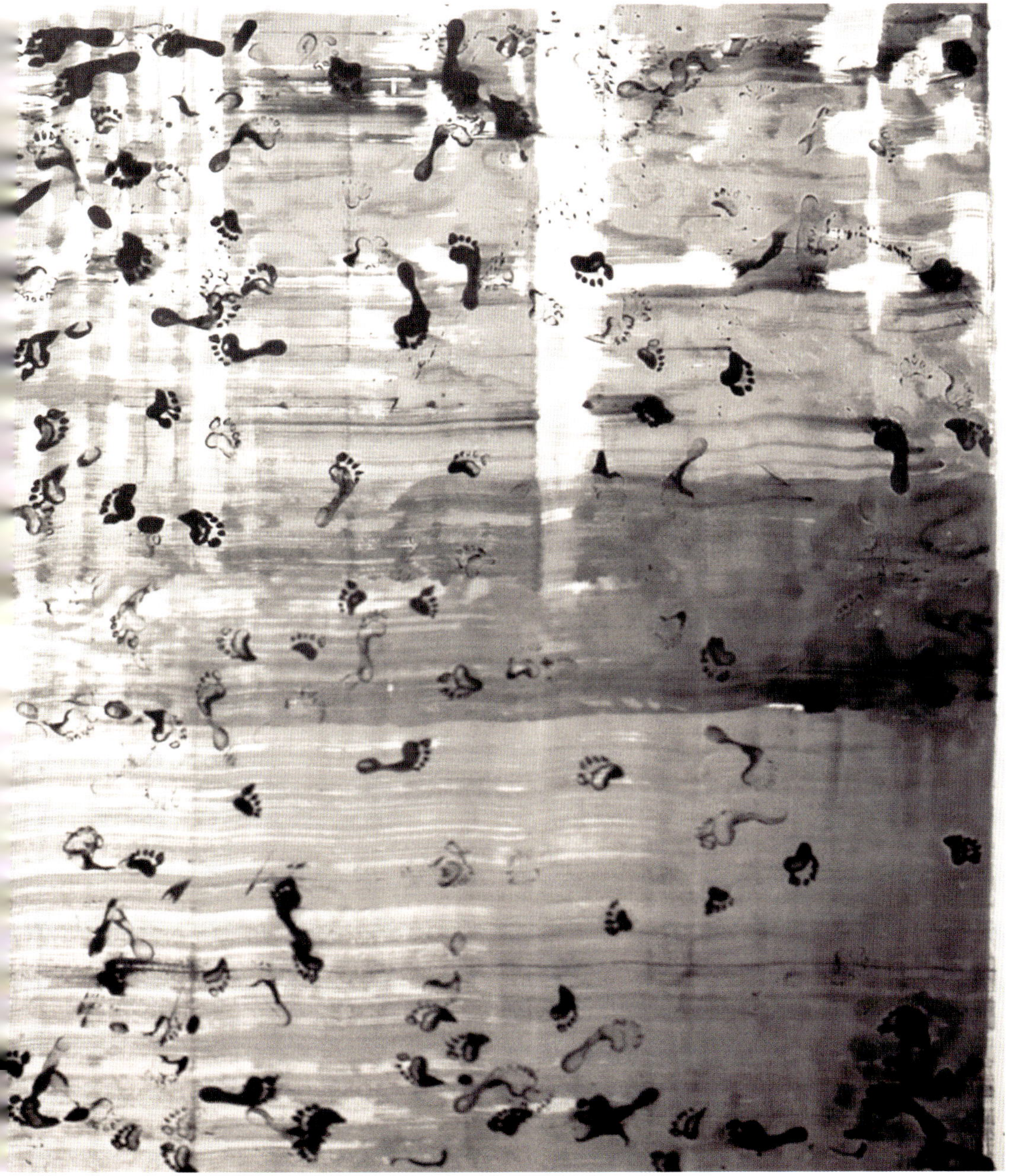

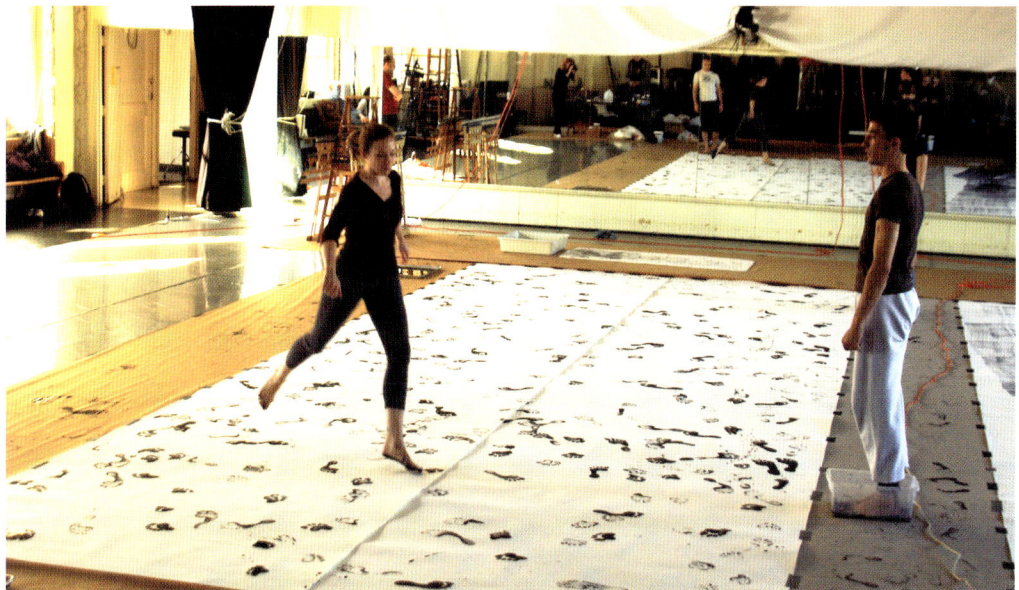

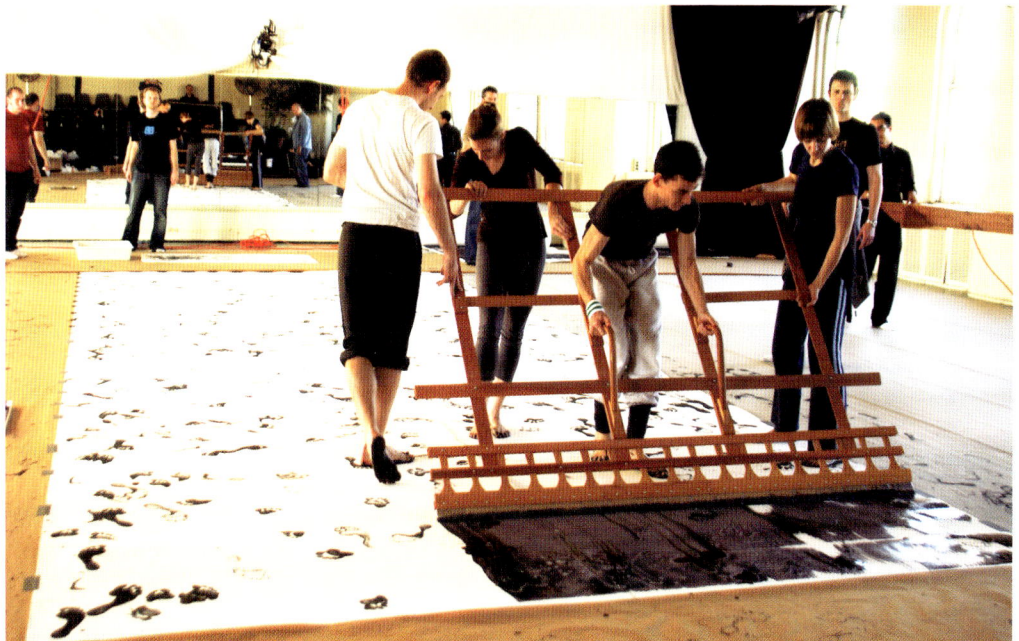

Top: Krista Nelson and Dylan Crossman
Photo: Audrey Seo

Bottom: (Holding brush, L-R) John Hinrichs, Krista
Nelson, Dylan Crossman, and Jamie Scott
Photo: Audrey Seo

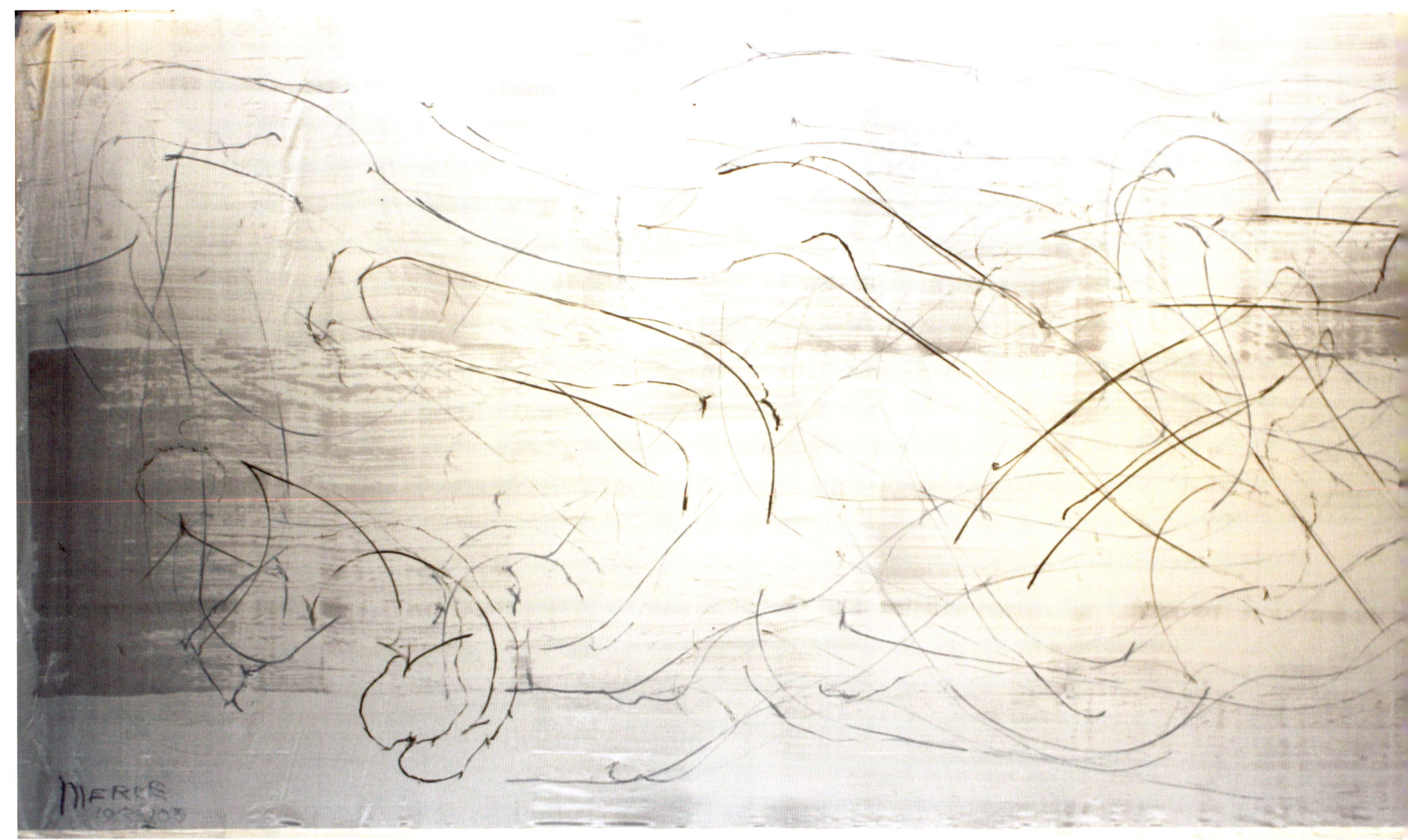

Merce Cunningham and the Repertory Understudy Dance Group with the Mountain Lake Workshop, *Dancers III*, 2008, a performance of *John Cage's STEPS: A Composition for a Painting*, water media on rag paper, 198 x 396 in. (502 x 1005 cm)

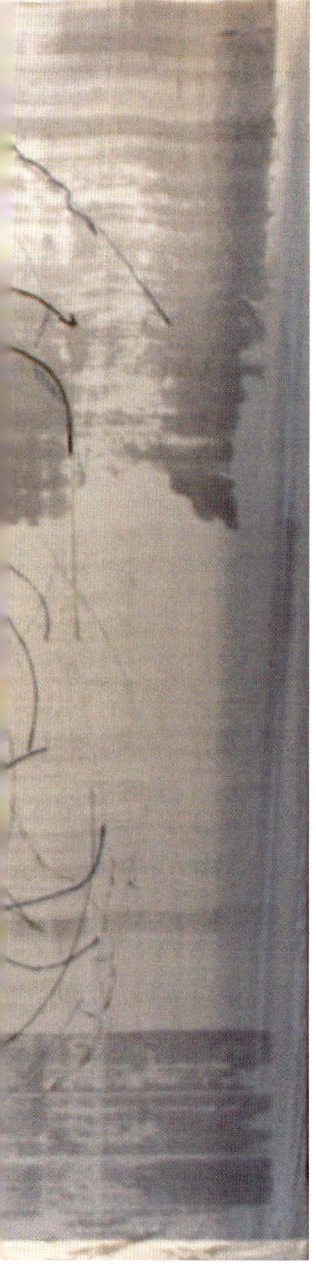

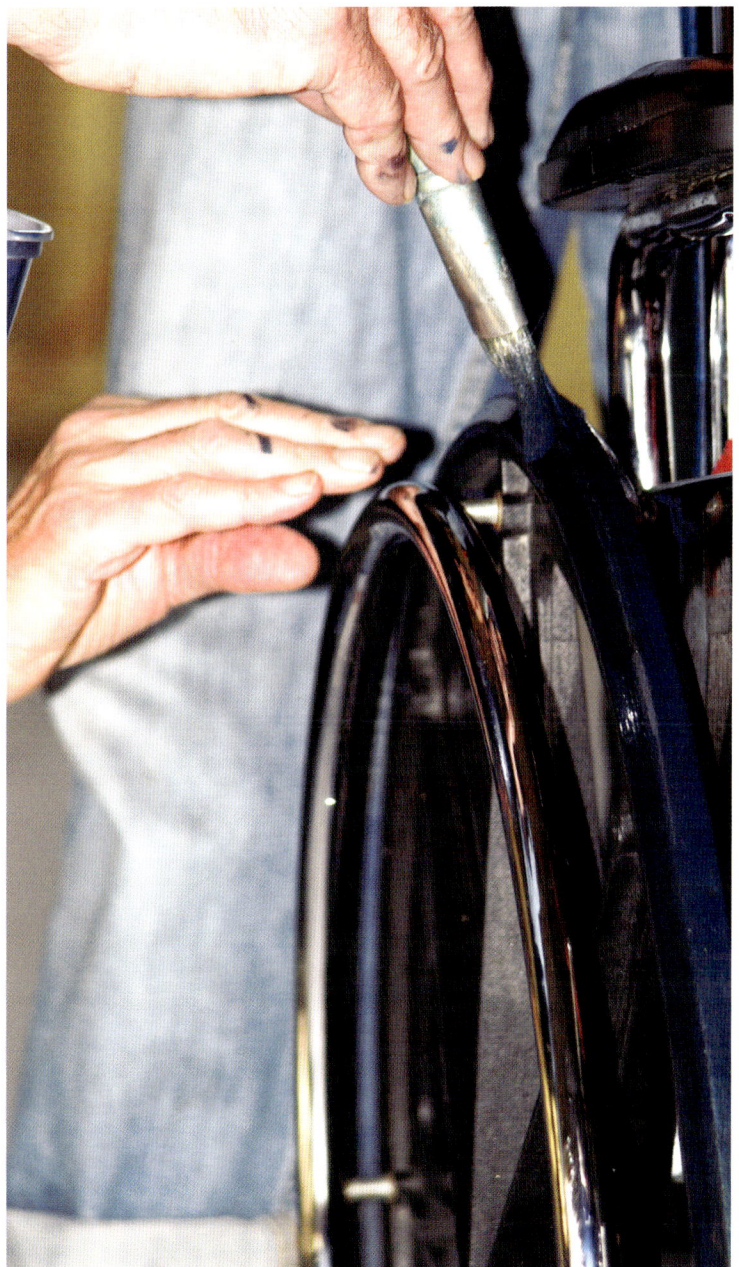

Inking the wheels of Merce Cunningham's wheelchair

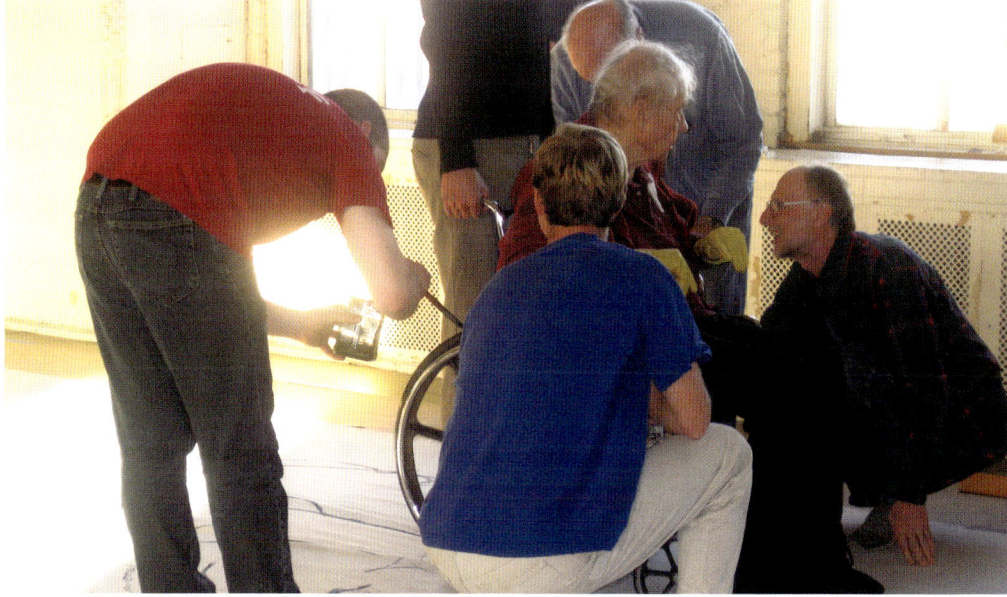

Photo: Audrey Seo

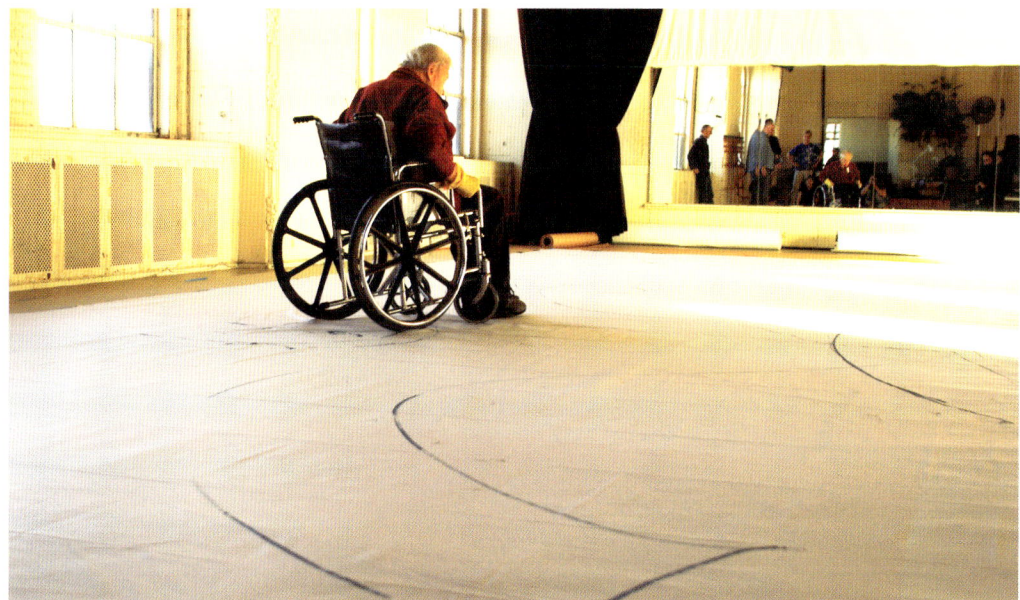

Photo: Simone Paterson

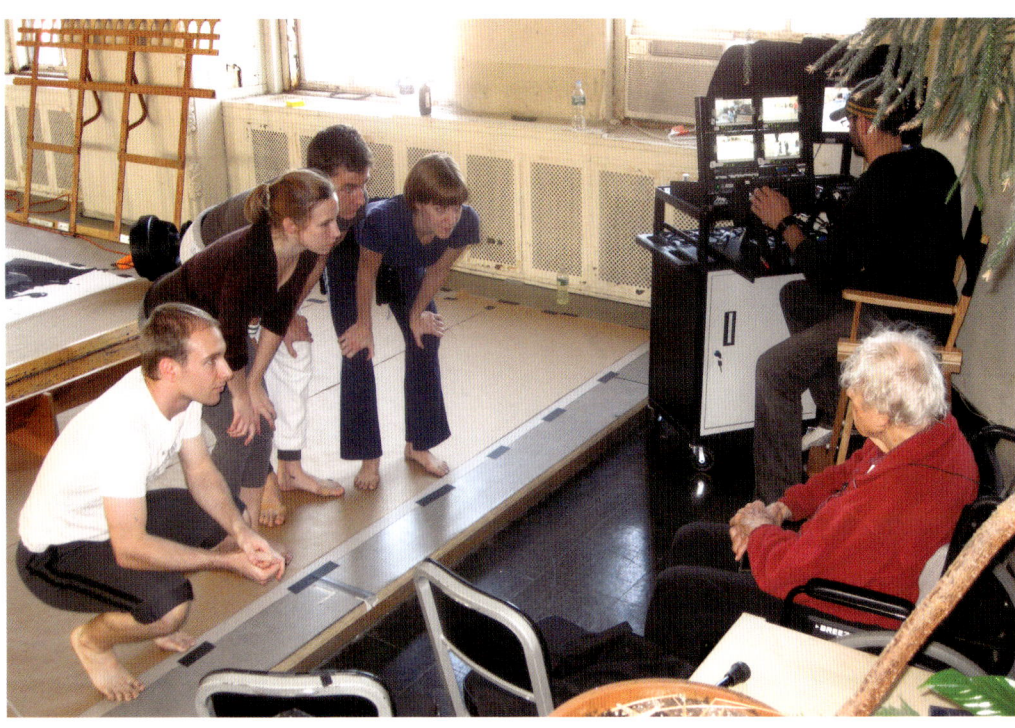

Dancers John Hinrchs, Krista Nelson, Dylan Crossman, and Jamie Scott receive instruction from Merce; videographer Christopher Young in the background
Photo: Audrey Seo

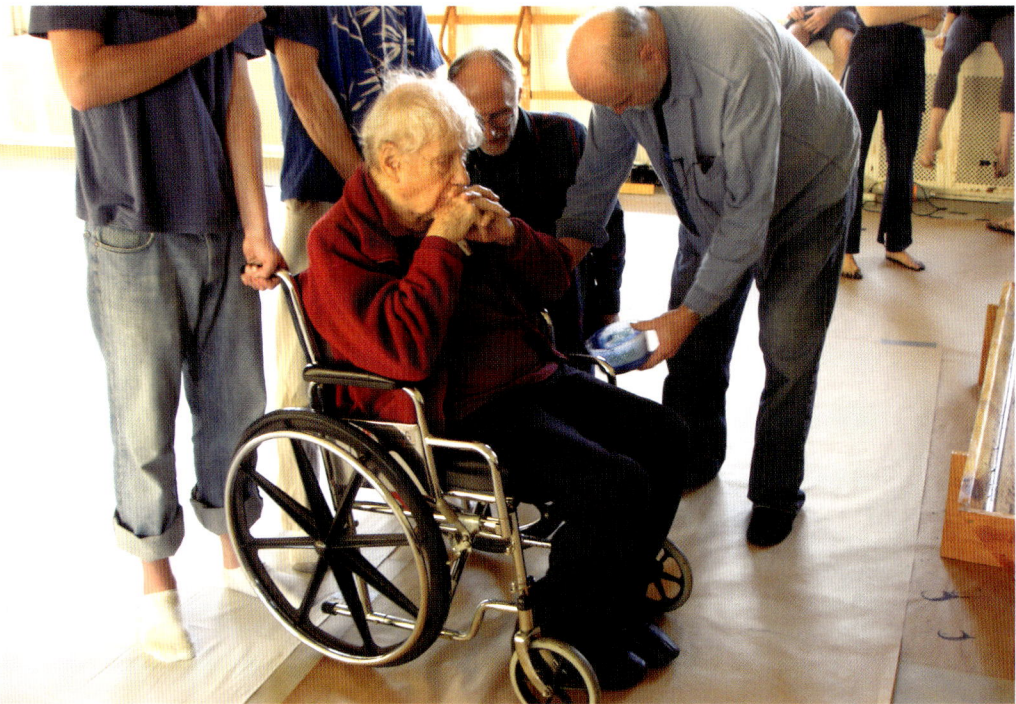

Photo: Nolan Doran

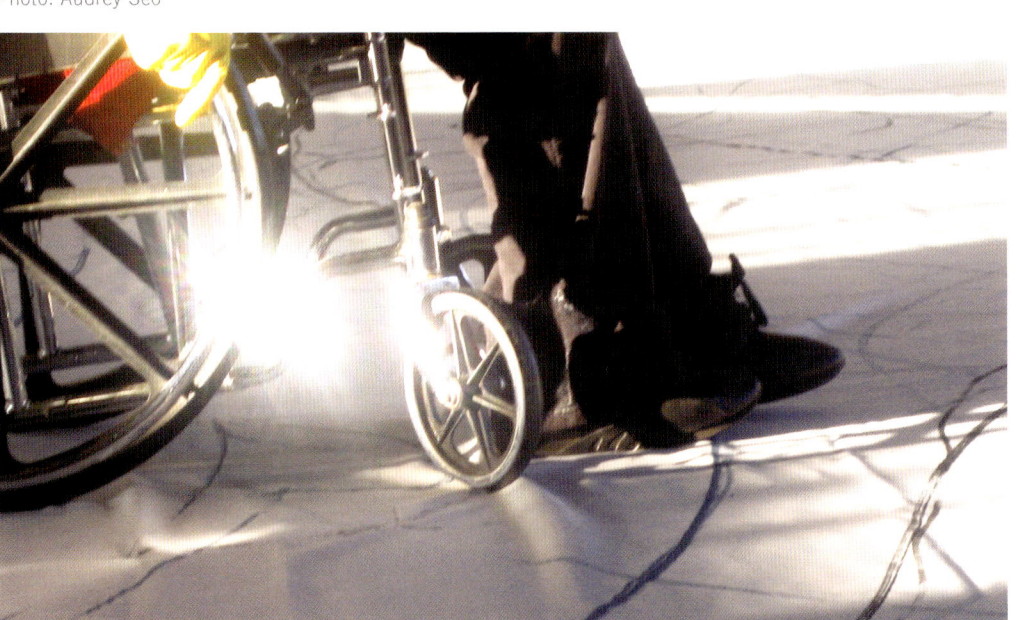

Photo: Audrey Seo

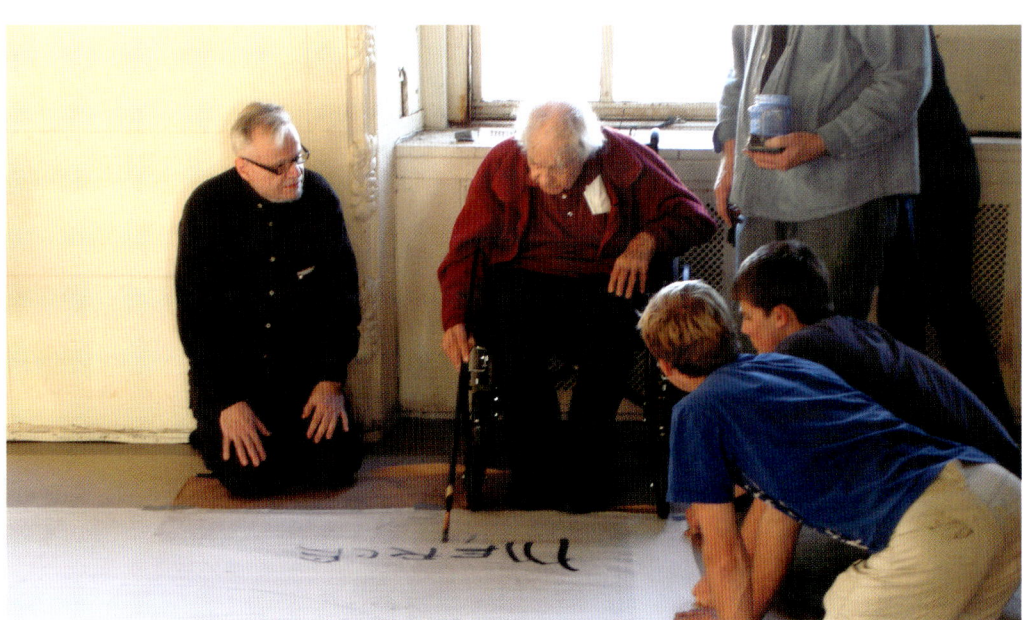

(Clockwise from left) Stephen Addiss, Merce Cunningham, Ray Kass (standing) Andrew Puhl, Matt Belay
Photo: Nolan Doran

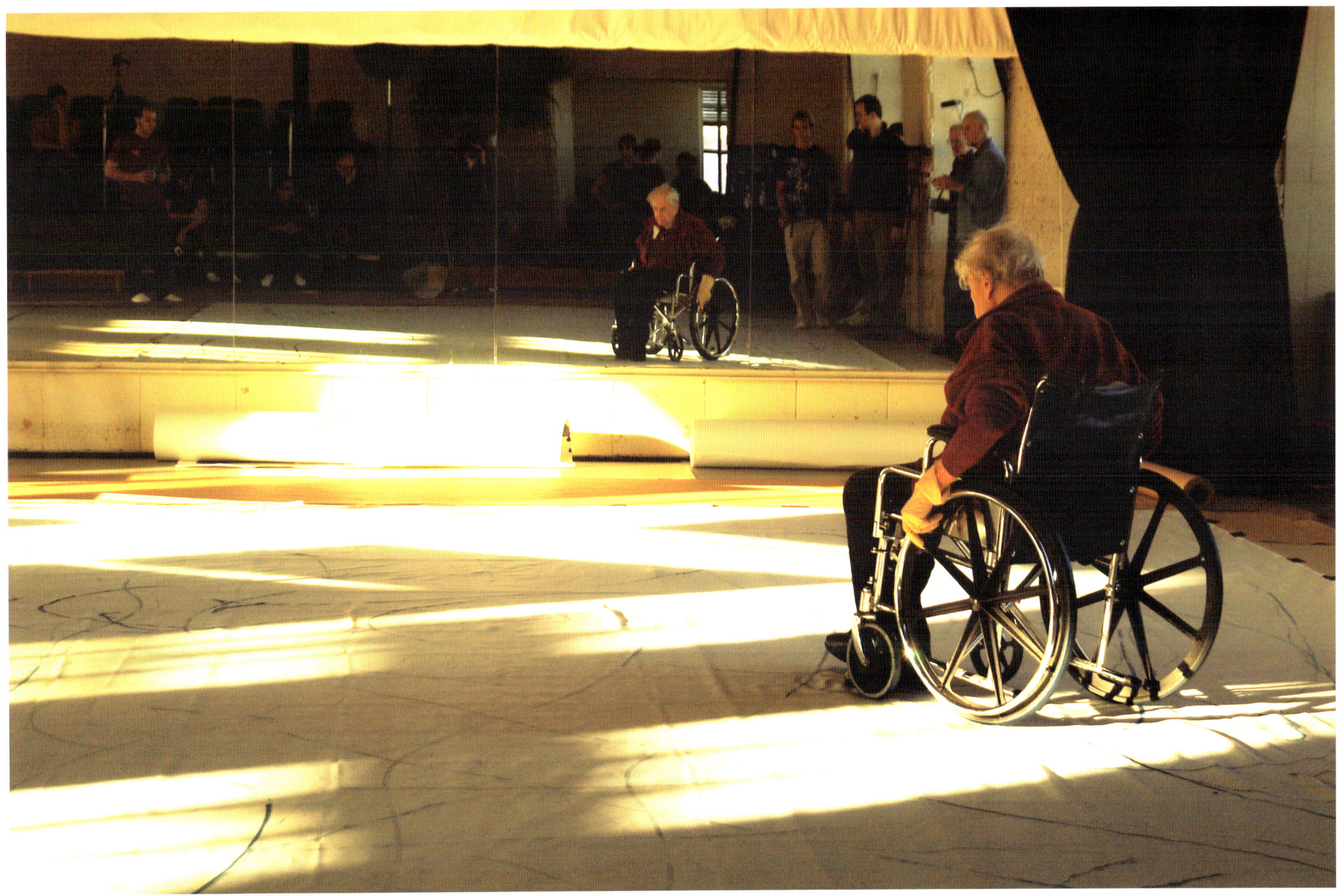

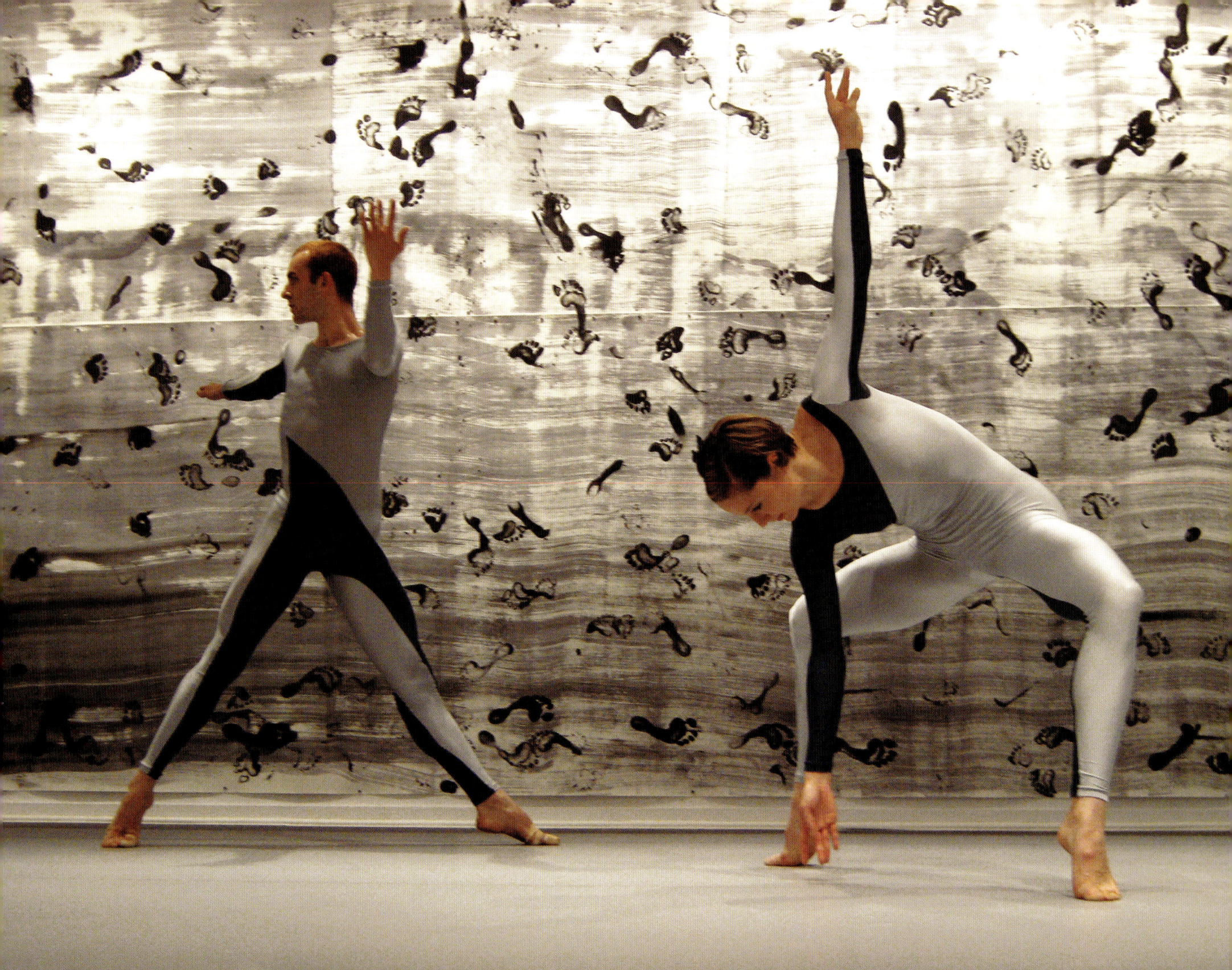

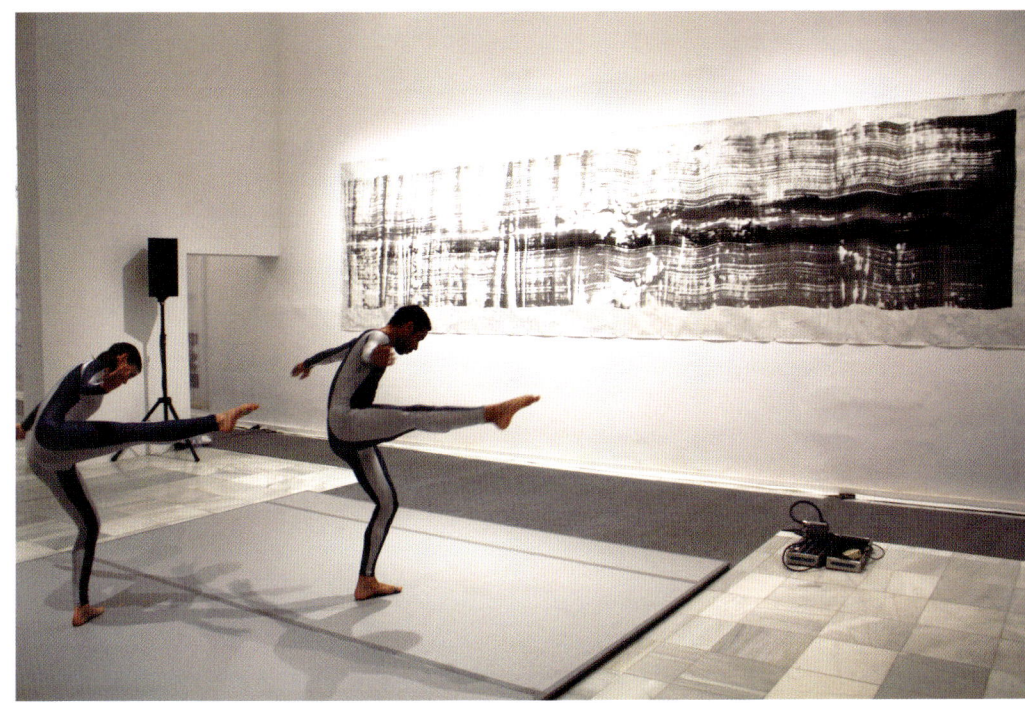

Marcie Munnerlyn and Rashaun Mitchell. Décor: Ray Kass, *Current III* (2009), Photo: Francis Thompson

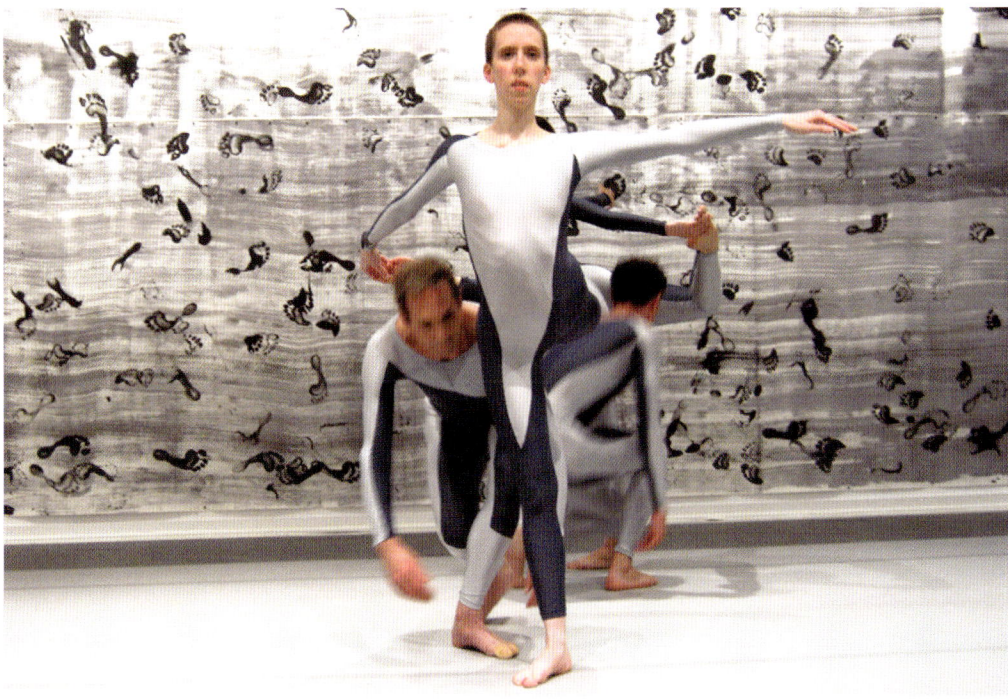

Julie Cunningham, Robert Swinston, Daniel Madoff (hidden), Emma Desjardins (hidden), Photo: Francis Thompson

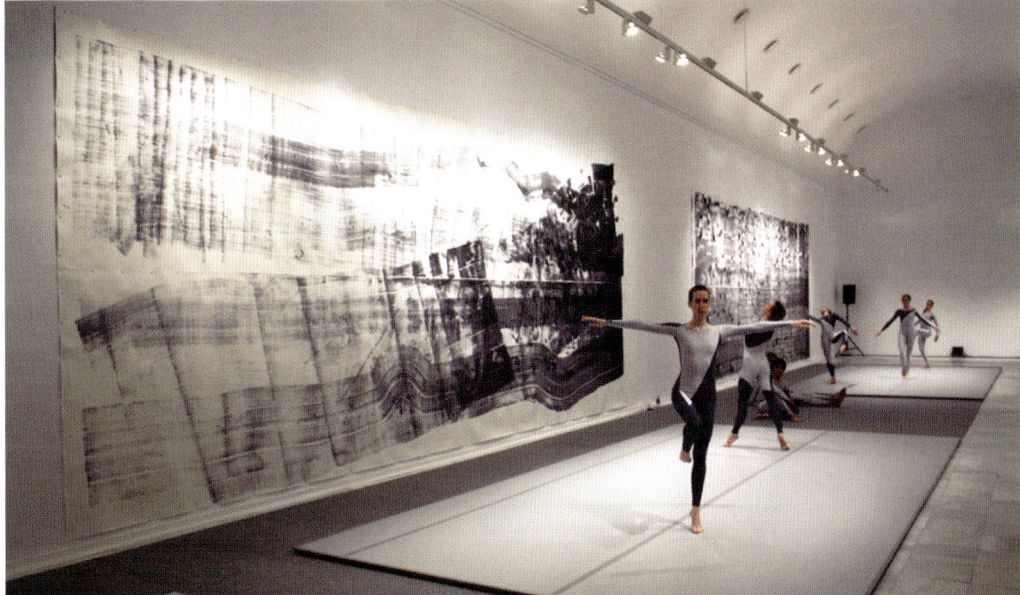

Merce Cunningham Dance Company. Décor: Cunningham Repertory Understudy Dance Group, *Dancers I and II* (2008) at Museo Nacional Centro de Arte Reina Sofia, Madrid, Photo: Francis Thompson

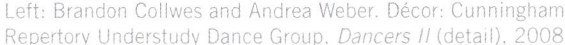

Left: Brandon Collwes and Andrea Weber. Décor: Cunningham Repertory Understudy Dance Group, *Dancers II* (detail), 2008

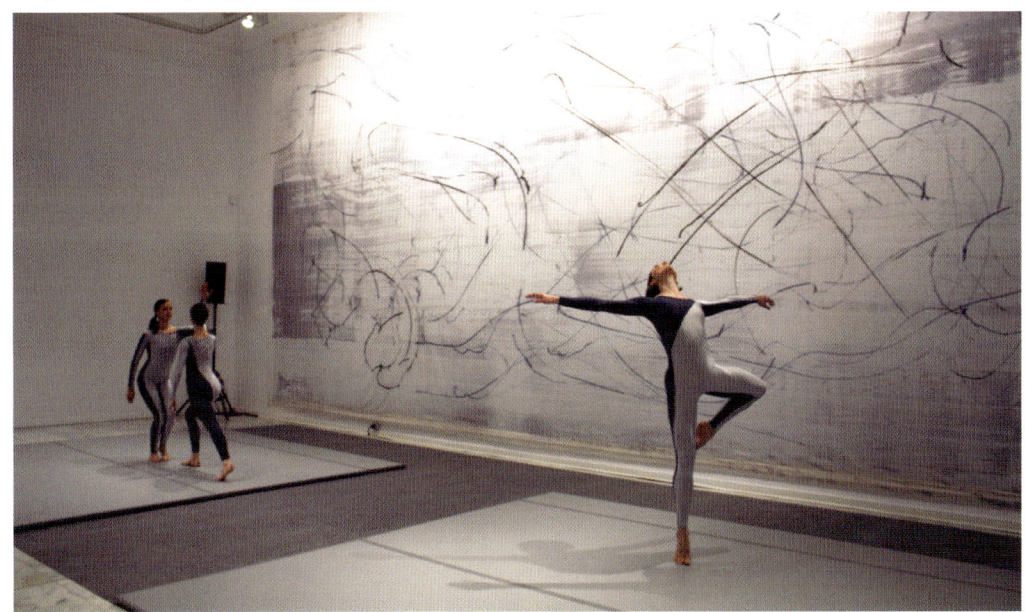

(L-R) Marcie Munnerlyn, Julie Cunningham and Andrea Weber. Décor: Cunningham Repertory Understudy Dance Group, Merce's solo performance of *Dancers III* (2008) at Museo Nacional Centro de Arte Reina Sofia, Madrid, Photo: Francis Thompson

# PERFORMANCES OF *STEPS* FOR JOHN CAGE'S CENTENNIAL YEAR

ROGER REYNOLDS

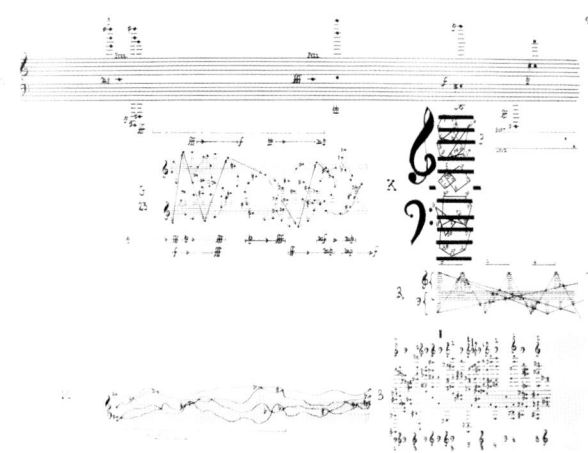

Before embarking on the organization of the John Cage Centennial Festival Washington, D.C., with Steve Antosca and my partner Karen Reynolds, I had been only tangentially aware of Cage's work as a visual artist.[1] His graphic scores, most particularly the epic effort that produced the 1957 score *Solo for Piano*, the central component of a larger construct titled *Concert for Piano and Orchestra*, had been, Cage indicated, a tribute to the pianist and composer David Tudor, who had been a dedicated (and perhaps even more disciplined) performer of Cage's music.

Cage's use of graphic provocation in this score was elaborated by prefatory notes inscribed with an exquisite pen and ink calligraphy. So it had already been evident from his score that Cage was observant, disciplined, artful, and meticulous about the ways in which he presented his ideas to the world. At the same time, it was equally clear that he did not and would not ever live a restrictive life. His curiosity and unique "aesthetic sensibility" caused him to be responsive to the world in continuously evolving ways. One should not look for or expect surface consistencies in his work. Surprisingly, painter and collaborator Ray Kass notes that Cage had said in 1983 (in reference to an exhibition of his etchings and drawings) that "All of these things take as a beginning that I can't draw"; this comment betrays a surprisingly limited definition of what it is to draw.

Kass had previously donated three Cage watercolors made at Mountain Lake to Washington's Phillips Collection, and I suggested to the collection's administration that it would be an appropriate and a valuable addition to the Cage centennial (JCDC) celebration that they mount a small show. They exhibited their three Cage watercolors along with

works by two Pacific Northwest artists, Mark Tobey and Morris Graves, with whom Cage had developed important friendships in Seattle in the late 1930s. It was a wonderful and fitting contribution to the Cage centennial events.

American University, one of the ten collaborating institutions for the JCDC festival, also made its large gallery in the Katzen Arts Center available. Its director, Jack Rasmussen, agreed immediately to mount a major exhibition of previous performances of *STEPS*. In addition, he and I visited the archives of Cage's publisher, the C. F. Peters Corporation in Queens, New York, and located letters and manuscript sketches for various musical works that were also displayed in the Katzen galleries.

Two culminating visual art experiences on the final day of our JCDC enterprise were workshops/performances of public events hosted at the University of California's Washington Center (UCDC) near DuPont Circle. Kass had devised a quite astonishing confrontation for our group of participants. I say "confrontation" because the interface involved one (or several!) elements that brought one — in a very personal and immediate way — to the edge of two quite distinct though deeply related "fields of opportunity." The first, Jiro Okura's intense "breathing lines" exercise, was both personal and also collaborative. Our actions mattered, but were not determinative. In fact, the inevitable variability of the outcome in relation to the task that was set for us was one of the formative qualities on which the exercise depends. In using the term "exercise" I may be understood to imply something less directed or immediately revealing than what we actually did on the afternoon of 10 September 2012.

As I experienced the "breathing lines" exercise, the participants were given a task that was, for the uninitiated, both simply described and arduously realized. Choose a brush (an act that will, of course, influence the outcome in ways that an inexperienced individual could not foresee) and using the ink provided and mixed as one wished, paint a line across a broad, textured paper surface in such a way as to cause the line to metaphorically "breathe" by increasing and decreasing the pressure applied by brush to paper as you proceed from the beginning to the end of your intended path. If you were the first to venture out onto the paper's surface, you were singularly adventurous, but also free of implied layers of interactive assessment. If one or more individuals had preceded you, then what you did was inevitably a combination of the alternating breadth of the line you produced and the influence of what was

[1] The festival as a whole altered the impressions that I had built up over decades of interaction with him, both as a person and to his diverse creation as a composer, performer, and writer.

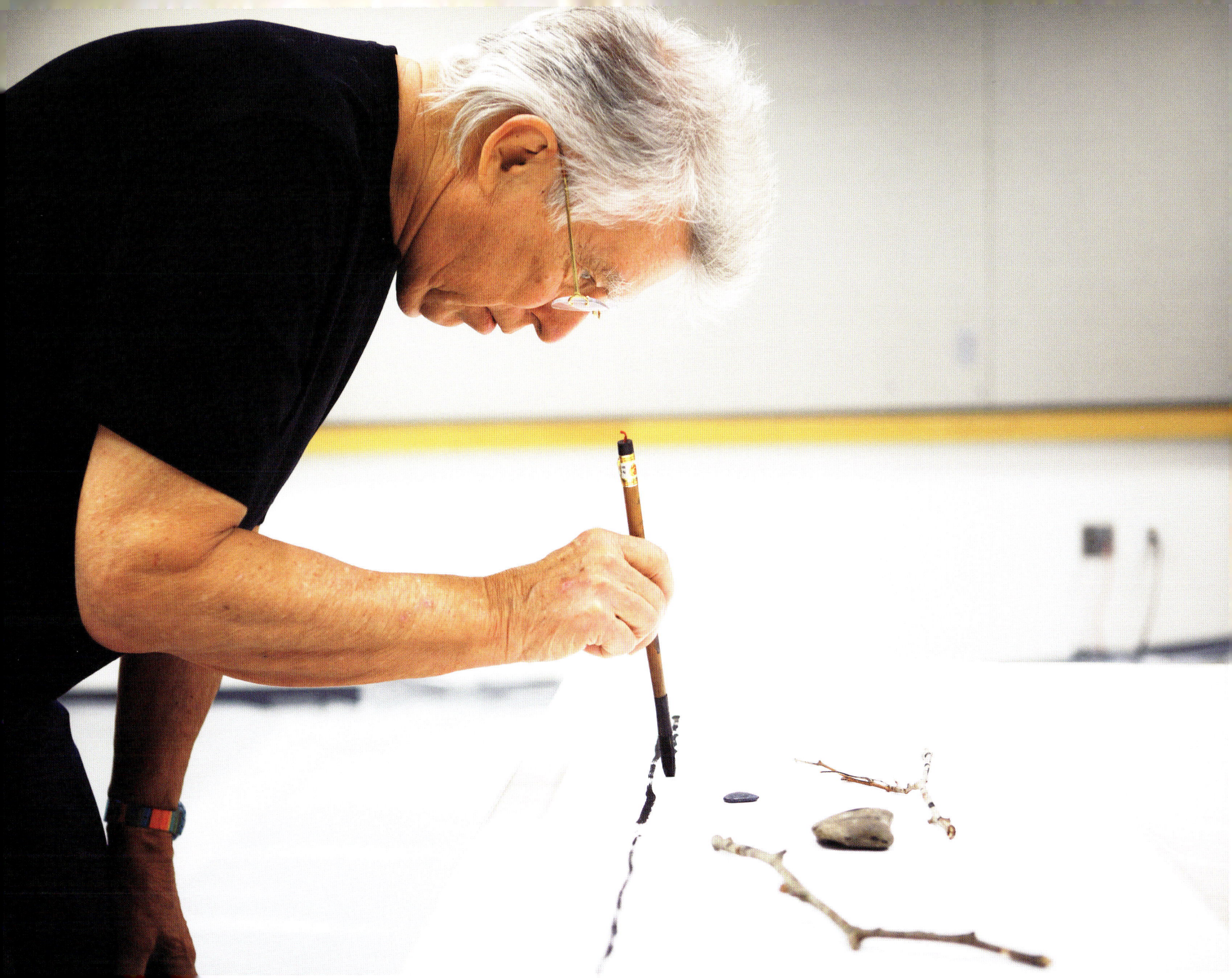

(below) Roger Reynolds about to encounter obstacles in realizing the "breathing lines" exercise.
Photo: Christopher Dobey

(next below) A finished and signed "breathing lines" exercise from the UCDC Cage Festival workshop/performance.
Photo: Christopher Dobey

Ray Kass displaying a completed "breathing lines" page from the JCDC festival event.
Photo: Christopher Dobey

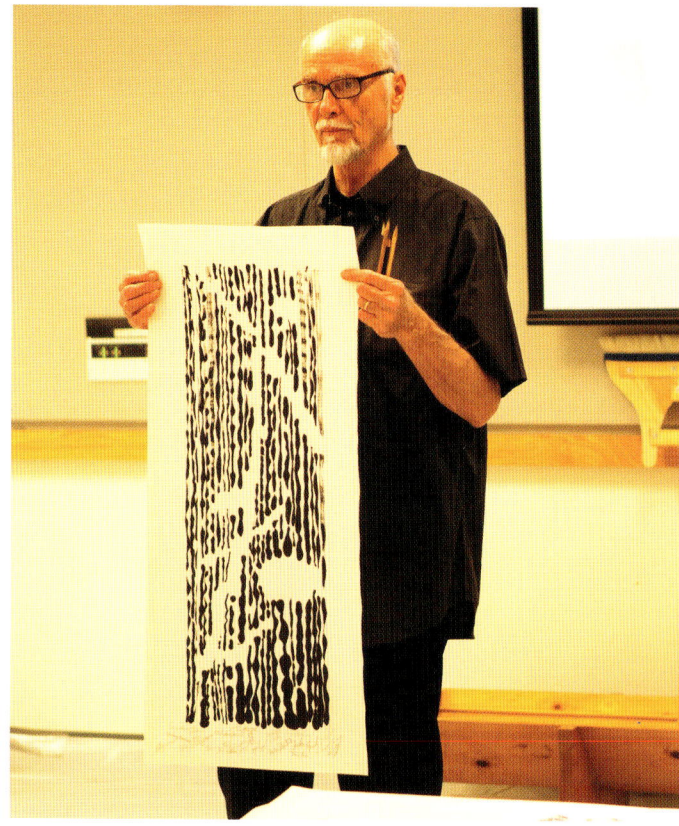

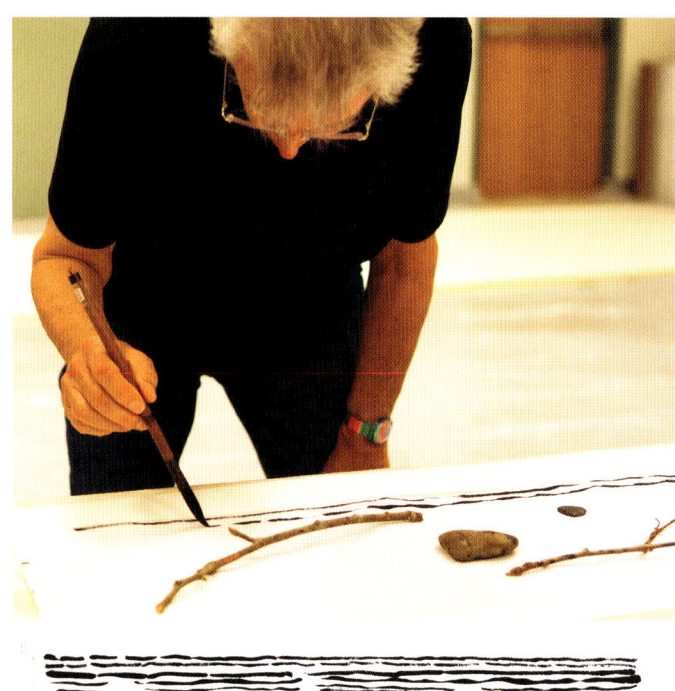

already "there." A sheet was completed when as many individuals as were needed to completely fill the paper with fluctuating lines had each made a contribution to a collaborative end. It was not a matter of expertise, but of thoughtful diligence.

For the final festival day workshop at UCDC, we had decided that there should be at least two performances of *John Cage's STEPS: A Composition for a Painting to Be Performed by Individuals or Groups* in order to ensure that the variability of potential outcomes could be appreciated by participants and observers. In the end, we were able to get the cooperation of American University cellist Nancy Snyder and two former Cunningham Dance Company dancers. As Kass had explained, the performers were free to approach their engagement as they chose, first creating a field of locally confined images with inked feet and then using brushes of various widths (up to 5 feet) to add washes of chosen density to overlay the smaller markings with broad, continuous pathways that were themselves subject to unpredictable irregularities. Preliminary to the use of the wide-swathed diagonals of the wash brush there would be markings created by bare feel that carried ink acquired by standing briefly in prepared trays at the paper's edges. Of course, as is the case with the individual trajectories of the waxing and waning brush trails, there is the influence of intentionality: one "goes" from a "here" to various "theres."

The Cunningham dancers performed an improvisatory duet titled *Steps with Arms* that was based on *Changing Steps*, a piece that Cunningham choreographed in 1973. Stepping out of trays of ink placed on the sides of the large paper, their feet left path-like intermittencies. One noticed that directed trajectories left a very different sort of mark than did pirouettes. Their approach to the culminating application of wide-brush washes led to a strongly colored and all-surface outcome.

Lacking the training that might prepare one for the more kinetic approach of the dancers, I had decided that Nancy and I might adopt a more bounded approach in our performance, and we began by laying out angular edge areas at diagonally opposite sides of the paper. We were both somewhat concerned about the possibility of making unintended markings by falling off-balance if we attempted something virtuosic. So we agreed upon a succession of large arcs, rendered (necessarily) while moving backwards within the confines of the corner markings.

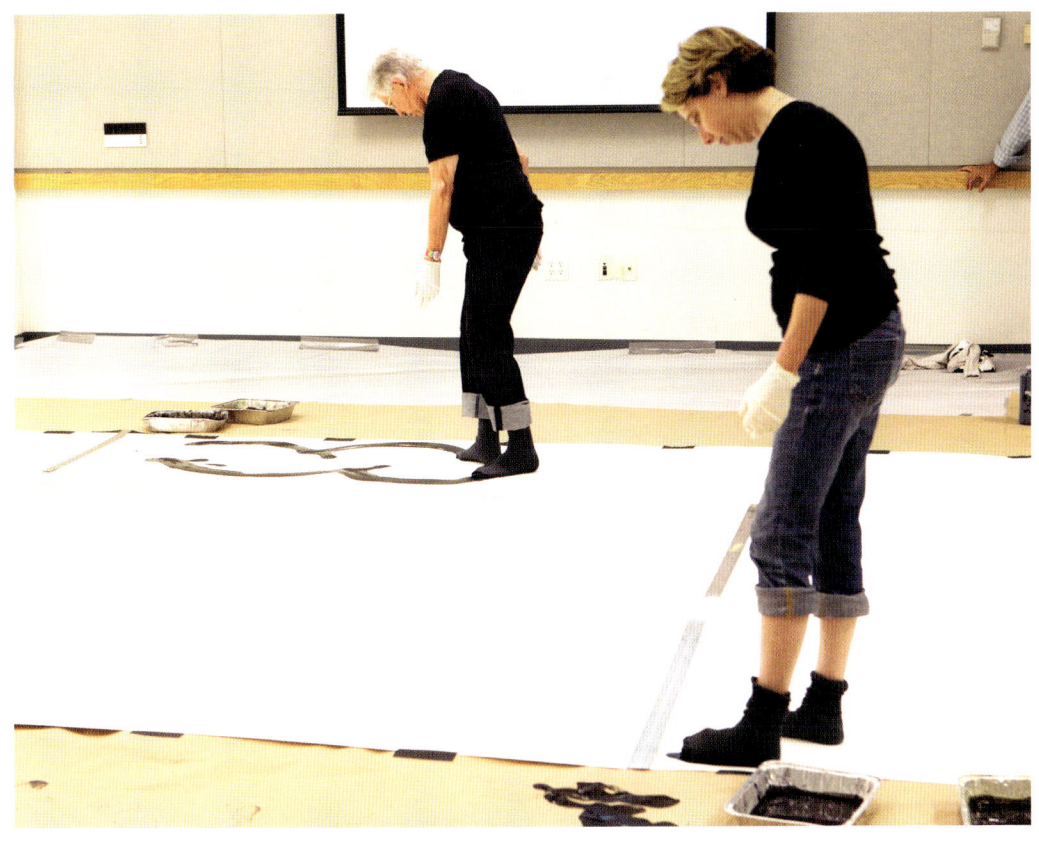

Nancy Snyder and Roger Reynolds beginning their version of *STEPS* as a part of the JCDC Festival at UCDC, Photo: Christopher Dobey

Former Cunningham Dance Company performers Jamie Scott (left) and Emma Desjardins (right) performing *STEPS* at a JCDC Festival event, Photo: Christopher Dobey

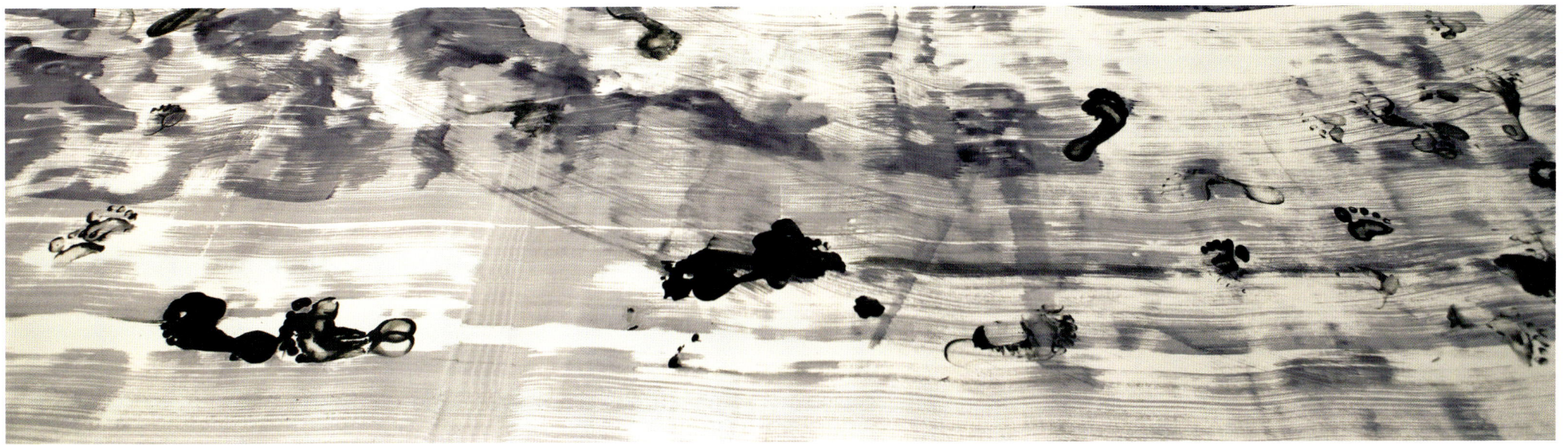

The completed image from the Cunningham Company dancers' performance of *STEPS* at a JCDC festival event , Photo: Christopher Dobey

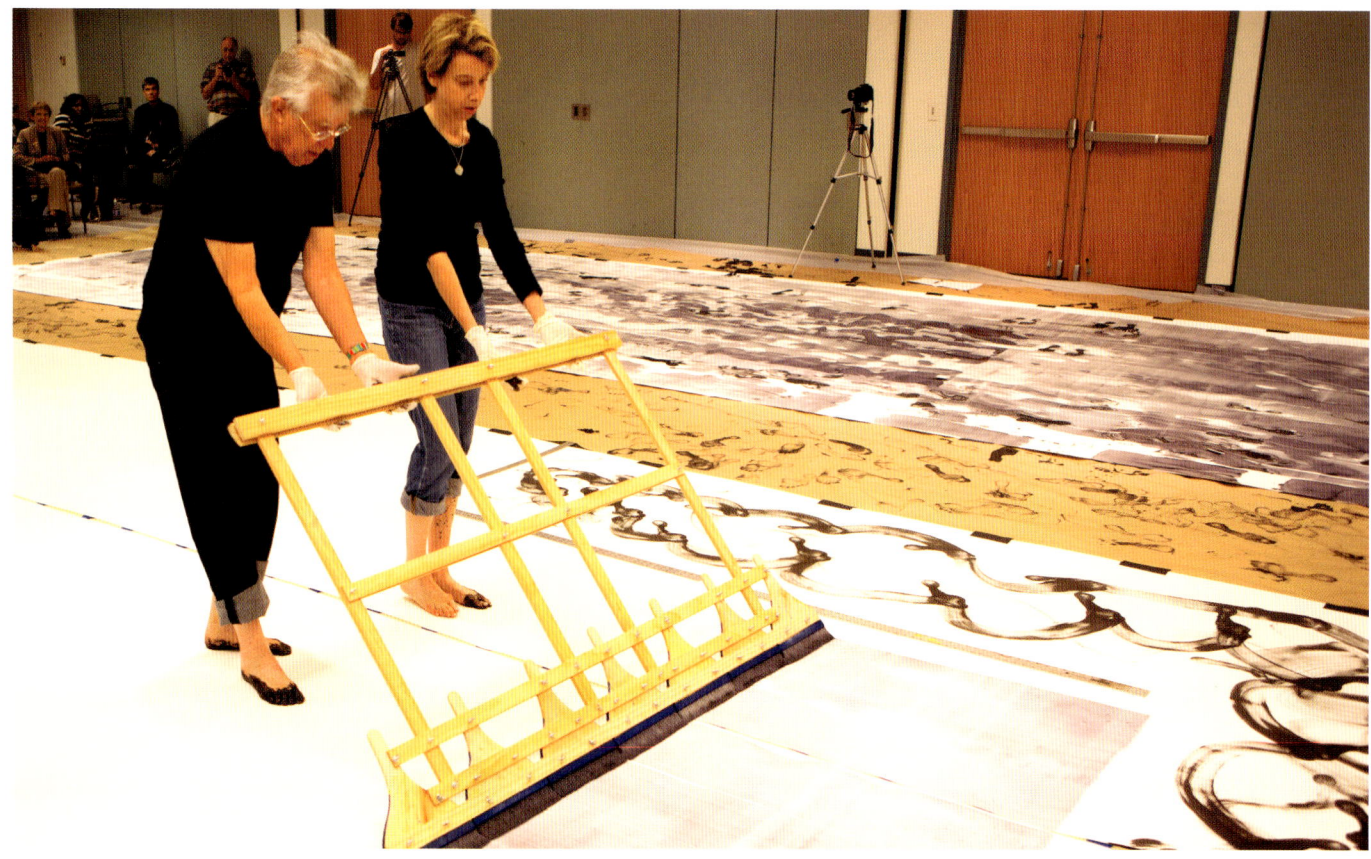

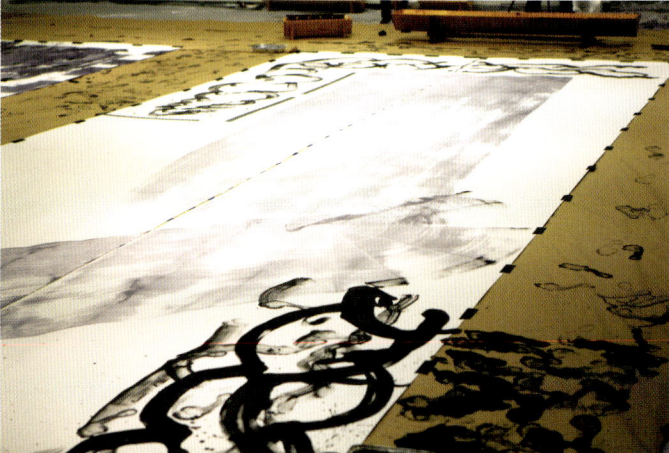

First dragging one's right foot in a convex arc, stabilizing oneself, and then doing the mirror opposite with the left foot, one achieved a dark, scalloped train, embellishing the opposing corners of the paper. We then found various ways of spattering the open spaces by launching ink with energetic, random gestures.

We loaded the wide brush with a light wash and embarked on several straight-line paths, either in parallel with the long edge of the paper or at an angle. I also used a 2-foot-wide brush with a very light wash in imitation of the dark arcs previously made with heavily inked feet. The outcome of our version was strikingly different than the textural "all-over" approach that the dancers had taken. The sensation of "performing" a gestural work of art on a massive scale led to a notably rich interplay of intention with chance, of control with acceptance. *STEPS* is, of course, best understood and experienced by performing it; but the scale and materials and collaborative process that it involves also make it, as a performance, engrossing to watch: implying, from a speculative perspective, questions of intention, predictability, serendipity, and, of course, the relishing of the ways in which the selected media — ink, brush, paper — provide, and indeed constitute, an inevitable content.

The frontier in the realm of aesthetic action and observation opened by *STEPS* — a realm in which the things used along with their inherent character interact with design and purpose — invites consideration. When one is faced with such an enormous expanse of toned white paper, the realm of aesthetic action and observation opened to performers implicitly engages them in an act of acceptance of the intended and the unexpected. The *STEPS* procedure has been so designated that its combination of the physical and the imagined produces something deeply meaningful. It is not only one's hand and arms that are engaged, but one's whole body and mind.

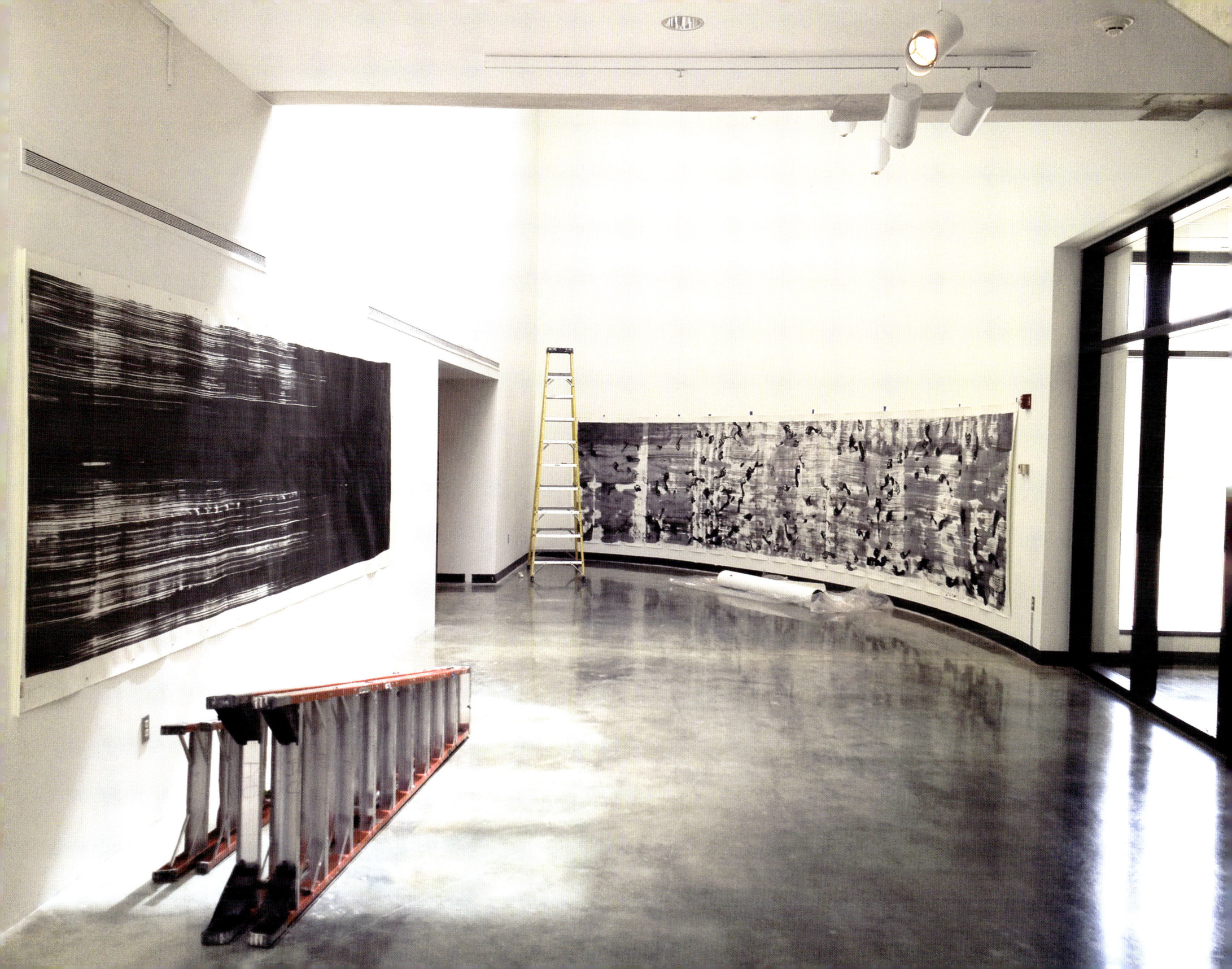

# DOROTHEA ROCKBURNE:
## *ANGULAR MOVEMENT*, 2012

Dorothea Rockburne painting *Angular Movement*, 2012 (a performance of *John Cage's STEPS: A Composition for a Painting to Be Performed by Individuals or Groups)*, at the National Academy Museum, NYC

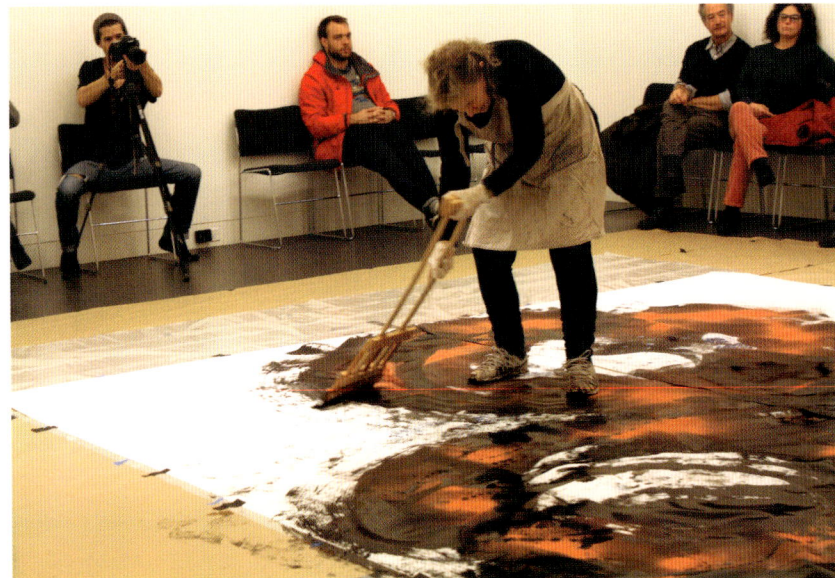

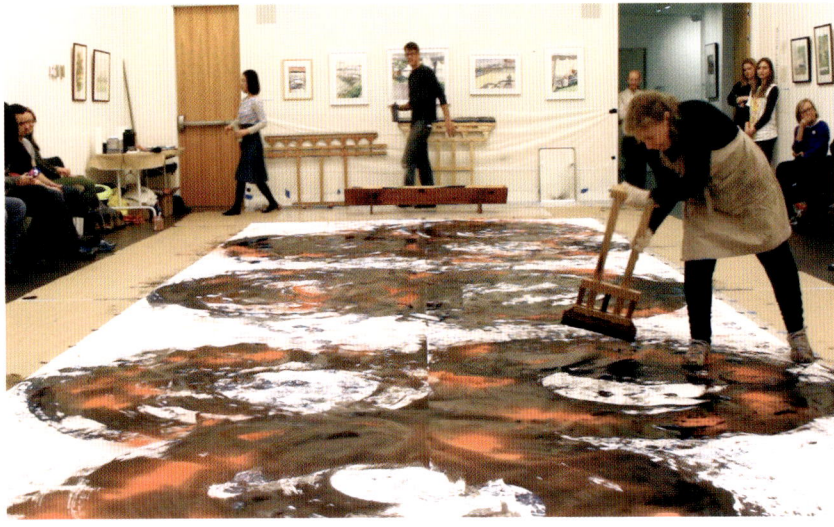

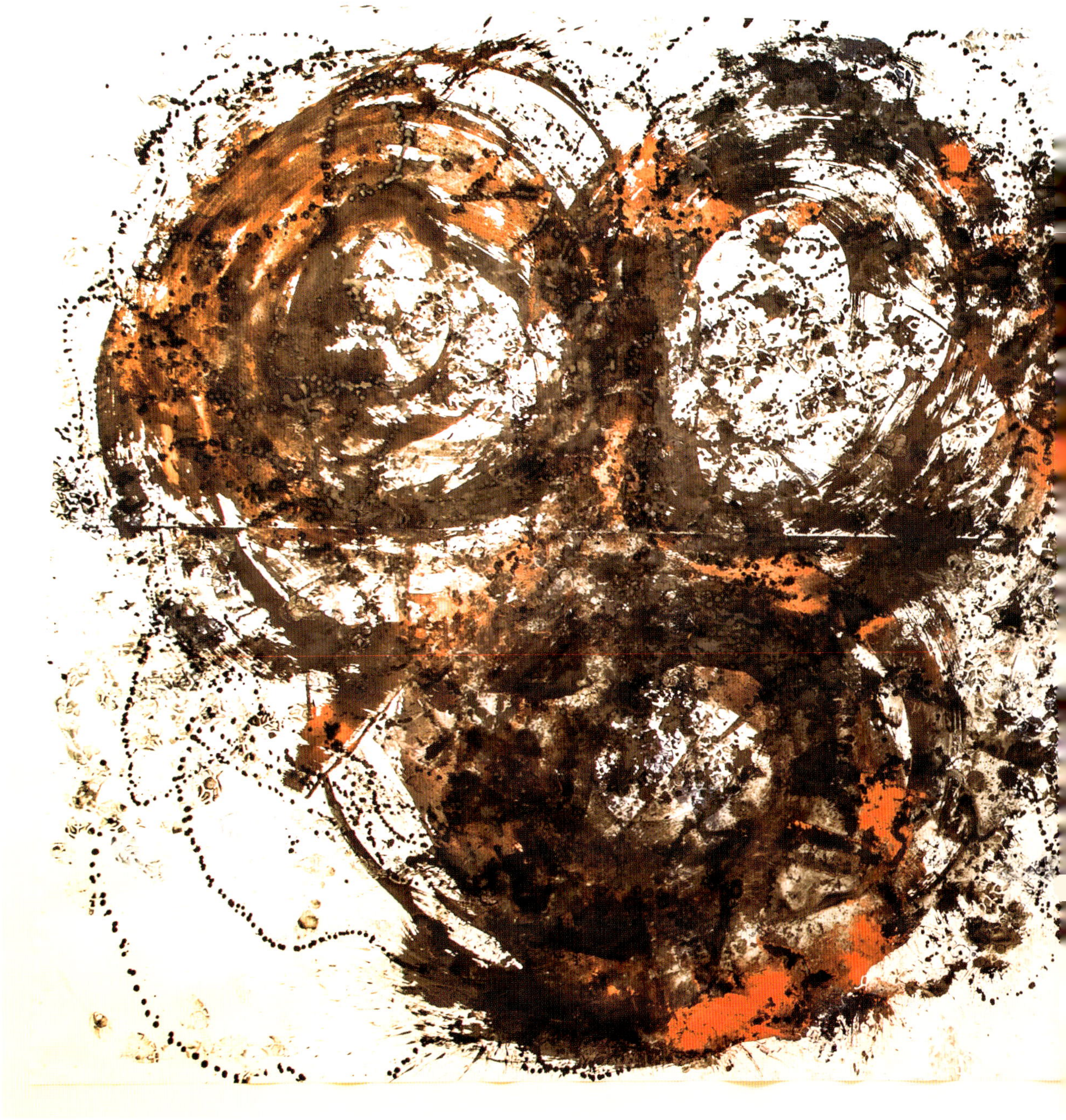

Dorothea Rockburne, *Angular Movement*, 2012, a performance of *John Cage's STEPS: A Composition for a Painting to Be Performed by Individuals or Groups*, ink, water media, copper, and mica on paper, 140 x 400 in. (356 x 1016 cm)

Photo: Jared Ladia, courtesy of the Taubman Museum of Art, Roanoke

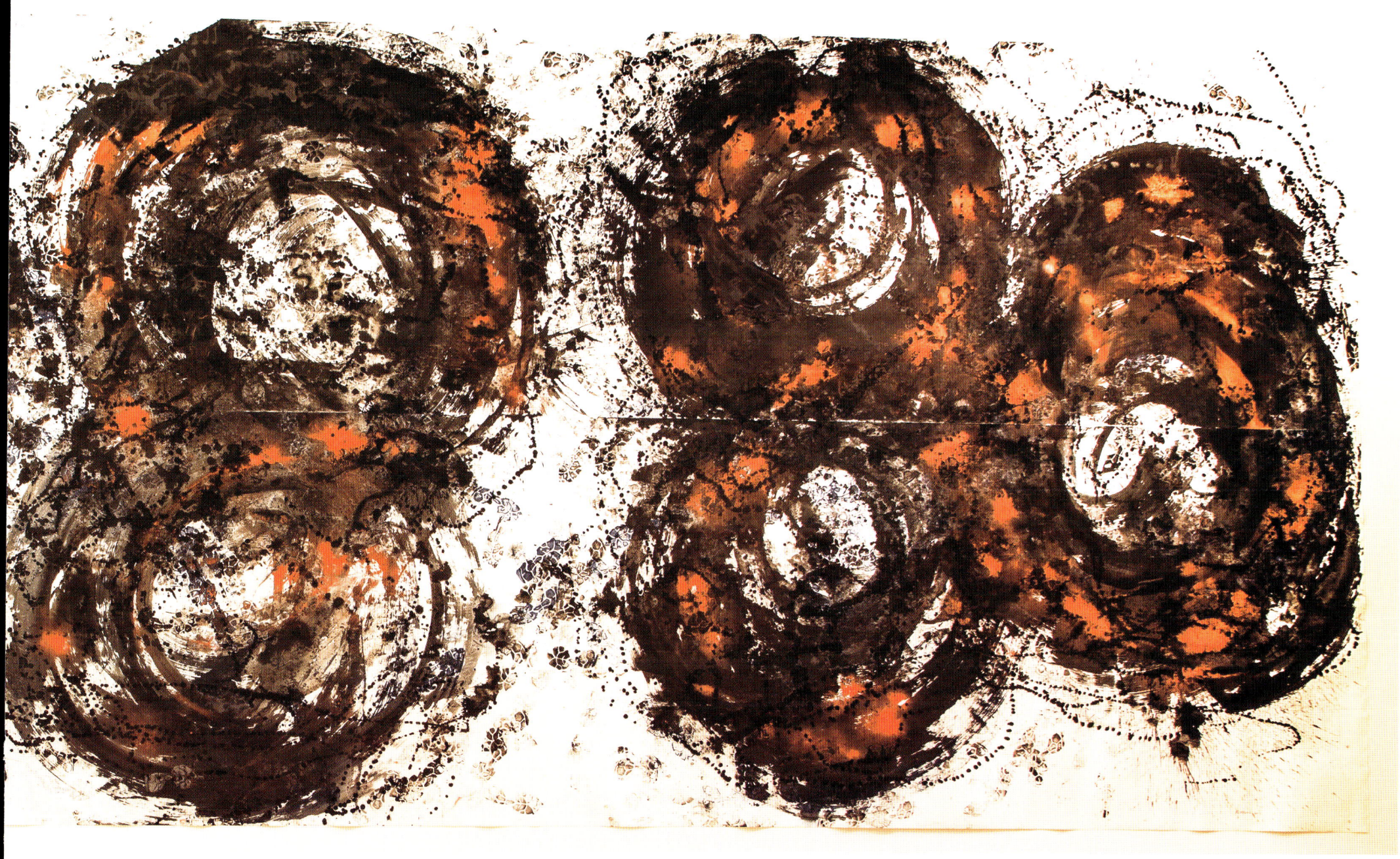

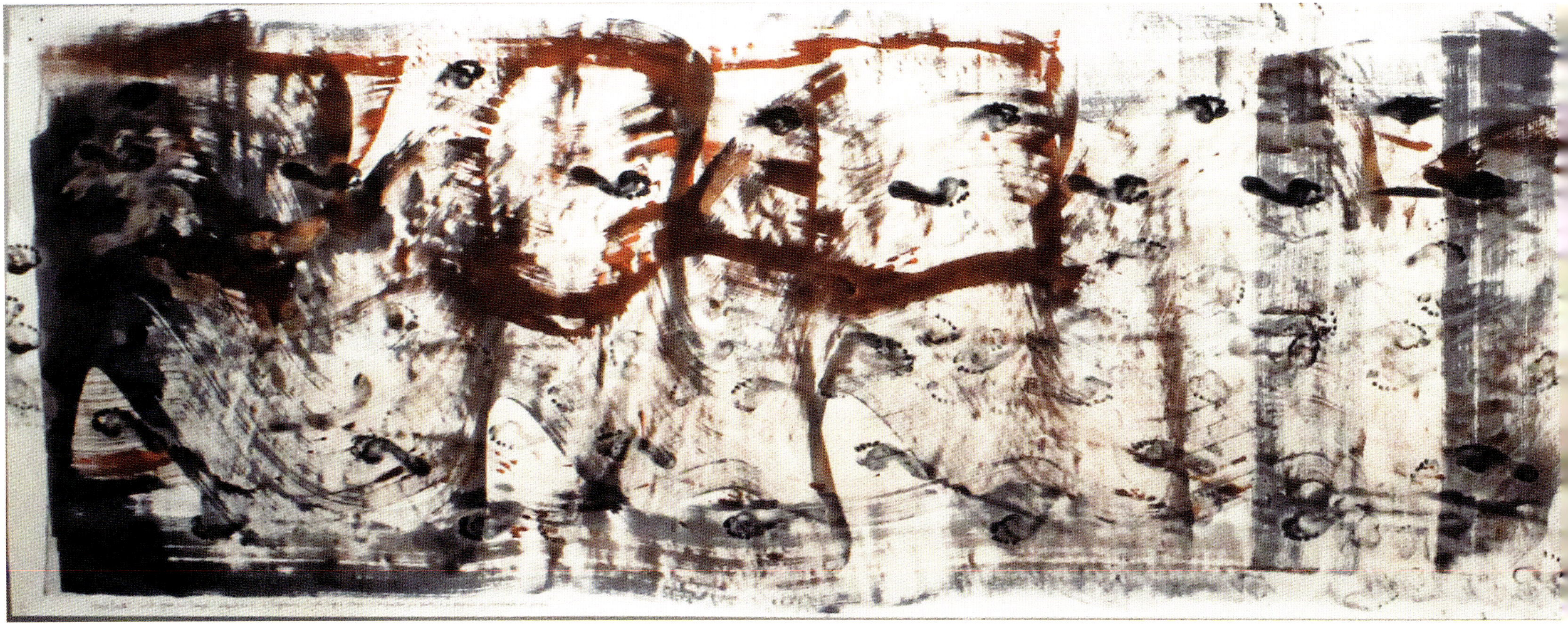

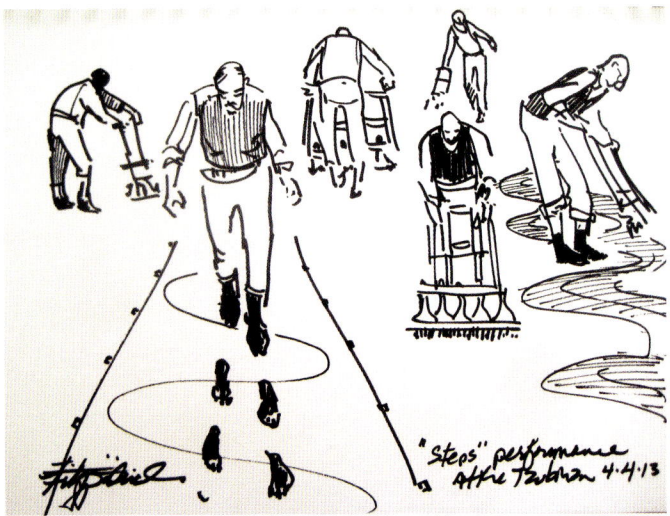

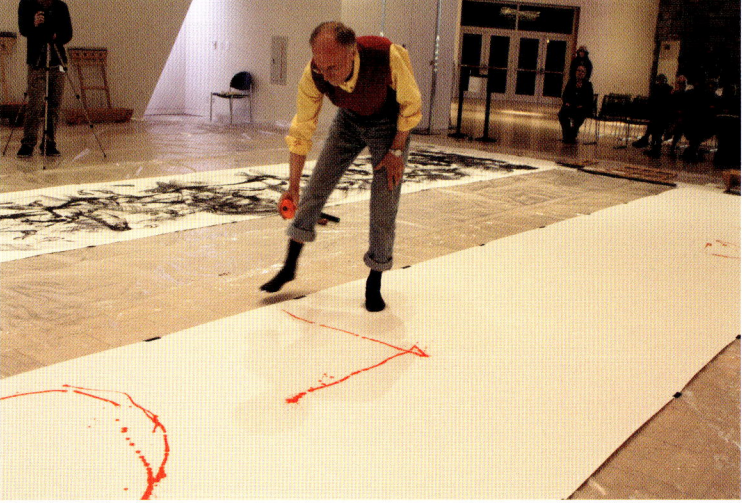

Eric Fitzpatrick, drawing of Howard Risatti's *STEPS* performance of *Circle, Square, and Triangle*, 2013, ink on paper

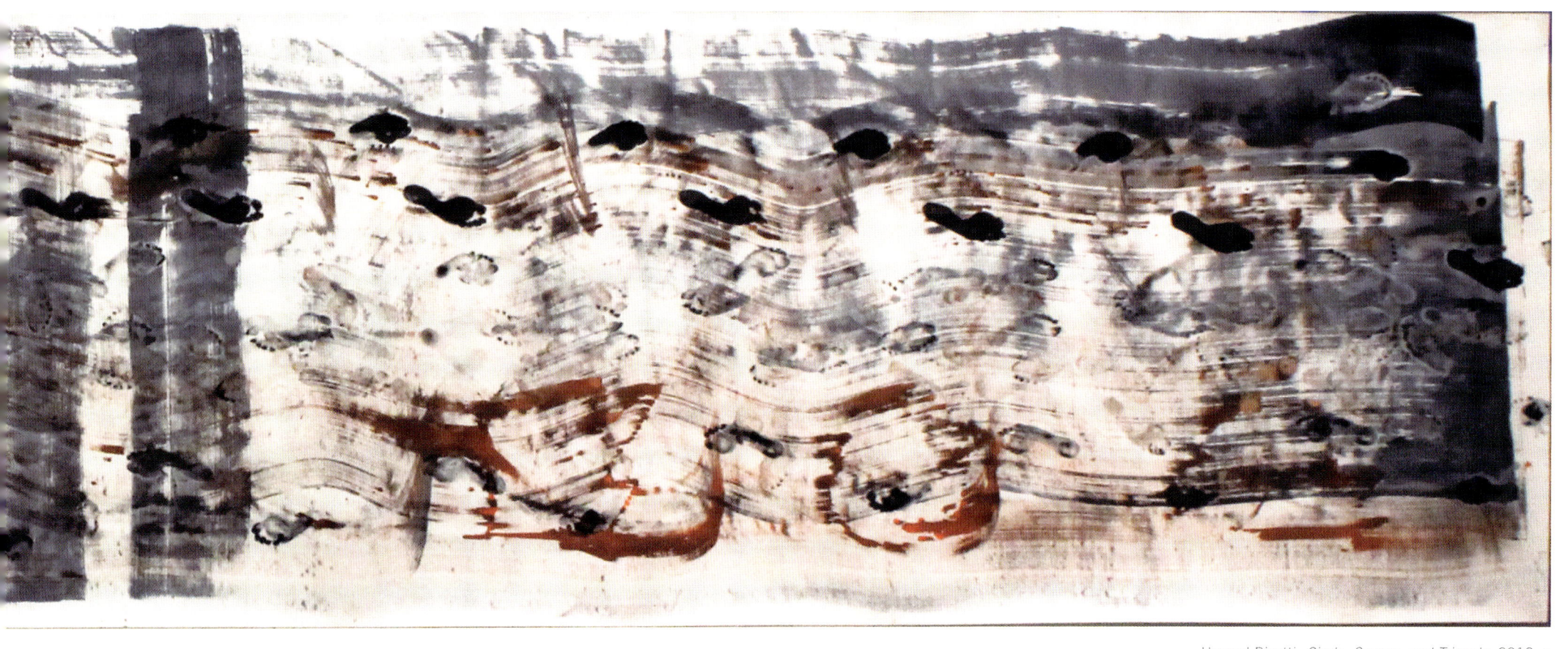

Howard Risatti, *Circle, Square, and Triangle*, 2013, a performance of *John Cage's STEPS: A Composition for a Painting to Be Performed by Individuals or Groups*, water media on rag paper, 72 X 360 in. (182.88 X 914.4 cm)

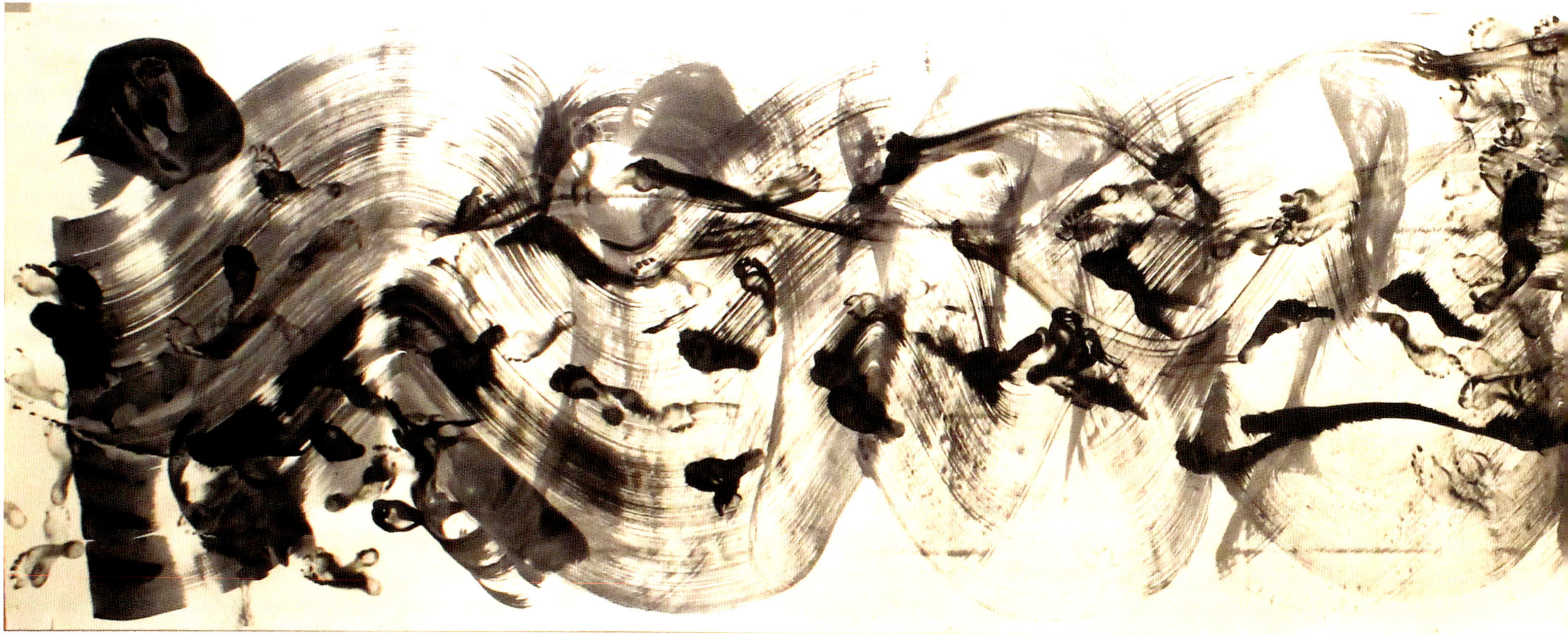

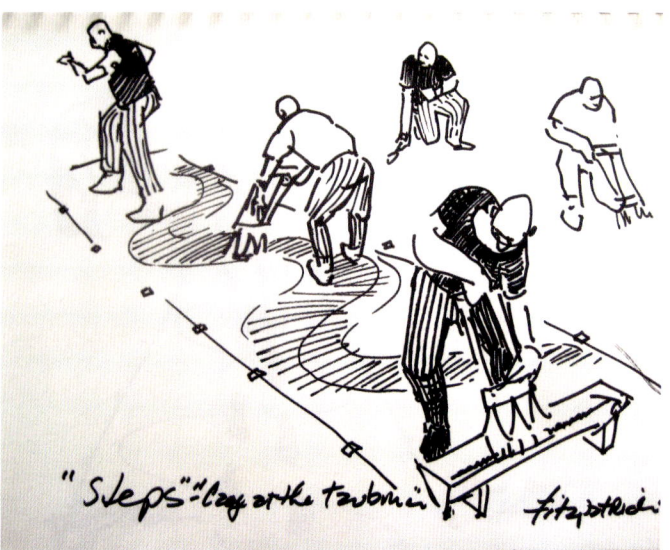

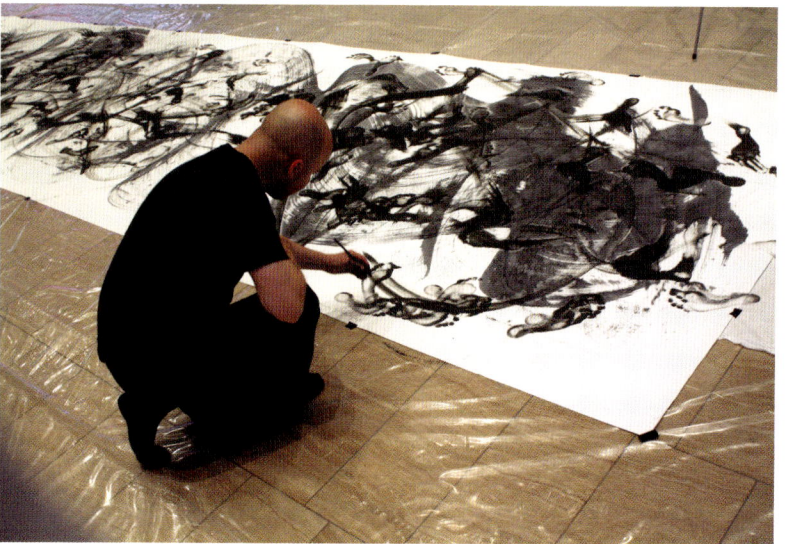

Eric Fitzpatrick, drawing of Scott Williamson's *STEPS* performance
of *Night by Silent Sailing Night*, 2013, ink on paper

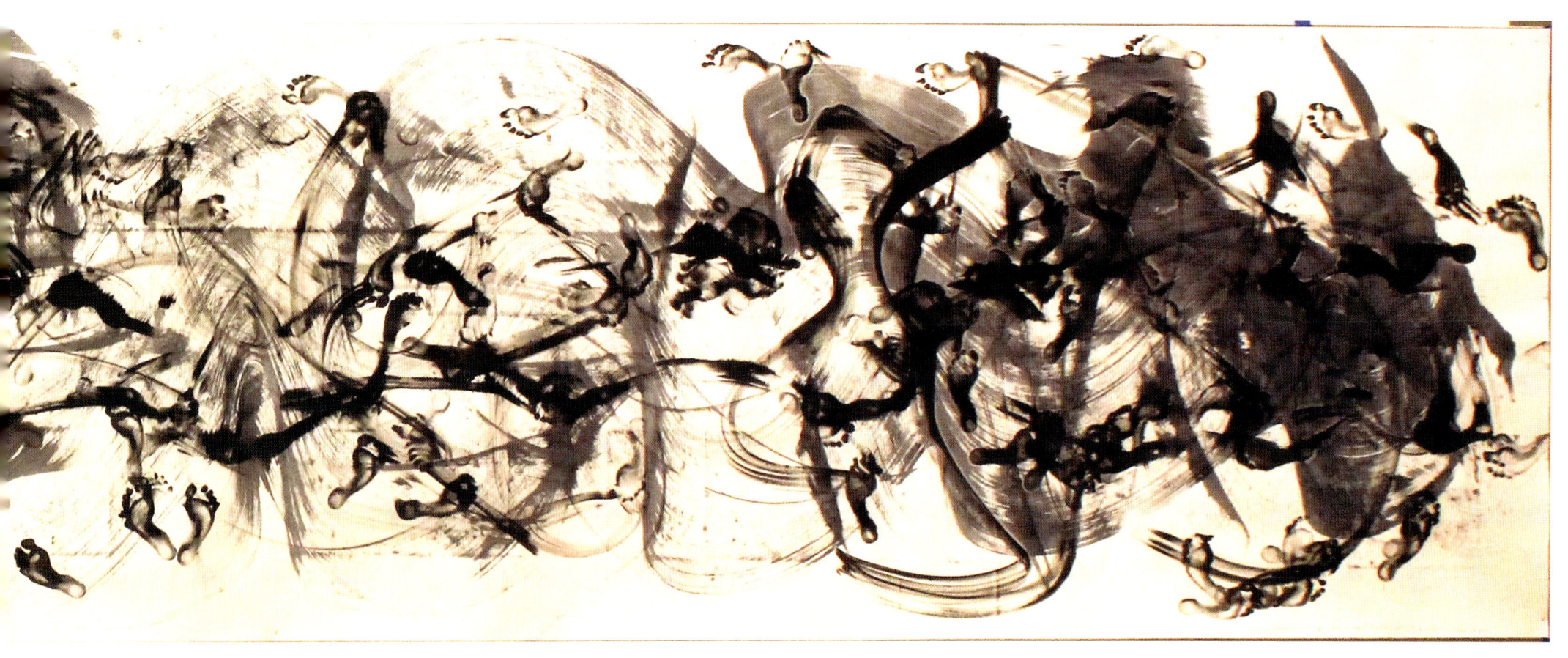

Scott Williamson, *Night By Silent Sailing Night*, 2013
a performance of *John Cage's STEPS: A Composition
for a Painting to Be Performed by Individuals or Groups*,
water media on rag paper, 72 x 360 in. (182.88 x 914.4 cm)

# MAKE *STEPS*, NOT …

**GEORG WECKWERTH**

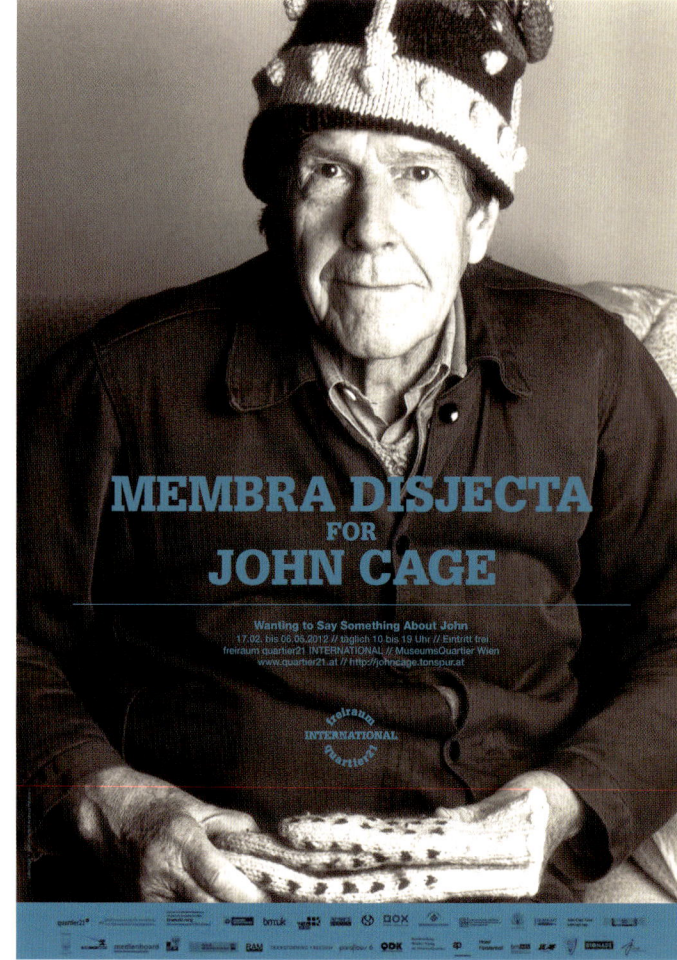

Exhibition poster for *Membra Disjecta for John Cage. Wanting to Say Something About John.*
© Q21/MQ & TONSPUR
Kunstverein Wien
Photo: Andreas Pohlmann

*Referring to "Make love, not war," the famous slogan against the Vietnam War and the Cold War, and to artists everywhere who adopted the slogan — such as Yoko Ono and John Lennon in their "Bed-In" performances and music.*[1]

*STEPS*: that short and striking name has been in my head since 2011. As a native German speaker, I consciously use the vivid Anglicism "step-by-step" with pleasure. Even more, the term has dogged me, in an absolutely positive sense, ever since I became aware of John Cage's *STEPS: A Composition for a Painting to Be Performed by Individuals or Groups*. The history of this multifaceted work began in 1989, and in this essay I will reminisce on my engagement with it in Austria and Germany.

In 2011, for the upcoming 2012 Cage centennial, I was organizing a major touring exhibition together with the Slovakian curator Jozef Cseres, who had had the good fortune of personally meeting John Cage in June 1992 in Bratislava, Slovakia, where Cage was lecturing; this was only a few weeks before Cage's death.[2] The exhibition, titled *Membra Disjecta for John Cage. Wanting to Say Something About John*, was shown in Vienna, Prague, and Ostrava and included works by more than sixty international artists. Numerous works from the exhibition are today installed in the Raum für Cage (Room for Cage), which I initiated as part of the world-renowned *John Cage*

*Organ Project* in Halberstadt, Germany. Among the artists in the exhibition was the U.S. painter and university professor Raymond (Ray) Kass, founder of the Mountain Lake Workshop.

In his artist's statement for the catalogue, Kass describes Cage as an alchemist who, in the last watercolors he did at Mountain Lake Workshop, tried "to transmute fire into water."[3] Before that, Kass notes that water played an essential role for Cage as a source and as the content or object in a body of visual work that developed over many years. I mention this because there will be more talk of water and other materials in due course, in connection with a workshop that Kass initiated during the run of our Cage centennial exhibition, which more than twenty thousand people visited between 17 February and 6 May 2012, in the MuseumsQuartier (MQ) Vienna.[4]

To clarify the workshop's prehistory in connection with Kass' one-month residency at MQ Vienna in March 2012, and in order to be able to grasp the significance of the workshop, it's necessary to introduce Kass' own contribution to *Membra Disjecta for John Cage*. His exhibit directly creates the bridge to Cage's *STEPS*. He showed a narrow length of nylon fabric several meters long, upon which at first glance an unusual Indian ink drawing could be seen. The drawing, in turn, was based on the notation for Cage's *STEPS*. Kass' work (pictured on p. 283) bore the title *For Merce Cunningham*, augmented by a previously written portion directly referring to Cage's composition: "A performance of John Cage's *STEPS: A Composition for a Painting to Be Performed by Individuals or Groups*" and a date: "performed on July 27, 2009."

As a matter of fact, I heard of *STEPS* for the first time when I was gathering exhibits for the Vienna exhibition. The previously unpublished notation for this 1989 composition by Cage, in conjunction with reproductions of the first performance, had an extraordinary impact on me from the start. (pictured on p. 285) I immediately grasped *STEPS* as a grand gesture and homage to each individual person and to us all collectively: as a manifestation of the spirituality and creativity that slumbers or blazes in each

[1] See: https://en.wikipedia.org/wiki/Make_love,_not_war; and https://en.wikipedia.org/wiki/Bed-In

[2] For Cage's lecture in the Slovakian Philharmonic in Bratislava (June 15–19, 1992) see the CD in the exhibition catalogue for the Cage centennial: *Membra Disjecta for John Cage. Wanting to Say Something About John*, edited by Jozef Cseres and Georg Weckwerth (DOX, Prague & GVUO, Ostrava: 2012).

of us, regardless of age, sex, origin, religion, inclinations, etc. — as indicator-like instructions for realizing the force and power of art. Kass recognized my fascination with *STEPS* and immediately suggested doing a workshop and carrying out a series of performances in Vienna. Needless to say, with me, he encountered an open door. I was tremendously excited by the idea of being present at the creation of new works on the basis of the *STEPS* notation and of being in a position to enable this to come about. The course of preparations for the several-days-long March 2012 workshop was accompanied by a deepening examination of *STEPS*. I would learn that *STEPS* consists of two very different versions, which only heightened my interest in Cage's ingenious composition.

The first version or "first notation" bears the title *STEPS: A Composition for a Painting*. Its notation spells out in great detail the collaboration with Kass and follows the format of Cage's own performance at the Mountain Lake Workshop carried out in Kass' studio in Christiansburg, Virginia, in 1989.

The title of the second version or "second notation" adds: *to Be Performed by Individuals or Groups*. At the invitation of Laura Kuhn, director of the John Cage Trust, Kass wrote official versions of the two notations in 2006.[5] The second notation allows the performer to select the materials used to carry out the performance, which can either be comparable to the materials Cage used or freely chosen — including the option of freely designing the performance or realizing it entirely on the basis of other media such as photography,

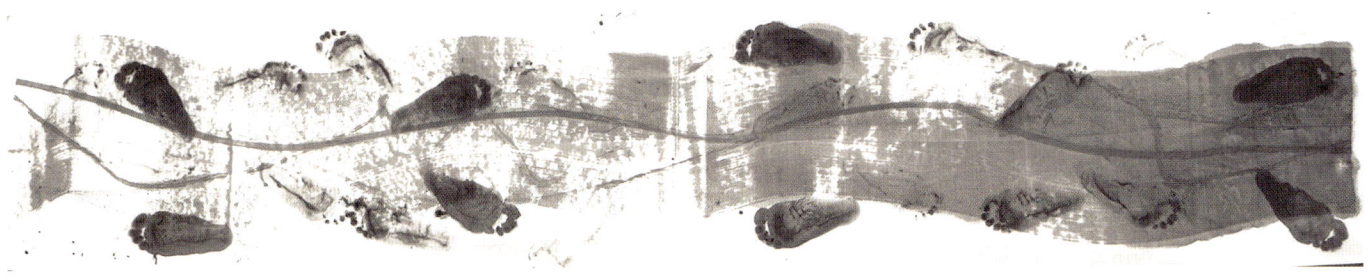

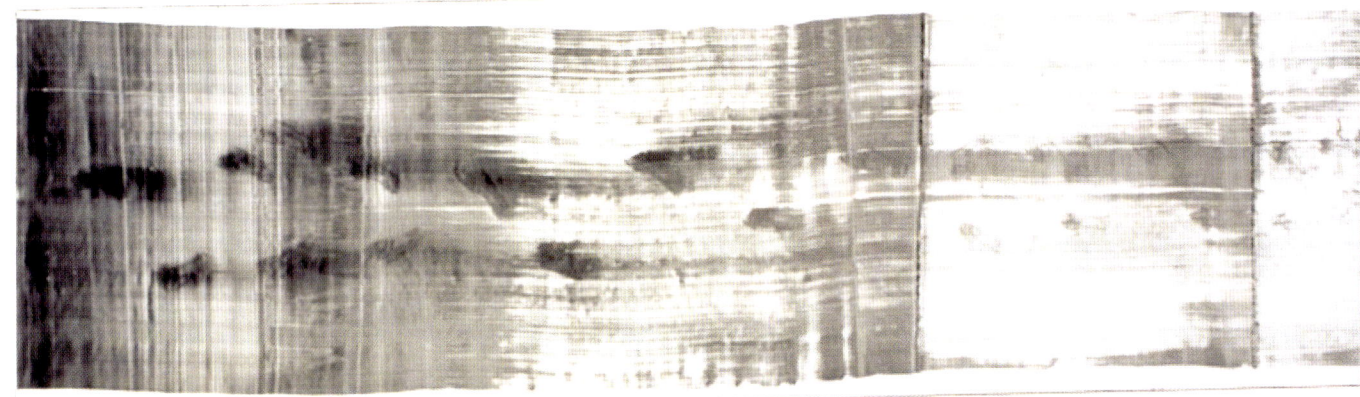

everything, which, like the precise, strict notation of the first version, is equally typical of Cage. But in order to dispel the notion that one can do just something or other, that just anything can be done." Additionally, the second notation has the decisive sentence: "The performance must be in the spirit of Cage's original *STEPS* performance."

[3] Ibid., p. 118.

[4] See exhibition blog at http://johncage.tonspur.at/

[5] The John Cage Trust, based at Bard College in New York, is the fiduciary administrator of John Cage's estate. Kuhn was a long-time Cage assistant. See http://johncage.org/

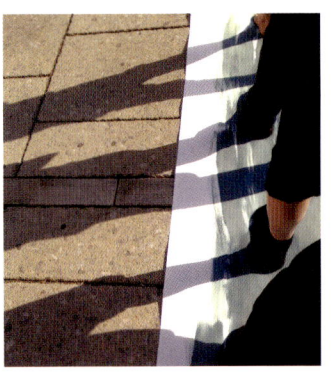
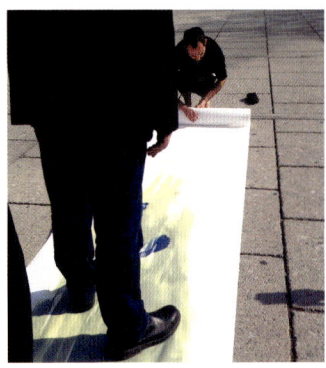

Tyler Adams, *Watery Walk*, 2012.
Photos: Georg Weckwerth

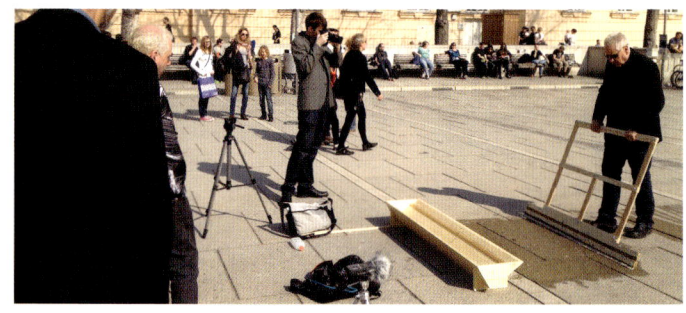

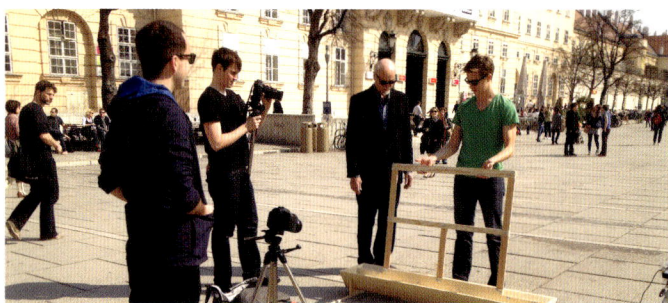

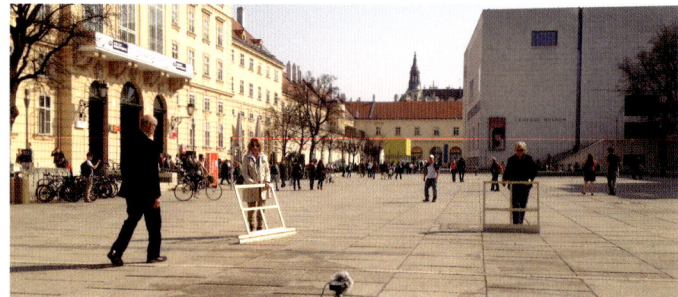

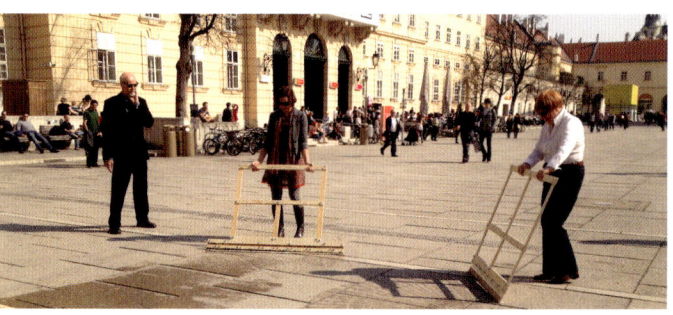

**Cut! Vienna, spring 2012:**

Twelve Performances of John Cage's *STEPS: A Composition for a Painting to Be Performed by Individuals or Groups*

The following is a list of *STEPS* pieces that were created in Vienna and Lower Austria during the Cage centennial year of 2012. All twelve performance events are listed in chronological order. Performers are indicated in bold type and, of the twelve events, some are presented in greater detail than others.[6]

**I. Vienna, March 22, 2012, MQ main courtyard**

The American sound artist Tyler Adams stands barefoot in bright spring sunshine, together with Arnold Dreyblatt, Ray Kass, and Georg Weckwerth, on an approximately five-meter-long ribbon of paper prepared with a sensitizer solution for cyanotype for his *Watery Walk — a performance of John Cage's STEPS (...)*. For a few minutes nothing happens as the four performers stand motionless.[7] Then one after another they step off the ribbon of paper, their footprints visible in the greenish coating on the paper.

**II. Vienna, March 22, 2012, MQ Electric Avenue**

The artists Nikola Tasic, André Wagner with his dog, Rhabarba, and Anna Watzinger, all students of digital art at the University of Applied Arts Vienna, realized *ONNRA — a performance of John Cage's STEPS (...)* in classical form, i.e., following the first notation of *STEPS*. Vienna, March 22, 2012, MQ Electric Avenue The media artist Ruth Schnell, professor and head of the digital art program at the University of Applied Arts Vienna,

and the artist Nita Tandon perform *Duo Through Chance — a performance of John Cage's STEPS (...)*, again following the original version.

**III. Vienna, March 24, 2012, MQ main courtyard**

Ray Kass and various public participants (Philipp Reichel, Clara Monti, Peter Kuthan, Grace Pardi and Beatrix Maier, Anna Watzinger and Arnold Dreyblatt, Igna Wakka and Laudy van Hettema, Erik Van Ree) perform Invisibility — a public introduction of the perform*ance of John Cage's STEPS (...)* solely with clear water, which had such great significance for Cage, on the pavement of the broad central plaza of Vienna's MuseumsQuartier.

**IV. Vienna, March 24, 2012, MQ main courtyard**

The U.S. singer and performance artist Sam Ashley imbues an empty white sheet of Fabriano paper with his shamanistic mysticism. It was an unusual and extraordinary performance in the midst of many astonished observers. The performance *As If It Would Have Happened Anyway — adapted for a performance of John Cage's STEPS (...)* is filmed; the piece now consists of a ten-minute live video with sound and the sheet of paper, later signed by Ashley.

**V. Vienna, March 24, 2012, MQ café-bar Kantine**

The Austrian poster artist, visual artist, performer, filmmaker, and writer Julius Deutschbauer sits alone at a table in the crowded Kantine for *abdecken, bügeln, reisen — a performance*

---

[6] For the Viennese workshop performances under the direction of Ray Kass and Georg Weckwerth, replicas of the painting utensils Cage used in his Mountain Lake Workshop in 1989 were built by Harald Hasler in the MQ carpenter's workshop in 2012. These utensils were also used in other *STEPS* performances carried out on the occasion of another Cage Centennial exhibition at the Museum der Moderne in Salzburg in 2012.

[7] Cyanotype, or iron blueprint, is one of the oldest monochrome photography techniques able to be carried out relatively simply and at low cost. It is exposed by sunlight or another UV light source (e.g. sun lamp) in a contact print process. See https://en.wikipedia.org/wiki/Cyanotype

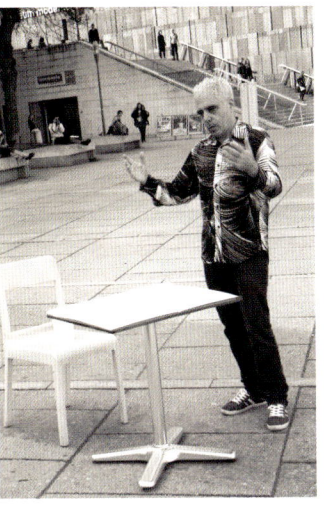
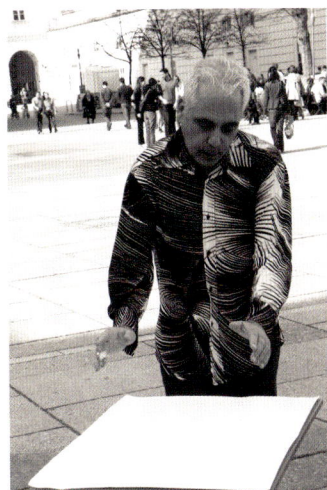
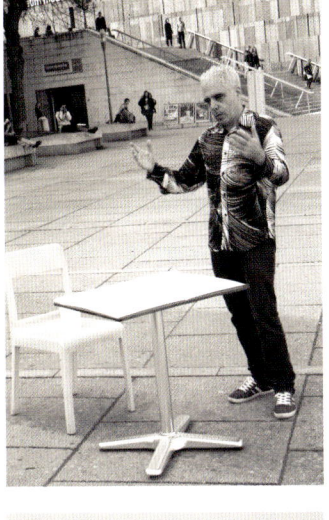
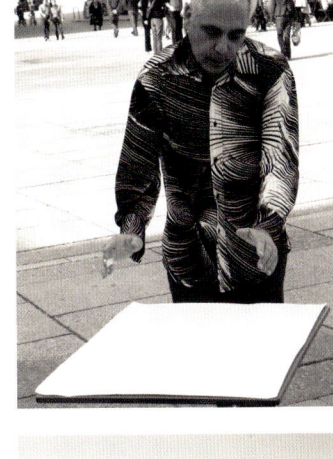
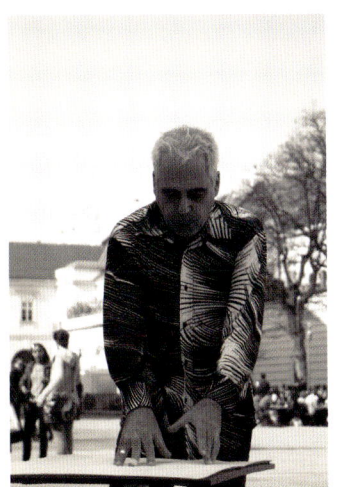
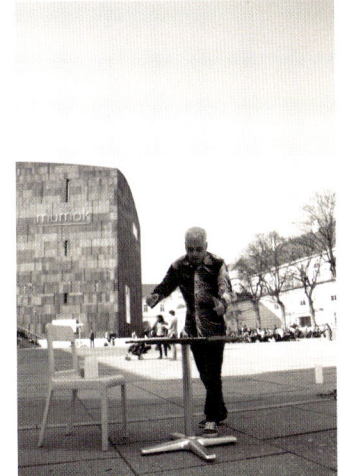

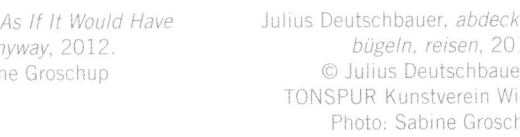
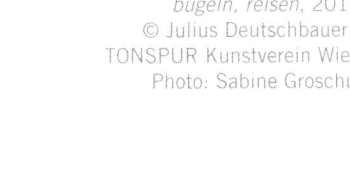

# John Cage's STEPS
### performed by Julius Deutschbauer

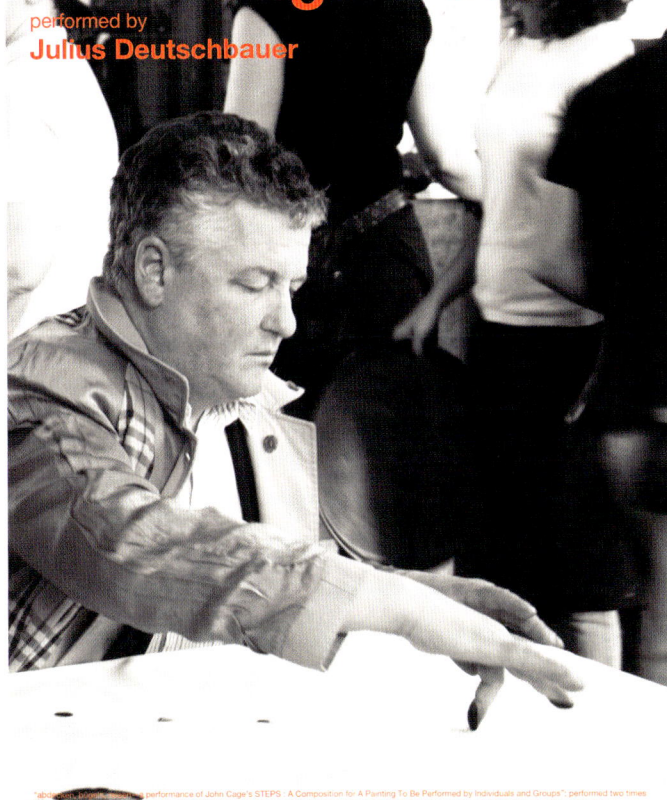

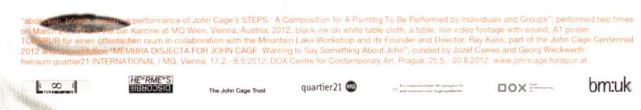

and middle fingers in a little porcelain bowl of black ink that also stands on the table. Then he quite intentionally walks his two ink-dipped fingertips over the white tablecloth. Then pauses. Witty! Inspired! Flashes through my head.

## VI. Vienna, March 24, 2012, MQ café-bar Kantine

Julius Deutschbauer repeats his journey. A second exhibit is created. Both performances, each less than five minutes, are filmed with a mobile phone and are now part of the work. Subsequently, Julius Deutschbauer creates one of his typical art posters. It bears the number 147 (by the end of 2016, there are already 186 posters) and is published in an edition of 1000. Its motif includes Sabine Groschup's black-and-white photograph of the artist as he takes leave of the performance. Deutschbauer's *STEPS* poster is a sought-after collector's item nowadays.

## VII. Lower Austria, March 25, 2012

The performance by Austrian artist, filmmaker, and writer Sabine Groschup takes us out of Vienna into a magnificent riverside forest on the Donau. While doing research for her film *(JC{639})* about the *John Cage Organ Project* in Halberstadt, her contribution to the exhibition *Membra Disjecta for John Cage*, she discovers Cage's *Mud Book: How to Make Pies and Cakes* which he published with Lois Long.[8] The small book would go on to play a special role for Groschup, inspiring her to develop an unusual workshop for children, which was well received in Vienna and later in Salzburg. So it's no surprise that the artist would also use soft, fresh earth for one of her two *STEPS* performances. She finds magnificently fresh mud

in the Donau woods near Stockerau, not far from Vienna. Right there, in front of many puzzled day-trippers on a sunny spring afternoon, in the company of Kass, Sam Ashley, Ian Cobb-Ozanne, who films the action, and Georg Weckwerth, she realizes *A "Picnic" for a Painting — a performance of John Cage's STEPS (...)*. The title refers to one of Groschup's favorite paintings, which she had already reprised in many variations: *Le déjeuner sur l'herbe* (Luncheon on the Grass) by Édouard Manet (1863).

of *John Cage's STEPS (...)*. The table is covered by a square white damask tablecloth. With the help of a pocket mirror, Deutschbauer daubs a concealer on his face and nose, then stands up and turns his classic trench coat inside out so that the typical Burberry pattern is visible. Then he irons the white tablecloth with an electric iron standing on the table and sits down again. He dunks the tips of his right index

8 John Cage and Lois Long, *Mud Book: How to Make Pies and Cakes* (hand printed by Simca Print Artists, Inc., Japan, 1983).

9 Wulf Herzogenrath and Barbara Nierhoff-Wielk, eds., *John Cage und ... Bildender Künstler–Einflüsse, Anregungen* (John Cage and ... Visual Artist — Influences, Ideas) (Cologne: DuMont, 2012), p. 295. For more on Lassnig, see https://en.wikipedia.org/wiki/Maria_Lassnig; and for Fischinger see https://en.wikipedia.org/wiki/Oskar_Fischinger

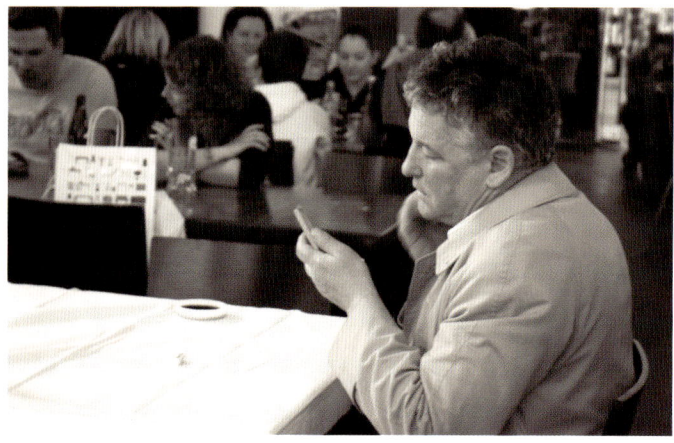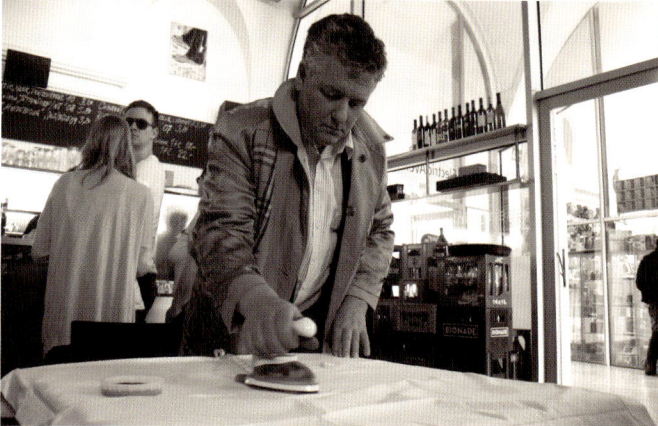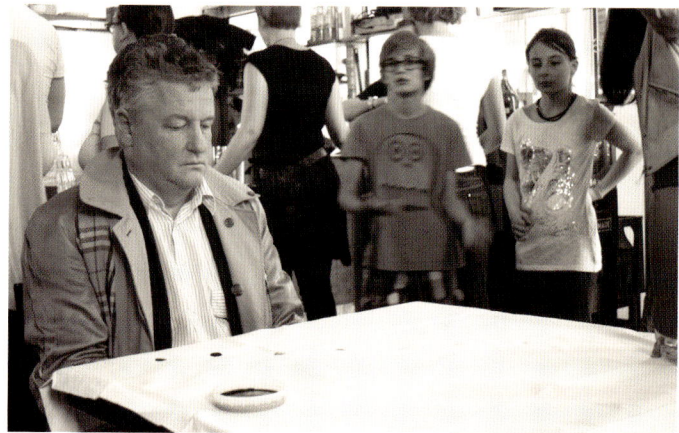

Julius Deutschbauer, *abdecken, bügeln, reisen*, Performance II, 2012. Photos: Sabine Groschup

### VIII. Lower Austria, March 25, 2012

In his impressive residence and studio in the middle of a woods near Jaidhof, at his drafting table with the video camera running, the renowned Austrian conceptual artist Franz Graf realizes *aroundrecording — a performance of John Cage's STEPS (...)*. The music lover and record collector places pre-selected recordings by John Cage under the camera, pulls the vinyl LP or the CD out of its cover, and, on a sheet of paper that has been laid on the table, traces circles around it with one or several pencils, eventually creating four, approximately two-meter-long narrow bands of paper with circle drawings. The experimental video with no sound shows the artist's hands both lying down and circling the round platters and discs, along with the smoke constantly rising from his glowing cigarette. Graf is concentrated and expressive in his typical way. The atmosphere is intense. I watch Kass and read in his eyes: We are in a special way in the presence of the spirit of John Cage. The subsequent tour, no longer part of the performance, of the Heurigen (the local winemakers' taverns) and our toasts to Cage and *STEPS* with exquisite wine are merely the icing on the cake.

### IX. Vienna, March 26, 2012, MQ rear courtyard

Ray Kass and his endearing assistant Ian Cobb-Ozanne, who joined him on the trip to Vienna, realize *Currents III —*

a performance of John Cage's STEPS (...) which follows the first notation. The work, done on Fabriano paper, ten meters long by three meters wide (32.8 feet x 9.84 feet), is the largest exhibit in the Vienna performance series and, apart from its sheer size, makes an impression with its rhythmic drawing.

### X. Vienna, March 26, 2012, MQ Electric Avenue

On transparencies of a type still in use today in analog animation films, **Sabine Groschup**, who was trained by Maria Lassnig, pays homage in her second *STEPS* performance to a pioneer of abstract film: the filmmaker Oskar Fischinger, who came from Germany and died in 1967 in Los Angeles, Cage's birthplace. Cage met Fischinger for the first time in the mid-1930s, and the latter would inspire Cage's view of sound; Cage was impressed by Fischinger's idea of an indwelling soul in all things that can be liberated by making the object produce sound.[9] As Cage himself put it: "He said that everything in the world has a spirit which is released by sound, and that set me on fire, so to speak."[10] For *A Tribute to Oskar F. — a performance of John Cage's STEPS (...)*, Groschup uses her red-sneakered feet to transfer three different hues of film color onto the approximately ten-square-meter "carpet of transparencies" consisting of nine sections. What she creates "step-by-step" is a huge mushroom — in homage, of course, to the mycologist John Cage.

### XI. Vienna, March 26, 2012, MQ rear courtyard

I contributed the twelfth and last performance of the Vienna series. I cite Cage's Happening *A House Full of Music* (1982) in the title and Robert Rauschenberg's famous *Automobile Tire Print* (1953) in the execution. At Rauschenberg's invitation, Cage had made the unusual painting by slowly driving his Model A Ford, as directed, over a strip of paper 7½ meters (24.6 feet) long placed on Fulton Street in Lower Manhattan (Rauschenberg had made the paper by gluing together twenty sheets). Although the front tire left just a slight trace, the rear tire created a deep, black impression because Rauschenberg had put paint in front of the rear tire. Here it must be added — thus closing the circle — that Cage composed *STEPS* in 1989 and performed it himself, for the first and only time, as an homage to Rauschenberg's *Automobile Tire Print* and as a Zen-inspired painting.

*A Car Full of STEPS (reminiscence of RR, JC, and a Model A Ford) — a performance of John Cage's STEPS (...)* was performed more than sixty years later in Vienna. At a late-night hour I cautiously drive my 1992 red Volvo 240 station wagon, lights on and with Glenn Gould playing Bach's *Goldberg Variations* on the sound system, up a 10-meter-long by 1½-meter-wide (33.8 foot x 9.84 foot) strip of paper that has been laid down on the MQ Vienna service alley. (Only the left tires are on the paper.) I turn off the motor and, with the safety brake on, I step in front

[10] Cage interview with Joel Eric Sueben (1983) reprinted in Richard Kostelanetz, *Conversing With Cage* (New York and London: Psychology Press, 2003), p. 8.

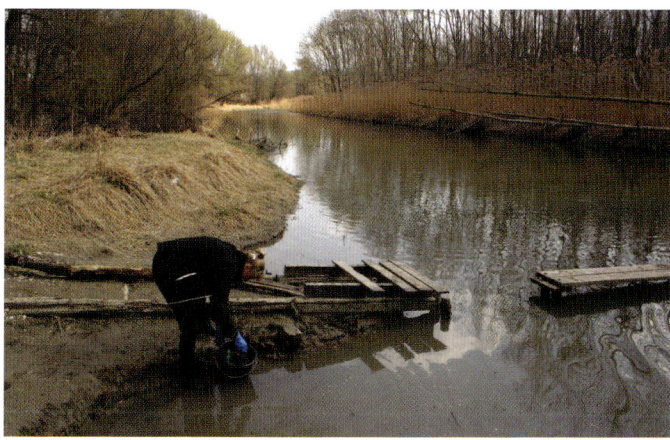
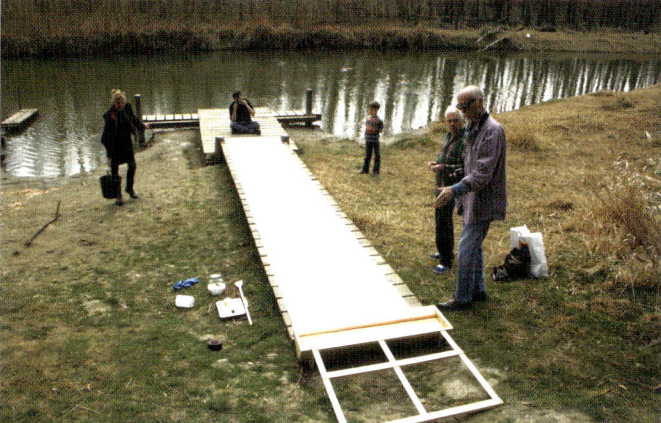
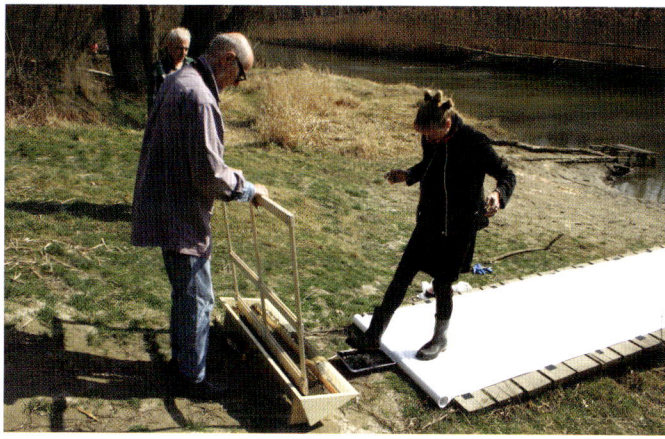
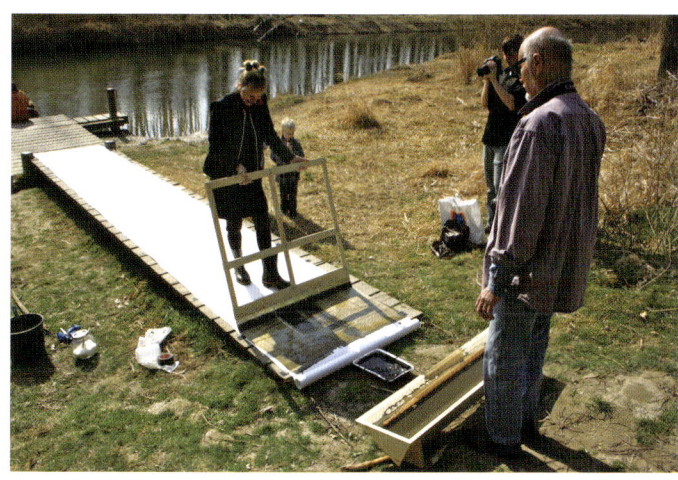
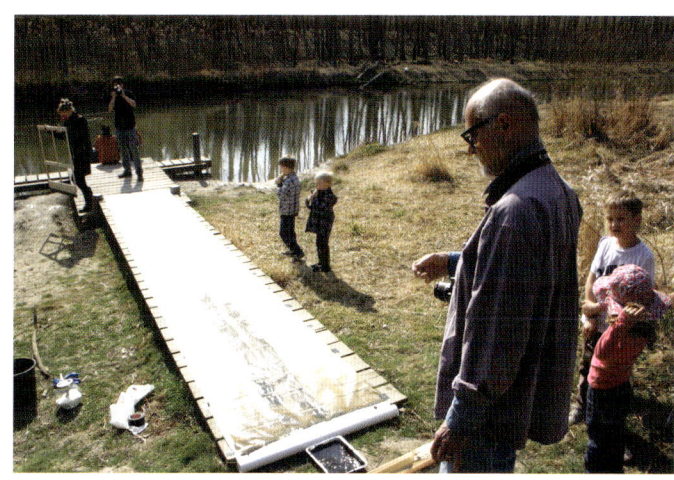
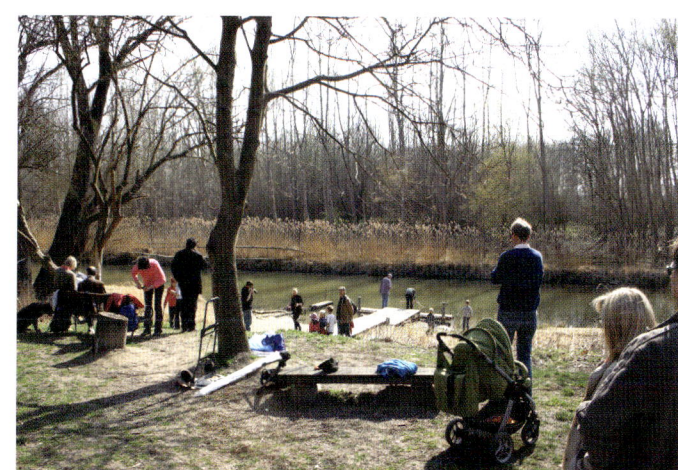

Sabine Groschup, *A "Picnic" for A Painting*, 2012. Photos: Georg Weckwerth

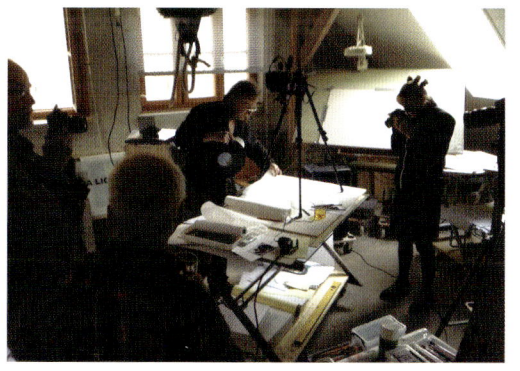
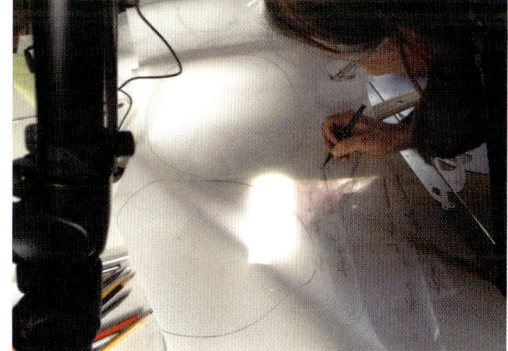
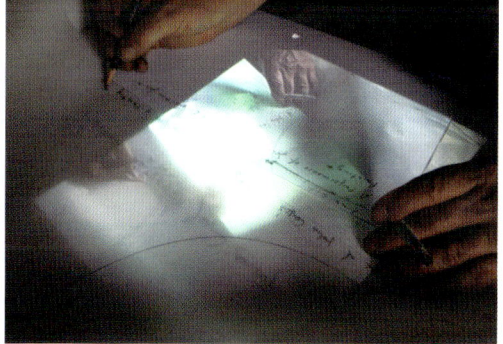
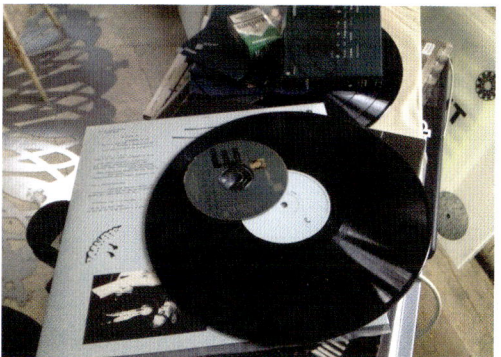

Franz Graf, *aroundrecording*, 2012. Photos: Georg Weckwerth

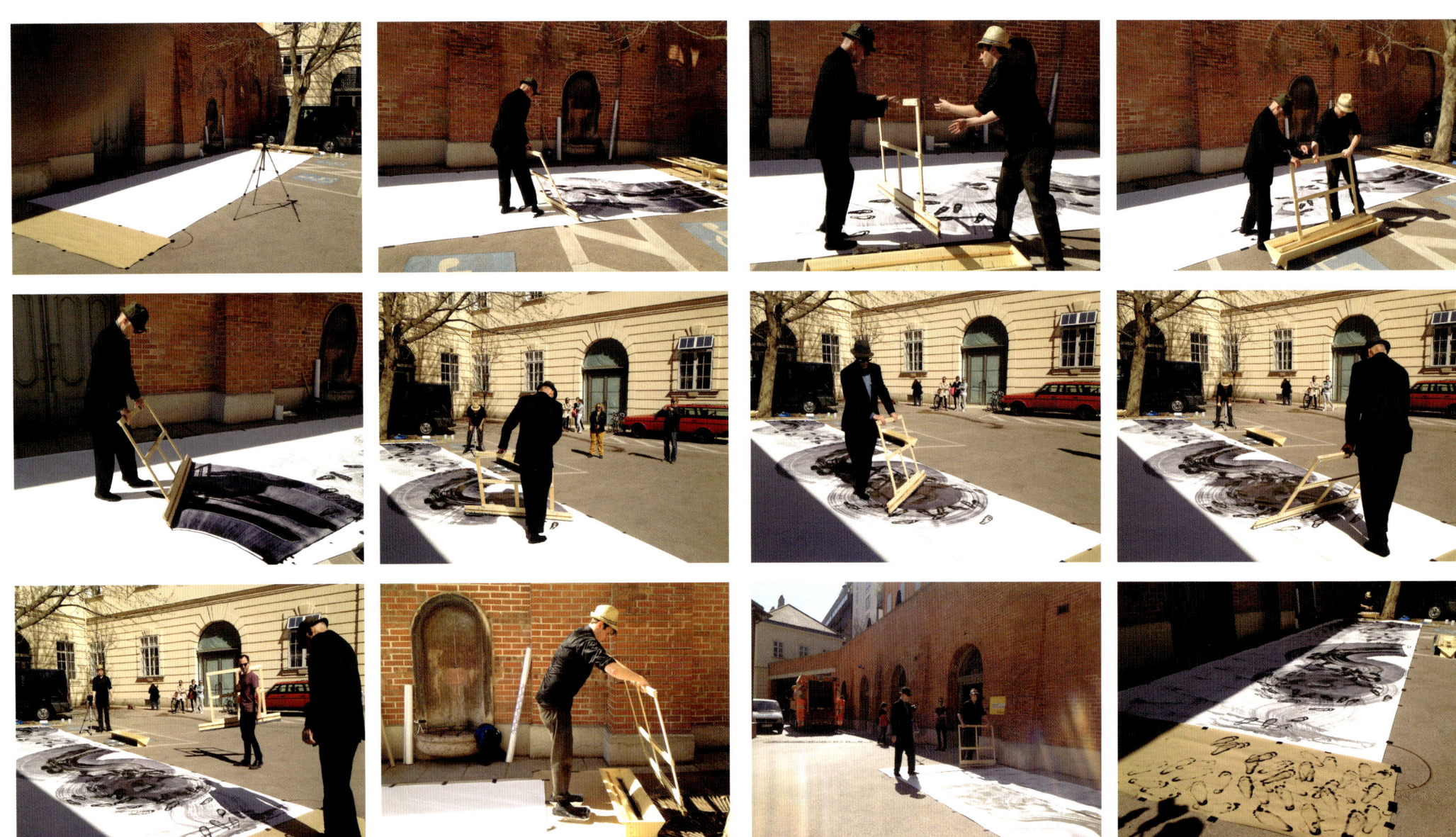

Ray Kass and Ian Cobb-Ozanne, *Current III*, 2012. Photos: Georg Weckwerth

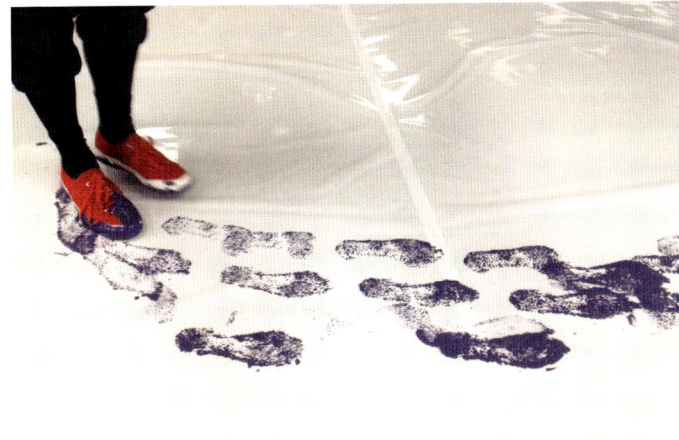
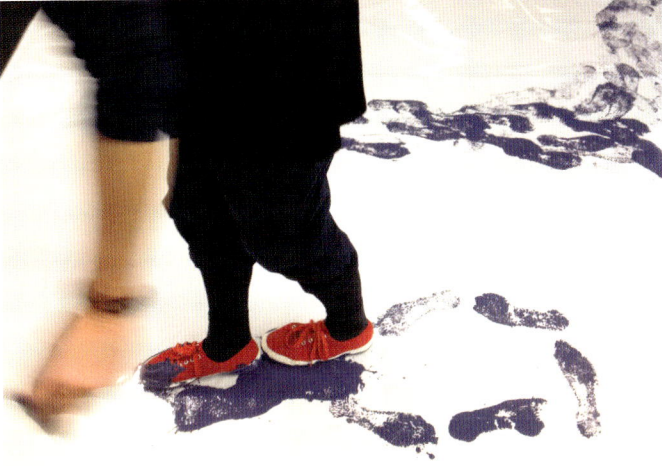
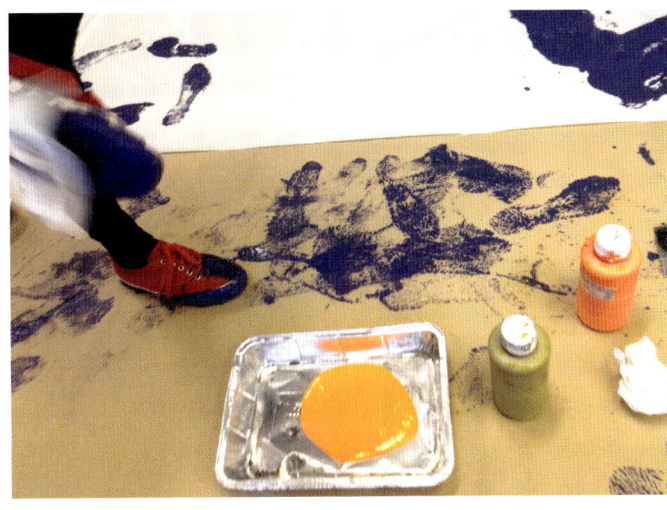
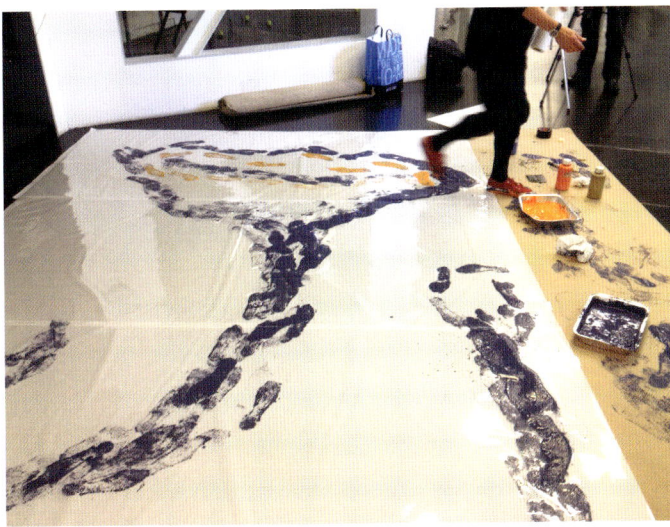
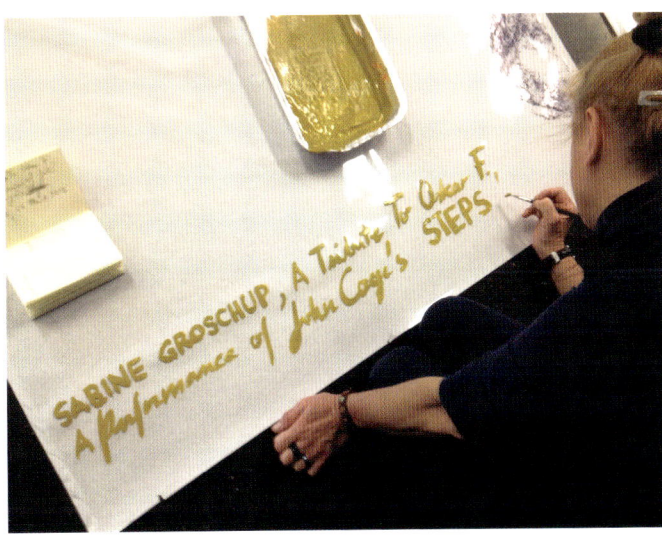
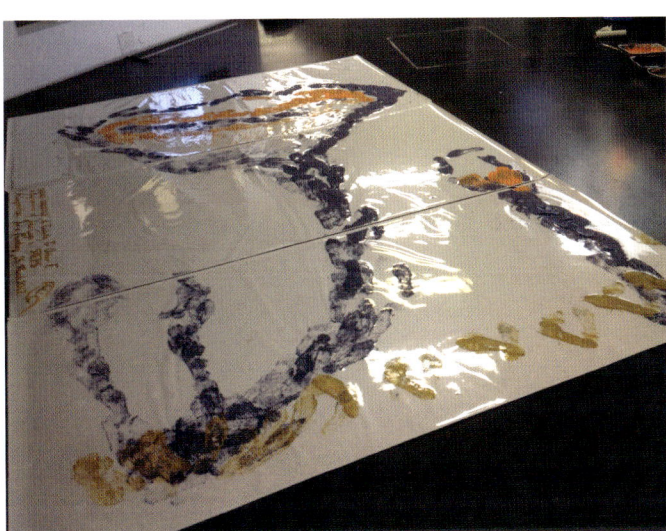

Sabine Groschup, *A Tribute to Oskar F.*, 2012. Photos: Georg Weckwerth

of the car and into two trays of ink as Ian Cobb-Ozanne, Ray's assistant, hands me the large *STEPS* brush, which I then dip into a trough of black ink. Ian then pours ink over the left front tire as Sabine Groschup drapes herself over the hood. Tyler Adams climbs onto the left rear bumper, and Bach is still playing as Ian releases the brake and shuts the door. With my back to the car, I start it moving with my rear end. It begins rolling backwards down the paper. "It's going fast," Sabine shouts. I keep on pushing the Volvo backwards over the paper, pulling the brush in front of me. In the process, I erase the traces of the performance at almost the very moment they are created, melding them into an impressive painting of the collectively experienced moment.[11]

[11] Video footage, clip I: https://youtu.be/boWWnX1qxjU; clip II:
https://youtu.be/GG2Ea7-YriA; https://www.youtube.com/results?search_query=TONSPUR+Kunstverein+Wien

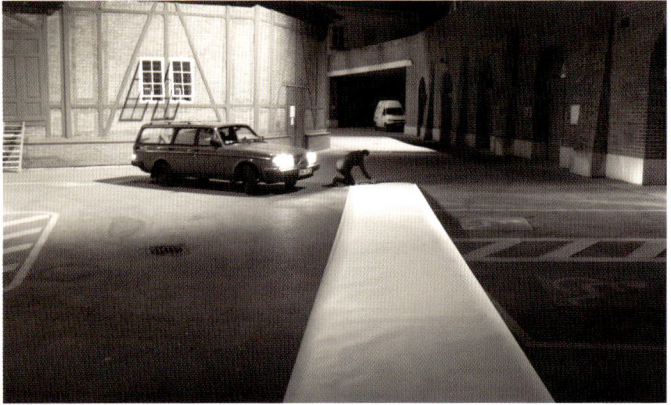

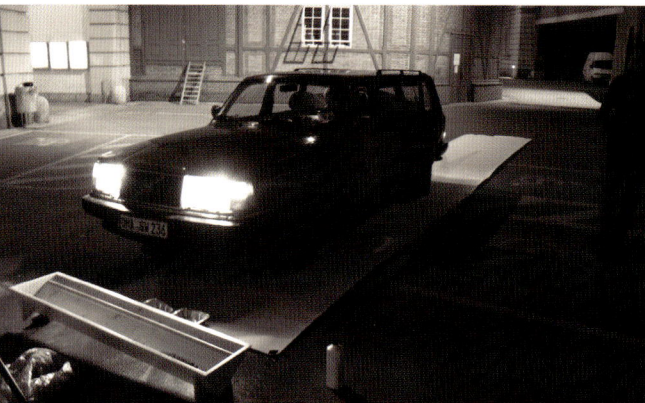

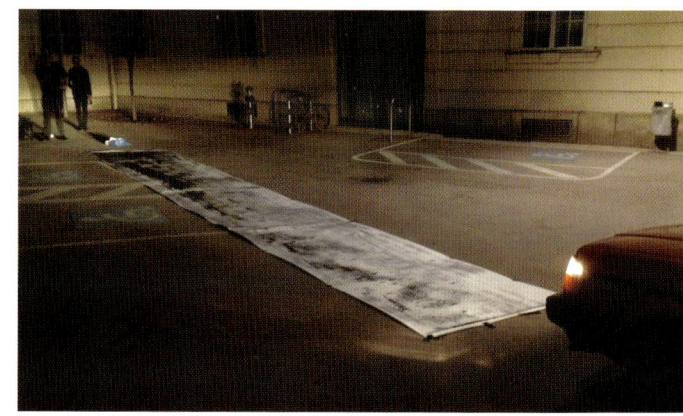

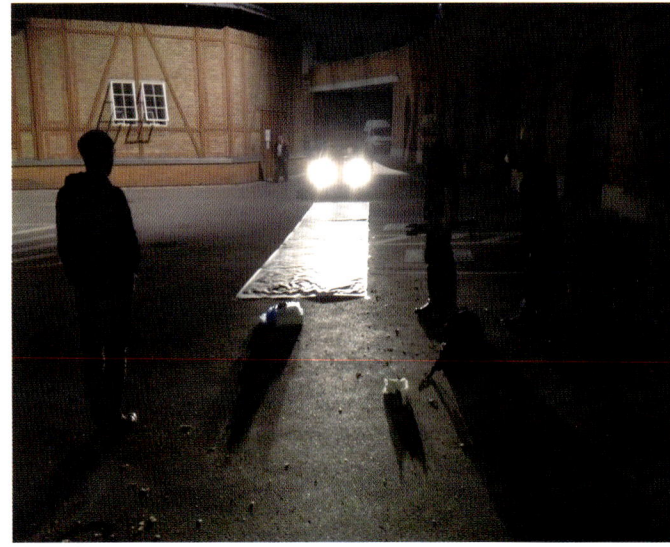

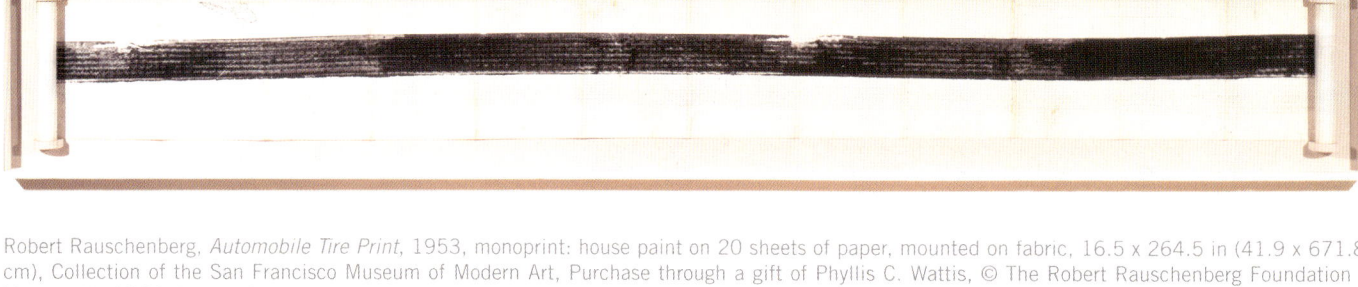

Robert Rauschenberg, *Automobile Tire Print*, 1953, monoprint: house paint on 20 sheets of paper, mounted on fabric, 16.5 x 264.5 in (41.9 x 671.8 cm), Collection of the San Francisco Museum of Modern Art, Purchase through a gift of Phyllis C. Wattis, © The Robert Rauschenberg Foundation / Licensed by VAGA, New York, NY.

(above & across) Georg Weckwerth, *A Car Full of STEPS (reminiscence of RR, JC, and a Model A Ford)* — (…), 2012. Photos: Sabine Groschup and Georg Weckwerth

**December 2016, shortly before the new year:**

The worldwide situation characterized by war, terror, expulsion, hatred of foreigners and populism, as well as the "me-first" mentality that is spreading like a virus, must be decisively faced. What is called for now is not mistrust, envy, mobbing, instigation, … but cosmopolitan life, the search for community and the cultivation of a spirituality that does not exclude but unites. The will and drive to think positively, to get things moving, to shape, to form, to create, to communicate … are important building blocks in our open and free society. The discovery of one's own creativity often accompanies them. I imagine that the renowned composer John Cage, a key figure of the Happening movement, while moving to activate the passion he developed painting at the Mountain Lake Workshop, and so manifesting his fascination with the elements fire, water, air, and earth through the visual arts, might have had those kinds of thoughts going through his head as he created *STEPS* — for himself and for us all. We ought to follow him — freely adapting Neil Armstrong's "That's one small STEP for a man …"[12] and also Yoko Ono and John Lennon's inspiring slogan, a variation of which has become the title of this essay.

**John Cage's *STEPS* in Halberstadt 2017**

On the occasion of the 25th anniversary of the death of John Cage on August 12, 1992, and his 105th birthday on September 5, 2017, the John Cage Organ Foundation Halberstadt extends an invitation for a "STEPS" workshop by Ray Kass and the Mountain Lake Workshop. The scene is the very same Halberstadt in Saxony-Anhalt, Germany, that has already gained worldwide recognition with the 639-year-long performance of John Cage's composition *ORGAN²/ ASLSP*, which began in 2001 and will end in 2640.

[12] On July 2, 1969 at 2:56:20 UTC, Neil Armstrong was the first person to step on the surface of the moon and said the famous words: "That's one small step for a man, one giant leap for mankind!"

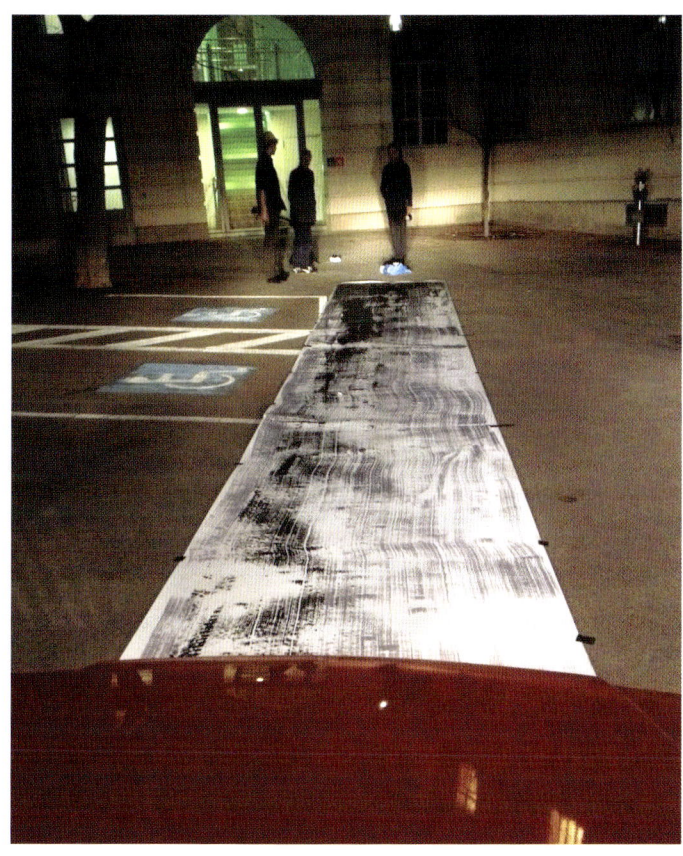

*A Car Full of Steps* (cont.)

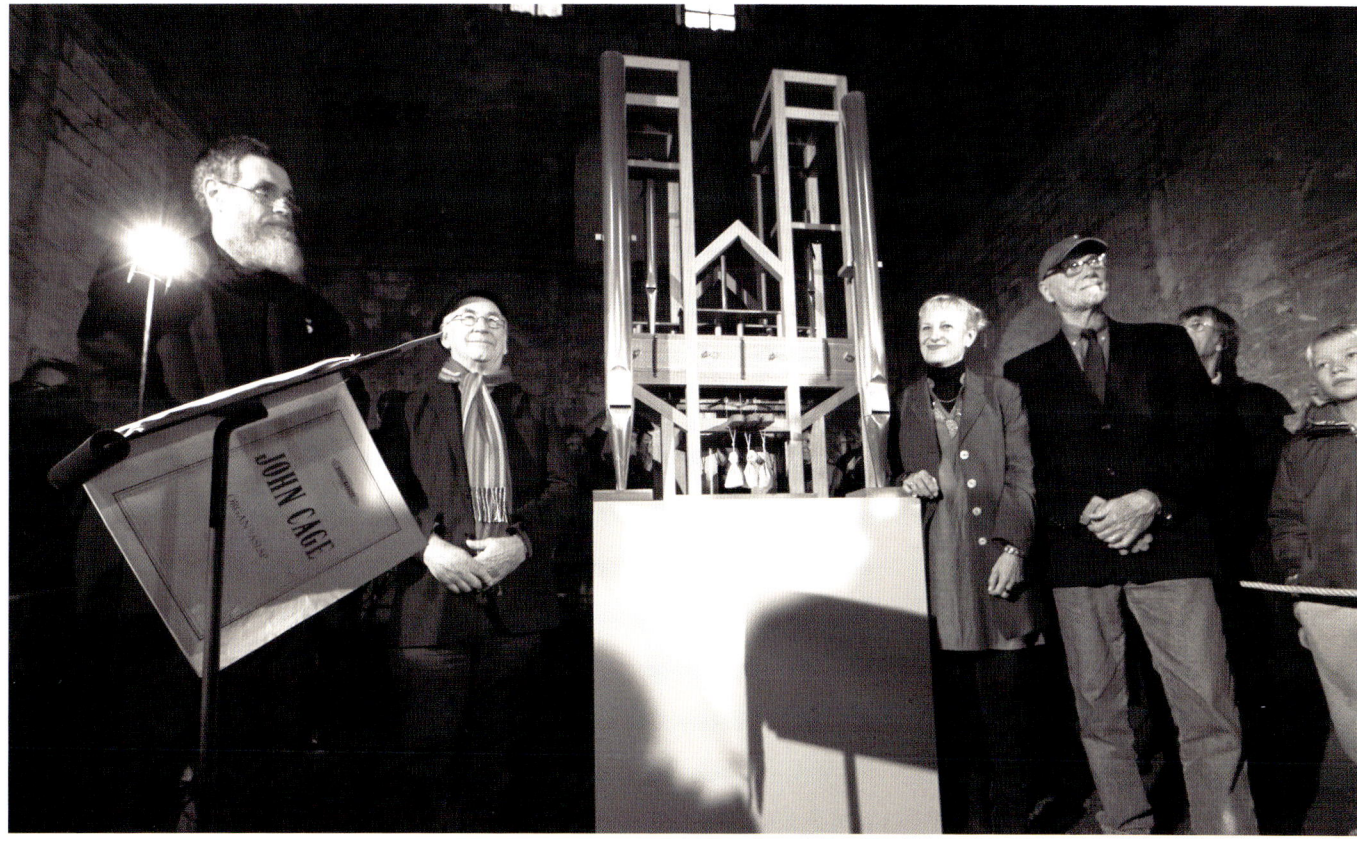

At left, with the score of *ORGAN² ASLSP* by John Cage: Rainer O. Neugebauer from the John Cage Organ Foundation. With (from l. to r.) Pierre Hébert, Sabine Groschup, and Ray Kass - all "organists" at the *Cage Project* 2013 sound change in the Burchardi Church in Halberstadt. Photo: Ronald Göttel

Halberstadt is where the poet, literary patron and collector Johann Wilhelm Ludwig Gleim was active, and where today the Gleimhaus houses the estate of this exponent of the German 18th-century enlightenment culture of friendship; it is also where Alexander Kluge, the filmmaker, writer, and co-founder of *New German Film*, was born and where the musical roots of Christian Wolff, one of the most influential composers of the American avant-garde around Cage and an intimate member of his circle, extend to his grandfather Leonard, a musician, composer, conductor, and violinist, and to his son Kurt, Christian's father, who was a renowned German publisher of expressionist literature.

Invited artists, members of the general public, and persons involved in the Cage Project will participate in performances of John Cage's *STEPS, A Composition for a Painting*. It is anticipated that art schools in the local area and universities of the arts throughout Germany and Europe will also collaborate. The workshop will culminate in a large-scale exhibition which will present a number of the 2012 Viennese *STEPS, A Composition for a Painting* pieces together with the works created in Halberstadt. Venues are the Haus für Cage (House for Cage) in the Burchardi cloister, the socio-politically significant church St. Martini of Halberstadt,

and public spaces in the city on the eastern border of the Harz National Park, which is known beyond German borders for the Halberstadt Cathedral Treasury, one of the most precious church treasures of the world. Curators for the project will be Ray Kass and Georg Weckwerth. The project director is Harriett Watts from the *John Cage Organ Project*.

# MdM SALZBURG
## *STEPS*, 2012

**RAY KASS**

The 100th birthday of the composer, musician, philosopher, writer, and thinker John Cage was celebrated all over the world. In cooperation with Wulf Herzogenrath and the Academy of Arts, Berlin, MdM (Museum der Moderne) Salzburg Director Toni Stooss organized an exhibition that focused on the visual oeuvre of John Cage, who greatly influenced art in the second half of the twentieth century.

Ray Kass was invited for a residency in Salzburg to deliver lectures and create performances of *John Cage's STEPS: A Composition for a Painting to Be Performed by Individuals or Groups*. The performances were documented by Mountain Lake Workshop assistants Luke Demarest and Ryan Dudik, who traveled to Vienna and Salzburg with Kass, and the videos can be viewed on the Mountain Lake Workshop website in the Workshops & Artists section entitled "John Cage's *STEPS*: The Centennial Year Compositions for a Painting." The five performances developed are pictured on the pages that follow and also described briefly in Appendix F.

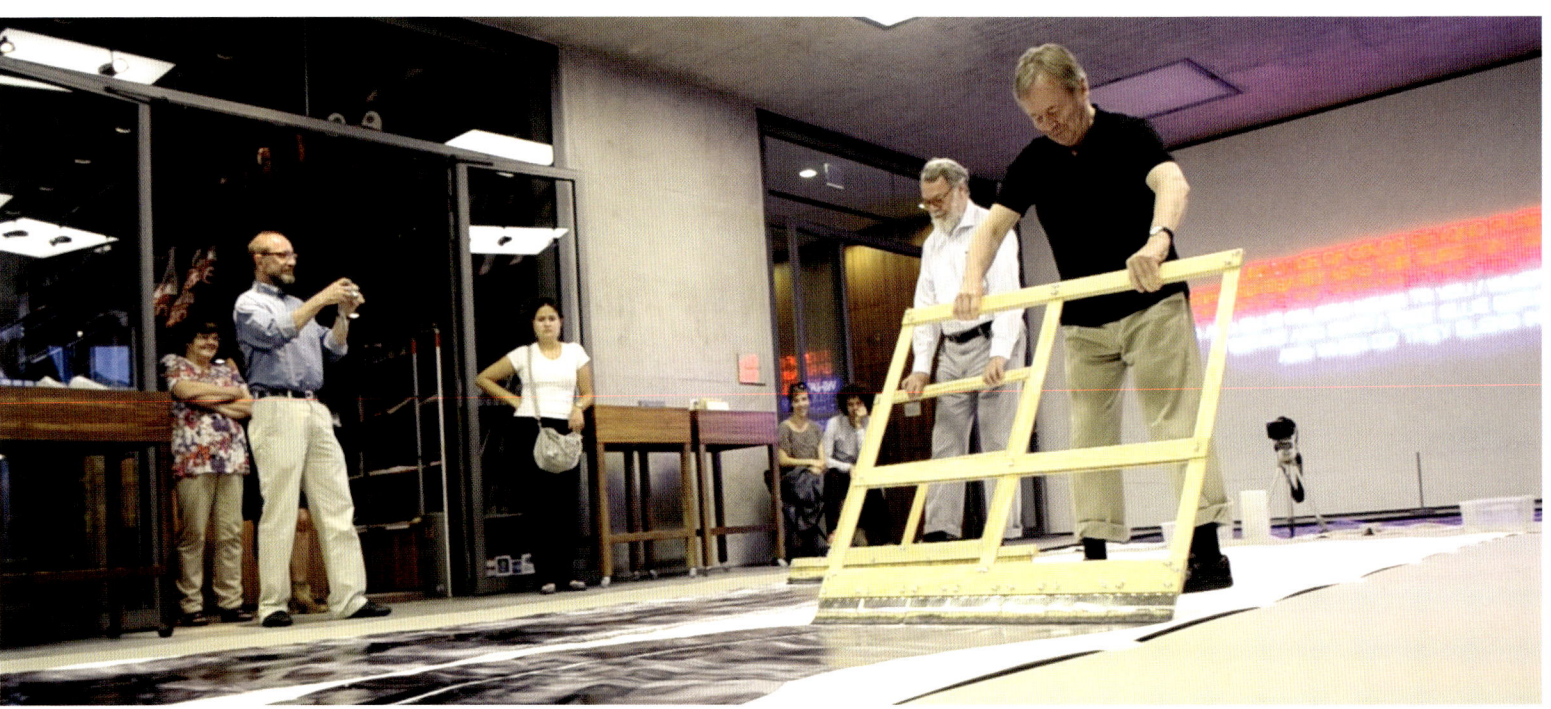

Toni Stooss and Wulf Herzogenrath, *John Cage's STEPS: Small and Tall Is Beautiful. In Friendship*, July 18, 2012, black ink and watercolor on two peices of white Fabriano paper, each 59 x 211 in. (150.8 x 537 cm)

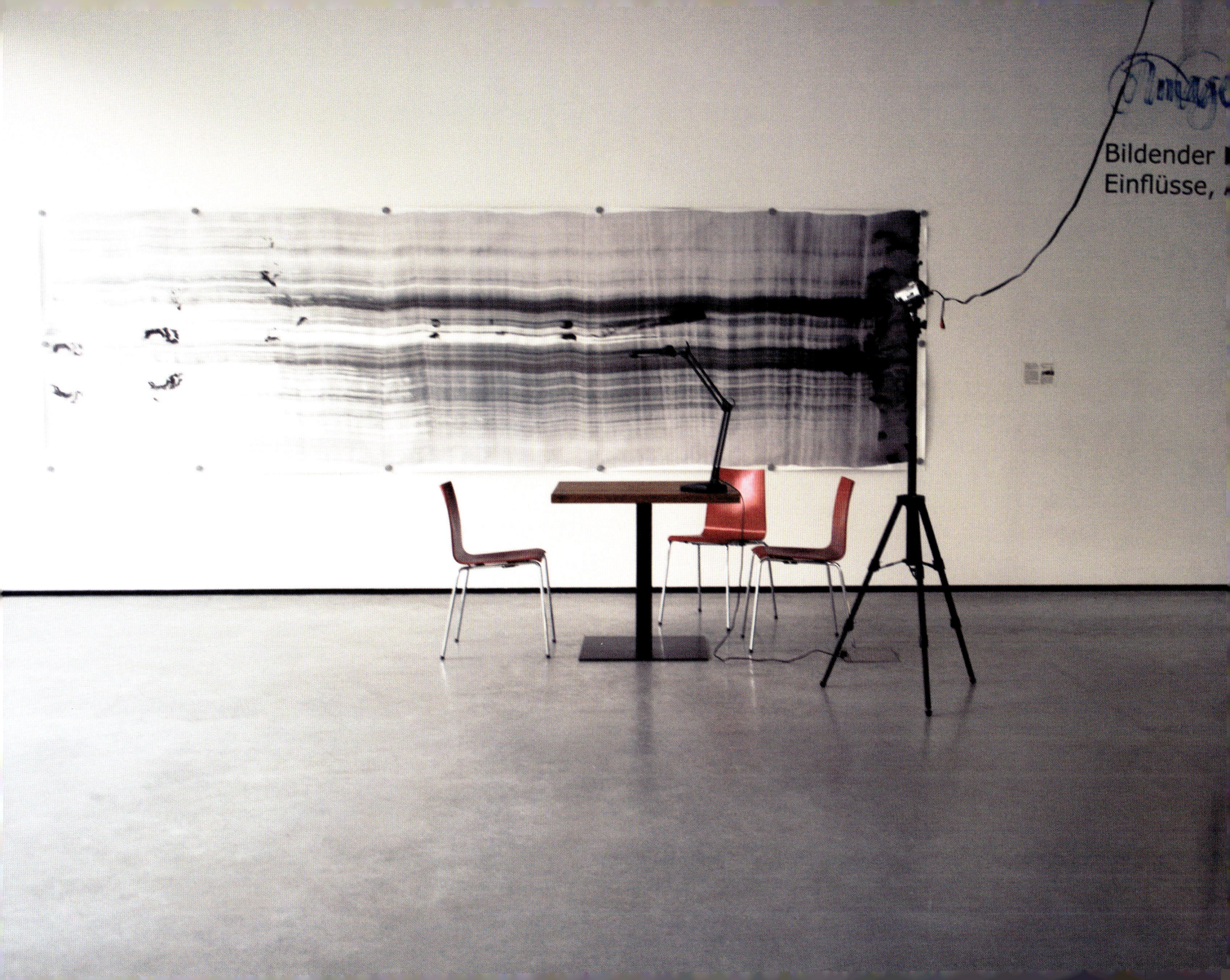

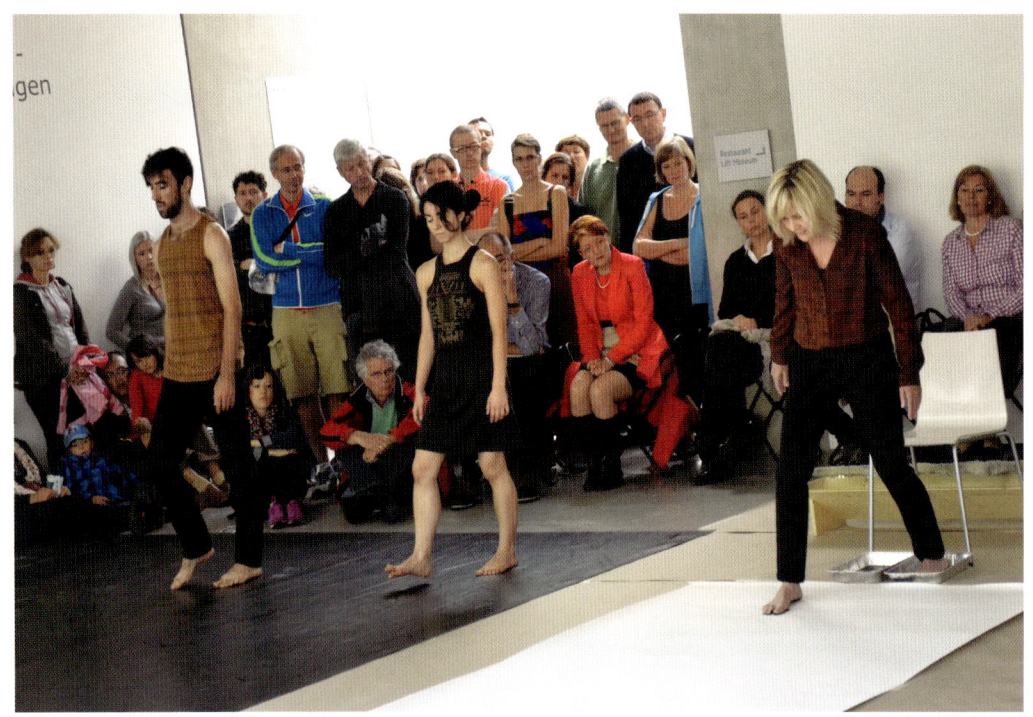
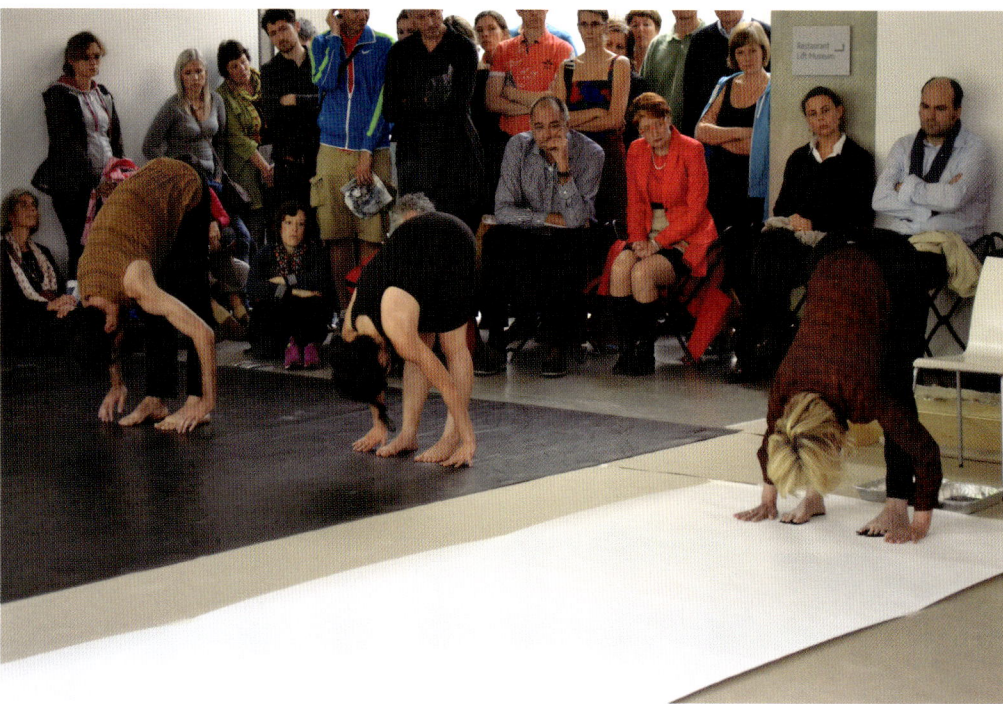
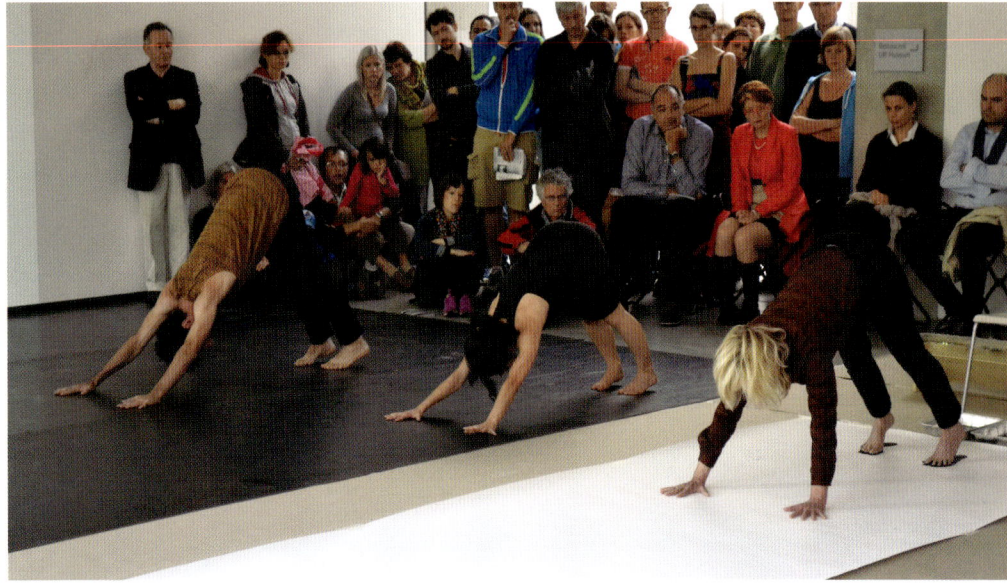
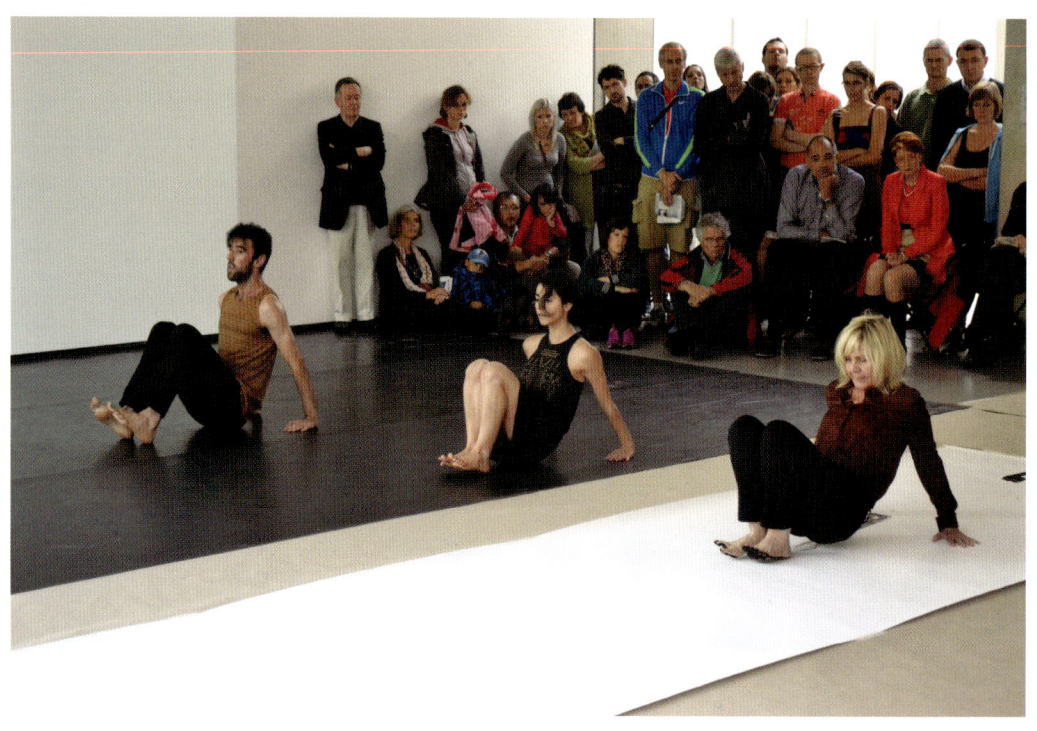

Susan Quinn and SEAD Dance Company, choreography by Jelka Milic, *Generations: A performance
of John Cage's STEPS: A Composition for a Painting to be Performed by Individuals or Groups*
Performers: Susan Quinn, Evandro Pedroni, Daniela Oliveira Faria, Evandro Pedroni.
Photos: Museum der Moderne, Salzburg

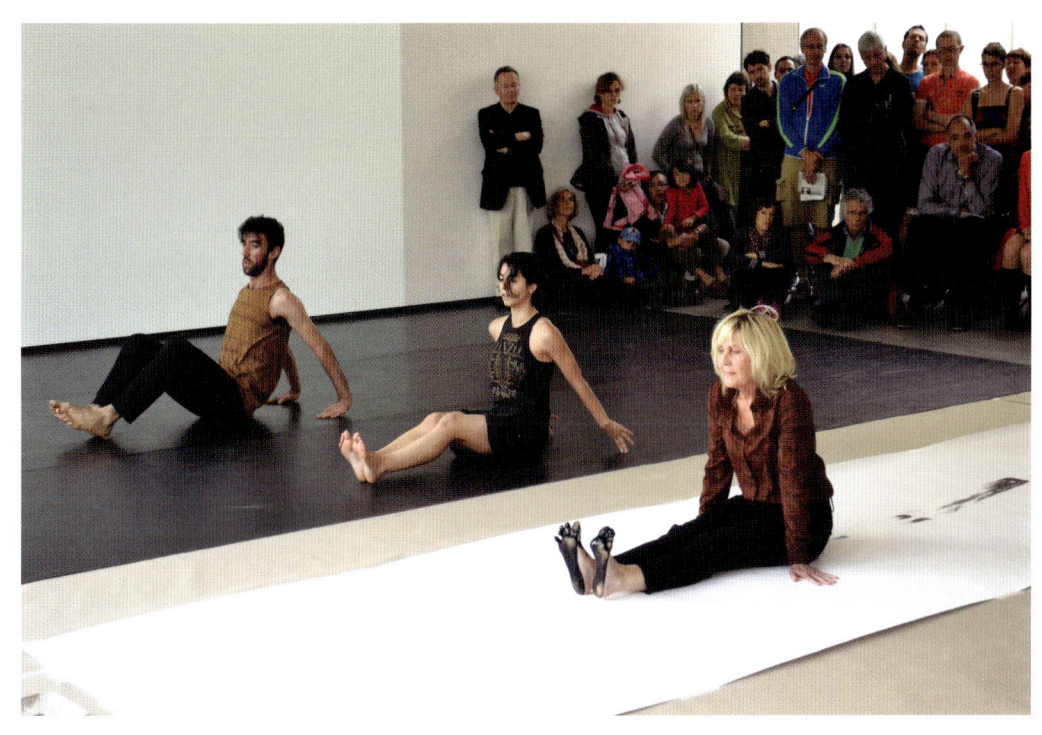
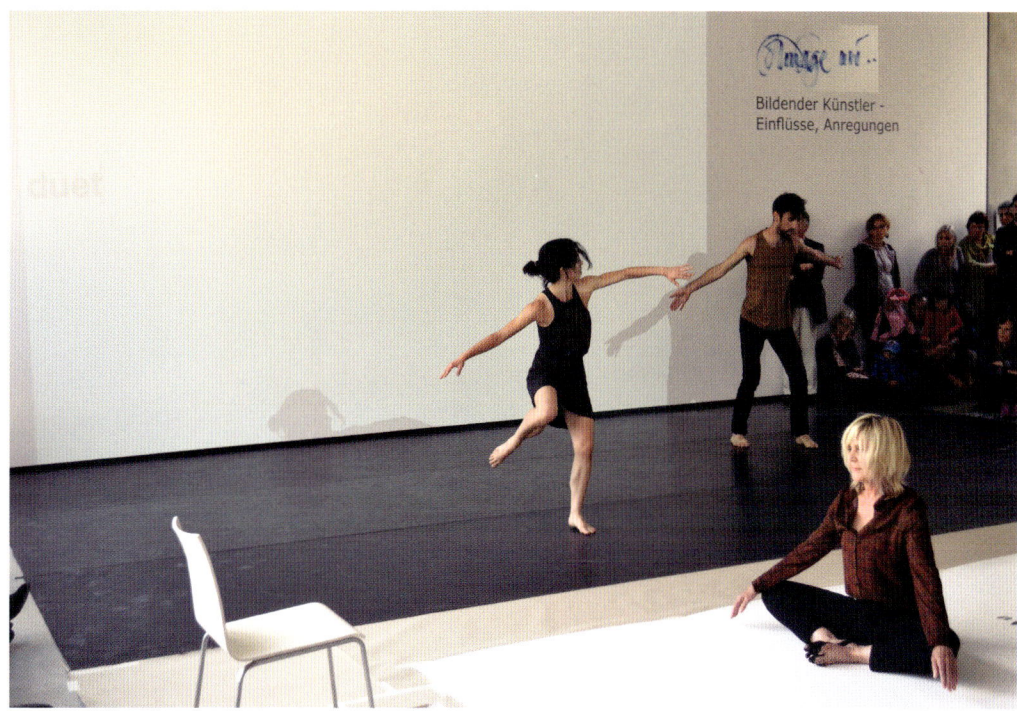
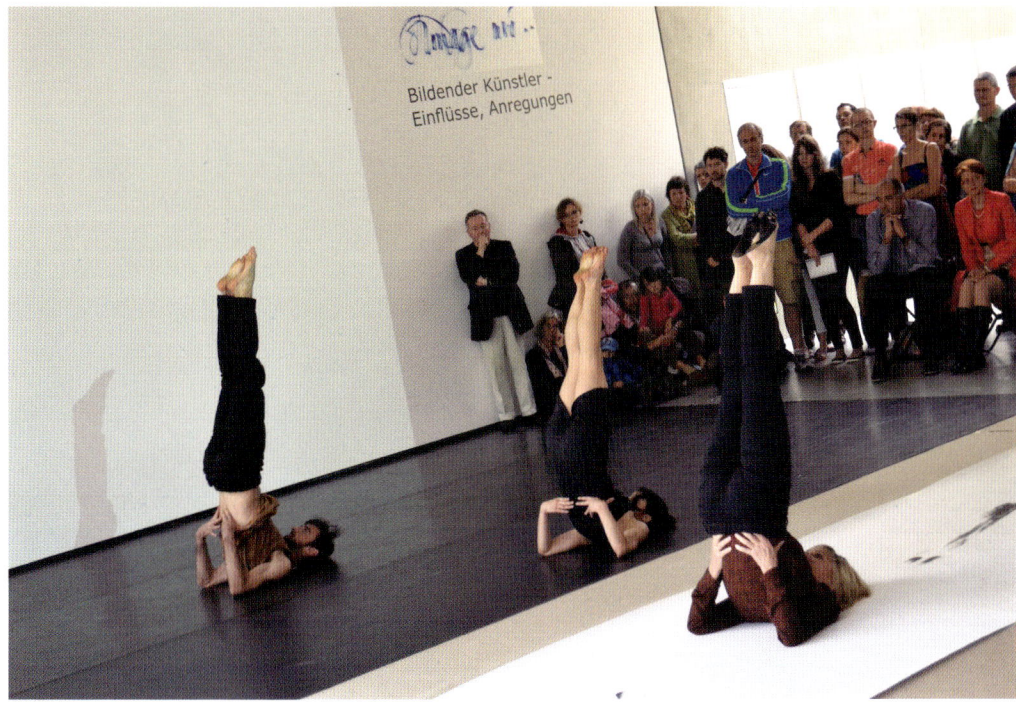
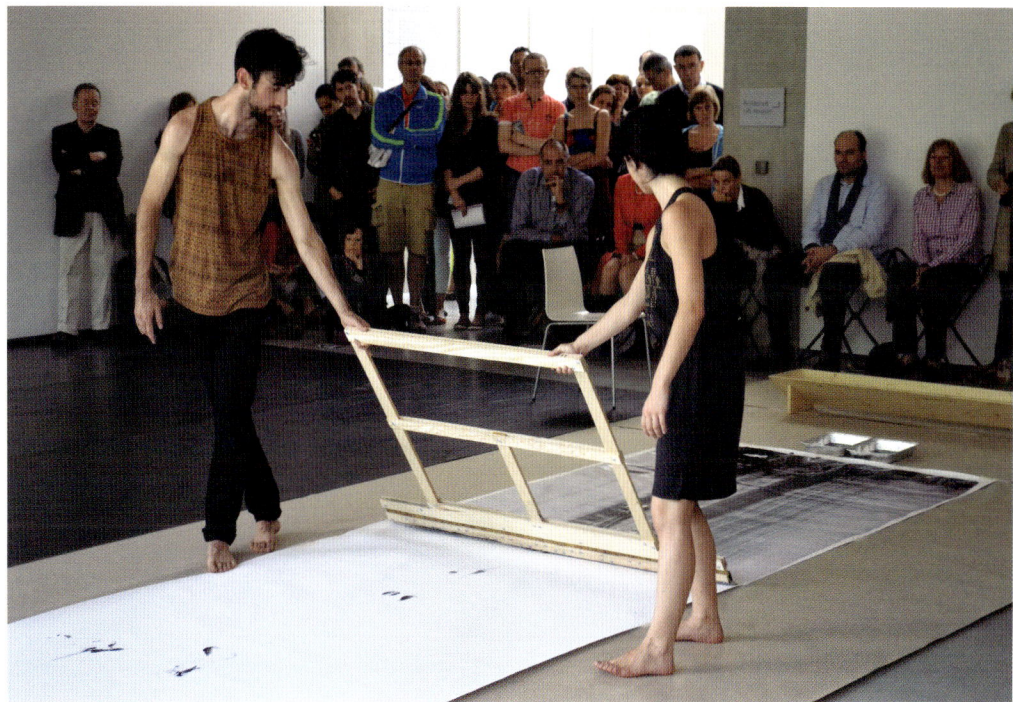

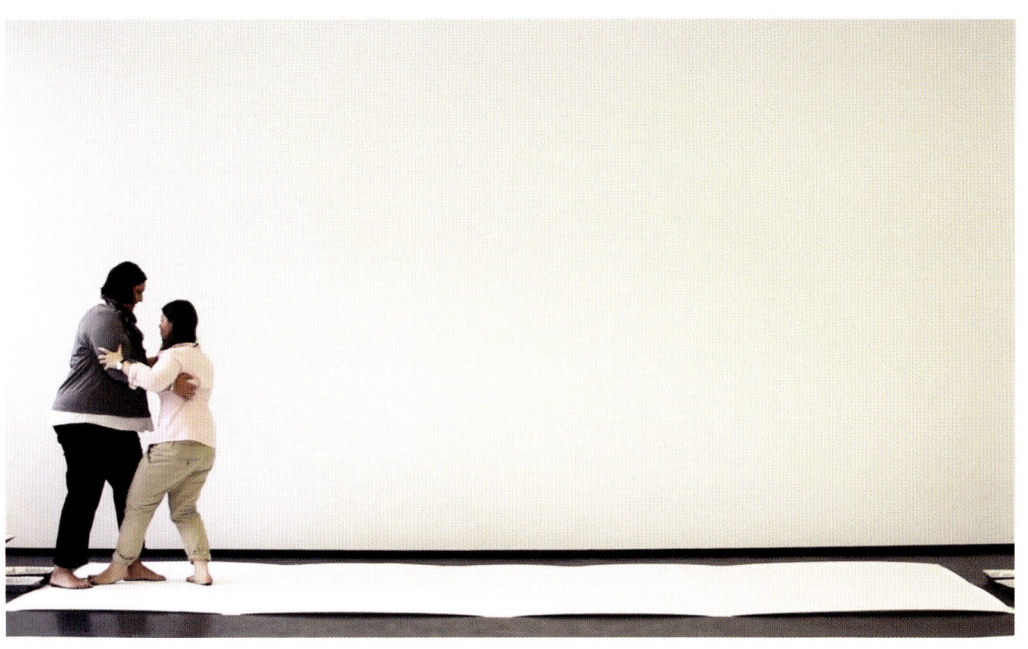
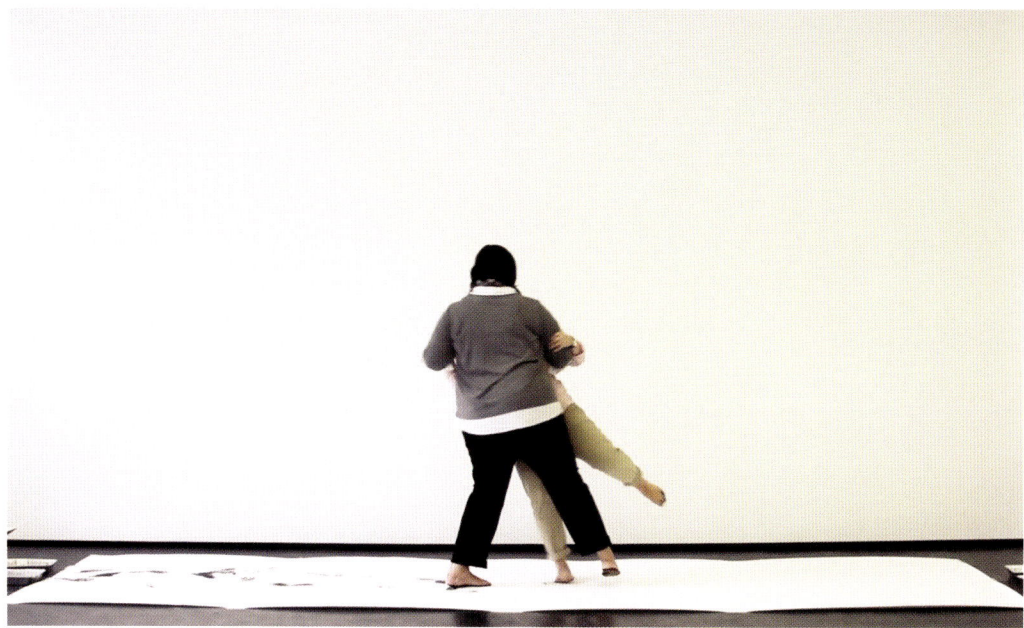
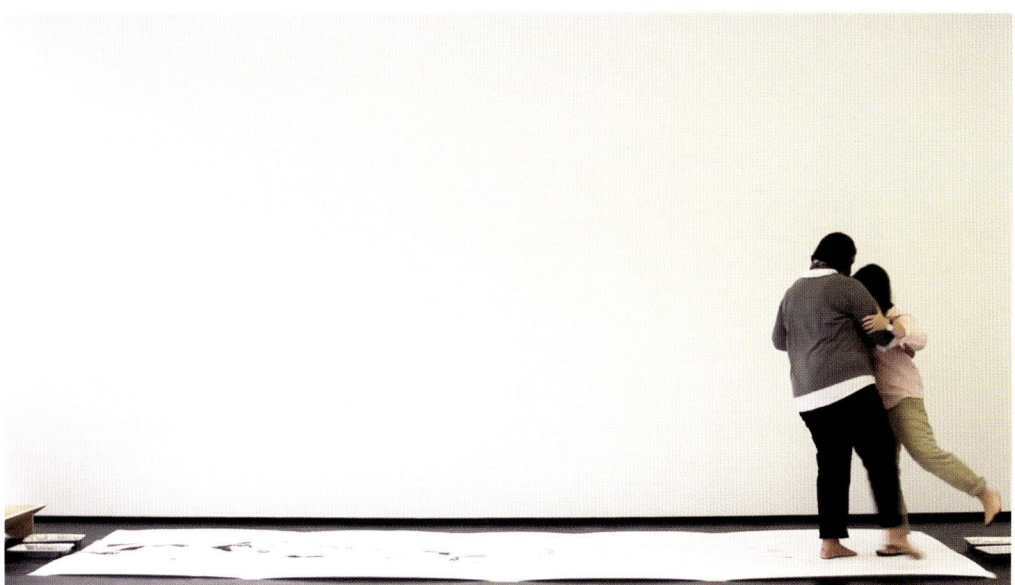
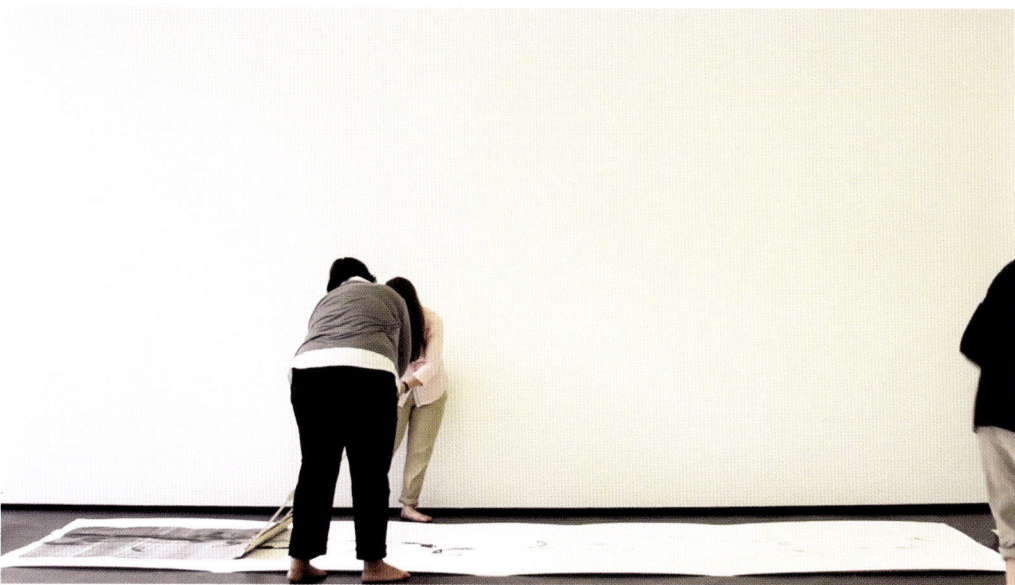

Tina Teufel and Martina Pohn, *Spelunking für John Cage*, 150 x 495.2 cm. (59 x 195 in.),
July 21, 2012

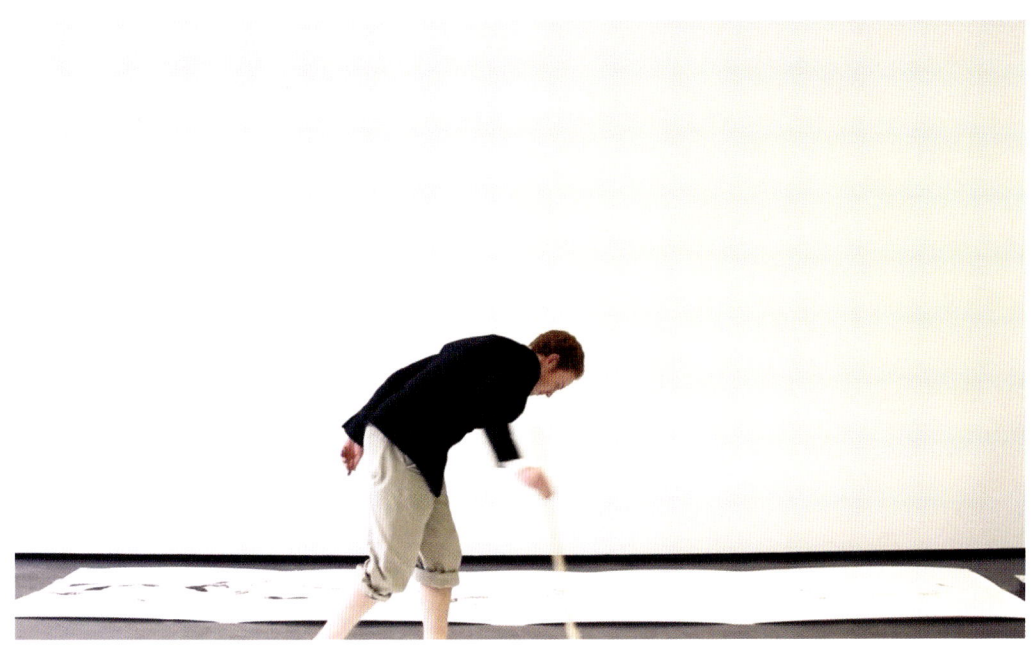
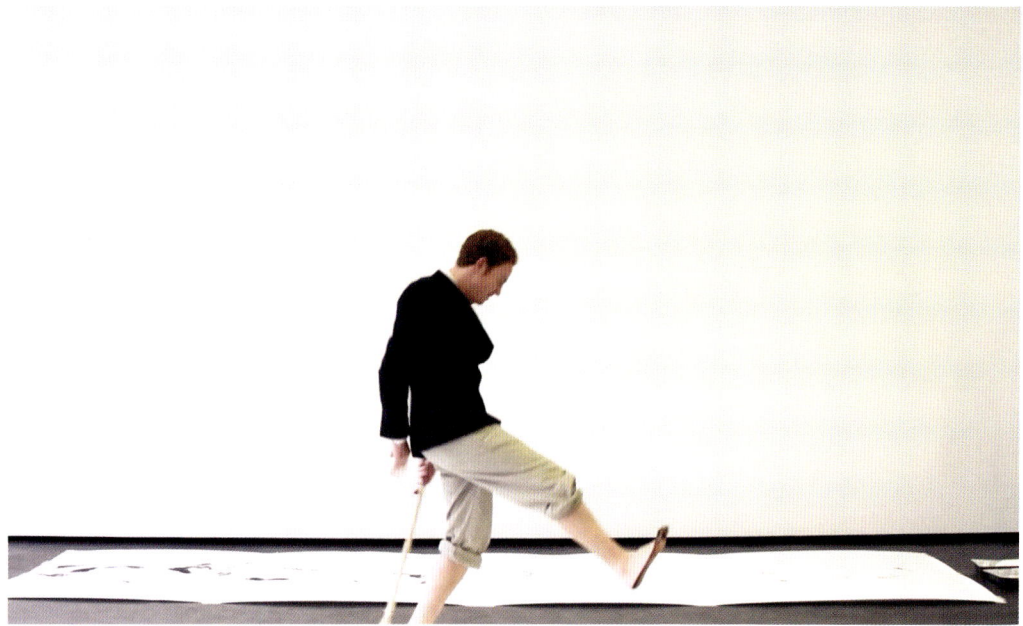
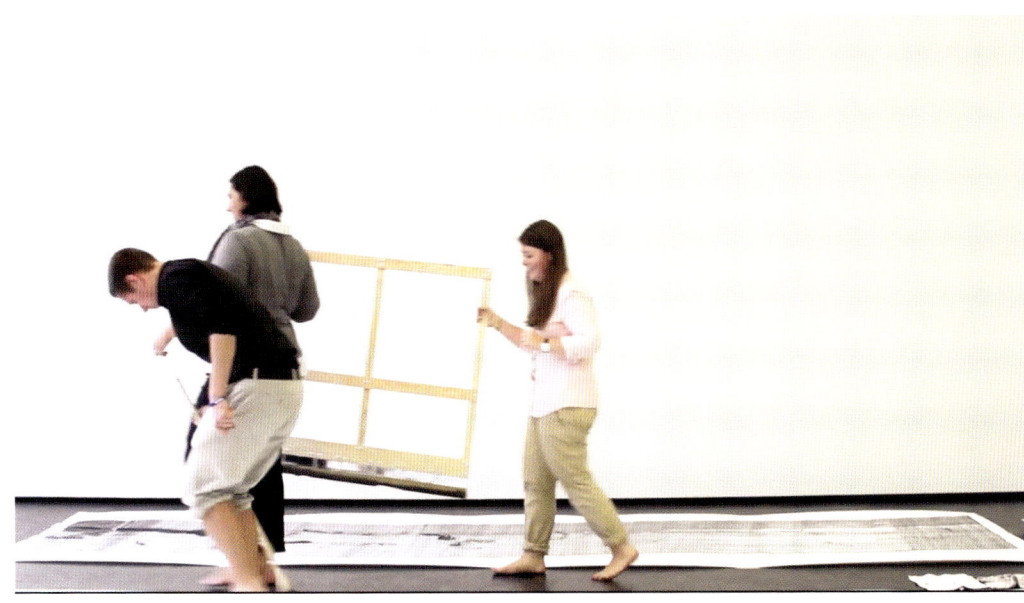
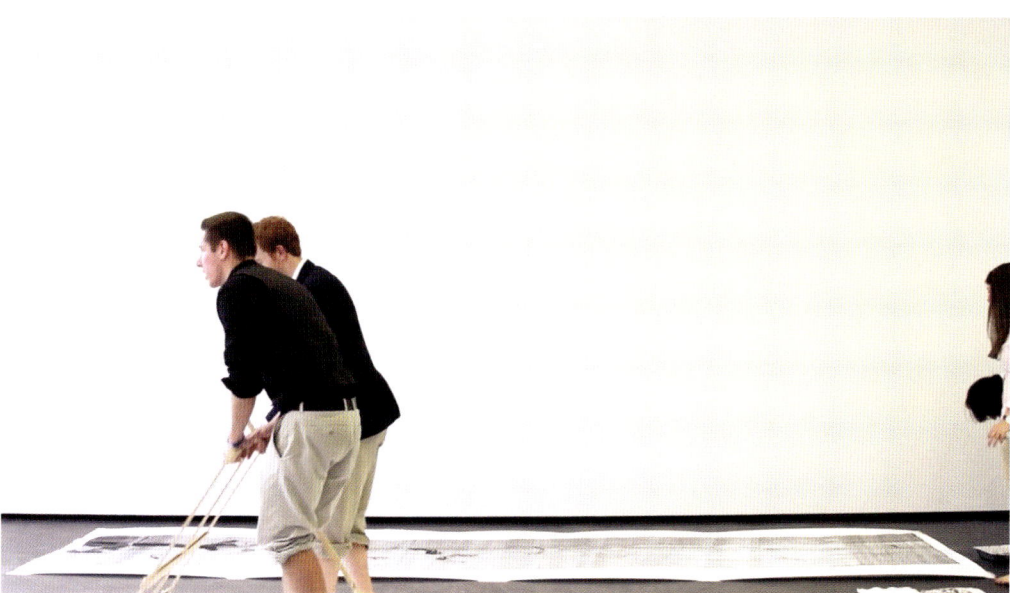

Ryan Dudik and Luke Demarest, *The Baumgartner: A Performance of John Cage's STEPS*, 150 x 568 cm (59 x 223.6 in.), July 21, 2012

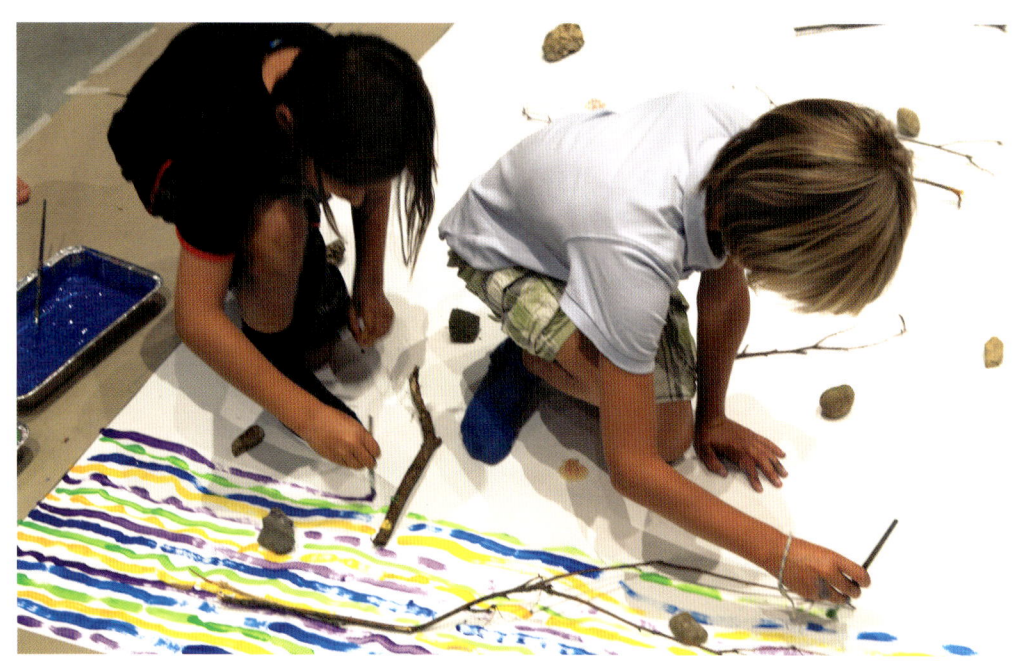
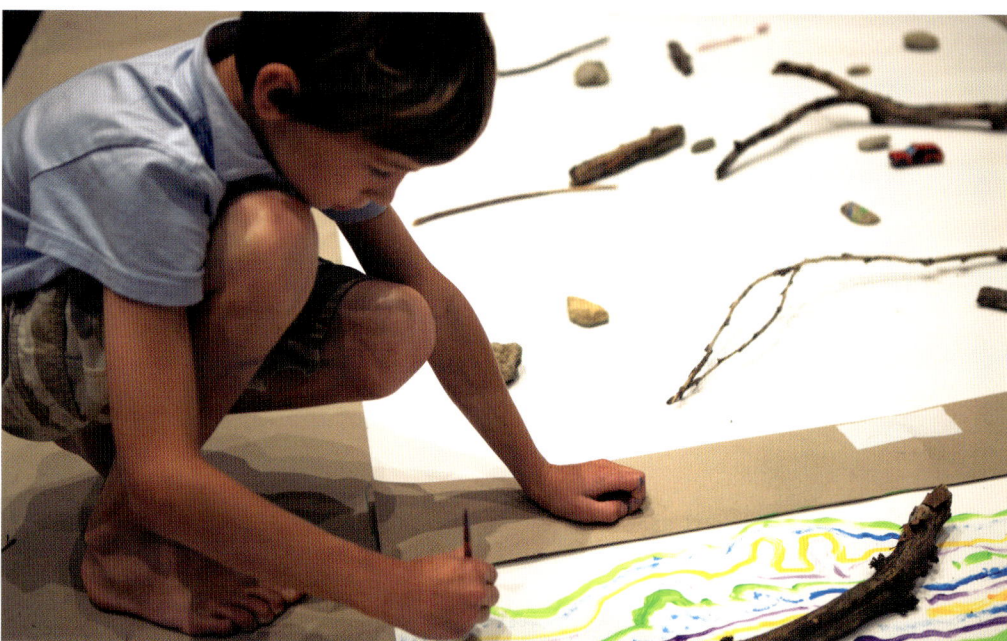
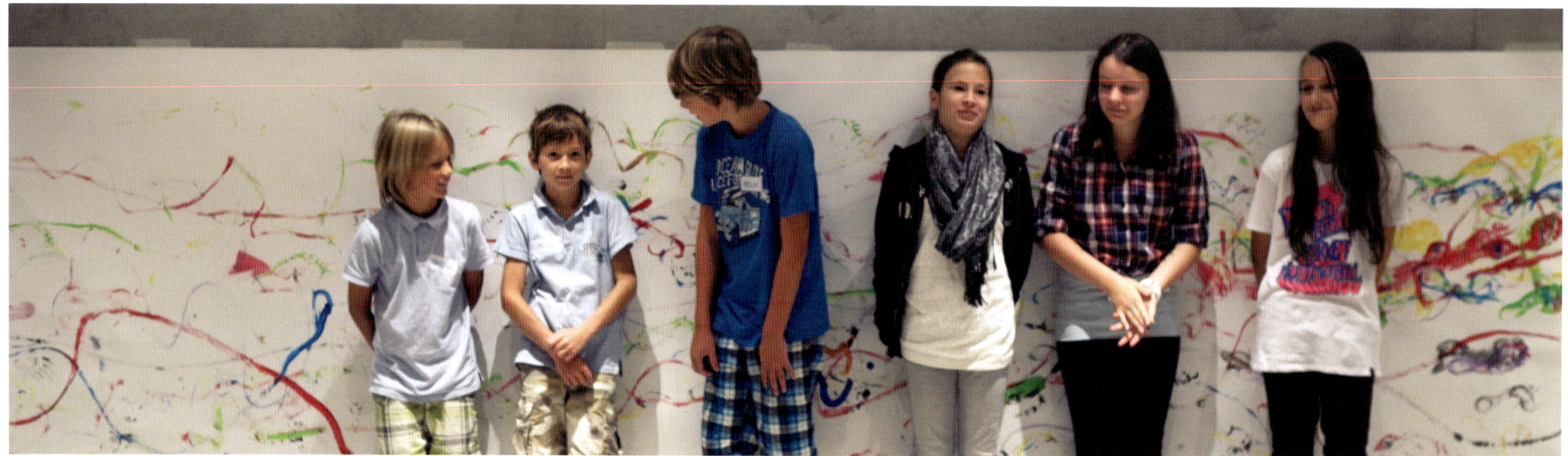

Participants' names are listed on page 335.

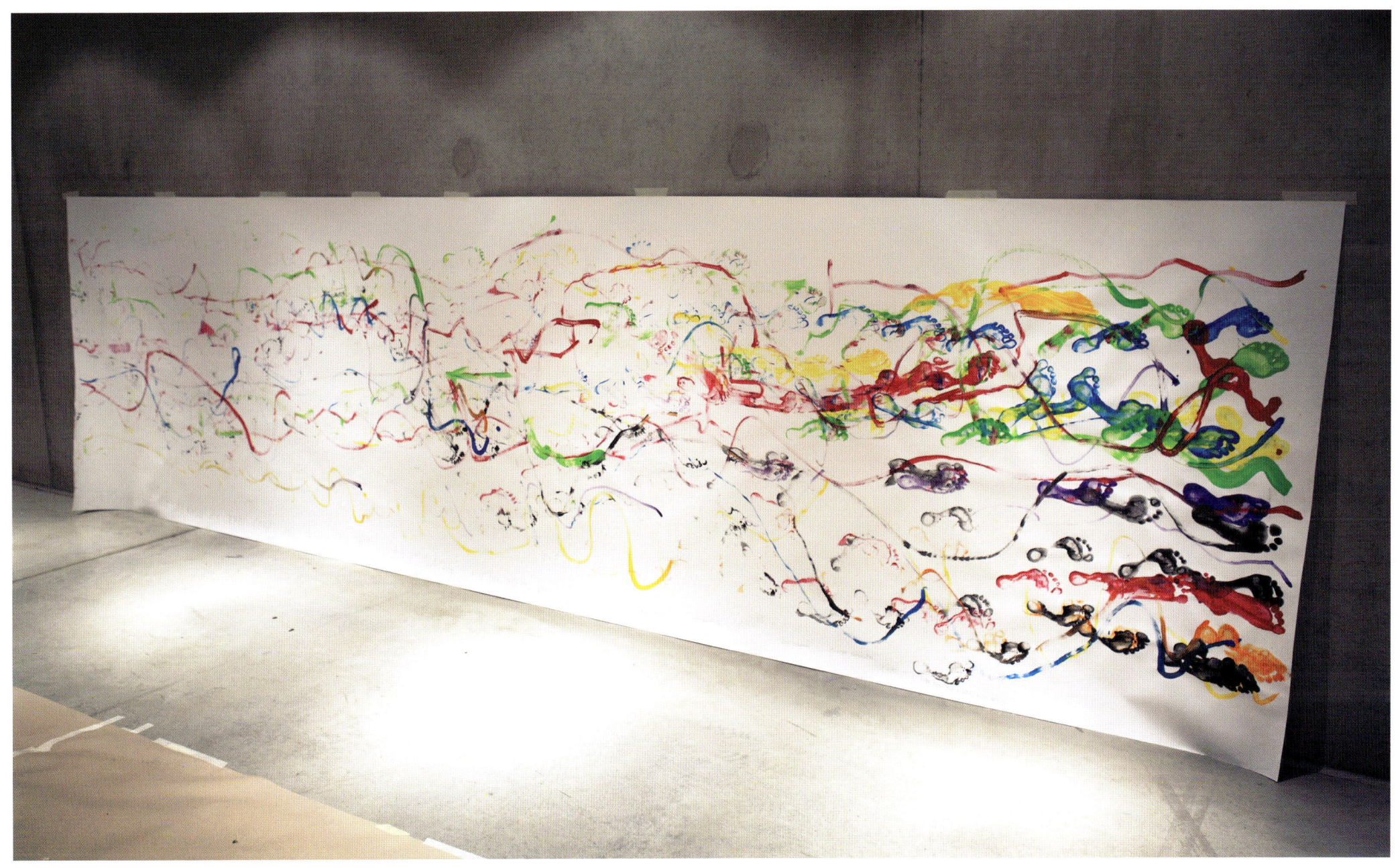

The Summer Children's Class at MdM, *A STEPS Variation of Jiro Okura's "Breathing Lines,"*
150 x 549.5 cm (59 x 216 in.)

Seven participants guided by their teacher, Theresa Weiss, and Mountain Lake Workshop
Director Ray Kass, July 19, 2012. Children assigned their own titles to the group piece

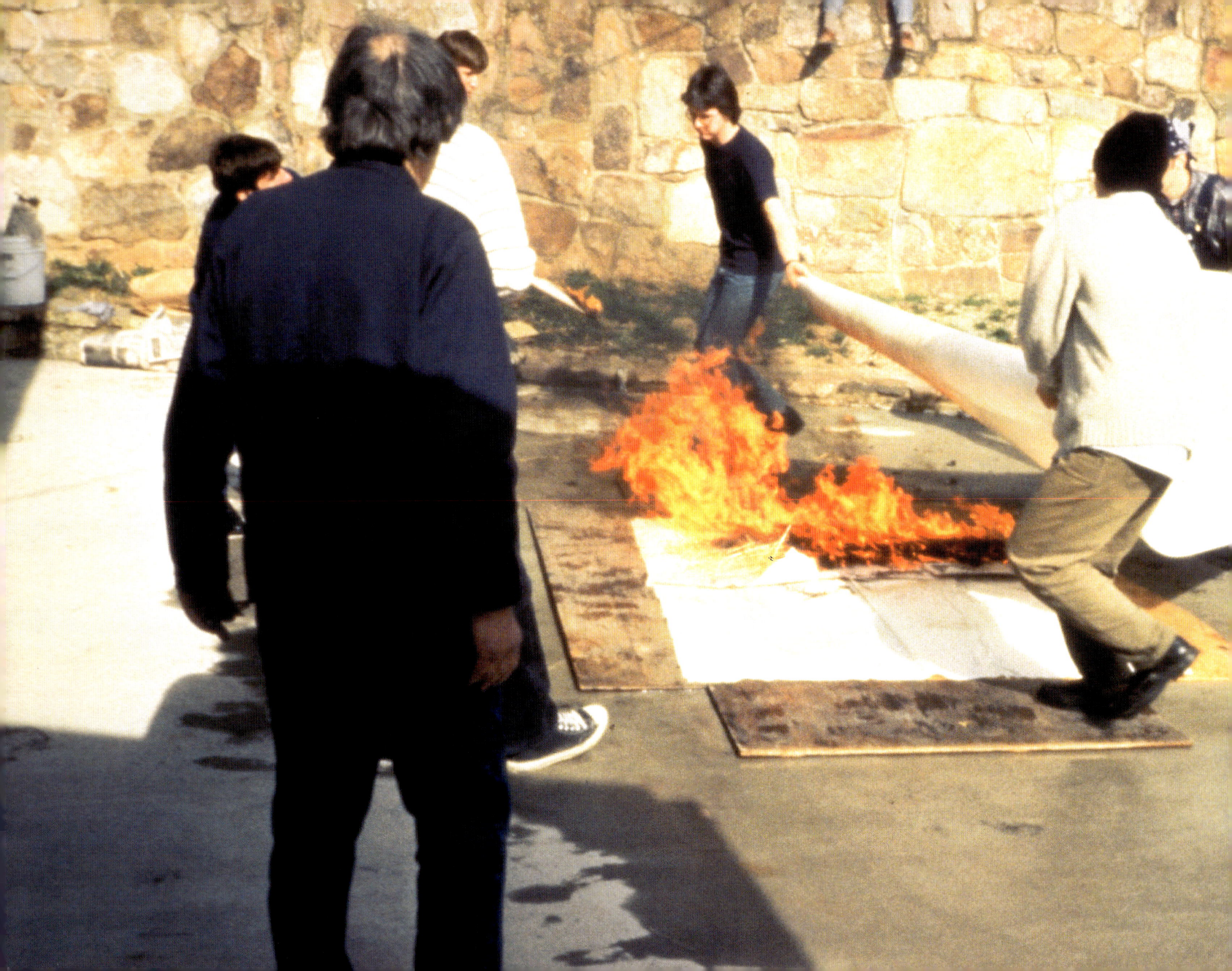

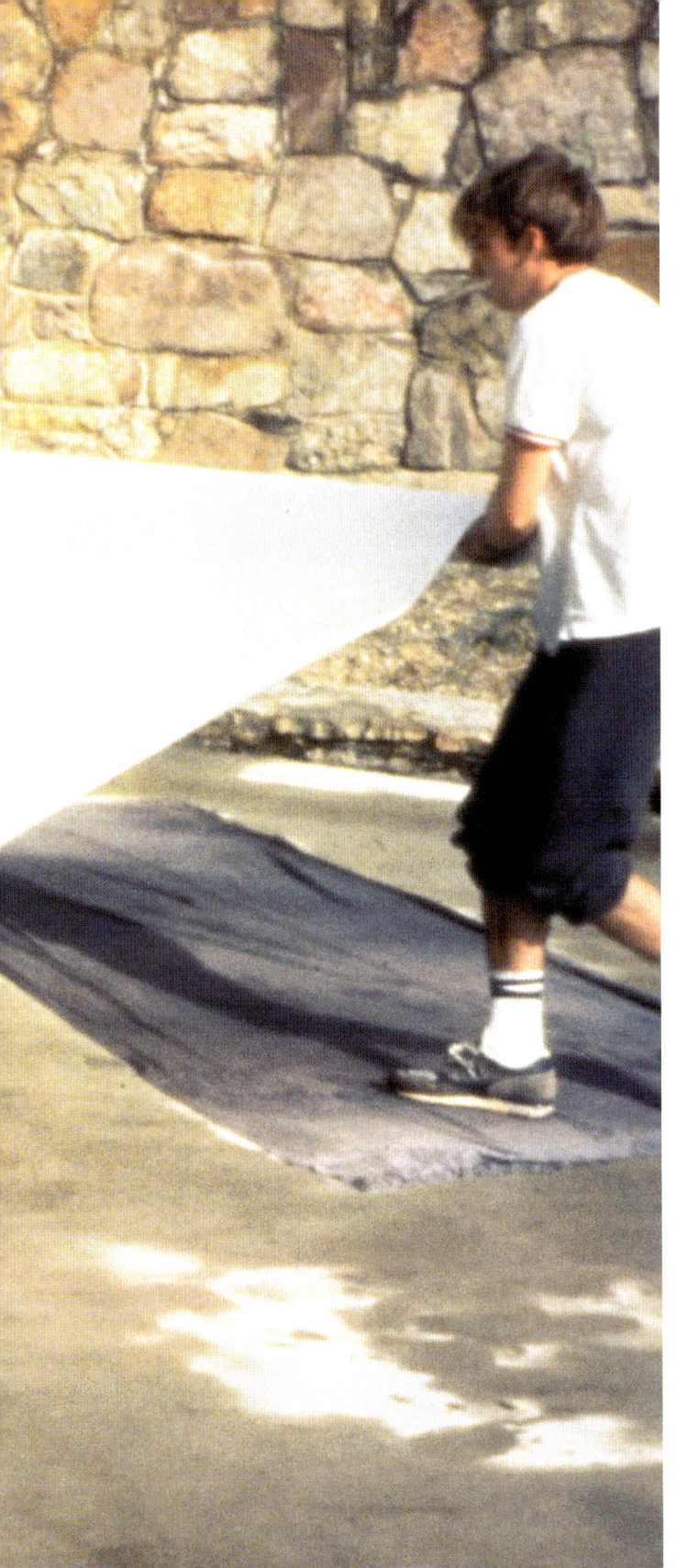

# XII
*Epilogue*

# MOUNTAIN LAKE AND THE COLLABORATIVE SPIRIT

HOWARD RISATTI

All of the Mountain Lake Workshops have had different emphases. Okura's were about meditation and the development of intuitive skills through repetitive actions as a kind of "bodily chanting." Some involved aspects of narrative as in Finster's workshop and Kelley's *Appalachian Trail Frieze* or a sense of nature at the cosmological level as in Cage's workshops. Other workshops also touched on nature and natural forces. Kass, Ukeles, and Pinkerton did so at the microbiological level by looking at microbial organisms, while Jackie Matisse explored natural forces like wind and gravity through the use of new technologies.

Despite these differences, what all of the workshops have in common is that they have been similarly structured around the collaborative process and various forms of chance and indeterminacy. These procedures, when combined with visionary themes and "landscape" elements from the microbial to the near grandiose, allow for the reconsideration of the issue of artistic control of the creative process. This is because the very idea of collaboration challenges the generally accepted notion of the artist as someone who works alone, isolated from the wider world. Collaboration shows how groups of individuals working together following mutually agreed-upon procedures can create genuine works of art that reflect a unity of ideas but, in their complexity and scale, as evident in Okura's *Screen Tachi* or Matisse's virtual *Kites Flying In and Out of Space*, may be beyond the scope and expertise of any single individual. At the same time, such works can still reflect the individual hand and mind through their idiosyncratic details. Moreover, at a more metaphorical

level, the collaborative process in which people work together toward a common goal reflects a creative communal "coming together" that in many ways symbolizes the nature of society itself and represents an important psychological "breakthrough" in how we think about our relationship to the world.

When combined with chance and indeterminacy, the collaborative process also offers a way to "let" unintended and unexpected things occur. The unintended and unexpected force the thoughtful viewer to confront the unfamiliar and to rely less on the psychological comfort and security that the already known provides. In this way one is encouraged to examine accepted relationships with things in the world, with normal patterns of "being," and to see them in a new light so that new concepts can develop that expand our understanding of ourselves as well as the world around us.

This was something that Cage had attempted to do with his music as early as 1952 when he composed *4'33"*. In the premier performance of this piece, often referred to simply as *Silence*, pianist David Tudor sat quietly before a piano on stage at Woodstock, New York, in late August of 1952 as the unintended and unexpected sounds of both nature and humans (wind in the trees, raindrops on the roof, and the usual audience noises) were allowed to comprise the "music." In *Silence*, a book of his lectures and writings published nearly a decade later in 1961, Cage argued that when one realizes that sounds occur whether intended or not, if one then turns to the unintended sounds, this is a psychological turning:

*this psychological turning leads to the world of nature, where, gradually or suddenly, one sees that humanity and nature, not separate, are in the world together. ...*[1]

Something of an analogous "psychological turning" has infused the spirit of the Mountain Lake Workshops, causing nothing less than a re-envisioning of the creative self's ability to conceptualize and create a deeper image and understanding of nature through a collaborative process that allows for chance and indeterminacy to occur.

As the workshops progressed, it became increasingly clear that the direction in which the collaborative process was going would merge the conception of nature (as envisioned by Coomaraswamy) with the imagery depicted in the work. The visual appearance of the works was now being generated by processes similar to those that the works intended to symbolize. This seems to be the unconscious effect of combining the collaborative process with chance and indeterminacy, of letting things happen that could not have been predicted at the outset of any of the individual workshops.

This re-envisioning of the artistic/creative self that precipitated toward this deeper image and conception of nature also had connections to the social, economic, and political issues that the ecology movement (e.g., Save the Planet) has made visible. In some respects this was the direct result of one of the motivational impulses of the Mountain Lake programs in their desire to respond to the broader social and political climate of

[1] John Cage, *Silence: Lectures and Writings* (Middleton, Connecticut: Wesleyan University Press, 1973), p. 5.

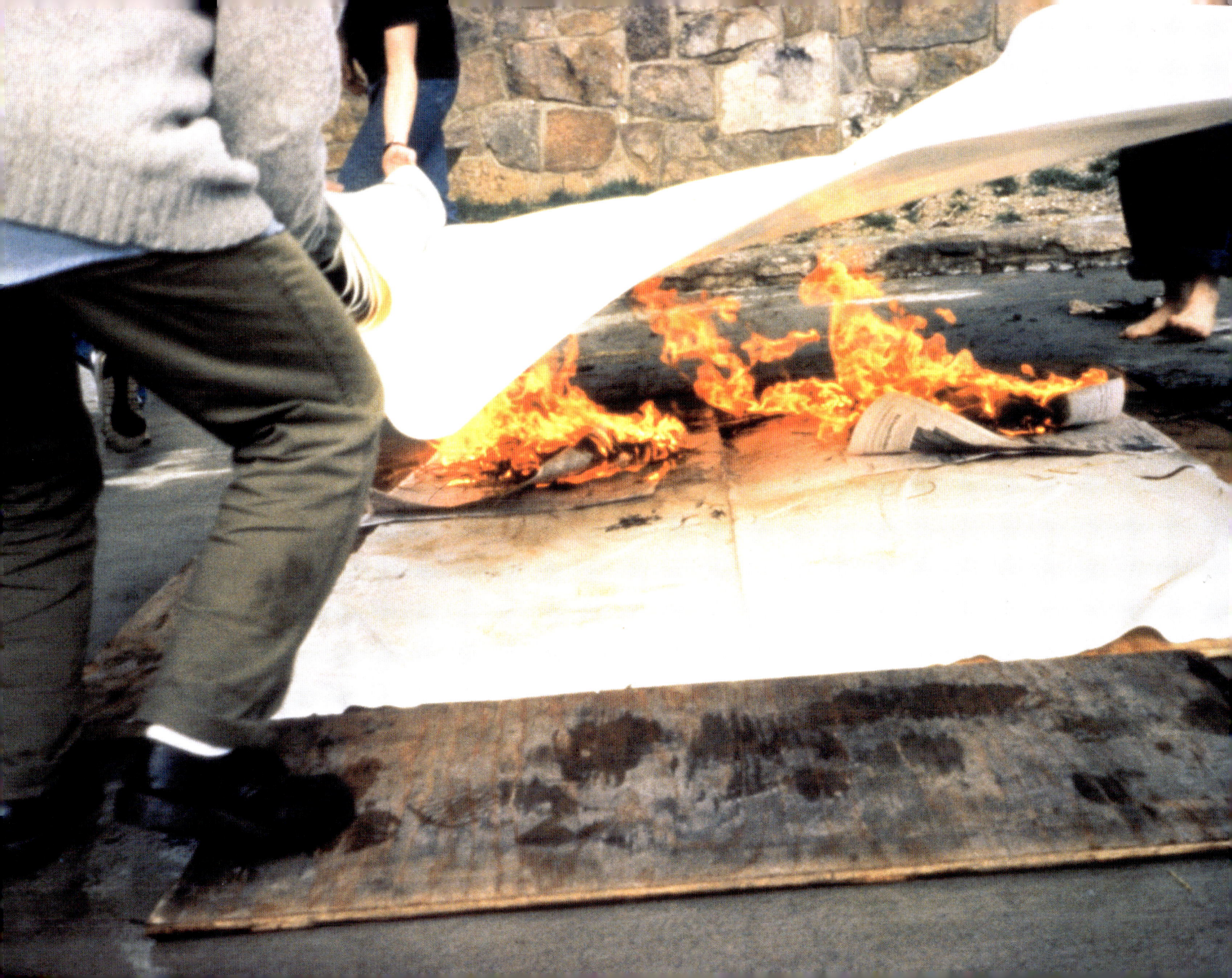

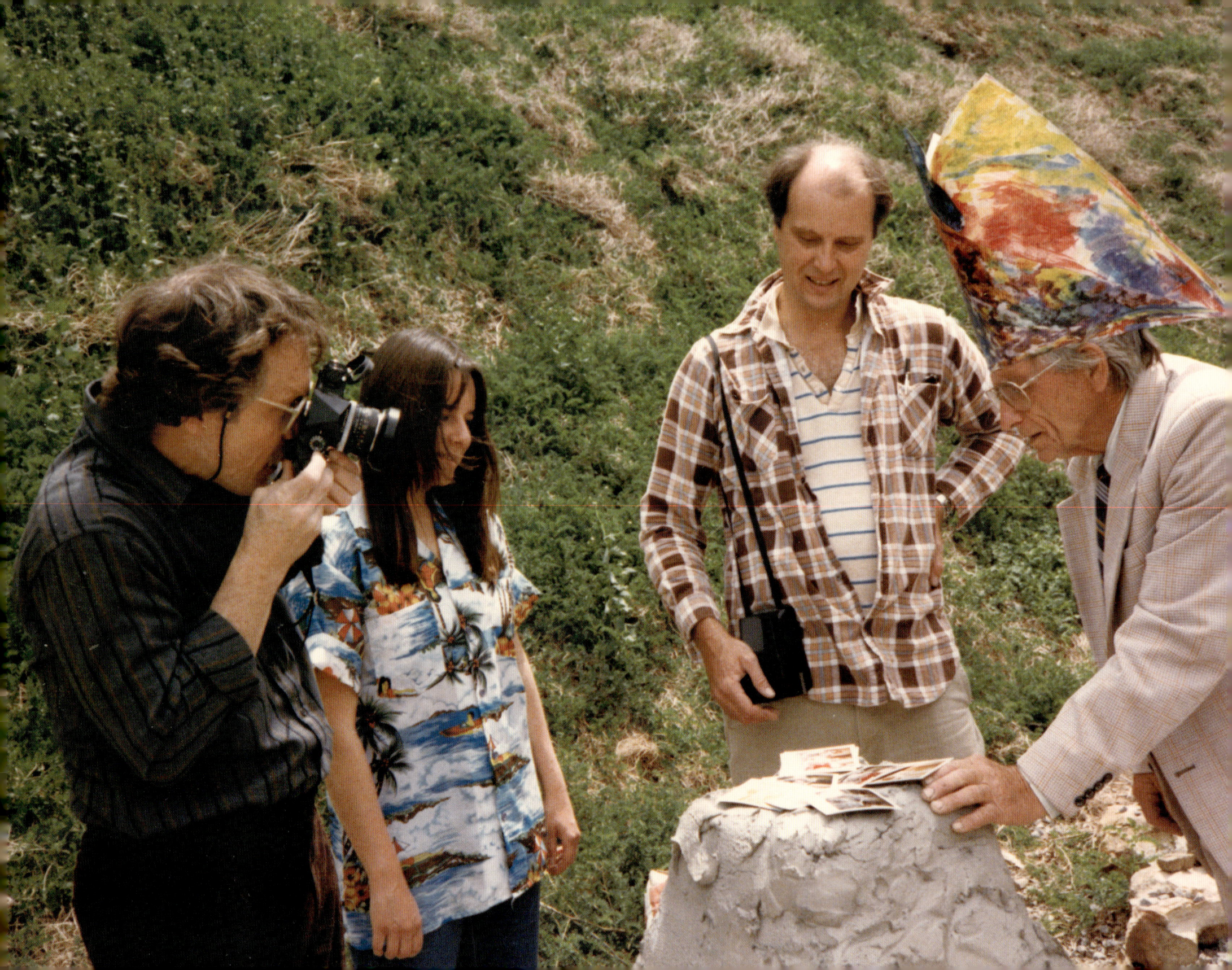

Late Modern and Postmodern society. As German philosopher Jurgen Habermas has observed, Postmodern society needs to develop a system of values that extends beyond the purely economic and entrepreneurial. "The life-world," he argues,

*has to become able to develop institutions out of itself which set limits to the internal dynamics and imperatives of an almost autonomous economic system and its administrative compliments.*[2]

Unease over various social and political issues (e.g., the environment, race, healthcare, gender identity) which today seem to intrude into our attention at every moment is evidence that attempts are being made to do just this. However, this climate of unease also betrays the very real difficulties involved in achieving these goals even today in the first decades of the new millennium.

Looking back it becomes clear that the imperatives of early-twentieth-century modern society were intimately linked to economic transformation because, in many ways, economic progress and social progress were thought to be synonymous, to be inextricably linked. American prosperity as well as the persistent Marxist experiments over the century are evidence of this and help explain why the modernist avant-garde waged such a heated battle in the cultural realm against what can be called "the authority of tradition." In the heady early days of Modernism, it was believed that the meaning and value of social goals could be determined and measured by — even equated with — economic values. In such a climate, the transformative

values of Modernism *were* economic *and* transcendent at one and the same time.

Today this equation no longer seems valid as economic interests seem to prevail over all other interests and values. As economic inequality increases, the economic system of late capitalism, which is transforming life relationships at every level, from the social to the environmental, has become an almost autonomous, self-justifying system in which higher, non–economically equatable goals seem devalued and increasingly difficult to defend; hence attacks on the humanities and liberal arts. As political economist Daniel Bell noted, already in 1978, in late capitalist society

*emphasis on accumulation [of wealth] has made that activity an end in itself ... [rather than] a means to the realization of virtue, a means of leading a civilized life.*[3]

In the decades following Bell's observations, the situation has deteriorated even more as economic inequality has grown to nearly unimaginable heights. And not surprisingly, the nature of culture itself has changed. Mid-twentieth-century discussions about low-brow, middle-brow, and high-brow culture and the values inherently reflected in such discussions seem completely antiquated today as society is increasingly being transformed and defined by commercial/pop culture and the economic interests of mass media. In short, nowhere in the equation "audience size = economic success" do transformative human values play a major role, something social media have not been able to overcome.

Seen from this perspective, it is clear that from the very beginning the topics that the Mountain Lake Symposium addressed and that are reflected in the Mountain Lake Workshops, topics about "aesthetics and morality," "art and society," and "art and conscience," were, in a subtle way, radically subversive and ahead of their time because they were never about how to flourish in art's economic realm (i.e., how to make money). And when participants were invited to the symposium programs, it became clear again and again that their willingness to participate was predicated on the seriousness and relevance of the topics under discussion as well as their respect for the ideas of the other participants.[4] As a result, a spirit of collaboration also developed in the programs as audience and speakers came together in a friendly exchange of ideas in an effort to make sense of the world.

Even addressing the narrower realm of art making itself, the symposium programs were clearly intended to engage larger cultural issues and values that went well beyond those of a late Modernist formalism and "stylistic competence"— Kuspit's idea of the "good enough artist" or the "aesthetic management" of form. But they should not be seen as an attempt to establish and promote a regional and local style in contemporary art. What the symposium and workshops attempted to frame and address is a very critical and pertinent question for art and one of increasing relevance today: What is or should be the role of art in society today?

This crucial question underlying all the Mountain Lake programs was developed as a context for art in the symposium through

[2] Jurgen Habermas, "Modernity Versus Postmodernity," *New German Critique* 22 (Winter, 1981), reprinted in Howard Risatti, *Postmodern Perspectives: Issues in Contemporary Art* (Englewood Cliffs, NJ: Prentice Hall; 1990), p. 64.

[3] Daniel Bell, "Modernism and Captialism," *Partisan Review*, vol. XLV, no. 2, 1978, p. 207. Perhaps this is why curators Neal Benezra and Olga M. Viso use the term "distemper" to allude to what they see as a "climate of unease in which a sense of anxiety and disaffection permeates the age." See *Distemper: Dissonant Themes in the Art of the 1990s*, 1996 exhibition catalogue, Hirshhorn Museum and Sculpture Garden, a Smithsonian Institution, Washington, D.C., distributed by Art Publishers, New York.

theoretical and critical discussions. It was then extended to the workshops as the philosophical rationale for their focus on "artists and locale" and "region and place." Because of this critical context, it would be mistaken to see the workshops as attacks on a New York art world that, for many people, has come to represent the economic mainstream and urban culture. Instead, the workshops should be understood as attempts to approach the question of art's role in society from a local level, from a level of experience that is as unmediated as possible — i.e., something as direct as the gathering of rocks by a river or the blessing and harvesting of trees in the woods. That the workshops demanded a high degree of competence and innovation in the manipulation of such materials showed that an art coming out of such an experience need not be intellectually or aesthetically retardataire, that such an art could be as good as the best of mainstream art.

When seen in this perspective, the workshops are, in a sense, "demonstration events" encouraging both artists and participants to seek ways to make a meaningful art out of their direct, localized experiences. Such experiences could well form the basis of a local/regional self which possesses a deeper psychological conception of place and environment, one based on real experiences untethered to the commercialism of mass culture.

This, the Mountain Lake "model" of the local/regional self, is based on a psychological turning or transformation in which the individual, in paying attention to his or her immediate environment, gains a new and deeper awareness of self and the

idea of place. And because of its psychological basis, such a self is not bound by or limited to a particular place or a specific geographic region. In this sense it can develop just as easily in New York City as in the rural landscape of Appalachia.

Because the art from the workshops is related to such a self, it is not an art that militates against the idea of a mainstream urban culture, but one that has attempted to realize itself parallel to and in harmony with a spirit of culture based on shared values that are not purely economic. Moreover, rather than uncritically accept the notion that an art, to be contemporary, must be intentionally and consciously avant-garde, the approach of the workshops is that art should stem from an informed and informing cultural activity in which shared meanings and values are created through collaborative experience of place and the art-making process. In this sense, the Mountain Lake Symposium and Workshops articulate what could be seen as a post avant-garde conception of art.

Through their emphasis on collaboration and chance, the Mountain Lake programs have attempted to open and explore a pathway to give the individual and collective imagination the potential to realize a meaningful and socially responsible relationship to the world around it through the aesthetic experience. It is in this way that the programs of the Mountain Lake Symposium and Workshop attempt to situate art within a larger realm of culture, a realm of culture that is cognizant of the social context in which art must exist in order for it to provide a meaningful experience for both makers and viewers.

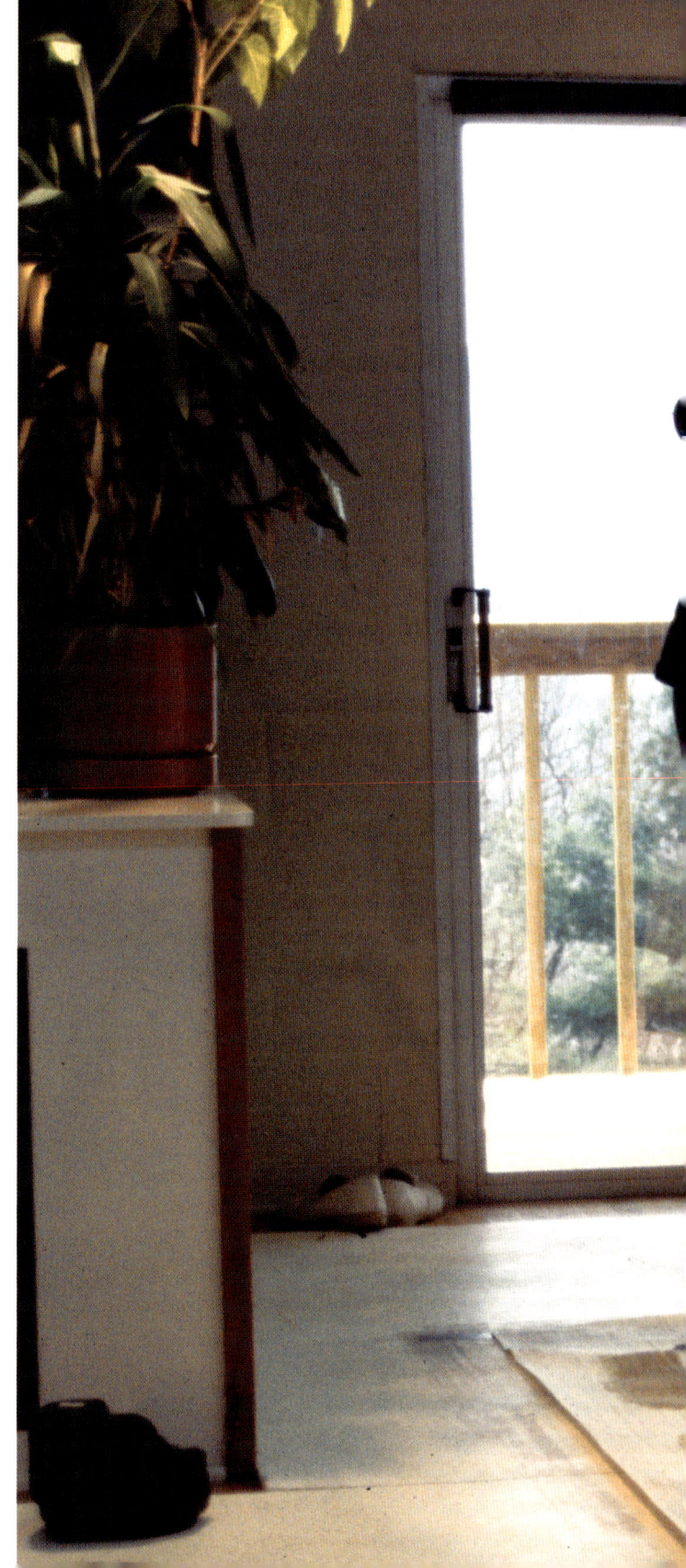

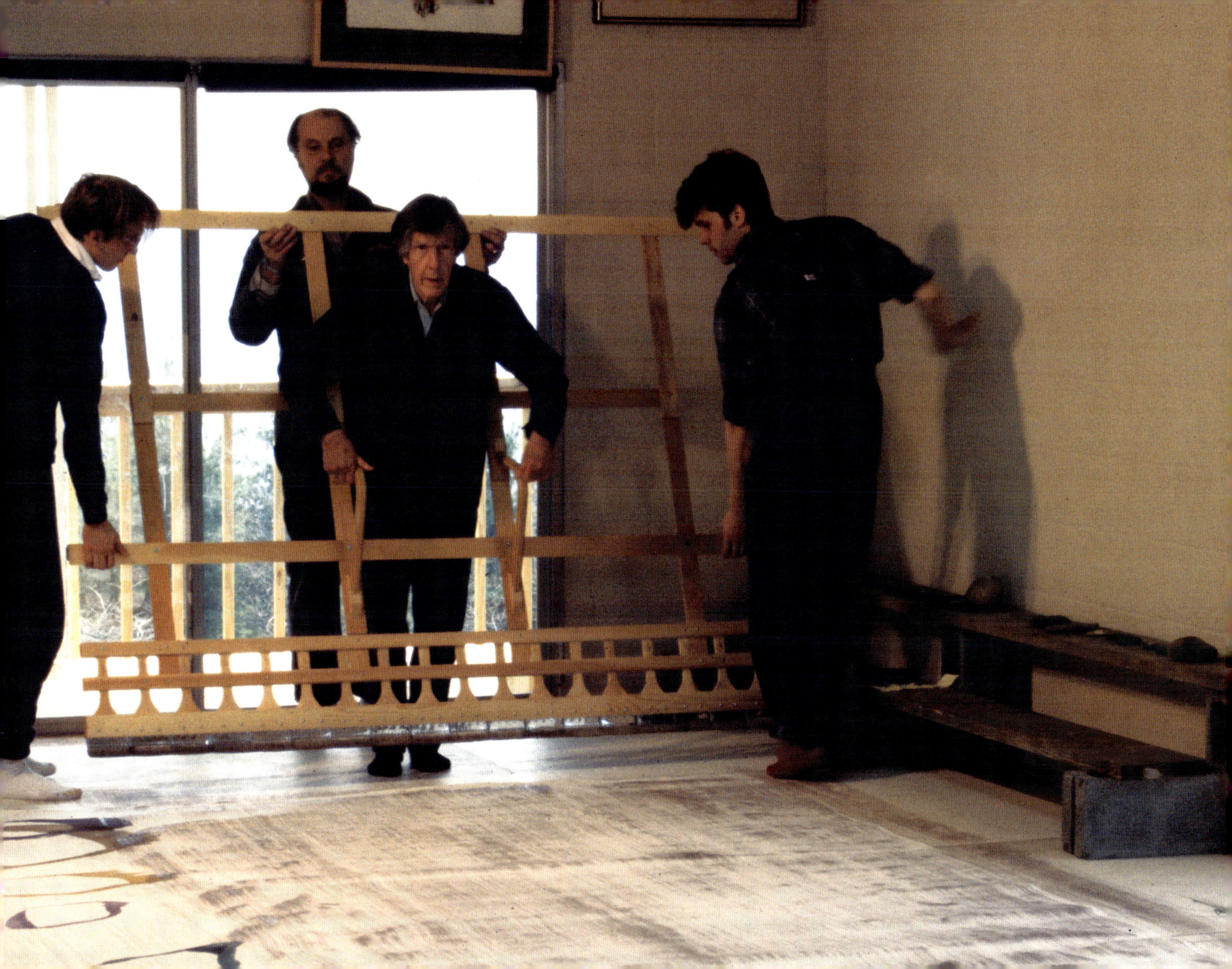

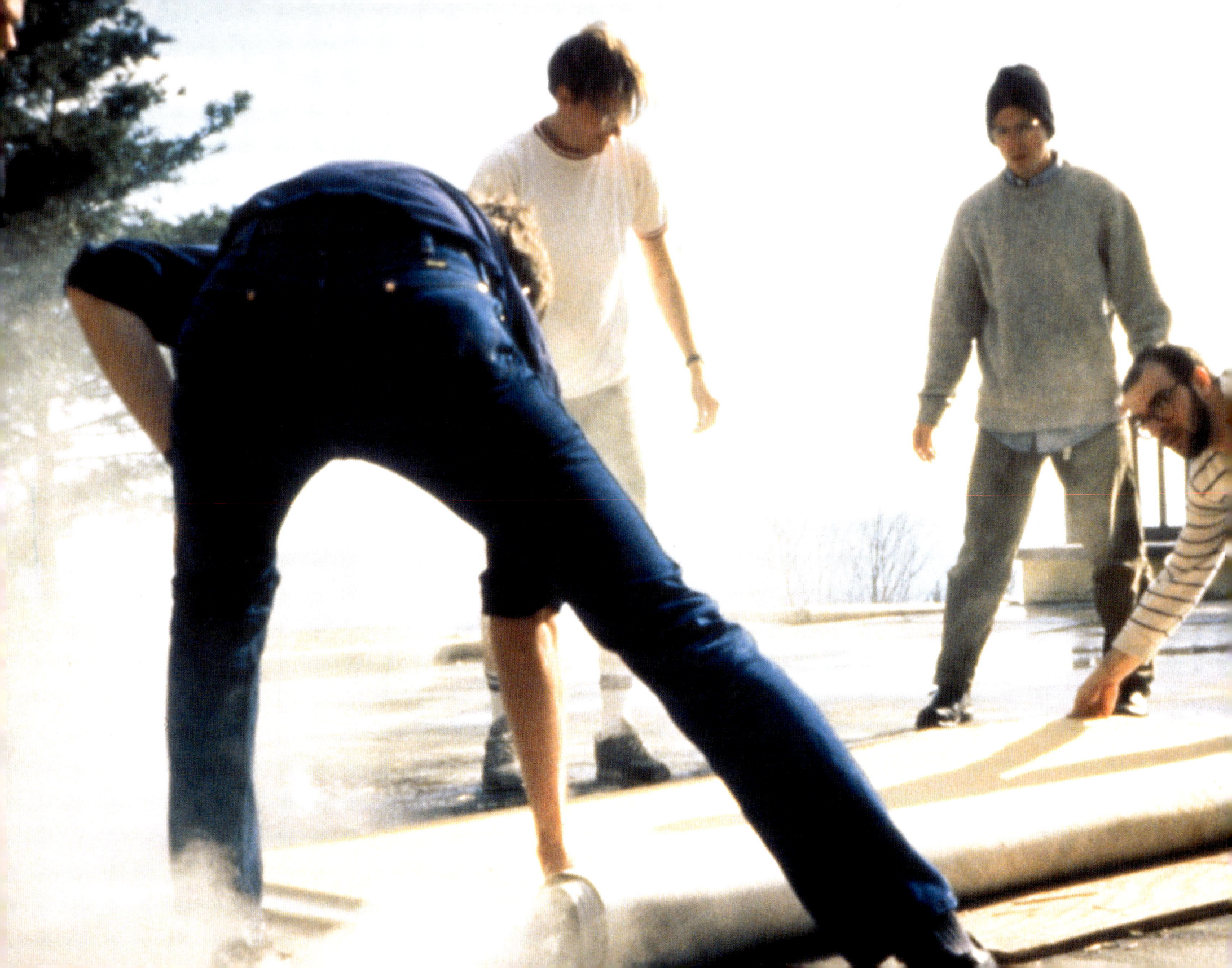

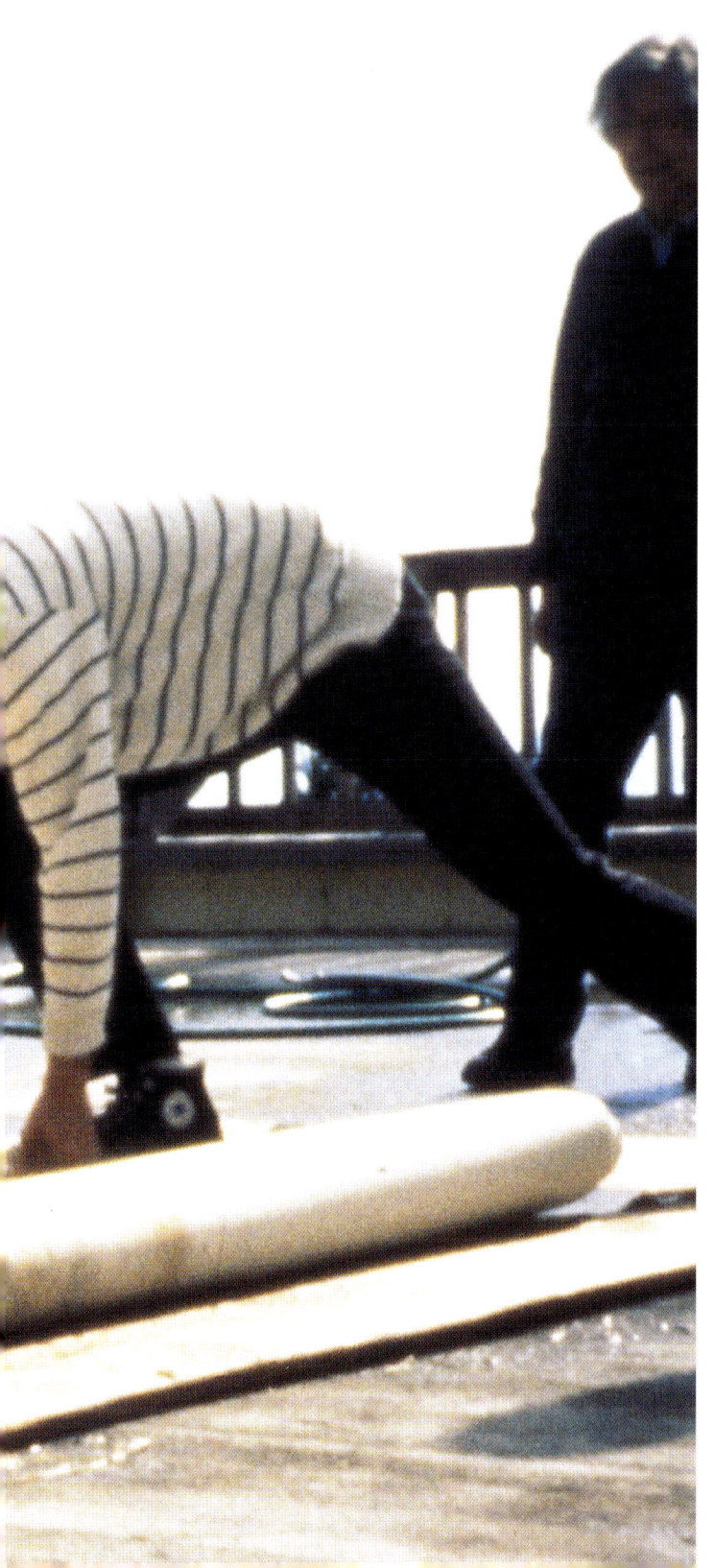

# APPENDIX A: MAKING SMOKED PAPER

RAY KASS

My experimentation with applying "smoke" imagery on paper (and other surfaces) began in 1989 and developed directly out of my collaborative experiences working with John Cage at Mountain Lake in 1983, '88, '89 and '90. Cage had employed fire marks in his work at Crown Point Press in Oakland by "branding" paper with a red-hot cast-iron teapot and by placing pieces of burning newspaper on print paper and then quickly passing everything through the printing press. The challenge at Mountain Lake Workshop was to develop new techniques more suitable to large pieces of paper and to extend the potential organic range of this imagery in correspondence with Cage's ongoing development of the New River watercolors.

We decided not to create the dark carbon marks that can be obtained by applying an acetylene torch with a low oxygen mix (as Yves Klein had done in his "fire paintings"). Instead we decided that a more natural, organic quality was desirable and experimented by burning dried weeds and grasses, hay, straw, discarded cloth — even steel wool. I discovered that clean, dry straw created the most distinct linear impressions and also imparted a rich range of warm tones to the paper.

After 1990, I discovered that it was possible to achieve more detailed smoke patterns and linear elements on the paper through repeated applications of the process. But before actually smoking the paper, I also began applying as many as seven or eight thin watercolor washes containing mica powder and pale, metallic hues to the paper, allowing distinct patterns of watermarks to dry into the paper to create another level of imagery.

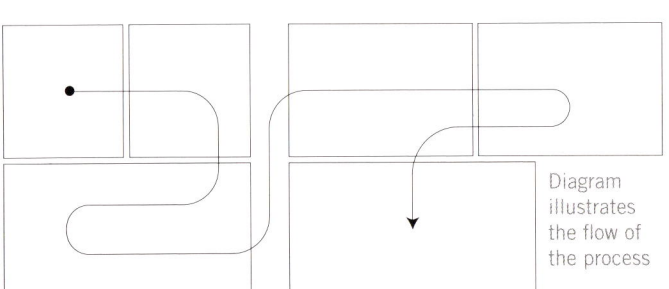

Diagram illustrates the flow of the process

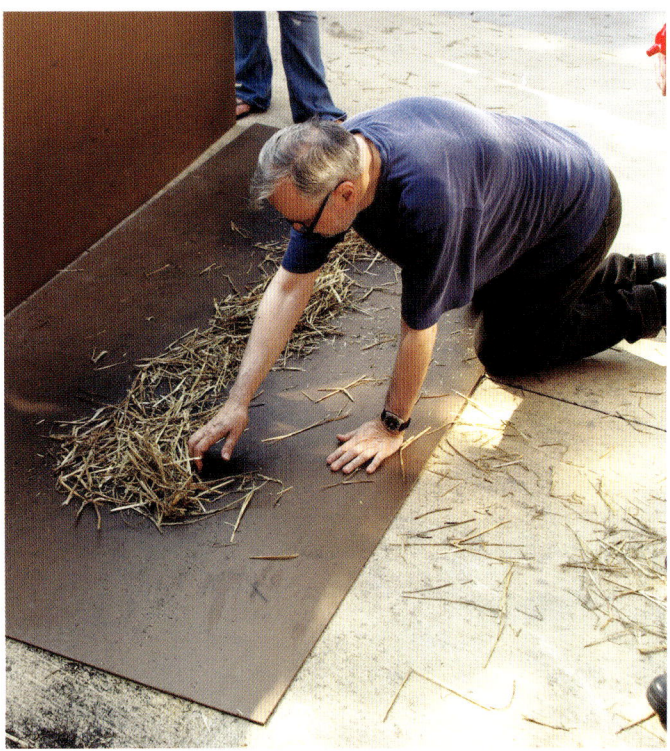

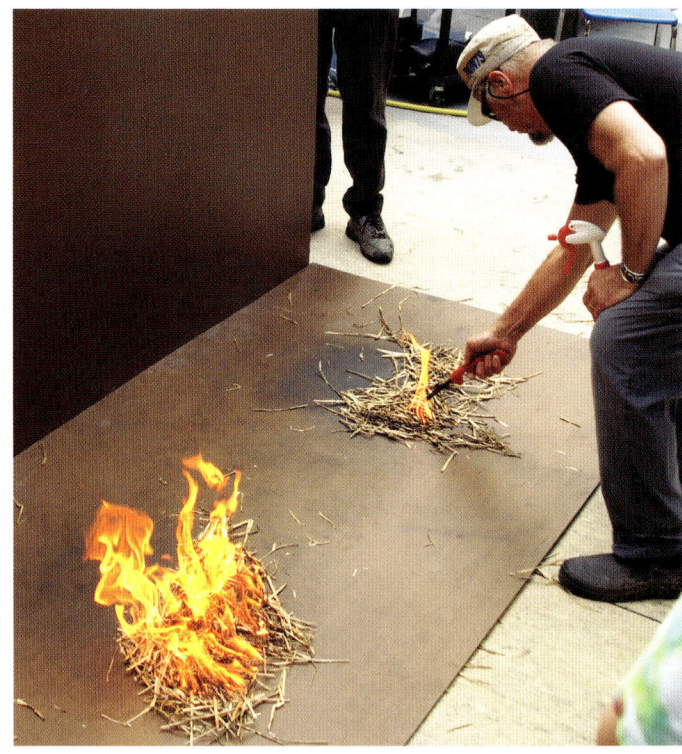

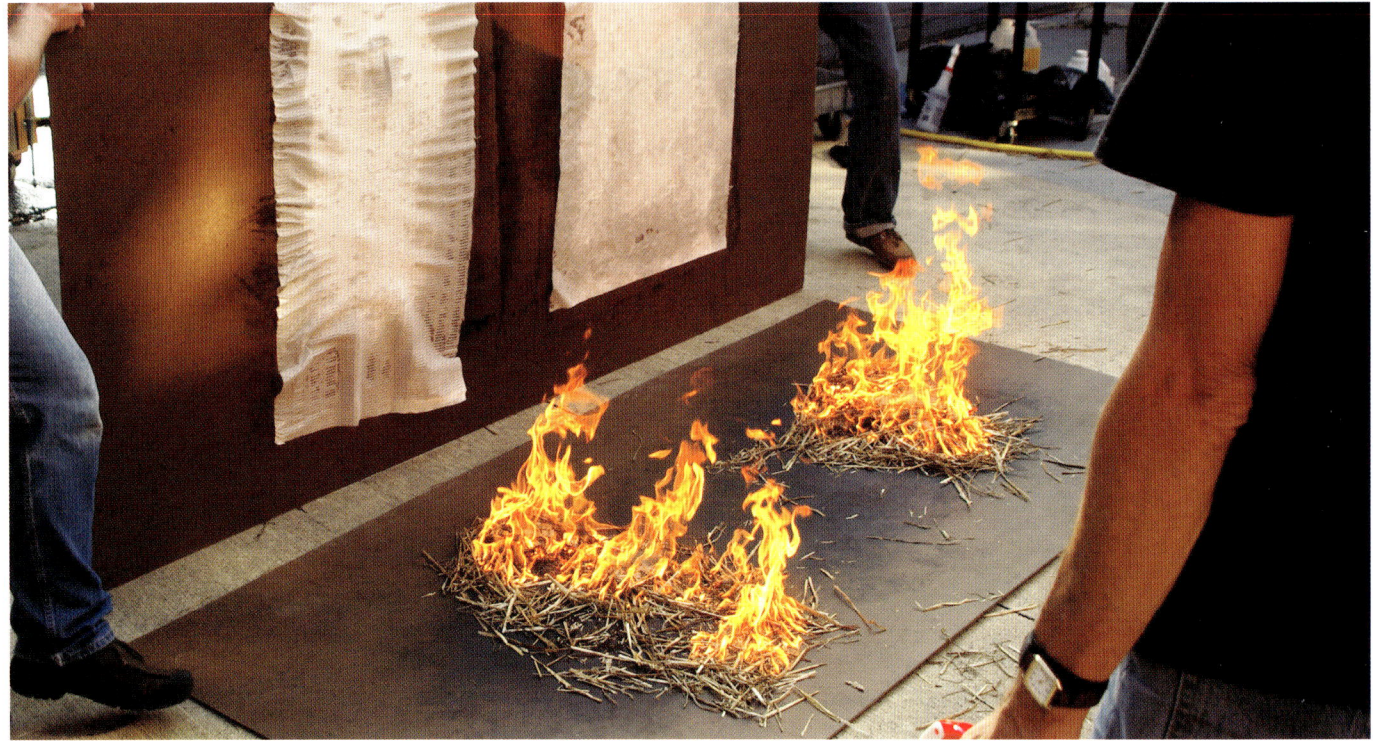

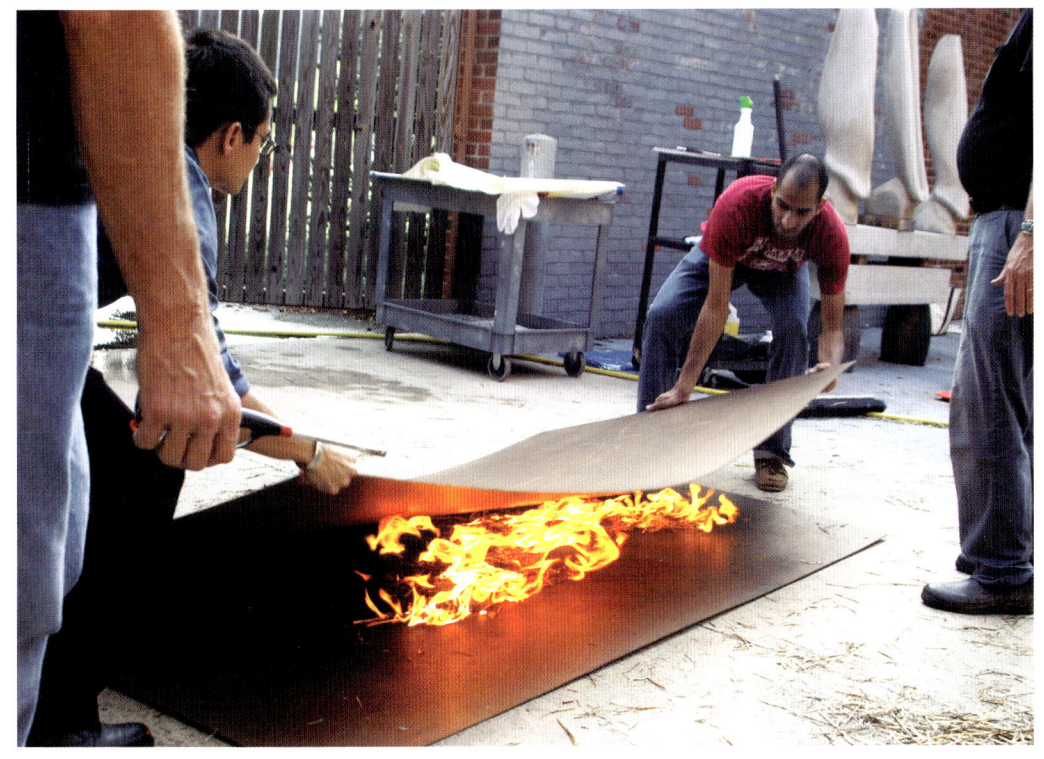

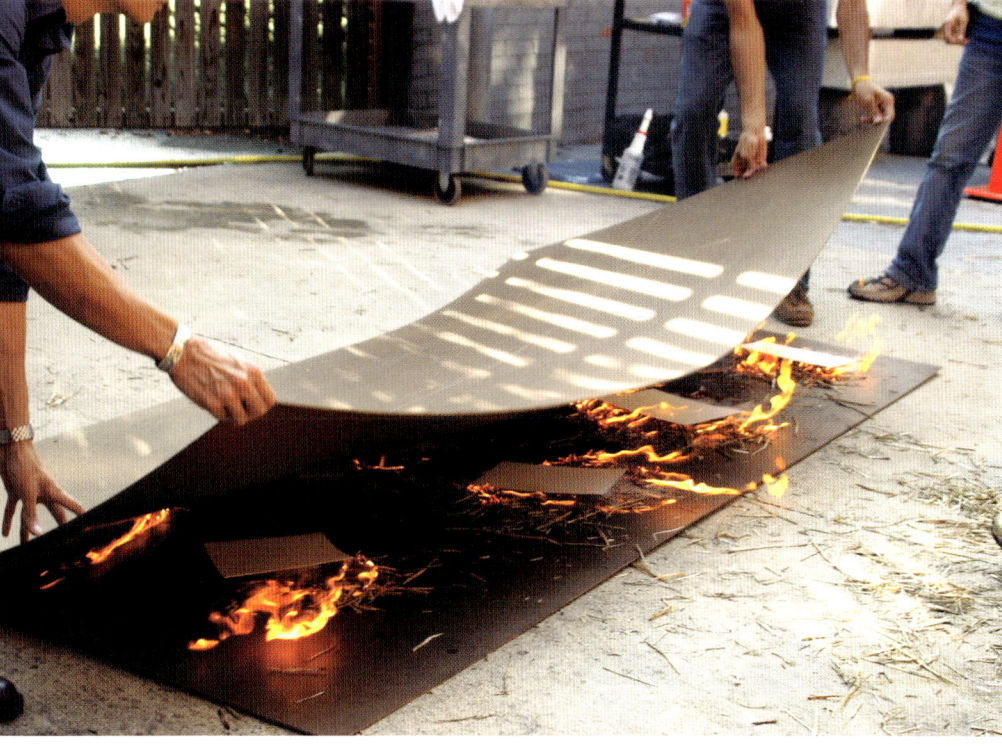

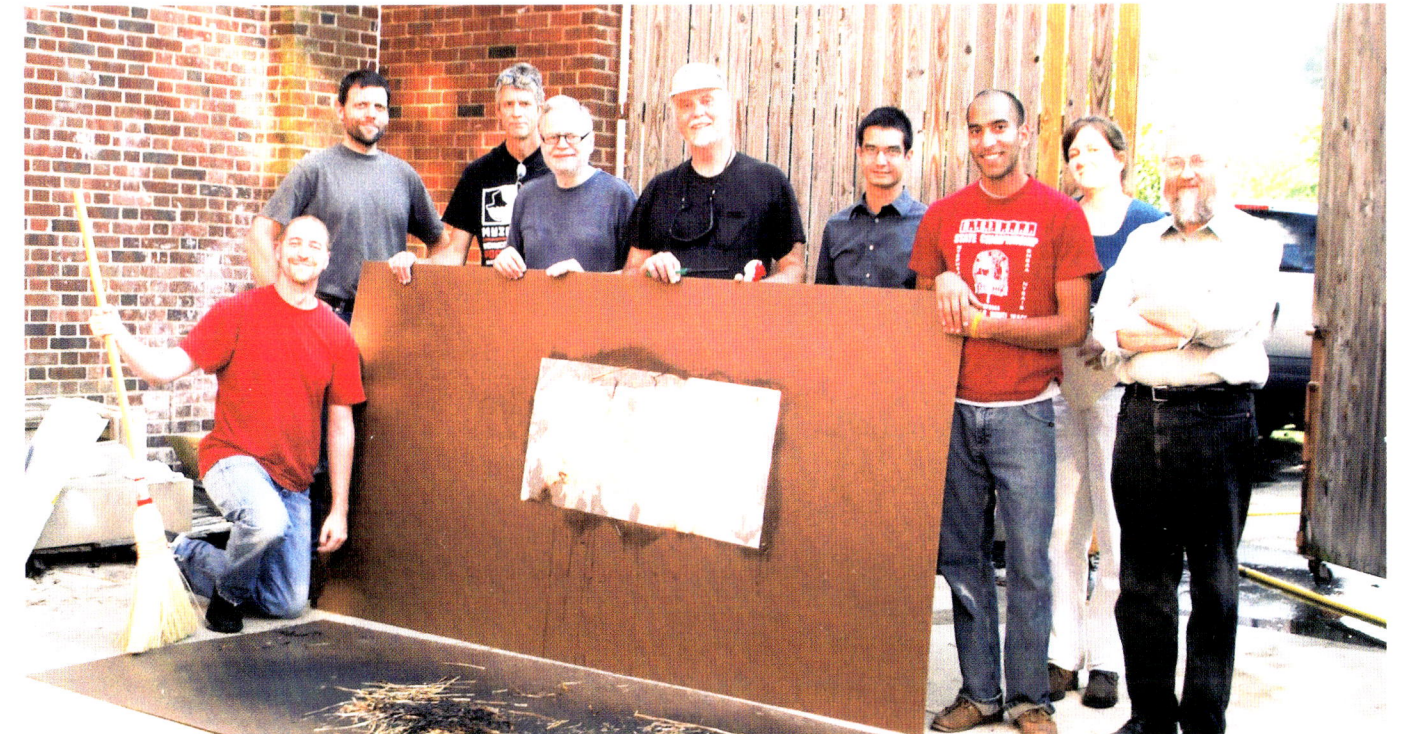

## THE PAPER SMOKING PROCESS

Dampened paper is quickly laid down over small patches of burning straw on a prepared Masonite[1] platform, and then the fire is immediately suffocated by laying another sheet of Masonite on top of the paper. The degree of wetness of the surface of the paper can determine a variety of effects in the resultant imagery. When the fire is completely extinguished, the papers are lifted from the Masonite, rinsed, and pinned to a rigid surface where they dry out and stretch and finally are wiped or polished with cotton or wool cloth.

The process requires five to six participants to run safely and efficiently.

[1] Masonite is "a type of hardboard made of steam-cooked and pressure-molded wood fibers in a process patented by William H. Mason." Wikipedia

# APPENDIX B: JOHN CAGE AND MERCE CUNNINGHAM: A HISTORY

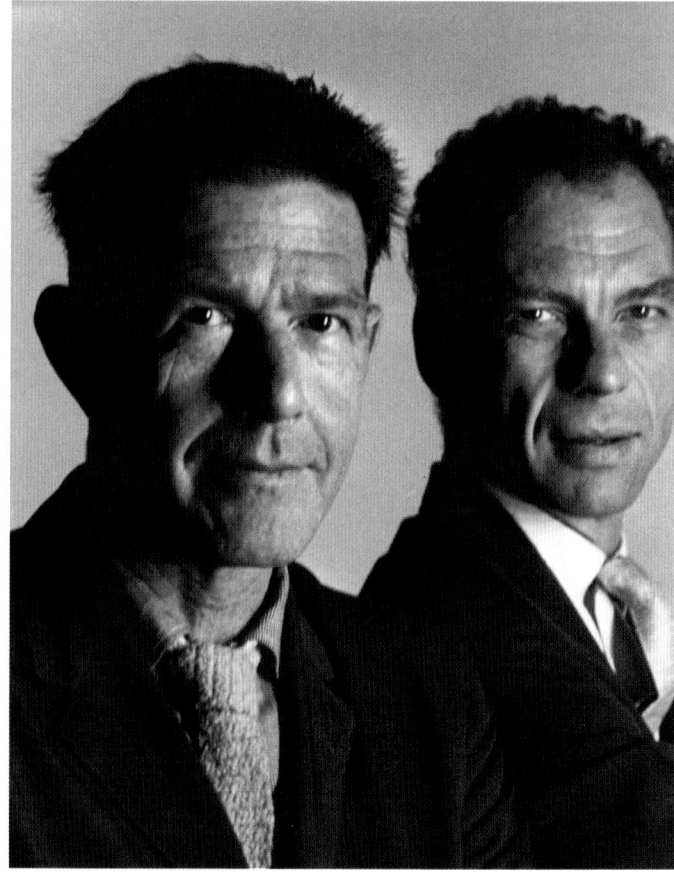

Merce Cunningham and John Cage were undeniably two of the most important figures in the arts to emerge in the American post WWII era. Cunningham, probably the most celebrated choreographer of the second half of the twentieth century, and Cage, one of the most influential composers of that period, had a profound and wide-ranging impact not only on their own respective fields of dance and music, but also on visual and Performance Art. Their shared investment in moving the American avant-garde forward, whether by the use of chance or advocating innovative forms of collaboration between artists, dancers, and musicians, dramatically changed the landscape of contemporary art. Cunningham and Cage first met in 1938 when Cage began working for Bonnie Bird at the progressive Cornish School in Seattle in a creative environment where area artists such as Mark Tobey and Morris Graves were working and exploring notions of Northwestern mysticism. Cunningham was a dance student at Cornish, Cage an accompanist and composer for Bird's dance classes. For both Cage and Cunningham these classes offered an important example of collaboration between dance and music that would become a model for their later endeavors.[1]

After pursuing independent paths for the next few years, Cunningham and Cage met again in New York City in 1942 and soon became both collaborators and partners. Cunningham, who had distinguished himself as a dancer, was urged by Cage to explore choreography, presenting in 1944 a performance of solo dance works accompanied by music by Cage that he would later consider his formative work as a choreographer. In the early '50s, they together developed and promoted a radical vision for music and dance, contending that the two art forms should be developed separately but performed simultaneously, so that they would be coexistent yet autonomous forms of expression.

Both Cage and Cunningham experimented with chance as a constitutive element in their compositions, embracing the *I Ching*, the Chinese "book of changes" that one is meant to consult after tossing a set of yarrow sticks (at first Cage used coins; then he consulted computer-programmed lists of random numbers) as a means of freeing their work from the constraints of predictability and personal preference.[2] They also shared a broad interest in Eastern philosophy, in particular Zen Buddhism, which at times manifested itself in their work in a sense of detachment or acceptance in the face of conflicting forces.

In 1953, the Merce Cunningham Dance Company gave its first performance at Black Mountain College in North Carolina where they met the young artist Robert Rauschenberg, who soon became an important collaborator, serving as artistic advisor for the dance company. Together these three artists became compelling exponents for the autonomy of theater arts. Each developed his part of their collaborations independently, often revealing the costumes, stage sets, and music to dancers only at the dress rehearsal or even on the night of the first performance. They also collaborated on other notable projects such as Rauschenberg's famous *Automobile Tire Print* of 1953, for which Cage drove his Model T across an expanse of paper.

It was through Rauschenberg that Cage and Cunningham met Jasper Johns in 1954. Cage, Cunningham, and Johns would, in turn, forge lasting bonds as well, mutually influencing each other. For instance, Cage's famous composition *4'33"*, in which the only sounds are of the natural environment and the rustling of the audience, was influenced by Rauschenberg's 1951 *White Painting* [three panel] in which the only images

in the painting were shadows cast by gallery viewers.[3] Johns would also serve as artistic advisor to the Merce Cunningham Dance Company, from 1967 to 1980. It was in honor of this important partnership that Johns created his celebrated *Dancers on a Plane* series, including the large-scale painting of this subject that he gave to Cage and Cunningham as a gift.

Although Cage passed away in 1992, he continued to have a lasting influence on Cunningham, who created innovative works up until his own death in July 2009. During the five decades they spent together, Cunningham and Cage developed a creative bond that was truly legendary, spurring each other on and inspiring successive generations of artists in diverse ways.

[1] See David Revill, *The Roaring Silence, John Cage: A Life* (New York: Arcade Publishing, 1992), pp. 56–57.

[2] Ibid., pp. 130–31.

[3] See Roni Feinstein, "The Early Works of Robert Rauschenberg: The White Paintings, The Black Paintings, and The Elemental Sculptures," *Arts Magazine* (Sept. 1986), p. 30. *White Painting* [three panel] is now in the collection of the San Francisco Museum of Modern Art (SFMOMA).

# APPENDIX C: JOHN CAGE
# AS A TEACHER

*Permit each person, as well as each sound, to be the center of creation.*

John Cage[1]

When I began to study with John Cage at the New School in New York City in the autumn of 1957, I had recently graduated with a degree in music composition from Harvard, and Cage was a shock. I realized very quickly that I either had to quit the class or open myself up to a much broader idea of music. Not that Cage insisted on his own views; in fact, he was an ideal teacher in that he never pushed himself forward nor held himself back. For example, he would talk about his own music only if someone asked; when someone did, he was very generous about sharing his ideas. I can best describe Cage as clear or transparent, and at the same time creative, funny, fascinating, and always ready to encourage his students' musical ideas and experiments.

Cage began teaching at the New School in 1956 and continued until 1960. He later explained that he felt a responsibility to make his musical ideas available since they were changing and certainly different from what students might find elsewhere.[2] As he stated in an oral interview,

*My plan was to in the first [class] explain to the students what I was doing. Then the next class was to find out what they were doing — and the class was conceived as people meeting one another. From those two classes on, there was no further teaching: it was doing work. Whoever had done any work would simply show it. Then we would all comment on it. I warned them that the only thing I would do in the way of teaching was if they were being too conservative, that I would suggest that they be more experimental.[3]*

Cage's catalogue description of the class was straightforward:

*Experimental Music, A course in musical composition with technical, musicological and philosophical aspects, open to those with or without previous training. Whereas conventional theories of harmony, counterpoint, and musical form are based on the pitch or frequency component of sound, this course offers problems and solutions in the field of composition based on other components of sound: duration, timbre, amplitude and morphology; the course also encourages inventiveness. [It will include] a full exposition of the contemporary musical scene in light of the work of Anton Webern, and present developments in music for magnetic tape (musique concrete, elektronische musik).[4]*

The one part of the description that was not often fulfilled was the last. Cage would discuss contemporary music when asked, but there was no systematic attempt to cover the entire field. As I recall, Cage began the first session with some remarks about his own work in music; he looked forward, he said, to our own experimentations. After that, most of the classes were taken up with works that students brought in; the only stipulation from Cage was that we must be able to perform them in class. As he later recalled, "I didn't want them making things that couldn't be done. Practicality has always seemed to me to be of the essence."[5] To perform our pieces, we could use the piano in the classroom plus an odd collection of mostly percussive instruments kept in a closet. In addition, we might bring in any form of sound-makers or we might simply use our voices. In some later classes, we tried out electronic music that we had created on tape. When there was not enough new music from students, Cage might describe what he was doing in his own compositions and/or have free discussions of new ways to create and organize sounds.

The classes usually had from six to ten members, many of whom (like myself) came term after term.[6] Several of these students were among the founders and lively spirits of the Fluxus movement which helped transform the art world in the 1960s with an emphasis upon multi-disciplined activities ("Happenings") and performance arts. Although there was no official connection, Cage's class also had a friendly relationship with the avant-garde Living Theatre of Judith Malina. Jackson Mac Low's *The Marrying Maiden: A Play of Changes* of 1958 (with music by Cage) had a long run there in 1960–61, and portions of my own one-act opera were performed at one point, along with other music by composers in Cage's class.

Looking back, I remember several things about the New School era, which was one of the few times that Cage taught in a regular class structure (although in my mind everything he did was a form of teaching). I was made an assistant to the classes, taking attendance and becoming a go-between between Cage and the administration. I recall one time in the late spring being told by the registrar to ask Cage if he would teach that summer, and if

[1] John Cage, *For the Birds* (Boston and London: Marion Boyars, 1981), p. 100.

[2] From an early 1960s interview with Clara Meyer, former dean at the New School, in Richard Kostelanetz, *John Cage: An Anthology* (New York City: Da Capo Press, 1991), p. 119.

[3] Smithsonian Archives of American Art, "Oral Interview with John Cage," interviewer: Paul Cummings, May 2, 1974, p. 19.

[4] New School for Social Research course catalogue, 1956.

[5] Quoted in Richard Kostelanetz, *Conversing with Cage* (New York City: Limelight Editions, 1988), p. 20.

[6] Toshi Ichiyanagi (born 1933) – married to Yoko Ono at the time; became a successful experimental composer, sometimes using traditional Japanese instruments in his compositions. Jackson Mac Low (1922–2004) – who eventually published twenty-seven books of his poetry and also created and exhibited works of visual art. Dick Higgins (1938–1998) – who later coined the word "intermedia" to describe his activities, which included writing, composing, visual arts, and publishing. Allen Kaprow (1927–2006) – a painter who helped to develop "Happenings" and was a leader in visually based performance art. George Brecht (1926–2008) – who began with an interest in film, and combined minimalist compositions

there were any classes he might like to add to his "Experimental Composition." The questions posed, Cage thought for a moment, and said he would like to teach mushrooms. I was worried that the registrar might scoff, but she said, "Fine," and it turned out that Cage, a noted mycologist, drew more students for that course than he did for music. His mushroom class, which consisted largely in hunting for mushrooms in the wilds of New Jersey, was a great success. (Cage was enough of a mushroom expert to win an Italian quiz show on this subject in early 1959.) [7]

Cage was very concerned with compositional structures in music, exploring possibilities other than the sonata form and other "Germanic" structures based upon thematic or harmonic development. For this reason he became interested in Erik Satie and in the fall of 1957 gave an entire class on his music, probably the first (and perhaps the only) time that this has ever been done. Why couldn't structure be based on time units, he wondered, or other possibilities? This interest in structure was to carry over to his visual art, which was almost entirely done at later points in his career, although I remember the visual fascination of his musical scores, which were much admired by his artist friends.

One significant event that took place during the New School years was the retrospective concert of Cage's music at Town Hall on May 15, 1958. Supported by his painter friends, this was the equivalent to the kind of retrospective more often given to visual artists. Typically for Cage, he was more interested in what he was now composing and his plans for the future than in pieces from his past, but the concert provided the audience a sonic window into the constant change and innovation in Cage's music from *Six Short Inventions* of 1933

to his latest piece, a premiere of his *Concert for Piano and Orchestra* of 1957–58. At that time an exhibition was also held of Cage's scores in the Stable Gallery (he was shown upstairs while a Rauschenberg exhibition was downstairs), and it attracted the first sustained attention to Cage's visual art.

When Cage was traveling or had other responsibilities, he turned his class over to the composers Morton Feldman and Earle Brown and (for one complete term) the electronic music composer Richard Maxfield. I found it fascinating that Maxfield worked for Westminster Records cutting the coughs out of live performance tapes so that the concerts could be issued on LP records. He then ran the coughs, which were now tiny snippets of tape, through filters to extract notes from the "white noise" of the coughs, which contained every pitch in uneven amplitudes. At this time tape music was in its very early days, and we were given an assignment to create our own music out of different lengths of tape. Since Cage was interested in space equaling time, tape music was a natural avenue for him, and us, to explore.

There was also a philosophical element of the New School classes since some of us wanted to discuss creativity and the purposes of music and the other arts. When asked, Cage talked about how he had learned from a dancer from India the traditional idea that the purpose of music is to quiet and sober the mind and make it receptive to divine influences. Cage also discussed the nine emotions expressed in the arts of India, four positive and four negative, with serenity at the center, to which the arts always returned. In his own music, Cage seemed to alternate between the most complicated pieces, such as *Williams Mix*, and the simplest, such as his *Suite for Toy*

*Piano* (1948). Perhaps these reflect his celebration of diverse life experiences as well as his interest in serenity at the center.

Cage also liked to note that the statement "art imitates nature" needed to be completed with "in her manner of operation." In other words, art does not copy nature, but following her manner of operation maintains an endless supply of egoless creation. Cage sometimes discussed his studies in Zen Buddhism with D. T. Suzuki at Columbia University, and I believe that they were extremely significant in his life. For example, Cage mentioned that sometimes he had no idea what Suzuki was talking about, but later, perhaps when walking in the woods, he would suddenly understand. This is much like a Zen student being given a *kôan* (meditation question) and reaching a deep understanding only when the intellectual process was transcended. Suzuki's teachings about moving beyond personal ego were particularly significant to Cage, it seems to me, and related directly to his music.

Most celebrated among Cage's compositions is *4'33"*, a work in which the pianist sits in front of a piano for four minutes and thirty-three seconds but does not actually play it. In my view, this is the ultimate music of non-ego — Cage wrote that it expresses "the acceptance of whatever happens in that emptiness."[8] It is also a teaching, because at a concert people are prepared to listen, and maybe, just maybe, if the performer does not play, they will learn to listen to all the other sounds that are always present. In other words, while this piece does not resemble music associated with Zen in Japan (such as the bamboo flute *shakuhachi*), it is nonetheless a Zen teaching of awareness.

in art and music with a career as a professional chemist. Al Hansen (1927–1995) – who developed performance pieces, Happenings, and collages, eventually founding an avant-garde art school in Cologne, Germany. Scott Hyde (born 1926) – a photographer who became one of the leaders in the use of his medium beyond commercial and exhibition formats.

[7] Cage appeared on the Italian quiz show *Lascia o Raddoppio* (Double or Nothing) in Milan in 1959 and won 5 million lire, about $8,000.00. Photos of Cage appeared in several issues of *La Stampa* newspaper in Turino in February 1959.

[8] Quoted in Richard Kostelanetz, *Conversing with Cage*, p. 188.

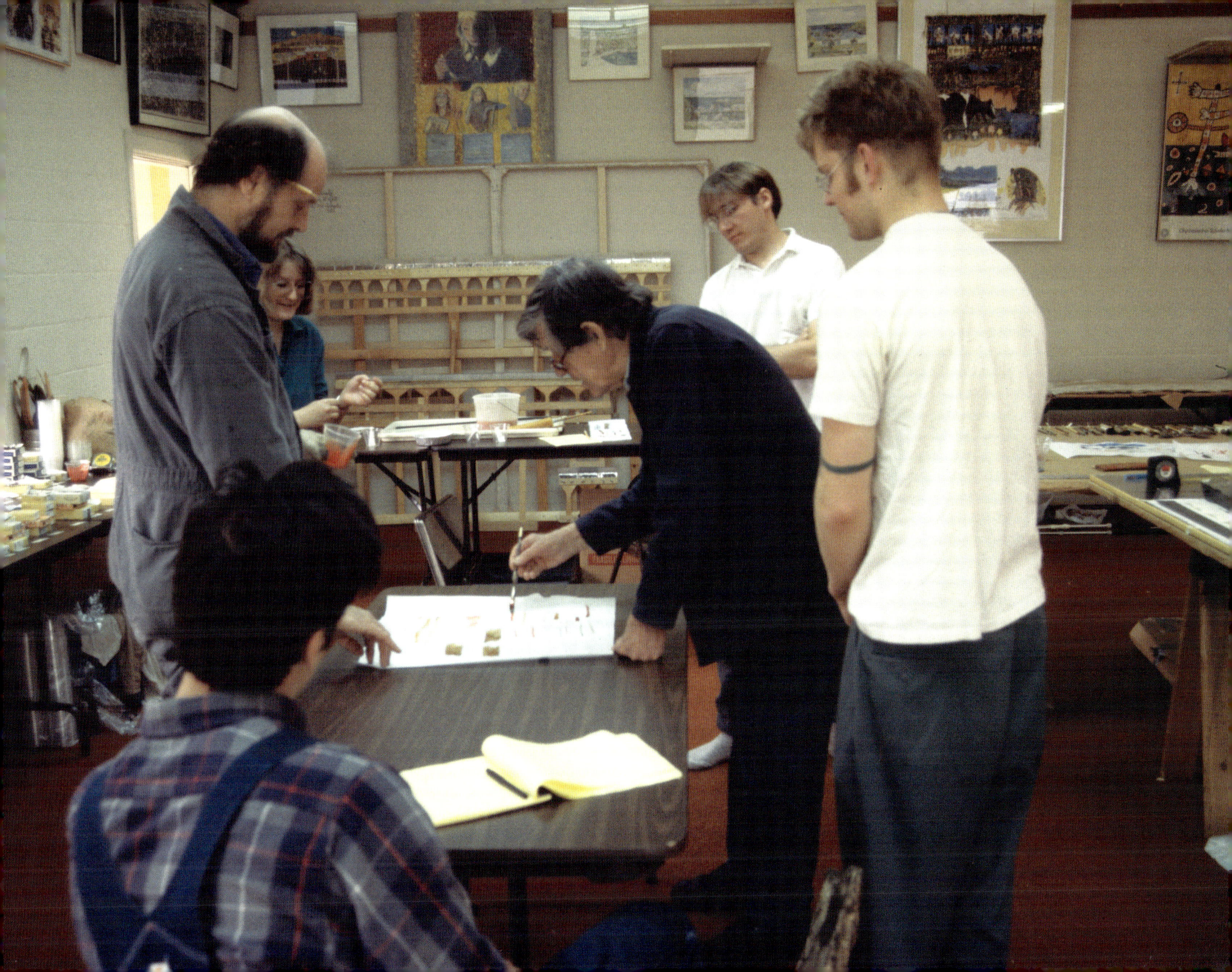

Following his attitude of not copying externals but seeking nature's "manner of operation," Cage did not meditate in the conventional sense, but tried to go beyond his own ego in composition through using chance methods. Most musicians were horrified. Critics complained that Cage was abandoning his responsibility towards what they considered to be the most important aspect of musical composition, personal choice. Yet in practice Cage had to make many choices in setting up the parameters in which chance could operate in each piece. It was the specifics — notes, durations, timbres, volume, and often the instruments — that were left to chance. Cage at this time used the ancient Chinese *I Ching* to generate random potentials. There was nothing sacred about this; Cage was delighted to switch to a computer-generated system of random numbers when it became available to him at a later moment. In either case, what most delighted him was that he did not know what a piece would sound like until the music was performed, and for many of his pieces, each subsequent time the result would be different.

The question of personality and ego came forth again in a discussion after a concert of new music that we had attended. Cage noted that after one piece, people murmured, "What a fine performer," while after another they said, "What marvelous music!" When he admired performers such as David Tudor, who played much of his piano music, it was because David used his amazing skill with total devotion to the music.

One story from the New School days that Cage discussed several times in later years involved teaching turning into learning, a process that Cage found vital.

*I was teaching a class at the New School for Social Research in New York and among the pupils was a Japanese composer Toshi Ichiyanagi and my thought of my responsibility as a teacher at that time was that I should spur this student on to greater heights of experimentation. We were approaching the Christmas vacation. I felt that would be a good time to sum up so to speak the work of the student during the previous months and give him something that would make his work go farther and in my terms as I was talking to Toshi telling him what to do he very quietly and looking straight ahead without looking at me and it was as though he were speaking to himself he simply said "I am not you."*[9]

Cage was, of course, delighted by this incident and believed that "Everyone deserves to have his own music, the music he freely chooses — whether or not he is a composer! And each person must be able to live in a way that suits him. ... [A]ll we can do is to leave space around each person. To be as careful as possible not to form any ideas about what each person should or should not do ... to strive to appreciate, as much as possible, everything he does do, even down to the slightest activities."[10]

This was the spirit that Cage infused into the class, and that led to so many of us coming back term after term. Although the course was entitled "Experimental Composition," for most of Cage's students it was not the musical elements that were most important, but the aura of free experimentation that he fostered. As Dick Higgins wrote, "the main thing was the realization of possibilities which made it easier to use smaller scales and a greater gamut of possibilities than our previous experience would have led us to expect."[11]

Certainly this was true in my own case; I had different ideas about musical composition than anyone else in the class. In addition, in the late 1950s my interest in utilizing traditional tonality in new ways was counter to the prevailing modern music aesthetic, but Cage's teaching and example gave me the confidence to follow my own path.

After his time at the New School, Cage very occasionally taught at universities but much more often gave individual lectures and talks. In the late 1960s he taught a course at the University of Illinois, and as he described it,

*The first thing I announced was that everyone in the class would get an A because I am opposed to the grading in schools. Well, when this got around the size of the class increased to 120 people who all wanted to have A's. Gradually, it settled down to about 80 people. ... My first talk to them explained my point of view. And that included the fact that we didn't know what we were studying. That this was a class in we didn't know what. And in order to make that clear we would subject the entire University Library to chance operations, to the* I Ching, *and each person in the class would read, say, five books or part of five books, if books were too long, and the* I Ching *would tell them which part to read ... and that way we would all have, I thought and they agreed, something to talk about, something to give one another. Whereas if we did as other classes do and all read the same book and knew what we were doing, then we could only be in a position of competing.*[12]

[9] John Cage, *I–VI* (Cambridge, MA: Harvard University Press, 1990), pp. 59–61.

[10] Cage, *For the Birds*, pp. 99–100.

[11] Quoted in *Cage: An Anthology*, p. 124.

[12] *Conversing with Cage*, p. 251

[13] John Cage, *M: Writings '67–'72* (Middletown, CT: Wesleyan University Press, 1973), p. 198.

[14] *Conversing with Cage*, p. 247.

[15] Ibid., p. 243.

[16] Ibid., p. 240.

[17] Ibid., p. 246.

[18] Ibid., p. 248.

Cage later wrote this event into one of his prose-poems,

*Subjected*
*university library to chance*
*operations. Eighty students read four*
*hundred books. Class became people.*
*Conversation.*[13]

At another point in his career Cage taught at Wesleyan University; in his musical composition class he introduced the students to the work of Marcel Duchamp. Because this was visual rather than directly musical, Cage commented, "It was received in an original way by each of the students — so that when the students brought compositions resulting from that information they were all different, whereas if the teaching had been more musical they would all have done more similar things. The fact that they were different was refreshing."[14]

More generally, Cage had several disputes with the traditional university system and even more with the limitations of universities as institutions, commenting that "The university itself is modeled on the idea of a prison, so you get used to the idea of prison already while you're being educated. ... The great trouble with universities is that they limit hours, schedule classes, arranging things so that you run from one thing to the other like an idiot. The first thing you should think of doing in a university is not to schedule things, because that isn't the way people live."[15] "Our whole education has been to stop singing and inspire cheating."[16]

Cage's second criticism was that universities confuse outward structure with inner process. "There is a tendency because of the structure of universities to think that if you enter a building marked 'Music' and go all the way through you'll come out a musician. This isn't true. ... [Instead] the matter of meeting people is very important. Finally, the meeting has to be with yourself. The university doesn't encourage meeting with yourself because it's constantly offering the opportunity to do something other than meet yourself."[17]

A third point of disagreement for Cage was the university hierarchy of teacher and student. Just as he was delighted by the episode with Toshi Ichiyanagi at the New School, Cage felt that "one wants to lose the distinction of teacher and student and to simply develop the notion of a society which has young people, older people, inexperienced people, experienced people, all willing to help one another. ... The teachers can learn much from the students ... just as the students can on occasion learn something from the teachers. But mutual learning will take place better if the distinction is obscured. It can only be obscured if the students give their work to themselves as well as to the teacher."[18] In this regard, Cage said that "I don't think the arts can be taught. I think that the process of teaching should be a meeting between the teachers and the students and in that exchange it is not certain who is going to learn."[19]

*Twelve*
*disciples. One teacher. One too*
*many.*[20]

Finally, Cage paradoxically stated that he supported both no university and an all-encompassing university. He echoed Thoreau's statement that the best government will be no government at all with the comment that "The best university will be that which is no university at all. And [Buckminster] Fuller says we want a university from which we never graduate. There is no question of graduating because the whole society has turned into a university — and what university is that? It's a place where one is allowed to do research on one hand, invention, creation, etc and/or all these things to affect one another and so make society lively. And if it were a good university who would want to graduate from it?"[21]

Cage's teaching philosophy was certainly idealistic, and yet if we are tempted to dismiss it as impractical, we have to realize that he became one of the most influential thinkers of the twentieth century, one from whom many of us have learned, perhaps primarily, to break free of traditional limitations.

Some of Cage's ideas on education may have come from a Zen tradition that learning does not have to come directly from what we traditionally call teaching, and may in fact be fundamentally impossible if it does not come from inside. There is a Zen anecdote in which a monk does not gain enlightenment until he gives up studying with his teacher; later, he is unexpectedly spiritually awakened when he is sweeping in front of his hut and a stone hits a culm of bamboo with a small but resonant sound. In one interview Cage commented that:

[19] Ibid. p. 247.

[20] Cage, *M: Writings '67–'72*, p. 210.

[21] *Conversing with Cage*, p. 248.

*This story occurs over and over in the annals of Zen Buddhism —
the student who comes to the teacher and begs him for
instruction. The teacher says nothing — he's just sweeping up
leaves. The student goes off into another part of the forest and
builds his own house; and when he is finally educated, what does
he do? He doesn't thank himself; he goes back to the teacher
who said nothing and thanks him. It's this spirit of not teaching
that has been completely lost in our educational system.*[22]

What then can this teaching by not teaching be? Despite his
voluminous writings and his many published interviews, we may
still see that Cage's major teachings are by example, through
his music, art, and poetry, and even more through his life. His
spirit of compassion in daily life was exhibited in such simple
acts as always answering his own phone, writing back to those
who wrote to him, sharing what he earned and was given, and
constantly experimenting, changing, and delving deeper into
his creative process while simultaneously subordinating his ego.
His remarkable openness to others was accompanied by a great
respect for creative people before him — especially Thoreau,
Joyce, Pound, Fuller, Satie, and Duchamp — and always enlivened
by his effortless curiosity, awareness, warmth, and humor.

I have been told that he often carried with him my 1989 book
*The Art of Zen*, with its many masterpieces of ink painting
and calligraphy by Japanese Zen Masters, and yet he never
imitated them. Instead, he found similar creative sources
that led to a celebration of the actual, suggesting the words
of the Chinese Master Yun-men, "Every day is a good day."

Indeed, as a composer, artist, poet, philosopher, provocateur,
and Zen layman, he was one of the few seminal figures of the
twentieth century to celebrate life. His very name can serve in
a grade schooler's form of mesostic that well describes him:

Joy

Optimism

Humor

Naturalness


Creativity

Artistry

Generosity

Energy

[22] Ibid., p. 241.

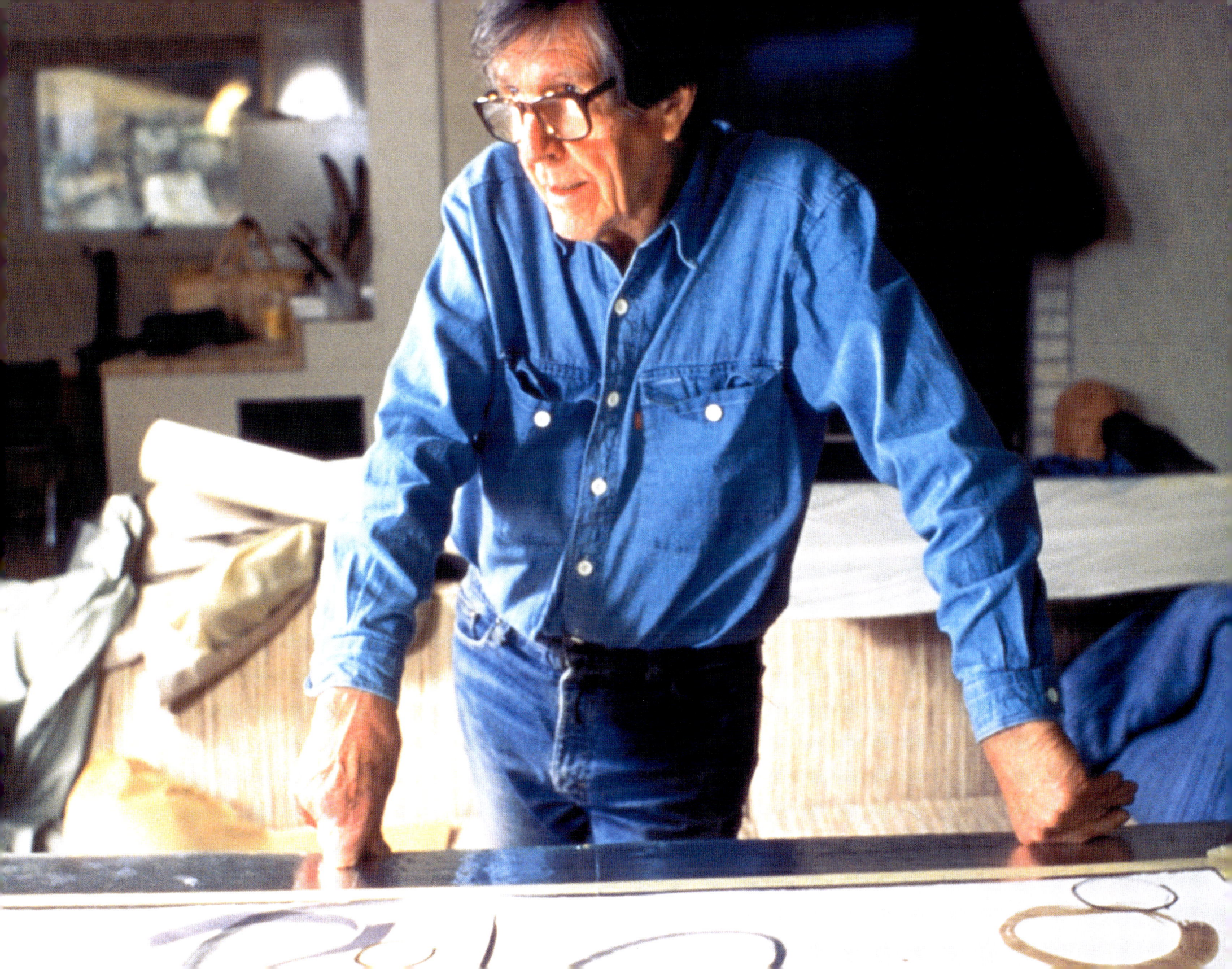

# APPENDIX D: HOWARD FINSTER'S RICHMOND "WORKOUT" — A REMINISCENCE

ANN OPPENHIMER

In 1983, on the way driving home from our first visit to Howard Finster at his Paradise Garden in Summerville, Georgia, my husband (William, known to all as "Boo") said, "We need to bring Howard to the University of Richmond for an exhibition and festival." At the time, we never imagined that this idea would change our lives forever.

The art department at the university approved the project, I applied for and received a grant from the Virginia Foundation for the Humanities, we began to make plans, and the project took on a life of its own. We had nearly a year to make it all happen.

Boo named the festival and exhibition — "Sermons in Paint" — the first use of this title, which has been appropriated without attribution many times since. We had purchased fifty pieces of Finster's art, so we had a head start on the exhibition. We arranged to borrow pieces from important Finster collectors Chuck and Jan Rosenak (who were conveniently packing to move from Maryland to New Mexico), from former Finster dealer Jeff Camp (who hired someone to deal with us as he and Finster had fallen out), from local collectors, and from the Library of Congress (which owned two significant Finster paintings).

Richmond writer Susan Hankla agreed to be co-editor of the catalogue. The staff of the Modlin Fine Arts Center at the university agreed to help with the exhibition. Even though I taught art history at the university, I had no experience in arranging for and installing an exhibition. Looking back, I can see that we made a few mistakes, but Howard was with us — so everything worked out fine in the end.

I contacted Bob Bishop, director of the Museum of American Folk Art; Alan Jabbour, director of the American Folklife Center at the Library of Congress; and Jane Livingston, associate director of the Corcoran Gallery of Art, requesting their participation in lectures during the festival. Susan Hankla arranged for her husband, Jack Glover, and his band, The East Virginia Toadsuckers, to perform with Finster (on the banjo) one night. We also scheduled Finster to give a talk at 1708 Gallery, an artists' cooperative in Richmond. Workshops (or "workouts," as Finster called them) would be held on two consecutive days at the University of Richmond. All events were free and open to all.

On October 30, 1984, Howard arrived by Greyhound bus, and Boo and I took him directly to the Modlin Center to see the exhibition, newly installed and ready for the festival to start the next day. Howard was noticeably moved to see older works that he had not seen in a long time. He looked carefully at each one, remembering it and making comments. Howard carried a small baby-food bottle in his pocket to use for spitting tobacco. He pulled it out and spat, then promptly dropped it on the gallery's marble floor, sending glass and spit in all directions. Boo turned pale and said, "Ann, you're on your own with this one," and I was happy to oblige.

Howard spent six nights in our home, and contrary to the claim of Glen C. Davies, who wrote in *Stranger in Paradise: The Works of Reverend Howard Finster* (2010), "Howard Finster takes a bath only once a month," Howard took a bath every day, filling the tub almost to the brim. "I like to take a good soak," Howard told us. Howard also played the piano every day, for his relaxation and pleasure.

To facilitate the workouts, Howard had brought his paper "dementions" (patterns) that he used to make wooden cutouts for the multiples that he then painted individually. He spread these dementions out in the art studio for university students, professors, and townspeople to use in constructing their own art works. Wonderful, imaginative, and unusual works were created by the many individuals who came to share those two days with the master artist. The University of Richmond provost eagerly participated, saying, "I'm letting the university run itself today!"

Howard freely shared the personal patterns that he had used over and over in various ways to make his own art. What other artist would have been this open and generous? He would even co-sign participants' work if requested.

After Howard's concert with the East Virginia Toadsuckers, a group of musicians gathered at our home — Jack Glover on piano, Howard on banjo, Mike Seeger on guitar, and Alan Jabbour on the fiddle. This was indeed a remarkable evening but, unfortunately, was not recorded for posterity.

Just before Howard's lecture at 1708 Gallery, he asked me to give him a signal when his time was up. "I always talk longer than anyone is able to listen," he said. We planned for him to speak for an hour and leave time for questions. When the hour was approaching, sitting on the front row I began to point to my watch. Howard continued to talk about his topic ("How to make money with your art"), and I kept

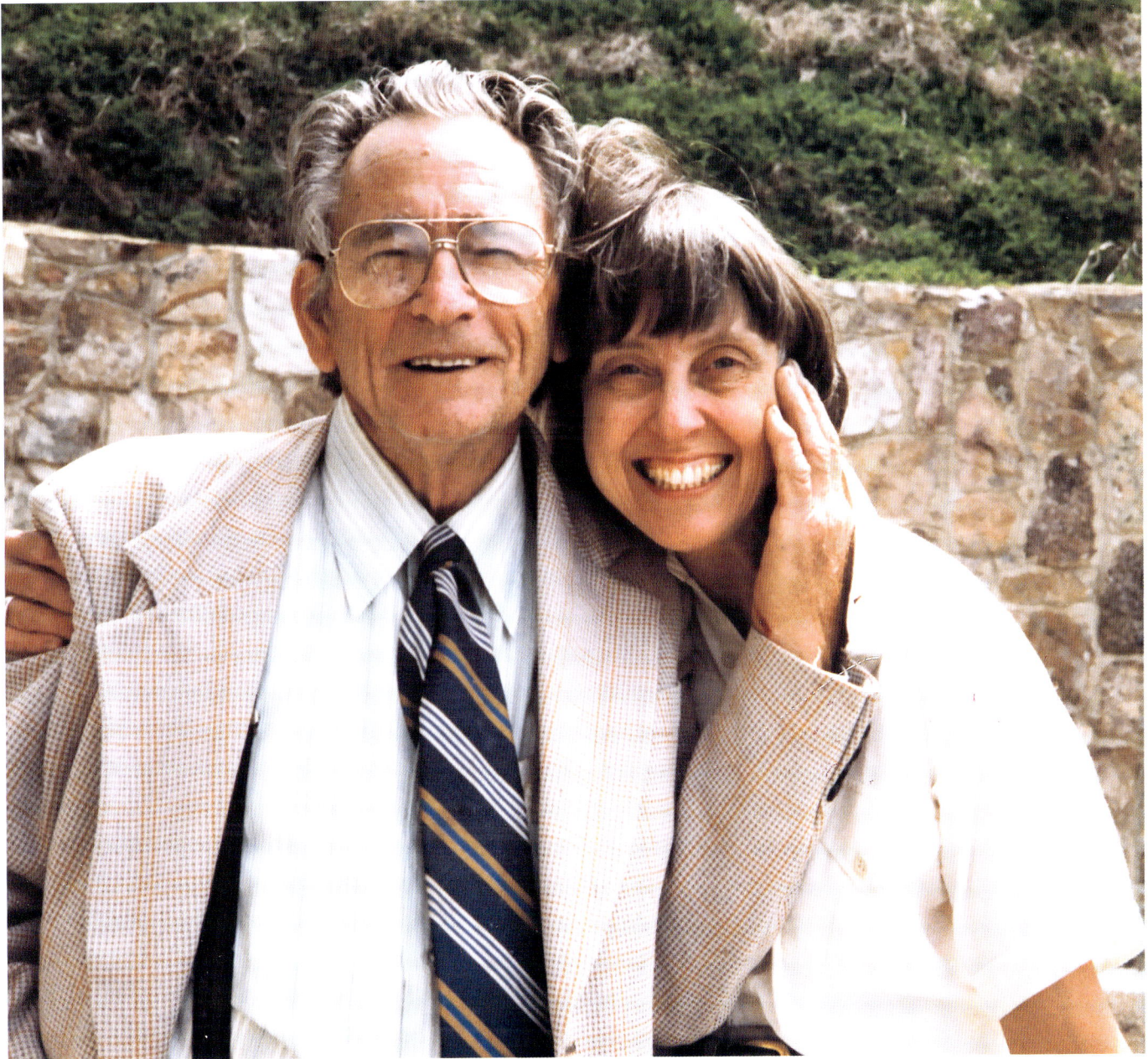

signaling. Finally, Howard stopped and said, "Miss Ann, are you telling me my fly is open?" Of course, this brought down the house, and Howard had the biggest laugh. "Everyone should laugh at least once a week," he liked to say.

In looking back through the photographs we made that week, I was struck by the smiling faces and happy demeanor of the participants. It was a magical week with Howard as the centerpiece. He had such a remarkable effect on everyone with whom he came in contact. He spread joy, love, and laughter with his ebullient and charismatic personality. One of his favorite and oft-quoted sayings, especially true at this Howard Finster Folk Art Festival, was "I never met a person I didn't love."

# APPENDIX E: BASICS OF BLOOMERY SMELTING

LEE SAUDER

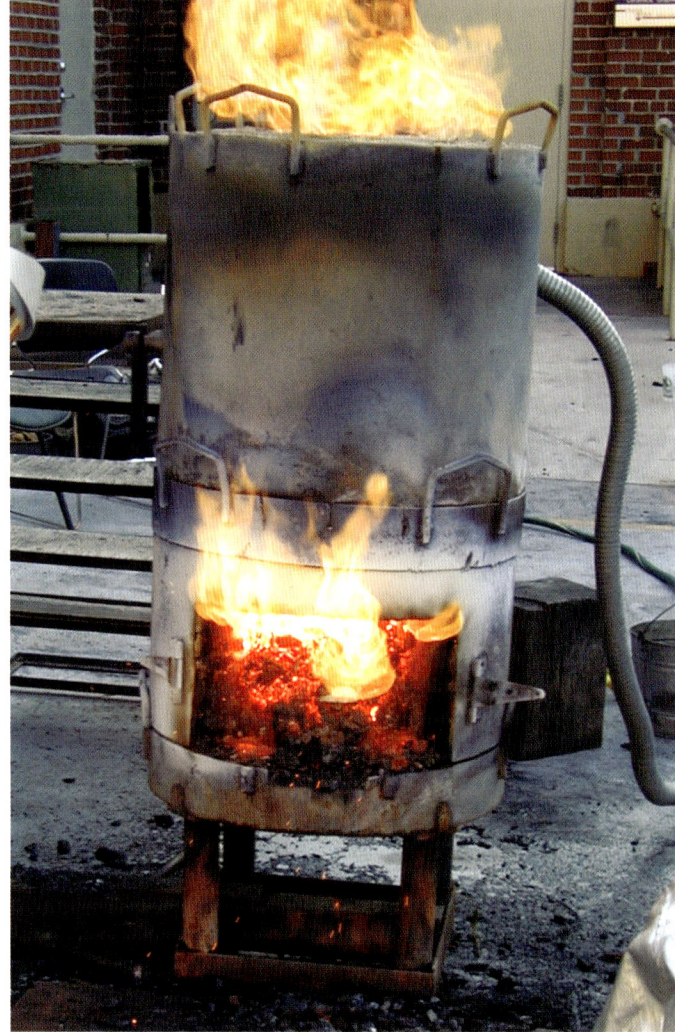

Lee Sauder's portable
iron "bloomery"

Inspired by accounts of African iron smelting and an account of the 19th-century iron industry in Rockbridge County, Virginia, the Rockbridge Bloomery began smelting iron from local ore in 1998. Modeled on the traditional African bloomery furnace, this method had been used to smelt iron on a small scale until the 15th century, when new technologies changed metallurgy and led to the demise of this essential process.

The bloomery process (also referred to as direct reduction) is the original method of producing iron. Operating on a small scale and at relatively low temperatures, it produced a sponge of malleable iron and slag that was forged directly into a wrought iron bar or billet. Furnaces varied greatly in form from shallow hearths to tall shafts. Beginning in medieval times, the bloomery was gradually supplanted by the blast furnace process, also referred to as indirect reduction.[1]

Iron and oxygen really love each other and are constantly trying to unite to form iron oxide (i.e., rust), the most common form of iron ore. At elevated temperatures, oxygen most handily unites with carbon. Putting iron oxide in a charcoal fire above 900°C with lots of carbon monoxide (CO) allows the carbon monoxide to grab oxygen from the iron oxide thereby creating carbon dioxide ($CO_2$) and leaving behind bits of pure iron. These particles of iron will fall into a bath of liquid slag in the bottom of the furnace, and float around until they stick together into a bloom.[2]

However, if there is enough carbon fuel to produce enough heat and carbon monoxide to reduce much iron from the ore, there also tends to be enough available carbon to combine with the

iron to make it unforgeable. By throwing in plenty of charcoal and running the furnace hotter, optimal reducing conditions in the stack of the furnace are achieved. Yes, the carbon particles that fall to the hearth are cast iron, but the slag bath decarburizes them (at least this is what I think happens). Besides fayalite, the slag also contains wustite (FeO). When the wustite comes in contact with the carburized iron, the carbon and oxygen combine, simultaneously decarburizing the existing metal and contributing more pure iron to the bloom. In this way we've progressed from 5-pound slaggy blooms to 20–40-pound dense blooms.

To build our furnaces, we used old hot water heaters. Besides being a convenient form, the steel skin is handy for welding on legs, *tuyeres*, handles, and such. Inside the shell is a layer of insulation and then a 3200°F castable. Leave an opening to insert the *tuyere* 8 or 10 inches above the bottom of the furnace and another at the level of the furnace floor to form a slag tapping arch. The interior diameter of our first furnace was 12 inches and that of the second 14 inches.[3] We tried several sorts of *tuyeres* and finally built a water-cooled *tuyere*, which works great.[4]

We are currently using a 150 CFM squirrel cage blower and an air gate to adjust flow. Bellows should work well if you've got lots of free labor. Probably the optimal set-up would be a variable speed/stroke piston. If you're really ambitious, some provision for preheating your blast will save some charcoal.

Before smelting, ore should be roasted in a wood fire or a gas forge.[5] Bring it to a nice red or low orange heat, and try to keep it there awhile without melting. Cool it down with

water to help the ore to shatter into smaller pieces, or just let it cool. The ore will now be more friable. Bust it up so that most of the pieces are fine to pea size. You'll see that the ore is now shot through with fissures that will be accessible to the furnace gases. It will probably also have changed color to red and hammer-scale gray, making any other bits

Excerpted from Lee Sauder, "The Basics of Bloomery Smelting" *The Anvil's Ring* (the quarterly of the Arist Blacksmith Association of North America, July 1999).

[1] The blast furnace operated on a larger scale and at higher temperatures, and produced molten cast iron which had to be further refined by eliminating carbon and reintroducing slag to create wrought iron. The blast furnace's advantages of producing large quantities and removing a higher percentage of iron from the ore outweigh the difficulty of this extra step.

[2] The slag is largely composed of iron, silicon (the major impurity in most iron ore) and oxygen combined into a substance called fayalite. About ten percent of the iron in the slag can be replaced with calcium without altering the slag's melting temperature. Limestone or oyster shells are the traditional sources of calcium. Manganese can also replace iron in fayalite.

[3] The first shaft was cast in a single piece, but removing the hot bloom through the top proved an ugly chore. The second furnace was built in sections that could be lifted off with an overhead hoist (tip o' the hat to Wally Yater for this idea) so the contents could be more easily removed, to allow further experimental changes, and to improve portability.

[4] The first *tuyere* was cast iron and melted immediately. Then we cast refractory tubes, which worked OK but had to be replaced every other smelt or so. The water-cooled, hollow *tuyere* with an interior diameter of ca. 1 inch opens directly into a water reservoir. This dimension is one of the primary determinants of air flow, especially if you use a low-pressure air source like a squirrel cage blower. Our current *tuyere* is 14" from horizontal. A removable peephole in line with the *tuyere* is entertaining, as well as vital for monitoring temperature and cleaning occasional blockages.

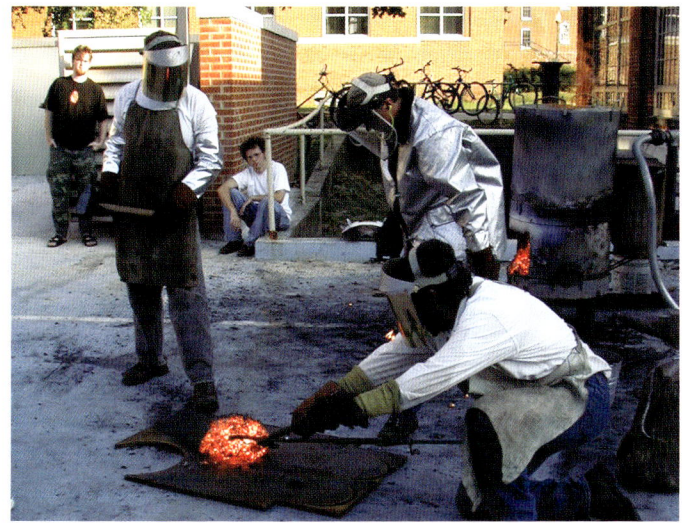
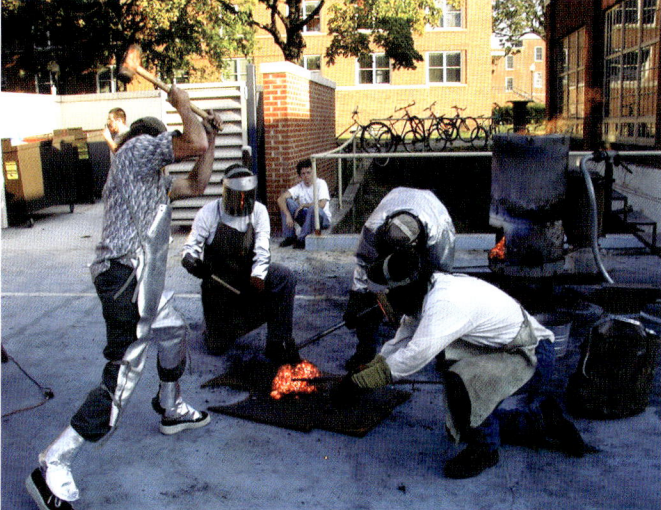
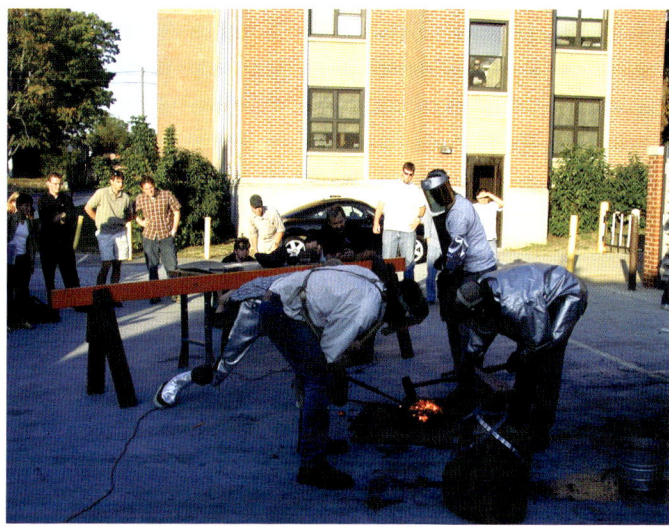

of sandstone, etc., easier to see and remove. If you got the heat just right, non-magnetic ores may convert to magnetite, allowing you to pick out the good stuff with a strong magnet.

Charcoal is the biggest part of the whole job if you're making it yourself. In my furnace, I'm burning 10–12 feed sacks of charcoal for every smelt. There are many ways of making charcoal but don't bother with anything except the retort method. Your charcoal will be better, and the retort burns some of the noxious fumes.[6] A flux is optional.

First, get the furnace hot.[7] To save charcoal, I stick the gas burner from my pipe forge into the slag tapping arch for about an hour before starting the charcoal. You can also start the preheat with wood. Then, leaving the tap arch open for draft, add the charcoal slowly until the fire burns up to tuyere level. Start the blast and add charcoal gradually until the furnace is full and keep it near full during the entire preheat. Our preheat time has been 4–5 hours in our furnace and uses the majority of the day's charcoal. When the smoke stops and the gases at the top of the furnace start to burn, you're ready for the first ore charge.

Fuel-to-ore ratio is one of the important variables, affecting temperature, efficiency of reduction, rate of burn, and

carburization. A ratio of 1:1 (by weight) is a good place to start. As the furnace burns down enough to allow a charge, add in the charcoal, followed by the ore. We have been adding ore in 15-pound charges. At this early stage, we tend to use a fairly gentle blast, increasing it during the course of the smelt. There is a limit to the total ore you can charge in your bloomery. In ours it seems to be about 60–80 pounds. The charging sequence could last anywhere from two to four hours. As your bloom and slag bath grow up to the level of the *tuyere*, you can prolong things by tapping some slag out.[8]

At a certain point, you may find the furnace's temperature will begin falling and you'll have difficulty keeping the *tuyere* cleared. You've reached the charge limit of the furnace. Add another bucket or so of charcoal, and burn the furnace burden on down to the bloom, which we hope has formed just below the *tuyere*. This post heat can take an hour or two.

The bloom will be an irregular spongy mass firmly attached to the furnace wall directly below the *tuyere* and extending most of the way across the furnace. Pry it loose however you can and pull it out. Ideally, your bloom will be spongy iron with slag in it. If not, it will be mostly spongy slag with little bits of iron in it. Try again.

When we've examined our blooms by spark testing, we have usually found a wide range of carbon content. The portion of the bloom nearest the *tuyere* is denser and higher in carbon content, receding to spongier, lower-carbon iron towards the periphery. If you want to make a knife or tool with this, you may want to try removing the high-carbon section now so you can work it separately. Spark testing may lead you to believe you've made cast iron, but don't panic yet. The cast may only be skin deep, and the included slag and the more oxidizing environment of forging will continue decarburizing the bloom with each heat.

We often begin working up the bloom immediately after smelting, using our bloomery with the top sections removed as a forge, moving later to the gas or coal forge for welding. At this stage, your object is compaction rather than forging. If you take a welding heat now, all your slag will run out of the bloom, leaving you with lots of separate pieces of sponge iron. Rather, take a series of orange heats and compact the bloom, beginning with fairly gentle blows. Watch out, slag will be squirting all over the place. You will note that the spongy character of the bloom causes it to neither conduct nor hold heat very well, requiring many short heats to work it. When it's compact enough to heat like iron and return energy to the hammer like iron, take a welding heat and go for it.[9]

[5] We have gotten iron ore by picking through the tailings of old iron mines in our area — ask local geologists, rockhounds, or your state Division of Mineral Resources. You may be able to find bog ore (iron oxide precipitated out of water in current or ancient swamps). I guess if worse came to worst, you could buy some.

[6] For info on charcoal making in a retort see Barrie Howard, *Making Charcoal and Coke* (Bradley, Il.: Lindsey Publications, 1982). Bust the charcoal up so the average piece is 1–2 inches across, and sift out the fines.

[7] You will be dealing with a very large, hot fire. Wear proper attire, taking special care of eyes and hands. In addition, cover hair when charging the furnace.

[8] Spectators (and believe me you'll have some) really like this part, but try to refrain from doing it too early or too often. Remember, slag is your friend. Of late, we have often found it unnecessary to block the tap arch at all, simply poking through the charcoal and cooled slag that accumulates there to tap, but have a firebrick handy to stop it up if need be.

[9] More information can be found on my website at www.leesauder.com. I see a lot of sculptural possibilities in the grain and crystal structures of the iron, and the potential for true escape from bar forms. And this process has definitely deepened and intensified my understanding, appreciation, and love for this material I've built my life around.

# APPENDIX F: MOUNTAIN LAKE WORKSHOP PROGRAMS

Following is a selection of programs that, in part or whole, may appear on video tapes in the Mountain Lake Workshop archival collection donated to the Library of Congress.

## 1980 PROGRAMS

*Spring Workshop: "Polaroid Photography"* (May 1980)
Marie Cosindas     Polaroid photographer, Boston, MA

*Mountain Lake Symposium I: "Moral Philosophy, Aesthetics, and Contemporary Art"* (Oct 1–3, 1980) (principal investigator, Ray Kass, and co-directed with John Link and Dr. Robert Porter)
Participants: John Dixon     Professor of art, UNC–Chapel Hill
Clement Greenberg     Critic, author, NYC
Giles Gunn     Professor of religion and American studies, UNC–Chapel Hill, NC
Donald B. Kuspit     Critic, professor of art history, SUNY–Stony Brook; contributing editor to *Art in America*; advisor in 1980 and to all subsequent symposia
Robert Pincus-Witten     Critic, professor of art, Queens College, NYC
Jan van der Marck     Art historian, Director, Center for the Fine Arts, Miami

## 1981 PROGRAMS

*Spring Workshops: "Landscape Painting"* (May 1981)
Susan Shatter     Painter, NYC
Jane Freilicher     Painter, NYC

*Fall Workshops: "Painting and Polaroid Photography"* (Sept 27–30, 1981)
Wayne Thiebaud     Painter, Sacramento, CA
Marie Cosindas     Polaroid photographer, Boston, MA

*Mountain Lake Symposium II: "Art Criticism/Social Criticism"* (Oct 9–11, 1981)
(co-directed by Trudie Grace)
Participants: Stanley Diamond     Poet, professor of anthropology, New School of Social Research, NYC
Rosalind E. Krauss     Professor of art, Hunter College, NYC; co-editor, *October* art journal
Donald B. Kuspit     Critic, professor of art history, SUNY–Stony Brook
Irving Sandler     Writer, professor of art history, SUNY–Purchase
Richard Schiff     Visiting professor of art history, University of Pennsylvania

## 1982 PROGRAMS

*Spring Artists' Conference* (May 14–17, 1982)

Clement Greenberg     Critic, NYC
Anthony Caro     Sculptor, London, England
Walter Darby Bannard     Painter, Princeton, NJ
Terry Fenton     Gallery Director, Edmonton, Canada

*Spring Workshops: "Painting and Polaroid Photography"* (May 13–14, 1982)
Walter Darby Bannard     Painter, Princeton, NJ
Marie Cosindas     Polaroid photographer, Boston, MA

*Mountain Lake Symposium III: "Art and Its Publics"* (Oct 7–9, 1982)
Participants: Donald B. Kuspit     Critic, professor of art, SUNY–Stony Brook
Gerald Graff     Critic, professor of English, Northwestern University
Derek Guthrie     Critic, publisher of *New Art Examiner*
Joseph Kosuth     Artist, critic, NYC
George Rochberg     Composer, professor of humanities, University of Pennsylvania
Ingrid Sischy     Critic, editor-in-chief, *ARTFORUM*

## 1983 PROGRAMS

*Spring Artists' Conference: "Environmental Variations"* (April 29, 30, May 1, 1983)
(co-directed with Linda McGreevy)
Participants: Mary Miss     Artist (site sculptor)
Carrie Rickey     Critic (art, film), The Village Voice
Nancy Holt     Environmental sculptor
Mary Beth Edelson     Multimedia artist/painter, performer

*Mountain Lake Symposium IV: "Media: Artists, Imagery, and Influences"* (Oct 13–15, 1983)
Participants: Thomas Lawson     Painter, critic (*REALLIFE magazine*)
Donald B. Kuspit     Critic, professor of art history, SUNY–Stony Brook
Russell Keziere     Critic, editor of *Vanguard* magazine, Vancouver, Canada
Howard Becker     Professor of sociology, Northwestern University, author of *Art Worlds*, Evanston, IL
Edward Paschke     Painter, teacher, Northwestern University, Evanston, IL

*Fall Workshop: "Painting and Polaroid Photography"* (Oct 5–8, 1983)
Participants: Robert Berlind     Painter, NYC
Marie Cosindas     Polaroid photographer, Boston, MA

*Mycological Foray* (Oct 5–8, 1983)
John Cage     Composer, NYC

Orson Miller                         Mycologist, professor of botany and
                            Curator of Fungi Virginia Tech, Blacksburg, VA
Ray Cowell                                British botanical illustrator

## 1984 PROGRAMS

*Spring Workshop: "Re-certification" Workshop and Symposium* (May 1984)
    Edna Love                    Pulaski County High School Art Department
    Martha Ireson                Pulaski County High School Art Department
    Leslie Willet                   Supervisor, Roanoke City Schools
    Virginia Tech                   Department of Art and Art History

*Conference: Technicron'84* (May 1984)
    Frank Kelly Freas        Visiting artist for Sci-Fi Art Conference at Virginia Tech

*Mountain Lake Symposium V: "Revisionism/Criticism: Directions
in Post-Modern Art and Architecture"* (Oct 25, 26, 1984)
Participants: Alan Colquhoun                         Architect; professor
                            of architecture, Princeton University;
                    author of *Essay in Architectural Criticism: Modern
                        Architecture and Historical Change* (MIT Press)
    Kenneth Frampton          Architect and historian; author of *Modern Architecture:
                    A Critical History* (1980) and "Towards a Critical Regionalism"
                (1983); Ware Professor of Architecture, Columbia University
    Serge Guilbaut                   Professor of art history, University
                            of British Columbia; author of *How New
            York Stole the Idea of Modern Art: Abstract Expressionism,
                        Freedom, and the Cold War* (U. of Chicago Press)
    Donald B. Kuspit          Critic, professor of art history, SUNY–Stony Brook
    Keith Sonnier                        Multimedia artist/sculptor
    Anthony Vidler                     Critic; professor of architecture,
                    Princeton University; author of numerous articles
                                on contemporary architecture

## 1985 PROGRAMS

*Spring Workshop: "The Howard Finster Workout"* (May 1985)
An art collaboration with the Reverend Howard Finster, resulting in more than
100 individual works now in the permanent collection of the Art Museum of

Western Virginia, expressing a wide range of Finster's "demential" images
as well as his inclusive aesthetic philosophy. An informal program in art
criticism and poetry accompanied this workshop, with participants:
    John Yau                                    Art critic and poet
    Jonathan Williams                Essayist and founder of the Jargon Society

*Mountain Lake Symposium VI: "Dislocated Sources: Historicism
in Post-Modern Art and Architecture"* (Oct 10–12, 1985)
Participants: John Baldessari                         A painter who has worked in
                        film, video, photography, and artists' books; professor,
                                California Instituteof the Arts, Santa
                                Monica. (unable to attend at the last minute)
    Dan Cameron                     Critic, writer (*Arts, Art in America, Artnews*)
    Douglas Davis            Video/film artist; critic (Newsweek, Art in America, others)
    Allan Greenberg                         Architect, New Haven, CN; author
                        of Design Paradigms in the 18th and 20th Centuries
                    and other theoretical writings on architecture; has taught
                        at Yale University, University of Pennsylvania
    Donald B. Kuspit          Critic, professor of art history, SUNY–Stony Brook
    Elaine A. King       Art historian, Director, Carnegie Mellon University Art Gallery,
                            corresponding editor, *Dialogue* magazine
    Carroll WilliamWestfall                         Professor of architectural
                            history, University of Virginia; author of The
                        *Two Ideal Cities of the Early Renaissance* and
                                *In This Most Perfect Paradise:
                        Alberti, Nicholas V, and the Invention of
                        Conscious Urban Planning in Rome, 1447–55*

## 1986 PROGRAMS

*Spring Painting Workshop* (April 1986)
    Katharine Porter                        Painter, NYC and Maine
    Susan Shatter                              Painter, NYC
    Andrew Tavarelli                        Painter, Boston and NYC
    Willem de Looper     Chief curator, The Phillips Collection, Washington, D.C.
*Exhibition: Intuitive Art: Three Folk Artists: Howard Finster, James
Harold Jennings, and Abraham Lincoln Criss* (April 1986)
Organized by the Mountain Lake Workshop and guest-curated by Ann
Oppenhimer, founder and director of the Folk Art Society of America.
Squires Gallery, Squires Student Center, Virginia Tech.

*Mountain Lake Symposium VII: "The Evaluative Process in Contemporary Art"* (Oct 17–18, 1986), Virginia Museum of Fine Arts, Richmond

Participants: Yve-Alain Bois — Author, curator, co-founder and co-director of *Macula* magazine; frequent contributor to art journals such as *Critique*, *October*, *Art in America*; associate professor of art history, Johns Hopkins University, Baltimore, MD

Suzi Gablik — Artist, critic, and author of *Has Modernism Failed?*, *Progress in Art*, and (with John Russell) *Pop Art Redefined*; frequent contributor to major art journals, and corresponding editor from London to *Art in America*

Allan Kaprow — Artist, writer; teacher, University of California, San Diego; credited with inventing the New York "Happenings" of the 1950s and '60s; has performed and exhibited extensively in the U.S. and abroad

Donald B. Kuspit — Critic, art historian, writer, professor of art history, SUNY–Stony Brook

Annette Michelson — Author; co-editor and co-founder with Rosalind Krauss of *October* magazine; professor of cinema studies, New York University; visiting professor, Yale University, Christian A. Johnson Professor of Art, Middlebury College, VT

*Exhibition: Rev. Howard Finster's Mountain Lake "Workout"* (Oct 1986), Roanoke Museum of Fine Arts, Roanoke, VA

## 1987 PROGRAMS

*Spring Painting Workshop* (May 1987)

Carol Goldberg — Painter, Washington, D.C.

*Mountain Lake Symposium VIII: "Making Psychoanalytic Sense of Art"* (Oct 29–31, 1987)

Participants: John E. Gedo, M.D. — Training and supervisory analyst, Institute for Psychoanalysis, Chicago; author of *Conceptual Issues in Psychoanalysis: Essays in History and Method* and *The Mind in Disorder: Psychoanalytic Models of Pathology*

Mary Mathews Gedo — Clinical psychologist and art historian in Chicago; essayist and author of *Picasso: Art as Autobiography*; editor of interdisciplinary series entitled *Psychoanalytic Perspectives on Art*

Jacques Leenhardt — Professor, Ecole des Hautes Etudes en Sciences Sociales; director, Groupe de Sociologie de la Littérature; president (France), International Association of Art Critics; Fellow, Institute for Advanced Studies Princeton, N.J.; author of *Lecture Politique du Roman* (1973) and *La force des Mots: Le role des intellectuels* (1982); editor, *Psychanalyse et Sociologie Comme Méthodes d'Etude des Phénomènes Historiques et Culturel* (1973); and author of many articles on theories of literary criticism, aesthetics, and sociology of culture

Charles V. Miller — Managing editor, *ARTFORUM*; former editor-in-chief of *Dialogue*, a cooperative art journal in Columbus, OH

Gerardo Mosquera — Curator; associate, Centro Wifredo Lam, Havana, Cuba; organized the Havana Biennial Exhibition; art critic, contributor to Cuban publications *Granma* and *Revolucion y Cultura*

Howard Risatti — Co-organizer, Mountain Lake Symposium; professor of art history, Virginia Commonwealth University, Richmond; Richmond editor, New Art *Examiner*; author of *Post-Modern Perspectives: Issues in Contemporary Art* (Prentice Hall, 1989)

Juan Pablo Bonta — Former professor, University of Buenos Aires; professor of architecture, University of Maryland; author of An *Anatomy of Architectural Interpretation* (Rizzoli, 1979), and *American Architects and Architectural Texts* (MIT Press, 1988); extensive lecturer in U.S., Europe, South America

Elaine A. King — Associate professor of art history and director, University Art Gallery, Carnegie Mellon University, Pittsburgh; curator, author of exhibition catalogues for *Mel Bochner 1973–1985* and *Elizabeth Murray: Drawings 1980–86*

Donald B. Kuspit — Critic; professor of art history and editor of Art Criticism journal, SUNY–Stony Brook; author of

*Clement Greenberg: Art Critic* (1979), *The Critic Is Artist: Intentionality of Art* (1984), *Leon Golub: Existentialist/Activist Painter* (1985)

Ellen Handler Spitz — Interdisciplinary scholar (art historian, aesthetician); research candidate at the Columbia Psychoanalytic Institute, NYC; author of *Art and Psyche* (1985)

## 1988 PROGRAMS

*Spring Workshop: John Cage (painting) workshop: New River Watercolors* (April 1988)

*Exhibition: John Cage: New River Watercolors* (Oct 1988)
A traveling exhibition and catalogue with essays by Julia Boyd, curator, and Ray Kass. Virginia Museum of Fine Arts, The Phillips Collection, Roanoke Museum, and Radford University.

*Mountain Lake Symposium IX: "Artists in Locale: Beyond a Regional Critique"* (Nov 18–20, 1988), Carnegie Mellon University, Pittsburgh, PA
Participants: Judith Russi Kirshner — Curator, critic, professor of art history, theory, and criticism, School of the Art Institute of Chicago; former curator at the Terra Museum of American Art and at the Museum of Contemporary Art, both in Chicago; has organized exhibitions on Vito Acconci, Gordon Matta-Clark, and contemporary artists in Chicago and elsewhere, including *Surfaces: Two Decades of Painting in Chicago*

Donald B. Kuspit — Critic, professor of art history, SUNY–Stony Brook

Jacques Leenhardt — Professor, Ecole des Hautes Etudes en Sciences Sociales; Director, Groupe de Sociologie de la littérature; President (France), International Association of Art Critics; Fellow, Institute for Advanced Studies, Princeton, N.J.; author of many articles on theories of literary criticism, aesthetics, and the sociology of culture

Charles V. Miller — Managing editor, *ARTFORUM*; former editor-in-chief of *Dialogue*, a cooperative art journal in Columbus, Ohio

Gerardo Mosquera — Curator; Associate, Centro Wifredo Lam, Havana, Cuba; organized the Havana Biennial Exhibition; art critic, contributor to Cuban publications *Granma* and *Revolucion y Cultura*

Tim Rollins — Artist, New York; director of K.O.S. (Kids of Survival), The Art and Knowledge Workshop, a South Bronx community action group. Exhibitions: "Aperto," 43rd Venice Biennale, Museum Für Gegenwartskunst, Basel, DIA Art Foundation, NY

Howard Risatti — Co-organizer, Mountain Lake Symposium; professor of art history, Virginia Commonwealth University, Richmond; Richmond editor, *New Art Examiner*; author of *Post-Modern Perspectives: Issues in Contemporary Art* (1990)

## 1989 PROGRAMS

*Winter Workshop: John Cage performs STEPS: A Composition for a Painting* (Feb 1989)
Painting workshop in Ray Kass' studio, Christiansburg, VA

*Spring Workshop: Alston Conley Fresco Workshop* (April 1989), Virginia Tech (partially funded by Mountain Lake Workshop)

*Summer Program: Rev. Howard Finster, "Pennville Workout" and "Visions of Another World" Workshop, Summerville, GA* (June 1989)

*Exhibition: Paradise Garden: Visions of Another World,* Gallery Rodeo, Beverly Hills, CA (designed by Mountain Lake assistant Peter Lau) (Oct 1989)

*Mountain Lake Symposium X: "Artists' Intentions: Enduring Values/ Discounted Goods"* (Nov 3–5, 1989), Mountain Lake Hotel
Participants: Suzi Gablik — Critic, author, artist; C. C. Garvin Visiting Endowed Professor of Art and Art History, VPI & SU, Blacksburg

Ronald Jones — Artist, critic, NYC

Donald B. Kuspit — Critic, author, professor of art history, SUNY–Stony Brook

Akram Midani — Professor of drama and art, Carnegie Mellon University, Pittsburgh

Charles V. Miller — Managing editor, *ARTFORUM*

Marcus Raskin — (present through a submitted paper)

Professor of public policy, George Washington
University; co-founder of the D.C. Institute for Public Policy; author
of works about public policy and progressive social change

Maureen Sherlock — Art historian, critical theorist, The School of the Art Institute of Chicago

Nancy Spero — Feminist artist, NYC
Sidney Tillim — Painter/critic, NYC

## 1990 PROGRAMS

**Wood Harvesting Ceremony** (Jan 2, 3, 1990)
Kyoto artist Jiro Okura visits for Wood Harvesting Ceremony in which
Ray Kass is appointed as a Shinto priest and conducts a Shinto Forest-
Blessing ceremony on Little Stone Mountain in Wise County, VA

**Spring Workshop: John Cage and the Mountain Lake Workshop – New River
Rocks and Washes and New River Rocks and Smoke Watercolors** (April 1990)

**Summer Workshop: Jiro Okura: Mountain Lake Screen Tachi
Workshop** (six weeks from June–Aug 1990)
Eight large folding screens carved by community participants and covered with
cashew oil paint calligraphy and artificial gold leaf. Portions of the screen are
in the permanent collections of the Art Institute of Chicago, the Saint Louis
Museum of Art, the Asian Art Museum in San Francisco, and Virginia Tech.

**Mountain Lake Symposium XI: "Decadence and Conscience: What Is Art
Doing?"** (Nov 3, 4, 1990), Virginia Museum of Fine Arts, Richmond
Participants: Lowry Burgess — Dean, College of Fine and Performing Arts, Carnegie Mellon University, Pittsburgh
Luis Camnitzer — Artist (sculptor), critic, NYC
Robert Colescott — Painter, Tucson, AZ
Donald Kuspit — Critic, author, professor of art history, SUNY–Stony Brook
Kay C. Larson — Critic, *New York* magazine
Charles V. Miller — Managing editor, *ARTFORUM*
Kay Rosen — Conceptual artist (painter), Gary, IN
Mierle Laderman Ukeles — Environmental artist
(installation sculptor); artist-in-residence, New
York City Department of Sanitation

**Art Criticism Workshop: Virginia Museum of Fine Arts** (Nov 2, 1990)
Conducted by Kay Larson and Donald Kuspit

## 1991 PROGRAMS

**Exhibition: Mountain Lake Screen Tachi**, The Southeastern Center
for Contemporary Art, Winston-Salem, NC (June–July, 1991)

**Spring Workshop: Ray Kass and the Mountain Lake Workshop, Broad Channel: The
Vorticella Polyptych and Writing on the River** (April–May 1991)
*Broad Channel* was installed in Newman Library of Virginia Tech and is now
in the permanent collection of the Nevada Museum of Art, Reno, NV

**Video: Broad Channel: Nebulae** (June–July 1991)
A documentary of the spring 1991 workshop for the purposes of making
a video for Virginia Tech's TV Satellite Outreach Program

**Exhibition: Ray Kass and the Mountain Lake Workshop**, Shelby
Gallery, Chelsea District, New York City (Sept–Dec 1991)

## 1992 PROGRAMS

**Spring Exhibition: Double Faces: Ray Kass and the Mountain Lake
Workshop**, Art Du Monde Gallery, New York City (April 1992)
An exhibition of double-sided polyptychal paintings utilizing chance-
generated imagery and hung from the ceiling with cables

**Summer Workshop: Shisendo Garden Painting Workshop** (June–Aug 1992)
Jiro Okura Mountain Lake painting workshop in single-brush Japanese-
style "Zen" *sumi-e* painting technique developed by Okura. During the
workshop, Okura made a painting as an homage to John Cage, who died
in NYC while the workshop was being conducted in Virginia.

**Fall Exhibition: Howard Finster Mountain Lake Exhibition and Workshop**
(Oct 1992) Virginia Film Festival, Charlottesville, VA. An exhibition of Howard
Finster's art works curated by Ray Kass and Brian Sieveking and installed at the
Second Street Gallery in Charlottesville during the film festival. Finster was the
guest artist and made the festival poster. He appeared in conference programs
with actor Robert Duvall, writer William Styron, and film critic Roger Ebert.

*Fall Workshop: "John's Place at Ripplemead."* Participants: Ray Kass and Stefan Gibson. Three photomontages created as an homage to John age for Musiktexte magazine (Cologne, Germany, 46/47, Dec 1992)

**1993 PROGRAMS**

*Spring Program: "Art & Collaboration" — Honors Course and Workshop*, Virginia Tech (spring semester, 1993)
A review of ten years of the Mountain Lake Workshop, including a special collaborative workshop in Kass' studio in which the *The Muscarelle Polyptych* was created.

*Exhibitions: Collaboration: Mountain Lake Workshop*, the Muscarelle Museum of the College of William and Mary, Williamsburg, VA (3 April–16 May, 1993)
The exhibition featured works by Cage, Kass, and Okura, including *The Muscarelle Polyptych*.

*Collaboration Workshop*: a special one-day Mountain Lake "Breathing Lines"painting workshop in the Muscarelle Museum conducted by Ray Kass with Jiro Okura and members of the Williamsburg community to coincide with the *Collaboration* exhibition.

*Workshop: Pyramid Atlantic and Helen Frederick*: P*aper-Making at the Mountain Lake Workshop* (June 1993)

*Exhibition: Helen Frederick — Works on Paper*, Armory Art Gallery, Virginia Tech. (June 1993). A Blacksburg Summer Arts Festival exhibition selected from The Pyramid Atlantic Workshop and curated by Ray Kass, to coincide with the Pyramid Atlantic Mountain Lake Workshop

**1994 PROGRAMS**

*Workshop and Exhibition: Methanogenesis: Mierle Laderman Ukeles and the Mountain Lake Workshop* (April 1994)
An interdisciplinary collaboration with Virginia Tech's Anaerobic Lab and microbiologist Dr. James G. Ferry. The resulting special exhibition was part of Blacksburg's 1994 Summer Arts Festival.
The exhibition and video documentary were subsequently on view at the Art Museum of Western Virginia in spring 1995, and at the Anderson Gallery (VCU) in Richmond, Virginia, Sept–Oct 1996.

*Workshop: Pathways: The Appalachian Trail Frieze* (summer1994).
Joe Kelley with Stefan Gibson and the Mountain Lake Workshop. A collaborative photography and drawing workshop and exhibition (Blacksburg Summer Arts Festival '94) sponsored by the U.S. Forest Service

**1995 PROGRAMS**

*Workshop and Exhibition: ROTO-OPTICS* (summer 1995). The Mountain Lake Workshop with Bruce McClure (an homage to Marcel Duchamp); a special collaborative community workshop based in Duchamp's retinal experiments to create a dazzling Armory Art Gallery, Blacksburg Summer Arts Festival exhibition

*Workshop: Pathways* (Sept 1995). An extension of the Appalachian Trail Frieze conducted by Carlton Sturges Abbott and Joe Kelley and the Mountain Lake Workshop; a hiking and drawing workshop to initiate future collaborations on the Blue Ridge Parkway. The event was sponsored in part by the National Linear Parks annual conference and the Virginia Tech Design Consortium and was planned to coincide with Carlton Abbott's exhibition in Virginia Tech's Armory Art Gallery entitled *Parts and Pieces*. (Aug 22–Sept 12, 1995)

**1996 PROGRAMS**

*Workshop: Methanogenesis*: Mierle Laderman Ukeles and the Mountain Lake Workshop (March 18, 19, 1996). A collaborative workshop for the conference and exhibition *Views From Ground Level*, Feb 26–Mar 22, 1996, Appalachian State University, Boone, NC

*Workshop: ROTO-OPTICS* (fall 1996). The Mountain Lake Workshop with Bruce McClure (an homage to Marcel Duchamp); a special collaborative workshop at the Anderson Gallery, VCU, Richmond, VA

**1997 PROGRAMS**

*Spring Program: "Ki no Ichiku"* (June, 1997). A special study in Japanese arts and crafts and architecture organized and directed by Peter Lau and Ray Kass. The program included the collaborative painting workshop "The Nisso Screen" with Jiro Okura and the Mountain Lake Workshop in Osaka

*Fall Workshop: M.C. Richards and the Mountain Lake Workshop: "Cosmos and Creation in Clay, Color, and Words"* (Oct 5–11). Drawing, ceramics, writing, and book-making with the eminent author of the landmark book *Centering: In Pottery, Poetry, and the Person* (1962).

## 1998 PROGRAMS

*Workshop: "Building a Paradigm in Wood, Earth, and Water"* (May, June 1998). Peter Lau and the Mountain Lake Workshop, sponsored by the Virginia Commission for the Arts and the Higo Garden. Completed projects: A Moon-Viewing Pavilion, a lily pond, a 40-foot rammed-earth wall, and related Japanese-style garden

*Summer Workshop: "Seeing the Dragon"* (June 1998). Michael Hofmann and the Mountain Lake Workshop. A workshop in *sumi-e Nanga* painting in which Hofmann painted *Under Mountain Lake Dragon.*

*Summer Exhibition: Souls on Garbage* (July 1998), Jiro Okura and the Mountain Lake Workshop. Exhibition at the Art Museum of Western Virginia in Roanoke.

## 1999 PROGRAMS

*Exhibition: "Water Mountain": Ray Kass and the Mountain Lake Workshop.* Exhibition in Kyoto, Japan (June–July 1999) and at Virginia Tech's Armory Art Gallery in 2000

*Fall Workshop and site-specific exhibition: "Relic Habitats"* (Aug 29– Sept 19, 1999) Colorado-based "eco artist" Lynne Hull and the Mountain Lake Workshop and outdoor site-specific exhibition, sponsored by Mountain Lake Hotel and the Virginia Commission for the Arts

## 2000 PROGRAMS

*Summer Workshop and Exhibition: Watercolor and traditional Asian paper mounting* (July 7–Sept 1, 2000). Workshop was conducted by Xiao Yan Gan. His exhibition, *Chinese Watercolor Scroll Paintings*, was at Armory Art Gallery, Virginia Tech, and was funded by the Blacksburg Summer Arts Festival and the Virginia Commission for the Arts.

*Summer Workshop and Exhibition: "Talking Walls and Sidewalks,"* a Mountain Lake Workshop directed by James De La Vega, a nationally recognized muralist and street artist from New York City's East ("Spanish") Harlem. The exhibition was presented in Virginia Tech's Armory Art Gallery and was accompanied by chalk and color-tape inscriptions on the campus and downtown sidewalks

*Summer Exhibition:* Jiro Okura's "Breathing Lines" workshop method used for the workshop *Souls on Garbage: Waterfalls*, directed by Ray Kass and Joe Kelley with display fabricated by Joe Kelley for the Summer Arts Festival exhibition at the William King Regional Arts Center in Abingdon, VA, curated by Tom Perryman.

## 2001 PROGRAMS

*Winter Workshop: Iron Forging Workshop* with Lee Sauder. In early February Ray Kass and a group of students visited Lee Sauder's studio on McLaughlin Street in downtown Lexington, Virginia where they met Cy Twombly who happened to be there. In the workshop they learned about iron forging and tried their hand at it under the supervision of Sauder.

*Fall Workshop: "Pyromancy": Forged Iron* (Oct 2001) A three-day workshop on traditional iron-forging process by the well-known Lexington, Virginia, sculptor and forged-iron specialist and blacksmith Lee Sauder. The collaborative sculpture developed in this workshop is in the permanent collection of the Taubman Museum of Art, Roanoke, VA.

*Workshop: Cy Twombly: Prices Fork Sculptures* (with Steven Bickley), a private workshop in foundry casting that extended from 2001 until early in 2004

## 2002 PROGRAMS

*Spring Workshop: Jackie Matisse, Kites Flying In and Out of Space* A workshop and "virtual reality" presentation in Virginia Tech's CAVE in April 2002. This project developed and traveled to international exhibitions in NYC and Chalon sur Saône, France, and to supercomputing conferences in France, The Netherlands, Brazil, and Italy in 2003–2004 and 2005.

*Workshop: Microcinema/Filmstreams* (Oct 2002) Workshop conducted by Bruce McClure in which cameras were put into the hands of participants who were then led on an investigatory journey exploring the surface of media imagery as it transitions between film, video, and digital realizations.

## 2003 PROGRAMS

*Spring Workshop and Exhibition: "Faces Figure"* (spring 2003) A painting workshop with Edinburgh-based figurative artist James Donnelly and Ray Kass. The completed installation was exhibited at Virginia Tech's Armory Art Gallery

*Workahop: Atelier du Lac* (early summer 2003) Montage paper-mounting workshop, Jacques Pourcher with Ray Kass and Dr. Ulriuke Kasper

## 2006 PROGRAMS

*Fall Workshop: "Smoked"* (Oct 2006)
A paper-smoking workshop conducted by Stephen Addiss, Ray Kass, and the Mountain Lake Workshop at the University of Richmond.

*Performance: Stephen Addiss performs John Cage's STEPS: A Composition for a Painting* at Capital One, Inc., West Creek Campus, Richmond, VA in Dec 2006. This is the inaugural performance of what has become known and performed as the "second notation" related to the original performance of *STEPS* by Cage in 1989. The two notations were written at the request of the John Cage Trust at Bard College in 2006.

## 2007 PROGRAMS

*Spring Workshop and Exhibition: "Faces"* (Feb 2007)
A drawing and Asian-style paper-mounting workshop at the Nevada Museum of Art in conjunction with the exhibition of Ray Kass' *Broad Channel: Writing on the River* (1991), now in the permanent collection of the Nevada Museum of Art, Reno, NV.

*Fall Workshop and Exhibition: "Smoked"* (Nov 2007)
Stephen Addiss and the Mountain Lake Workshop at Virginia Tech conducted a paper-smoking workshop along with an exhibition at Virginia Tech's Armory Art Gallery of Addiss' works on "smoked" paper and his *Sumi-e I* and *Sumi-e II*, his two performances of *John Cage's STEPS: A Composition for a Painting to Be Performed by Individuals or Groups*.

*Fall Workshop: John Cage's Zen Ox-Herding Pictures* (Nov 2007)
In reviewing the paper towels John Cage used to wipe his brush during his watercolor workshops in 1988, Ray Kass suggested they should take Cage's advice and make something out of them; organizing the 50 paper towels into groups of ten they began working together on the workshop project that later resulted in J*ohn Cage's Zen Ox-Herding Pictures*

## 2008 PROGRAMS

*Spring Workshop: Jiro Okura's "Breathing Lines"* (April 2008)
A workshop at the Jefferson Center, Roanoke, Virginia, as a fund-raising event to benefit CASA (Court-Appointed Special Advocates for Children), co-hosted by Virginia's First Lady, Anne Holton

*Fall Performances: Merce Cunningham and the Cunningham Dance Foundation Repertory Understudy Group* (Oct 23, 2008)

Four of the understudy dancers and Merce Cunningham created *Dancers I*, *Dancers II*, and *Dancers III*, three performances of *John Cage's STEPS: A Composition for a Painting to Be Performed by Individuals or Groups*, Cunningham Dance Studio, Greenwich Village, NYC.

## 2009 PROGRAMS

*Spring Exhibition: John Cage's Zen Ox-Herding Pictures*
An exhibition created by Stephen Addiss and Ray Kass at the Mountain Lake Workshop: an exhibition and publication (Braziller, NY, 2009) coordinated with the Harnett Museum of the University of Richmond Museums

*Exhibition: Current I and Current II: Ray Kass and the Mountain Lake Workshop*
*Current I* (118 in. x 396 in., ink and water media on fabric voile) and *Current II* (72 in. x 287 in., water media and mica on rag paper) are two performances of *John Cage's STEPS (1989): A Performance for a Painting to be Made by Individuals or Groups* (2006). *Current II* was exhibited at the Museo Nacional Centro de Arte Reina Sofia, Madrid, Spain (May 6–9, 2009)

*Exhibition: Performances of John Cage's STEPS: A Composition for a Painting to Be Performed by Individuals or Groups* (May 6–9, 2009)
Merce Cunningham and the Repertory Understudy Group's *Dancers I*, *Dancers II*, and *Dancers III* (Merce's final solo performance), created at the Cunningham Dance Studio with Ray Kass and the Mountain Lake Workshop in 2008, were presented along with Ray Kass' *Currents II* as backdrops/decor for "Events" performances by the Merce Cunningham Dance Company at the Museo Nacional Centro de Arte Reina Sofia, Madrid, Spain, May 6–9, 2009.

NOTE: Cunningham's *Dancers III* was backdrop for the musicians at the commemorative 67th St. Armory event, and *Dancers II* was subsequently exhibited at Lincoln Center as part of the overall programming for Merce Fair, a day-long tribute to Merce Cunningham.

*Fall Exhibition and Workshop: The Mountain Lake Symposium and "Virginia Pathways" Workshop*. Directed by Joe Kelley and Ray Kass, with Dr. Simone Paterson, Montgomery County Regional Museum (Lewis Miller Museum of Art), Christiansburg, Virginia. An exhibition and accompanying workshop and educational program about the activities of the Mountain Lake Workshop in southwestern Virginia since 1980. Included documentary materials related to the art criticism conference, and small works by various visiting workshop artists as well as by local participants in the programs.

## 2010 PROGRAMS

*Winter Workshop: A Workshop Based on Jiro Okura's "Breathing Lines"* (November, 2010). University of Richmond in association with the Virginia Museum of Fine Arts Canvas Group.

## 2011 PROGRAMS

*Fall Workshop: "Metempsychosis: Photography, Laser Imagery, and Painting"* (Oct 2011). A workshop with Jessie and Sally Mann and Liz Liguori, including *Metempsychosis STEPS*, a performance of *John Cage's STEPS: A Composition for a Painting to Be Performed by Individuals or Groups*.

## 2012-13 PROGRAMS for John Cage Centennial Year

*Exhibition with Accompanying Public Program: Membra Disjecta for John Cage. Wanting to Say Something About John* (Feb 17–May 6, 2012) An exhibition at freiraum quartier21 INTERNATIONAL, MuseumsQuartier Wien, curated by Jozef Cseres and Georg Weckwerth in cooperation with TONSPUR für einen öffentlichen raum

*Eleven performances in Vienna and Lower Austria of John Cage's STEPS: A Composition for a Painting to Be Performed by Individuals or Groups* (list compiled by Georg Weckwerth and Ray Kass). Organized by Georg Weckwerth, artistic director, TONSPUR for a public space / Sound works at MQ in Vienna; and Ray Kass, founder and director of the Mountain Lake Workshop of the Virginia Tech Foundation. Special thanks to Harald Hasler, master craftsman of the MQ Cabinet Shop, who constructed the big brushes and troughs that were used in the performances. We are grateful for his important contribution to this project. Listed in chronological order:

*1*
Tyler Adams, *Watery Walk — a performance of John Cage's STEPS* performed in open air by Tyler Adams, Arnold Dreyblatt, Ray Kass, and Georg Weckwerth, on March 22, 2012, at MQ Wien (Vienna), Austria, using cyanotype sensitizer on white Fabriano paper, 40 x 197 in. (101 cm 60 x 500 cm)

*2*
Nikola Tasic, André Wagner with his dog Rhabarba, and Anna Watzinger realized *ONNRA — a performance of John Cage's STEPS* in cooperation with the University of Applied Arts Vienna on March 22, 2012, at MQ Wien (Vienna), Austria, using black ink and watercolor on white Fabriano paper, 59 x 247 in. (150.8 x 627.8 cm)

*3*
Ruth Schnell and Nita Tandon performed *Duo Through Chance — a performance of John Cage's STEPS* in cooperation with the University of Applied Arts Vienna on March 22, 2012, at MQ Wien (Vienna), Austria using black ink and watercolor on white Fabriano paper, 60 x 163 in. (150.4 x 413.4 cm)

Ray Kass and public participants performed I*nvisibility — A public introduction of the performance of John Cage's STEPS* in the open air on the plaza at MQ (Museum Quartier 21) with clear water on the pavement stones. Public participants included: Philipp Reichel, Clara Monti, Peter Kuthan, Grace Pardi and Beatrix Maier, Anna Watzinger and Arnold Dreyblatt, Igna Wakka and Laudy van Hettema, and Erik Van Ree.

*5*
Sam Ashley performed *As If It Would Have Happened Anyway* — adapted for a performance of *John Cage's STEPS* in the open air on March 24, 2012, at MQ Wien (Vienna), Austria; mystic energies implied on an empty piece of white Fabriano paper plus live video footage with sound, 21.5 x 27.25 in. (54.7 x 69 cm)

*6*
Julius Deutschbauer performs a*bdecken, bügeln, reisen — a performance of John Cage's STEPS*, performed two times on March 24, 2012, in the bar Kantine at MQ Wien (Vienna), Austria, using black ink on white tablecloth, live video footage with sound, a table (80 x 80 cm), A1 poster, 35.43 in. x 35.43 in. (90 cm x 90 cm)

*7*
Sabine Groschup performs *A "Picnic" for a Painting — a performance of John Cage's STEPS* on March 25, 2012, in the lowland riparian forest near Stockerau in Lower Austria using water and mud out of the Danube River and black ink on white Fabriano paper, 40 x 275.59 in. (101.6 x 700 cm)

*8*
Franz Graf realizes *aroundrecording — a performance of John Cage's STEPS* by drawing around vinyl records and CDs of John Cage's music on March 25, 2012 in the house of the artist in the countryside of Lower Austria near Jaidhof; with pencil on two pieces of transparent paper and two pieces of white paper plus live video footage without sound, 13 x 70.5 in. (33 x 179 cm), 17.91 x 76.18 in. (45.5 x 193.5 cm), 17.91 x 77.55 in. (45.5 x 197 cm) , 12.99 x 84.09 in. (33 x 213.6 cm)

**9**

Ray Kass and Ian Cobb-Ozanne realize *Current III — a performance of John Cage's STEPS* on March 26, 2012, at MQ Wien, Vienna, Austria using black ink and watercolor on two pieces of white Fabriano paper, each 59.37 x 393.7 in. (150.8 x 1000 cm)

**10**

Sabine Groschup performed *A Tribute to Oskar F. — a performance of John Cage's STEPS* on March 26, 2012, at MQ Wien (Vienna), Austria; using Vallejo film color on foil, 141.73 x 106.29 in. (360 x 270 cm), cut into nine pieces, each 47.24 x 35.43 in. (120 x 90 cm)

**11**

Georg Weckwerth performed *A Car Full of STEPS (reminiscence to RR, JC, and a Model A Ford) — a performance of John Cage's STEPS*, with Tyler Adams, Ian Cobb-Ozanne, and Sabine Groschup, on March 26, 2012, at MQ Wien (Vienna), Austria, using black ink, watercolor, and car tire traces on white Fabriano paper, 59.37 x 216.92 in. (150.8 x 551 cm)

**Five performances** of J*ohn Cage's STEPS: A Composition for a Painting to Be Performed by Individuals or Groups* performed at the Salzburg Museum of Modern Art (MdM) in July 2012:

**1**

Toni Stooss and Wulf Herzogenrath — *John Cage's STEPS: Small and Tall Is Beautiful. In Friendship*, July 18, 2012 using black ink and watercolor on two pieces of white Fabriano paper, each 59 x 211 in. (150.8 x 537 cm)

**2**

Summer Children's Class at MdM — *Jiro Okura's "Breathing Lines" STEPS*, performance of *John Cage's STEPS* in which seven children, guided by their teacher, Theresa Weiss, and Mountain Lake Workshop Director Ray Kass, incorporated Okura's "breathing lines" into their *STEPS* performance (July 19, 2012). Each child assigned their own title to the group piece, which is 59 x 216 in. (150 x 549.5 cm)

    Carla Franchetti, *14 malende Füße* (14 painting feet)
    Sandro Hofbauer, *Der Rückwärtsgang der bunten Füße* (The reverse of the colorful feet)
    Charlotte Fink von Finkenheim, *Die Fußabdrücke der sieben Kinder* (The footprints of the seven kids)
    Sebastian Weiss Bunter, *Rückwärtsgang* (Colorful reverse)
    Nikolas Weiss, *Bunte Füße* (Colorful feet)
    Lorenz Rinner, *Die betrunkenen Füße* (The drunken feet)
    Olivia Rinner, *Zu Fuß* (By foot)

**3**

Susan Quinn and SEAD Dance Company, choreography by Jelka Milic — *Generations, a performance of John Cage's STEPS*, July 21, 2012, 59 x 206 in. (150 x 524 cm)

**4**

Tina Teufel and Martina Pohn — *Spelunking für John Cage, a performance of John Cage's STEPS*, July 21, 2012, 59 x 195 in. (150 x 495.2 cm)

**5**

Ryan Dudik and Luke Demarest — *The Baumgartner, a performance of John Cage's STEPS*, July 21, 2012, 59 in. x 223.6 in. (150 cm x 568 cm)

\*

*Performance: Jiro Okura's "Breathing Lines"* (Sept 10, 11:00 a.m. and 3:00 p.m.). Held at the University of California Washington Center, conducted by Ray Kass, Luke Demarest, Ryan Dudik, and the Mountain Lake workshop with community participants, for the final day of the Washington D.C. John Cage Centennial Festival (Sept. 4–10, 2012).

Participants: Roger Reynolds, Linda Lowery, Karen Reynolds, Ryan Dudik, Andrea Hull, Florence Brodkey, Rodger Rak, James Chute, Takako Okura, Luke Demarest, David Mills, Alexis Descharmes, Janine Green, Marcia Ristaino, Patricia Moss, Larry Oleniak, Debbi Wins, Ariana Childs Graham, Kathleen Lane, András Goldinger, Joanne Kent, Emma Desjardins, Jamie Scott, and Ed Bisese.

**Two performances of John Cage's STEPS: A Composition for a Painting to Be Performed by Individuals or Groups** at the University of California Washington Center, Sept. 10, 2012, as part of the week-long Washington John Cage Centennial Festival:

**1**

Jamie Scott and Emma Desjardins — *STEPS with Arms, a performance of John Cage's STEPS* following the "arm duet" portion of Merce Cunningham's 1973–75 choreographed composition *Changing Places* using black ink and water media on two connected rolls of toned rag paper (142 in. x 360 in.)

**2**

Roger Reynolds and Nancy Snyder, *Within a Frame, a performance of John Cage's STEPS*, using black ink and water media on two connected rolls of toned rag paper (142 in. x 360 in. approx.)

*Performance: Dorothea Rockburne performs Angular Movement, a performance of John Cage's STEPS* (142 x 393 in.) at the National Academy Museum, NYC, Dec 1, 2012. Ray Kass assisted by Jeffrey Cornwell, Anderson Cornwell, Dylan Goodwin, Luke Demarest, and Ryan Dudik

*Seattle STEPS: Disintegrating Loop, 12 Parameters, and 24 Breaths: three performances of John Cage, STEPS: A Composition for a Painting to Be Performed by Individuals or Groups*, presented by the Wayward Music Series at the Chapel Performance Space, Seattle, WA, Dec 14, 2012
Director: Jarrad Powell; Video Artist: Robert Campbell; Choreography and Performance: Beth Graczyk; and Set Design: Reilly Sinanan
Movement Performers: Beth Graczyk, Corrie Befort, Shannon Stewart, Alia Swersky, and Mary Margaret Moore
Musicians: Angelina Baldox, trumpet; Stuart Dempster, trombone; Julio Lopez, violin; Roger Nelson, piano; Jarrad Powell, percussion; and Paul Taub, flute; with Jessica Kenney, conductor
Music: *Atlas Eclipticalis* (1961) and *Winter Music* (1958) by John Cage
Videography and Post Production: Danielle Allinice, Destiny Reidel, and Reilly Sinanan

*Spring Performances: Two performances of John Cage's STEPS: A Composition for a Painting to Be Performed by Individuals or Groups*: *Circle, Square, and Triangle*, performed by art historian Howard Risatti using water media on rag paper (72 in. x 360 in.); and *Night by Silent Sailing Night*, performed by Scott Williamson, director of the Roanoke Opera using water media on rag paper (72 in. x 360 in.), Taubman Museum of Art, April 4, 2013.

## 2013 PROGRAMS

*Spring Workshop: "Three Graces."* Sally and Jessie Mann and Liz Liguori, with Sam Krisch and the Mountain Lake Workshop: photography, laser and digital imagery, and painting. This project received support from the Virginia Commission for the Arts and the Reynolds Gallery, Richmond, Virginia.

*Exhibition: Metempsychosis, Three Graces, and Sam Krisch's Day-Off:*
Photomontage exhibition at Capital One campus, Glen Allen, VA. *Metempsychosis* was exhibited at the Reynolds Gallery, Richmond, VA in Oct 2013.

## 2016 PROGRAMS

*Spring Exhibition: John Cage's Zen Ox-Herding Pictures* (Set III), exhibited in Innsbruck at the Museumspartner – Die Kunstspedition, Sebastian-Kneipp-Weg 17, 6020 Innsbruck, Austria.

## 2017 PROGRAMS

**Paper-Smoking Workshop: Christiansburg, Virginia, May 6, 2017** – A special workshop to smoke the 21 panels that comprise *Notations*; a mural-size painting by Ray Kass, with assistance from Elise Gill and Maddie Kopjanski.

Workshop particpants: Scott Bristow, Carol Burch-Brown, Kevin Concannon, Margo Crutchfield, Luke Demarest, Dominique Francesca, Ray Kass, Joe Kelley, Alys McAlpine, Liz Liguori, Derek Parks and Brennan Young. The paper was sized and cut by Nicolaas Baudoin.

**Halberstadt STEPS Performances at St. Burchardi Cloister: October 2 - 7, 2017**

Sponsored by the John Cage Organ Project: to commemorate the announcement by Nicholas Riddle, President, Editions Peters Group, of the publication of the notation: J*ohn Cage, STEPS, A Composition for Painting*

Anticipated performers are composers Alvin Curran, Achim Freyer and Dieter Schebel, and Edition Peters CEO Nicholas Riddle, Laura Kuhn, director of the John Cage Trust, John Cage Organ Foundation members Rainer O. Neugebauer, Christof Halleger and Hans and Uschi Hermann, and performances by refugees in honor of their solitary journey of Hope.

A special exhibition of *STEPS* performance-paintings curated by Ray Kass and Georg Weckwerth will open on September 7, 2017 at the Manor House in St. Burchardi Cloister. St. Burchardi is the site of the John Cage's *ORGAN2ASLP (As Slow AS Possible)* for Organ that began playing in 2001 and is to continue for 639 years, ending in 2640.

**17 PERFORMANCES IN HALBERSTADT IN SAXONY-ANHALT, GERMANY IN 2017**

Commissioned by the **John Cage Organ Foundation** Halberstadt in collaboration with the **John Cage Trust, Edition Peters Group,** the **Mountain Lake Workshop** and **TONSPUR** Kunstverein Wien.

On occasion of the publication of the notation *John Cage, STEPS, A Composition for a Painting* announced by Nicholas Riddle, CEO of Edition Peters Group. Commemorating John Cage's *STEPS,* the original performance of the painting (Collection Kunsthalle Bremen) realized in collaboration with Ray Kass, in Kass' studio in Christiansburg, Virginia, USA on February 3, 1989.

The performances were accompanied by exhibition of STEPS performances created in Vienna and Halberstadt since 2012.
Organizer: Harriett Watts, John Cage Organ Project Halberstadt
Curator: Georg Weckwerth, TONSPUR Kunstverein Wien
Cage-Haus Halberstadt (CHH) of the John Cage Organ Foundation, Am Kloster 1, 38820 Halberstadt, Oct. 3–29, 2017.

www.aslsp.org

*1*
**Rainer O. Neugebauer,** *My First Steps (STEPS test):* A performance of *John Cage's STEPS, A Composition for a Painting;* performed on Oct. 3, 2017 at Cage-Haus Halberstadt next to the Burchardi Church, Germany; 2017, black ink and water color on brown painter's masking tape, 400 x 80 cm (157.48 x 31.50 in.).

*2*
**Ray Kass and various public participants,** *Invisibility:* A public introduction of the performance of *John Cage's STEPS, A Composition for a Painting;* performed open air by Volker Bürger & Thomas Rimpler from the Halberstadt City Parlament, artist Sabine Groschup among others on Oct. 3, 2017 on the plaza before the City Hall of Halberstadt, Germany; 2017, clear water on the paving stones.

*3*
**Saadet Che Demir & Fadi Al Jasser,** *All In Steps:* A performance of *John Cage's STEPS, A Composition for a Painting;* performed open air on Oct. 4, 2017 on the courtyard of the Burchardi cloister next to the Cage-Haus Halberstadt, Germany; 2017, black ink and water color on white Fabriano paper, 150.8 x 1000 cm (59.37 x 393.70 in.).

*4*
**Ursel Huelsdell & Hans-Hermann Richter,** *Fast + Furious:* A performance of *John Cage's STEPS, A Composition for a Painting;* performed open air on Oct. 4, 2017 on the courtyard of the Burchardi cloister next to the Cage-Haus Halberstadt, Germany; 2017, black ink and water color on white Fabriano paper, 150.8 x 1000 cm (59.37 x 393.70 in.).

*5*
**Christof P. Hallegger & Rainer O. Neugebauer,** *Steps For A Society Without Fear:* A performance of *John Cage's STEPS, A Composition for a Painting;* performed open air on Oct. 4, 2017 on the courtyard of the Burchardi cloister next to the Cage-Haus Halberstadt, Germany; 2017, black ink and water color on white Fabriano paper, 150.8 x 1000 cm (59.37 x 393.70 in.).

*6*
**Ray Kass & Dylan Goodwin,** *A Heap Of Living:* A performance of *John Cage's STEPS, A Composition for a Painting;* performed on Oct. 5, 2017 at Cage-Haus Halberstadt next to the Burchardi Church, Germany; 2017, black ink and water color on white Fabriano paper, 150.8 x 1000 cm (59.37 x 393.70 in.).

*7*
**Laura Kuhn & Nicholas Riddle,** *Ein Gesamtschrittwerk:* A performance of *John Cage's STEPS, A Composition for a Painting;* performed on Oct. 5, 2017 at Cage-Haus Halberstadt next to the Burchardi Church, Germany; 2017, black ink and water color on white Canson paper, 110 x 1000 cm (43.30 x 393.70 in.).

*8*

**Dieter Schnebel,** *273 Steps for John Cage:* A performance of *John Cage's STEPS, A Composition for a Painting;* performed by walking and counting and same time drawing on three pieces of corrugated fiberboard while the musician **Heidi Steger** played a new composition by Dieter Schnebel on an Accordion on Oct. 5, 2017 at Cage-Haus Halberstadt next to the Burchardi Church, Germany; 2017, Edding® permanent marker in blue, red and yellow (each marker installed on a wodden staff of 1 Meter length) on three pieces of brown corrugated fiberboard, each 80 x 500 cm (31.49 x 196.85 in.) plus a score with a composition for accordion and a text in German, surface in total 240 x 500 cm (94.48 x 196.85 in.).

*9*

**Sabine Groschup,** *Nadeltanz (Needle Dance):* A performance of *John Cage's STEPS, A Composition for a Painting;* performed by doing embroidery on a handkerchief by Ray Kass on Oct. 6, 2017 at Cage-Haus Halberstadt next to the Burchardi Church, Germany; 2017, embroidery, black ink, water color and Lascaux Studio Bronze on handkerchief, 46 x 46 cm (18.11 x 18.11 in.).

*10*

**Alvin Curran,** *Hat jemand meinen Hirtenstab gesehen?* ("In praise of everything that walks"): A performance of *John Cage's STEPS, A Composition for a Painting;* performed open air Oct. 6, 2017 on the grounds of the Burchardi Cloister before the Cage Haus Halberstadt next to the Burchardi Church, Germany; 2017, black ink and watercolor on white Fabriano paper plus a shepherd's crook handmade by the artist, 150.8 x 1000 cm (59.37 x 393.70 in.).

*11*

**Arnold Dreyblatt,** *380 Steps:* A performance of *John Cage's STEPS, A Composition for a Painting;* performed by walking in a circle of ten music stands and reading a text installed on 380 pieces of paper in A5 formate and let each piece fell down on the ground after reading it on Oct. 6, 2017 at Cage-Haus Halberstadt next to the Burchardi Church, Germany; 2017, black ink and water color on white Fabriano paper plus ten black music stands, type Adam Hall SMS 2 mounted with a set of 380 A5 cards installed with the text "An introductory Essay to the Doctrine of Sounds containing some proposals for the improvement of acoustics, as it was presented to the Society of Dublin November 12, 1683 by Archbishop Narcissus March," app. 400 x 400 cm (157.48 x 157.48 in.).

*12*

**Roberto Paci Dalò,** *Waterfire:* A performance of *John Cage's STEPS, A Composition for a Painting;* performed by drawing in a full opened Moleskine® Japanese Album installed with electronics to amplify the sound of drawing and same time playing sound samples from the computer on Oct. 6, 2017 at Cage-Haus Halberstadt next to the Burchardi Church, Germany; 2017, pencil, water-soluble graphite, watercolour, Album closed: 21.6 x 13.3 x 1.3 cm (8.50 x 5.23 x 0.51 in.), Album opened: 21.6 x 328 cm (8.50 x 129.13 in.).

*13*

**Kalle Laar,** *Pinocchio Playing Cage Backwards:* A performance of *John Cage's STEPS, A Composition for a Painting;* performed by walking around a working table with 14 installed sound objects and toys incl. a Pinocchio puppet framed by a pencil drawing, activating each sound object for a minute and telling a personal story connected to it on Oct. 6, 2017 at Cage-Haus Halberstadt next to the Burchardi Church, Germany; 2017, sound objects and toys, white Fabriano paper, working table 180 x 60 x 75 cm (70.86 x 23.62 x 29.52 in.).

*14*

**Achim Freyer,** *Schrittfolgen 30917 (Für Dieter Schnebel):* A performance of *John Cage's STEPS, A Composition for a Painting;* performed on Sep. 30, 2017 in the house of the artists in Tatti, Groseto, Italien; 2017, Acrylic on canvas plus video footage with sound, 100 x 100 x 2.5 cm (39.37 x 39.37 in.).

*15*

**Angélica Castelló,** *ELECTROALTAR for John Cage, siete rezos* (Halberstadt version): A performance of John Cage's STEPS, A Composition for a Painting; performed by setting up an audio-visual installation dedicated to John Cage, then switching on in seven steps different light elements of the installation and playing on a Petzold Flute on Oct. 6, 2017 at Cage-Haus Halberstadt next to the Burchardi Church, Germany; 2017, empty television body ø 55, electronic scrap, plaited magnetic tape, tablecloth, table 80 x 80 x 75 cm (31.50 x 31.50 x 29.52 in.).

*16*

**Uwe Bressnik,** *Seven Steps To Heaven* (SSR 189): A live-recording of seven performances of *John Cage's STEPS, A Composition for a Painting;* performed by keeping a record of the seven performances of Cage's *STEPS* by Sabine Groschup, Alvin Curran, Arnold Dreyblatt, Kalle Laar, Roberto Paci Daló, Angélica Castelló and his own on Oct. 6, 2017 at Cage-Haus Halberstadt next to the Burchardi Church, Germany; 2017, silver liner on cardboard, acrylic paint, paper, acrylic, watercolors, 75 cm (29.5 in.).

*17*
**Georg Weckwerth,** *"Is this a flag or a painting?"* (A tribute to Jasper Johns): A work in progress performance of *John Cage's STEPS, A Composition for a Painting;* performed by designing a flag together with the Vienna based grafic designer Astrid Seme for the Halberstadt workshop #JohnCageSTEPS, organizing the production of the flag, installing by hand a 6 Meter long flagstaff at the chimney on the roof of the Cage-Haus Halberstadt next to the Burchardi Church with the great help of **Christof Hallegger, Kay Lautenbach** and **Willi Maynicke** on Oct. 4, 2017, and finally raise the STEPS flag; the take down of the flag and its installment inside of the Cage-Haus Halberstadt will take place on John Cage's 108th birthday on Sep. 5, 2020 as part of the 14th sound change in the Halberstadt performance of John Cage's *ORGAN²/ ASLSP* in the Burchardi Church next to the Cage-Haus Halberstadt of the John Cage Organ Foundation; 2017–2020, a Vispronet® flag produced by Sachsen Fahnen GambH & Co. KG Dresden plus photos, 150 x 250 cm (59.05 x 98.43 in.).

# CONTRIBUTORS

*Stephen Addiss* is Tucker-Boatwright professor emeritus at the University of Richmond. He has a special interest in the conjunction of text and image, as in Zen painting, literati painting, and haiku painting (*haiga*).

His own haiku as well as translations from the Japanese have appeared in many journals and books, and his calligraphy, ceramics, and paintings, including haiga, have been exhibited in China, Japan, Taiwan, Singapore, Korea, England, France, Germany, Austria, and many American venues. His many authored or co-authored books include *The Art of Zen*; *How to Look at Japanese Art*; *77 Dances: Japanese Calligraphy*; *The Art of Chinese Calligraphy*; *John Cage: Zen Ox-Herding Pictures* (with Ray Kass); *A Haiku Menagerie*; *Haiga: Haiku-Painting*; *Haiku People*; *A Haiku Garden*; *Haiku Humor*; *Haiku Landscapes*; *Haiku: An Anthology of Japanese Poems*; and *The Art of Haiku*.

*Steven Bickley* is professor emeritus of art at Virginia Tech and is a regionally and nationally recognized sculptor. Notable regional exhibitions of his work include a solo exhibition in the sculpture garden at The Phillips Collection. His work has been included in over 120 national and regional exhibitions.

He has also been a fabricator of large-scale works since 1974 and is currently working with Santiago Calatrava and Beverly Pepper on national and international projects. d

He collaborated with Chas Fagan on the entrance sculpture to the Reagan Airport and with Cy Twombly on bronze castings between 2001 and 2004.

*Tom Coffin* is a fine artist exploring the medium of virtual and augmented reality currently employed by the Emerging Analytics Center at the University of Arkansas at Little Rock. He is a graduate of the Pennsylvania Academy of the Fine Arts, the School of the Art Institute of Chicago, and the Electronic Visualization Laboratory (EVL) at the University of Illinois at Chicago. Upon completion of his studies at EVL, he assisted in the commercialization of the CAVE, a projection-based virtual reality technology. Tom Coffin has exhibited his virtual reality work at the Ars Electronica Center, SIGGRAPH, and numerous institutions with CAVE or CAVE-like facilities. His most current work is an Augmented Reality Artwork (ARt) entitled Glass Slag. Images and downloadable App can be found at: www.appliedvr.com

*Alston (Stoney) Conley* is an associate professor of practice in art at Boston College and former curator of the McMullen Museum of Art. He is a painter who has received grants from the Massachusetts Cultural Council, the National Endowment for the Arts, and the Fulbright Program (a grant to Italy), and fellowships to the Fine Arts Work Center in Provincetown and the Ballinglen Arts Foundation, Ireland. For the last decade he has made paintings and collages. These images capture light and the natural world and reflect a sense of place. In the late 1970s and '80s he painted in fresco, making murals and panels. He learned, and later taught, fresco at the Skowhegan School of Painting and Sculpture in Maine.

*James Donnelly* is a Glasgow, Scotland-based painter who graduated from the Edinburgh College of Art in 2000. His work incorporates his oil paintings on deep acrylic in fully designed gallery installations.

*Jane M. Farmer* is an independent curator, formerly of Washington, D.C., who lives in New Mexico. She worked at the National Museum of American Art under Joshua Taylor and has organized traveling exhibitions and artist exchanges for various organizations including the Smithsonian Traveling Exhibition Service and the Crossing Over Consortium. Farmer chaired the Museum Education Roundtable and was a co-founder of the Paper Road/Tibet project, an organization working to reestablish the traditional art of hand papermaking displaced by China's incursions into Tibet. She served on the board of Pyramid Atlantic from 1982 to 2004 and has been an advisor to the board of Hand Papermaking since 1996. She has published numerous exhibition catalogues, reviews, and articles.

*Gary "Chico" Harkrader* is an artist who lives and exhibits his paintings in Roanoke, Virginia. He has said, "A canvas or found object represents a stage for me to explore the visual attributes of light, color, form, and movement. Past experiences, present environment, and experimentation with mixed media allow me to echo my passion, peace, or pleasure."

*Taro Hatanaka* is a Tokyo-based Architect currently working at an Urban Planning and Civil Engineering firm in Jakarta, Indonesia.

*Rachel Talent Ivers* is the executive director of the Longwood Center for the Visual Arts at Longwood University in Farmville, Virginia. Before coming to Longwood University in 2014, she was the director of exhibitions and curatorial affairs at the Museum of Art, Fort Lauderdale.

*Ulrike Kasper* is a teacher, art historian, author, and independent curator who lives in Paris. She holds a PhD in art history from Université Paris I – Panthéon-Sorbonne. In addition to teaching at the Parisian campuses of the Institute of European Studies, Skidmore College, George Washington University in Paris, and the Institut d'histoire de l'art de Chatou, she has taught at Paris III – Sorbonne Nouvelle for over ten years. She is a lecturer on contemporary art and interdisciplinary subjects at the Musée d'art moderne et contemporain de Saint-Étienne and at the museums of fine arts in Lyon and Chambéry. She has written three books: *John Cage: Un artiste dans son temps* (2009); *Écrire sur l'eau: L'esthétique de John Cage* (2005), and *L'art contemporain pour les Nuls* (2014).

*Joe Kelley* is an artist who lives in Blacksburg, Virginia. He began volunteering in the Mountain Lake Workshop in 1990 as an assistant in John Cage's workshop New River Rocks and Smoke. Later that same year he worked closely with Japanese sculptor Jiro Okura to help create the carved walnut panels of the *Mountain Lake Screen Tachi*, and subsequently worked as an assistant for Mierle Laderman Ukeles' workshop, Methanogenesis. Kelley produced his own workshop, The Appalachian Trail Frieze, with assistance from Stefan Gibson, in 1994. He has remained a constant supporter of and participant in the Mountain Lake Workshop to the present.

*Ashley Kistler*, an independent curator and editor, has been an integral part of the Richmond arts community with a curatorial career spanning over 30 years. Her numerous exhibitions and catalogues have featured a wide range of work by regional, national, and international artists. She served as director of VCUarts Anderson Gallery from 2008 to 2015, and as curator of the Visual Arts Center of Richmond from 1999 to 2008. From 1984 to 1999, Kistler held various curatorial positions at the Virginia Museum of Fine Arts, most recently as associate curator of modern and contemporary art.

*Sam Krisch* is a Roanoke, Virginia–based fine art photographer known for his dramatic landscapes and whimsical and experimental iPhone photographs. He has exhibited throughout the United States at museums, universities, art centers, and commercial galleries. He teaches workshops in iPhone photography and creativity and has directed community art ventures. He has also curated photographic exhibitions at the Taubman Museum in Roanoke and been the juror for national photography exhibitions.

*Donald Kuspit,* one of America's most foremost art critics, is Distinguished Professor Emeritus of art history and philosophy at the State University of New York at Stony Brook. Besides a PhD in Philosophy, having studied under Theodor W. Adorno in Frankfort, Germany (1963), he has a Ph.D. in art history from the University of Michigan (1971) and the equivalent in psychoanalysis from New York University (1990s). In 1979, being dissatisfied with the state of contemporary criticism, he co-founded and edited the journal Art Criticism at Stony Brook. A hallmark of his critical discourse, found in the literally hundreds of catalogue essays, articles, and books he has authored, is its wide ranging approach to art, engaging art on many levels

including the historic, philosophic, and psychoanalytic. He is a recipient of the College Art Association's Frank Jewett Mather Award for Distinction in Art Criticism (1983).

*Peter Lau* currently resides in Atlanta and works as a vice president of construction for Hines, an international real estate developer based in Houston. He was principal assistant to Ray Kass and the Mountain Lake Workshop from 1988 to 1991, during which time he worked under John Cage (1988, 1989, and 1990), Howard Finster (1989), and Jiro Okura (1990). After receiving his BA in architecture from Virginia Tech in 1991, he embarked on a cultural exploration of Kyoto to learn more about traditional architecture and carpentry. Over a period of seven years, he immersed himself in the traditional design culture of Japan, beginning with a two-year apprenticeship with a master carpenter and concluding with three years of practical training under one of Kyoto's best-known architects specializing in the revitalization of traditional Japanese architecture.

*Liz Liguori* is a multimedia artist from Brooklyn, New York, who works in photography, lighting, sculpture, video, and environmental installations. Liguori earned her MFA in Creative Technologies from Virginia Tech in 2017 and her BFA in Studio Art from Drew University in 2001. Liguori's process-driven work is a reexamination of high and low technologies and their relationship to art.

*Jessie Mann* is a painter, writer, conceptual artist, and doctoral student. Her research is on the cognitive neuroscience of virtual neurorehabilitation. Mann's paintings have been featured in various galleries and national publications. Mann is engaged in an ongoing collaboration with photographer Len Prince, which deals expressly with the phenomenology of the collaborative subject in art. Selections from this series, entitled "Self Possessed," are in the permanent collections of The Art Institute of Chicago, the Getty Museum, and The Florida Museum of Photographic Arts. Mann is currently engaged in a collaboration with artist Liz Liguori that pushes the boundary between painting and photography. Their "electromagnetograms,"

produced with laser beams and chemically painted photo paper, address photography's latent abstract and painterly tendencies and, conversely, painting's light-capturing action.

*Bruce McClure's* film work, which has been shown nationally and internationally, including in two Whitney Biennials, is about re-experiencing and documenting film, video, and digital media. His early work was based in Marcel Duchamp's "Roto Optics" and displayed the psychedelic effect of spinning disks bathed in flickering strobe lights. The work for which he first received widespread recognition employed hand-modified film material, objectifying the film itself as the subject of its own projection, and was accompanied by his own performance format for its unique display.

*Alwyn Moss* is a Blacksburg, Virginia, writer and artist who grew up in New York City. She has been an editor for *Mademoiselle* magazine, has free-lanced fiction and nonfiction to other national magazines and journals, and has published a biography of Dr. Margaret Mead (*Shaping A New World*, 1963). An environmental activist, her more recent published writings grow out of her studies with Thomas Berry and are devoted to the "great work" of preserving the life, the natural environment, and the beauty of our planet. She met M.C. Richards at a workshop in North Carolina and discovered that they shared similar approaches to art and a belief in the values of Rudolf Steiner's anthroposophy and Waldorf education.

*Ann Frederick Oppenhimer* is a writer and editor who lives in Richmond, Virginia, where she taught art history at the University of Richmond for 17 years and organized the 1984 exhibition *Sermons in Paint: A Howard Finster Folk Art Festival* and was co-editor, with Susan Hankla, of the exhibition catalogue. In 1987 she founded the Folk Art Society of America with her husband, William Oppenhimer, and is executive director; and she is editor and publisher of the society's journal, *Folk Art Messenger*. She is on the advisory board of Paradise Garden Foundation in Summerville, Georgia.

*Mason Peterson* is a an alumnus of the design program at Virginia Tech. He was raised on a small-scale organic farm in Abingdon, Virginia, where he acquired a passion for hard work and detail-oriented projects. The opportunities he has been given throughout his life and career have led to his passion for education and desire to teach design. He has made an important contribution to the design of this publication. masonjackp.com

*Jerrie Pike* is a retired art historian who holds an MA from Oberlin College and a PhD in Classical art from the University of Iowa. She has presented papers at various scholarly conferences including SECAC, the Southeastern College Art Conference. Her interest in Jiro Okura's work coincides with her interest in the art of bonsai design. She established Higo Garden Bonsai, a bonsai nursery and gardens in Christiansburg, Virginia, where she lives and practices and teaches the art of bonsai. More information is available at: higogardenbonsai.com

*Kathy Pinkerton* lives in Blacksburg, Virginia, and Savannah, Georgia, and has taught in the art department at Virginia Tech. She received an MFA in painting from Radford University and studied papermaking at the Penland School of Crafts and Pyramid Atlantic Art Center. She has made large-scale commissioned wall pieces out of intensely colored paper pulp and is currently working with found objects.

*Roger Reynolds* is a composer, writer, producer, and mentor, pioneer in sound spatialization, intermedia, and also algorithmic concepts. His Pulitzer prize–winning "Whispers Out of Time," for string orchestra, mused on a poem by John Ashbery. The intermedial evening, FLiGHT, explores the human aspiration to fly — with string quartet, projected imagery, and a performed text that stretches from Plato to Michael Collins. C. F. Peters publishes Reynolds's music; his manuscripts are housed in a Library of Congress special collection and at the Sacher Foundation. He seeks the satisfactions of experiencing unanticipated connections, bringing the elevating capacity of music

into public spaces, and engaging with others to discover new amalgamations of sensation and insight that can "improve the human experience."

*Lee Sauder* has been blacksmithing since 1974 and working as a full-time professional smith from 1981. Since 1998 his focus and passion has been rediscovering the lost art of bloomery smelting and making sculpture from the resulting iron. He has shared his knowledge in workshops and demonstrations from California to Maine, and overseas in England, Italy, Burkina Faso, and Sudan. His work has been published in both art magazines and scientific journals. He lives and works at the end of a long dirt road on the south slope of House Mountain in Rockbridge County, Virginia. www.leesauder.com/

*Brian Sieveking* is a painter, professor, print publisher, and curator living in Roanoke, Virginia. His paintings and prints explore the blurring of history, myth, and religion, especially in relation to vernacular and pop culture in the South. The creative, critical, and documentary work that he began with Howard Finster has continued and expanded to include many folk and outsider artists including Georgia Blizzard, James Harold Jennings, Mose Tolliver, and Jimmy Lee Sudduth. He is currently writing a history of roadside dinosaur parks.

*Georg Weckwerth* is an independent curator and artistic director and curatorial manager of TONSPUR PASSAGE, Vienna's first permanent venue for sound art, located in the MuseumsQuartier museum complex of the former Hapsburg Imperial Residence in Vienna, Austria. Since 2003 Weckwerth has been collaborating with the eminent sound engineer Peter Szely in creating an innovative presence for "sound art" installations throughout Europe. In 2012 he co-curated (with Jozef Cseres) *Membra Disjecta for John Cage: Wanting to Say Something About John*, a special centennial celebration traveling exhibition of John Cage's music and visual artworks, which premiered at MuseumsQuartier and then traveled to Salzburg and Prague.

*David Whaley* is a designer and photographer living in Richmond, Virginia. His work has won numerous national and international awards. He serves as Director of Design for Longwood University.

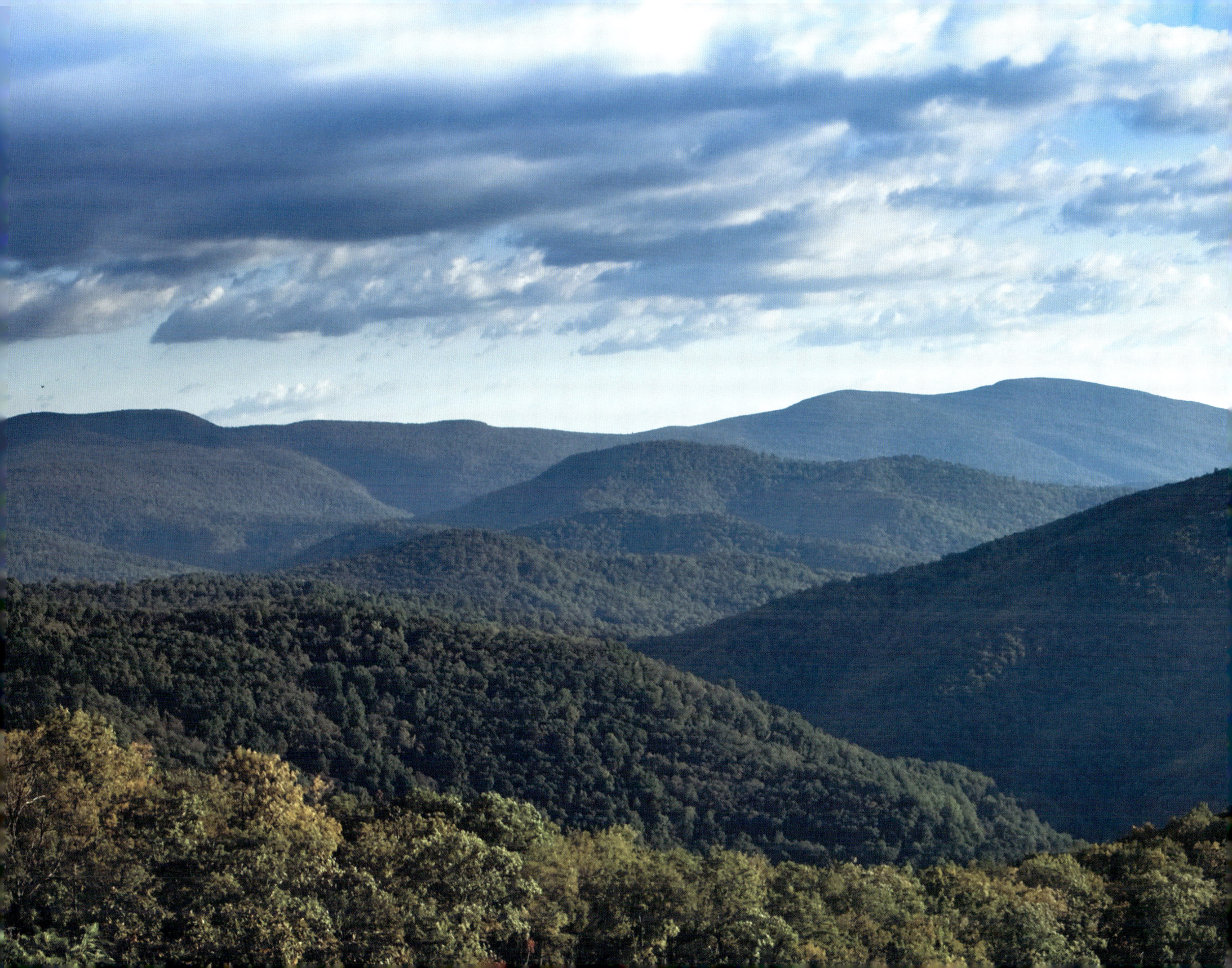

# INDEX

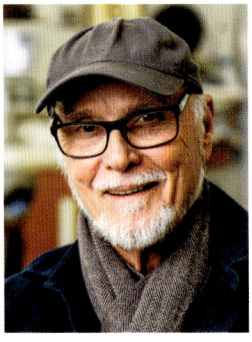

**Ray Kass** is a widely exhibited artist whose paintings are represented by Garvey/Simon ART ACCESS in New York City and the Reynolds Gallery in Richmond, Virginia. He is professor emeritus in the School of Visual Arts at Virginia Tech and founder and director of the Mountain Lake Workshop, a collaborative, community-based art project drawing on the cultural, environmental, and technological resources of the New River Valley and the Appalachian region. His publications include *The Sight of Silence: John Cage's Complete Watercolors* (2011), *John Cage: Zen Ox-Herding Pictures* (with Stephen Addiss) (2009), and *Morris Graves: Vision of the Inner Eye* (1983). More information is available at www.raykass.com and mountainlakeworkshop.org.

Photo by David Franusich

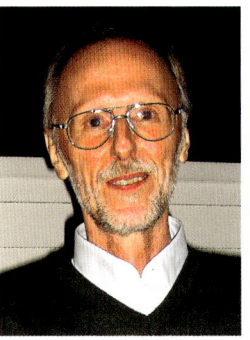

**Howard Risatti** is emeritus professor of contemporary art and critical theory in the Department of Art History at Virginia Commonwealth University, where he also was chair of the Department of Craft/Material Studies from 2001 to 2005. His writings have appeared in many journals, and his books include *New Music Vocabulary* (1975); *Postmodern Perspectives: Issues in Contemporary Art* (1998); and *The Mountain Lake Workshops: Artists in Locale* (1996). He co-authored with Kenneth Trapp *Skilled Work: American Craft in the Renwick Gallery* (1998). His latest book is *A Theory of Craft: Function and Aesthetic Expression* (2007).

Photo courtesy Howard Risatti

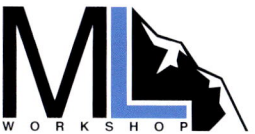

This book was published on the occasion of *Rural Avante Garde: The Mountain Lake Experience,* an exhibition organized by the Longwood Center for the Visual Arts at Longwood University.

EXHIBITION SCHEDULE

August 23 – December 23, 2018
Gregg Museum of Art & Design
1903 Hillsborough Street
Raleigh, North Carolina 27607

January 26 – March 24, 2019
Pinkard Gallery, Maryland Institute College of Art
1401 West Mount Royal Avenue
Baltimore, Maryland 21217

November 16, 2019 – March 8, 2020
Longwood Center for the Visual Arts
129 North Main Street
Farmville, Virginia 23901

ENDPAPER

Smoking the paper for John Cage's *New River Rocks and Smoke,* 1990

IMAGES

Unless otherwise noted, all images of John Cage and his art works © John Cage Trust; all images of Merce Cunningham and the Merce Cunningham Dance Company © Merce Cunningham Trust; Wayne Thiebaud's Mountain Lake Landscape appears courtesy of the artist, the Virginia Historical Society, and VAGA; Robert Rauschenberg's *Automobile Tire Print* appears courtesy Robert Rauschenberg Foundation, the San Francisco Museum of Modern Art, and VAGA; images of Cy Twombly's Untitled appears courtesy Cy Twombly Foundation and the Menil Collection. Reproduction of scores by John Cage by permission of C.F. Peters Corp. © Edition Peters
Unless otherwise noted, all other images of Mountain Lake Symposium and Workshop events and artworks © the credited artists or Ray Kass and the Mountain Lake Workshop.

TEXT

All contributors retain copyright to their individual texts.
The compiled volume is © Longwood Center for the Visual Arts, Longwood University, Ray Kass, and Howard Risatti

BOOK DESIGN

Mason Peterson and David Whaley, Director of Design, Longwood University

PRINTING & BINDING

Asia Pacific Offset, China

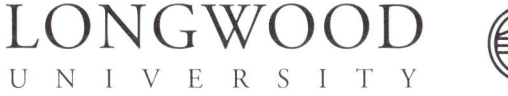

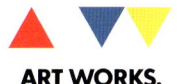

ISBN: 978-0-9978381-0-7
Library of Congress Control Number:  2017954813

Distributed by the University of Virginia Press

This exhibition is supported in part by an award from the National Endowment for the Arts. To find out more about how National Endowment for the Arts grants impact individuals and communities, visit www.arts.gov.

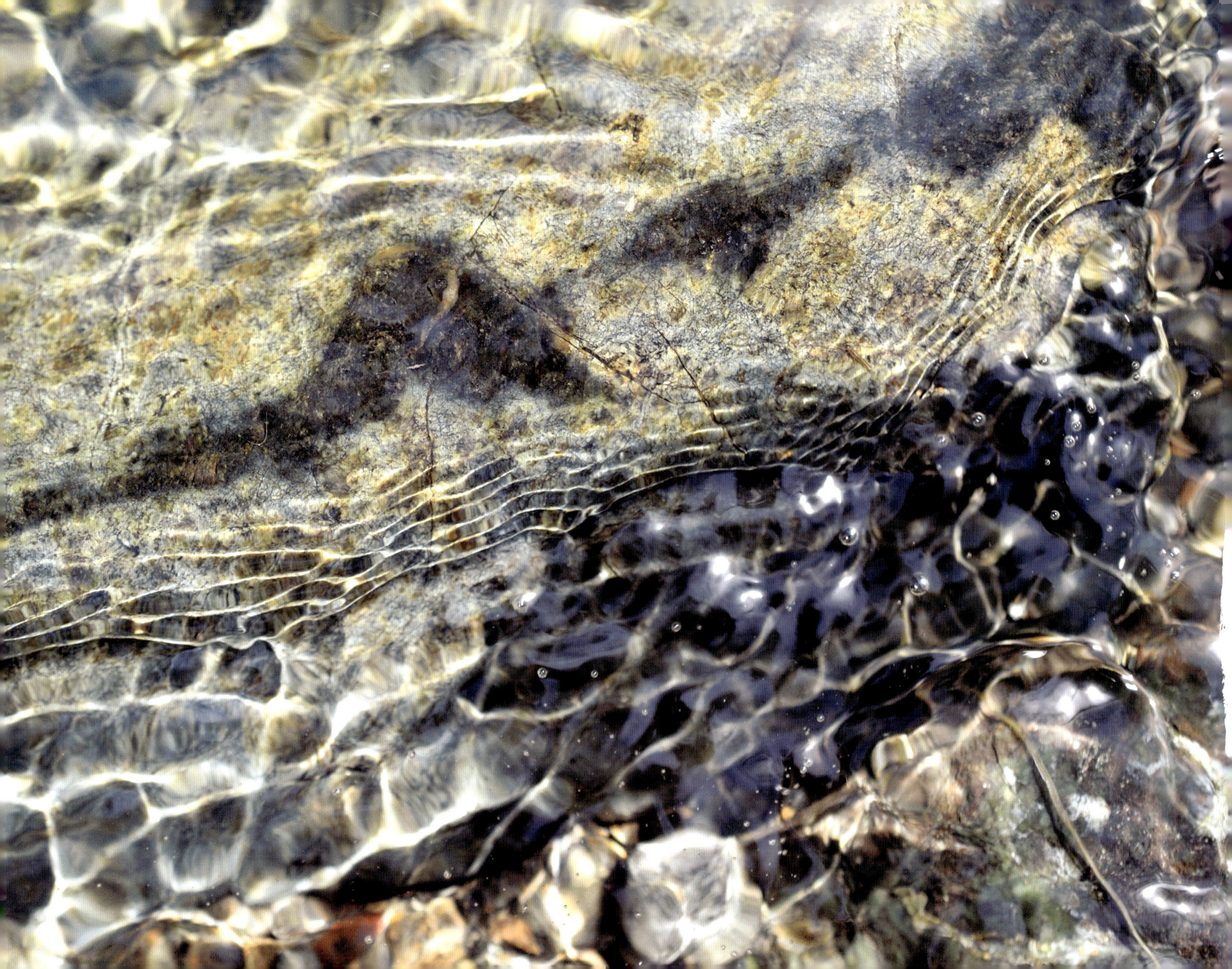